THE ROUTLEDGE RESEARCH COMPANION TO ANTHONY TROLLOPE

Bringing together leading and newly emerging scholars, *The Routledge Research Companion to Anthony Trollope* offers a comprehensive overview of Trollope scholarship and suggests new directions in Trollope studies. The first volume designed especially for advanced graduate students and scholars, the collection features essays on virtually every topic relevant to Trollope research, including the law, gender, politics, evolution, race, anti-Semitism, biography, philosophy, illustration, aging, sport, emigration, and the global and regional worlds.

Deborah Denenholz Morse is Vera W. Barkley Term Professor of English at the College of William & Mary, USA.

Margaret Markwick holds an honorary fellowship at the University of Exeter, UK.

Mark W. Turner is a professor of English at King's College London, UK.

THE ROUTLEDGE RESEARCH COMPANION TO ANTHONY TROLLOPE

Edited by Deborah Denenholz Morse, Margaret Markwick and Mark W. Turner

LONDON AND NEW YORK

First published 2017
by Routledge
2 Park Square, Milton Park, Abingdon, Oxon OX14 4RN

and by Routledge
711 Third Avenue, New York, NY 10017

Routledge is an imprint of the Taylor & Francis Group, an informa business

© 2017 selection and editorial matter, Deborah Denenholz Morse, Margaret Markwick and Mark W. Turner; individual chapters, the contributors

The right of Deborah Denenholz Morse, Margaret Markwick and Mark W. Turner to be identified as the authors of the editorial material, and of the authors for their individual chapters, has been asserted in accordance with sections 77 and 78 of the Copyright, Designs and Patents Act 1988.

All rights reserved. No part of this book may be reprinted or reproduced or utilised in any form or by any electronic, mechanical, or other means, now known or hereafter invented, including photocopying and recording, or in any information storage or retrieval system, without permission in writing from the publishers.

Trademark notice: Product or corporate names may be trademarks or registered trademarks, and are used only for identification and explanation without intent to infringe.

British Library Cataloguing in Publication Data
A catalogue record for this book is available from the British Library

Library of Congress Cataloging-in-Publication Data
A catalog record for this book has been requested

ISBN: 978-1-4094-6204-0 (hbk)
ISBN: 978-1-315-61273-7 (ebk)

Typeset in Bembo
by Apex CoVantage, LLC

To

Ann Donahue

CONTENTS

List of figures   *xi*
Notes on the contributors   *xii*
Acknowledgements   *xix*
Anthony Trollope: An overview   *xx*

    Introduction   1

PART I
Political settings   **13**

  1 Trollope and politics   15
      Lauren M.E. Goodlad and Frederik Van Dam

  2 Trollope and the state   35
      Michael Martel

PART II
Culture and gender   **49**

  3 Trollope the feminist   51
      Deborah Denenholz Morse

  4 Anthony Trollope's conduct-book fiction for men   63
      Hyson Cooper

  5 Women, violence, and modernity in *The Way We Live Now*   72
      Mary Jean Corbett

6	Marital law in *He Knew He Was Right* Suzanne Raitt	84
7	Legitimacy and illegitimacy Jenny Bourne Taylor	100
8	Trollope and material culture Margaret P. Harvey	111
9	"Within the figure and frame and clothes and cuticle": Trollope and the body Sophie Gilmartin	120

PART III
Critical theory — 135

10	Trollope's tragedy James Kincaid	137
11	"As a matter of course": Trollope's ordinary realism Jonathan Farina	142
12	Rethinking marriage: Trollope's internal revision Helena Michie	154
13	Affective Trollope: marshaling the feelings in *Orley Farm* Suzanne Keen	166
14	Forms of storytelling, repetition, and voice in Anthony Trollope's *Kept in the Dark* Helen Lucy Blythe	177
15	Trollope writes Trollope Margaret Markwick	190
16	Trollope and Darwin Lauren Cameron	201

PART IV
Illustration studies — 211

17	Trollope and illustration Paul Goldman and David Skilton	213

18	Trollope's picturesque chroniclette and John Millais: portrait of the artist as a young swain *Robert Polhemus*	239

PART V
Trollopian preoccupations   261

19	"Fiery shorthand": Trollope's Irish novel *Robert Tracy*	263
20	"The clever son of a clever mother": Anthony and Frances Trollope *Elsie Michie*	274
21	Legal culture *Ayelet Ben-Yishai*	285
22	Trollope and aging *Kay Heath*	295
23	Trollope and literary labour *Kate Osborne*	306
24	Trollope and field sports *Heather Miner*	315

PART VI
Creed and cant   323

25	Rethinking Trollope and anti-Semitism: gender, religion, and "the Jew" in *The Way We Live Now* *Anna Peak*	325
26	Can you forgive him?: Trollope, Jews, and prejudice *Steven Amarnick*	336
27	Anthony Trollope's religion *J. Jeffrey Franklin*	347

PART VII
Global Trollope   361

28	Irish questions: Ireland and the Trollope novels *Gordon Bigelow*	363

29 Place and topicality: *La Vendée* and Trollope's novels of regional change   378
Nicholas Birns

30 Trollope and emigration   388
Tamara S. Wagner

31 "So wild and beautiful a world around him":
Trollope and Antipodean ecology   399
Grace Moore

32 "Yams, salt pork, biscuit, and bad coffee": food and race in
The West Indies and the Spanish Main   412
Michelle Mouton

33 Trollope and global modernity   423
Mark W. Turner

Index   *435*

FIGURES

17.1	Lord Lufton and Lucy Robarts, by John Everett Millais	220
17.2	"Was It Not a Lie?" by John Everett Millais	222
17.3	The Crawley Family, by John Everett Millais	225
17.4	Lady Lufton and the Duke of Omnium, by John Everett Millais	227
17.5	"Mark," She Said, "The Men Are Here," by John Everett Millais	228
17.6	Mrs Gresham and Miss Dunstable, by John Everett Millais	230
17.7	Never Is a Very Long Word, by John Everett Millais	232
17.8	Monkton Grange, by John Everett Millais	233
17.9	"It's All the Fault of the Naughty Birds," by John Everett Millais	235
18.1	*A Private View at the Royal Academy, 1881*, by William Powell Frith	247
18.2	"Was It Not a Lie?" by John Everett Millais	249
18.3	*The Order of Release*, by John Everett Millais	251
18.4	*Portrait of a Girl*, by John Everett Millais	254

CONTRIBUTORS

Steven Amarnick is editor of *The Duke's Children: First Complete Edition*, published by the Folio Society, and curator of "Anthony Trollope: The Art of Modesty," at the Fales Library, New York University. He is a professor of English at Kingsborough Community College, City University of New York.

Ayelet Ben-Yishai teaches Victorian and postcolonial literature in the Department of English at the University of Haifa. With degrees in both law and literature she has published extensively on their intersection, especially in the novels of Anthony Trollope. In addition to her book, *Common Precedents: The Presentness of the Past in Victorian Law and Fiction* (Oxford, 2013), articles on Trollope and/or Victorian law and literature have appeared in *Nineteenth-Century Literature*, *Nineteenth-Century Contexts*, *The Cambridge Companion to Anthony Trollope*, and in *The Journal of Law, Culture and the Humanities*.

Gordon Bigelow is a professor and former chair of the English department at Rhodes College in Memphis, Tennessee, where he was presented the Clarence Day Award for Excellence in Teaching in 2010. He is the author of *Fiction, Famine, and the Rise of Economics in Victorian Britain and Ireland* (2003) and co-editor with John O. Jordan of *Approaches to Teaching Dickens's Bleak House* (2009). His essays have appeared in *Novel*, *LIT*, *ELH*, and *Harper's*, as well as in the *Cambridge Companion to Anthony Trollope* and the 2014 collection *Global Legacies of the Great Irish Famine*.

Nicholas Birns is the author of *Understanding Anthony Powell* (University of South Carolina Press, 2004) and the co-editor of *A Companion to Australian Literature Since 1900* (Camden House, 2007), which was named a CHOICE Outstanding Academic Book of the year for 2008. His book *Theory After Theory: An Intellectual History of Literary Theory from 1950 to the Early 21st Century* appeared from Broadview in 2010 and is now widely used in classrooms, and his monograph *Barbarian Memory: The Legacy of Early Medieval History in Early Modern Literature* came out with Palgrave Macmillan in 2013. *Contemporary Australian Literature: A World Not Yet Dead*, a major overview of contemporary fiction from Down Under, appeared from Sydney University Press in 2015. Co-edited projects on teaching Australian and New Zealand Literature and Roberto Bolaño as world literature are under contract with the Modern Language Association and Bloomsbury respectively. He has contributed to the *New York Times Book Review*, *The Hollins*

Critic, Exemplaria, Arizona Quarterly, MLQ, and many other journals and edited anthologies. He is the editor of *Antipodes: A Global Journal of Australian/NZ Literature*.

Helen Lucy Blythe is a professor of nineteenth-century British literature at New Mexico Highlands University. She is the author of *The Victorian Colonial Romance with the Antipodes* (Palgrave Macmillan, 2014) and several articles on the works of Anthony Trollope.

Lauren Cameron is a lecturer at the University of Iowa, where she teaches courses in rhetoric and literature. She earned her PhD in 2013 from the University of North Carolina at Chapel Hill. Her previous scholarship on nineteenth-century British literature and science has appeared in *Nineteenth-Century Literature, Victorian Literature and Culture, Nineteenth-Century Contexts*, and *Victorians Journal of Culture and Literature*. Her dissertation and current book project is titled "Renegotiating Science: British Women Novelists and Evolution Controversies, 1826–1876."

Hyson Cooper has recently relocated to Boston after eleven years of teaching at Temple University in Philadelphia; she now teaches in the Liberal Arts Department at Berklee College of Music. Her research interests primarily concern Victorian masculinity, with a particular focus on Trollope.

Mary Jean Corbett is a university distinguished professor of English and affiliated with the Women's, Gender, and Sexuality Studies Program and the Department of Global and Intercultural Studies at Miami University. She is the author of *Representing Femininity: Middle-Class Subjectivity in Victorian and Edwardian Women's Autobiographies* (Oxford, 1992); *Allegories of Union in Irish and English Writing, 1790–1870: History, Politics, and the Family from Edgeworth to Arnold* (Cambridge, 2000); and *Family Likeness: Sex, Marriage, and Incest from Jane Austen to Virginia Woolf* (Cornell, 2008). Her current research explores late-Victorian contexts for the life and writing of Virginia Woolf.

Jonathan Farina is an associate professor of nineteenth-century English literature at Seton Hall University, where he also directs the Center for Literature and the Public Sphere and teaches intellectual history in the Honors Program. He is finishing a book, *Everyday Words and the Character of Nineteenth-Century British Prose*, which examines ordinary stylistic tics as signatures of a pervasive epistemology of character, a form of knowledge that supplemented the referential fact. He has published articles on Dickens, Trollope, Eliot, and others in *Dickens Studies Annual, Victorian Studies, Victorian Literature and Culture, Victorians, Victorian Periodicals Review, RaVoN*, and elsewhere.

J. Jeffrey Franklin is a professor of English and associate vice chancellor for undergraduate experiences at the University of Colorado Denver. He is the author of *Serious Play: The Cultural Form of the Nineteenth-Century Realist Novel* (UPenn, 1999), *For the Lost Boys* (poetry, Ghost Road Press, 2006), and *The Lotus and the Lion: Buddhism and the British Empire* (Cornell, 2008, and Munshiram Manoharlal, 2009). His essays have appeared in *Cahiers victoriens & édouardiens, ELH, Journal of Religion and Literature, Literature Compass, Nineteenth-Century Literature, Victorians Institute Journal, Victorian Literature and Culture, Victorian Review*, and *The Ashgate Companion to Spiritualism and the Occult in the Nineteenth Century*. He has completed two new manuscripts, *Spirit Matters* (scholarly) and *What Is* (poetry). He lives in Denver with his wife, Judy Lucas.

Sophie Gilmartin is a reader in nineteenth-century literature at Royal Holloway, University of London. She has written on blood relations and nation in her book *Ancestry and Narrative in Nineteenth-Century British Literature* (Cambridge UP), and co-authored with Rod Mengham

Thomas Hardy's Shorter Fiction: A Critical Study (Edinburgh UP). For Penguin Classics, she edited Trollope's *The Last Chronicle of Barset*. Currently she is writing a book on Cape Horn and Victorian women navigators.

Paul Goldman is currently an honorary professor in the School of English, Communication and Philosophy at Cardiff University. He was formerly an associate fellow at the Institute of English Studies in the School of Advanced Study at University of London. He has published extensively on Victorian illustration, including *Beyond Decoration: The Illustrations of John Everett Millais* (British Library, 2012), *Victorian Illustrated Books 1850–1870: The Heyday of Wood-Engraving* (British Museum Press, 1994), *Victorian Illustration: The Pre-Raphaelites, The Idyllic School and the High Victorians* (Lund Humphries, 1996, second edition revised 2006), *John Everett Millais: Illustrator and Narrator* (Lund Humphries 2004), and as editor with Simon Cooke, *Reading Victorian Illustration 1855–1875* (Ashgate, 2012). With the same co-editor in the press is *George du Maurier: Beyond Svengali* (Ashgate, 2016). In other directions, he has published *Looking at Prints, Drawings and Watercolours: A Guide to Technical Terms* (British Museum Press and J. Paul Getty Museum, 1988, revised and enlarged edition, 2006) and *Master Prints Close-Up* (British Museum Press, 2012).

Lauren M. E. Goodlad is a Kathryn Paul Professorial Scholar of English, Criticism & Interpretive Theory at the University of Illinois, Urbana, where she is also Provost Fellow for Undergraduate Education. Her recent publications include *The Victorian Geopolitical Aesthetic: Realism, Sovereignty, and Transnational Experience* (Oxford, 2015); *The Ends of History*, a co-edited special issue of *Victorian Studies*; and *Worlding Realisms*, a special issue of *Novel: A Forum on Fiction*.

Margaret P. Harvey is a doctoral candidate at Rice University. Her work focuses on inquiries into gendered concepts of value in political economy, material culture, and reproductive labor by authors from the mid- to late nineteenth century. In her dissertation she examines how Victorian ideas and thinking about value intervened and intersected with debates about and depictions of the woman question.

Kay Heath is a professor of English and assistant dean of liberal arts at Georgia Gwinnett College. She is the author of *Aging by the Book: The Emergence of Midlife in Victorian Britain* (SUNY, 2009) as well as various articles on Victorian literature, culture, and aging.

Suzanne Keen is Thomas Broadus Professor of English and dean of the college at Washington and Lee University, where she teaches the novel in English and narrative. Keen's books include *Victorian Renovations of the Novel: Narrative Annexes and the Boundaries of Representation* (1998); *Romances of the Archive in Contemporary British Fiction* (2001); *Empathy and the Novel* (2007); and most recently, *Thomas Hardy's Brains: Victorian Psychology, Neurology, and Hardy's Imagination* (2014), which was shortlisted for Phi Beta Kappa's Christian Gauss Award.

James Kincaid, still reportedly at large, is author (he says) of *The Novels of Anthony Trollope* and some other scholarly books and articles. He has turned in the past years to writing novels and short stories, areas in which he is less likely to do harm.

Margaret Markwick, from the University of Exeter, is a Victorianist with special interest in gender studies, narratology, and the Victorian church. Her first full-length study of Trollope was *Trollope and Women* (Hambledon and Trollope Soc., 1997). Her second monograph, *New Men in Trollope: Rewriting the Victorian Male*, was published by Ashgate in November 2007, and *The Politics of Gender in the Novels of Anthony Trollope: Readings for the Twenty-First Century*, co-edited with

Contributors

Deborah Denenholz Morse and Regenia Gagnier, was published by Ashgate in 2009. *Trollope Underground*, a collection of essays co-authored with Deborah Denenholz Morse, is forthcoming. She has contributed widely to other collections of essays, and is currently exploring the relationship between the development of Anglican thought and the expression of religious belief in the mid-Victorian novel.

Michael Martel is a PhD candidate in English at the University of California, Davis. His dissertation, "Anytown UK: the Local State of Victorian Fiction," explores how novelistic form helped coordinate a widespread dispersal of state authority across England's local institutions. He has published on Anthony Trollope and state figuration in *Victorians: A Journal of Culture and Literature*.

Elsie Michie is a professor and chair of the English Department at Louisiana State University. Her books include *Outside the Pale: Cultural Exclusion, Gender Difference, and the Victorian Woman Writer* (Cornell, 1993), *The Vulgar Question of Money: Heiresses, Materialism, and the Novel of Manners from Jane Austen to Henry James* (Johns Hopkins, 2011), the essay collection *Victorian Vulgarity: Taste in Verbal and Visual Culture* (co-edited with Susan David Bernstein, Ashgate, 2009), and editions of Frances Trollope's *The Lottery of Marriage* (Pickering and Chatto, 2011) and *Domestic Manners of the Americans* (Oxford, 2014). She is currently working on a book entitled *Trollopizing the Canon* that explores Frances Trollope's impact on canonical Victorian writers from Charles Dickens to George Eliot.

Helena Michie is the author of numerous books and articles on Victorian culture and gender studies. She has recently published, with Robyn Warhol, *Love Among the Archives: Writing the Lives of Sir George Scharf, Victorian Bachelor* (Edinburgh, 2015). Other books include: *Victorian Honeymoons: Journeys to the Conjugal* (Cambridge, 2006); *The Flesh Made Word: Female Figures and Women's Bodies* (Oxford, 1987); *Sororophobia: Differences Among Women in Literature and Culture* (Oxford, 1991); and as co-author, with Naomi R. Cahn, *Confinements: Fertility and Infertility in Contemporary United States Culture* (Rutgers, 1997). She is the co-editor, with Ronald Thomas, of the essay collection *Nineteenth-Century Geographies: The Transformation of Space from the Victorian Age to the American Century* (Rutgers, 2002). She teaches courses in feminist theory, literary theory, and Victorian literature and culture. She also teaches classes and workshops on professional writing.

Heather Miner (PhD, Rice University, 2013; MA, University of Virginia, 2007) is an instructor and advisor at Lewis & Clark College in Portland, Oregon, and specializes in nineteenth-century British literature and culture, with particular research interests in Victorian ecocriticism, architecture, and heritage studies. She has published articles in the *Victorian Review*, *Victoriographies*, *Nineteenth-Century Gender Studies*, and the *Virginia Quarterly*. Currently, she is researching her first monograph, entitled *Saving Place: Nineteenth-Century Environmentalism and Cultures of Conservation*.

Grace Moore's *Dickens and Empire* was shortlisted for the NSW Premier's Award for Literary Scholarship in 2006. She is the author of *The Victorian Novel in Context* and editor of *Pirates and Mutineers of the Nineteenth Century* and (with Andrew Maunder) *Victorian Crime, Madness, and Sensation*. She is a senior research fellow at the Australian Research Council's Centre for Excellence in the History of Emotions and lectures in literary studies at the University of Melbourne. Her most recent work is on Australian settlers and bushfires, and she is also working on a project on Dickens and emotion.

Contributors

Deborah Denenholz Morse is the Vera W. Barkley Term Professor of English and inaugural fellow of the Center for the Liberal Arts at The College of William and Mary. She is the author of *Women in Trollope's Palliser Novels* (1987) and *Reforming Trollope: Race, Gender, and Englishness in the Novels of Anthony Trollope* (Ashgate, 2013). She is the co-editor of the collections *The Erotics of Instruction* (with Regina Barreca, 1997), *Victorian Animal Dreams: Representations of Animals in Victorian Literature and Culture* (with Martin Danahay, 2007), and *The Politics of Gender in Anthony Trollope's Novels* (with Margaret Markwick and Regenia Gagnier, 2009). She is co-editor (with Diane Long Hoeveler) of two collections on the Brontës, *The Blackwell Companion to the Brontës* and *Charlotte Brontë: Time, Space and Place*, both forthcoming in 2016. She has published essays on the Brontës, Trollope, Gaskell, Maxine Hong Kingston, A. S. Byatt, Mona Simpson, Kay Boyle, Elizabeth Coles Taylor, Hesba Stretton, Catherine Cookson, and within animal studies.

Michelle Mouton is a professor of literature at Cornell College, where she teaches Romantic and Victorian literature. Publications and research interests include elections and legislative politics in the works of Anthony Trollope, Margaret Oliphant, George Eliot, and George Meredith; nineteenth-century liberalism and the Second Reform Act; and the intersections between nineteenth-century food and travel writing.

Kate Osborne is a PhD candidate at King's College London. She works on the early to mid-Victorian novel, and is particularly interested in representations of writing technologies, the circulation of data, and literacy.

Anna Peak teaches in the Intellectual Heritage Program at Temple University. Her work has appeared in *Victorian Literature and Culture*, *Victorian Review*, and *SEL: Studies in English Literature, 1600–1900*. Her current book project, *Not a Universal Language: Musical Aesthetics and Literary Formalism*, argues that British aestheticism may be redefined in terms of its self-conscious creation of a musical aesthetic that implicates British aestheticism in the racial theories of the time and that directly influenced the literary formalism of the early twentieth century. A second project, *The Victorian Invention of China*, traces the growth of Sinophobia in nineteenth-century England with relation to social class, arguing that Sinophobia was shaped not only by the lower classes but also by the upper and educated classes.

Robert Polhemus, the Joseph S. Atha Professor in Humanities and English, Emeritus, at Stanford University, is the author of a pioneering twentieth century study of Trollope, *The Changing World of Anthony Trollope* (1968); *Comic Faith: The Great Tradition from Austen to Joyce* (1980); *Erotic Faith: Being in Love from Austen to D. H. Lawrence* (1990); *Critical Reconstructions: The Relationship of Life and Fiction: Essays in Honor of Ian Watt* (co-edited with Roger Henkle, 1994); and *Lot's Daughters: Sex, Redemption, and Women's Quest for Authority* (2005). He is at work now on three projects: a book on Woody Allen, *Hate Woody, Late Woody, Great Woody*; a study of moral conflict between religion and works of art, *Devices to Root Out Evil: Faith and Art*; and a work on the muralist Jose Clemente Orozco's *Epic of American Civilization* (*Orozco: The Epic of American Civilization*), one of the very greatest twentieth-century works of American art.

Suzanne Raitt is a chancellor professor of English at the College of William & Mary. Her books include *May Sinclair: A Modern Victorian* (Oxford, 2000), *Vita and Virginia: The Work and Friendship of V. Sackville-West and Virginia Woolf* (Oxford, 1993), and *Virginia Woolf's "To the Lighthouse"* (St Martin's, 1990). She also co-edited a collection of essays with Trudi Tate called *Women's Fiction and the Great War* (Oxford, 1997), and in 1995 she published an edited collection of essays on lesbian criticism, *Volcanoes and Pearl Divers* (Onlywomen Press). Editions include a

Norton Critical Edition of Virginia Woolf's *Jacob's Room* in 2007, Katherine Mansfield's *Something Childish and Other Stories* for Penguin in 1996, and Virginia Woolf's *Night and Day* for Oxford World's Classics in 1992. She has published numerous essays and articles in journals, including *Modernism/modernity* and *History Workshop Journal*, and for twelve years, she was on the editorial collective of *Feminist Studies*. She is currently working on a scholarly edition of Virginia Woolf's *Orlando*, co-edited with Ian Blyth, for Cambridge University Press; and completing a series of articles on waste and efficiency in British culture in the late nineteenth and early twentieth centuries.

David Skilton is a professor emeritus at Cardiff University. He is a productive critic and editor of Trollope's work, and one of the founders of illustration studies as a distinctive discipline.

Jenny Bourne Taylor is a professor emerita in English literature at the University of Sussex, UK. Her publications include *In the Secret Theatre of Home: Wilkie Collins, Sensation Narrative and Nineteenth-Century Psychology* (Routledge, 1988; revised edn, Victorian Secrets, 2014); ed., *The Cambridge Companion to Wilkie Collins* (Cambridge, 2006); with Margot Finn and Michael Lobban, *Legitimacy and Illegitimacy in Nineteenth-Century Law, Literature and History* (Palgrave Macmillan, 2010), and ed. with John Kucich, *The Oxford History of the Novel in English, vol. 3, The Nineteenth-Century Novel 1820–1880* (Oxford, 2012). Her essays on Trollope include: 'Bastards to the Time: Legitimacy as Legal Fiction in Trollope's Later Novels' in *The Politics of Gender in Anthony Trollope's Novels* (Ashgate, 2009), and 'Trollope and the Sensation Novel' in *The Cambridge Companion to Anthony Trollope* (Cambridge, 2011).

Robert Tracy is a professor emeritus of English and Celtic studies at the University of California, Berkeley, where he has taught for fifty years. He has been a visiting professor of American literature at the University of Leeds, of Russian literature at Wellesley, and of Irish literature at Trinity College, Dublin. His publications include recent articles on Dickens, Trollope, Seamus Heaney, and Brian Friel, and on Irish sculptors Oliver Sheppard and Seamus Murphy; *Trollope's Later Novels* (1978); editions of works by Synge, Trollope, Le Fanu, and Flann O'Brien; *Stone* (1981), a translation from Russian of Osip Mandelstam's *Kamen'*; and *The Unappeasable Host: Studies in Irish Identities* (1998). He is a founder and a past president of the American Conference for Irish Studies, Western Division, and was president of the Dickens Society during 2008–9.

Mark W. Turner is a professor of English at King's College London, where his teaching interests include nineteenth-century literature/culture and queer studies. He has long-standing research interests in the work of Anthony Trollope and is the author of *Trollope and the Magazines: Gendered Issues in Mid-Victorian Britain* (2000), in addition to a number of articles and chapters in books. He is the co-editor, with John Stokes, of the scholarly edition of Oscar Wilde's journalism for the Oxford English Texts collected works series (2013), and has edited a number of essay collections, including most recently, *The News of the World and the British Press, 1843–2011* (edited with Laurel Brake and Chandrika Kaul, 2016).

Frederik Van Dam is a postdoctoral research fellow at the University of Leuven (KU Leuven) and the Research Foundation Flanders (FWO). He is the author of *Anthony Trollope's Late Style: Victorian Liberalism and Literary Form* (Edinburgh, 2016) and is currently working on a literary history of nineteenth-century diplomacy. In the context of the Trollope Bicentennial Conference, of which he was the principal organiser, he also created a film about J. Hillis Miller, *The Pleasure of that Obstinacy*.

Contributors

Tamara S. Wagner obtained her PhD from Cambridge University and is currently an associate professor at Nanyang Technological University in Singapore. Her books include *Financial Speculation in Victorian Fiction: Plotting Money and the Novel Genre, 1815–1901* (2010) and *Longing: Narratives of Nostalgia in the British Novel, 1740–1890* (2004), as well as the edited collections *Consuming Culture in the Long Nineteenth-Century* (2007), *Antifeminism and the Victorian Novel: Rereading Nineteenth-Century Women Writers* (2009), *Victorian Settler Narratives: Emigrants, Cosmopolitans and Returnees in Nineteenth-Century Literature* (2011), and *Domestic Fiction in Colonial Australia and New Zealand* (2014). Wagner's current projects include *Victorian Narratives of Failed Emigration: Settlers, Returnees, and Nineteenth-Century Literature in English* (forthcoming in 2016) and research into Victorian infancy.

ACKNOWLEDGEMENTS

So many of us can recall who first pointed us toward Anthony Trollope, and we, the editors, would like to thank Christopher Herbert, who influenced Deborah Denenholz Morse in her early days, Mary Saunders, who first introduced Mark W. Turner to his novels, and John Letts, who encouraged Margaret Markwick when she first set out to write about Trollope's works.

We are grateful to the Bridgeman Art Library and Peter Nahum Ltd for permission to use their image of Sir John Everett Millais's *Portrait of a Girl*, and to Tate Britain for their permission to use their image of *The Order of Release*, again by Sir John Everett Millais. We gratefully acknowledge Martin Beisly's generosity in giving us his image of *A Private View at the Royal Academy, 1881*, by William Powell Frith, and permission to use it. And we are grateful also to our institutions, the College of William & Mary, Williamsburg, USA, the University of Exeter, UK, and Kings College London, UK, for their support.

And finally, we are, as ever, grateful for the computer technology skills of Charlie Morse and Chris Markwick, who turned this collection of essays into a book.

ANTHONY TROLLOPE
An overview

Trollope wrote forty-seven novels, four travel books, four biographical studies, five collections of short stories, and three collections of non-fiction sketches, in addition to a range of journalism. Not all of that extensive output is listed here. The "Chronological List of Trollope's Works," in N. John Hall, *Trollope: A Biography* (Clarendon, 1991), 560–2, remains an excellent source for the full publication details of Trollope's works.

1815	Born in Keppel Street, Bloomsbury, London, son of Thomas Anthony Trollope, a barrister, and Frances Milton ("Fanny") Trollope, an author.
1816	Trollope family moves to Harrow.
1823	Attends Harrow School as a day student, an experience recalled bitterly in *An Autobiography*.
1827	Attends Winchester College. His mother moves to America, initially to join a settlement in Tennessee, but quickly moves on, setting up a store in Cincinnati.
1828	Father and brother Tom join his mother in America, leaving Anthony entirely alone for six months.
1830	Returns to Harrow School, due to family's financial insecurity.
1832	Fanny Trollope's *Domestic Manners of the Americans* is published and provides much needed financial support for the family.
1834	Trollope family moves to Bruges, Belgium, to escape the consequences of bankruptcy.
1834–41	Works as a junior clerk in the General Post Office in London. Older brother Henry dies in December 1834; father dies in Bruges, October 1835; and younger sister, Emily, dies in Hadleigh in 1836.
1841–5	Moves to Ireland, as deputy postal surveyor. Begins writing novels and takes up foxhunting, which becomes a lifelong passion.
1844	Marries Rose Heseltine, with whom he has two children, Henry Merivale and Frederick James Anthony.
1847–8	Publishes his first novels, *The Macdermots of Ballycloran* (1847) and *The Kellys and the O'Kellys* (1848), both set in Ireland and which speak to contemporary politics. Neither does well.

1851	After a postal mission to England and the Channel Islands, recommends the development of the now-famous pillar box for the collection of post.
1855	Publishes *The Warden*, the first of what becomes the Barsetshire chronicles, a series of six novels set in the imaginary county of Barset. Writes *The New Zealander* and begins writing *Barchester Towers*.
1857	Publishes *Barchester Towers* and *The Three Clerks*.
1858	Publishes *Doctor Thorne*, and undertakes a postal mission to Egypt, the Holy Land, Malta, Gibraltar, Spain, the West Indies, and Central America, which provides significant material for travel stories and travel books.
1859	Publishes his first travel book, *The West Indies and the Spanish Main*. Moves to Waltham House, Waltham Cross, Hertfordshire.
1860	Begins serialization of *Framley Parsonage* in *Cornhill Magazine*, edited by his literary hero, William Makepeace Thackeray. Henceforth, nearly all of his novels are conceived of, and many published in, serial or part-issue form. During the 1860s, Trollope established his pattern of literary labour, writing every morning, from 5:30 to 8:30, at the rate of 1,000 words per hour, before heading off to work at the Post Office. In Florence, where his brother lived, meets the American Kate Field, with whom he forms a lasting and important friendship.
1861	Publishes *Framley Parsonage* in volume form, along with the short story collection based on his travels, *Tales of All Countries*. The novel *Orley Farm* is serialized in monthly parts from March 1861 to October 1862.
1862	*The Struggles of Brown, Jones and Robinson* serialized in *Cornhill*. Publishes the travel book *North America*. Becomes a member of the Garrick Club.
1863	*Tales of All Countries, Second Series* published. Fanny Trollope dies.
1864	Publishes *The Small House at Allington* in volume form, after serialization in *Cornhill*. Begins publishing *Can You Forgive Her?* in monthly numbers, the first of what becomes the Palliser series, about the machinations of the Commons, influential political families, and London Society.
1865	Along with a group of others, including G. H. Lewes, helps to found the liberal *Fortnightly Review*, which becomes an important liberal voice of the higher journalism, and for which he provides the inaugural serial, *The Belton Estate*, and some journalism, including the important article, 'On Anonymous Journalism.' Starts writing hunting, travel, and clerical sketches for the newly founded London evening paper, the *Pall Mall Gazette*, all of which are later published in volume form.
1866–7	Publishes *The Last Chronicle of Barset*, the last of the Barsetshire novels, in weekly numbers, before publishing it in volume form in 1867.
1867	Resigns from the Post Office; publishes *The Claverings* and *Lotta Schmidt and Other Stories*.
1867–70	Edits the monthly shilling magazine *St. Paul's*, where he serialized two novels, *Phineas Finn* and *Ralph the Heir*, a series of short stories collected as *An Editor's Tales* (1871), and some journalism.
1868	Unsuccessful bid as the Liberal candidate for Beverley in the House of Commons. Travels to the United States.
1869	*He Knew He Was Right* published, after appearing in weekly penny part-issue numbers.
1870	Publishes *The Commentaries of Caesar* and *The Vicar of Bullhampton*.

1871–2	Begins serializing *The Eustace Diamonds* in the *Fortnightly Review*. Moves from Waltham Cross to Montagu Square, London. Makes the first of two extended trips to Australia to visit his son Fred, also taking in New Zealand and the United States. Meets Fred's fiancée, Susan Ferrand. His letters about his travels, signed "Antipodean", appear in the *Daily Telegraph* in 1871.
1873	*Australia and New Zealand* published, based on his travels. *Phineas Redux* begins serialization in the *Graphic*.
1874	Monthly numbers of *The Way We Live Now* begin, before volume publication in 1875. *Lady Anna* published, after serialization in the *Fortnightly Review*, and the short Australian novel *Harry Heathcote of Gangoil* published, after appearing as a Christmas story in the *Graphic*.
1875	Second trip to Australia to visit his son Fred, also including visit to Rome, Naples, and Ceylon. *The Prime Minister* begins to appear in monthly shilling numbers, before publication in four vols in 1876. Begins writing *An Autobiography*.
1877	*The American Senator* published, after serialization in the monthly magazine *Temple Bar*. Travels to South Africa.
1878	Travel book *South Africa* published, along with *Is He Popenjoy?*, after serialization in *All the Year Round*.
1879	Publishes a short biography of Thackeray, along with *John Caldigate*, previously serialized in *Blackwood's Magazine*, and *Cousin Henry*, previously serialized in the *Manchester Weekly Times* and the *North British Weekly Mail*.
1880	*The Duke's Children* published, after serialization in *All the Year Round*, along with *The Life of Cicero*.
1882	*Mr. Scarborough's Family* is serialized in *All the Year Round* before being published in volume form in 1883. Dies in London on December 6, after suffering a stroke during a jovial dinner party.
1883	*An Autobiography* published posthumously, along with two novels, *The Landleaguers* and *An Old Man's Love*.

INTRODUCTION

In the late 1960s through the 1970s, a few intrepid scholars – Robert Polhemus, Ruth apRoberts, James Kincaid, Juliet McMaster, Reginald Terry, and Robert Tracy – arguably changed the way Anthony Trollope's work was subsequently read. Hitherto, Trollope was assumed too frequently to be a Victorian novelist of huge popular appeal, but of no academic significance. This generation of critics refocused our attention, emphasizing not just his skilled craftsmanship but also his substantial and nuanced art. Since then Trollope has received the long-overdue attention his work demands, as scholars have increasingly recognised how his writing is illuminated by the perspectives of disciplines across the humanities, social sciences – and of late the natural sciences, particularly Darwin studies. Today, Trollope is examined from the point of view of economic theory, sociology, emerging scientific thinking in psychology, gender studies, critical theory, ecocriticism, and postcolonial studies, plus very new ideologies, such as food studies and illustration studies, emerging fields where Trollope is a central source of material. With breadth of scholarship has also come a new depth in terms of close reading and analysis of Trollope in relation to narrative theory and technique.

Although Trollope scholarship took some time to gather force, he has always been, as he remains, among the most popular Victorian novelists with a wide range of readers. Although he was not the first of our great writers to publish an autobiography (John Stuart Mill's autobiography had been published in 1873), it is certainly true that *An Autobiography* whetted his audience's appetite for greater detail of his life. Trollope assiduously defended his right to privacy, and that of other celebrated writers,[1] and destroyed so much – like all his letters from Kate Field, and his journals – which might put flesh on the well-known bones of his life, such as the impoverishment of his parents, his misery at school, his mother's rescuing of the family finances with her pen, his career in the Post Office, and his prodigious output as one of his time's favourite novelists. In 1913, T.H.S. Escott, working from notes made face-to-face with Trollope, brought out *Trollope, His Originals and Associates*. Eminently readable, Escott is particularly strong on details of Trollope's life in Ireland. This was followed in 1927 by the belle-lettrist bibliographer Michael Sadleir's *Anthony Trollope: A Commentary*, which fleshed out so much of Fanny Trollope's until then unexplored life, while relying heavily on Escott for the detail of Anthony Trollope's life. While his critiques of the novels lack much depth, Sadleir does sterling work in keeping the thirty-five novels not in the Barchester or Palliser sequences in the public eye.

Introduction

In 1972, James Pope Hennessy published the first of the modern full-length biographies of Trollope. It must be said that much of the length of his book consists of accounts, largely plot-retelling, of the novels, with little to add to Sadleir in the way of factual detail of Trollope's life, though he is strong on Irish background. As N. John Hall points out, the work is marred by inaccuracy, and he pulls him up for the lack of notation, and the perfunctory bibliography of Trollope's works.[2] Three years later came C. P. Snow's beautifully presented *Trollope: An Illustrated Biography*. Snow differs from Escott and Pope Hennessy in accepting at face value Trollope's own account of his childhood misery: "twenty years of neglect and humiliation" (p. 11). Brief as it is, Snow does address Trollope's career as a civil servant, and turned up good evidence about his contribution to the development of postal services.

The most thorough investigation of Trollope and his years of public service is to be found in Robert Super's *Trollope in the Post Office* (1982), a work he followed up in 1988 with a full-scale biography, *The Chronicler of Barsetshire: A Life of Anthony Trollope*. Super's version of Trollope's schooldays, in contrast to Snow's, plays down the humiliation of the constant floggings, and quickly moves on to Trollope's career in the Post Office. This is meticulously recounted, and is the backdrop to Super's very full descriptions of each writing project as it is published. Like Snow, Richard Mullen in *Anthony Trollope: A Victorian in His World* (1990) accepts Trollope's version of his schooldays, though he dwells more on the probable comparative happiness of his first eight years before he went to Harrow. Mullen's work is half as long again as Super's, largely accounted for by the plethora of sociological and cultural detail of the times Trollope lived in. N. John Hall's *Trollope: A Biography* was published in 1991. Hall's now standard edition of Trollope's letters had been published in 1983, and his editorial work there shows. His account of Trollope's adult life is fastidious; his empathy for his subject reflected in his lifetime study. Victoria Glendinning's *Trollope* (1992), while encompassing the same material, uses the vantage of her own gender to examine more revealingly Trollope's ambivalences about the aspirations of women, and her own Yorkshire origins enhance her reading of Rose Heseltine, given what scanty information there is about her. This plethora of major works on Trollope's life is a testament not only to his popularity but also to his enduring interest as a quintessential liberal Victorian.

Our research companion seeks to capture both the breadth of scope and the depth of analysis in contemporary Trollope scholarship, and, to that end, we have enlisted a combination of established Trollopians alongside newer critical voices. We have tried to be as unprescriptive as possible, encouraging scholars to think in new directions as they wish. Thus some of the most well-established Trollope critics have been given the opportunity to think in wholly new ways. James Kincaid, best known for his work on Trollope's comedy, has here written on Trollope and late-Romantic theories of tragedy. Robert Polhemus, celebrated for his work on Trollope in relation to the changing currents of his times, explores the meaning of art and the artist in Trollope's work and life. Robert Tracy, recognised for his work on Trollope's late fiction, here considers Trollope's first novel, *The Macdermots of Ballycloran*. In other words, we have sought to ensure that the work of generations of Trollope scholars is recognised in the volume, while encouraging ever new scholarship to emerge.

We think this approach has resulted in a selection of essays which portrays both the status and the state of Trollope studies today, and where it is going tomorrow. All of the essays in the volume locate their arguments within a review of the literature on Trollope in its subject area as well as making an original contribution to Trollope scholarship. This has been an important part of our remit, to ensure that the essays are useful in providing an overview of a topic, while also ensuring that new ideas emerge that will shift the debates in Trollope studies in future. Our hope is that we have created an indispensable resource for Trollope scholars, one that will delight as well as instruct them for many years to come, both representing all the good work that has already been done and pointing the way forward to new work yet to come.

Introduction

We have organized the *Companion* into seven separate sections: "Political Settings"; "Culture and Gender"; "Critical Theory"; "Illustration Studies"; "Trollopian Preoccupations"; "Creed and Cant"; and "Global Trollope." These intentionally broad sections are neither absolute nor defining – some essays might sit happily in other sections – but they do provide meaningful ways of organizing the diverse work on Trollope that scholars currently undertake. These sections also, to some extent, reflect some of the more significant intellectual moves in literary studies in the past generation. The importance of both gender and critical theory, for example, which is so striking in many essays, has its roots extending back decades, to the work of feminist and deconstructivist scholars, whereas a more recent emphasis on global issues extends the work of postcolonial criticism, ecocriticism, and other fields of study. These sections are not the final word, but rather help to map a wide array of subjects, approaches, and critical points of view.

Political settings

While conventionally Trollope's reputation as a "political" novelist rests with the "Palliser" series, Lauren Goodlad and Frederik Van Dam show how it is in the Barchester novels that we can first trace Trollope's view of the old world order being "shouldered out" by new movements in the metropolis. Goodlad and Van Dam offer a chronological study to trace the development of his radicalism through the concept of the "divided mind", melding issues of realism and liberalism. In unpeeling Trollope's description of himself as an "advanced conservative Liberal", they uncover him expressing pro-union and anti-slavery views; he endorses the campaign for universal state education, and dismisses the Tories as all hocus-pocus and conjuring tricks. They finish with a rare examination of *The Landleaguers*, Trollope's final and unfinished novel.

In contrast, Michael Martel seeks to demonstrate a conscious link between Trollope's professional grasp of the principles of a universal postal service and his understanding of the reach of the state into all the functions of government, a concept he calls "addressability". Using concepts of metonymy, Martel shows Trollope's serial fictions and the intertwining of characters from different novels in the series deepens Trollope's presentation of a state quietly but purposefully pursuing the common good.

Culture and gender

In the famous Frith painting, *A Private View at the Royal Academy, 1881*, Trollope is standing by two women and a young girl, perhaps watching his fellow viewers as he simultaneously writes something down in a notebook. As Frith's representation of the novelist suggests, Trollope was a close observer of his fellow human beings. Among the most acutely observed elements of Victorian culture and society are the tensions gender ideals and realities generated in both men and women. *The Routledge Research Companion to Anthony Trollope* explores Trollope's responses to varied issues of gender, from his observations upon masculine prerogative through his sympathies with women's desire for equality with men to his tolerance of homosexuality in some of his fiction. Trollope's art reveals an intricate and at times conflicted vision of what Robert Polhemus long ago termed the "changing world" of Victorian England, in which agitation for women's rights and reassessments of masculinity were both significant aspects of that change. The first half of Deborah Denenholz Morse's essay is concerned with tracing the legacies of Trollope scholarship on women, from Henry James's commentary in *Partial Portraits* that Trollope's girls were always "delightfully tender, modest, and fresh" to Christopher Herbert's, Margaret Markwick's, and Morse's own readings of Trollope as sympathetic to women's awareness of their unequal state under the law of the land, to the extent that Morse calls Trollope a "feminist". In the second half of her essay, Morse locates Trollope's exposure of the misogyny of impotent, diseased upper-class manhood in the lesser-known novels *The Claverings* (1867), *Sir Harry Hotspur of Humblethwaite* (1870), and *Is He Popenjoy?* (1878). Morse argues that Trollope continues to expand the critique of his culture's entrenched gender biases in these less celebrated works through his "depiction of the thought processes of upper-caste males and his dissection of masculine privilege in Victorian culture and society. In his critique of the lassitude and misogyny of aristocratic Englishmen coupled with his loving depiction of vibrant women – including an actress and a stablekeeper's granddaughter – Trollope interrogates the masculine prerogatives that underlie English civilization."

Hyson Cooper, in "Anthony Trollope's Conduct-Book Fiction for Men," looks at a more positive vision of Trollope's male characters. Cooper examines Trollope's emphasis upon masculine feeling and its role in a man's conduct as a gentleman. Cooper argues that Trollope cares more about what men *feel* about what they do than about what they actually do – and that this is true for men of all social classes. In analyzing Trollope's representations of men, Cooper emphasizes Trollope's nuanced creations: "Trollope's men are not divided into those who would never dream of behaving badly and those who choose not to behave well, thus giving readers an easy choice of whom to emulate; instead Trollope takes us deep into the process by which men who explore their feelings arrive at courses of behavior."

Mary Jean Corbett's essay, "Women, Violence, and Modernity," pursues another avenue in examining the relationship of the sexes in Trollope's fiction, as she investigates the grounds of male violence against women in *The Way We Live Now* in relation to Trollope's stance on women's rights. Corbett sees Trollope as ambivalent about a modernism that includes the domestic violence of the ruthless financier Augustus Melmotte, even if it also includes the freedom of Hetta Carbury to marry the man she loves rather than be compelled to marry her avuncular cousin Roger Carbury for family convenience. Ultimately, Corbett argues, even in subordinating the "women's plots" to the Melmotte narrative, "*The Way We Live Now* demonstrates, quietly but persistently, that particular forms of violence continue to attend the entry of young women into the courtship practices and marriage systems of modern life."

Suzanne Raitt's essay, "Marital Law in *He Knew He Was Right*," argues that many of Anthony Trollope's novels explore the dynamics of marriage in all their complexity, but few are as focused on the energies of marital failure as *He Knew He Was Right*. Her essay reads the novel in the context of nineteenth-century marital law reform, arguing that the novel is a sustained engagement with some of the most complex and controversial aspects of the divorce debate, including the definition of marital cruelty, the double standard, and mothers' rights to custody of their children. As Raitt argues about the divorce debate's influence, "it is this profoundly adversarial model of marital breakdown that shapes both Trevelyans' attitudes to their conflict." Through the three other couples in the novel who strive for equality in their marriages, however, by the end of the novel, Raitt believes that "the defensive, adversarial model that emerges from the 1857 Act is supplanted by a different, more joyful version of the modern, in which marriages are resilient because the parties to them are free to disobey, to err and to be forgiven. In a world like that, there would be no need for divorce."

Jenny Bourne Taylor's essay, "Legitimacy and Illegitimacy," also deals with Victorian law as it is imbricated with gender. Bourne Taylor, like Raitt, looks at the novels in the context of Victorian law; as she explains, "debates on marriage law reform did not lead to any improvement in the legal situation of illegitimate children – indeed the 1857 Matrimonial Causes Act (which condoned the husband's, but not the wife's adultery) was underpinned by entrenched anxieties about the threat of adulterine bastardy to hereditary estates." She examines several novels from all periods of Trollope's career, from *Doctor Thorne* (1858) through *Ralph the Heir* (1871), *Lady Anna*

Introduction

(1874), *Is He Popenjoy?* (1878), and *Mr. Scarborough's Family* (1883), that "form part of Trollope's recurrent interrogation of the competing claims of contract, blood and intimacy; that is, formal law, dynastic imperative and emotional bonds – those often contradictory ties that make up the family, but which are most clearly focused through the problematically legitimate heir." Bourne Taylor's essay plumbs the intricate relationship between gender and legitimacy in arguing that Trollope's novels explore and ultimately question the societal assumptions that conventionally underlie this connection.

"Trollope and Material Culture," Margaret Harvey's essay, shifts the focus to the period before marriage and the relation between material objects and female identity. Harvey argues that "objects and descriptions of material culture often appear around and in tandem with descriptions of female subjectivity and gendered notions of value." She examines wedding trousseaux in particular in three novels spanning twelve years of Trollope's career: *Framley Parsonage* (1861), *He Knew He Was Right* (1869), and *The Eustace Diamonds* (1872). In all of these works, Harvey finds that Trollope questions the function of material objects in defining a woman's identity and discredits the possibility of "material culture and commodified goods to grant women the kind of value and agency that they so desperately seek and deserve."

In "Trollope and the Body," Sophie Gilmartin explores Trollope's fascination with portraying the actual bodies of his male and female characters, whether they blush from desire or act in violence. Trollope is always aware of bodies in space, bodies moving or standing still, bodies gesturing, flushing with colour, trembling with fear or anger. Gilmartin illuminates the subject of Trollope and the body by looking at depictions of characters' bodies, including Lucy Robarts's desiring body in *Framley Parsonage* (1861), George Vavasor's violent movements in *Can You Forgive Her?*, and in *The Way We Live Now*, Hetta Carbury's newly modern woman's body, moving through London on foot and on the omnibus to visit her rival, Winifred Hurtle, or to meet her lover, Paul Montague. About Hetta's body as it navigates London "unprotected", Gilmartin states that Trollope "describes new women who are less circumscribed by the distancing hoops of the crinoline, who are freer in their movements and independence, and he describes also new men who emerge in the period to meet and respond to these women in his novels of emergence."

Critical theory

Trollope's smooth-flowing, seamless prose had seemed to defy deep analysis until Michael Riffaterre's groundbreaking 1982 essay, "Trollope's Metonymies," demonstrated the richness that flowed when once the acuity of critical theory penetrated that resistant surface. This selection of essays, by applying several discrete interventions of critical theory to Trollope's texts, uncovers remarkable subtleties in his prose style, his narrative techniques, and his gender-awareness.

James Kincaid's deadly serious purpose to make us reread comic romance as Nietzschean tragedy is wrapped in a security blanket of eloquent and deceptive light-heartedness. His exploration of "that roar which lies on the other side of silence" takes us into Josiah Crawley's internalisation of Silenus's existential pit, along with Roger Scatcherd, Plantagenet Palliser, Louis Trevelyan, Lily Dale, and, ultimately, Phineas Finn, reinterpreted here as the man who is brought face-to-face with the empty, purposeless world of politics he has chosen to live in.

Jonathan Farina's original and witty essay focuses on Trollope's use of "of course". Critiquing other critics who have accepted at face value the adage that Trollope's style is rooted in the commonplace, Farina takes the phrase "of course" and examines the myriad ways it occurs, and the multitude of layers of meaning he incorporates into this "prosaic", everyday phrase. His close reading of *Rachel Ray* demonstrates Trollope knowingly manipulating and ironising Rachel viewing the sunset with Luke so that the ordinary becomes the extraordinary.

Helena Michie is similarly alive to the characteristic shape of Trollope's sentences, and his fascination with the art of thinking. She identifies the centrality of internal revision: small changes, verbal and syntactical, in consecutive sentences that build up to a specifically Trollopian form of realism in his representation of the process of thinking. "Free indirect discourse", where the point of view of the text segues between character and narrator and between a plurality of narrative voices almost indistinguishably, is the key element of her theoretical framework. On this she builds close readings of the interiority of Alice Vavasor, Caroline Waddington, and Lily Dale, with some revelations about Trollope's style and technique, and his response to women prone to "deep thought".

Building on the theorising of Dorrit Cohn's representations of consciousness, and using *Orley Farm* as her source, Suzanne Keen takes us through an erudite exploration of the way Trollope manipulates the passionate feelings of both his characters and his readers. Focusing on theories of "free indirect discourse", she sets out her concepts of internalised narration and instrumental thought in the manner in which Trollope speaks of Lady Mason and her suffering. She finishes with a reappraisal of Henry James which is refreshingly sympathetic and appreciative, after an era when it has been fashionable to disregard his contribution in favour of the formalist schools.

Helen Lucy Blythe's study of the narratology of *Kept in the Dark*, with its interest in the Russian formalists and their theories of *sjuzhet*, has clear affinities with Keen's microanalysis. Blythe's focus is the exclusion of Cecilia Western from the telling of her own story, from narrative authority. Grounding her study in the critical structures of astutely observant early reviewers, she shows how narratology has finally put a name to their practical techniques, in the face of James and his twentieth-century followers. Blythe's analysis finishes on a staunchly feminist point, asking, "What does it mean for a woman to be constructed, read, and interpreted by men, and how difficult is it for a woman to take control of her own story?", a recurrent theme of the "Culture and Gender" section of this volume.

Margaret Markwick has written an exploration of the narratology of Trollope's four biographies and the *Autobiography* to discover an experimental Trollope well ahead of his time. For while biographies in his era were conventionally three-volume cradle-to-the-grave behemoths, Markwick discovers a biographer writing powerful first-person narratives, playing with chronology, and employing defamiliarisation techniques that are strikingly modern. She views his forays into life-writing through the prism of Borges's short essay "Borges and I", to conclude that Trollope, like Borges, has a fine appreciation of the subtleties of the relationship between an authorial "I" and the existent narrator.

Darwin's *Origin of Species* was first published in November 1859, just as Trollope was transferring back to the mainland from Ireland, and just as he became embedded into the literary and scientific milieu of men's clubs and magazines. Lauren Cameron bolsters the arguments for Trollope's familiarity with Darwinian thought by exploring women from his Palliser novels – all written after the *Origin of Species* – as he explores the limits of variations and the adaptive or destructive decisions that women like Alice Vavasor, Emily Wharton, Mabel Grex, and Isabel Boncassen make.

Illustration studies

The very new field of research of illustration studies, pioneered by David Skilton and Julia Thomas at the Centre for Editorial and Intertextual Research at Cardiff University, has particular resonance for Trollope studies, as the next two essays show. The section begins with an expansive essay by Paul Goldman and David Skilton, joining forces here to give a theoretical framework to the relationship between illustration and text, focusing particularly on the symbiosis between

Introduction

Trollope and John Everett Millais. They are pioneering the new field of illustration studies, how the meaning of an illustrated work is generated by both visual and verbal elements – the bimedial text. To this end, they closely examine six of the illustrations for *Framley Parsonage*, revealing a richness of cultural reference, and note the self-conscious interplay between novelist and illustrator in *Orley Farm*, when the narrator refers back not to his text but to an earlier illustration: the bimedial text indeed.

Offering a very different slant is Robert Polhemus's essay, "Trollope's Picturesque Chroniclette and John Millais", which opens with a warning against trying too hard to unify our readings across Trollope's vast oeuvre. Reading too broadly leads to overgeneralizations about his work, and Polhemus encourages readers to look closely, often at unsuspecting moments. By example, the focus of his essay is on the little discussed, perhaps even seldom noticed, art subplot in *The Last Chronicle of Barset*, in which Trollope draws on his close relationship to the Pre-Raphaelite John Everett Millais (a friend and an illustrator of Trollope's fiction) in depicting a painter's love for his model. For Polhemus, this subplot amounts to a novel-within-a-novel that is actually "a major piece of fiction", in which "the novelist is working in the new territory . . . exploring the where, how, and why of the processes that produce art." Polhemus's detailed, enlightening close attention to these chapters in the novel show us that through Trollope's writing of Millais, we are better able to understand and interpret both Trollope and Millais.

Trollopian preoccupations

There is a frequent critical misconception by casual mis-readers of Trollope that the extent of his output does not reveal a breadth of interest. As the essays gathered in "Trollopian preoccupations" indicate, nothing could be further from the truth. Trollope was voraciously curious, and while his fiction may appear to cover similar ground in terms of class and gender, the themes, ideas, and images which preoccupy him are wide-ranging. Trollope's imagination and intellect were capacious.

Trollope's love affair with hunting extends from the beginning of his literary career, as we see in one of his earliest novels, set in Ireland, *The Kellys and the O'Kellys* (1848). In fact, Ireland was another of Trollope's great loves. As a junior civil servant in the Post Office, he lived there for ten years and his first novels sought to capture his intimate experience of Irish life. Robert Tracy's essay discusses Trollope's Irish fiction in relation to the "Irish novel" in the nineteenth century. He notes that Trollope would have known Irish literature (in English), extending back to Maria Edgeworth, whose *Castle Rackrent* was a particular influence on his first novel, *The Macdermots of Ballycloran* (1847). An account of the descending fortunes of a landowning family in County Leitrim, "prisoners of Ireland's past and present," according to Tracy, the novel "joined the conversation about Ireland that Maria Edgeworth began." Trollope remained enamoured of Ireland, long after he returned to England to live, and Ireland reappears in later fiction, though, as Tracy suggests, never quite with "so sure a touch, such confident insight" as in *The Macdermots*.

Elsie Michie's essay reads "the careers of Frances and Anthony Trollope as a sequence that runs from 1832, when she published her first book, to 1882, when he died while working on novels that would be published posthumously" to provide "a window onto transmutations in the uses of cleverness over a fifty-year period." Critics of both writers frequently described them and their novels as "clever," though in meaningfully different ways, and it's a term used pointedly by both Trollopes in their fiction. What emerges is a shift from pejorative sense of cleverness, linked to the vulgar pursuit of wealth, to a more socially positive sense, "associated with the valuing of work and intellectual accomplishments."

As the son of a failed barrister, Trollope's continued interest in representing lawyers and thinking about the law may not be surprising. Since Rowland McMaster's and Coral Lansbury's pioneering work in the 1980s, there has been a steady stream of critical readings of Trollope, not least in relation to the field of "law and literature" studies. Ayelet Ben-Yishai seeks to shift the terms of that critical history somewhat, to show the ways Trollope is less interested in "the law," as a singular, universal, monolithic category or institution, and more concerned with its historically specific and "always-shifting complexities." For Ben-Yishai, Trollope's fiction reveals the plurality of legal discourse in the period, and Trollope's "obsession with the law" is "akin . . . with the plurality and dynamic nature of Englishness itself."

In an essay that touches on a wide range of Trollope's fiction, Kay Heath focuses attention on issues relating to aging in Trollope: the tipping point for spinsters; "age-disparate" relationships; gender and aging; (im)potency and old men. Trollope began writing later than most, and perhaps had a particular maturity when it came to questions of aging, which he depicts with care and sensitivity throughout his career. As for his own awareness of aging, he never allowed old age to slow him down and, as Heath notes, resisted the call of retirement: "As to that leisure evening of life, I must say that I do not want it. I can conceive of no contentment of which toil is not to be the immediate parent."

A lifelong commitment to "toil" is the subject of Kate Osborne's essay on Trollope and literary labour. Those who know little else about Trollope know this: he wrote a great deal, which some early critics found to be too much of a good thing. Trollope's extensive oeuvre – which arises partly from what Osborne identifies as the writer's "consistency" and "efficiency" – and his frank discussion of literary labour in *An Autobiography* have been at the centre of discussions of Trollope and authorship. Osborne seeks to shift our focus to the fiction, to explore the way Trollope's representation of literary labour in his fiction was linked closely to other forms of labour. In Trollope's fiction as in his life, writing was an important and valuable kind of work.

Heather Miner's essay on Trollope and field sports reminds us of perhaps Trollope's greatest pleasure. Those who know only a little about Trollope know that he loved the hunt, and his writing is full of exciting scenes connected to horses and hounds. Miner reads Trollope's hunting scenes in relation to the wider, shifting cultural discourse about field sports and about the status of animal/human relations to argue that the hunt is imagined in complex ways that prevent any simplistic understanding of hunting as "escapist or nostalgic." For her, it is through Trollope's depictions of hunting scenes that he is able "to articulate the concerns of rural communities and social cohesion." Perhaps more surprisingly, Miner suggests that in Trollope's mid-career novels, hunting "is emblematic of Victorian modernity in the urbanizing nation."

Creed and cant

Trollope's writing career covers a period of great religious reassessment and prejudice, and these next three essays explore that prejudice from multiple angles, examining the prejudice against Jews in Victorian society and its expression in the characters he creates, and prejudice within the Protestant church in general and the Anglican church in particular. *The Way We Live Now* is regularly read as anti-Semitic, but Anna Peak's essay not only refutes this but also identifies a narrative voice exposing the sophistry of anti-Semitism, both in the fluidity of assumptions about Melmotte and in the shallow, knee-jerk responses of the Longestaffe family to the one honest person with integrity in the business world, Mr Breghert. Steven Amarnick, from a similar brief, builds his argument on a close reading of the rarely explored novella *Nina Balatka*, moving on to *Rachel Ray*, *Phineas Finn*, and *Redux*, and finishing with an examination of *The Prime Minister*, and the imposition of Jewishness onto Ferdinand Lopez. Like Peak, he is clear that it is the society he so accurately portrays that is anti-Semitic; it is society that is at pains to read Jewish features in Madame Max and Lopez. Rachel Ray speaks of those "who talk most of Christian charity . . . yet who think evil of people", a sentiment redolent of Matthew Arnold's exhortation "to see things as they really are", Amarnick's final assessment of Trollope's deeply and sincerely held belief in the novelist's duty of truth and moral leadership. The section finishes with J. Jeffrey Franklin's layered exploration of prejudice in dissenting creeds and in the Church of England, examining *The Vicar of Bullhampton* for his evidence of the established Church being as riven with intolerance and fanaticism as the dissenting factions in the Nonconformist sects around it. Franklin's overview of the arguments of all parties leads him to the conclusion that the true practice of the Christian faith and doctrine is to be found not in its priesthoods but outside, in the humblest of its practitioners.

Global Trollope

Readers of Trollope have long appreciated his outward-looking vision. While Trollope is perhaps still best known for his depictions of local and regional milieu – whether Barchester or London – his localism is far more globally concerned than that of most of his contemporaries. Trollope was a great traveller, more widely travelled than Dickens, George Eliot, Thackeray, and virtually all of his contemporaries, and he explored in detail the edges of empire and beyond as it was spreading across the globe at mid-century. Working for the Post Office took him abroad, first to Ireland, where he worked for ten years (1841–51) and which was so formative on the development of his fiction and his thinking, and then on extended trips to the West Indies, North America, Australia, and South Africa, in addition to trips to Europe. His extensive travels produced a significant body of travel literature – lengthy tomes entitled *The West Indies and the Spanish Main* and *Australia and New Zealand* (1859), for example – and short stories located in, among other places, Costa Rica, Palestine, and Egypt. The familiar young men and women of Trollope's courtship plots frequently find themselves adrift, at sea, isolated, and otherwise challenged when located abroad. Trollope's global encounters also inform his novels, with significant plots and scenes located in the places where he had travelled – Australia in *John Caldigate* (1879) and *Harry Heathcote of Gangoil* (1874) to name but two.

Recent critical interests in literary and cultural studies – postcolonial critiques, globalization studies, transatlanticism – have ensured that interest in "global Trollope" is increasing. Indeed, a number of the contributors to this volume have been formative in shaping how we think about Trollope's engagements with the nineteenth century beyond Britain, in relation to national identity, gender, race and ethnicity, and other concerns. The recent *Cambridge Companion to Anthony Trollope* included several essays that focus explicitly, in one way or another, on aspects of Trollope's experiences and treatment of "abroad." The work gathered here extends our thinking in new directions.

Trollope's first two novels, *The Macdermots of Ballycloran* (1847) and *The Kellys and the O'Kellys* (1848), were set in Ireland, where the author was working for the Post Office as a surveyor. This work required him to walk postal route after postal route, ensuring the postal system was both fluent and efficient, and it offered him a detailed knowledge of the country that informs his early novels. Gordon Bigelow's essay begins by noting the strangeness of Trollope's Irish novels – in part due to Trollope the Englishman writing as informed outsider about the Irish, in the wake of the famine – which never struck a chord with contemporary readers. He charts a critical history of the Irish novels, and invites us to think about them in relation to the development of the realist novel in national terms. Bigelow ends by arguing for an outward-looking understanding of this body of fiction. "Trollope's work," Bigelow suggests, "can advance our thinking about the relation of the English and the Irish novel, and perhaps our broader view of western Europe in relation to the world history of the novel. What is required is a sociological criticism expansive enough to consider the colonial borders Trollope's oeuvre crosses."

Nicholas Birns, who has long been interested in Trollope and the Antipodes and questions of place and identity more broadly, explores the significance of place and regionalism in Trollope through close examination of *La Vendée: An Historical Romance* (1850), a novel about royalists and republicans, set during the French Revolution in 1793, when regionalism and attachments to place had particularly acute meanings. Birns compares this early novel to the later novels, *Rachel Ray* (1863) and *Cousin Henry* (1879), and shows how an intense affiliation with place and location is pivotal in Trollope's shift from counterrevolutionary to reformist liberal thinking.

The crossing of borders, and in particular the question of emigration, is central to Tamara Wagner's essay. In a wide-ranging essay that explores some of the travel literature and a number of the novels, including *The Three Clerks* (1858), *Lady Anna* (1874), *Harry Heathcote of Gangoil* (1874), and *John Caldigate* (1879), Wagner argues that the often uneasy realism of Trollope's writing about settler life leads to new possibilities in the emigration plot in nineteenth-century fiction. Emigration provides Trollope with an opportunity to experiment with generic expectations and to rework "popular representational strategies." Heralding new ways of reading Trollope, Wagner suggests that "new transatlantic studies approaches, developments in postcolonial studies, widening comparative analyses, and, above all, renewed attention to genre formation" will produce "new readings of Trollope's changing evocation of emigration to and return from settler spaces [that] offer a different perspective on his fictional world." Also focused on Trollope's encounter with Australia and New Zealand, Grace Moore's fascinating essay on "Antipodean ecology" concentrates our attention on colonized lands and landscapes. Unlike his account of West Indian landscapes, Trollope's "position on Antipodean flora and fauna is surprisingly nuanced," she suggests, and does not always "conform to prevailing ideas of mastery." Not always consistent in his views of colonial landscapes across his works, Trollope was nevertheless a sensitive writer much of the time, with a strikingly ecologically aware sensibility.

Michelle Mouton and Mark W. Turner each in their different ways consider Trollope in relation to the emerging systems and technologies of nineteenth-century global modernity – new postal and communication routes, new methods of commodity transport, and new global flows. Mouton brings recent developments in "food studies" critique to bear on Trollope's *West Indies* and argues that Trollope's mission to streamline the British postal system led to his keen awareness of food *as* a system, thereby increasing his awareness of global food production, distribution, and consumption. Trollope's comments on racial inferiority in that travel book – where we find some of his most problematic and disturbing comments – can be read in relation to the history of food and the capitalist expansion of the food industry, in the context of colonialism. According to Mouton, "for Trollope, a post-emancipation, global food system would continue to feed English appetites while sustaining the health and wealth of its colonies." However, "this future could occur, in the West Indian and Central American context, only with the continued manual labour of non-European, non-White, colonial subjects on Europe's behalf." Turner's essay is similarly interested in global networks, global movement, and, in particular, global spread. He looks at some of Trollope's short stories and Australian fiction in order to suggest new ways of understanding Trollope, the man and his writing, in global contexts which frequently can be disturbing and unsettling. What becomes of Englishness when it is "located" abroad?

Notes

1 See Markwick, "Trollope Writes Trollope," in this volume.
2 N. John Hall, *Nineteenth-Century Fiction*, Vol. 27, No. 4 (Mar., 1973), pp. 477–80.

Works cited

Dever, Carolyn, and Lisa Niles, eds. *The Cambridge Companion to Anthony Trollope.* Cambridge: CUP, 2011.
Escott, T.H.S. *Anthony Trollope: His Work, Associates and Literary Originals.* London: John Lane, The Bodley Head, 1908.
Glendinning, Victoria. *Trollope.* London: Hutchinson, 1992.
Hall, N. John. *Trollope: A Biography.* Oxford: Clarendon Press, 1991.
Mullen, Richard. *Anthony Trollope: A Victorian in His World.* London: Duckworth, 1990.
Pope Hennessy, James. *Anthony Trollope.* London: Phoenix Press, 1971.
Riffaterre, Michael. "Trollope's Metonymies." *Nineteenth Century Fiction,* Vol. 37, Dec. 1982. 272–92.
Sadleir, Michael. *Trollope: A Commentary.* London: Constable, 1928.
Snow, C.P. *Trollope: An Illustrated Biography.* London: Herbert Press, 1991.
Super, R.H. *Trollope in the Post Office.* Ann Arbor: U of Michigan Press, 1981.
———. *The Chronicler of Barsetshire: A Life of Anthony Trollope.* Ann Arbor: U of Michigan Press, 1988.

PART I
Political settings

1

TROLLOPE AND POLITICS

Lauren M. E. Goodlad and Frederik Van Dam

In a scene near the end of *Barchester Towers* (1857), as Francis Arabin struggles to declare his feelings for Eleanor Bold, the tongue-tied pair discusses Ullathorne, the Thorne family's antiquated home. When Eleanor says that "old-fashioned things are so much the honestest," Arabin demurs: "It is strange," he says, "how widely the world is divided on a subject which is . . . so close beneath our eyes. Some think that we are quickly progressing towards perfection, while others imagine that virtue is disappearing from the earth." When Eleanor asks him what *he* believes, he replies, "I hardly know whether . . . [we] lean more confidently than our fathers did on those high hopes to which we profess to aspire" (ch. 48).

Nestled in a chapter called "Match-Making," the exchange may seem like a mere device through which two nervous lovers consummate a long-delayed courtship plot. Yet, if we pause to reflect on the Barchester novels, we recognize Arabin's somber uncertainty as the underlying mood of a comic series that works to ironize, humanize, and domesticate the forces of radical change – but not to arrest them or wish them away. Arabin's evocation of a world "divided" between heralds of progress and prophets of doom thus anticipates the author who famously described himself as "an advanced, but still a conservative Liberal" (*Autobiography* ch. 16).

These indications of a "divided mind" have made the political cast of the Victorian era's most accomplished political novelist something of a conundrum. According to John Hagan, Trollope's "ambivalence" pervades his fiction: "Throughout the whole body of his work instinctive or emotional conservatism continually clashes" with the more "liberal bent of his temperament" (2). But where Hagan finds conflict, other scholars discern conservatism, ideologically and/or formally. As John Halperin sees it, Trollope's "essential conservatism is deep-rooted and consistent – much more consistent than his vague and spasmodic liberalism" (*Trollope* 14). This position tallies with James Kincaid's notion of Trollope's comic conservatism, Jane Nardin's feminist claim that "*Barchester Towers* is a profoundly conservative novel" (382), and George Levine's assertion that Trollope's fiction, unlike the experimental works of Dickens, the Brontës, or George Eliot, "confirms things as they are" (203).

As Julian Wolfreys has noted, Trollope's Palliser novels mark a transition in political fiction from the early-Victorian industrial concerns of Dickens, Gaskell, and Kingsley to the middle-class terrain of "identity-as-problem" in "a condition of rapid flux" (62). Thus, for Patrick Brantlinger, Trollope exemplifies realism's turn toward depoliticizing "disillusionment" and "loss of critical energy" (208). In his influential Foucauldian reading of *Barchester Towers*, D. A. Miller suggests that Trollope's "Novel as Usual" typifies a social world that lacks police because their normalizing powers have "been subsumed" (111). More recently, Fredric Jameson has adduced Trollope to argue that mid-century realism loses its ability to represent capacious histories as politics devolves into the "specialized" subject matter of "those institutionalized genres which deal with" Parliament (*Antinomies* 272; cf. 217).

In this chapter we propose that Trollope's politics are both more coherent and less ostensibly reactionary the more one abandons the assumption of a simple "liberalism" for which Trollope's "realism" provides the obvious formal complement. In making this case, we join David M. Craig in affirming that "advanced conservative Liberalism" (Trollope, *Autobiography* ch. 16) was an important expression of its time that does not reduce to conservative politics. Nonetheless, to grasp "Trollope and politics" is no simple or singular task. On the one hand, it calls on scholars to explore the political contours of the age of Palmerston, Gladstone, and Disraeli as well as the distinctly civic and historicist dimensions of the liberalism Trollope embraced. On the other hand, to capture Trollope's achievement as a political novelist one must elucidate the complexity of his historically sensitive and formally diverse oeuvre. Thus, while Trollope's Barsetshire fiction marked the invention of a genre to evoke an emergent modern nation and empire, his formally restless Palliser novels befit the later and more vexatious stages of the author's encounter with that dynamic history. The challenge for scholarship is, thus, to calibrate Trollope's "political unconscious" with the formal conventions and material textures that each work sets in motion.[1] If, as Kincaid proposed, "No one has ever been able to decide whether" Trollope's "views are liberal or conservative" (*Novels* 17), the reason may be partly the under-recognized formal heterogeneity of his oeuvre.

In what follows we pursue this argument first by plumbing Barsetshire's historicist core and then tracing the advent of a new novelistic affect, parliamentary desire, with the launch of the Palliser novels. From there we move to the actually existing politics of Trollope's times and their impact on the series that made him the era's premiere political novelist. A closing section describes how the author's later works cap a long career in which persistent formal experimentation seeks out new ways of rendering the civic dimensions of Victorian politics against a backdrop of world-historical forces and metropolitan change.

"How Englishmen have become what they are"

Though Trollope's reputation as a political novelist understandably rests on the Palliser novels, their prologue is the series of provincial fiction that elevated him to the rank of a leading author in the 1850s and 1860s. The occasion for Barsetshire was the unprecedented pressure of modern forces on the hallowed ideal of a sovereign English history, including the globalization of capital and culture; the acceleration of technology, commerce, and finance; the gradual rise of a territorial empire; and world-scale conflicts, such as the Crimean War and Indian rebellion (alluded to in the pages of *Barchester Towers* and *Framley Parsonage* [1861] respectively). Far from a reactionary bulwark, this serial portrait of a fictional county, published over a dozen years, offered a formally sophisticated, ethnographically thick, and ideologically nuanced response to an age in transition. Trollope's verisimilitude, however, should not be mistaken for the "direct, mechanical mirroring" that Georg Lukács, one of the twentieth century's most influential critics of realism, associated with "human values" overcome by "the commodity structure of capitalism" (*Studies* 93, 63). Rather, Trollope's Barsetshire novels portray a modern nation imbued with a still palpable ethico-cultural richness: a holistic foundation on which to assert that "buying and selling" is not – or not yet – the "noblest work of an Englishman" (*Doctor* ch. 1).

Barsetshire's cultural work can thus be compared to the historicity Lukács praised in the fiction of Walter Scott and Honoré de Balzac. Like Scott's Waverley novels, the Barsetshire series answers a world besieged by modernizing change with a vision of history's unifying power. By emphasizing heirloom legacies, such as Barchester's cathedral or the Greshambury arms, Trollope indexes a form of property that accumulates ethico-cultural worth in excess of individual possession or abstract economic value.[2] The holistic social world he evokes resists the kind of progress that, as Elaine Hadley notes, privileged abstraction, deracination, and atomism over "common cultural embedment in rituals and customs" (5). Thus, while mid-century England was part of a multi-ethnic nation, sprawling commercial network, and expanding territorial empire, Trollope's series sets out to explain "more truly than any written history can do, how Englishmen have become what they are" (*Doctor* ch. 1).

Trollope began his literary career by trying out classic forms, including Scott's signature historical fiction.[3] It was not until his fourth novel, *The Warden* (1855), that he devised a modern genre that blended the formal conventions of comedy, satire, historical fiction, courtship narrative, clerical novel, and provincial romance. *The Warden* demonstrates that though Septimus Harding is undeniably the beneficiary of a "snug sinecure" (ch. 3), he is also a dutiful pastor. As it subtly concedes the legitimacy of moderate reform, the novel shows that the law, the supposed compass of a secular modernity, fails to provide comprehensive judgments on questions of ethical ownership and conduct. The overarching effect of *The Warden* is, thus, neither a reactionary pull toward the past nor a fruitless "stalemate between radicalism and conservatism" (Brantlinger 207). It is, rather, a complex historicism of the kind Lukács described when he upheld Balzac's *Comédie Humaine* as a form of realism that depicts the *"present as history"* (*Historical* 83).

In fact, the Trollopian stance that some critics mistake for contradiction is explicitly dialectical. "In almost every [English] bosom," Trollope wrote, "there sits a parliament in which a conservative party is ever combating to maintain things old, while the liberal side of the house is striving to build things new. . . . Bit by bit, very slowly, . . . the old wood is dragged away, and the new plantations are set in order" ("Public" 157). Although the quotation derives from an 1865 article on public schools, its germ is *The Warden*'s rumination on the established church: "Who without remorse can batter down the dead branches of an old oak without feeling that they sheltered the younger plants?" asks the narrator (37). Such metaphors anticipate Trollope's analogy in *Phineas Finn* (1869) between parliamentary reform and a coach that must be driven forward by liberals against the "drag" of conservatives (ch. 35).[4] Thus, when Arabin tells Eleanor that he "hardly knows" what the future bodes, he neither chooses "preservation" nor depicts "forward movement as destruction" (Kincaid, "*Barchester*" 596). Instead, Arabin's uncertainty bespeaks the condition of the modern historical subject – one who recognizes his immersion in advancing time, yet perceives that history's movement has outstripped the individual capacity to control, prevent, or predict.

Narrative form provides another means through which Trollope's fiction registers these lived dimensions of modernity in motion. Barsetshire's "present as history" inflects marriage plots (e.g., Lady Lufton's eventual acceptance of Lucy for her daughter-in-law), narratives of development (e.g., Mark Robarts's nearly disastrous social-climbing or John Eames's thwarted *Bildung*[5]), and resonant spatial motifs (e.g., the unpretentious grace of the Allington estate, or the vicarage at St. Ewold's, which prompts no less a bastion of tradition than Archdeacon Grantly to press for a makeover). By such means, the Barsetshire novels break down the opposition between transformation and preservation. They show that while openness to change offers no guarantee of progress, a reactionary clinging to the past is, at best, the choice of quaint eccentrics like the Thornes of Ullathorne. Nonetheless, this recognition of historical flux refuses nihilistic indifference, ludic postmodernism, or unbridled will-to-power. Holistic and dialectical, the Barchester imaginary repels the atomizing effects of mercenary marriage, moral posturing, and rank dishonesty. To flourish in Barsetshire is to adapt one's life in history through ethical reflection, sober self-knowledge, and duty to others mediated by both respect for the past and care for the future. This is as much Mr. Harding's stance in ceding Barchester's deanship to a younger man as it is Mr. Arabin's in accepting the position.

As a novel centered on the value of historic heirlooms, *The Warden* is, perhaps, the most Scott-like of Trollope's series. By contrast, *Barchester Towers* is the novel that most intensely engages the "present as history." One of the few Victorian authors who set his novels in the present day, Trollope began writing *Barchester Towers* during the Crimean War. The result is a novel saturated with "images of warfare" (Sutherland, "Introduction," *Barchester* xvii). Geopolitical crisis is domesticated through a comic contest between the established clerical elite and a cadre of Evangelical pretenders. The consequent tussle between old guard and new, high church and low, hangs unresolved until the courtship plot culminates in the long-awaited match between Eleanor and Arabin.

Writing anonymously in the *Westminster Review*, George Meredith hailed *Barchester Towers* as the "cleverest novel of the season," declaring that, in Anthony Trollope, "we have a caustic and vigorous writer, who can draw men and women, and tell a story that men and women can read" (326–7). Meredith's praise for Trollope's "masculine delineation of modern life" (327) was likely inspired by the family of Dr. Stanhope. Recalled from Italy by the new bishop, this cantankerous rector returns with his daughter Charlotte, his bohemian and possibly homosexual son, and a second daughter, la Signora Madeline Neroni, who is an exoticized siren separated from the abusive Italian husband who has maimed her.[6] These exceptional characters help Trollope to inject the spice of erotic intrigue into his tale of episcopal scrimmage. As Arabin and Slope fall under the spell of a married temptress, both contemplate proposals to Eleanor. Yet, in the novel's most remarkable turn, the self-same Signora exercises a "most singular disinterestedness" when she shepherds Eleanor and Arabin toward wedlock (ch. 45). In doing so, she aligns herself with history's forward motion.

It follows that the Bold-Arabin marriage may not be the wholesale capitulation to patriarchy that some scholars allege in citing the figure of the "parasite" ivy that "grow[s] and prosper[s]" only once it has "found its strong wall" (ch. 49). As one critic puts it, Trollope achieves "resolution and stability" through an "image of physical frailty", which contrasts "weak but beautiful women" to "supporting men" (Purdy 63). Such a reading ignores the fact that Eleanor Bold – whose surname marks the empowered status of widowhood – is neither weak nor frail. That Trollope's young widow is both richer and more sexually experienced than the man she marries[7] makes it likely that the "parasite" passage, like much else in the book, is at least slightly tongue-in-cheek.

Authoritative though he is, Eleanor's new husband is a forty-year-old virgin who nearly followed "the great Newman" to a life of celibacy (ch. 20). Having spent his formative years regarding women as "children," this recovering Tractarian lacks "any idea" that a mature woman might "either actuate his conduct or influence his opinion" (ch. 20). Thus, while Madeline teaches him "to heed his own longings for pleasure, the flesh, and relationship" (Polhemus 185), Eleanor transforms his experience of female intellect. Far from a case of feminine frailty feeding off manly strength, *Barchester Towers* offers an English variation on the continental *Bildungsroman* in which experienced women guide men's entrées to the social world.

Trollope's tendency to align female characters with sexual maturity and a life in history may bring to mind Bruce Robbins's discussion of the erotic patroness – a recurrent figure in works by Rousseau, Balzac, and Flaubert. According to Robbins, the relation between male protagonists and female patrons in these narratives shows how the modern desire for democracy must be sexualized and sublimated. In thus "nourishing and redirecting" the erotic passions they incite, these *Bildungsroman* cultivate the "citizenly desire necessary to the emergence of a democratic state" (24). *Barchester Towers* affirms this pattern: for while Arabin's maturation is but a single thread in a multiplot structure, the novel ends by stabilizing the modern historical condition without pretending to halt its movement.

Thus, when *Barchester Towers* makes mature female society a fixture of modern life, outside and inside the marital relation, it channels men's political desire away from the solitary "apostle" (ch. 20) and toward the socially embedded citizen. This civic understanding of politics recurs throughout Trollope's works, exemplifying a republican strain in nineteenth-century political culture that flourished through multiple channels – from the legacies of Aristotle, Machiavelli, and James Harrington, through Eliot's *Romola* (1862–3), Elizabeth Barrett Browning's poetry, and (as we shall see) Trollope's own *The Life of Cicero* (1880). Paradoxically, however, while the political impulse of Trollope's clerical fiction is decidedly civic, the rather more somber terrain of his political novels suggests the precarity of civics in a modern world.

Parliamentary desire

In his essay "On Sovereignty" (1867), Trollope evokes the kind of venerable organic history that his Barsetshire novels uphold. Just as *The Warden* places Barchester's cathedral at the center of its ethical imaginary, so the essay likens Britain's political constitution to Salisbury cathedral. As a symbolic sovereign, the British monarch, like the "tower and spire" of an ancient church, enjoys a position of perfection that no actual government can achieve. "It might be said," writes Trollope, "that Parliament did not know its own mind" or that "the minds of men were vacillating. But though the change were made twenty times . . . no one would say that the sovereign had vacillated" (87). In this way the monarchy, like the spire of Salisbury cathedral, signifies the historic grandeur of sovereignty as opposed to its workaday functions or practical effects.

"On Sovereignty" appeared in the October 1867 issue for *Saint Paul's Magazine*, a journal whose editorship Trollope assumed after his retirement from the Post Office. The same issue included the first instalment of *Phineas Finn*, the second in the series of Palliser novels, which would eventually establish Trollope as the leading political novelist of his day. At the time, England's most accomplished political novelist, Benjamin Disraeli, was busy shaping Parliament's history outside the pages of fiction. In the summer of 1867, as Trollope finished the story of his Irish member, Disraeli led the Tories in passing the reform bill that famously "dished the Whigs."[8] His trilogy of Young England novels – *Coningsby* (1844), *Sybil* (1845), and *Tancred* (1847) – evokes a Tory vision of the British constitution, which reinvents feudal romance for a modern and imperial age. By contrast, the "advanced conservative Liberal" constitution glimpsed in *Barchester Towers* presages the rather different breed of political novel that soon became synonymous with Trollope.

As we will see, the Palliser novels diverge in several ways from Barchester's characteristic features. Yet, it is worth noting that the heirloom institutions that mitigate modern uncertainty in the earlier series are still salient in *Can You Forgive Her?* (1864–5), the first of the Pallisers. To be sure, the courtship plots of this novel are less ebullient than the couplings that close the Barsetshire novels. But *Can You Forgive Her?* recalls those works in centering on Alice Vavasor's long-deferred union with John Grey, while describing Palliser's marriage to Lady Glencora. Subtending these plotlines is the depiction of Parliament as the secular complement to a great cathedral. As the narrator describes "that more than royal staircase" that leads "to those passages and halls which require the hallowing breath of centuries to give them the glory in British eyes which they shall one day possess," Trollope portrays the House of Commons, rebuilt after fire in 1834, as a living legacy from which "the world's progress" flows (ch. 45).

But it is not only Parliament's substitution for the Church that marks the Palliser series' onset. *Can You Forgive Her?* also features a new ingredient that signals the shift to high-stakes metropolitan politics: the presence of a pervasive desire for the excitements and rewards of a parliamentary career – or what *An Autobiography* more solemnly describes as "the highest object of ambition to every educated Englishman" (ch. 16). By its nature, parliamentary desire redirects politics from the public good to individualized questions of who can participate and under what terms. At the uppermost echelons, such desire informs Plantagenet's need for "that colossal wealth" and "expansive expenditure" so "necessary to our great aristocratic politicians" (ch. 23). Yet, Trollope's fiction, in contrast to Disraeli's, does not romanticize a particular scion's calling to invigorate the nation's political life. Instead, parliamentary desire infects a host of ambitious men as well as the women they court. One thus finds it at work in George Vavasor, whose failed political career ends in inglorious exit to the United States, as well as in Jeffrey Palliser, the cousin who would prefer Parliament to New Zealand were it not clear that politics would "get [him] terribly into debt" (*Can* ch. 25). Already we see the outlines of what Christopher Harvie perceives as a central theme: "the rise into Parliament of ambitious but impecunious young men" (90). Such characters, including Phineas, Frank Greystock in *The Eustace Diamonds* (1872), and Frank Tregear in *The Duke's Children* (1880), must feed their political aspirations with the fortunes of the women they aim to marry.

Thus, while each Palliser novel entails significant formal variations, all entwine courtship, money, and politics to make parliamentary desire the fuel of an expanding democracy, commercial power, and empire. The wish to enter what Jacques Berthoud calls "the acknowledged centre of national life" (xix) is as much the story of an Irish doctor's son or a mysterious Portuguese speculator as of a wealthy patrician's passion for statesmanship. It is also the story of the women they wed. Whereas Madame Max declares undying love for the Irish member whose reputation and life she saves in *Phineas Redux* (1874), Glencora embraces the "dull dignity" of her husband's calling with keen reluctance (*Can* ch. 24). Her own parliamentary desire fixes on the rakish Radical, Burgo Fitzgerald.

As the most female-centered of the Pallisers, *Can You Forgive Her?* pairs Glencora's unruly passion with the triangulated desire that Alice feels toward her cousin George as well as his sister Kate – a woman who, without impropriety, can "attach herself on to George's political career, and obtain . . . all that excitement of life which Alice desired for herself" (ch. 23).[9] Putting her fortune at George's disposal, Alice entreats him to afford her the "honour and glory of marrying a man who has gained a seat in the Parliament of Great Britain!" (ch. 32). In a concluding chiasmus, these two stories of deferred parliamentary desire intersect. As Palliser temporarily puts private affairs ahead of public, departing London on a journey that leads to the birth of an heir, he persuades the reluctant Grey that a life in Parliament can be both "useful" and "good" (ch. 77). Hence, just as Glencora, happy in expectant motherhood, reconciles herself to a husband whose "mouth waters" over blue books (ch. 73), so Alice finds that Grey's abject lack of parliamentary desire is "in the process of being cured" (ch. 77).

The most plangent desire, however, is the narrator's. In a memorable aside, the narrator pauses to ask his "male friend and reader" if he has ever "confessed," at the entrance to Parliament, "that Fate has been unkind" in denying him "the one thing" that he has most "wanted." With an almost startling intimacy, he admits, "I have done so and as my slow steps have led me up that more than royal staircase . . . I have told myself, in anger and in grief, that to die and not to have won that right of way, though but for a session . . . is to die and not to have done that which it most becomes an Englishman to have achieved" (ch. 45). A few months after the appearance of these words, Trollope closed the Barsetshire series. By the time he began writing *Phineas Finn*, he was editing *Saint Paul's* in the hopes of himself ascending that more than royal staircase. As Sutherland notes, the editor's stipend would provide Trollope with the kind of independence Phineas lacks while giving him "a platform outside the House" for himself and his allies ("Introduction," *Saint* n.p.).

This vision of sating parliamentary desire while being "useful" and "good" was dashed by the fateful candidacy for Beverley in 1868. As many scholars have noted, the Liberal Party's interest in this Tory stronghold was not to win but to expose corruption and disqualify the seat. Yet, despite knowing that he had been called on to wage a losing battle, Trollope seemed to hope that Beverley's working men would reject Tory bribes in favor of progressive Liberal proposals, such as affordable education and disestablishment of the Church in Ireland (Super 251–4; Halperin, *Trollope* 115–26).[10] Less noticed is the fact that Trollope suffered this crushing disappointment as Disraeli became the acknowledged leader of the Tory party – a matter that was increasingly to influence the author's political writings inside and outside of fiction.

"Advanced" conservative liberalism

So far we have suggested that Trollope's most politically salient works are more formally nuanced and politically sophisticated than previous scholarship has acknowledged. To develop that case further, it is necessary to describe two key challenges for research. The first concerns the complexity of Victorian-era politics. The Liberal Party that came into being in the 1850s was a motley alliance of upper-class Whigs, middle-class enthusiasts of political economy, and radicals of various stripes, including those whose quest for equalitarian democracy would eventually draw them to socialism and the Labour Party. At the same time, Conservatism began reinventing itself in the 1860s under the charismatic leadership of Disraeli – a rival author whose politics Trollope decried as "hocus pocus" and "conjuring tricks" (qtd. in N. Hall, *Trollope* 395). Hence, while Trollope saw Conservatism as a crucial check – a "repressive action," like the breaks on a coach, to offset the danger of headlong advance – he regarded the era's most influential Tory as a "political intriguer" who had abandoned conservative principles in the interests of party "dominion" (*Autobiography* chs. 16, 10).

The second difficulty concerns the author himself. As Robert Hughes observes, though Trollope is "seriously political to a degree unmatched by any other major nineteenth-century British novelist, his political ideas are distressingly hard to define" (33). To be sure, literary fiction seldom proffers a reliable index of an author's political opinions – or vice versa – and Trollope, whose Palliser novels manufacture the politics they depict, is no exception. Nonetheless, despite "the sense of a man literally bursting with opinions" (Craig 355), Trollope kept his views surprisingly private. We know, for example, that Thackeray's letters in 1848 suggest sympathies for revolutionary France (Cole); that the Brownings embraced the Italian *Risorgimento*; that Dickens's correspondence vilified the rebels during the Indian "mutiny"; that both Dickens and Ruskin defended Governor Eyre's brutal repression in Morant Bay; that Matthew Arnold regarded working-class unrest in Hyde Park as a dangerous anarchy to be sternly repressed. By contrast, discerning Trollope's views on such topics requires an inferential approach. While one need not conclude that Trollope "had very few political ideas" (Brantlinger 209), the task of contextualizing "advanced conservative Liberalism" remains challenging, even after decades of scholarship.

When the term "advanced Liberal" came into usage in the 1860s, it described allies of the Liberal Party who sought significant expansion of the franchise beyond the middle-class male electorate constituted in 1832. Among the best-known "advanced" Liberals of the day were John Stuart Mill (a Radical member of Parliament between 1865 and 1868) and John Morley (the young Millean disciple who became editor of the *Fortnightly Review*). In *An Autobiography*, Trollope commended Morley for his "admirable patience, zeal, and capacity" while at the same time indicating that the journalist's "much advanced" viewpoints were more radical than his own (ch. 10). In *Phineas Finn*, Mill appears when a frustrated Violet Effingham becomes disenchanted with the "charms" of matrimony. Instead of marrying a politician, she declares, "I shall knock under to Mr. Mill, and go in for women's rights" (ch. 51). Trollope, who satirized feminism in *He Knew He Was Right* (1869), can hardly be taken to have endorsed the female franchise. Nonetheless, Violet's nod to Mill's amendment, which was debated while Trollope was writing *Phineas Finn*, exemplifies the novel's subtle assimilation of the events that led to the Second Reform Act.

One suspects that Trollope would have appreciated Mill's proposals for using education to offset the leveling effects of a democratic franchise.[11] Trollope's campaign speeches, according to Halperin, were radical in holding that "every poor man should have brought within his reach the means of educating his children, and that those means should be provided by the State" (qtd. in *Trollope* 120). Like Mill, moreover, Trollope believed that the secret ballot, though endorsed by most Radicals, would deplete civic virtue. As a candidate in 1868, he supported Mill's bid for reelection as the member for Westminster – the same seat that Augustus Melmotte wins (as a Tory) in *The Way We Live Now* (1875). When Mill invited Trollope to dine, the author declared that "Stuart Mill was the only man in the whole world" who could tempt him to "leave [his] own home on a Sunday." The meeting, however, was "only a moderate success" (Anonymous, "Anthony" 55).[12]

In *An Autobiography*, Trollope remarks on the tendency of many Britons during the Civil War to support the Confederacy even though the "Southern cause was bad" (ch. 9). The author, writes Halperin, was "[a]lmost alone among Englishmen" in supporting the North ("Trollope" 150). Thus, at a time when Gladstone and Russell upheld the Confederacy (Campbell 168–76), Trollope's pro-Union sentiments aligned him with advanced Liberals like Mill. To be sure, Trollope's views on race were complicated and, in contrast to Mill's, marked by the theories of racial difference, which were becoming mainstream in the 1860s.[13] But on one key point his position was clear: "slavery has been a curse," he wrote (*North* ch. 3). Still, when the Eyre controversy erupted in 1866, Trollope appears to have been silent even though his friend Charles Buxton was the first to chair the Jamaica committee that Mill eventually led. His fiction may have been more responsive: according to Deborah Denenholz Morse, *He Knew He Was Right*, written while the effort to prosecute Eyre was still under way, "is imbued . . . with the memory of European intertwinings of race, gender, and imperialism" (*Reforming* 112).

It is easier to gauge the author's positions on Ireland (the subject of Gordon Bigelow's chapter in this volume) even though on Irish matters Trollope was far more conservative than Mill or even Gladstone. Whatever his views on policy, however, Trollope's novels strike a blow against rising anti-Irish prejudice in the age of Fenianism. Thus, an early review of *Phineas Finn* regretted that the title character is a sympathetic youth instead of a "leery, cunning, old, corrupt Irish type of member," of the sort "whose low, mischievous influence" has "injured [the] country perhaps more than the Fenians" ("Mr. Trollope's"). Trollope counters such prejudice by making Laurence Fitzgibbon an "Irish stereotype" against which Phineas bodies forth "manly independence" (Corbett 123).

According to Patrick Lonergan, Phineas recedes in the later Palliser novels because the rising support for Irish tenant right and Home Rule made it difficult to portray an Irishman whose politics adhered to the author's conservative views on these topics. Indeed, Lonergan speculates that real-life debates over tenant right influenced the conclusion of *Phineas Finn*: when Phineas travels to Ireland to "investigate the Land Question," writes Lonergan, he is compelled to break with his party and resign from politics (151). Tenant right was a complicated issue that pitted troubling colonial conditions against foundational beliefs in the ownership of property. Whereas English landlords could be seen as hereditary stewards, their Irish counterparts, descended from conquerors, were often absentee owners whose treatment of tenants was egregious.[14] Thus, while the Irish Land Acts of 1870 and 1881 reduced landlords' power, Gladstone, despite his "aristocratic" politics (Steele 45), saw them as a victory for "historical and traditional rights" (qtd. in Steele 45). By contrast, Mill's *England and Ireland* (1868) urged the purchase and redistribution of Irish land, premised on the conviction that land was the possession of society at large. Trollope, however, writing on Gladstone's timid bill in an 1870 essay, declared himself sanguine on the matter of Irish landlords and unperturbed by Fenianism. Singling out Bright as the instigator behind reform, he noted that Mill's "visionary, impracticable, and revolutionary" scheme "was doubly dangerous" in coming "from a man with world-wide reputation for wisdom" ("Mr. Gladstone's" 621).

If Trollope's "advanced" credentials are, thus, limited, the point to bear in mind is that the majority of Liberals in the 1860s either opposed democracy outright or sought to curtail its effects. Such Liberal conservatism was abetted by Palmerston, whose long leadership lasted until his death in 1865, at the age of eighty. As Walter Bagehot wrote in *The Economist*, Palmerston's death closed an epoch in which "moderate Liberals" and "moderate Conservatives" converged in supporting the status quo ("Effect" 1066). Palmerston's passing enabled pro-reform moderates, such as Gladstone and Russell, to seek common cause with "extreme" allies, such as the Radical John Bright (ibid.). Their modest Reform Bill of 1866 prompted anxious Liberals to worry that the party's new leaders would "go farther than they wanted" (ibid.). In actuality, Gladstone sought to enfranchise only that portion of workers who exercised "self-control, respect for order, patience under suffering, confidence in the law, [and] regard for superiors" (qtd. in Tyler 441) – in other words, those who, by definition, "deferred to the better judgment of their social and political 'superiors'" (ibid.).

The most outspoken opposition to Gladstone's bill came from "Adullamite" Liberals, such as Robert Lowe, who described lower-class voters as "impulsive, unreflecting, and violent people" given to "venality," "ignorance," "drunkenness, and facility for being intimidated" (74).[15] As Bagehot argued in *The English Constitution* (1865–7), a democratic franchise would transform the House of Commons from a deliberative body into the instrument of a mass electorate managed through party machinery (cf. Parry 214–5). In *Culture and Anarchy* (1867–8), Arnold recommended "the best ideas of [the] time" to counteract such narrow tendencies ("Culture" 53). James Fitzjames Stephen made a similar case: if liberalism expanded "popular power" without elevating "the general tone of public life," it would result in "permanent degradation" ("Liberalism" 73).

As an "advanced conservative Liberal," Trollope thus stakes out a position to the Left of the Adullamites and to the Right of Radicals (e.g., Bright) whose object was manhood suffrage. According to an anonymous writer in the Tory publication *John Bull*, terms such as "Liberal-Conservatives and Conservative-Liberals" had become commonplace in an era that saw "moderate and honest men of both parties" adopting convergent viewpoints ("What Mean"). Though the observation can be compared to Bagehot's remarks, *John Bull* further affirmed Disraeli's boast that the 1867 Act had "broken" the Liberals' "monopoly" on reform (qtd. in "Dishing"). *John Bull* thus diverged from the kind of Tory conviction that prompted Robert Cecil, the future Lord Salisbury, to decry the apostasy of Derby and Disraeli. Their conservative "surrender," he thundered in the *Quarterly Review*, had outstripped every instance of "recklessness," "venality," and "cynicism" in the annals of Parliament (540). "Those who have trusted to the faith of public men, or the patriotism of parliamentary parties, or the courage of aristocratic classes, must now find other resting-places on which to repose their confidence" (553). Here was an influential Tory (and future prime minister) to affirm Trollope's sense of Disraeli's perfidy while vindicating his belief that the core principle of Conservatism was "combating to maintain things old." As Trollope himself wrote, Liberals and Conservatives "regard the whole human race from a different point of view" ("Whom" 541). Conservatives believe that "the welfare of the world depends" on the very social differences that Liberals seek to diminish (*Autobiography* ch. 16).

In *The Prime Minister* (1876), Sir Alured Wharton presents an unflattering instance of this Conservative type – a "proud, ignorant man" who "thought the assertion of social equality" to "amount to the taking of personal liberty." Nonetheless, while Alured "read little or nothing," he "could not tell a lie" or "do a wrong" (ch. 13). The novel thus contrasts his unenlightened rigidity to the flexile falseness of the Disraeliesque Ferdinand Lopez and, by extension, to Disraeli's conduct in breaking the Liberal "monopoly" on reform. *An Autobiography* is explicit on this point: whereas the Liberal equalitarian, wary of "sudden disruption," may pronounce himself "glad" of "a Conservative opponent" – thus inhabiting the stance of an advanced conservative Liberal – to *feign* equalitarianism for party gain is to take the path of the "charlatan" (ch. 16).

The "advanced conservative Liberal" thus rejects the homogenization of parties. His purpose is to affirm political dialectics – within parties but also between them – as the sign of a healthy civic culture and organic social history. If the delineation of this liberal subject evokes the tensions immanent in a particular historical moment, the intention is neither to universalize that subject nor to collapse the terms of an agonistic political structure (which, to the contrary, are to be valued almost as much as liberal principles themselves). Yet, as a self-description, Trollope's qualified association with "advanced" liberalism suggests a position potentially closer to Mill's than to Arnold's or Bagehot's. Indeed, Trollope seems to diverge as well from his friend George Eliot, whose title character in *Felix Holt: The Radical* (1866) is a working man who does not seek the vote. To be sure, Trollope's precise stance on reform may possibly have resembled that of Gladstone – whose 1866 bill Mill described as "far more moderate than is desired by the majority of reformers" ("Representation" 60–1). Yet, while Gladstone makes working-class *deference* the key qualification for citizenship, Trollope stresses *equality*. As Lady Glencora declares, to be a "Liberal at heart" is to embrace equality as "the gist of [one's] political theory" (*Can* ch. 14). Trollope's non-fictional writings concur. Whereas the Conservative seeks to maintain social hierarchy, the Liberal believes "inequality to be itself a thing bad" ("Whom" 541).

Derived from an essay that upholds Gladstone as the answer to Tory government, Trollope's claim that inequality is "bad" is hardly a call for socialism or even social democracy. The author's piecemeal thoughts on the topic may seem to amount to little more than a tenuous ideal, as when Palliser describes "equality" as a "millennium . . . so distant that we need not even think of it as possible" (*Prime* ch. 48). Isolated in this way, Palliser's creed may seem to support Hayden White's critique of a liberalism that imagines utopia only to project it into "the remote future, in such a way as to discourage any effort in the present to realize it precipitately" (25). Applying this observation to the Palliser novels, Lynette Felber writes that conservatism "would perpetuate the status quo," while liberalism "has faith in the possibility of progress" (443).

But is this a sufficient optic for assessing Trollope's politics? Plantagenet's alienated condition in *The Prime Minister* bespeaks a novel split between a narrative of failed political compromise and a fraudulent outsider's tragic descent toward suicide. Palliser's position, according to Harvie, is that of "a fallible man conscious of the distance of his own life both from the practice of the parliamentary system and from his own ideals" (98). As an assessment of Trollope's non-fiction, moreover, White's formulation cannot account for the author's conviction that inequality is "bad." Hence, limited though it is, the advanced conservative Liberal's response to poverty involves significantly more than affirming the possibility of progress. While Trollope rejects the revolutionary "desire to set all things right by a proclaimed equality," he regards the "tendency towards equality" as a modern fact and, moreover, proclaims the "feeling of injustice" and "consciousness of wrong" that animate his own politics in furtherance of that tendency (*Autobiography* ch. 16). We have seen how Trollope campaigned on the issue of state-funded education for the poor – a measure Halperin calls "needlessly provocative" and "gratuitously Radical" (*Trollope* 120). Rather than gratuitous, Trollope's radicalism on the matter of education suggests that – contra Halperin – the author's "deep-rooted" convictions are at times "advanced" in quite meaningful ways.

Consider, too, how in *North America* (1862), Trollope's encounter with the vastly different material conditions of the American West prompts him to praise the "manly dignity" of the emigrant settler. Unlike the English cottier who is his counterpart, the American settler "is his own master, standing on his own threshold" (*North* 128). On the one hand, this "rough fellow" farms for "dollars" – not the rooted connection to place that ensures Barsetshire's historicity. On the other, his manly "ease" resembles that of "a lettered gentleman in his own library" (*North* 128). Thus, while Trollope prizes the heirloom culture of provincial England, from the standpoint of the American West, he finds it impossible to dignify the laboring-class dependence on which Barsetshire's social edifice depends – a structure in which 60 percent of land was owned by 4,000 people in a population of 20 million (Steele 43). We might even say that the Trollope who comes across in these reflections is "a fallible man conscious of the distance of his own life . . . from his own ideals."

Given these equalitarian strains, it is worth comparing Trollope to T. H. Green, a younger advanced Liberal whose writings influenced New Liberalism at the turn of the century. Green's holist and collectivist liberalism – premised on a Hegelian and civic notion of positive freedom – anticipates the social democracy of the postwar era. As Green observed in a well-known 1881 speech,

> When we speak of freedom as something to be so highly prized, we mean a positive power or capacity of doing or enjoying something worth doing or enjoying, and that, too, something that we do or enjoy in common with others. We mean by it a power which each man exercises through the help or security given him by his fellow-men, and which he in turn helps to secure for them. When we measure the progress of a society by its growth in freedom, we measure it by the increasing development and exercise *on the whole* of those powers of contributing to social good with which we believe the members of the society to be endowed.
>
> (199)

Green's civic equality, in addition to the franchise, entails educational and economic opportunities sufficient to enable "citizens as a body to make the most and best of themselves" (199). This definition of freedom derives from Hegel's *Sittlichkeit* (ethical life), which holds that citizenship reconciles the individual's liberty with participation in and development through the community. Such collectivism makes individual poverty inimical in diminishing "*the whole* of those powers of contributing to social good."

It would be misguided, of course, to overstate the likeness between Trollope, whose political writings are scant, and Green, an Oxford professor of moral philosophy whose works exerted a significant influence on twentieth-century social thought. Nor, for that matter, is our purpose to suggest that communitarian social democracy necessarily delivers the balance of individual and social freedoms that Green's speech invokes. The comparison is important, however, because it helps us to see how firmly Trollope distinguishes between two strains of Radicalism that, via the Palliser novels, we might designate as the Radicalism of Turnbull versus the Radicalism of Monk.

In *Phineas Finn*, the narrator disparages Turnbull, a demagogic orator whose politics are founded on "generalities" and a kind of Everlasting No: "It was his business to inveigh against existing evils," to "cut down forest-trees," while having "nothing to do with the subsequent cultivation of the land" (*Phineas* ch. 18). The negative liberty that such Radicalism enshrines exemplifies the free trade philosophy that helped to usher in Corn Law repeal in the 1840s. Though it was originally associated with Cobden and Bright, free trade doctrine became a solid plank of the Liberal Party in the Palmerston era. In *Phineas Finn*, Turnbull, "the great Radical of the day" – a character often regarded as a caricature of Bright – believes in "free trade in everything except malt" (ch. 18).[16] Free trade of this kind privileged the narrow liberties of "entrepot trade" while having few "implications for other parts of the economy," let alone "civic equality" (Breuilly 113). Such negative liberty contrasts with the Greenian vision of a holistic community that ensures the positive "capacity of doing or enjoying something worth doing or enjoying." Underlying free trade, in other words, is the atomistic social ontology particular to influential strands of Enlightenment political philosophy: for example, Locke's possessive individual, Hobbes's anarchic state of nature, and the *homo economicus* of Bentham's felicific calculus. The limitations of this atomized abstraction of the modern subject eventually prompted Mill to abandon Bentham's philosophy. Mill's growing interest in history and sociology, his civic and social variations on utilitarian ethics, and his revisions to the *Principles of Political Economy* (1848) informed the intellectual fabric in which liberal collectivism, socialism, and the politics of the Labour Party emerged at the end of the century.[17]

It thus behooves us to recall that Joshua Monk (another "JM" with a first name that seems to riff off "John Stuart"), is, like Mill, alternatively described as an "advanced Liberal" and "Radical" (*Phineas* ch. 14). The Radicalism of advanced Liberals like Mill and Green – in contrast to the free trade Radicals of an increasingly conservative Liberal Party – helped to inspire the New Liberalism of L. T. Hobhouse, J. A. Hobson, and, eventually, John Maynard Keynes.[18] More palpable in Trollope's day, Mill's signal parliamentary virtues, like Monk's, are his uncompromising independence and unswerving civic ethos. Notably, then, in *Phineas Finn*, it is Monk who helps Phineas understand tenant right and who takes Glencora's lead in affirming equality; though the rhetoric of equality may "frighten" and "mislead" us, says Monk, the "wish of every honest man" must nonetheless be "to assist in lifting up those below him" (ch. 14). It is a sentiment much like Trollope's in *An Autobiography*.

To be sure, though Mill, like Monk, was "a thin, tall, gaunt man, who had devoted his whole life to politics" (*Autobiography* ch. 14), he was neither the scion of a commercial family, a long-serving member of Parliament, nor a cabinet minister. Like many characters in the Palliser novels, Monk is the portrait of a "living political character," not a "living man" (ch. 20). The point, therefore, is less to insist that Mill is the single inspiration for Monk than to demonstrate how Trollope's writing valorizes parliamentary independence, a holistic and civic vision of the nation, and an ethically vital "tendency towards equality." These characteristic features of "advanced conservative Liberalism" may be as useful in explaining why Mill sought to meet Trollope as why Monk is the mentor and guiding conscience of *Phineas Finn*.

The Palliser novels

Trollope's deepening pessimism in the years after 1868 is sometimes attributed to the author's demoralizing bid for Parliament (e.g., Cockshut; Halperin, *Trollope* 111). Yet, the bleak political imaginary at work in *The Eustace Diamonds*, *The Way We Live Now*, and *The Prime Minister* suggests a complicated historical landscape. Reforms in banking since the 1850s had created a credit economy conducive to "commercial profligacy" (*Autobiography* ch. 20). Imperial shocks like the

Jamaica controversy were becoming recurrent features of a metropole that preferred to regard itself as the benign arbiter of trade. The formalization of empire in India (and later Africa) favored a Tory party that believed Britain's workers were "proud of belonging to an Imperial country" (Disraeli 528–9). Whereas the Liberal Party of the 1850s had stood forth as a "ruling force" (Parry 167), by the time of *The Duke's Children*, Liberalism was foundering over imperial contradictions and Conservatism had begun to show the resilience that persists in our own day.[19] The election of 1868 had already demonstrated that workers could vote for Tory candidates: but the heavy Liberal losses of 1874 left Radicals like Green "almost stunned" by defeat (qtd. in Tyler 455).

In the Palliser novels, the preponderant sign of this changing metropole is formal heterogeneity. We have seen how, in *Phineas Finn*, Irish questions interrupt the political *Bildungsroman*'s classic fusion of courtship and statecraft. The next work in the series, *The Eustace Diamonds*, subverts that genre entirely. The scene of Lizzie's tale of pilfered jewels – like that of *The Way We Live Now* – is the London metropolis: a growing center of global finance and imperial policy. These novels exemplify the *naturalistic narrative of capitalist globalization*: a new Trollopian genre in which the forces of capitalist and imperial expansion visibly transmogrify the English lifeworld. While such novels conjure insidious foreigners to personify these injurious effects, they also generate a countervailing sense of ethical and political crisis to haunt such scapegoating (Goodlad, *Victorian Geopolitical*).

According to Harvie, Trollope's recurring characters map Britain's political constitution in the tense period before and after the Second Reform Act. Thus, while Phineas dominates the second and fourth novels, Palliser's arc begins in *Can You Forgive Her?*, plays off against Lopez's in *The Prime Minister*, and concludes in *The Duke's Children*. Taken as a whole, the Palliser series ponders how an aristocratic ruling class might adapt itself to govern this brave new metropole. Can Parliament assimilate the most exemplary of the ambitious outsiders that modernity so plentifully furnishes? Whereas Phineas represents the kind of rejuvenating otherness they do well to embrace, Frank Greystock in *The Eustace Diamonds* is a more troubling figure. "Honesty goes about with a hang-dog look about him," he tells his cousin Lizzie, while "Dishonesty carries his eyes high" (ch. 53). Greystock raises the possibility that honesty is a quaint relic that aspiring politicians cannot afford to embrace. The return of Phineas in the next instalment is more optimistic. Yet, while *Phineas Redux* is less darkly naturalistic, it resumes the hero's *Bildungsroman* only to interrupt it anew with a sensational murder, courtroom, and bigamy plot. By the end, Phineas is cleared of guilt and securely engaged to Madame Max. His charismatic speech in Parliament calls out Tory opportunism and checks the Liberal Party machinery in a single stroke. If this is a notable victory for political honesty, it is also Phineas's last major act in the series.

One of the salient features of *The Prime Minister*, the fifth of the Pallisers, is the increasing signs of a growing anti-Semitism among Liberals in the years of Disraeli's leadership. When Disraeli's policies in the 1870s favored geopolitical interest over defense of Christians in the Ottoman Empire, they stoked an anti-Jewish animus that saturates much of Trollope's later writing (Wohl). Like *The Way We Live Now*, *The Prime Minister* tells the story of a racialized outsider who threatens Britain's moral condition. Moreover, as Michael Ragussis writes, the novel stages an imaginative reversal during Disraeli's second ministry: Lopez, the secret Jew who "fails to win a seat in Parliament, is the epitome" of "moral bankruptcy," while Trollope's fictional prime minister is "the truest nobleman in all England'" (258; cf. Cheyette). Nonetheless, Lopez is no stock character like Emilius, the crypto-Jewish villain of *The Eustace Diamonds*. In fact, it is possible to read Lopez as one whose story tells against English prejudice (Gagnier).[20]

In the final Palliser novel, the Conservatives are led by Sir Timothy Beeswax, another "conjurer" who does "not know the meaning" of true "patriotism" (ch. 21). *The Duke's Children*, however, is less a parliamentary narrative than a reflection on Palliser's marriage from the standpoint of an altered political landscape. The most elegiac of the series, the novel finds the widowed duke struggling to countenance his children's marriages to the kinds of outsiders who created dramatic tension in earlier works. While Silverbridge chooses an American heiress, Mary will marry Frank Tregear, another ambitious Tory. The novel (and series) thus closes with a conversation in which Palliser and Silverbridge discuss Mary's new husband: "Perhaps what surprised me most," says Palliser, "was that he should have looked so high. . . . But now I will accept that as courage which I before regarded as arrogance" (ch. 80). As a reward for this tolerance, Palliser learns that his son will not defect to the Tories, as he had feared. Moreover, the duke himself returns to government in a symbolic role: the same character who enters the series as a "laborious man," notable for his "industry" (*Can* ch. 24), closes it as a kind of national heirloom, like the spire of a cathedral. As George Butte writes, *The Duke's Children* evokes "the pain of history." In a way that recalls us to Arabin, Palliser's melancholic affect befits the condition of the conscientious modern subject resigned to finding his way in a world that has seemed to leave him behind.

Later works

When the Liberals returned to power in 1880, Gladstone's support for Home Rule alienated many former supporters, including Trollope and, ironically, Bright. That the author was challenged by both Disraeli and Gladstone goes some way toward explaining the formal restlessness that continues to pervade his later fiction.[21] We have seen how *The Way We Live Now* typifies a new Trollopian naturalism.[22] The narrator's angry and satirical tone recalls the essays of Thomas Carlyle – the writer whose polemical style Trollope had parodied in *The Warden* (ch. 15) and whose "lamentations" he continued to deprecate in his autobiography. Nonetheless, discussing the later novel, Trollope wonders whether a world "retrograding from day to day" can "be considered to be in a state of progress" (ch. 20).

Though less naturalistic than *The Way We Live Now*, *The American Senator* (1877) pursues a critique of individualism familiar to Trollope's fiction as far back as *The Warden*. The title character has come to England to study English customs. As Ruth apRoberts notes, the "Senator as a device" recalls the "classical critical mode" of Montesquieu and Oliver Goldsmith (173); but the novel's vision of Britain is decidedly modern. Trollope's propertied classes are epitomes of selfishness: like Arnold's barbarians ("Culture" 106ff), they know how to seize property, but not how to cultivate it for the benefit of others. This degraded heirloom culture is symbolized by the disruption of local tradition. On "hunting mornings all the lands of the county," the narrator declares, "are the property of the hunt" (ch. 18) – a holistic gesture that is wrecked when a disgruntled tenant poisons a fox (cf. Trotter). Likewise, in *Is He Popenjoy?* (1878), a mismanaged estate is revived through the discovery of an industrial commodity: coal. Trollope again echoes *Culture and Anarchy*, in which Arnold derides Britons for taking coal rather than culture as the basis for greatness ("Culture" 64). Both novels portray a rudderless nation without any exemplary protagonist; they criticize liberal modernity without advocating the remedies of the mid-Victorian era's aging sages – whether Carlyle's hero-worship, Ruskin's Gothic aesthetics, or Arnold's more liberal-minded turn to Culture.

As we have seen, Trollope's own ideals tended toward civic republicanism, a tradition of political thinking that emphasizes public participation and the positive freedom to develop citizen character (Pocock). Significantly, then, Trollope affirmed this turn to civics in late non-fictional works such as "Cicero as a Politician" (1877) and *The Life of Cicero*, both of which portray the ancient Roman as an antidote to atomized individualism. As "sincere, as he was also self-denying" (*Life* 1, ch. 1), Trollope's Cicero admonishes his brother to "study the welfare of all over whom he stands in the position of master" (1, ch. 11). Though freedom in an age of slavery could not be "absolute" (1, ch. 1), "liberty," Trollope writes, was "very dear to" Cicero, not only for his own sake but also "as a privilege for the enjoyment of others" (1, ch. 3).

Of course, it is one thing to admire a republican ethos and another to transport it into the pages of realist fiction. Consider Lord Hampstead in *Marion Fay* (1882) – a Radical and republican who has made it his mission to oppose the abuses of his own rank. The novel's opening pages suggest a political *Bildungsroman* like *Coningsby* or *Phineas Finn*. Instead of politics, however, Hampstead's quest for equality soon focuses on Marion, the sickly daughter of a Quaker clerk. As Hampstead's misguided desire to "make a property of" her (ch. 51) hastens Marion's illness, political *Bildung* is thwarted by the hero's selfishness and the heroine's death.

In *The Fixed Period* (1882), a dystopian satire and science fiction (recounted by a first-person and possibly unreliable narrator), civic republicanism is a mere façade. The novel's setting is Britannula, a late-twentieth-century colony on the Australian continent that has just asserted its independence from Great Britain.[23] Its premise is a law that mandates compulsory euthanasia at the age of sixty-eight: the so-called Fixed Period. Although President John Neverbend, the originator of the law, imagines the Fixed Period as an ennobling civic project, Trollope's narrative makes clear that the overzealous Neverbend is motivated by the desire for control and utility – a perverse blend of Benthamite utilitarianism and biopolitics (Foucault). At the conclusion of the work, Britannula, a former Crown Colony, must be annexed by Britain.

Trollope continues to ponder republican politics in his last (and incomplete) work, *The Landleaguers* (1883). The novel begins as a naturalistic depiction of Ireland during the agrarian troubles of the late 1870s and early 1880s. Gradually, however, the focus shifts from Irish revolutionaries to metropolitan liberalism as the narrator articulates a critique of Gladstone's land reforms much like Trollope's own. Instead of making land the property of tenants, the narrator suggests, citizenship should be based on the classical notion of land as an absolute form of property – precisely the kind of ownership Mill rejected. Yet, while the novel's Irish politics are conservative, its treatment of poverty points to an advanced Liberal understanding of citizenship as that which requires the positive freedom to thrive. Given its incompletion, it is impossible to be sure of the novel's intended form or content. Split between a defense of Irish landlords and an adumbration of social welfare, *The Landleaguers* may, perhaps, contain an unfulfilled dialectical impulse, or it may return us to the notion of Trollope's "divided mind." What is clear in either case is that Irish locality and the colonial relation that subtends it amplify the estranging effects of a fiction already struggling to connect to a modern political history in motion.

Notes

1 See Jameson, *Political*, as well as Felber, who adopts the term.
2 On Barchester's notion of "heirloom sovereignty" see Goodlad, *Victorian Geopolitical*, chapters 3 and 4.
3 According to Bigelow, Trollope's two early Irish novels "flip through every available convention of narrative, testing and then discarding each in turn as the particular social and economic structure under discussion challenges the premises on which those narrative conventions rely" (104). On *La Vendée*, Trollope's early historical romance, see Birns in this volume as well as Faulkner, who observes that, "Unlike Scott, Trollope cannot envision people and places whose prototypes are not actually before him" (162).
4 Cf. Craig 359–60. According to Butte, Trollope tries "to reconcile needs of the future with loyalties to the past within a generally liberal commitment" (214). Whereas Butte chooses "balancing" to describe this position, our preference for *dialectics* emphasizes the transformative process through which future "needs" and past "loyalties" shape one another's history.
5 On Eames, see Langbauer's essay on the Trollopian "hobbledehoy."
6 Bertie's preference for the homosocial companionship of "some youngster" whom he regales with "an account . . . of some of the pastimes of the Eastern clime" (*Barchester* 2:160) builds on the orientalist association of the East and homosexuality (see Markwick, 69–72; Flint 106–7).
7 On Trollope's widows, see Noble.

8 For example, "Dishing."
9 Morse reads the relationship between Kate and Alice as a displacement of Kate's quasi-incestuous feelings for George (*Women*). For Marcus this homoerotic bond is a kind of female marriage.
10 Trollope's Beverley experience is reflected in *The Way We Live Now* when Melmotte runs for Parliament as a Tory: "Some unfortunate Liberal was to be made to run against him, for the sake of the party," the narrator says, "but the odds were ten to one on Melmotte" (ch. 35). See also *Ralph the Heir* (1870–1) for an electoral plotline that echoes Beverley and, for a close reading of that novel, Tracy.
11 Summarizing, Tyler writes that Mill "continued to advocate literacy and numeracy qualifications, as well as championing a system of plural voting based on educational achievement . . . [H]e support[ed] some of the more extreme and apparently more democratic measures including votes for women and proportional representation" (441–2). According to Parry, however, proportional representation was a means to "safeguard the rule of the educated" (209).
12 The review contrasts Mill's "modesty and courtesy" to Trollope's "blustering," adding, "It was a relief to get the bull safely away from the china shop" ("Anthony" 55–6). In his edition of Trollope's letters, Hall attributes the review to Morley; see *Anthony* 598, note 7.
13 This is especially true of the travel writings, which have been discussed by postcolonial scholars, including C. Hall and Gikandi. For scholarship on Trollope and race that works across fiction and non-fiction, see Goodlad, *Victorian*, chapters 3 and 4.
14 On related scholarship by Hadley and Maurer, see Bigelow's chapter in this volume.
15 The term Adullamite, deriving from the biblical Cave of Adullam in which David sought refuge from Saul, denotes an oppositional band, temporarily exiled from political power.
16 On Bright and Turnbull, see Dinwiddy.
17 On Mill's increasingly progressive economic agenda, see Ashcraft.
18 For an earlier window on radicalism that is not quite Monkian or Turnbullian, see *Rachel Ray* (1863), ch. 26.
19 On the crisis of liberal imperialism during this period, see, for example, Mantena.
20 On Trollope's complicated attitude toward Jews see also Peak and Amarnick in this volume.
21 For the argument that Trollope's later novels were an attempt to develop a new aesthetic, committed to analogically related plots and designed to "celebrate order," see Tracy 57. Other stylistic innovations in Trollope's late novels serve to articulate a form of subjectivity in which the individual element, agency, has been erased, which is an index of Trollope's growing doubts about the viability of liberalism; see Van Dam.
22 For other readings of this important late novel see Anderson; Hensley; Morse, "The Way"; and Van.
23 See Alessio for a comparison to Edward Bulwer Lytton's *The Coming Race* (1871) and Birns, who likens the work "to the Latin American genre of *novella del dictador*" (191).

Works cited

Alessio, Dominic. "A Conservative Utopia? Anthony Trollope's *The Fixed Period* (1882)." *Journal of New Zealand Literature* 22 (2004): 73–94. Print.
Anderson, Amanda. "Trollope's Modernity." *ELH* 74.3 (2007): 509–34. Print.
Anonymous. "Anthony Trollope." *Macmillan's Magazine*, 49 (November 1883): 47–56. Print.
Anonymous. "Dishing the Whigs." *Spectator* (10 August 1867): 6. <http://archive.spectator.co.uk/article/10th-august-1867/6/-dishing-the-whigs>.
Anonymous. "Mr. Trollope's New Magazine." *Spectator* (5 October 1867): 20. <http://archive.spectator.co.uk/page/5th-october-1867/20>.
Anonymous. "What Mean the Terms Conservative and Liberal?" *John Bull* 42.2 (21 September 1867): 652. Print.
apRoberts, Ruth. *The Moral Trollope*. Athens: Ohio University Press, 1971. Print.
Arnold, Matthew. "Culture and Anarchy." *Culture and Anarchy and Other Writings*. Ed. Stefan Collini. Cambridge: Cambridge University Press, 1993. 53–211. Print.
———. "Culture and Its Enemies." *Cornhill Magazine* 16.20 (July–December 1867): 36–53. Print.
Ashcraft, Richard. "John Stuart Mill and the Theoretical Foundations of Democratic Socialism." *Mill and the Moral Character of Liberalism*. Ed. Eldon J. Eisenach. University Park: Pennsylvania State University Press, 1998. 169–89. Print.
Bagehot, Walter. "The Effect of the Political Events of 1867 upon the Minds of Moderate Liberals." *The Economist* (21 September 1867): 1066–7. Print.

———. *The English Constitution*. 1865–7. Ed. R.H.S. Crossman. Ithaca: Cornell University Press, 1963. Print.

Berthoud, Jacques. "Introduction." Trollope, *Phineas Finn*. vii–xx. Print.

Bigelow, Gordon. "Anthony Trollope's Famine Economics." *Global Legacies of the Great Irish Famine: Transnational and Interdisciplinary Perspectives*. Ed. Marguérite Corporaal, Christopher Cusack, and Lindsay Janssen. Bern: Peter Lang, 2014. 103–18. Print.

Birns, Nicholas. "Trollope and the Antipodes." *The Cambridge Companion to Anthony Trollope*. Ed. Carolyn Dever and Lisa Niles. Cambridge: Cambridge University Press, 2010. 181–95. Print.

Brantlinger, Patrick. *The Spirit of Reform: British Literature and Politics, 1832–1867*. Cambridge: Harvard University Press, 1977. Print.

Breuilly, John. "Variations in Liberalism: Britain and Europe in the Mid-Nineteenth Century." *Diplomacy and Statecraft* 8.3 (1997): 91–123. Print.

Brown, Wendy. *States of Injury: Power and Freedom in Late Modernity*. Princeton: Princeton University Press, 1995. Print.

Butte, George. "Trollope's Duke of Omnium and 'The Pain of History': A Study of the Novelist's Politics." *Victorian Studies* 24.2 (1981): 209–27. Print.

Campbell, Duncan Andrew. *English Public Opinion and the American Civil War*. London: Royal Historical Society, 2003. Print.

Cecil, Robert (Viscount Cranborne). "The Conservative Surrender." *Quarterly Review* 123.246 (October 1867): 533–65. Print.

Cheyette, Bryan. *Constructions of "the Jew" in English Literature and Society: Racial Representations, 1875–1945*. Cambridge: Cambridge University Press, 1996. Print.

Cockshut, A. O. J. *Anthony Trollope*. 1955. London: Methuen, 1968. Print.

Cole, Sarah Rose. "National Histories, International Genre: Thackeray, Balzac, and the Franco-British Bildungsroman." *Romanticism and Victorianism on the Net* 48 (2007). <http://www.erudit.org/revue/ravon/2007/v/n48/017436ar.html?vue=resume>.

Corbett, Mary Jean. "'Two Identities': Gender, Ethnicity, and Phineas Finn." *The Politics of Gender in Trollope: New Readings for the Twenty-First Century*. Ed. Regenia Gagnier, Deborah Denenholz Morse, and Margaret Markwick. Aldershot: Ashgate Press, 2009 117–30. Print.

Craig, David M. "Advanced Conservative Liberalism: Party and Principle in Trollope's Parliamentary Novels." *Victorian Literature and Culture* 38.2 (2010): 355–71. Print.

Dever, Carolyn, and Lisa Niles, ed. *The Cambridge Companion to Anthony Trollope*. Cambridge: Cambridge University Press, 2010. Print.

Dinwiddy, J. R. "Who's Who in Trollope's Political Novels?" *Nineteenth-Century Fiction* 22.1 (June 1967): 31–46. Print.

Disraeli, Benjamin. "Conservative Principles: April 3, 1872." *Selected Speeches of the Late Right Honourable the Earl of Beaconsfield*. Ed. T. E. Kebbel. Vol. 2. London: Longmans, Green, 1882. 490–535. Print.

Eliot, George. *Felix Holt: The Radical*. 3 vols. London: Blackwood, 1866. Print.

Faulkner, Karen. "Anthony Trollope's Apprenticeship." *Nineteenth-Century Fiction* 38.2 (1983): 161–88. Print.

Felber, Lynette. "The Advanced Conservative Liberal: Victorian Liberalism and the Aesthetics of Anthony Trollope's Palliser Novels." *Modern Philology* 107.3 (2010): 355–71. Print.

Flint, Kate. "Queer Trollope." *The Cambridge Companion to Anthony Trollope*. Ed. Carolyn Dever and Lisa Niles. Cambridge: Cambridge University Press, 2010. 99–112. Print.

Foucault, Michel. *The Birth of Biopolitics: Lectures at the Collège de France 1978–79*. 2004. Trans. Graham Burchell. Ed. Michel Senellart. Basingstoke: Palgrave Macmillan, 2008. Print.

Gagnier, Regenia. "Conclusion: Gender, Liberalism and Resentment." *The Politics of Gender in Trollope: New Readings for the Twenty-First Century*. Ed. Regenia Gagnier, Deborah Denenholz Morse, and Margaret Markwick. Aldershot: Ashgate Press, 2009. 235–48. Print.

Gagnier, Regenia, Margaret Markwick, and Deborah Denenholz Morse, ed. *The Politics of Gender in Anthony Trollope's Novels*. Aldershot: Ashgate Press, 2009. Print.

Gikandi, Simon. *Maps of Englishness*. New York: Columbia University Press, 1996. Print.

Goodlad, Lauren M. E. *The Victorian Geopolitical Aesthetic: Realism, Sovereignty, and Transnational Experience*. Oxford: Oxford University Press, 2015. Print.

———. *Victorian Literature and the Victorian State: Character and Governance in a Liberal Society*. Baltimore: Johns Hopkins University Press, 2003. Print.

Green, T. H. *Lectures on the Principles of Political Obligation and Other Writings*. Ed. Paul Harris and John Morrow. Cambridge: Cambridge University Press, 1986. Print.

Hadley, Elaine. *Living Liberalism: Practical Citizenship in Victorian Britain.* Chicago: University of Chicago Press, 2010. Print.
Hagan, John. "The Divided Mind of Anthony Trollope." *Nineteenth-Century Fiction* 14.1 (1959): 1–26. Print.
Hall, Catherine. "Going a–Trolloping: Imperial Man Travels the Empire." *Gender and Imperialism.* Ed. Clare Midgley. Manchester: Manchester University Press, 1998. 180–99. Print.
Hall, N. John, ed. *The Letters of Anthony Trollope.* Stanford: Stanford University Press, 1983. Print.
———. *Trollope: A Biography.* Oxford: Oxford University Press, 1991. Print.
Halperin, John. "Trollope and the American Civil War." *Clio* 13.2 (Winter 1984): 149–55. Print.
———. *Trollope and Politics: A Study of the Pallisers and Others.* London: Macmillan, 1977. Print.
Harvie, Christopher. *The Centre of Things: Political Fiction in Britain from Disraeli to the Present.* London: Unwin Hyman, 1991. Print.
Hensley, Nathan. "Mr. Trollope, Lady Credit, and *The Way We Live Now.*" *The Politics of Gender in Trollope: New Readings for the Twenty-First Century.* Ed. Regenia Gagnier, Deborah Denenholz Morse, and Margaret Markwick. Aldershot: Ashgate Press, 2009. 147–60. Print.
Hughes, Robert. "'Spontaneous Order' and the Politics of Anthony Trollope." *Nineteenth-Century Literature* 41.1 (1986): 32–48. Print.
Jameson, Fredric. *The Antinomies of Realism:* London: Verso, 2013. Print.
———. *The Political Unconscious: Narrative as a Socially Symbolic Act.* Ithaca: Cornell University, 1981. Print.
Kincaid, James. "*Barchester Towers* and the Nature of Conservative Comedy." *ELH* 37.4 (December 1970): 595–612. Print.
———. *The Novels of Anthony Trollope.* Oxford: Clarendon, 1977. Print.
Langbauer, Laurie. "The Hobbledehoy in Trollope." *The Cambridge Companion to Anthony Trollope.* Ed. Carolyn Dever and Lisa Niles. Cambridge: Cambridge University Press, 2010. 113–27. Print.
Levine, George. *The Realistic Imagination: English Fiction from Frankenstein to Lady Chatterley.* Chicago: University of Chicago Press, 1981. Print.
Lonergan, Patrick. "The Representation of Phineas Finn: Anthony Trollope's Palliser Series and Victorian Ireland." *Victorian Literature and Culture* 32.1 (2004): 147–58. Print.
Lowe, Robert. *Speeches and Letters on Reform.* 2nd ed. London: Bush, 1867. Print.
Lukács, Georg. *The Historical Novel.* Trans. Hannah Mitchell and Stephen Mitchell. Lincoln: University of Nebraska Press, 1983. Print.
———. *Studies in European Realism: A Sociological Survey of the Writings of Balzac, Stendhal, Tolstoy, Gorki and Others.* Trans. Edith Bone. London: Hillway, 1950. Print.
Mantena, Karuna. "The Crisis of Liberal Imperialism." *Victorian Visions of Global Order: Empire and International Relations in Nineteenth-Century Political Thought.* Ed. Duncan Bell. Cambridge: Cambridge University Press, 2007. 113–35. Print.
Marcus, Sharon. "Contracting Female Marriage in Anthony Trollope's *Can You Forgive Her?*" *Nineteenth-Century Literature* 60.3 (2005): 291–325. Print.
Markwick, Margaret. "Out of the Closet: Homoerotics in Trollope's Novels." *The Politics of Gender in Trollope: New Readings for the Twenty-First Century.* Ed. Regenia Gagnier, Deborah Denenholz Morse, and Margaret Markwick. Aldershot: Ashgate Press, 2009. 61–76. Print.
Meredith, George. "Belles Lettres and Art." *Westminster Review* 68.134 (October 1857): 585–604. Print.
Mill, John Stuart. *England and Ireland.* London: Longmans, 1868. Print.
———. "Representation of The People [2], 13 April 1866." *Collected Works of John Stuart Mill.* Volume 28. *Public and Parliamentary Speeches (November 1850–November 1868).* Ed. John M. Robson and Bruce L. Kinzer. Toronto: University of Toronto Press, 1988. 58–68. Print.
Miller, D. A. *The Novel and the Police.* Berkeley: University of California Press, 1988. Print.
Morse, Deborah Denenholz. *Reforming Trollope: Race, Gender, and Englishness in the Novels of Anthony Trollope.* Aldershot: Ashgate Press, 2013. Print.
———. "The Way He Thought Then: Modernity and the Retreat of the Public Liberal in Anthony Trollope's *The Way We Live Now.*" *BRANCH* <http://www.branchcollective.org/?ps_articles=deborah-denenholz-morse-the-way-he-thought-then-modernity-and-the-retreat-of-the-public-liberal-in-anthony-trollopes-the-way-we-live-now-1873>.
———. *Women in Trollope's Palliser Novels.* Rochester: University of Rochester Press, 1987. Print.
Nardin, Jane. "Conservative Comedy and the Women of *Barchester Towers.*" *Studies in the Novel* 18.4 (1986): 381–94. Print.
Noble, Christopher S. "Otherwise Occupied: Masculine Widows in Trollope's Novels." *The Politics of Gender in Trollope: New Readings for the Twenty-First Century.* Ed. Regenia Gagnier, Deborah Denenholz Morse, and Margaret Markwick. Aldershot: Ashgate Press, 2009. 177–92. Print.

Parry, Jonathan. *The Rise and Fall of Liberal Government in Victorian Britain*. New Haven: Yale University Press, 1993. Print.

Pocock, J. G. A. *The Machiavellian Moment: Florentine Political Thought and the Atlantic Republican Tradition*. Princeton: Princeton University Press, 1975. Print.

Polhemus, Robert M. *Comic Faith: The Great Tradition from Austen to Joyce*. Chicago: University of Chicago Press, 1980. Print.

Purdy, Daniel. *Narrative Bodies: Toward a Corporeal Narratology*. New York: Palgrave Macmillan, 2003. Print.

Ragussis, Michael. *Figures of Conversion: "The Jewish Question" and English National Identity*. Durham: Duke University Press, 1995. Print.

Robbins, Bruce. *Upward Mobility and the Common Good: Toward a Literary History of the Welfare State*. Princeton: Princeton University Press, 2009. Print.

Sadleir, Michael. *Trollope: A Commentary*. 3rd ed. London: Oxford University Press, 1961. Print.

Steele, E. D. *Irish Land and British Politics*. Cambridge: Cambridge University Press, 1974. Print.

Stephen, James Fitzjames. "Liberalism." *Cornhill Magazine* 5.25 (1862): 70–83. Print.

Super, R. H. *The Chronicler of Barsetshire: A Life of Anthony Trollope*. Ann Arbor: University of Michigan Press. 1988. Print.

Sutherland, John. "Introduction." Trollope, *Barchester Towers*. vii–xxviii. Print.

———. "Introduction." Trollope, *Writings in Saint Paul's Magazine*. n.p. Print.

Tracy, Robert. *Trollope's Later Novels*. Berkeley: University of California Press, 1978. Print.

Trollope, Anthony. *The American Senator*. 1877. Ed. John Halperin. Oxford: Oxford University Press, 1999. Print.

———. *An Autobiography*. 1883. Ed. Michael Sadleir and Frederick Page. Oxford: Oxford University Press, 1999. Print.

———. *Barchester Towers*. 1857. Eds. Frederick Page and Michael Sadleir. Oxford: Oxford University Press, 2009. Print.

———. *Can You Forgive Her?* 1864–5. Ed. Andrew Swarbrick. Oxford: Oxford University Press, 2008. Print.

———. "Cicero as a Politician." *The Fortnightly Review* 21.124 (April 1877): 495–515. Print.

———. *Doctor Thorne*. 1858. Ed. David Skilton. Oxford: Oxford University Press, 2000. Print.

———. *The Eustace Diamonds*. 1872. Ed. W. J. McCormack. Oxford: Oxford University Press, 1983. Print.

———. *The Fixed Period*. 1882. Ed. David Skilton. London: The Trollope Society, 1997. Print.

———. *Framley Parsonage*. 1861. Ed. David Skilton and Peter Miles. London: Penguin, 1985. Print.

———. *The Landleaguers*. 1883. Ed. David Skilton. London: The Trollope Society, 1995. Print.

———. *The Last Chronicle of Barset*. 1867. Ed. Stephen Gill. Oxford: Oxford University Press, 1980. Print.

———. *The Letters of Anthony Trollope*. Ed. N. John Hall. Stanford, CA: Stanford University Press, 1983. Print.

———. *The Life of Cicero*. 2 vols. London: Chapman and Hall, 1880. Print.

———. *Marion Fay: A Novel*. 1882. Ed. R. H. Super. Ann Arbor: University of Michigan Press, 1985. Print.

———. "Mr. Gladstone's Irish Land Bill." 1870. Trollope, *Writings* 620–30. Print.

———. *North America*. New York: Harper, 1862. Print.

———. "On Sovereignty." 1867. Trollope, *Writings* 76–91. Print.

———. *Phineas Finn*. 1869. Ed. Jacques Berthoud. Oxford: Oxford University Press, 2008. Print.

———. *The Prime Minister*. 1876. Ed. David Skilton. Harmondsworth: Penguin, 1996. Print.

———. "Public Schools." *Fortnightly Review* 2 (October 1, 1865): 476–87. Print.

———. *The Way We Live Now*. 1875. Ed. John Sutherland. Oxford: Oxford University Press, 1986. Print.

———. "Whom Shall We Make Leader of the New House of Commons?" 1868. Trollope, *Writings*. 531–545. Print.

———. *Writings for Saint Pauls Magazine*. Ed. John Sutherland. New York: Arno, 1981. Print.

Trotter, Jackson. "Foxhunting and the English Social Order in Trollope's *The American Senator*." *Studies in the Novel* 24.3 (1992): 227–41. Print.

Tyler, Colin. "T. H. Green, Advanced Liberalism and the Reform Question 1865–1876." *History of European Ideas* 29.4 (2003): 437–58. Print.

Van, Annette. "Ambivalent Speculations: America as England's Future in *The Way We Live Now*." *Novel: A Forum on Fiction* 39.1 (2005): 75–96. Print.

Van Dam, Frederik. *Anthony Trollope's Late Style: Victorian Liberalism and Literary Form*. Edinburgh: Edinburgh University Press, 2016. Print.

White, Hayden. *Metahistory: The Historical Imagination in Nineteenth-Century Europe.* Baltimore: Johns Hopkins University Press, 2014. Print.
Wohl, Anthony S. "Dizzi-Ben-Dizzi: Disraeli as Alien." *Journal of British Studies* 34.3 (July 1995): 375–411. Print.
Wolfreys, Julian. "The Nineteenth-Century Political Novel." *A Companion to the Victorian Novel.* Ed. William Baker and Kenneth Womack. Westport: Greenwood, 2002. 49–67. Print.

2
TROLLOPE AND THE STATE

Michael Martel

In 1851, looking to establish a comprehensive mail system, the British Post Office dispatched a struggling novelist to survey possible mail routes in rural Britain. Having gained expertise in such labor while in Ireland, Anthony Trollope dove headfirst into his English surveying. "It was the ambition of my life," Trollope recollects, "to cover the country with rural letter-carriers" (*An Autobiography*, ch. 5). An arduous task, extending the postal network into the provincial backwaters of the nation: riding forty miles a day and visiting every nook in western Britain, Trollope determined the length of carriers' routes, arranged them to include as many hamlets and villages as possible, and calculated the cost-effectiveness of the potential route against the promised volume of mail (Super 21). Trollope's account of his surveying highlights a set of protocols that will become critical to his fiction's portrayal of the Victorian state. Trollope characterized his state position as that of a "beneficent angel" bringing a "more regular delivery of letters" to regions previously served in "an irregular manner" (*Autobiography*, ch. 5). Surveying integrates otherwise isolated persons and locales into a comprehensive network. The state coordinates, but it does so through a paradoxical appearance. To gather information for new postal routes, Trollope had "to startle" inhabitants "into the revelations which I required them to make for their own good" (*Autobiography*, ch. 5). Noticeable though he must be, Trollope nevertheless remains a mystery to rural Britons: "the angelic nature of my mission was imperfectly understood" because "I . . . did not allow as much time as was necessary to explain" it (ibid.). A conspicuous yet enigmatic outsider bringing order to a disordered nation: retrospectively, Trollope casts the postal surveyor as emblematic of the state as it had appeared in his fiction for nearly three decades.

We encounter the state everywhere in Trollope's novels. Small wonder, then, that Trollope has garnered extensive attention in Victorian state studies, a particularly fruitful subfield of literary scholarship concerned with literature's intersection with the state and governance.[1] Chronicling the "clerico-political world" (*Barchester Towers*, ch. 52), Trollope's fiction abounds with Church of England clergy, secretaries from the civil service, and members of Parliament and the government. In novel after novel we witness the internecine struggles over pastoral responsibilities, the bureaucratization of the civil service, and partisan fracases over government control. By focusing on such disputes, literary historians have brought to light Trollope's engagement with individual components of the state. For such scholarship, the specificity of the state depends upon its focalization through typically male, professional characters: clergymen, civil servants, and politicians.

The whole of the state thereby seems reducible to parts like the civil service, the Church of England, and Parliament and its government.[2]

And yet for all its prominence we rarely learn what the state does. What Trollope's contemporary Walter Bagehot called the efficient secret of the British Constitution – the executive organs of the nation state performing "the work of government" (5) – appears in Trollope's novels only indirectly through figurative tropes. Trollope carries out a literary project scholars now recognize as crucial to the realist novel's role in developing the modern state during the Victorian period. Portraying the state as both noticeable and opaque, Trollope imagines a state that functions best when it slides into the background of everyday life. Postal routes, highways, sewers, weights, and measures: these mundane aspects of the state pervade the lives of Victorians as so much white noise, despite their importance. The realist novel, argues Bruce Robbins, makes visible such a routine yet vital state. Unlike Charles Dickens, who uses caricatures like the Circumlocution Office to visualize the state and thereby establish a vantage point from which it can be criticized and rejected, Trollope's novels echo the very form of the state they depict. Conspicuous in its characterization yet obscure in its day-to-day operations, the state in Trollope's fiction appears much as it would in the everyday lives of his Victorian and contemporary readers.

Using literary forms that simultaneously evoke and elide the complexity of the Victorian state, Trollope draws much from the postal system. Like postal addresses, metonymy, which Trollope uses to characterize state officials and recurring series characters, abstracts complex information – persons, localities, and entire systems of power – into truncated forms that can then be circulated with broader networks. Literary form, therefore, is not simply a vehicle for narrating the intersection between the representation of the state and its routine activities. It serves as the means whereby Trollope first mimics the form of the state as it appears to his readers and then repeats the state's ongoing effort to reform its multitudinous parts into a working order. Functioning like addresses, the state characters of Trollope's fiction coordinate disparate departments, institutions, and domains into a figure of the state. Through this figure, Trollope acclimates readers to a state increasingly permeating their everyday lives. Having integrated rural Britain into the state as a postal surveyor, Trollope the novelist naturalizes such a state for a skeptical public.

Representative state: governance and the everyday

Recent scholarship describes the Victorian state as nearly synonymous with governance, or in the jargon, governmentality – the rationalities, protocols, and technologies involved in attempts to shape deliberately any aspect of others' or one's own behavior according to a set of norms and for a variety of ends (Dean 10). Pushing back against Victorian studies' overreliance on Foucauldian "discipline" (in which social controls are internalized to the degree that they seem natural and inescapable), Lauren Goodlad argues that Michel Foucault's notion of governmentality offers us a more flexible and apt model of Victorian power relations. For Goodlad, the problem with Victorianists' overreliance upon discipline is that as "a totalizing paradigm in which human subjectivity is reduced to the effect of an inescapable mode of domination" it overshadows the Victorians' own imagining of themselves "as citizens of a self-governing nation and heirs to ancient constitutional liberties" (*Victorian Literature* 2–3). Instead, governmentality, with its emphases on purportedly free subjects and indirect rule, offers scholars a better framework for Victorian England. Governmentality, accordingly, reconfigures our definition of the state. Rather than a monolithic institution locatable in Whitehall, the Victorian state forms a dispersed and nearly unlocalizable array of state and non-state actors because of its ostensible commitment to ideals of individual liberty and a less-is-more theory of government. In Goodlad's words, "Britain's ruling classes strove to govern *indirectly*: to implement parliamentary power in ways that encouraged self-help, philanthropy, volunteerism, and local government" (ibid. 14). The Victorian state's indirect governance arose from its balance of such philosophical liberalism and modes of pastoral rule. On the one hand, liberal governance stipulated that one governs best by governing least, a formula that cordoned off from the state entire swaths of the social fabric; on the other hand, pastoral modes of rule, such as self-help societies and charity organizations, enabled the state to indirectly intervene into these domains (Maurer 15). Offering an encyclopedia of the state's indirect interventions into everyday life, Trollope's fiction enables us to understand the Victorian state as analogous to the totality of such extensive alliances. As we see in Trollope's fiction, even in its more circumscribed forms the Victorian state attempted to facilitate, indirectly, the "free" activity of domains purportedly separate from it – the economy, populations, individual character, and the domestic.

Long concerned with financial swindles – from Nathaniel Sowerby's duplicitous dealings with Mark Robarts in *Framley Parsonage* (1861) to the predatory speculations of Augustus Melmotte and Ferdinand Lopez in *The Way We Live Now* (1875) and *The Prime Minister* (1876) – Trollope rarely has the state intervene, either to protect unsuspecting victims like Mark or to punish perpetrators like Lopez. But Trollope's state is not strictly *laissez-faire*. In Trollope's fiction, the state plays the dual role of economic umpire and facilitator. It regulates local economic activities through inspection and funds them through grants-in-aid. Much of *The Three Clerks'* (1857) depiction of governance focuses on the state's role as an arbitrator in local economies. In that novel, Alaric Tudor's meteoric rise through the civil service starts with his successful inspection of and report on the Wheal Mary Jane mine in Cornwall. Without directly intervening in the self-governance of the mine, the Department of Woods and Forests instead settles "some disputed point as to the boundaries and privileges of certain mines" (ch. 7). Such inspection and arbitration exemplify the central state's intervention into local affairs during the early and mid-Victorian periods (Eastwood 162).

Alaric's unethical speculation in Wheal Mary Jane mining shares – unethical because the value of the shares depends upon the very report Alaric pens – also suggests the dangers involved in such indirect intervention. Increasingly, the Victorian state turned to grants-in-aid as a mechanism for facilitating the nation's economy (Bellamy 24–25). The Exchequer distributed these grants, also known as "subventions," to local authorities for the purposes of developing the infrastructures needed to bolster local economies and support the health of populations. While having early nineteenth-century antecedents, especially the funding of estate drainage following parliamentary enclosures, grants-in-aid increased during the later half of the century as the state tried to develop stronger controls over local affairs. John Fletcher's land drainage bill in *The Prime Minister* typifies this practice. Fletcher's bill proposes that the Exchequer will "lend money to the parishes" for "draining bits of common land" (ch. 37). Once they drain the land, the parishes will sell it to farmers, who will "increase the cereal products of the country," thereby increasing England's competitiveness in the international grain market. The profits from these sales will in turn fund the local poor rates and public health projects, both of which facilitate the health of marginalized populations. "Parliament can do such a thing," asserts Fletcher, "not because it has any creative power of its own, but because it has the command of unlimited capital." Operating according to the logic of liberal governance, the state, regardless of party affiliations like those of the Conservative Fletcher or the Liberal Plantagenet Palliser, provides the funds to build the infrastructure needed for agricultural and biological prosperity.

The Victorian state as imagined by Trollope also indirectly shapes individual character and the domestic sphere. As a privileged term in Trollope studies, character has garnered extensive attention by scholars interested in Trollope's engagement with the state. Typically this scholarship explores Trollope's characterization of state agents. Through his idealized portrayals of civil servants and clergymen, Trollope sought to restore public confidence in the state. Racked by its disastrous handling of the Crimean War (1853–1856) and a long-standing reputation for nepotism, the civil service was in great need of such restoration mid-century. By characterizing the ideal civil servant as a mixture of genteel disinterestedness and enterprising self-interestedness, Trollope suggested that the civil service could, in Goodlad's words, "sublimate the nation's bold entrepreneurial spirit by integrating it within the crucial imagining of a 'classless class of well-bred men'" (*Victorian Literature* 120). Similarly, Laura Rotunno argues that with his postal novel, *John Caldigate* (1879), Trollope attempted to promote public trust in the ideals of the civil service (95). Addressing readers skeptical about the state's commitment to equal opportunity and social progress, *John Caldigate* offers Samuel Bagwax, the altruistic postal official who saves the novel's eponymous hero from bigamy charges and is rewarded with a promotion. Similarly, clergymen like Septimus Harding and Josiah Crawley play the Arnoldian pastor, a classless best self striving to foster the good conduct of impoverished and marginalized flocks.

Beyond imagining the ideal civil servant, Trollope's fiction also sought to create that very paragon. This process extends to the state what David Skilton calls Trollope's "chief subject" – the modeling through fiction of how to make life choices enabling one to live a morally and economically fulfilling life in an imperfect world (128). As Nicholas Dames and Frederik Van Dam demonstrate, Trollope's representation of the career provided a template for the growing army of state bureaucrats fictionalized in *The Three Clerks*' Charley Tudor, *The Small House at Allington* (1864) and *The Last Chronicle of Barset*'s (1867) Johnny Eames and Adolphus Crosbie, and *Marion Fay*'s (1882) George Rodon. As a narrative pattern, the career mediates social energy, "making of 'vocations' or 'ambitions' a path more amenable to rationalization" after the Crimean War and the Trevelyan-Northcote report uncovered the woefully inept administration of the civil service (Dames 249). In both of these lines of criticism, individual character solidifies through the indirect aid of the state. Exemplars like Bagwax and the figure of the career offered civil servants what Elaine Hadley calls "liberal formalism," a code of conduct outlining "*how* one ought to think but not precisely *what* to think" (10).

Following the same imperative to bolster activities beyond it, the state also gives shape to the domestic through infrastructures, which provide its material and legal conditions of possibility. In this facet of Trollope's novels, the state mediates non-state actors' domestic relations to each other and their social worlds. Critics like Richard Menke, Catherine Golden, and Kate Thomas have demonstrated how in Trollope's novels state infrastructures like the post give shape to the everyday lives of characters. Using literary forms like the postal plot – in which postal accessories like postmarks, stamps, postman, and pillar boxes drive narrative action (Thomas 30) – Trollope imagines how the state's postal system structures social relations into imagined communities, such as the nation (Thomas 38). Trollope repeatedly stages this process by emphasizing the role of the postal system in securing good marriages. Across Trollope's oeuvre, the penny post, when used properly, facilitates marriage plots. Alice Vavasor returns to John Grey after inculcating proper postal conduct in *Can You Forgive Her?* (1864–1865); in *The Eustace Diamonds* (1872) Lucy Morris and Frank Greystock's courtship sours and sweetens depending upon their use of the post. Even existing marriages are patched up through the post. Plantagenet and Glencora Palliser restore their fraught marriage in part through their postal communications with the old Duke of Omnium in *Can You Forgive Her?* Beyond the ubiquity of the postal system, Trollope's political novels also position the state as guarantor of property ownership, a similarly infrastructural imagining of the state. Through what Sara Maurer calls vicarious enjoyment – wherein legal owners need "to be joined to the dispossessed in order to have someone who might enjoy their prosperity in their place" (12) – Trollope portrays the state as indirectly facilitating the everyday social relations of Britons by securing their requisite legal parameters.

While offering insights into Victorian England's fraught balance of individual liberty and the perceived need for greater governmental intervention, existing scholarship has elucidated only a fragmentary version of Trollope's state. By and large the disparate components of the state remain isolated from each other in critics' discussions of Trollope. The civil service, the government, the post, and so on have received thorough investigation, their varied dimensions brought into sharp focus. Without an account of how Trollope threads these pieces together, scholarship may, at times, repeat the central dilemma of Victorian governance: the proliferation of government, either by the central state or local governments, ever threatened disorder and unevenness. Some regions would be quick to modernize their government, adopting new technologies for policing, public health, and transportation, while others would begrudgingly cling to old practices and old infrastructures. Faced with such disorder, many Victorians advocated for stronger mechanisms of centralized and/or national control. Writers like John Stuart Mill, Walter Bagehot, and Trollope imagined alternative models of the state capable of drawing this disarray to order.[3] In part, their work theorized the state as one prominent component in a larger field of government, a way of thinking that anticipates the political theorists Peter Miller and Nikolas Rose. Miller and Rose argue that the state is "a way in which certain technologies of government are given a temporary institutional durability and brought into particular kinds of relations with one another" ("Political Power Beyond the State" 56). Such is the state envisioned by Mill, Bagehot, and, especially, Trollope: an institutional framework that shapes a jumble of different technologies of government into stable form, therein making them accountable to representative politics. Victorians called this state "representative government."

Literary historians have begun to investigate the relationship between the state and literature in terms that resonate with the Victorians' emphasis on representative government. They have taught us that the modern state operates largely in the background of our lives. As bridges and highways, sewers and waterworks, parks and libraries benefit our lives, we fall prey to what H. G. Wells called "state blindness": the inability to perceive the state as pervading our lives. In representative governments like the one Victorian Britain was fast becoming, the invisibility of the state presents an acute problem: public control and oversight of the state are dependent upon the state's visibility and yet the state's effectiveness relies upon its ability to fade into obscurity. In libertarian political climates like Victorian Britain, representation of the state becomes paramount to the state's continued expansion. Representative government concerns not only the political representation of citizens to the state but also the representation of the state to its citizens. The realist novel, with its privileging of the quotidian, became a critical tool for such mediation. In their attempts to depict the everydayness of Victorian culture, Trollope's novels were exceptionally poised to track the intersections between his readers' lives and the rapidly expanding state. Beyond the ways illuminated by previous critics (and summarized earlier), how Trollope's fiction offers an image of the state as the combination of individual components has, however, only recently flitted onto Victorianists' radars. Lauren Goodlad and I have begun to grapple with the ways Trollope's realism uses figurative language to transform Victorian governance's heterogeneity into a cohesive whole retrospectively designated as "the state." Much as the individual components of the state function by fading into the background, so too does the state in its entirety. The task of the realist novel, therefore, is to give new shape to the state. Unlike previous Trollope scholarship, which sees the state as only metonymic to its individual parts, the rest of this chapter demonstrates how across his career Trollope figures the state as a whole that is always also localized in its parts. He does so, I argue, by using the state's protocols to transform the litany of civil servants, departments, and infrastructures into the figure "the state."

Figures of the state: character and metonymy

Tracking the state's indirect interventions into the economy, health of populations, individual character, and the domestic sphere, Trollope's fiction attempts to garner his readers' trust in and acclimation to a rapidly transforming state. He does so in a manner resonant to the state. As Goodlad recently argued, Trollope interrogated imperialism by depicting it as the "great Parliamentary bore" – a conspicuous yet obfuscating topic of parliamentary debate (*The Victorian Geopolitical Aesthetic* 96). While a critical component of the British state, imperial administration attempted to gain autonomy from representative, political oversight by obfuscating its activities in an avalanche of technical jargon (*The Victorian Geopolitical Aesthetic* 101). *The Eustace Diamonds* (1872) interrogates such mystification through the figure of the Indian Sawab, who serves as "a figural marker of a political-imperial map" (115). As a figure for the imperial state, the Sawab not only links narratives about party politics, marriage, empire, and ownership, but also reiterates the very procedures of the Victorian state. He is conspicuous as an emblem of imperial rule and yet an obscure minor figure, a "non-character." This paradoxical representation, I argue, is a key characteristic of Trollope's figuration of the Victorian state, which follows the same representational logic.

As a formal procedure, what does it mean to figure the state? At bottom, such figuration entails coordinating an array of otherwise isolated parts into an apparent whole. In rhetorical terms, such figuration is synecdochical: "the state" stands in for its individual parts – officials, offices, departments, and so on. As Timothy Mitchell theorizes, without such a synecdoche the state's welter of components would remain perceptually isolated (94). We can see the basic form of this troping in Charles Dickens's Circumlocution Office. As what Dickens calls "the Whole Science of Government," the Circumlocution Office condenses the state into a single, localizable figure that can be more readily criticized and, ultimately, rejected. Trollope, however, never uses such figuration, which within the realist novel ossifies and immobilizes the state. Rather, Trollope figures the state through metonymy, synecdoche's close cousin. In Trollope, individual components stand in for the state without coalescing into a monolithic figure, "the state." Instead, each component is both part and whole. As metonymy, Trollope's figurative state remediates the protocols of the historical Victorian state the better to portray the latter's paradoxically dispersed situatedness: the state is limited and therefore everywhere. If for Dickens synecdoche pins down the state the better to reject it, for Trollope metonymy scatters the state even as it locates it in individual characters and settings.

This paradoxical quirk of Trollope's state derives from the postal system. Following the creation of national penny postage in 1839, the British Post rapidly expanded both in volume and in scale. Trollope's surveying is one instance of the general procedure whereby the state attempted to manage such expansion. By a system of addresses and mail routes, the state brought to order the prevailing disorder of the emerging postal system. This involved a two-step process: first transform persons and locations into addresses and then situate those addresses within an open-ended network of other addresses. This process, which postal historians designate by the neologism "addressability," enabled the British postal system to become the most efficient and voluminous mail system in the world by the mid-Victorian period. As a pattern for organizing individual entities – persons, locations – into a complex, ordered system, addressability was a highly portable protocol. Mid-Victorian civil service reforms followed this same pattern; they transformed individual departments into three-tiered divisions of labor that became interchangeable with other departments, thereby standardizing and unifying the entire civil service (Perkin 9). In the same manner, late nineteenth-century local government reforms first homogenized individual counties, parishes, and boroughs and then linked them together in a nationwide system of governance.

Addressability, in other words, was more than a protocol for the postal system. It served as a general procedure whereby the modern British state organized itself.

The affordances of such a pattern were not limited to the state, however. Pattern is another word for form, as Caroline Levine points out; as the *"arrangement of elements,"* form operates by *"ordering, patterning, or shaping"* (3) – all terms with which historians describe the Victorian state.[4] More than mere correlation between the state and literary form is at play here. After all, like Trollope surveying rural Britain, form travels (Levine 4–5). Addressability, as the two-part process of renaming and reconnecting, structures Trollope's figuration of the state. Addressability offered Trollope's fiction patterns for organizing the state's seemingly isolated parts into a cohesive whole. What Menke argues about *The Three Clerks* and the civil service can be extended to Trollope's figuration of the state overall: Trollope "uses the Post Office as a scheme for organizing the representation of real life" (56–57). Just as Trollope the postal official does in the anecdote I began with, Trollope's novels construct the state as a networked entity comprising nodes and their connections – addresses and routes, civil servants and departments, departments and the civil service, and so on, a cascade of interlocking parts and wholes. Like addresses, Trollope's state characters become metonymic for their positions within the state, a figurative status that enables Trollope to circulate them within a broadening figuration of the state.

Trollope's state characters all feel the pressure of institutional conformity. For Trollope, the ideal civil servant was an individual adaptable to the rigors of the individual department within which he worked. Of Charlie Tudor, the youngest of the titular *Three Clerks*, Trollope remarks, "he was easily malleable, and he took at once the full impression of the stamp to which he was subjected" (ch. 2). While such plasticity renders Charlie susceptible to the mildly corrupting influences of the boisterous Internal Navigation Office, it also enables him to become the novel's lone career civil servant. In an age of civil service reform following the debacles of the Crimean War, Charlie's malleability suggested that the state needed to produce officials fitted to its requirements, instead of, as reformers like Stafford Northcote and Sir Charles Trevelyan argued, using entrance examinations to find them ready-made. In regards to the state, Trollope's is a prescriptive notion of character rather than a descriptive one: an official's character is changeable and not an expression of that individual's intrinsic nature. As Colón, Dames, and Craig have demonstrated in regards to the Church of England, the civil service, and parliamentary politics, prescriptive character appears throughout Trollope's exploration of the state. It encapsulates the central tension of Trollope's professional plots: characters' expression of individual will and their adherence to a collective institutional order. Septimus Harding and the Church of England, Johnny Eames and the Income Tax Office, Phineas Finn and the Liberal Party, Bagwax and the General Post Office: across Trollope's long career, the state's individual departments operate according to the conflict between individual actors and the imperatives of the collective order. At stake in this conflict, however, is not so much the autonomy of the individual official but rather the state's legibility. A metonymic process underlies this issue of autonomy and malleability. Through plots such as those of fledgling politician Phineas Finn's, Trollope turns a rhetorical trope into a procedure whereby individuals come to stand in for parts of the state. We can read the eponymous undersecretary's stand for Irish tenant rights in *Phineas Finn* (1869), for instance, as a resistance to becoming a metonymy for the state. In later novels, having returned from a political exile spurred by his Irish tenant rights stand, Phineas Finn and his vote – his expression of individuality – become indexes of the Gresham and Omnium governments. Phineas becomes that metonymy for the government he resisted in *Phineas Finn*: "the honourable member" (ch. 38). Part stands in for the whole, officials for the state, Phineas for the government.

An official's adaptability entails becoming a metonym for a portion of the state. And yet, metonymy alone does not figure the state in Trollope's fiction. Phineas Finn, government official, does not represent the entirety of the British state, but rather its parliamentary component, the Liberal Gresham government. Similarly, Bishop Proudie and Gregory Hardlines stand in for branches of the state, the Church and the civil service, not the entire multifaceted state they help compose. In the same way that the government, the Church, the civil service, and the postal system do not form, on their own, "the state," individual metonymies in Trollope's fiction do not figure the state in its entirety. Rather they do so only when they are all coordinated together.

Configured state: addressability and the series novel

To fully grasp how Trollope uses individual characters to figure the state we must now return to the idea of "addressability." Within Trollope's fiction state officials become the addresses of the departments for which they work. Characters in Trollope's novels operate by the very protocols of the post's system of addressability, wherein individuals and locations were abstracted into addresses circulatable within the postal system. Much as a character becomes a metonym for the portion of the state for which he labors, an address is metonymic of the coupling of individuals to locations. The peculiar metonymy of both Trollope's characters and addresses proceeds through a condensation of complex information into compact discursive units. A person or a location becomes represented by the address, which has meaning only within the context of the postal system. Analogously, in Trollope's fiction a state department becomes condensed into a character, whose name can then situate that department in relation to others, similarly crystalized in individual characters. Addressability's play between metonymy and coordination is crucial to Trollope's figuration of the state. It enables his fiction to link the seemingly isolated and otherwise opaque components of the Victorian state into a legible whole.

When characters form addresses – by becoming metonymies enabling the mapping of a complex network of other metonymies – their links give shape to the Trollopian state, a scattered yet unified array. It is therefore no accident that Mr. Monk, Trollope's ideal government official in his balance of independence and official duty (Craig 368), is a recurring series character. Trollope's series fiction seems an obvious foil to the discursive abbreviation of the address: a loose baggy monster entailing two intertwined series of six triple-decker novels totaling over 7,000 pages written, published, and originally read over two decades. Yet this expansive, open-ended writing achieved its cohesion through types of writing of a very different scale: the short, truncated reappearances of main characters, the textual recurrence of which performs the sort of contraction the address made routine. As Stephen Wall, Lynette Felber, and Laurie Langbauer have demonstrated, Trollope's series novels are riven by the tension between the boundedness of individual novels and open-endedness of the series they form. Eschewing the continuation of plots across novels, Trollope's series fiction coheres through a complex network of repeating characters, the recognition of whom, in Wall's estimate, depends upon intimacy between reader and character established over the long durée of the series (132). In other words, Trollope's series novels meet their generic imperative to coordinate semiautonomous parts without closure by means of a novelistic addressability built through recurring, self-referential characters. Recurring characters function as addresses: abridged, abstracted representations of fully fleshed-out figures circulating within a new system. Protagonists reappear in the abbreviated form of the minor character, thereby enabling the series reader to link the current novel with previous ones. And through such metonymic characterization, which operates upon characters plucked from the governing classes, Trollope's series readers can thread the various components of the state into a cohesive and dispersed figure of the state.

Cohering like a postal system, Trollope's series fiction serves as an optimal vehicle for figuring the state. The bulk of these novels' characters represent Britain's governing institutions: Harding,

Doctor Grantly, and Josiah Crawley the clergy; Johnny Eames and Adolphus Crosbie the civil service; Mr. Monk, Phineas Finn, and Plantagenet Palliser both government and Parliament. The series novel's adoption of addressability enables Trollope to figure the state as a heterogeneous entity dispersed over time, space, and institutional contexts. Scattered as it may be, however, such a state's cohesion is legible when characters gather.

A recurring character's legibility in these instances reiterates the curious appearance of the Victorian state – at once conspicuous and opaque, a tension generated by the difference between series and non-series reading. Take the appearance of Archdeacon Grantly and Bishop Proudie at the close of *Doctor Thorne* (1858). When filling out the guest list for Mary and Frank Gresham's wedding, Trollope has Grantly, whose clerico-political war with evangelical-leaning Proudie formed one-half of *Barchester Towers* (1857), perform the ceremony instead of the bishop of nearby Barchester: "A hint had even been given, that his lordship would himself condescend to perform the ceremony, if this should be wished . . . but that work had already been anticipated by a very old friend of the Greshams. Archdeacon Grantly, the rector of Plumstead Episcopi, had long since undertaken this part of the business" (ch. 47). To the series reader this exchange replays the internecine struggles of *Barchester Towers*. However, *Doctor Thorne*'s characterization strips *Barchester Towers'* clerico-political conflict of its political specificity, therein turning Grantly and Proudie into metonymies for the Church, not just their factions within it. For a non-series reader, the state is conspicuous and opaque – these are clearly stand-ins for the Church yet its internal conflicts are illegible. Through this metonymy, moreover, Trollope can overlay governing regimes atop one another, at least for his series readers. Unlike with the novel's other clerical figures, such as Caleb Oriel, whom we may see as partially emblemizing the Church, through the tension between *Doctor Thorne*'s curtailed characterization of Grantly and Proudie and their deep portraiture across the entire Barsetshire Chronicles the series reader glimpses the clergymen's embeddedness within a local network of governance. Standing in for a portion of the state, the clergymen fill out the dramatis personae of local ruling elites, including the old Duke of Omnium and Lord de Courcy. The central state, represented by Grantly, Proudies, and the Church, allies itself with the local state, the aristocracy ruling rural Barsetshire, in order celebrate the union of the professional and landed classes, represented by Mary Thorne and Frank Gresham. As recurring characters in *Doctor Thorne*, Grantly and Proudie serve as addresses locating the central state within the governing landscape of provincial Britain.

Moving both from the state's margins to its center and from the Barsetshire novels to the Palliser novels, we see a similar procedure of metonymy and coordination. While he composes the Barsetshire novels' cast of characters from the rural governing classes – clergy, landlords, and magistrates – Trollope populates the Palliser series with recurring figures aligned with the central state: parliamentarians, cabinet ministers, and government officials. The links tethering these components of the state function through the same formal mechanisms developed in the Barsetshire novels. Trollope's figuration of the state is most apparent in *The Prime Minister* (1876). In this novel, not only does Trollope's characteristic addressability run wild – the novel is peppered with recurring characters from the Barsetshire and Palliser series – but also the novel turns the challenges of series reading into an analogy for governing a global state from a distant center. In *The Prime Minister*, the figuration of the state challenges both readers and characters. Through the narrative of the Duke of Omnium premiership, Trollope intimates that because such state rule depends upon bureaucratic forms of abbreviated yet prolific writing, it is best ruled when its administers behave like postal surveyors – which is also to say, as series readers. Despite occupying the very center of a centralized governing institution, the duke is confronted with a ministry populated by figures reduced to mere names and locations within the state. He must learn to supplement these addresses with characterological depths gleaned through years of previous intimacy. Reading his ministry like a series novel, the duke gains the ability to see through the metonymic characterization of his ministers to the state fanning out as a collocated totality. The duke's narrative suggests that the ability of a centralized state to govern across the globe depends upon the post's protocols of addressability.

The Omnium Coalition is built entirely out of recurring characters. Because both the series reader and the duke are familiar with most of these characters, *The Prime Minister* can embed their address-like form into the novel's action itself. The duke relates to his ministers through the form of the Trollopian recurring character:

> There was Mr. Monk with his budget, and Lord Drummond with his three or four dozen half rebellious colonies, and Sir Orlando Drought with the House to lead and a ship to build . . . and Lord Ramsden with a codified Statute Book.
>
> *(ch. 27)*

The duke's ministers appear as addresses: names and locations within the larger system of the state. Monk, Drummond, Drought; the Exchequer, the admiralty, Parliament: all the prime minister knows about each minister and his labor is concentrated into a name and office. The duke knows what they do, not how they do it. Metonyms for the work they oversee and the forms of writing that that work involves, these recurring characters, inserted into the duke's narrative, challenge centralized state authority. As long as the duke sees his ministers as just metonymies for their departments, his state remains a Leviathan with its head lopped off. But as recurring characters like Phineas Finn these figures also hold the promise of a comprehensive vision of the whole state – if, however, the duke can learn how to read them.

In his relationship with Phineas Finn, the duke spends *The Prime Minister* developing the same type of intimacy Trollope's series readers had long established with Phineas through their reading of the novels *Phineas Finn* and *Phineas Redux* (1874). Through his wife Glencora's close friendship with Marie Finn, the duke has private channels of information differing from the bureaucratic dispatches of the state characterizing his interaction with the rest of his government. Not unlike a serialized series novel, bit by bit Glencora feeds the duke tidbits of extra-professional information – how the Finns travel, how Phineas fares in Ireland, and so on. Ostensibly "private," this supplementary information adds depth to Phineas's character as colonial secretary for Ireland and, later, First Lord of the Admiralty. Such depth is possible, moreover, because of its series-like form: incremental installments accumulating slowly over the course of several years. Through official dispatches and Glencora's gossip, the duke learns to read Phineas as if he were a series character, eventually establishing the ground for previously unimaginable intimacy. Reflecting on a peculiarly gregarious duke toward the end of the Coalition, Phineas wonders, "Looking back he could hardly remember that he had in truth ever conversed with the Duke . . . But now [the Duke] smiled, and . . . very soon fell into the ways of a pleasant country host" (ch. 68).

More is at stakes than friendship, of course. Through the channels forged by such series-reading-like intimacy, the duke gains insight into the works of two branches of the imperial state – the colonial secretary for Ireland and the Admiralty. Postal surveyor-like reading practices provide the duke an intensive and extensive vision of the state he otherwise lacks. Read like a recurring series character, Phineas serves as the duke's window into a bureaucratically opaque state, a vista lacking from the duke's interaction with the treasury or the postal service, branches overseen by Mr. Monk and Barrington Erle. Intimate with Phineas, the duke learns about the demands of his offices – constant travel between London and Ireland (ch. 11) and prolonged tours of the empire's ports of call (ch. 42).

Insights such as the duke's radiate outwards as well. Having gained the capacity to peer into the characterological and institutional depths of the state's metonymic figures, the prime minister can thread those figures into the larger network forming the state. Although Leviathan does not regain its head entirely – the Omnium Coalition is short-lived following the duke's maturation as premier – it nevertheless can comprehend the intricate relations between its parts. No longer viewing the state as if it were an itemized cabinet list, the duke grasps the state as a complex collocation of self-governing parts. The state, having cohered through the duke and *The Prime Minister*'s figuration, becomes a functioning totality, or, as Lady Glencora describes the duke's state, "'a world going on very smoothly'" (ch. 63).

The Trollopian state

Through the protocols for figuration afforded by the postal system, Trollope's fiction elucidates the depth and breadth of the Victorian state. Operating according to the logic of liberal governance, the Trollopian state indirectly intervenes in the economic, biological, ethical, and domestic lives of Trollope's characters by providing the conditions of possibility for the realization of those dimensions' potential. Trollope's adoption of addressability's protocols augments this deep portraiture of the state. Through metonymy, Trollope's novels bind the state's individual institutions into a cohesive whole. Trollope, in so figuring the state, echoes the state's appearance as a representative government – it is at once conspicuous and obscure, both in fiction and in reality. Trollope's remediation of these characteristics helps evince public faith in the state. Holding a mirror to the state, Trollope makes it accountable to his readers, but in a manner that renders it routine. Casting flashes of an idealized state through characters like Bagwax and the Plantagenet Palliser, Trollope's novels then allow the state to fade into the background of his ever-accumulating details of everyday Victorian life. Readers can then come to trust the state. When combined with portrayals of the state's effective rule – Harding's benign yet ill-fated wardenship, Bagwax's postal heroics, the Omnium Coalition's economic stewardship – this opacity evinces the state's self-rule as desirable (Martel). State figuration, in other words, suggests to readers that when freed from political micromanagement, gentlemanly civil servants like Monk and Finn can best carry on their routine duties. In so doing, Trollope articulates an alternative model of representative government. As Christopher Harvie demonstrates, lacking a written constitution, British politics and government arguably depended upon the political novel, which, along with constitutional historians and philosophers like Bagehot and J. S. Mill, gave shape to constitutional practices (4). For a novelist famously wary of public indifference to the politics of the state (Halperin 168), figuration was a potent device for modeling a representative government according to the premises of liberalism.

Notes

1. For a useful overview of this literary scholarship, see Amanda Claybaugh, "Government Is Good." I will discuss Victorianist inquiries into the state and literature at length in the next section.
2. For work on the civil service see Shuman, Goodlad (*Victorian Literature*), Dames, Ruth, and Sullivan; on the Church of England, Colón; and on Parliament and the government, Hadley, Van Dam, Felber ("Advanced Conservative"), Craig, and Goodlad (*Victorian Geopolitical*).
3. For Mill's elaboration of such centralized, national control, see the chapter "On Local Representative Bodies" in *Considerations on Representative Government* (1861). For Bagehot's similar model, see the chapter "The Cabinet" in *The English Constitution* (1867).
4. For Patrick Joyce, the liberal state, as a set of activities dispersed across an array of institutions, can be best grasped by "recognizing the interaction, the patterning, of these practices of ordering that resistance *and* the coherence of what I called governmental rationalities, or strategies of governmental power, can be

realized" (*Rule of Freedom* 11). Peter Miller and Nikolas Rose also define governance in the same terms: "Governing involves . . . the ordering of activities and processes" ("Governing Economic Life" 42). Of the Victorian state and its depiction by novelists, Pamela K. Gilbert argues that Charles Dickens portrays London as "an unmanageable jumble . . . to impose order upon" (*Mapping* 112).

Works cited

Bagehot, Walter. *The English Constitution*. London: Chapman and Hall, 1867.
Bellamy, Christine. *Administering Central-Local Relations, 1871–1919: The Local Government Board in Its Fiscal and Cultural Context*. Manchester: Manchester UP, 1988.
Claybaugh, Amanda. "Government Is Good." *Minnesota Review* 70 (2008): 161–8. Print.
Colón, Susan. *The Professional Ideal in the Victorian Novel: The Works of Disraeli, Trollope, Gaskell, and Eliot*. New York: Palgrave Macmillan, 2007.
Craig, David M. "Advanced Conservative Liberalism: Party and Principle on Trollope's Parliamentary Novels." *Victorian Literature and Culture* 38 (2010): 355–71. *JSTOR*. Web. 7 January 2015.
Dames, Nicholas. "Trollope and the Career: Vocational Trajectories and the Management of Ambition." *Victorian Studies* 45.2 (2003): 247–78. *JSTOR*. Web. 28 September 2013.
Dean, Mitchell. *Governmentality: Power and Rule in Modern Society*. London: SAGE, 1999.
Dickens, Charles. *Little Dorrit*. 1857. Ed. Stephen Wall and Helen Small. New York: Penguin, 2003.
Eastwood, David. *Government and Community in the English Provinces, 1700–1870*. New York: St. Martin's Press, 1997.
Felber, Lynette. "The Advanced Conservative Liberal: Victorian Liberalism and the Aesthetics of Anthony Trollope's Palliser Novels." *Modern Philology* 107.3 (2010): 421–46. *JSTOR*. Web. 23 July 2013.
———. *Gender and Genre in Novels Without End: The British Roman-Fleuve*. Gainesville, FL: UP of Florida, 1995.
Gilbert, Pamela K. *The Citizen's Body: Desire, Health, and the Social in Victorian England*. Columbus, OH: Ohio State UP, 2007.
———. *Mapping the Victorian Social Body*. New York: SUNY Press, 2004.
Golden, Catherine. *Posting It: The Victorian Revolution in Letter Writing*. Gainesville: UP of Florida, 2009.
Goodlad, Lauren. *The Victorian Geopolitical Aesthetic: Realism, Sovereignty, and Transnational Experience*. Oxford: Oxford UP, 2015.
———. *Victorian Literature and the Victorian State: Character and Governance in a Liberal Society*. Baltimore: Johns Hopkins UP, 2003.
Hadley, Elaine. *Living Liberalism: Practical Citizenship in Mid-Victorian England*. Chicago: University of Chicago Press, 2010.
Halperin, John. *Trollope and Politics: A Study of the Pallisers and Others*. London: Macmillan, 1977.
Harvie, Christopher. *The Centre of Things: Political Fiction in Britain from Disraeli to the Present*. London: Unwin Hyman, 1991.
Joyce, Patrick. *The Rule of Freedom: Liberalism and the Modern City*. New York: Verso, 2003.
———. *The State of Freedom: A Social History of the British State Since 1800*. Cambridge: Cambridge UP, 2013.
Langbauer, Laurie. *Novels of Everyday Life: The Series in English Fiction, 1850–1930*. Ithaca: Cornell UP, 1999.
Levine, Carolyn. *Forms: Whole, Rhythm, Hierarchy, Network*. Princeton: Princeton UP, 2015.
Martel, Michael. "Figuring the State: Representative Government and Paralipsis in Anthony Trollope's Palliser Novels." *Victorians: A Journal of Culture and Literature* 128 (Fall 2015): 117–38.
Maurer, Sara L. *The Dispossessed State: Narratives of Ownership in Nineteenth-Century Britain and Ireland*. Baltimore: Johns Hopkins UP, 2012.
Menke, Richard. *Telegraphic Realism: Victorian Fiction and Other Information Systems*. Stanford: Stanford UP, 2009.
Mill, John Stuart. *Considerations on Representative Government*. London: Parker, Son, and Bourn, 1861.
Miller, Peter, and Nikolas Rose. "Governing Economic Life." In *Governing the Present: Administering Economic, Social, and Personal Life* (pp. 26–52). New York: Polity, 2008.
———. "Political Power Beyond the State: Problematics of Government." In *Governing the Present: Administering Economic, Social, and Personal Life* (pp. 53–83). New York: Polity, 2008.
Mitchell, Timothy. "The Limits of the State: Beyond Statist Approaches and Their Critics." *The American Political Science Review* 85.1 (1991): 77–96. *JSTOR*. Web. 11 April 2012.

Perkin, Harold. *The Rise of Professional Society: England Since 1880.* New York: Routledge, 1989.
Robbins, Bruce. *Upward Mobility and the Common Good: Toward a Literary History of the Welfare State.* Princeton: Princeton UP, 2007.
Rotunno, Laura. *Postal Plots in British Fiction, 1840–1898: Readdressing Correspondence in Victorian Culture.* New York: Palgrave Macmillan, 2013.
Ruth, Jennifer. *Novel Professions: Interested Disinterest and the Making of the Professional in the Victorian Novel.* Columbus: Ohio State UP, 2006.
Shuman, Cathy. *Pedagogical Economies: The Examination and the Victorian Literary Man.* Stanford: Stanford UP, 2000.
Skilton, David. "The Construction of Masculinities." In *The Cambridge Companion to Anthony Trollope.* Ed. Carolyn Dever and Lisa Niles, pp. 128–41. Cambridge: Cambridge UP, 2011.
Sullivan, Ceri. *Literature in the Public Service: Sublime Bureaucracy.* New York: Palgrave Macmillan, 2013.
Super, R. H. *Trollope in the Post Office.* Ann Arbor: University of Michigan Press, 1981.
Thomas, Kate. *Postal Pleasures: Sex Scandal, and Victorian Letters.* Oxford: Oxford UP, 2012.
Trollope, Anthony. *An Autobiography.* New York: Oxford UP, 2008.
———. *Barchester Towers.* New York: Oxford UP, 2008.
———. *Doctor Thorne.* New York: Penguin, 2004.
———. *Phineas Finn.* New York: Oxford UP, 2011.
———. *Phineas Redux.* New York: Oxford UP, 2011.
———. *The Prime Minister.* New York: Oxford UP, 2011.
———. *The Three Clerks.* New York: Harpers & Brothers, 1860. Internet Archive. Web. 13 August 2015.
Van Dam, Frederik. "Character and the Career: Anthony Trollope's Phineas Finn and the Rhetoric of the Victorian State." *English Text Construction* 2.1 (2009): 91–110. Print.
Wall, Stephen. "Trollope, Balzac, and the Reappearing Character." *Essays in Criticism* 25.1 (1975): 123–44. Web. 11 January 2014.
Wells, H. G. *The Future in America: A Search After Realities.* New York: Harper & Brothers, 1906.

PART II

Culture and gender

3

TROLLOPE THE FEMINIST

Deborah Denenholz Morse

In 1968, Robert Polhemus in *The Changing World of Anthony Trollope* first seriously challenged the prevailing critical view that Trollope was unprogressive in his attitudes toward women. Polhemus's argument relies heavily on Trollope's pervasive sympathetic depiction of his female characters' psychology. This emphasis is also central to Juliet McMaster's *Trollope's Palliser Novels*, which gives particular attention and admiration to the brilliance and sensitivity of Madame Max Goesler (later Mrs. Finn) in the examination of "the mind in the process of decision." Ruth apRoberts's touchstone essay, "Emily and Nora and Dorothy and Priscilla and Jemima and Carry" considers Trollope's portrayal of remarkable women resisting their gender oppression in the magisterial novel of marital estrangement, *He Knew He Was Right* (1869). Christopher Herbert's *Trollope and Comic Pleasure* declares that Trollope is "the leading and most sympathetic student of women in contemporary fiction" (75). Arguing for Trollope's essential feminism as he analyzes Trollope's debt to Renaissance and Jacobean comedy, Herbert claims that for Trollope, "to improve women's standing in the world . . . would be to rejuvenate erotic pleasure" (68).

But it was not always thus in Trollope studies, or with commentators upon his work. Henry James declared in *Partial Portraits* that "Trollope settled down steadily to the English girl; he took possession of her, and turned her inside out . . . She is always definite and natural. She plays her part most properly . . . She has not a touch of the morbid, and is delightfully tender, modest and fresh."[1] Michael Sadleir in *Trollope: A Commentary* (1927) echoes James's assessment that Trollope's ideal woman is "modest of mien, low-voiced . . . claiming nothing of equality, she achieves supremacy" (382–3). In 1956, Mario Praz declares in "Anthony Trollope" in *The Hero in Eclipse in Victorian Fiction*, "Trollope's novels are designed to encourage gentle, modest, not very passionate girls" (271). Praz nevertheless comments upon Trollope's portrayals of passionate behavior as having "a vehemence and a truth that we meet with in no other Victorian except Emily Bronte" (298), a remark that surely describes the passionate Lily Dale in *The Small House at Allington* (1864), Emily Trevelyn and her sister Nora Rowley in *He Knew He Was Right* (1869), or desperate Lady Laura Standish in the Phineas novels (1869, 1874) at least as accurately as it describes Trollope's male characters like fiery Lord Chiltern or indeed Phineas Finn himself in the Phineas novels, or the intense, eccentric Josiah Crawley in *The Last Chronicle of Barset*.

Following the lead of Sadleir and Praz, the author of the germinal *Anthony Trollope: A Critical Study* (1955), A.O.J. Cockshut, in *Man and Woman: A Study of Love and the Novel, 1740–1940* (1977), still insists – although he is writing during the Second Wave of Feminism – upon

Trollope's adherence to his society's gender conventions: "Trollope's assumption of polarity of sexual roles . . . with its manifold implications about contrasting roles in the family, in work and in society, was for Trollope simply an obvious assumption of common sense" (152). George Levine's influential work on the realist novel in *The Realistic Imagination* (1983) acknowledges Trollope's "complicated and sensitive but thoroughly masculine perception of the difficulties of being a woman in so arbitrarily constructed a society." At the same time, however, Levine locates "that special angle from which Trollope sees with cynical warmth," which "reduces reality for any woman to marrying and having two children and being honest with an honest husband" (10, 15).

My own *Women in Trollope's Palliser Novels* (1987), a feminist study of Trollope, analyzes Trollope's progressively flexible – and increasingly feminist – responses in his urban chronicle (1864–1880) to the Victorian woman question. In analyses of Trollope's women, I find in particular that Trollope approves of women who are strong mentally and physically, regardless of social class – a clear flouting of class-based cultural ideals that prescribed upper-class women as ideally weak, tender, and pliable. Other works on gender issues that were published at about the same time or in the following years include: Jane Nardin's *He Knew She Was Right* in 1989; Robert Polhemus's chapter on Phineas's erotic career and his arrival at his mature love of Madame Max in *Erotic Faith* (1990); William Cohen's "Trollope's Trollop" in *Sex Scandal* (1996), which discusses "sexual unspeakability" (160) and gendered property in *The Eustace Diamonds*; Margaret Markwick's *Trollope and Women* and pathbreaking *New Men in Trollope's Novels* (2007); Mark W. Turner's pioneering analysis of the "gendered space" (7) of Victorian periodicals, the homosociality of the gentlemen's clubs (including Trollope's Reform Club), and the latent homoerotics in stories like "The Turkish Bath" in *Trollope and the Magazines* (2000); Richard Dellamora's "Stupid Trollope" (2001), on Trollope's struggle with schoolboy homoerotics and its influence on the Trollopian gentleman, his chapter analyzing homosocial bonding and anti-Semitism in *The Prime Minister* in *Friendship's Bonds* (2004), and his *Victorian Studies* review of Sharon Marcus's book, "Friendship, Marriage, and *Between Women*" in *Victorian Studies* (2007); Mark Forrester's "Redressing the Empire: Anthony Trollope and British Gender Anxiety in "The Banks of the Jordan" in *Imperial Desire* (2005), the first scholarship following Turner's groundbreaking book and Dellamora's work to acknowledge Trollope's heterodox responses to deviant sexualities; Sharon Marcus's chapter on coded same-sex love in *Can You Forgive Her?* (*Between Women*, 2007); Kate Flint's "Queer Trollope" and David Skilton's "The Construction of Masculinities" in *The Cambridge Companion* (2011); and the 2009 collection *The Politics of Gender in Anthony Trollope's Novels* (Markwick, Morse, & Gagnier), based on the 2006 Exeter conference "Trollope & Gender."

The only volume on Trollope and gender, this collection includes thirteen essays that are essential reading for any contemporary consideration of the subject, under the rubrics of "Sex, Power, and Subversion," "Imperial Gender," "Genderised Economics," and "The Gender of Narrative Construction." The collection includes: Robert M. Polhemus on Trollope's relationship with the beautiful American feminist, lecturer, and actress Kate Field, delving into the influence of their older man–young woman friendship as an influence upon Trollope's fiction; Kathy Alexis Psomiades on marriage laws and the "tyranny of the sexual contract" in *He Knew He Was Right*; Markwick's "Out of the Closet," which builds upon Forrester's work and Markwick's own *New Men* and serves as background to Kate Flint's "Queer Trollope"; Lauren M. E. Goodlad's analysis of Trollope's gendered responses to Indian issues in *The Eustace Diamonds*; Anca Vlasopolos's critique of gender and history in *Sir Harry Hotspur of Humblethwaite*, which influences the argument of my own chapter on that novel in *Reforming Trollope*; Mary Jean Corbett's exploration of gender and Irish ethnicity in the Phineas saga; Jenny Bourne Taylor on illegitimacy, the law, and Trollope's fiction, especially the little-noticed *Ralph the Heir*, *Lady Anna*, and *Is He Popenjoy?*; Nathan Hensley's analysis of economics and gender in *The Way We Live Now*; Helen Lucy Blythe on the colonial aesthetic in relation to gender in Trollope's short Antipodean fiction "Catherine Carmichael"; David Skilton on gender and narrative "portraiture"; Steven Amarnick's revelations about Trollope's original, much longer, manuscript of *The Duke's Children*; Elsie B. Michie on gender and wealth in relation to Miss Dunstable in the Barsetshire series; Christopher S. Noble's examination of Trollope's often powerful widows; Regenia Gagnier on gender and liberalism; and my work on gender, race, and imperialism in *He Knew He Was Right*.

This *Routledge Research Companion to Anthony Trollope* offers other essays that focus upon Trollope and gender. Hyson Cooper, "Anthony Trollope's Conduct-Book Fiction for Men," examines how Trollope emphasizes masculine feeling and its role in a man's conduct as a gentleman. Hyson Cooper's essay in this *Companion* emphasizes that "Trollope takes us deep into the process by which men who explore their feelings arrive at courses of behavior." Mary Jean Corbett's essay in this volume, "Women, Violence, and Modernity," interrogates the grounds of male violence against women in *The Way We Live Now* in relation to Trollope's stance on women's rights. Corbett sees Trollope as ambivalent about a modernism that includes the domestic violence of the ruthless financier Augustus Melmotte as well as the freedom of Hetta Carbury to marry the man she loves rather than be compelled to marry her avuncular cousin Roger Carbury for family convenience.

Most of the recent scholarship on Trollopian gender relations argues that Trollope's attitude toward women was more sympathetic and intricate than his blunt pronouncements – such as *North America*'s 'The best right a woman has is the right to a husband' – suggest. In Markwick's *New Men in Trollope's Novels*, she explores Trollope's affinity with what we might now term 'feminized men' – men who are loving, involved fathers and who are fully appreciative of intelligent women and sensitive to their just desire for equality in marriage. Some of the most recent scholarship on Trollope and gender, Markwick's "Out of the Closet" and *New Men*, and later, Flint's "Queer Trollope," discovers sympathetic portrayals of homoerotics and sensitivity to deviant sexualities, especially in Trollope's more experimental short fiction. Marcus's chapter in *Between Women* instead argues for a conflicted but ultimately more conservative Trollope in her analysis of *Can You Forgive Her?* (1864–65), the first novel in the Palliser series, as she demonstrates how Trollope codes female same-sex attraction as heterosexual desire in the aftermath of the debates over the 1857 Matrimonial Causes Act.[2] My *Reforming Trollope* (2013) finds a much more liberal Trollope as it explores his evolving critique of Victorian gender relations in response to English history and contemporary politics, viewing *Sir Harry Hotspur of Humblethwaite* (1870) in light of the Second Reform Bill and 1860s women's rights agitation and connecting *Ayala's Angel* (1881) to the approach to the 1882 Married Women's Property Act. I also examine Trollope's changing responses to the call for reform in women's rights in relation to imperialist issues in *He Knew He Was Right* (1869) and *Doctor Wortle's School* (1881), and in relation to a racialized marriage plot in *Lady Anna* (1874).

Yet Trollope's insistent critique of gender ideals in Victorian culture has certainly not been fully explored, if only because of his plethora of novels. Especially in lesser-known fictions, little has been written about Trollope's engagement with his culture's gender politics, in particular with the oppressions of Victorian women and their attempts to maintain their integrity and independence despite the privileges of Victorian men. In three novels from different points of his career that are not a part of either the Barsetshire chronicle or the Palliser series nor one of the other magisterial novels, such as *Orley Farm* (1861), *He Knew He Was Right* (1869), or *The Way We Live Now* (1875) – *The Claverings* (1867), *Sir Harry Hotspur of Humblethwaite* (1870), and *Is He Popenjoy?* (1878) – Trollope continues to expand the critique of his culture's entrenched gender biases. In the following analysis of these less celebrated Trollopian novels, I am concerned with Trollope's depiction of the thought processes of upper-caste males and his dissection of masculine privilege in Victorian culture and society. In his critique of the lassitude and misogyny of aristocratic Englishmen coupled with his loving depiction of vibrant women – including an actress and a stablekeeper's granddaughter – Trollope interrogates the masculine prerogatives that underlie English civilization. Thus, Trollope's critique of gender is imbricated with a critique of social class and nationhood.

"Wish you were dead": gender and violent thought crime in Anthony Trollope's novels

> In ordinary society, George Hotspur was bright, and he was proud of being bright. With this woman he was always subdued, always made to play second fiddle, always talked like a boy; and he knew it. He had loved her once, if he was capable of loving anything, but her mastery over him wearied him, even though he was, after a fashion, proud of her cleverness, and he wished that she were, – well, dead, if the reader choose that mode of expressing what probably were George's wishes. But he had never told himself that he desired her death. He could build pleasant castles in the air as to the murder of Captain Stubber, but his thoughts did not travel that way in reference to Mrs. Morton.[3]

In Anthony Trollope's powerful short novel, *Sir Harry Hotspur of Humblethwaite* (1870), the reprobate heir to the title of a baronetcy thinks thus about his energetic, talented mistress, who later becomes his wife, the future Lady Hotspur. It is a strikingly dark thought that jars the reader, not least because in expressing the languid George Hotspur's unconscious desires, Trollope's narrator is so determinedly understated and casual: "he wished that she were, – well, dead, if the reader choose that mode of expressing what probably were George's wishes." All through the novel the narrator expresses respect and pity for Lucy Morton, a successful actress who is both sexually involved with and financially supports the impecunious, dissolute George Hotspur: "there had come upon him a blasé look, and certain outer signs of a bad life, which, however, did not mar his beauty, nor were they always apparent" (ch. 5). The narrator tells us that Lucy Morton "was in every respect superior to the man she had condescended to love" (ch. 11). George is "a brute, unredeemed by any one manly gift; idle, self-indulgent, false, and without a principle. She was a woman greatly gifted, with many virtues, capable of self-sacrifice, industrious, affectionate" (ch. 22). Trollope exposes the violent hatred underlying George's chilling – if not consciously acknowledged – wish for "industrious" Lucy's death as the male desire to extinguish a woman who makes him feel inadequate in his masculinity not least because she has so much more vital energy than he does – including, it is implied, sexual energy.

As Victorian women struggled for their political rights in the 1860s and 1870s, Trollope responded in his fiction with an interrogation of his society's masculine prerogatives. A part of this critique occurs in scenes in which an enervated upper-class man commits the thought crimes Adela Pinch discusses in *Thinking About Other People in Nineteenth-Century British Writing* (2010). Unlike Pinch's example of desperate Gwendolen Harleth's wish for her tyrant husband Grandcourt's death in *Daniel Deronda*, however, the thought crimes in which Trollope's weak male characters desire the death of a wife or mistress who challenges their privileged status are not realized – and in that very impotence to effect imagined violence upon their wives and mistresses inheres a part of Trollope's gender critique.

George Hotspur's idea of "noblesse oblige" is not that privilege has its duties and responsibilities, but that he deserves all the good things of the world without working for them:

> He was living in a bachelor's set of rooms, at this time, in St. James's Street, for which, it must be presumed, that ready money was required. During the last winter he had horses in Northamptonshire, for the hire of which, it must be feared, that his prospects

as heir to Humblethwaite had to some degree been pawned. At the present time he had a horse for park riding, and he looked upon a good dinner, with good wine, as being due to him every day, as thoroughly as though he earned it. That he had never attempted to earn a shilling since the day on which he had ceased to be a soldier, now four years since, the reader will hardly require to be informed.

(ch. 5)

George is in one sense a measure of crumbling feudal dominion, accelerated by the two Reform Bills that took away the prerogative of control from the landed classes. Trollope must have been thinking of the Second Reform Bill as he wrote *Sir Harry Hotspur*, just a year after the passage of the momentous piece of legislation that widened the franchise to many working-class men in England (and to no Englishwomen), and to about two in five of all males in England and Wales. As Victoria Glendinning states when discussing Trollope's *The Way We Live Now* (1875), written in 1873–1874, only a few years after *Sir Harry Hotspur*, Trollope's "picture of the weakened, dishonoured English upper class was not misjudged."[4] Born between the Reform Bills – George is "something under thirty years of age" – George can be interpreted as the diseased scion of a blighted class. He has no work, no duties – nor does he want any.[5]

Although George wishes Lucy Morton dead, it is the death of his cousin and betrothed Emily Hotspur that he actually precipitates. George has utterly charmed Emily with his sophisticated gentlemanly demeanor and good looks. He is her first love, and she is entirely inexperienced with the devious Georges of the Victorian world. Although he is a black sheep in the family, disreputable and a known scapegrace, George is at first encouraged by the elder Hotspurs in his courtship of his cousin Emily so that the Hotspur lands and wealth that the daughter will inherit might be joined to Cousin George's inheritance of the baronetcy. George, however, remains not only a black sheep but a black sheep of a deep dye indeed, a cardsharp who cheats a poor man of his money and then lies about it afterwards to Emily's father, Sir Harry.

Before he shows his darkest colors, however, George is helped along by not only Emily and Lucy but also Lady Altringham, all of whom are energetic on his behalf. Lady Altringham constantly exhorts George to bestir himself to win the great prize of Emily Hotspur, each time George is minded to give up: "She was in earnest about it. To her it was a matter of great moment that this great heiress should marry one of her own set, and a man who wanted money so badly as did poor George" (ch. 18). Lady Altringham even writes a "rough copy" of a love letter to Emily for him, and "he had copied her ladyship's words verbatim" (ch. 18). He has neither originality nor sincerity: the letter begins "Dearest Emily" and ends with the declaration that he desires "to see the girl I love better than all the world" (ch. 18). After George wins Emily and then nearly loses her through the discovery of his perfidy, Sir Harry prescribes him a course of "purification" at the isolated Hotspur estate of Scarrowby, only because of Emily's urgent pleas that her fiancé be given another chance to repent of his wicked ways in the pursuit of his own pleasures. Emily thinks that at Scarrowby, he will "be made clean by the fire of solitude and the hammer of hard work" (ch. 21), and she encourages George to exert himself in learning his duties as future head of the Hotspurs while at Scarrowby, and to pursue a course of reading in the evenings. But all of this "hard work" appals the lackadaisical, completely self-indulgent George, who thinks "it did seem to him that Scarrowby was a kind of penal servitude to which he was about to be sent with his own concurrence. The scent of the cleanliness was odious to him" (ch. 21). The name of Scarrowby is richly suggestive. It evokes the saint and the martyr, even perhaps the flagellant. Clearly Cousin George does not want his soul to be "harrowed" or "scoured clean," rigorous actions of purification. He refuses as well to be "harrowed" in the sense of "troubled" or "bothered" by disturbing the ease and torpor of his life. Finally, George will not reflect upon his life and feel sorrow and spiritual scarring. It is all just too much work.

George's aversion to "the scent of cleanliness" is one clue Trollope gives the reader that George is, in fact, unclean – that his lack of energy may come in part from disease. That disease is most likely syphilis, as other evidence in the novel suggests. As I argue in *Reforming Trollope* about Sir Harry's incessant fears of his pure daughter's contamination: "Sir Harry knows what kind of man George Hotspur is, and what his dissolute manner of life might have bred in his body as well as in his degraded soul" (74). Margaret Markwick has written extensively of Trollope's portrayals of syphilitic men in *New Men in Trollope's Novels* (92–95, 159). George is the first of three weak upper-class men I will discuss who most likely have contracted syphilis as a result of their dissolute sexual habits. George does not die as do these other two men in *The Claverings* and *Is He Popenjoy?*, and he will inherit, albeit perhaps briefly, the title of baronet. However, like his counterparts in these other novels, he does not produce a healthy heir – indeed, we hear of no children from his union – and we are left to surmise that George's venereal disease added to sexual lethargy has prevented even vital Lucy Morton from conceiving.

George at last abandons Emily, takes Sir Harry's offered money, and rejoins his more comfortable and accepting mistress: "he could say what he chose to Lucy, and smoke in her presence, own that he was fond of drink, and obtain some sympathy for his 'book' on the Derby" (ch. 21). The actress insists that he write a letter renouncing his fiancée. He is so enervated that he cannot write the letter himself, so she, like Lady Altringham before her, composes it, and he simply repeats her words in his own handwriting: "Then he turned himself wearily to her writing-desk, and copied the words which she had prepared for him" (ch. 22). George has no creativity in him at all, while Lucy can not only act quite well – she is to perform Lady Teazle that very night in *A School for Scandal*, a role that is perhaps an index to her strong will – but also compose a lacerating epistle to her genteel rival: "He hoped that his cousin might be made happy by a splendid alliance" (ch. 22).

Emily Hotspur is stunned with George's betrayal, and she at last realizes that "he had never loved her" (ch. 22). She is never able to recover, despite her hale constitution – emphasized early on in the novel. She punishes herself relentlessly for her poor judgment, goes out in all weathers, and resists a return to the Hotspur estate that has been the very ground of her deep loss, and she chooses to remain in exile. She dies abroad in Lugano, not long after the marriage of George and Lucy. Emily, however, is energetic even in her unbending self-castigation and will to die, while the last image we are offered of George is one of dissolution and lassitude:

> In April they were married, and she must be added to the list of women who have sacrificed themselves on behalf of men whom they have known to be worthless. We need not pursue his career further; but we may be sure, that though she watched him very closely, and used a power over him of which he was afraid, still he went gradually from bad to worse, and was found at last to be utterly past redemption . . . to eat and to drink was all that was left to him . . . There are such men; and of all human beings they are the most to be pitied. They have intellects; they do think; the hours with them are terribly long; – and they have no hope!
>
> *(ch. 24)*

The perceived challenge to privileged male status that Lucy Morton represents in *Sir Harry Hotspur of Humblethwaite* is somewhat differently portrayed in the slightly earlier novel *The Claverings* (1867). In this novel, Sir Hugh Clavering is a cold, mean-spirited husband whose dislike of his wife, Hermione, increases when his feeble son and heir, Hughy, dies. The fact that Sir Hugh introduces his sister-in-law, Julia Brabazon, to the likely syphilitic Lord Ongar, her future husband, suggests that Sir Hugh's social circle not only countenances but also indulges in the male debauchery that leads to Lord Ongar's gruesome death. Sir Hugh himself then most likely gives his poor son, Hughy, his weak constitution and his heritable, fatal disease. This account is even more probable when one learns that an earlier daughter, Meeny, born to them has also died in infancy, "at little more than twelve months old," as Hermione reminds the kindly rector's wife, Mrs. Clavering, her relation through marriage. Sir Hugh's response to his daughter's death is to refuse the energy it would take to remember: "he only shook his head and went out of the room. He has never spoken one word of her since that. I think that he has forgotten Meeny altogether, – even that she was ever here."[6] Sir Hugh does not have the generative energies to produce another child – and his line will die out. Despite his almost certain knowledge of his own responsibility for his son's frailty, Sir Hugh refers to his son as his wife's child after little Hughy dies, as if Hermione and not he himself is to blame for the ill health that results in Hughy's death.

With his hopes of an heir for his estate gone, Sir Hugh resolves to be even more cruel to Hermione – whom the Shakespeare-loving Trollope almost certainly named for the ill-used wife of *A Winter's Tale*. This Hermione is not publicly accused of infidelity by her husband, but instead Sir Hugh tries to foist her upon her widowed sister, Lady Ongar, so that he can avoid the upkeep of his family estate, Clavering Park. He threatens to shut up Clavering Park entirely and send his wife to his smaller property, Moor Hall, in a part of Devonshire "which is perhaps as ugly, as desolate, and as remote as any part of England" (ch. 35). Although Hermione has come to regard Clavering Park itself "as a prison," she "had heard much of Moor Hall, and dreaded it as the heroine, made to live in the big grim castle low down among the Apennines, dreads the smaller and grimmer castle which is known to exist somewhere higher up in the mountains" (ch. 35). The comparison of Hermione to an imprisoned fairytale or gothic heroine of course makes it clear that Hugh is the domestic tyrant as ogre, as gothic villain:

'You're very, very cruel.'
'You said that before.'
'And I'll say it again. I'll tell everybody; so I will. I'll tell your uncle at the rectory, and he shall speak to you.'
'Look here, Hermy . . . if I find you telling tales about me out of this house, and especially to my uncle, or indeed to anybody, I'll let you know what it is to be cruel.'
'You can't be worse than you are.'
'Don't try me; that's all.'

(ch. 35)

Sir Hugh Clavering's hatred and avoidance of his family estate is in itself a condemnation in the moral universe of Trollope's fiction. As Juliet McMaster states, Trollope "is imbued with a deep respect for the values that are rooted in the land."[7] Trollope's favored characters in the Barsetshire series – the final novel of which, *The Last Chronicle of Barset* (1867), was published the same year as *The Claverings* – have sufficient energy to keep up their estates properly. From Frank Gresham (*Doctor Thorne*) through Lord Lufton (*Framley Parsonage*), Squire Dale (*The Small House at Allington*), and Archdeacon Grantly and his son Henry (*The Last Chronicle of Barset*), whether ancient landed gentry or new landowner, those who care for the land and attend to its responsibilities – from tenants to the preserving of foxes – are to be respected in Trollope's fictional world. Lord Chiltern of *Phineas Finn* (1869), the second of the urban Palliser series of novels, redeems his previously violent behavior by his careful nurturing of foxes and his excellence as master of hounds for the Brake Hunt. Darker characters in Trollope's fiction – for instance, the debt-laden Whig MP Nathaniel Sowerby of Chaldicotes in *Framley Parsonage* – sometimes lose their estates because they have not expended the energy necessary to maintain them, but instead have squandered money in gambling and high living in London. Sowerby's negligence toward Chaldicotes, about which he belatedly realizes he feels strongly, is matched by his casual use of his friends, such as the trusting Reverend Mark Robarts, whom he nearly ruins. It is not accidental that Robarts is actively succored by his old university friend and devoted landowner, Lord Lufton, who will also act responsibly toward the other people he loves, including Robarts's sister Lucy, whom he will insist upon marrying despite his mother's opposition to her middle-class origins.

Sir Hugh, however, leaves Hermione alone at Clavering Park very soon after the death of their son. His cruel neglect at this saddest of familial moments is of course an index to his hard, selfish nature. His cold, sterile home life in a shuttered, gloomy house would have been anathema to Trollope. As R. C. Terry tells us in *Anthony Trollope: The Artist in Hiding*, "The home where all's accustomed, ceremonious meant much to Trollope and in his fiction often represents order and stability in an uncertain world" (42). Hermione knows Sir Hugh is entertaining violent thoughts about her upon his return for a brief sojourn before going off again to his pleasures elsewhere: "I sometimes think . . . I will not submit to it any longer. Of course he would be mad with rage, but if he were to kill me I should like it better than having to go on in this way. I'm sure he is only waiting for me to die." The wife is right in her surmises about her entirely selfish husband, who, "according to the teachings of his whole life," sees no reason for Hermione to exist:

> What had his wife done for him, that he should put himself out of the way to do much for her? She had brought him no money. She had added nothing by her wit, beauty, or rank to his position in the world. She had given him no heir. What had he received from her that he should endure her commonplace conversation, and washed-out, dowdy prettinesses?
>
> (ch. 35)

"How to Dispose of a Wife" is Trollope's title for the chapter following Sir Hugh's departure from Clavering Park to prepare in London for his forthcoming yachting trip to Norway. In this chapter, Sir Hugh visits Hermione's widowed sister, Lady Ongar (formerly Julia Brabazon), at her handsome London lodgings. It is his purpose to slough off the "burden" (ch. 38) of his wife as well as to facilitate the sale of Lord Ongar's estate to his relations, since Julia now avoids Ongar Park, inherited after her depraved husband's death. Julia, who has been ostracized since her return to England from the Continent largely because Sir Hugh, her closest male relation, has not been willing to exercise himself on her behalf when she is slandered as an unchaste wife, is unflinching in exposing his real intention of "ridding yourself of her [Hermione's] society" (ch. 38). To Sir Hugh, Hermione is human waste now that she cannot reproduce. However, it is Sir Hugh rather than the supposedly frail Hermione Trollope soon disposes of, when the cruel husband is drowned along with his brother Archie in a yachting accident resulting from his hubris, even as the other sailors are rescued. Thereafter, Hugh's widow lives a somber but companionable life with her sister Lady Ongar, freed by Sir Hugh's death from his abuse and neglect.[8]

Even in his very late novels, such as *Is He Popenjoy?* (1878), Trollope writes about the violent thoughts that are a matter of course to privileged men, such as the degenerate Marquis of Brotherton. The marquis's young son is dying, almost certainly because the marquis himself is syphilitic; even when his son is very ill, the marquis and his servant frequent the brothels of London.[9]

The child is conceived with an Italian woman who may have been his wife or his mistress at the time, and the main plot of the novel centers around Popenjoy's questionable legitimacy. In a story in which nearly everyone is waiting for the little Italian Popenjoy's death and some are openly or secretly desiring it, the debilitated marquis is almost alone in the novel in lacking the energy to desire anything. As he confides to his nearly equally debauched mentor, the country gentleman Mr. De Baron,

> 'I think I made a mistake, De Baron, in not staying at home and looking after the property.'
> 'It's not too late now.'
> 'Yes, it is. I could not do it. I could not remember the tenants' names, and I don't care about game. I can't throw myself into a litter of young foxes, or get into a fury of passion about pheasants' eggs. It's all beastly nonsense, but if a fellow could only bring himself to care about it, that wouldn't matter. I don't care about anything.'
> 'You read.'
> 'No, I don't. I pretend to read – a little. If they had left me alone I think I should have had myself bled to death in a warm bath. But I won't now. That man's daughter won't be Lady Brotherton, if I can help it.'[10]

Lord Brotherton wants the death of a Roman Stoic after a life of Epicurean hedonism. Although during the peer's entirely self-absorbed life he has not previously cared much about producing an heir, the marquis would like to "cut out" his devoted younger brother Lord George Germain and his beautiful wife, Mary (daughter of Dean Lovelace, Dean of Brotherton), who is pregnant. Although the marquis doesn't "care about anything," he would like to damage the prospects of Lord George and at the same time get back at "that man's" daughter. The marquis especially hates the dean because he was thrashed by the much older man when the marquis insulted Mary, calling her a whore. For most of the novel after that beating, the marquis is even more debilitated. His inert body is particularly evident in the fight scene, juxtaposed to the vigorous dean's "fury":

> The Marquis fell like a heap into the fender, with his back against the top bar and his head driven farther back against the bricks and iron. There, for a second or two, he lay like a dead mass.
>
> Less than a minute had done it all, and for so long a time the Dean's ungoverned fury had held its fire. What were consequences to him, with that word as applied to his child ringing in his ears?
>
> *(Vol. 2, ch. 41)*

It seems that the marquis might have vitality enough just to commit adultery – but in fact he has just enough spark for risqué conversation. The marquis flirts with Adelaide Houghton – who hopes to bring down the Germain marriage herself but fails to entangle Lord George – by speculating that they might create an heir together if only his Italian wife and her English husband were dead. First the marquis confides in Mr. De Baron, Adelaide's father, that "I like her. If my wife would die, and he would die, we might get up another match, and cut out Lord George after all" (Vol. 2, ch. 52). The casual enormity of these dark thoughts confound even the worldly host: "This speculation was too deep even for Mr. De Baron, who laughed, and shuffled himself about, and got out of the room" (Vol 2, ch. 52). At the same country house soirée, the marquis asks Adelaide "if the coast were clear I wonder whether you'd take me now," after he has assured her that "I don't mean that you should have murdered anybody." When Adelaide replies that "the coast isn't clear, Lord Brotherton," the marquis declares, "No, by George. I wish it were; and so do you too, if you'd dare to say so" (Vol. 2, ch. 52).

But the marquis does not marry again. At this very country house-party, he hears of Popenjoy's death – which is followed soon afterwards by his own death. In Trollope's portrayal of this diseased lord's violent thoughts coupled with his enfeebled body, Trollope culminates his fiction's exposé of the misogyny that underlies the male fear of women's power. Trollope also suggests through the marquis's particular hatred for pregnant Mary Lovelace Germain, granddaughter of a stablekeeper, how imbricated are violence against women and violence against the working classes during the decades when both these groups struggled most fiercely for their political rights. It is Mary – known for her waltzing, for dancing the daring Kappa-Kappa, and for her effervescent high spirits, as well as for her beauty and fidelity to her husband – whose plebeian energies and healthy son triumph over the viciousness of the old male order represented by the debilitated marquis.

In progressive explorations of Trollope's views on women's character, psychology, and rights, most scholars have come to think that Trollope was not only intensely interested in Victorian women but also increasingly aware of the gendered strictures of his society, and often critical of these limitations. Critics writing today tend to believe that Trollope was responsive to the agitation for women's rights, although they differ in their conclusions as to the degree of that response. Sharon Marcus's essentially conservative view of Trollope's feminism might be balanced by Margaret Markwick's and my own arguments about his essential liberalism in sympathizing with reforms that would expand women's rights under the law. In any event, all of the scholars who have recognized Trollope's sympathies with deviant sexualities – Turner, Cohen, Dellamora, Forrester, Markwick, Flint – have also uncovered a moral and aesthetic flexibility in Trollope that argues for at the very least his willingness to imagine and consider greater erotic freedoms for all men and women in his culture and society.

Notes

1 Quoted in Donald Smalley, *Anthony Trollope: The Critical Heritage* (London: Routledge and Kegan Paul, 1969), 542.
2 See also Morse, *Women*, for an earlier reading of the triangulation of Alice-George-Kate Vavasor as coding incestuous desire.
3 Anthony Trollope, *Sir Harry Hotspur of Humblethwaite*, ed. N. John Hall (Oxford: Oxford University Press, 1991), ch. 11.
4 Glendinning, *Anthony Trollope*, 432. *The Way We Live Now* is Trollope's most expansive vision of a dissolute and sometimes vicious and rapacious upper class, most notable in figures like the young Sir Felix Carbury, a liar, sponge, gambler, and eventual attempted rapist of the pretty country girl Ruby Ruggles. Of the young aristocrats in the novel, only Lord Nidderdale shows some decency and kindness, especially when he aids Marie Melmotte just after her father Augustus Melmotte's grand fraud is discovered and Melmotte commits suicide.
5 See Morse, *Reforming Trollope*, ch. 3.
6 Anthony Trollope, *The Claverings*, ed. David Skilton (Oxford: Oxford University Press, 1986), ch. 20.
7 "Trollope's Country Estates" in *Centenary Essays*, ed. John Halperin, 70.
8 Andrew Wright in *Anthony Trollope: Dream and Art* comments upon Trollope's depiction of the "exhausted idleness" (135) of all the Claverings, including the flawed hero Harry, who eventually inherits Clavering Park along with the family title.
9 See P. D. Edwards, *Anthony Trollope: His Art and Scope*, 79: "It is hinted that his conduct offstage is even more disgraceful, that he scours the fleshpots of the Haymarket each night in company with his servant and that he has spies in his pay both at Brotherton and in London."
10 Anthony Trollope, *Is He Popenjoy?*, ed. John Sutherland (Oxford: Oxford University Press, 1986), Vol. 2, ch. 52.

Works cited

Amarnick, Steven. "Trollope at Fuller Length: Lord Silverbridge and the Manuscript of *The Duke's Children*." In *The Politics of Gender in the Novels of Anthony Trollope: New Readings for the Twenty-First Century*. Ed. Margaret Markwick, Deborah Denenholz Morse, and Regenia Gagnier. Aldershot, England: Ashgate Press, 2009.

apRoberts, Ruth. "Emily and Nora and Dorothy and Priscilla and Jemima and Carry." In *The Victorian Experience: The Novelists*. Ed. Richard A. Levine. Athens, OH: Ohio University Press, 1976.

Blythe, Helen Lucy. "The Rough and the Beautiful in 'Catherine Carmichael': Class and Gender in Trollope's Colonial Aesthetic." In *The Politics of Gender in the Novels of Anthony Trollope: New Readings for the Twenty-First Century*. Ed. Margaret Markwick, Deborah Denenholz Morse, and Regenia Gagnier. Aldershot, England: Ashgate Press, 2009.

Cockshut, A.O.J. *Man and Woman: A Study of Love and the Novel, 1740–1940*. London: Collins, 1977.

Cohen, William. *Sex Scandal: The Private Parts of Victorian Fiction*. Durham, NC: Duke University Press, 1996.

———. "Skin: Surface and Sensation in Trollope's 'The Banks of the Jordan.'" In *Embodied*. Minneapolis: University of Minnesota Press, 2009.

Corbett, Mary Jean. "Two Identities: Gender, Ethnicity, and Phineas Finn." In *The Politics of Gender in the Novels of Anthony Trollope: New Readings for the Twenty-First Century*. Ed. Margaret Markwick, Deborah Denenholz Morse, and Regenia Gagnier. Aldershot, England: Ashgate Press, 2009.

Dellamora, Richard. "Friendship, Marriage, and *Between Women*." Book Review Forum. In *Victorian Studies* 50.1 (Autumn 2007), 67–74.

———. "The Lesser Holocausts of William Gladstone and Anthony Trollope." In *Friendship's Bonds: Democracy and the Novel in Victorian England*. Philadelphia: University of Pennsylvania Press, 2004.

———. "Stupid Trollope." *Victorian Newsletter* 100 (Fall 2001), 22–6.

Edwards, P. D. *Anthony Trollope: His Art and Scope*. New York: St. Martin's Press, 1977.

Flint, Kate. "Queer Trollope." In *The Cambridge Companion to Anthony Trollope*. Ed. Carolyn Dever and Lisa Niles. Cambridge: Cambridge University Press, 2011.

Forrester, Mark. "Redressing the Empire: Anthony Trollope and British Gender Anxiety in 'The Banks of the Jordan'." In *Imperial Desire: Dissident Sexualities and Colonial Literature*. Ed. Philip Holden and Richard J. Ruppel. Minneapolis and London: University of Minnesota Press, 2003.

Gagnier, Regenia. "Gender, Liberalism, and Resentment." In *The Politics of Gender in the Novels of Anthony Trollope: New Readings for the Twenty-First Century*. Ed. Margaret Markwick, Deborah Denenholz Morse, and Regenia Gagnier. Aldershot, England: Ashgate Press, 2009.

Glendinning, Victoria. *Anthony Trollope*. London: Penguin, 1994.

Goodlad, Lauren. "Anthony Trollope's *The Eustace Diamonds* and 'the Great Parliamentary Bore.'" In *The Politics of Gender in Anthony Trollope's Novels*. Ed. Margaret Markwick, Deborah Denenholz Morse, and Regenia Gagnier. Aldershot, England: Ashgate Press, 2009.

Hensley, Nathan K. "Mister Trollope, Lady Credit, and *The Way We Live Now*." In *The Politics of Gender in the Novels of Anthony Trollope: New Readings for the Twenty-First Century*. Ed. Margaret Markwick, Deborah Denenholz Morse, and Regenia Gagnier. Aldershot, England: Ashgate Press, 2009.

Herbert, Christopher. *Trollope and Comic Pleasure*. Chicago: Chicago University Press, 1986.

James, Henry. "Anthony Trollope." *Partial Portraits*. In *Anthony Trollope: The Critical Heritage*. Ed. Donald Smalley. New York: Barnes and Noble, 1969.

Levine, George. *The Realistic Imagination: Fiction from Frankenstein to Lady Chatterley*. Chicago: University of Chicago Press, 1983.

Marcus, Sharon. *Between Women: Friendship, Desire, and Marriage in Victorian England*. Princeton & Oxford: Princeton University Press, 2007.

Markwick, Margaret. *New Men in Trollope's Novels: Rewriting the Victorian Male*: Aldershot. England: Ashgate Press, 2007.

———. "Out of the Closet: Homoerotics in Trollope's Novels." In *The Politics of Gender in Anthony Trollope's Novels: New Readings for the Twenty-First Century*. Aldershot, England: Ashgate Press, 2009.

———. *Trollope and Women*. London: The Trollope Society, 1997.

Markwick, Margaret, Deborah Denenholz Morse, and Regenia Gagnier, eds. *The Politics of Gender in Anthony Trollope's Novels: New Readings for the Twenty-First Century*. Aldershot, England: Ashgate Press, 2009.

McMaster, Juliet. "Trollope's Country Estates." In *Trollope Centenary Essays*. Ed. John Halperin. New York: St. Martin's Press, 1982.

———. *Trollope's Palliser Novels: Theme and Pattern*. London: MacMillan, 1978.

Michie, Elsie. "A Woman of Money: Miss Dunstable, Thomas Holloway, and Victorian Commercial Wealth." *The Politics of Gender in Anthony Trollope's Novels*. Ed. Margaret Markwick, Deborah Denenholz Morse, and Regenia Gagnier. Aldershot, England: Ashgate, 2009.

Morse, Deborah Denenholz. *Reforming Trollope: Race, Gender, and Englishness in the Novels of Anthony Trollope*. Aldershot, England: Ashgate, 2013.

———. "'Some Girls Who Come from the Tropics': Gender, Race, and Imperialism in Anthony Trollope's *He Knew He Was Right*." In *The Politics of Gender in Anthony Trollope's Novels: New Readings for the Twenty-First Century*. Ed. Margaret Markwick, Deborah Denenholz Morse, and Regenia Gagnier. Aldershot, England: Ashgate Press, 2009.

———. *Women in Trollope's Palliser Novels*. Ann Arbor, MI: UMI Research Press, 1987. Reprinted Boydell & Brewer/University of Rochester, 1991.

Nardin, Jane. *He Knew She Was Right: The Independent Woman in the Novels of Anthony Trollope*. Carbondale: Southern Illinois University Press, 1989.

Noble, Christopher S. "Otherwise Occupied: Masculine Widows in Trollope's Novels." In *The Politics of Gender in the Novels of Anthony Trollope: New Readings for the Twenty-First Century*. Ed. Margaret Markwick, Deborah Denenholz Morse, and Regenia Gagnier. Aldershot, England: Ashgate Press, 2009.

Pinch, Adela. *Thinking About Other People in Nineteenth-Century British Writing*. Cambridge: Cambridge University Press, 2010.

Polhemus, Robert. "(A)genda Trouble and the Lot Complex: Older Men-Younger Women Relationships in Trollope." *The Politics of Gender in Anthony Trollope's Novels*. Ed. Margaret Markwick, Deborah Denenholz Morse, and Regenia Gagnier. Aldershot, England: Ashgate Press, 2009.

———. *The Changing World of Anthony Trollope*. Berkeley & Los Angeles: University of California Press, 1968.

———. "The Mirror of Desire: Anthony Trollope's *Phineas Finn/Phineas Redux* (1869–74)." In *Erotic Faith: Being in Love from Jane Austen to D. H. Lawrence*. Chicago: University of Chicago Press, 1990.

Praz, Mario. "Anthony Trollope." In *The Hero in Eclipse in Victorian Fiction*. Ed. Angus Davidson. London: Oxford University Press, 1956.

Psomiades, Kathy. "*He Knew He Was Right*: The Sensational Tyranny of the Sexual Contract and the Problem of Liberal Progress." In *The Politics of Gender in Anthony Trollope's Novels*. Ed. Margaret Markwick, Deborah Denenholz Morse, and Regenia Gagnier. Aldershot, England: Ashgate Press, 2009.

Sadleir, Michael. *Trollope: A Commentary*. New York: Farrar, Strauss, 1947.

Skilton, David. "The Construction of Masculinities." In *The Cambridge Companion to Anthony Trollope*. Ed. Carolyn Dever and Lisa Niles. Cambridge: Cambridge University Press, 2011.

———. "Depth of Portraiture": What Should Distinguish a Victorian Man from a Victorian Woman?" In *The Politics of Gender in the Novels of Anthony Trollope: New Readings for the Twenty-First Century*. Ed. Margaret Markwick, Deborah Denenholz Morse, and Regenia Gagnier. Aldershot, England: Ashgate Press, 2009.

Smalley, Donald. *Anthony Trollope: The Critical Heritage*. London: Routledge and Kegan Paul, 1969.

Terry, R. C. *Anthony Trollope: The Artist in Hiding*. London: Macmillan, 1977.

Trollope, Anthony. *The Claverings*. Ed. David Skilton. Oxford: Oxford University Press, 1986.

———. *Is He Popenjoy?* Ed. John Sutherland. Oxford: Oxford University Press, 1986.

———. *Sir Harry Hotspur of Humblethwaite*. Ed. N. John Hall. Oxford: Oxford University Press, 1991.

Turner, Mark W. *Trollope and the Magazines: Gendered Issues in Mid-Victorian Fiction*. London: Macmillan, 2000.

Vlasopolos, Anca. "The Weight of Religion and History: Women Dying of Virtue in Trollope's Short Fiction." In *The Politics of Gender in the Novels of Anthony Trollope: New Readings for the Twenty-First Century*. Ed. Margaret Markwick, Deborah Denenholz Morse, and Regenia Gagnier. Aldershot, England: Ashgate Press, 2009.

Wright, Andrew. *Anthony Trollope: Dream and Art*. London: Macmillan, 1983.

4
ANTHONY TROLLOPE'S CONDUCT-BOOK FICTION FOR MEN

Hyson Cooper

At the opening of his 1870 lecture "On English Prose Fiction as a Rational Amusement," Anthony Trollope told his audience that "A man must, I think, have but a sorry existence upon whose bosom is forced a conviction that he gets his bread by doing evil and not good in the world" (*Four Lectures* 94). Trollope is speaking in defense of his own profession as a novelist, but the claim is one that pervades his fiction in his treatment of men in all walks of life. The belief expressed in that moment is significant to my discussion of masculinity in Trollope mainly for two reasons. First, it suggests that a man's own *feelings*, rather than any rules or customs external to himself, are his best and truest guide to his behavior. And second, it is inclusive of all men, regardless of class, age, education, religion, or any other mode of categorization. My aim in this essay is to show that for Trollope, a man is defined first and foremost by what he feels, and only secondarily by what he does. Or rather, what a man does is less worth noting, for Trollope, than the feelings that led him to do it. In this way, Trollope was writing what I call conduct book fiction for men, in which men are encouraged to examine and sort out their own feelings and act according to their dictates before all else; at the bottom of this we always find the position indicated by the above quotation, that no man who follows his less noble impulses can ever be contented. Trollope's men are not divided into those who would never dream of behaving badly and those who choose not to behave well, thus giving readers an easy choice of whom to emulate; instead Trollope takes us deep into the process by which men who explore their feelings arrive at courses of behavior.

For the more than twenty years since Michael Roper and John Tosh in *Manful Assertions* began to explore the implications of "[m]aking men visible as gendered subjects" in the study of British masculinity, scholarly treatment of Victorian men has tended to focus on behavior, both in terms of defining what behavior makes a man (or in some cases, a gentleman), and examining how such behavior is first learned and then maintained. In *Dandies and Desert Saints: Styles of Victorian Manhood*, James Eli Adams identifies modes of Victorian masculinity in the form of highly visible icons, an approach which again emphasizes behavior over feelings. More recently, Henry French and Mark Rothery in *Man's Estate: Landed Gentry Masculinities, c. 1660 – c. 1900* remark that for the class and period they cover, "Parents and children negotiated the meaning of the fundamental masculine values of virtue, honour, authority, independence, and self-command," going on to say that "It was then up to young gentry men to translate such values into value-judgements, diagnostics, and stereotypes by which they could navigate their way through a complex, contradictory, and confusing social world" (2). These approaches, while highly useful to the work of historicizing British masculinity, require us to look out through male eyes at the world around, rather than turning the gaze inward to the feelings men must examine in order to process influences, role models, rules, and customs external to themselves. For Trollope, I argue, this inward gaze is indispensable to an understanding of the behavior it leads to.

While Trollope himself was ostensibly mostly concerned with *manliness*, a term he uses frequently, I am deliberately focusing instead on *masculinity*, a term not yet current in Trollope's time. In *Manliness and Masculinities in Nineteenth-Century Britain*, Tosh identifies the difference between the two, as used in the nineteenth century and the present day: "Whereas manliness was treated essentially as a social attainment in the gift of one's peers, masculinity is an expression of personal authenticity, in which being true to oneself counts for much more than conforming to the expectations of others" (2–3). It is the latter concept that is of most use to my argument. Tosh's definition of Victorian manliness is in keeping with Trollope's claim that he wanted his novels to convey that "a man will be honoured as he is true, and honest, and brave of heart" (*Autobiography* Ch. 8). It would seem that if masculinity expresses what is personal to oneself, and manliness is granted to a man by his peers, then manliness is an end to which masculinity is the means. In the words of Margaret Markwick, one scholar who has explored Trollope's treatment of men's feelings, "Trollope's masculinity is explicitly grounded in a man being in touch with his nurturing side. Men need to learn the language which puts feelings into words" (13). The focus of this essay will be Trollope's portrayal of the process that must take place *before* a man can reach the point identified by Markwick; before a man can put his feelings into words he must discover what they are. While Markwick is concerned with the ways in which "[e]xpressing love for one's children and closeness to them in practical and physical ways will bring a satisfaction that transcends the exercise of power in public and political life," I am concerned with Trollope's analysis of men's feelings in situations in which a man is faced with difficult decisions that no one can make for him, and cannot make them until he has sorted out his own feelings as the only reliable guide to his behavior.

I focus my discussion on particular male characters from two of Trollope's novels: Sir Peregrine Orme of *Orley Farm* (1862) and Mountjoy Scarborough of *Mr Scarborough's Family* (1883). I have chosen these novels and these characters for a few key reasons: they come from widely removed points in Trollope's writing life, the two men differ a good deal in personality, lifestyle, and situation, and while these characters come from novels that have received much critical attention, as characters they have received very little. In addition, and most importantly, they are male characters whose feelings, as guide to their conduct, receive lengthy and detailed treatment from their creator.

In the events surrounding Sir Peregrine Orme, Lady Mason's elderly champion in *Orley Farm*, Trollope creates a perfect storm of the feelings of a man and his need to examine them. Sir Peregrine is a true gentleman and irreproachably manly, and also remarkably innocent. In his seventies, although Sir Peregrine is "conceited as to his experience of the world and the wisdom which he had thence derived" (Ch. 3), he is nonetheless so tender and chivalrous to women that he can scarcely believe a woman capable of a crime even when she has personally confessed it to him, and well into the story his creator remarks that it "was strange how that old man should have lived so near the world for seventy years, should have taken his place in Parliament and on the bench, should have rubbed his shoulders so constantly against those of his neighbours, and yet have retained so strong a reliance on the purity of the world in general" (Ch. 56). At the start of the novel, Sir Peregrine's life is such as to foster and indulge these foibles so as to see him contentedly through old age to death. The people closest to him are his son's widow Mrs Orme, a likeable Angel in the House who has lived with him as a daughter since the death of her husband a year into her marriage, and his grandson Perry, one of Trollope's most promising hobbledehoys, who respects and emulates his grandfather and will clearly grow up to be a credit to the family soon enough. Sir Peregrine is "a man whom it was by no means difficult to lead," and "amenable to flattery," but as he is cocooned by his relatives' love and his servants' loyalty, we should have no reason to fear for him in his old age (Ch. 3).

Sir Peregrine's tranquility is ruffled at this time by his neighbor Lady Mason, an attractive forty-seven year-old widow he has known for many years. Lady Mason had been charged some twenty years before with forging the codicil to her husband's will that left her son the property called Orley Farm, but was not convicted. When the case is reopened by a vengeful former tenant at the start of the novel, Sir Peregrine takes Lady Mason's innocence for granted, sets himself up as her greatest champion, and offers her his and his daughter-in-law's countenance as a shield against public opinion while the case awaits trial. In championing Lady Mason, Sir Peregrine falls wholeheartedly and irrevocably in love with her, and she accepts his proposal of marriage with gratitude, but also some misgivings. When she realizes the harm that would be done him as her husband should the case go against her, she discovers that the only way to persuade him to end the engagement is to confess her guilt to him herself. While her confession is regarded by Sir Peregrine and those who love him as noble and self-sacrificing, it is nonetheless a blow from which the chivalrous and trusting old man is unable to recover.

In causing the venerable Sir Peregrine to fall in love with a lady he has long known, only to learn that she is a criminal, Trollope has created a situation that can only end unhappily for all parties. The love story of Sir Peregrine Orme and Lady Mason is not Trollope's only account of a man falling in love in his maturity, but nowhere does he probe the wound more deeply. In making Sir Peregrine so manly and such a perfect gentleman both in thought and deed, with seventy years credit as such, Trollope puts the issue of a man's behavior out of the question. Of course Sir Peregrine will behave as becomes a man and an English gentleman, and therefore Trollope can spend nearly all of the space he allots to Sir Peregrine in probing and anatomizing his feelings.

In doing so, Trollope strikes an exquisite emotional balance, establishing that Sir Peregrine's vulnerability is in safe hands, and so are we. Sir Peregrine's feelings regarding Lady Mason are treated by Trollope with humor but never with ridicule, with compassion that is never patronizing, with tenderness that never grows maudlin or sentimental, and without passing either approval or judgment. This mode of authorial treatment creates a safe space for Sir Peregrine's feelings, and therefore for his masculinity. In sorting through and articulating Sir Peregrine's complex and conflicted feelings while still treating him with respect as a man, Trollope establishes that such emotional conflict is not only normal but also becoming to a man. Trollope's conduct book fiction for men thus refuses to gloss over the process of taking a hard look at difficult feelings, and using them as a guide to behavior.

In his psychological portrait of Sir Peregrine, Trollope deploys two main strategies: authorial interpretation of Sir Peregrine's feelings, and Sir Peregrine's own thoughts on what he will do about them. The first strategy makes a path for our sympathy with the second. When Sir Peregrine is first contemplating whether to propose to Lady Mason, Trollope treats his ruminations with gentle, rueful humor, remarking that "I and my readers can probably see very many reason why he should not; but then we are not in love with Lady Mason . . . We are not chivalrous old gentlemen, past seventy years of age, but still alive, keenly alive, to a strong feeling of romance" (Ch. 35). Trollope's narrative strategy in this passage, as Markwick says of a similar passage in another novel, "hints at an alliance between the narrator and his reader, and implies a reader now converted to the narrator's cause" (69).[1] Trollope's phrasing reminds us of both Sir Peregrine's strengths and his foibles, while the inclusive "we" credits us with sharing Trollope's own level of sympathy with his character, compelling us to acknowledge Sir Peregrine's masculinity without giving his behavior carte blanche.

By bringing us so deeply into the hard emotional work necessary for Sir Peregrine to persuade himself of the rightness of seeing his love for Lady Mason through to marriage, Trollope enlists our sympathy for Sir Peregrine's ultimate decision, after Lady Mason's shattering confession, to pass on the management of his estate to his grandson. When Sir Peregrine realizes that "he was no longer fit for a man's work, and that it would be well he should abandon it," the reader is able to perceive this as the outcome not merely of the passing of time and the natural order of things, but of an emotional battle over what makes a man masculine in the sense defined by Tosh. Christopher Herbert has asserted that the precipitate disclosure of Lady Mason's guilt "artfully throws the full, sustained weight of narrative interest where it belongs: on Sir Peregrine's inward struggle with a situation that, as he now recognizes all too clearly, has torn him away from his usual moorings and seems to require of him that he renew himself in some essential way" (139); his passing the management of the estate to Perry while he himself is still hale and of sound mind is one way that he attempts to do this. When Trollope tells us that Sir Peregrine "had ventured to love" and "had been terribly deceived," that he "had ventured his all upon [Lady Mason's] innocence and her purity . . . and he had lost," we know better than his actions alone might tell us, exactly what that cost him (Ch. 59).

In the second half of the novel, Trollope lingers over three significant epochs in Sir Peregrine's inner life, further elucidating the emotional cost of his unfortunate love affair with Lady Mason: his initial response to her confession, his emotional state during her trial, and their last meeting. Trollope makes Sir Peregrine rather than Lady Mason the center of emotional interest in the immediate aftermath of her confession, granting us access to his interiority alone. Trollope takes us step by step through the rapid cycle of Sir Peregrine's reaction, as he goes from blank incomprehension to an intense and urgent need for clarity (no matter how painful) to concern for Mrs Orme to a sincere desire still to be of service to Lady Mason to a clear conviction that now he cannot possibly marry her. Two actions on his part reveal a good deal of what he is going through: that he seeemingly unconsciously reverts to calling her "Lady Mason" rather than "Mary" and that only when "he felt her hand tremble in his" does he realize that he has been holding it the whole time that "all these thoughts pressed upon his brain." A moment before this realization he had been justifying to himself his need to extend Lady Mason's confidence to include Mrs Orme, as "[t]he weight of these tidings would be too much for him, if he did not share them with someone" (Ch. 45). Sir Peregrine is not the sort of man to make a boast of either his feelings or his judgment, and he keeps them to himself at this time because to communicate them to Lady Mason would be to increase her own burden of unhappiness; but while she may not know all that he feels, Trollope sees to it that we do.

It is during Lady Mason's trial that Trollope shows us the outcome of the brutal spate of emotions that assails Sir Peregrine upon hearing Lady Mason's confession, and that outcome is that her generosity toward him awakens and enforces his own toward her. His feeling that she has behaved nobly to him trumps any feeling that as a criminal she should be shunned. He chafes horribly during the days of her trial, which he does not attend, instead awaiting a daily report from Perry. Their conversations on the subject are painful for them both, as Perry strives to be both honest and gentle, and his grandfather strives not to show unseemly eagerness while probing for the information he craves. It is in detailing Sir Peregrine's private thoughts when Perry has left him alone, however, that Trollope lets us see the internal work he has done, to see to it that his own feeling can match Lady Mason's in generosity:

> Had he married her, and gone with her proudly into the court, – as he would have done, – and had he then heard a verdict of guilty given by the jury . . . it would have killed

him. He felt, as he sat there, safe over his own fireside, that his safety was due to her generosity . . . His head would have fallen low before the eyes of those who had known him since they had known anything, and would never have been raised again. In his own spirit, in his inner life, the blow had come to him; but it was due to her effort on his behalf that he had not been stricken in public . . . Let her be ever so guilty, . . . she had behaved very nobly to him. From him at least she had a right to sympathy.

(Ch. 70)

The process of focusing on how he feels toward Lady Mason's generosity also leads him to acknowledge, both to himself and to Mrs Orme, that he still loves her, and wishes it were still possible for them to marry; somewhat paradoxically, this is what makes it safe for him to pay her a farewell visit after her trial. He is guided by the need to look after his wounded feelings rather than by rules of conduct; it is because he has faced his feelings honestly that he is self-aware enough to keep them in check. In their farewell scene, Sir Peregrine first greets her as Lady Mason, then calls her "Mary" three times and "my love" once; he sits close beside her as they talk and kisses her forehead before he goes. Yet we know that no love affair will be revived between them, even though Trollope has told us that moments before their last meeting Sir Peregrine had still been wishing he could marry her:

[H]e could hardly bring himself to confess that it was impossible . . . It seemed to him that he might yet regain his old vitality if he could wind his arm once more about her waist, and press her to his side, and call her his own. It would be so sweet to forgive her . . . to teach her that there was one at least who would not bring up her past sin, even in his memory.

(Ch. 79)

In acknowledging these feelings to himself, Sir Peregrine cannot now be bowled over by them; his feelings toward Lady Mason may have suffered a relapse, but his awareness of them is the very reason his actions regarding her will remain steady.

By elucidating Sir Peregrine's deepest unspoken feelings so thoroughly, Trollope enlists our sympathy more powerfully than if we merely saw his actions from the outside in. In other words, if we were shown Sir Peregrine's choices in terms of what his culture prescribed he must do, we would certainly see him as an exemplar of Victorian manly and gentlemanly virtues, but we would see no more. But because Trollope allows us to see his choices from the inside looking out, his masculinity comes through as well as his manliness, as he faces the struggle to learn who he is based on what he feels, and to abide by that. As Robert Polhemus puts it, Sir Peregrine

finds gradually that the impact of Lady Mason's sin and retribution deepens his capacity for pity, for love, and for grief. It is not so much the actual content of the words which he comes at last to speak about her that makes them so moving; it is rather what these words tell about him and the way they bring home the quiet, but remarkable transformation of his moral consciousness.

(80)

It is worth noting that when we are told what Sir Peregrine *thinks* and what he *says*, we find him expressing himself in terms of how he must act, what he must do. His creator has taken upon himself to articulate what Sir Peregrine *feels*, wherein lie both his masculinity and his heroism.

In sorting through the male characters in *Mr Scarborough's Family*, one finds only two to admire for true Trollopian manliness: Mr Scarborough's conscientious lawyer Mr Grey, and the young Harry Annesley, who wins the love of the loyal and attractive heroine Florence Mountjoy. The rest of the men are an assortment of scoundrels, cads, prigs, gamblers, hobbledehoys, and liars. Critical attention to this novel has hitherto shown most attention to the towering Mr Scarborough, whose physical courage and ethical defiance on his deathbed are equally astounding, and his opposite Mr Grey, characterized by unfailing gentlemanly conduct and respect for law. Throughout the novel Trollope offers searching treatment of what the male characters feel or are unable to feel, but for the purposes of this discussion I focus on the feelings of Mr Scarborough's elder son Mountjoy, and to a lesser extent, by way of contrast, Mountjoy's younger brother Augustus. In his portrait of the sullen, self-destructive gambler Mountjoy Scarborough, Trollope explores how far even a modicum of honorable feeling may take a man with few or no other redeeming qualities.

The central plot of *Mr Scarborough's Family* is the story of a rich man's determination to defy the laws of entail. Unbeknownst to anyone but his own long-deceased wife, John Scarborough had married his wife a second time before the birth of his second son, and secretly retained the proofs of both ceremonies, both of which took place in obscure continental locations. His elder son Mountjoy also happens to be his favorite, but when Mountjoy's compulsive gambling threatens to bankrupt the estate, Mr Scarborough produces the "proof" that he had married his wife only after Mountjoy's birth, thus rendering Mountjoy illegitimate and the post-obits held by his creditors worthless. At this time Mr Scarborough is on his deathbed, facing a series of operations and amazing everyone with his physical courage. His younger son Augustus, now the heir in tail, forces Mountjoy's creditors to settle for a fraction of what they are owed, but then sets about making himself so disagreeable to his father that Mr Scarborough produces proof of his real first marriage, thus reinstating Mountjoy as the heir. Mountjoy's feelings throughout the novel are understandably bitter, but while he is certainly upset at finding he will not inherit the estate, what galls him the most is the slur cast on his late mother's name by making her out to have been his father's mistress before she was his wife. Perhaps the most significant difference between the two brothers, and the main source of our lack of sympathy for Augustus, is that Augustus remains impervious to any such feeling.

Mountjoy's fiercely protective attitude toward his mother's posthumous reputation is the one thing that gains him any support from Mr Grey, and it takes him surprisingly far. The embattled Mr Grey spends the novel torn between desire to uphold the law, and a combination of disgust and admiration for the Scarborough men; he is also not entirely free from curiosity as the case takes its twists and turns. A sullen, arrogant, aimless gambler like Mountjoy is exactly the sort to repel Mr Grey, and while Grey would much prefer to have nothing to do with him, he is much softened by the expression of Mountjoy's feelings on the subject of his mother. In describing Mountjoy to his daughter, Grey declares him "unfit to have any money in his hands" and "little better than a lunatic" (Ch. 20). When the two men are in conference together later on, however, and Mr Grey cannot deny that as far as he can see the story against the late Mrs Scarborough must be true, he finds himself coming over to Mountjoy's side, emotionally speaking:

> The cloud sat very black upon Mountjoy Scarborough's face, and the blacker it sat the more Mr Grey liked him. If something could be done to redeem from ruin a young man who so felt about his mother, – who so felt about his mother, simply because she had been his mother, – it would be a good thing to do. . . . Mr Grey knew [the story] was true; but he could not on that account do other than feel an intense desire to confer some benefit on Mountjoy Scarborough.
>
> (Ch. 40)

One noteworthy aspect of this scene is that while Mountjoy's feelings are deep and intense as well as noble, he is unable to express them at all in words, or accurately by his face and body language, and yet Mr Grey knows how to interpret them due to his own ability to feel. Mountjoy is only able to state gruffly that he does not believe the story and cannot forgive his father, and to scowl and sulk. As R. D. McMaster puts it, Mountjoy's "state of mind is complex . . . Property, legality, self-interest do not weigh heavily with him; filial sentiment for his mother does" (145). Mr Grey's first glimpse of Mountjoy's feelings had come in an earlier scene, when we are told that Mountjoy "would never believe, he said, that his mother was – Then he turned away, and in spite of all that had come and gone, Mr Grey respected him" (Ch. 37). It takes a sensitive, right-feeling, and perspicacious man like Mr Grey to see past Mountjoy's scowl to the feelings behind it; Grey sees that Mountjoy is hurt as well as angry, and that his hurt stems from self-forgetful feelings of chivalry and filial loyalty. The full impact that this understanding has on Mr Grey is shown several chapters later, when he relents so far toward this "lunatic" who should not be trusted with money that he pays Mountjoy's newest small gambling debt, incurred with a bit of pocket money his father had given him on condition that it would not go toward cards (Ch. 49). Clearly, neither Grey nor Mountjoy is behaving wisely in this – Mountjoy had broken his promise and now Grey is enabling him – but the impression left behind is of both men earning their masculinity by following the dictates of their feelings, even if unwisely.

Mr Scarborough appears to have had very little respect for his wife himself, making it all the more remarkable that his son's enduring respect for her should have a softening effect on him, even as it had on Mr Grey. Certain hints – not least the fact that she seems to have meekly submitted to his demand for a second wedding before the birth of her second child – suggest that the late Mrs Scarborough had little self-will, and was regarded by her husband as his creature, with no rights of her own. We are told that he had always been "very fond" of women while yet regarding them as "only something better than dogs," and that "when a woman rose to a way of thinking akin to his own, she was no longer a woman to his senses" (Ch. 21). From this and from the fact that he seems to remember his wife with affection (despite his disregard for her posthumous reputation), we may infer that she was the very model of unquestioning obedience and self-effacement. Mountjoy, however, seems to have acquired a very different attitude toward women, and to have got hold of the notion that the women of a man's own family at least are deserving of honor and respectful treatment, simply by virtue of their relation to him. As Jane Nardin puts it, "Scarborough [the elder] doesn't believe in rules of conduct, but only in unfettered benevolence. Hence he is logically precluded from teaching his sons to obey the precepts of common morality, to respect the law, or even to defer to the mores of their society" (132). If Nardin is right, then Mountjoy's chivalry toward his mother is all the more admirable. In another novel, *Is He Popenjoy?* (1878), Trollope had remarked that "A man must be very degraded indeed if his wife be not holy to him" (Ch. 35). Mountjoy seems to have a similar feeling toward his own mother, a feeling the elder Mr Scarborough had not held toward her as a wife.

Mr Scarborough's opinion of the law as "a perplexed entanglement of rules got together so that the few might live in comfort at the expense of the many" (Ch. 21) is the ostensible reason for his plot to foil the entail of his estate – that, and a genuine desire that the property whose value he had so increased should remain intact; yet if these were truly the chief motivators behind his actions, he would be happy for Augustus to inherit the estate, no matter how pestilential his personality. After all, making his business-minded younger son the heir would both defy the law and secure the property. What happens instead is that Mr Scarborough is both disgusted by Augustus's treatment of him and duly touched by the finer feelings of Mountjoy, which at last sway him away from his wish to thwart the law in order to thwart Augustus instead. Mr Scarborough's arrogantly patriarchal attitude toward women does not, in the end, stop him from preferring Mountjoy's masculinity to Augustus's. Augustus deeply offends his father by implying that he should die and get out of the way, and then neglecting him, but when Mountjoy tells Mr Scarborough off for slandering his mother, we are told that "[h]e rather liked his son for standing up for his mother, and was by no means offended at the expression of his son's incredulity" (38). As Coral Lansbury has remarked, "It is not within [Mr Scarborough's] power to alter the characters of his two sons, but he does succeed in seeing how they would behave if he were dead" (173).

In *Mr Scarborough's Family*, the masculinity that prevails at the end strikes a blow for pure feeling over proper action. The fate of the Tretton property is the cause that drives most of the novel's action, and yet it is left open at the end. Mountjoy inherits the full property free of encumbrance, but he is haunted by his erstwhile creditors, and self-destructively inclined to fall straight back into his former habits; he even seems inclined to use his abortive, one-sided affair with his cousin Florence as an excuse for doing so. We are left with no sense that the property has been rescued, nor that Mr Scarborough's elaborate plot has had its intended effect. What has triumphed, however, is admirable masculine feeling. The filial Mountjoy has materially triumphed over the greedy, self-serving Augustus. Trollope gives little hope for the estate's prosperity, but instead seems to ask, what good could Mountjoy's better feelings not do, if coupled with right action? And what good can Augustus's business sense ever do, if not guided by right feeling?

In both *Orley Farm* and *Mr Scarborough's Family*, Trollope makes the risky move of leaving his right-feeling men unfulfilled and unhappy. Sir Peregrine Orme's hale old age descends rapidly into decrepitude once he is disenchanted of his unconsummated love for the criminal Lady Mason. Mountjoy Scarborough inherits a prosperous and unembarrassed estate while yet in his twenties, but remains so wretched in his deep dissatisfaction with himself and his personal life – seeing the girl he loves marry another, the doors of the best clubs closed against him – that he seems actually to intend ruin for himself and the property. Yet these men receive much sympathy and even approval from their creator – and we are invited to follow that lead – in light of the pure masculinity of their feelings. In the bitter endings of these two novels, Trollope seems to say that for men of any age and background, right feeling that leads to an unhappy ending is better than the other way around.

Note

1 For a thorough close reading of how Trollope explores masculinity by way of his narrative approach, see Margaret Markwick, *New Men in Trollope's Novels*, pp. 61–82.

Works cited

Adams, James Eli. *Dandies and Desert Saints: Styles of Victorian Masculinity*. Ithaca: Cornell UP, 1995.
French, Henry and Mark Rothery. *Man's Estate: Landed Gentry Masculinities, c. 1660–c. 1900*. Oxford: Oxford UP, 2012.
Herbert, Christopher. *Trollope and Comic Pleasure*. Chicago: U of Chicago P, 1987.
Lansbury, Coral. *The Reasonable Man: Trollope's Legal Fiction*. Princeton: Princeton UP, 1981.
Markwick, Margaret. *New Men in Trollope's Novels: Rewriting the Victorian Male*. Aldershot: Ashgate, 2007.
McMaster, R. D. *Trollope and the Law*. London: Macmillan, 1986.
Nardin, Jane. *Trollope and Victorian Moral Philosophy*. Athens: Ohio UP, 1996.
Polhemus, Robert M. *The Changing World of Anthony Trollope*. Berkeley: U of California P, 1968.
Roper, Michael and John Tosh, eds. *Manful Assertions: Masculinities in Britain Since 1800*. London: Routledge, 1991.
Tosh, John. *Manliness and Masculinity in Nineteenth-Century Britain: Essays on Gender, Family and Empire*. Harlow: Pearson, 2005.

Trollope, Anthony. *An Autobiography*. 1883. Eds. Michael Sadleir and Frederick Page. Oxford: Oxford UP, 1950.

———. *Four Lectures*. 1938. N.p.: Folcroft, 1969.

———. *Is He Popenjoy?* 1878. Ed. John Sutherland. Oxford: Oxford UP, 1986.

———. *Mr Scarborough's Family*. 1883. Ed. Geoffrey Harvey. Oxford: Oxford UP, 1989.

———. *Orley Farm*. 1862. Ed. David Skilton. Oxford: Oxford UP, 1985.

5

WOMEN, VIOLENCE, AND MODERNITY IN *THE WAY WE LIVE NOW*[1]

Mary Jean Corbett

In its well-known discussion of *The Way We Live Now* (1875), the novel Anthony Trollope was composing even as he was also "formulating his views on the art of writing fiction" (Sutherland 473), the last chapter of *An Autobiography* (1883) both classifies the novel as a satire on "the commercial profligacy of the age" and calls attention to its "exaggerated" features (ch. 20). Perhaps aiming to redress a perceived imbalance in its tone, Trollope professes, on the one hand, some liberal faith in "progress," in that "comfort has been increased," "health has been improved, and education extended" (ch. 20); these comments, as N. John Hall notes, sound the same note of faith in amelioration that Bishop Yeld articulates in the novel itself (Hall 387; ch. 55). On the other hand, as James Kincaid first established, *An Autobiography* also makes some very pointed observations about "dishonesty magnificent in its proportions" as an actual feature of contemporary life (Kincaid 127). "Can a world, retrograding from day to day in honesty, be considered to be in a state of progress?" (ch. 20), Trollope asks, making the familiar, here tacit claim that one best measures "progress" by gauging the moral and ethical character of the nation.

"That men have become less cruel, less violent, less selfish, less brutal" (ch. 20), as *An Autobiography* asserts, would signify improvement within the civilizational framework so dear to Trollope and his contemporaries, in which both the "primitive" and the "progressive" were assessed in good part by the condition and treatment of women. Early anthropologists, such as Henry Maine and John McLennan, indexed the development of civil society over time by tracing a long, slow movement away from the routinized violent capture of women, who were once putatively shared by men in common, to modern, contractual, monogamous marriage.[2] But is the cruelty, violence, selfishness, and brutality that men demonstrably visit upon women in *The Way We Live Now* – as part of that system of subordination that John Stuart Mill identified as "a single relic of an old world of thought and practice exploded in everything else" (qtd. in Psomiades 34) – an instance of what the novel exaggerates in its effort to make its satirical point? Or are the autobiographer's remarks on "progress" undercut by the violence against women that the novel narrates?

Trollope's caginess, in both the novel and the memoir, might make it hard to decide. In measuring the mixed tenor of the times in *An Autobiography*'s final chapter, without particular reference to the status of women, he asserts that his own character as a satirist – whose "very desire . . . to do his work energetically makes him dishonest" (ch. 20) – partially aligns him with the rampant falsity he critiques in modern life. In both the actions of so many characters in *The Way We Live*

Now and the events that it narrates, Trollope owns that he has departed from his commitment to realistic representation in that "[t]he vices implied are coloured so as to make effect rather than represent truth" (ch. 20). Yet in that commonplace distinction between using color for dramatic "effect" and documenting an unvarnished "truth," we can grasp the way in which Trollope's narrative strategy gives the lie to *An Autobiography*'s more confident remarks on the diminishing cruelty, violence, selfishness, and brutality of modern life. The anti-progressive elements within modernity, including the contemporary status of women, haunt Trollope's novel in myriad ways. They are frequently but not entirely subordinated, both temporally and spatially, to the dramatic effects achieved in the "now" of the Melmotte plot, even as "the novel's general ambience is dominated," as Christopher Herbert observes, "by violence and fear" (*Trollope* 178).

Trollope's ambivalent comments about "progress" help to illuminate why *The Way We Live Now* shifted shape – or "switche[d] genres" (Kincaid 169) – over the course of its composition, subordinating some aspects of the novel's critique to others. What he referred to in the advance layouts as the "Carbury novel" became ever more steadily the Melmotte novel, as John A. Sutherland notes in documenting "large changes of emphasis" from Trollope's initial plans (481). The "three more or less equivalent nuclei" (Sutherland 476) of the complex multiplot novel gave way to a more intensely conceived focus on the rise and fall of the financier; "speculative writing and marriage schemes" (McGann 139), each mainly associated with women (and especially with the character of Lady Carbury), feature as somewhat subordinate elements within the overarching theme of the novel as it evolved. In the *Autobiography*'s highlighting of Melmotte's "magnificent" dishonesty as the key feature of the novel's satirical critique, then, Trollope might also seem to consign violence to an earlier, less progressive phase of English life: for "there can be no doubt" (354), according to the autobiographer, that "the way we live now" marks an improvement on the past.

By reframing the novel over its course, Trollope might be understood both to minimize the question of women's status and, more specifically, to relegate instances of men's violence against women to a marginal status within the text. Instead of pursuing the multiplot focus, he diagnoses the ills of what we now call modernity by collating multiple instances of a different symptom. And, following Trollope's lead, most recent critical evaluations of the novel have also focused on the Melmotte plot as the chief index of his critique. "The social and financial systems" that the novel describes, in Paul Delany's words, "resemble each other in having uncoupled their exchange function from any ultimate standard of value" (29). From Lady Carbury's epistolary efforts to cadge good reviews for her bad book (ch. 1), to her son Felix's lack of "repugnance at declaring a passion which he did not feel" (ch. 2), to the Longestaffes' inability "to pay anybody anything that they owed" (ch. 6): the novel points to falsity and misrepresentation as the governing condition of the age, epitomized by both the substitution of "unsecured paper" for "real bank notes" (ch. 10) at the Beargarden and the analogous substitution of "the floating of the railway shares" for "the construction of the railway" (ch. 10). Although Rebecca Stern usefully reminds us that "the tendency to represent economic trouble in social terms" (9) both pre- and postdates Trollope's times, it is fair to conclude, with Amanda Anderson, that "the forces of modernity have infiltrated all aspects of life in this commercial, speculative, cosmopolitan society" as Trollope conceives it, so that "representatives of the traditional ethos are more fully on the defensive" (526). Thus even though the stalwart Roger Carbury eschews the lure of the modern in his commitment to "England's 'heirloom' roots" (Goodlad 439), just hunkering down at Carbury Manor cannot insulate him from economic and cultural change, which arrives without his consent in the form of (relatively) new neighbors. "The grandeur of the Longestaffes and the too apparent wealth of the Primeros" depress both the real and the symbolic value of his estate, despite the fact that like his father, Roger "had never owed a shilling that he could not pay" (ch. 6). As

Nathan K. Hensley sums it up, "finance, writing, and marriage have all degenerated into the realm of suspicious fiction" (149–50).

But is violence against women one of "the forces of modernity" or a survival of "primitive culture"? Does it emerge in *The Way We Live Now*, as Sharon Marcus suggests that it does in *Can You Forgive Her?* (1864–65), alongside "the civilizational narratives" so as "to portray sexual equality as a form of false progress that unleashes a savagery curable only by a return to a traditional rule of force in which men govern women" (228)? Even in subordinating the "women's plots" to the Melmotte narrative, I will argue, *The Way We Live Now* demonstrates, quietly but persistently, that particular forms of violence continue to attend the entry of young women into the courtship practices and marriage systems of modern life, as a number of recent feminist critics have also observed. Considering the horror of Lady Carbury's married life, Monica Rydygier Smith notes that "[a]t first, the physical assault of women is recounted as part of an embedded narrative of past events . . . situated before the 'now' of the novel's title," even as the novel goes on to "equat[e] it with real conditions . . . as a facet of the contemporary world" (13). By chapter 77, in which we watch Melmotte attack his daughter Marie, "[v]iolence in the home is no longer presented as part of a distant and unsavoury past, . . . but actualized in the narrative 'now'" (Smith 20), a representational turn that Lisa Surridge dates to the passage of the Divorce Act in 1857, after which both the newspaper press and domestic fiction enhanced "the public visibility of spousal assault" (Surridge 8) among the middling classes.[3] Considering Felix Carbury's attempted rape of Ruby Ruggles, a narrative event I will discuss in more detail ahead, Elizabeth Bleicher calls attention to how, subtly yet stringently, the narrator's "shift in language from an almost facetious irony to grim reportage mirrors the descent in the couple's negotiation from flirtation into the violence of a back alley assault" (555). In this light, the dramatic "effects" of the Melmotte plot take precedence over but do not cancel out the more muted "truth" of violence against women that the narrative partially relegates to the past of its older female characters, in the backstories afforded to Lady Carbury and Winifred Hurtle, if not to the unnamed woman who gave birth to Marie Melmotte.

In what follows, I build on the work of these and other feminist analysts of the novel to explore the narrative trajectories of those unmarried female characters – Hetta Carbury, Georgiana Longestaffe, Marie Melmotte, and Ruby Ruggles – whose familial and sociosexual relationships constitute their chief means of participating in the novel's speculative economy. Albeit to different degrees and in different registers, violence attends the oscillation of all these female protagonists between the coercive, indeed anti-progressive claims of the fractured family units to which they belong and the less patently coercive, putatively progressive sphere associated with individual desire and the fictions of romance. As Marcus notes, "[t]o make marriage contractual," from the liberal individualist perspective associated most closely with John Stuart and Harriet Taylor Mill, "was to differentiate it from the savagery that all sides in the marriage debates identified as anathema" (217). Yet in the narrative present, and not just in the narrated pasts of the aristocratic Lady Carbury and the American Winifred Hurtle, young Englishwomen enter into marriage and modernity by and through the very experience of violence that some contemporary observers associated with the "savage" past that a "civilized" present had purportedly progressed beyond. The dark heart of metropolitan modernity that Trollope's novel both conceals and exposes, I will suggest, registers that contradiction, not as a dramatic "effect" but as a partially occluded, painful "truth."

***

From the points of view of most of the unmarried women in the novel, the experience of modernity differs significantly from that of men, in that the family apparatus tethers them more tightly to class and status in patriarchal forms. "Of infinitely less importance than her brother" (ch. 2), the narrator sarcastically remarks, Hetta tells her "'old-fashioned'" cousin-suitor Roger

Carbury that she and her mother "'belong to a newer and worse sort of world'" (ch. 8) than the one that he seeks to salvage – and that, if she were to become his wife and their children's mother, she would be charged with reproducing. That her "face was a true index of her character" (ch. 2) serves visibly to demonstrate, however, that Hetta's "character" (in both senses of the term) has been constituted through a not-yet-outmoded formation for femininity: if "the complexities of credit undid simple oppositions between intrinsic, real value on the one hand and the smoke and mirrors of finance on the other" (McGann 141) in the Melmotte plot, then Hetta is one of the few characters in the novel that almost entirely signifies as the real thing. Despite her resistance to Roger's repeated offers, she nonetheless aligns herself in part with that older world at the outset by representing herself as subject to her mother's authority, telling Roger that "'[i]f mamma chooses to go to the Melmottes' I shall certainly go with her. If that is contamination, I suppose I must be contaminated'" (ch. 8). What Wendy S. Jones contends of Marie Melmotte's movement over the course of the novel is thus, arguably, also the case in Hetta's plot: "it is only through [her] desire to marry the man she loves, and her opposition to her [family] on this issue, that she finds her sense of her own personhood" (136). By the end of the story, the once-dutiful Hetta has become "disposed to do battle with her mother and her cousin," "would not submit her own feelings to their control," and is "savage to the point of rebellion against all authority" (ch. 90). Taking an independent, unauthorized action that marks her, in her own mind, as "emancipated from control" (ch. 91), she resolves to "appeal to Mrs Hurtle" (ch. 91) to verify Paul's claims.

On the verge of the first and only meeting between Paul's two lovers, then, Trollope's use of the word "savage" to characterize Hetta's resistance to familial coercion connects these "rivals" in a fleeting but provocative way. Granted, Hetta's subjection to Lady Carbury's authority and values appears relatively mild, especially if we compare it with, say, the virtual imprisonment of the title character of *Lady Anna* (1874), published just before *The Way We Live Now*. Here Anna's ill-used mother – driven to a kind of madness by the consequences of her treatment at the hands of her faithless husband – ill-uses her daughter in turn, going so far as to threaten her life and attempt to murder her lover.[4] Nevertheless, what makes Hetta "savage" at this late point in the book is the collision between her emergent sense of herself as a free agent, or liberal individual, who seeks to make her own marital choice and the various ties and snares that her family, including her cousin-suitor, deploy to trap her within their marriage plot for their own ends. Having avoided both the "contamination" of the Melmotte world and the related contamination of the mercenary cousin-marriage her mother desires for her,[5] Hetta takes her life into her own hands, in a gesture that brings her as close to the position occupied by the American Winifred Hurtle – "the wild cat" (ch. 38; ch. 66) who has protected herself from men's violence by using violence in her own defense – as she will ever be.

At the other end of the spectrum, albeit unlike Hetta in almost every other respect, Georgiana Longestaffe also conceives herself – and is conceived by her sole suitor, Ezekiel Brehgert – as "emancipated from control," but only after ten years' experience of the London marriage market, which has assisted in depreciating her value.[6] Within the narrated action of the novel, she comes to comprehend that her value is declining even further according to the company she now keeps, through a metaphorical treatment of her status that echoes the novel's financial focus. More fully subject than the much-younger Hetta to the marriage market and its "contamination," Georgiana "had been more admired" than her elder sister Sophia during her first years on the London scene, "and boasted among her friends of the offers which she had rejected. Her friends on the other hand were apt to tell of her many failures. Nevertheless she held her head up" (ch. 17), despite being "not very highly born, not very highly gifted, not very lovely, not very pleasant," and – most importantly – having "no fortune" (ch. 32). She is subjected both to her father's authority, which ultimately consigns her to the Melmottes' company for purposes of his own, and to her brother's "freedom," which she and her sister "were aware . . . he had already used so . . . as to impoverish himself" (ch. 13); indeed, Dolly's decision to play hardball with his father about the sale of the Pickering Park estate precipitates Georgiana's increasingly desperate efforts to find someone to marry. But if her own actions and those of her male relatives partially "emancipate" her, Georgiana's status as a (relatively) free agent diminishes what little value might still accrue to her "as a Christian lady of high birth and position" (ch. 79).

When her father breaks his promise that they will return from the country to Bruton Street, Georgiana threatens "'to run off with the first man that will take me, let him be who it may,'" whether "'a London tradesman'" or "'some horrid creature from the Stock Exchange'" (ch. 21). But in less than a week's time, as a function of staying with the Melmottes, she sees her own market value plummet, just at the very moment when the railway "share prices take off and Melmotte's credit appears limitless" (McGann 149). From the "little flirtations . . . meaning nothing" that had once characterized her encounters with him, "Lord Nidderdale's manner to her had been quite changed," for in "none of them had he spoken to her as he spoke when he met her in Madame Melmotte's drawing-room. She could see it in the faces of people as they greeted her in the park – especially in the faces of the men" (ch. 25). Having "always carried herself with a certain high demeanour," Georgiana depreciates so rapidly that even the apathetic Dolly remonstrates with her; after staying with the Melmottes for just "a few days . . . she understood that others understood that she had degraded herself" (ch. 25) and is consequently treated with "a want of respect" (ch. 32). These terms clearly register Georgiana's sense of her (sexual and gendered) fallenness in the eyes of men – and perhaps also recall Ruby Ruggles's "understand[ing] that there was a degradation which it behoved her to avoid" (ch. 18) in her dealings with Felix Carbury, lest she decline in value and respectability through a loss of virginity.

Unlike the "savage" Hetta, then, Georgiana experiences the limits of her mobility and autonomy not in being denied her choice of suitor but in recognizing the contingency of her condition, as "the faces" of others mirror back to her the loss of status and value she experiences. She thus aims to slip the noose by engaging herself to Brehgert, without her parents' knowledge or consent, understanding that by doing so she must "go down into another and a much lower world" (ch. 65). Yet as the narrator aptly states at the end of a chapter in which her parents and sister ostracize her and she begins to feel intense regret for losing caste, "it is very difficult for a young lady to have done with her family" (ch. 78). Failing to appreciate Brehgert's appreciation for her and despite her strategic "tolerance" for Jews, when Brehgert's financial value drops, she writes the letter that leads him to drop her.[7]

Georgiana's perception of her new "want of respect" from others in the specular economy of London society – at which she arrives even before she contracts her projected alliance with Brehgert – marks her as a far more experienced observer of and knowing participant in that society than either Hetta Carbury or Marie Melmotte: she is almost if not quite an avatar of such Jamesian figures as Serena Merle, Kate Croy, and Charlotte Stant.[8] But it also makes her far less capable of acting independently of the structures that constitute both her social milieu and the straitened subjectivity that arises from it. Whereas Hetta's sense that she is "emancipated from control" leads her to take action as the individual desiring subject she has become, via her passion for Paul and her resistance to familial authority, Georgiana's experience of emancipation, far from enabling her to chart her own course, reveals her to be fully subject to "the faces" of others, entirely lacking in a "sense of her own personhood" (Jones) apart from desiring what other women of her class desire, a house in London and "being the season in town" (ch. 79). Small wonder, then, as Anderson highlights in her reading of the "plain speaking" in Brehgert's first letter, with its allusion to her potential reproductive role, that Georgiana looks "round the room" "as though to see whether any one was watching her as she read it" (ch. 79). And small wonder, too, that Georgiana's final narrative act is to elope with "the curate of the next parish" (ch. 95) on the morning of her younger sister's wedding: "'Of course it is a come-down to marry a curate,'" Lady Pomona comments, "'but a clergyman is always considered to be decent'" (ch. 95). In saving what little face she has left, Georgiana manages to arrest her own downward spiral just in the nick of time.

***

Although the narrator tells us early on that both Longestaffe daughters "felt themselves to be slaves, bound down by the dullness of the Longestaffe régime" (ch. 13), he reserves the use of the terms "trafficked" and "trafficking" to characterize Marie Melmotte's experience "with the Nidderdales and Grassloughs" when she is "at once thrown into the matrimonial market" upon arrival at her new Grosvenor Square address (ch. 11). This bit of plain speaking on the narrator's part follows directly from his concise narration of Marie's backstory. Born on a "dirty street in the German portion of New York" to a "poor, hardly-treated woman who had been her mother" (but not, apparently, Melmotte's wife) and uncertain as to that mother's "fate" both during and after the sea voyage to Hamburg, "she had run about the streets . . . very hungry, sometimes in rags," and with only "a dim memory of some trouble into which her father had fallen" that had led to his "absence" (ch. 11). She gains a stepmother, becomes a Jew, moves from Frankfurt to Paris, becomes a Christian, and is taken to London via Brighton, this last phase of "the migration" being "effected with magnificence" (ch. 11). In a virtual parody of "the international theme" that features so prominently in his own work (and is also taken up by Henry James), Trollope here crosses the narrative of the new-world heiress's arrival in the old world with that other transatlantic narrative of forced "migration."

Marie's narrated past experience thrusts the relatively insulated Longestaffe daughters' experience into sharp relief, impugning their claim to feel like "slaves," while recalling the novel's use of the term "emancipated" in reference to both Hetta and Georgiana. And the narrative also casts Marie's own trajectory as a coming to consciousness, a recognition that she is *not* enslaved that arises from an experience the narrator implicitly aligns with enslavement. Initially "overwhelmed by the sense of her own position" (ch. 4) in London society just before Madame Melmotte's ball, so much so that she "had been prepared to take [Nidderdale] at her father's bidding," she "had only not been wretched because she had not as yet recognized that she had an identity of her own in the disposition of which she herself should have a voice" (ch. 4). "Bewildered," "confused," "troubled," "with no enjoyment in her present life," her one hope for her immediate future is clearly predicated on the pattern of her immediate past: she "had come solely to this conclusion, that it would be well for her to be taken away somewhere by somebody" (ch. 11). Yet in the emergence of that "identity of her own," Marie "still had been conscious of a desire to have some hand in her own future destiny": she "was beginning to feel that it might be possible to prevent a disposition of herself which did not suit her own tastes" (ch. 11) and, after meeting Felix, to obtain one that would.

That Marie Melmotte and Ruby Ruggles each "hears a love tale" from the same man in successive chapters, and that each also "builds castles in the air" (ch. 18; cf. ch. 17) regarding her romance with Felix, indicates Trollope's concerted effort to illustrate, across differences of class and status, the fictions that these characters both generate and are generated by.[9] Here Herbert's wise remark about Trollope's novelistic aims bears consideration: the novelist "conceives the social order not as the backdrop for the adventures of his characters . . . but as the primary subject of his fiction" (*Culture* 267), for it is indeed "the social order" that *The Way We Live Now* is most invested in representing. As is obvious to any reader of the novel, Trollope builds up significant parallels among his female characters that direct our attention to their structural similarities, a recurring tactic within his fiction that brings together figures otherwise differentiated by class and status: the "fallen" Carry Brattle and the "jilt" Mary Lowther of *The Vicar of Bullhampton* (1870), for example, do not need to meet or interact for readers to perceive that each has, in a class-specific way, transgressed key norms for female sexuality.

Yet if Trollope creates and foregrounds many such parallels in *The Way We Live Now* – as in giving Hetta Carbury a chapter in which she, too, "hears a love tale" (ch. 18) – then he also meaningfully differentiates among the conditions and consequences that each of the unmarried female characters faces. For example, while the narrator resorts to free indirect discourse to tell us that the Longestaffe daughters "felt themselves to be slaves," implying some potential dissent from their judgment, he deploys direct narratorial address in using the terms "trafficked" and, much later, "chattel" (ch. 77) to describe Marie's position in relation to her father. By contrast with Georgiana on the one hand, for whom only an actual house in town will do, and more like Ruby Ruggles on the other, whose Felix-fantasies demonstrate "her ignorance as to the reality of things" (ch. 18), Marie's castles in the air "were bright with art and love, rather than with gems and gold" (ch. 17); her relative indifference to material wealth and repeated rejections of her father's plan to marry her into aristocratic circles for his own ends also align her with the relatively impoverished Hetta. Something of an heiress herself, in that Daniel Ruggles has promised to settle £500 on her when she marries John Crumb, Ruby Ruggles similarly "had a will of her own which gave infinite trouble to her grandfather" (ch. 18); so, too, does Marie's willfulness increasingly trouble her father. But by actually settling money on Marie and then treating her as if she had no will (aside from doing his), Melmotte ironically makes one of his key mistakes. During the narrated scene in which he beats her, with which the narrator elects not to "harrow [his] readers by a close description," even the threat of "cutting her up into pieces . . . after a most savage fashion" (ch. 77) cannot shake Marie's determination to withhold her signature and resist his demand. Treating her merely as a means of securing the money that he continues to think of as "his," rather than understanding that her legal possession of the money enables her to articulate and prosecute her own will, Melmotte commits the criminal act of forgery that both Cohenlupe and Brehgert so readily detect and about which they choose to remain silent.

But in Ruby's case, Trollope's narrator takes the position that Daniel Ruggles's efforts to curb or correct her "will" – to treat her as insensate property rather than the sensate conveyor of property between men that marriage would make her – are not so much wrong in themselves as wrongly executed: "Poor Ruby Ruggles," as he apostrophizes her, "who was left to be so much mistress of herself at the time of her life in which she most required the kindness of a controlling hand!" (ch. 18). Declaring herself not "'willing'" to marry John Crumb (ch. 33), Ruby's bid for emancipation leads her to flee the decided unkindness of Daniel's verbal and physical abuse. First Daniel "cuffed" (ch. 33) her; then he calls her, among other things, a "'nasty, ungrateful, lying slut'" (ch. 33) in her suitor's presence. Then, in the narrated past action of the subsequent chapter, the narrator reports that after John Crumb and Joe Mixet had left his house, Daniel had "struck her, and pulled her by the hair, and knocked her about" (ch. 34). This is, in my view, the most graphic and immediate scene of domestic violence of the novel: even though it is narrated in the past tense, unlike the scene between Marie and her father mentioned earlier, the narrator gives us here that "close description" of blows that the arguably more harrowing (because more prolonged and pervasive) past experiences of the novel's married women, Lady Carbury and Winifred Hurtle, do not receive. Perhaps the novel details Ruby's treatment at some length because the beating Daniel gives his granddaughter could readily be assimilated to available middle-class stereotypes of both working-class life and "primitive" culture. Most importantly, however, even if *The Way We Live Now*, like other Trollope novels, goes on to "condemn the overt violence the narrative associates" (Marcus 249) with Daniel's effort to force Ruby to honor the marriage contract he has negotiated with John Crumb, it does not abjure the necessity of that "controlling hand."

Ruby's emancipation from patriarchal control leads directly to further sexual danger, averted only by the intervention of a male protector. As Smith argues, on escaping from Daniel – whom Roger Carbury thinks "a violent brute" (ch. 44) – Ruby "faces an equally dire threat in London: Felix, whose genteel manners afford no security from rape" (21). At the juncture in the novel when Ruby's "aristocratic and vicious lover" finds her "not at once amenable to his arguments" – that spending the night with him would be "a preferable arrangement for her" than going back to Mrs. Pipkin's – and thinks euphemistically "that a little gentle force might avail him" (ch. 71) where words have failed, "a controlling hand" does indeed make itself felt. Described by the narrator at his first appearance as "willing to thrash any man that ill-used a woman," John Crumb "would certainly be a most dangerous antagonist to any man who would misuse a woman belonging to him" (ch. 33). On Sutherland's interpretation of them (485), Trollope's plans for the novel show that Felix was to die at John's hands as a result of having "dragged Ruby into the passage" (ch. 71) outside the music hall; instead, John prevents Ruby's rape and only sends Felix to the hospital.

But that Ruby "belongs" to John is underlined, I believe, in how the narrative point of view takes us to the scene of the attempted sexual assault. At the opening of this chapter, entitled "John Crumb Falls into Trouble," John arrives at Mrs. Pipkin's house, which Ruby has just left to meet Felix; discusses the situation with her aunt and her aunt's lodger, Mrs. Hurtle; leaves the house (and the narrated action) at midnight, while the two women continue to talk as they await Ruby's arrival; but returns just thirty minutes later with Ruby and two policemen. Then the narrator turns back in time to tell us what has happened during that half hour from John's point of view. As he walked toward his inn, he "heard a woman scream, and knew that it was Ruby's voice"; heard more words of protest and another scream; "rushed after the sound, and . . . saw Ruby struggling in a man's arms" (ch. 71). Narrating the lead-up to John's rescue of Ruby through the ears and eyes of this singularly inarticulate character, Trollope also turns the plot comic – sparing Felix's life, representing Ruby as vehement in Felix's defense, carting John off to jail without his uttering a word of protest.[10] And in that turn, Trollope also aims to direct readerly sympathy toward John as both the hero of the piece and the injured party, soliciting our attention to his position even in the chapter's title, in which it is his fall, rather than the assault on Ruby, that presumably warrants the reader's attention. Although John had declined all mercenary interest in her fortune (ch. 33), Trollope's way of narrating these events still casts Ruby as something like his possession, in need of his protection and, after this incident, properly – if reluctantly – subjected to her fate as his wife, and his unborn child's mother, under his "controlling hand."

***

While my analysis has by no means exhaustively detailed the ways that women live in the "now" of the novel, it has demonstrated the significant attention – across important differences of class and status – that the narrative pays to the conditions that attend the movements of its unmarried female figures, who all marry, or plan to marry, by novel's end. Their distinct plots intersect when each character articulates and enacts resistance to the designs of others. Although the assertion of a will of one's own has different consequences for each of the four, with Marie and Ruby subjected to physical assault while Hetta and Georgiana are not, taken as a group their fictive experiences would seem to indicate the persistence of the "primitive" within the civilized, which Trollope had, in *An Autobiography*, disavowed.

Most feminist analysts have traced that disavowal to an ambivalence in Trollope's fiction – as in the contemporary discourses it transmits and transforms – about the changing status of women in his own time, an ambivalence that has left its mark on his subsequent readers. Deborah Denenholz Morse's 1987 identification of "two camps" among Trollope's critics – divided between those who argue for "his essential conventionality" (*Women* 1) and others who insist on his progressive commitments – still holds true today, although most analysts now (including Morse herself) would locate the tensions and contradictions attending women's status as endemic to his culture and context rather than uniquely particular to the biographical Trollope. Moreover, by locating his putative feminist sympathies in relation to emergent contemporary legal and political debates over women's position, feminist critics read his work as responsive to the times. Like Morse, Jane Nardin calls attention to how Trollope's ideological position shifted over the course of a long career by juxtaposing an image of a helpless maiden rescued from male violence by a male protector in *La Vendée* (1850) with the active capacity for self-defense demonstrated twenty-five years later by Winifred Hurtle in *The Way We Live Now*, where "the objectified woman is seen clearly as a target of sexual violence – and no longer does a heroic protagonist automatically appear to rescue her" (xvi). And like Nardin, Margaret Markwick dates that change of ideological position to the mid- to late 1860s, as he responds to Eliza Lynn Linton's essay on "The Girl of the Period" in his representation of the French sisters in the 1869 *He Knew He Was Right* (95–102). Rather than argue for a fully "progressive" or an entirely "conservative" Trollope, then, feminist readers now emphasize his special awareness of women's disabilities and capacities, his simultaneous resistance and attraction to shifting norms for femininity, even while acknowledging that he may well have continued to believe to the end of his life, as he infamously wrote in *North America* (1862), that "the best right a woman has is the right to a husband" (326; vol. 1, ch. 18).

In constituting a husband as a woman's "right," Trollope both participates in and parodies the liberal discourse of the woman question, which typically advocated for the extension of other "rights" – education, economic opportunity, equal status under the law, and suffrage – to unmarried and married women alike. For "rights," in Trollope's idiom, also always entail "duties"; for both men and women, freedoms are, or ought to be, necessarily circumscribed by constraints. And that concept continues to shape his view of marriage, even in the post-divorce era.[11] Marcus correctly asserts that Trollope's narrators typically "advocate individualism, which mandates romantic love as the basis for marriage and requires that a woman freely choose her mate," even as they also "uphold male superiority and parental authority as traditional powers that can legitimately limit female autonomy" (240). With more than a hint of irony, Kathy Alexis Psomiades concludes her reading of *He Knew He Was Right* with the comment that "what makes modern women different from their primitive counterparts is that they . . . get to choose who carries them off" (43–44). But in *The Way We Live Now*, this "conflict between liberal and patriarchal ideals of marriage," which Jones calls "the paradigmatic contradiction for women within Victorian society" (11), emerges as violence or savagery, which is not only visited upon but also constitutive of the female protagonists; for as Smith contends, male violence – deemed entirely incompatible with a father or any man's "duties" – comes into play "when women strive to assert their own needs and interests" (17) in laying claim to their right to choose, even to choose wrongly.

In this novel, only the "weak and vapid" Hetta Carbury, as Trollope describes her in *An Autobiography* (ch. 20), gets the man of her choice, putatively because her love for Paul Montague – a "pure emotional responsiveness that cannot be broken down into its logical determinants" (Jones 134) – makes that choice not only "for" Paul but also "against" an endogamous union with Roger. As I argued earlier, in the interlude between learning about Paul's relationship with

Winifred Hurtle and conquering her doubts about his fidelity through her interaction with the other woman, Hetta's liberal pursuit of her choice to its normative closure in marriage simultaneously makes her, too, "savage to the point of rebellion against all authority," and legitimately so, from the narrator's perspective. The resistance that she meets with from others in prosecuting her desire – with "desire" itself understood, in Jones's terms, as based in emotion rather than logic or reason or an abstract conception of "rights" – leads her to rebel by slipping out of the house, just as first Ruby, then Marie, and finally Georgiana all do, making use of their bodily access to modern modes of transport and communication to execute their plans, whether successful or not, for escaping from one man's control right into another's. Although marital violence does feature in Hetta's familial backstory as part of Lady Carbury's "violent ill-usage" (ch. 2) at her husband's hands, the physical violence to which a father or a grandfather subjects Marie or Ruby when she seeks to achieve her desire does not feature in Hetta's own (fatherless) plot, or in Georgiana's, for that matter.

Hetta's power of choice signifies as "modern" – that is, especially as measured against the failed quests of Marie and Ruby, whose aspirations to fuller self-determination Trollope qualifies through tropes of class and racialization that attach to their putative male "protectors." Entirely focused on their own rights to the exclusion of their paternal duties, Augustus Melmotte and Daniel Ruggles are tarred with the same brush, collapsing the differences between them into a shared figure of patriarchal tyranny, which in resorting to brute force to break a young woman's will only intensifies the resistance it seeks to master. Although "patriarchal power over daughters who are of age is . . . legally limited" (Psomiades 38), legal protections, as we still know, go only so far; "patriarchal power" can make itself known – and quite literally felt – in a variety of forms. The most that either Marie or Ruby can hope for, in place of "castles in the air" or further beatings, is husbandly "protection" from the violence of other men: the traditional compensation that coverture offers to married women in exchange for the money settled upon them, in these instances, by the very men who beat them. The novel ultimately indicts these figures, I would suggest, for not adhering to the conception of patriarchal responsibility that it uniquely identifies with the stalwart but outdated Roger Carbury, who most resists "the forces of modernity" (Anderson) and insists upon the primacy of duties over rights, who eschews violence and force even as he is relentlessly associated with the values and ideals of a non-progressive past. In this respect, then, Trollope's ambivalence about the liberal discourse of women's rights might be more accurately glossed as an unyielding and unchanging conception of men's duties.

Notes

1 My chief debt in this essay is to the students who worked through *The Way We Live Now* with me, five chapters at a time, and whose independent projects deepened and enhanced my knowledge of Trollope's *oeuvre* during an undergraduate seminar I conducted at Miami University during the spring semester of 2013. I am grateful to them for their patience and intelligence.
2 For differences between Maine and McLennan on the question of the primitive and the progressive, see Psomiades 34–6.
3 Although Surridge's book focuses on marital violence, it is an invaluable resource for considering the representational and legal contours of male violence against women (as well as children and animals) in the period, and includes a chapter on *He Knew He Was Right* (165–86). For another literary study that considers marital violence specifically in relation to the sensation novel, see Tromp.
4 For an important recent reading of this novel, see Morse, *Reforming Trollope,* ch. 2, esp. 53–6.
5 In adhering to an aristocratic marriage strategy for consolidating wealth, despite Hetta's lack of fortune, Lady Carbury puts her daughter in the position of Jane Austen's Fanny Price, but her daughter's lack of romantic love for Roger gives this projected union a very different feel than it has in *Mansfield Park*. As Durey has demonstrated, "the thought of cousins marrying obviously played on Trollope's mind" once contemporary scientists and anthropologists "had raised the convention as a possible problem" in the

1860s and 1870s; thus "none of the potential cousin unions in the main plots of his five novels written after 1875 exchanged wedding bands" (140–1). For more on cousin-marriage in the nineteenth century, see Corbett, *Family Likeness*, esp. 32–50.

6 Georgiana's age makes her a little less likely, at least in her suitor's eyes, to be entirely dominated by her family's wishes. Striking a note that clearly offends his intended in the first of his two letters to her, Brehgert asserts, "you are to a certain degree emancipated by age from that positive subordination to which a few years ago you probably submitted without a question" (ch. 79).

7 As Cohen writes, "Georgiana's apparently liberal protest against religious prejudice is a convenient fiction in defense of her own envious despoliation of her family, her would-be suitor, and herself" (301).

8 I owe this observation to Deborah Denenholz Morse.

9 Trollope assigns to these two aspiring dreamers the same habit of counterfactual "castle-building" – that "dangerous mental practice" (*An Autobiography* ch. 3) – that he claims to have practiced as a boy and a young man, although as Bleicher points out, Ruby and Marie derive their fantasies from reading (bad) fiction (551) while Trollope remains silent on the textual inspiration for his own imaginative exploits.

10 That turn also recalls the comically violent subplot of *He Knew He Was Right* where, in Psomiades's words, "the violence that is specifically refused in the colonial plot," "the patriarchal plot," "and in the Trevelyan plot . . . appears in the form of the knife-wielding Camilla French" (39–40).

11 For a pertinent example, see my discussion of Trollope's use of marriage as an analogy for the political union of Ireland and England in *Phineas Finn* (1869) in *Allegories of Union* (148–51).

Works cited

Anderson, Amanda. "Trollope's Modernity." *ELH* 74 (2007): 509–34. Print.

Bleicher, Elizabeth. "Lessons from the Gutter: Sex and Contamination in *The Way We Live Now.*" *Victorian Literature and Culture* 39 (2011): 545–62. Print.

Cohen, William A. "Envy and Victorian Fiction." *NOVEL* 42 (2009): 297–303. Print.

Corbett, Mary Jean. *Allegories of Union in Irish and English Writing, 1790–1870: Politics, History, and the Family from Edgeworth to Arnold*. Cambridge: Cambridge UP, 2000. Print.

———. *Family Likeness: Sex, Marriage, and Incest from Jane Austen to Virginia Woolf*. Ithaca: Cornell UP, 2008. Print.

Delany, Paul. *Literature, Money, and the Market: From Trollope to Amis*. Houndmills: Palgrave, 2002. Print.

Durey, Jill. "The Church, Consanguinity, and Trollope." *Churchman* 122 (2008): 125–46. Web. 31 July 2013.

Goodlad, Lauren M. E. "Trollopian 'Foreign Policy': Rootedness and Cosmopolitanism in the Mid-Victorian Global Imaginary." *PMLA* 124 (2009): 437–54. Print.

Hall, N. John. *Trollope: A Biography*. Oxford: Clarendon P, 1991. Print.

Hensley, Nathan K. "Mister Trollope, Lady Credit, and *The Way We Live Now.*" In *The Politics of Gender in Anthony Trollope's Novels: New Readings for the Twenty-First Century*. Ed. Margaret Markwick, Deborah Denenholz Morse, and Regenia Gagnier. Burlington, VT: Ashgate, 2009. 147–60. Print.

Herbert, Christopher. *Culture and Anomie: Ethnographic Imagination in the Nineteenth Century*. Chicago: U of Chicago P, 1991. Print.

———. *Trollope and Comic Pleasure*. Chicago: U of Chicago P, 1987. Print.

Jones, Wendy S. *Consensual Fictions: Women, Liberalism, and the English Novel*. Toronto: U of Toronto P, 2005. Print.

Kincaid, James. *The Novels of Anthony Trollope*. Oxford: Clarendon P, 1977. Print.

Marcus, Sharon. *Between Women: Friendship, Desire, and Marriage in Victorian England*. Princeton: Princeton UP, 2007. Print.

Markwick, Margaret. *Trollope and Women*. London: The Hambledon P, 1997. Print.

McGann, Tara. "Literary Realism in the Wake of Business Cycle Theory: *The Way We Live Now* (1875)." *Victorian Literature and Finance*. Ed. Francis O'Gorman. New York: Oxford UP, 2007. 133–56. Print.

Morse, Deborah Denenholz. *Reforming Trollope: Race, Gender, and Englishness in the Novels of Anthony Trollope*. Burlington, VT: Ashgate, 2013. Print.

———. *Women in Trollope's Palliser Novels*. Ann Arbor: UMI Research Press, 1987. Print.

Nardin, Jane. *She Knew She Was Right: The Independent Woman in the Novels of Anthony Trollope*. Carbondale: Southern Illinois UP, 1989. Print.

Psomiades, Kathy Alexis. "*He Knew He Was Right*: The Sensational Tyranny of the Sexual Contract and the Problem of Liberal Progress." In *The Politics of Gender in Anthony Trollope's Novels: New Readings for the*

Twenty-First Century. Ed. Margaret Markwick, Deborah Denenholz Morse, and Regenia Gagnier. Burlington, VT: Ashgate, 2009. 31–44. Print.

Smith, Monica Rydygier. "Trollope's Dark Vision: Domestic Violence in *The Way We Live Now*." *Victorian Review* 22 (1996): 13–31. Print.

Stern, Rebecca. *Home Economics: Domestic Fraud in Victorian England*. Columbus: The Ohio State UP, 2008. Print.

Surridge, Lisa. *Bleak Houses: Marital Violence in Victorian Fiction*. Athens: Ohio UP, 2005. Print.

Sutherland, John A. "Trollope at Work on *The Way We Live Now*." *Nineteenth-Century Fiction* 37 (1982): 472–93. Print.

Trollope, Anthony. *An Autobiography*. 1883. Ed. Michael Sadleir and Frederick Page. Oxford: Oxford UP, 2008. Print.

———. *La Vendée*. Ed. W. J. MacCormack. New York: Oxford UP, 1994. Print.

———. *Lady Anna*. 1874. Ed. Stephen Orgel. Oxford: Oxford UP, 1990. Print.

———. *North America*. 2 vols. 1862; rpt. London: Dawsons of Pall Mall, 1968.

———. *The Vicar of Bullhampton*. 1870. New York: Dover, 1979. Print.

———. *The Way We Live Now*. 1875. Ed. Sir Frank Kermode. New York: Penguin, 1994. Print.

Tromp, Marlene. *The Private Rod: Marital Violence, Sensation, and the Law in Victorian Britain*. Charlottesville: U of Virginia P, 2000. Print.

6

MARITAL LAW IN *HE KNEW HE WAS RIGHT*

Suzanne Raitt

On 18 July 1839, John Copley, 1st Baron Lyndhurst, opened a debate on the Custody of Infants Bill in the House of Lords. As part of his impassioned appeal to his peers to vote for the bill, Lord Lyndhurst told the lamentable stories of several women who had lost custody of their children to cruel or abusive fathers. Under the terms of the new bill, these women would have the right to petition the courts for access to their children, and for custody of children under the age of seven.

> In the first case that he should refer to, the father was a French emigrant, who married a woman possessed of some landed property, yielding 700l. a-year. A settlement was made on him on their marriage of the interest of 200l. in the event of his surviving his wife. They had one child, which was an infant at the breast at the time that he referred to. The husband was dissatisfied with the settlement, and endeavoured to induce his wife to make a will in his favour. There were reasons which induced her to refuse him. What did he do? He immediately threatened to take possession of the child, and take it to the continent by law. The child was not weaned, and the mother, in the greatest distress and agony, thought she had a right to it under the circumstances, and made her escape to her mother's. The father got hold of the child by stratagem, which made it necessary for the mother to make an application to the Lord Chancellor for relief. The case was heard by Lord Eldon; he said he was powerless, and the mother was obliged to see her child put in the care of a stranger.
>
> *(House of Lords Debate, Custody of Infants, 18 July 1839, c. 488)*

This story, complete with its affecting rhetoric about a woman whose infant was snatched almost from her breast, was, in Lord Lyndhurst's view, fairly typical. The strategy of most defenders of the Custody of Infants Bill was to argue that the current legal situation – in which women had no right to either access to or custody of their children – frequently punished virtuous and worthy women, and rewarded cruel and profligate men. Lord Lyndhurst warned that, under the current legislation, men like the husband in the case he described were able to use their wives' affection for their children for their own ends:

> It was not for him to describe the situation of a woman ardently and devotedly attached to her offspring under such circumstances as those the cases he had cited divulged; it

was not for him to point out the harshness and cruelty of the law, which enabled a husband to make use of those very affections as a means of torture, to enable him to extort unjust concessions from his wife.

(House of Lords Debate, Custody of Infants, 30 July 1838, c.773)

In Anthony Trollope's *He Knew He Was Right*, serialized between October 1868 and May 1869, Louis Trevelyan, maddened by his failure to control his wife, uses exactly the tactics described by Lord Lyndhurst thirty years earlier: he threatens his wife Emily with the loss of her child if she refuses to obey him, and finally, after a false report of an encounter between Emily and the man Louis suspects of being her lover, he abducts the child from a cab under cover of darkness. Emily has no legal power to challenge his paternal authority, even though the 1839 Act to Amend the Law Relating to the Custody of Infants gave women the right to petition for custody of their children, since technically she is the deserting spouse.[1] In the novel, a magistrate explains that she could apply to the court for custody, and that the court would probably grant it,

> unless it were shewn that the wife had left her husband without sufficient cause. The magistrate could not undertake to say whether or no sufficient cause had here been given; [. . .]. It appeared, – so said the magistrate, – that the husband had offered a home to his wife, and that in offering he had attempted to impose no conditions which could be shewn to be cruel before a judge.
>
> *(He Knew Ch. 61)*

His advice is that Emily is powerless under the law, and eventually she concedes to all her husband's demands, apologizing for a sin she did not commit and devoting herself to her dying husband. "My nails have been dragged out," she tells her skeptical sister Nora, "and I have been willing to confess anything" (*He Knew* Ch. 95). For his part, Louis, who has not received the affection and comfort he hoped for from his silent and depressed child, finally returns him to his mother "[i]n mercy to the boy [. . .]; – in mercy to the boy if not to his mother" (*He Knew* Ch. 84), and resigns himself to his wife's care.

Trollope has frequently been read as an uncomplicated novelist of the ordinary and the everyday, whose prolificacy undermines any pretensions he might have had to greatness. One of the earliest reviewers of *He Knew He Was Right* complained, "We do not think it very high art to reproduce the ordinary daily conversation of commonplace people at breakfast, dinner, or even when washing their hands or brushing their hair" ("Belles Lettres" 303). In the last fifty or so years, however, this dismissive attitude has given way to a more nuanced awareness of the complexities of much of Trollope's work. Robert Polhemus in *The Changing World of Anthony Trollope* reoriented critics' attention when he identified conflict as one of the central themes of Trollope's novels ("he makes his characters realize the world's uncertainty and the conflicting forces of tradition and innovation in their lives," 3). In the 1970s, Ruth apRoberts and James Kincaid identified a "more strikingly modern, tougher, more ironic and complex" Trollope, arguing that his novels explored what apRoberts called "situation ethics" (apRoberts, *Moral* 52) in a "slippery world, totally without certainty, one which can appear to be simply absurd" (Kincaid 151). The avuncular, studiously superficial observer of human life described by Henry James in 1883 was firmly cast aside in favor of a more circumspect and cynical chronicler. Criticism of *He Knew He Was Right* – which even Henry James admitted attained "a conspicuous intensity of the tragical" (129) – was energized by the idea of this new, darker Trollope. The assertion by Polhemus (164), apRoberts ("Emily" 87), and Kincaid (153) that the plight of women is often at the heart of what Kincaid called Trollope's "tentative and mixed form" (21) signaled the beginning of a series of significant, challenging readings of the novel. Polhemus noted that Louis Trevelyan's obsession with his wife's fidelity registered a wider Victorian "panic at the idea of equal sexual freedom for women" (164); apRoberts read the novel as a response to a series of failed women's rights bills that were introduced in Parliament during the 1860s ("Emily" 91–2); and Kincaid asserted that Trollope's novels are largely about "the terrible risks women run" (154–5). In 1980, Simon Gatrell argued that *He Knew He Was Right* uses *Othello* to explore Trollope's "growing uncertainty whether society is capable of coping with the drive to power of the individual," especially in the context of the "institutionalized [. . .] mastery [. . .] of husband over wife" (100). Building on this insight, Christopher Herbert in a wide-ranging and influential essay showed that the novel is a "masterly unravelling of the ideological mystification" at the heart of the "nineteenth-century bourgeois ideal of marriage" (455): "much of the seeming irrationality of Emily's behavior [. . .] proves to be evidence of just how clairvoyantly she has traced the hidden anomalies in her marriage contract" in which she is required to collaborate "in her own disenfranchisement" (460). Elaborating on this insight, a few years later Jane Nardin included *He Knew He Was Right* in a list of Trollope's "feminist tragedies" (202–3); Margaret Markwick in 1997 continued to identify the contradictions between Trollope's conventionality and his sympathy for women; and Helen Goodman explored the tension in the novel between the disempowerment of wives and the more forgiving "codes of middle- and upper-class gentlemanliness" (Goodman 65). However, not all readers of Trollope's form of patriarchy felt so pessimistic about the message of *He Knew He Was Right*. More optimistically, Wendy Jones described Trollope, author and narrator, as an advocate of "gentle patriarchy" (408); and Kathy Psomiades in 2009 argued that the novel shows that Trollope continued to believe in the possibility of happy marriages in which "self-regulation makes law irrelevant" (39). Most recently, Deborah Morse has highlighted the colonial dimensions of the novel, reading it as a response to the Morant Bay Rebellion of 1865. Emily is coded as "the slave who rebels against her master and usurps his authority" (120), while the White Englishman who has "bought" her goes mad.

Critical discussion of the novel's focus on the social predicament of women intersected in the late 1970s with the emerging "law and literature" movement, to which Trollope's work was central. As Nicola Lacey explains, the law and literature movement grew out of the idea that "literary works [were] historical artifacts closely linked to developments in law and policy" (10), and Ayelet Ben-Yishai, in an influential essay, describes Trollope as "a perennial favorite in law-and-literature scholarship" (155). Valentine Cunningham, claiming that "Trollope exemplifies to a quite startling extent the Victorian novel's intimacy with legal matters" (93), shows how many of Trollope's plots revolve around issues of inheritance and the transmission of wealth and property. Coral Lansbury, in the first (1981) book-length study of "legal Trollope," similarly observes that "legal forms and legal reasoning serve to shape and inform Trollope's published work" (24); and five years later Rowland McMaster, in *Trollope and the Law*, agreed with Cunningham that Trollope was interested above all in land law and inheritance law: the "plots of his novels repeatedly turn on points of law" (1).

Oddly, however, neither Lansbury, McMaster, nor Cunningham gives extended attention to *He Knew He Was Right*, even though specific pieces of legislation are mentioned or invoked more than once in the novel (see, e.g., the magistrate's opinion on custody law, earlier). As Oberhelman points out (798), two chapter titles explicitly invoke the law: Chapter 38, "Verdict of the Jury – 'Mad, my Lord,'" and Chapter 98, "Acquitted." Some critics briefly mention specific pieces of legislation in their discussions of *He Knew He Was Right*. Ruth apRoberts refers in passing to various parliamentary bills, including the Married Women's Property Act ("Emily" 91); McMaster alludes to Caroline Norton, the 1839 Custody of Infants Act, and the Married Women's Property Acts (23); Wendy Jones briefly discusses debates over the Married Women's

Property Bill as a context for the novel (401); and Cunningham cites the 1839 Custody of Infants Act, and Trollope's familiarity with the plight of his mother's friend, Rosina Bulwer, whose children were taken from her in 1838 (Cunningham 104; Devey 130–1), as influences on the plot of *He Knew He Was Right*. David Oberhelman writes at length about the 1843 M'Naghten Rules in his discussion of the novel's "response to the wider cultural debate over the relationship between madness and legal responsibility" (791). But Lisa Surridge is the only critic to give substantial consideration to the looming presence of the divorce court in *He Knew He Was Right*, arguing in *Bleak Houses* that the novel "takes as its primary theme the intense scrutiny of marital conduct by the divorce court and the newspaper" (165), and exploring the novel's definition of marital cruelty.

Indeed, there is little in the story of the Trevelyans' marriage that would have been unusual in the Court of Chancery or in the new Court for Divorce and Matrimonial Causes, set up in the wake of the 1857 Act to Amend the Law Relating to Divorce and Matrimonial Causes in England. As Lord Lyndhurst had feared, the passage of the 1839 Custody of Infants Act, one month after he opened debate on its final version, made it only marginally easier for women to gain custody of their young children. Roderick Phillips notes that in "its formal respects the legalization of divorce was carried out timidly" (420), and the reform of custody law was similarly cautious. Any woman "against whom Adultery [had been] established" had no right to access to or custody of her children, and even virtuous mothers were at the mercy of the courts to decide their fate (*Infant Custody Act* cl. 4). For a novel in which no one ever actually goes to court, *He Knew He Was Right* is remarkably detailed in its citation of divorce and custody law. Even in the absence of a legal divorce, it can certainly be classed as employing the "failed-marriage plot" that Kelly Hager identifies in novels from the eighteenth and nineteenth centuries (14), and which Helen Goodman claims "gained force from the mid-nineteenth century onwards" (47). But *He Knew He Was Right* differs from other Victorian "failed-marriage" novels, such as *The Tenant of Wildfell Hall* (1848), *Hard Times* (1854), *East Lynne* (1861), *The Evil Genius* (1886), and *Jude the Obscure* (1895) (to name just a few), in its detailed engagement with the processes and language of legal divorce proceedings: the gathering of evidence, the consultation with lawyers, the employment of detectives, and the framing of the marital breakdown in language that is likely to stand up in court. As Bozzle says, "I don't think it's ripe yet for the court, but we'll have it ripe before long" (*He Knew* Ch. 45). *He Knew He Was Right* suggests that the mere existence of the divorce court – set up in 1858, only ten years before the novel was written – is profoundly destabilizing, especially to fragile couples. Trollope was not a lawyer, of course, but as Lansbury and McMaster have shown, he had a keen interest in the law, and many friends who were distinguished lawyers (McMaster 10); and like all English men and women, he could read salacious details of recently heard divorce cases, full of legal terminology, every day over breakfast. After 1857, the London *Times* reported daily on the proceedings of the Court for Divorce and Matrimonial Causes, sometimes at great length. Other newspapers – the *Pall Mall Gazette* and the *Evening News*, for example – routinely featured the previous day's divorce cases on their front page, and in 1857, a newspaper devoted entirely to coverage of the divorce court, *The Divorce Court Reporter*, was founded (Leckie 64, 68). As Leckie notes, "the divorce court publications were [. . .] delivered to every middle-class home that subscribed to a newspaper" in what she describes as a "new technology of publicity, visibility and surveillance" (66, 71). In *He Knew He Was Right*, Louis Trevelyan reads newspaper reports of divorce cases with increasing horror as he contemplates his wife's supposed infidelity:

> Could it be that she was so base as this – so vile a thing, so abject, such dirt, pollution, filth? But there were such cases. Nay, were they not almost numberless? He found

> himself reading in the papers records of such things from day to day, and thought in doing so he was simply acquiring experience necessary for himself.
>
> *(He Knew Ch. 38)*

In fact, of course, what he is acquiring is an increasingly paranoid obsession with wives' iniquities. As McMaster has remarked, the law in this novel is "a nether world meticulous in its catalogues of detail but claustrophobic, insane, attuned to Trevelyan's creeping madness" (20). The law cannot help Emily Trevelyan; but it cannot help Louis Trevelyan either.

It is not only the infiltration of the language of the divorce courts into the characters' consciousness that reveals the centrality of matrimonial legislation to the novel's narrative and ideological structure, however. At issue also is the multiplicity – and sometimes the incompatibility – of the roles married women must play within the family. Even in the heated debates over the 1839 Custody of Infants Acts, the sanctity of motherhood was never challenged. As Elisabeth Rose Gruner has argued, "this potentially progressive law, which recognized women as legal and familial subjects in their own right, did so only by redefining them solely in terms of motherhood" (307). Women's maternity became their only source of political power, and it also represented a kind of bedrock of feminine identity – something unassailable even at its most troubled. In *He Knew He Was Right*, with all its nuances, Priscilla, Charles Glascock, and Mrs. Bozzle all express the view that women's capacity to give birth to and to suckle their children is enough to stop any argument about women's rights as mothers in its tracks.[2] Even Louis believes that "a mother's love was more imperious, more craving in its nature, than the love of a father" (*He Knew* Ch. 27). But sanctifying and reifying motherhood in this way – especially in the age of widespread wet-nursing – produced some dangerous ideological contradictions. Mothers were usually also wives, and sometimes they were unloving ones. As Edward Sugden, later 1st Baron St. Leonards, said during a debate on an early version of the Custody of Infants Bill, the bill

> would enable a woman, though divorced from her husband by the deepest crime which a wife could commit, to demand and have access to her children, and for this plain reason, that she was a parent [. . .] a woman who had thus misconducted herself and disgraced her family did not cease to be a parent because she had forgotten the duties and perhaps even lost the title of a wife.
>
> *(House of Lords Debate, Second Reading of the Custody of Infants Bill, 14 February 1838, c. 1117)*

Members of Parliament had to manage the potential coexistence within one woman of the adulterous wife (or the "fallen" single woman) and the devoted mother. As we have seen, such a complex ideological tension was represented crudely in the legislation in bans on the award of access or custody to mothers who had been found guilty of adultery; but Anthony Trollope at least knew it was more complicated than that. The narrator's inconsistent attitude toward Emily in *He Knew He Was Right* seeks to contain the anxiety expressed by Edward Sugden about women's many functions within the family, and the special quality of their love for their children. Emily is at various times (and sometimes at the same time) suspected adulteress; deserter; wronged wife; abandoned mother; and finally, at her nadir, the mother who is bereft of her children. As if in despair at resolving the contradictions between her different roles, the novel abandons the effort – tellingly only after Louis has taken her son to Italy – and transforms Emily into a tragically de-sexed and self-sacrificing figure whose only responsibility is caring for her infantilized husband and baby son. As one of the novel's earliest reviewers put it, the conception with which, as we believe, Mr. Trollope clearly set out, of Mrs. Trevelyan, – the conception of a self-willed, haughty, steely woman, whose little feeling for her husband and easily wounded self-love were even more the cause of the whole tragedy than her husband's conceit and weakness, melts away into something which it is almost impossible to define.

(Rev. of *He Knew He Was Right*, 707)

At the very end of the novel, Emily clings to the belief that her husband has forgiven her and that she has been reinstated in his mind as a virtuous wife and a loving mother, but the reader is given no such assurance. "'He declared to me at last that he trusted me,' she said, – almost believing that the real words had come from his lips to that effect" (*He Knew*, Ch. 98). Can a sexually desirous and assertive woman ever be at the same time a dutiful wife? *He Knew He Was Right* ultimately avoids the question, transforming Emily into an asexual mother to both her husband and her child.

When Trollope started to write *He Knew He Was Right*, in the winter of 1867, the new divorce law had been in operation for a little less than ten years. Among its innovations were the creation of a new, secular court to handle divorce cases (previously handled by the Ecclesiastical Courts and the House of Lords); the establishment of a new legal category called "judicial separation"; and a revision of the legal grounds for divorce. After 1857, a husband could petition on grounds of his wife's adultery, and a wife on grounds of her husband's adultery and one other offense (incest, bigamy, rape, sodomy, bestiality, cruelty, or desertion for at least two years) (*Divorce Act* cl. 85). Central to the conceptualization of the law was the desire to keep couples together. As John Arthur Roebuck, Liberal MP for Bath, noted in the House of Commons on 7 February 1860, the 1857 Act "not only determined whether a man should be divorced from his wife, but it went further, and declared why he should be divorced, and by that means it affected public morality" (House of Commons Debate, *Court for Divorce and Matrimonial Causes*, 7 February 1860, c. 621). Its defenders saw the act, paradoxically, as a way of improving sexual conduct and upholding the sanctity of marriage.

In addition, as Allen Horstman observes, every divorce that was granted in Victorian England was adversarial, since if a couple agreed that they wanted to get a divorce, it would not be granted (81). The 1857 Act went to some lengths to prevent couples from filing jointly for divorce, outlawing collusion, condonation, and connivance.[3] If it were found that a couple had indulged in any of these, the court would refuse to grant them a divorce (*Divorce Act* cl. 29, 30, 31). Nonetheless, there was still so much anxiety about collusive divorces that in 1860, an amendment was passed to the 1857 Act which allowed the attorney general, acting through the Queen's Proctor, to investigate the possibility of collusion and to prevent the divorce if collusion was established (*Act to Amend* cl. 7). Even more strangely to twenty-first-century eyes, if the petitioner him- or herself was found to be adulterous, the court would refuse to grant a divorce, with the curious result that marriages in which both spouses were unfaithful were indissoluble (*Act to Amend* cl. 31). In other words, in couples where husband and wife were united in their lack of commitment to the marriage, a divorce would not be granted. If a couple did get divorced, it meant that someone had won.

It is this profoundly adversarial model of marital breakdown that shapes both Trevelyans' attitudes to their conflict. Even in the early stages of their disagreement, husband and wife are equally reluctant either to acknowledge wrongdoing or to apologize, even when they are uncomfortably aware that they may have done wrong. "As [Louis] walked to and fro among his books downstairs, he almost felt that he ought to beg his wife's pardon. [. . .] He would do so, he thought, but not exactly now" (*He Knew* Ch. 1). For her part, Emily decides she will apologize only if her husband comes to her first:

> She very much wished that he would come, and had made up her mind, in spite of the fierceness of her assertion to her sister, to accept any slightest hint at an apology which her husband might offer to her. To this state of mind she was brought by the consciousness of having a secret from him, and by a sense not of impropriety on her own part, but of conduct which some people might have called improper in her mode of parting from the man against whom her husband had warned her.
>
> (*He Knew* Ch. 2)

In spite of her discomfort with her own behavior, Emily has difficulty admitting that she is not entirely blameless, and when her husband in his anger fails to come to her room at just the right moment, she abandons her plan to say she is sorry, telling herself petulantly, "'If he chooses to be cross and sulky, he may be cross and sulky'" (*He Knew* Ch. 2). Neither spouse is willing to accept blame or to yield to the other, pitting them against one another from the outset. The reader is warned in the first few pages that there may be conflict ahead: "As Lady Rowley was the first to find out, he liked to have his own way. / 'But his way is such a good way,' said Sir Marmaduke. 'He will be such a good guide for the girls!' / 'But Emily likes her own way too,' said Lady Rowley" (*He Knew* Ch. 1). Temperamentally, both Trevelyans are inclined to dig their heels in.

This adversarial attitude is cemented and intensified as soon as Louis starts to employ Bozzle to watch Emily and find out whether she continues to see Colonel Osborne. As Lisa Surridge points out, Bozzle "invokes the language of lawyers, proof, and cross-examination, and thereby represents the intrusion of the court system into the private home" (170). From his first encounter with Bozzle, Louis feels "defiled" by contact with him: "He knew that he was having recourse to means that were base and low, – which could not be other than base and low, let the circumstances be what they might" (*He Knew* Ch. 19). Louis understands that as soon as Bozzle gets involved, the truth no longer matters. Bozzle's job is to find evidence of Emily's adultery; for him there is no chance that she is innocent.

> Mr. Bozzle was, of course, convinced that the lady whom he was employed to watch was – no better than she ought to be. That is the usual Bozzlian language for broken vows, secrecy, intrigue, dirt, and adultery. It was his business to obtain evidence of her guilt. There was no question to be solved as to her innocency.
>
> (*He Knew* Ch. 33)

Bozzle's cynicism drives his obsession with gathering evidence, irrespective of the truth: "Bozzle was very careful, and full of 'evidence'" (364); and he is sure he knows what happened during Colonel's Osborne's ill-advised visit to the Outhouses' home:

> "Of course he went there to see [Emily], and it's my belief he did. The young woman as was remembered says he didn't, but she isn't on the square. They never is when a lady wants to see her gentleman, though they comes round afterwards, and tells up everything when it comes up before his ordinary lordship."
>
> (*He Knew* Ch. 45)

Bozzle discounts even the testimony of those he has enlisted as witnesses, like the Outhouses' maid, when it does not reinforce his certainty of Emily's – and every woman's – guilt. He is confident that the maid will change her account in court, and that is enough for him. He even begins to displace Emily in Louis's emotional universe: "The only person who had been true to him was Bozzle" (*He Knew* Ch. 32). The faint echo of Emily's marriage vow in "true to him" suggests that Bozzle is now Louis's chosen intimate, akin to his wife. He will tell Emily's story and Louis is no longer interested in what his wife might have to say – unless she agrees with Bozzle. The stock characters of Victorian divorce cases – the wronged husband, the adulterous wife, and the neglected child – have overwhelmed the private narratives of Louis's and Emily's lives.

> Trevelyan would have given all that he had to save his wife; would, even now, have cut his tongue out before he would have expressed to anyone – save to Bozzle – a suspicion that she could in truth have been guilty; [. . .] and yet he expected it, believed it, and, after a fashion, he almost hoped it.
>
> *(He Knew Ch. 38)*

With the arrival of Bozzle and his contaminating closeness to the divorce court, the Trevelyans' marriage is effectively over for both spouses, as if any contact with the idea of divorce destroys any chance at reconciliation. Louis now hopes for proof of Emily's guilt so that he can win the tragic battle that is marriage, and Emily, for her part, no longer loves Louis once Bozzle and all he stands for has intruded on her life: "She had clung to her love in some shape, in spite of the accusations made against her, till she had heard that the policeman had been set upon her heels" (*He Knew* Ch. 60). It is this violation of the most intimate areas of her life that finally destroys her feelings for her husband as a man.

The multiple roles played by parents within a family, and the complicated disruption of those roles once a marriage is eroded by struggles over power, are acknowledged in one of the changes in the legal landscape introduced by the 1857 Act. Even though, as I have shown, the act constructed divorce as an adversarial process between two warring spouses, it also began to recognize that divorces break up families, not just couples. Before 1857, a husband who wished to petition for divorce on the grounds of adultery first had to sue his wife's lover in a common law court. This action, for trespass, assault, and criminal conversation (or crim. con., as it was universally called), would, if successful, result in damages being awarded to the husband. As Ann Sumner Holmes points out, central to this process was "the idea that a husband had a property interest in his wife; her adultery decreased the value of that interest" (605). The 1857 Act did away with the requirement for a crim. con. verdict and associated damages. Instead, a husband could include in his petition a claim for damages from a proven adulterer, but the court would decide how they would be distributed:

> the Court shall have power to direct in what Manner such Damages shall be paid or applied, and to direct that the whole or any Part thereof shall be settled for the Benefit of the Children (if any) of the Marriage, or as a Provision for the Maintenance of the Wife.
>
> *(Divorce Act cl. 33)*

The 1857 Act acknowledged for the first time that children were the silent parties in any divorce case, and attempted to provide for their future. It even gave authority to the court to "make Provision regarding the Custody, Maintenance, and Education of Children," slightly loosening the stranglehold of paternal control (*Divorce Act* cl. 18). In stipulations such as these, the 1857 Act cautiously began to imagine how to protect all parties to a divorce in their reconfigured lives, wrestling a modicum of power away from fathers and recognizing that when a household broke up, everyone who lived in it was affected. Furthermore, it implicitly addressed the needs and responsibilities of the divorcing spouses as parents, as well as husband and wife, recognizing that a divorce reshapes not only the roles played by each party in the dissolving household but also all the ways in which those roles interact.

This insight structures *He Knew He Was Right* from the very beginning. Emily — if not Louis — understands early on that not only her security but also that of her baby is threatened by her conflict with her husband.

> And then there came a horrible thought. What if the child should be taken away from her? If this quarrel, out of which she saw no present mode of escape, were to lead to a separation between her and her husband, would not the law, and the judges, and the courts, and all the Lady Milboroughs of their joint acquaintance into the bargain, say that the child should go to his father?
>
> *(He Knew Ch. 5)*

Edward Sugden had predicted in the February 1838 House of Commons debate on the Custody of Infants Bill that women would feel bound to their husbands by their offspring: "The great tie which prevents the separation of married persons is their common children. A wife was, in general, glad to have that excuse for submitting to the temper of a capricious husband" (House of Commons Debate, Second Reading of the *Custody of Infants Bill*, 14 February 1838, c. 1115). But in Emily's case, the excuse does not have the desired effect. In spite of her fear of losing her baby, she refuses to submit to her husband's caprices: her commitment to being a good mother to her child is not matched by a commitment to sustaining her identity as a compliant — including as a sexually compliant — wife. As the quarrel develops, Emily's intransigence contributes to its intensification. The narrator describes her as "hard, dignified, obedient, and resentful" (*He Knew* Ch. 6), and "hard and cold" (*He Knew* Ch. 6). "The husband had perhaps been more in the wrong than the wife," he comments cautiously, "but the wife, in spite of all her promises of perfect obedience, had proved herself to be a woman very hard to manage" (*He Knew* Ch. 9). Noting that if she really wanted to please her husband, she could have received Colonel Osborne in a way that would have "quelled all feeling of jealousy in her husband's bosom," the narrator is somewhat uncertain in his apportionment of blame. Even Emily's sister Nora, who later in the book becomes something of a free spirit, is anxious about Emily's recalcitrance, telling her that she is "so wrong" (*He Knew* Ch. 1), imploring her to tell Louis about the arrangement she has made with Colonel Osborne for her father to return to England (*He Knew* Ch. 2), and exhorting her a few pages later, "pray, pray, do what he tells you" (*He Knew* Ch. 3). We have seen that Emily is uncertain about the propriety of her conduct with Colonel Osborne early on in the book (see earlier, *He Knew* Ch. 2), and when later he writes to her asking if he can visit her in Nuncombe Putney, Emily is again conscious of her own disingenuousness in allowing him to come because he is "her father's oldest friend":

> She knew that he was wrong to speak of coming to Nuncombe Putney; but yet she thought that she would see him. She had a dim perception that she was standing on the edge of a precipice, on broken ground which might fall under her without a moment's warning, and yet she would not retreat from the danger. Though Colonel Osborne was wrong, very wrong in coming to see her, yet she liked him for coming. [. . .] she liked the excitement of the fear.
>
> *(He Knew Ch. 20)*

Emily's willingness to contemplate engaging in conduct that she knows is provocative is presented sympathetically by the narrator, who offers a lengthy explanation of the emotional and romantic deprivations of her life at Nuncombe Putney: "Reader, you may believe in her [. . .] where is the woman, who, when she is neglected, thrown over, and suspected by the man that she loves, will not feel the desire of some sympathy, some solicitude, some show of regard from another man?" (*He Knew* Ch. 20). But even if the narrator believes he can persuade his English readers to forgive Emily her recklessness, in other respects, Emily is emphatically not like other English women. She is dark-skinned, physically robust "as are some girls who come from the tropics," and she is never "weary" of dancing or riding her horse (*He Knew* Ch. 1). As Deborah Morse has argued, Emily's recalcitrance is not only a result of her own temperament, nor is it simply the consequence of a marital culture in 1860s England in which different forms of marital conflict – including wifely insubordination – were newly and sensationally visible in daily newspaper reports from the divorce court (see Leckie Ch. 2). Emily's willingness to take emotional and sexual risks causes her bemused husband to "reflect upon the voluptuous woman he has married as perhaps not quite the kind of pure English matron that he deserves" (Morse 123). In an echo of the confusions of the parliamentary debates over infant custody in the 1830s, and over divorce in the 1850s, Emily's complexity confounds Louis's conventional ideas about women and their duties. If she challenges his authority, and flirts (however cautiously) with another man, does he still owe her something as her husband?

Even Louis, however, never questions Emily's competence and capacities as a mother. She is consistently presented as both loving and protective toward her son. As we have seen, her first thought when she contemplates separating from Louis is the possibility of separation from her baby. While she is still living with little Louey, she is affectionate and tender: "He kicked, and crowed, and sputtered, when his mother took him, and put up his little fingers to clutch her hair, and was to her as a young god upon the earth" (*He Knew* Ch. 11). She repeatedly threatens to cling to him and never let go if Louis tries to abduct him, telling Lady Milborough desperately, "I will cling to him so that he cannot separate us" (*He Knew* Ch. 11); and when Louis has taken custody of the child, she visits him with her mother but says nothing "of a scheme which she had half formed of so clinging to her boy that no human power should separate them" (*He Knew* Ch. 67). Her reunions with the child are tender and poignant: in Willesden, "Mrs. Trevelyan had now thrown aside her bonnet and her veil, and was covering her child with caresses" (*He Knew* Ch. 67), and in Casalunga, "She tore off her bonnet, and then clinging to the child, covered him with kisses. 'Louey, my darling! Louey; you remember mamma?'" (*He Knew* Ch. 79). She even offers to "sleep on the boards beside his cot" rather than be parted from him (*He Knew* Ch. 79). In spite of the fact that Emily knowingly risks separation from her child in her dealings with Colonel Osborne, neither the narrator nor any of the characters ever impugns her character or conduct as a mother. Whatever she may lack as a wife, as a mother she is unassailable.

This certainty that only the most hardened reprobate could fail to love her own children – already embodied in the provisions of the 1839 Infant Custody Act – proves in the end to be the salvation of the moral and social confusions of *He Knew He Was Right*. As Christopher Herbert has described, the novel fully inhabits the contradictions of its era, attempting to "fuse [. . .] two antithetical ideals [. . .] into a single ideological structure, thus creating a domestic culture necessarily and deeply equivocal, full of potential tension" (Herbert 451). Related to those two antithetical ideals – male supremacy and companionate marriage – are the multiple, contradictory roles that Emily uneasily plays for the first half of the novel. She is a virtuous wife, but, as we have seen, she does allow herself to behave in ways that "some people might have called improper" (*He Knew* Ch. 2). She is a devoted mother, but her devotion to her child does not stop her playing with fire in her relationship with her husband. For the first third of the novel at least, the narrator is unsure where to place the majority of the blame for the breakdown of the marriage, and the arrival of Bozzle only complicates matters further, since the nuances are obscured by his allegiance to a crude and coercive narrative of female guilt. At the point in the narrative when Emily is living with the Outhouses, the novel seems as stuck as Emily herself. As Herbert notes (458–9), the Trevelyans at times seem to be fighting over nothing (except the question of who will win), and no resolution is anywhere in sight.

This impasse is broken by Louis's most outrageous act of all, the abduction of his son through a stratagem and under cover of darkness. At first, he attempts to take little Louey openly, backed by the strong arm of the law. But his lawyer, Mr. Bideawhile, who has been wearying of him for quite some time, is equivocal: "nothing could be done about the child till Mr. Trevelyan should return to England; – and [. . .] he could give no opinion as to what should be done then till he knew more of the circumstances" (*He Knew* Ch. 45). Undaunted, Louis sends Bozzle to the Outhouses' house, where Emily and her son are living, "armed with the due legal authority" in the form of a letter claiming "possession of the body of my child" (*He Knew* Ch. 52), but even Bozzle is now acting against his own best instincts and the advice of his wife. "The child shan't come here," she tells him. "It ain't the regular line of business, Bozzle; and there ain't no good to be got, never, by going off the regular line" (*He Knew* Ch. 59). When Louis does return to England, Mr. Bideawhile simply refuses to do anything (*He Knew* Ch. 52). In typically craven fashion, Bozzle organizes the kidnapping only because he wants the fee and because the law backs up Louis's claim (*He Knew* Ch. 61), but the narrator makes clear that he does so uncomfortably and without conviction. He directly challenges the premise of the act he is so fond of quoting (the 1839 Infant Custody Act, *He Knew* Ch. 59) when he tells Louis not to take the baby abroad: "Think twice of it, Mr. T. The boy is so young, you see, and a mother's 'art is softer and lovinger than anything. I'd think twice of it, Mr. T., before I kept 'em apart" (*He Knew* Ch. 62). After he utters these words, Bozzle all but vanishes from the narrative. The abduction of little Louey prompts even the few friends that were left to him to abandon not only Louis and his cause but also the novel itself.

As Louis is more and more shunned – including by the narrator, who after the abduction tends to assign blame only to Louis, calling him "evil" (*He Knew* Ch. 93) and "mad" (Ch. 98) – Emily's tragic predicament as she mourns her lost child mutes the reproaches of others. Staggering against the railings of the hotel, screaming with grief, Emily attains the lofty status of Niobe, weeping for her children. When she resists Louis's pleas to relent during her visit to Willesden, the narrator is silent, calling her only a "poor woman" (*He Knew* Ch. 67) and a "young mother in her great affliction" (*He Knew* Ch. 67). Only Louis clings to the idea that she is "obstinate" (*He Knew* Ch. 67), a view that the narrator now refuses to endorse. In her sorrow, bereft of her baby, Emily is no longer "hard" or "resentful," as she was described earlier in their sad story (*He Knew* Ch. 6); instead she is presented as a woman bereaved, dressed in "black, from head to foot" and wearing a "thick veil" (*He Knew* Ch. 79). Broken by the treatment she has received from her husband, Emily has become the victim, rather than a contributor to the deterioration of her marriage, and her child's desolation even at their reunion in Casalunga only increases her pathos:

> He was cowed and overcome, not only by the incidents of the moment, but by the terrible melancholy of his whole life. He had been taught to understand [. . .] that the former woman-given happinesses of his life were at an end.
> *(He Knew* Ch. 79)

The child's misery intensifies the feeling that Louis is cruel and at fault in separating mother and son. The detailed and loving presentation of the ailing child presents the reader with a scenario in which the undeniably innocent are punished for the failings of others. The injustice of this strengthens the reader's feeling that Louis's behavior has crossed a line.

Emily's transformation from troublesome wife to sanctified mother intensifies as she travels to Italy to see her husband and her son. Ironically, this happens only when, absorbed in her grief, she ceases to care about being "true" to her husband.

> As she had been travelling [to Casalunga], she had determined that she would say anything that he wished her to say, make any admission that might satisfy him. That she could be happy again as other women are happy, she did not expect; but [. . .] she might live with him and do her duty, and, at least, have her child with her.
>
> (He Knew Ch. 79)

During her first encounter with Louis in Casalunga, she still balks at telling him a lie, in spite of her resolution:

> "Tell me what you want me to say, and I will say it," she said.
>
> "You have sinned against me," he said, raising her head gently from his shoulder.
>
> "Never!" she exclaimed. "As God is my judge, I never have!" As she said this, she retreated and took the sobbing boy again into her arms.
>
> (He Knew Ch. 79)

Although Emily "retreats" into her role as mother, she is not yet ready to abandon her attempts to be a wife who tells the truth to her husband – that is, a wife who respects her husband and their intimacy enough not to lie to him. In Christopher Herbert's terms, at this point, Emily still clings to her belief in the ideal of companionate marriage. But as the novel wears on – and significantly, out of earshot of the reader, who is never privy to the scene – she eventually gives in, abandoning once and for all her belief in a marriage in which husband and wife can trust each other. She tells Nora,

> I have told him quite simply that it was all my doing, – as that I have been in fault all through, [. . .] What does it all matter? He had suffered so, that I would have said worse than that to give him relief. The pride has gone out of me so, that I do not regard what anybody may say.
>
> (He Knew Ch. 95)

The loss of Emily's "pride" is also the loss of her belief in her marriage and in her husband as a man and as a companion. She no longer has a sense of herself as a wife, except in so far as she still has a duty to the husband toward whom her feelings are now primarily protective and maternal.

> As she thought of him she tried to interrogate herself in regard to her feelings. Was it love, or duty, or compassion which stirred her? [. . .] She had loved him as Nora now loved the man whom she worshipped and thought to be a god, doing godlike work in the dingy recesses of the D.R. office. Emily Trevelyan was forced to tell herself that all that was over with her. Her husband had shown himself to be weak, suspicious, unmanly, – by no means like a god.
>
> (He Knew Ch. 86)

Emily's disillusionment with Louis's manhood is replaced by an impulse to protect him in his extreme vulnerability (compare this with Nora's desire that her husband be a "staff" on which she can lean [*He Knew* Ch. 13]): "her woman's heart was melted with softness as she thought of the condition of the man to whom she had once given her whole heart. [. . .] she remembered only his weakness" (*He Knew* Ch. 85); "nothing should entirely separate her from him, now that he so sorely wanted her aid" (*He Knew* Ch. 86); "There is nothing a woman will not forgive a man, when he is weaker than herself" (*He Knew* Ch. 93). In a development that echoes that in other Victorian "failed-marriage" novels, Emily in the final stages of her relationship with Louis abandons the role of erotic partner, becoming Louis's self-sacrificing, asexual mother and nurse, and treating him, we are told, "like a child" (*He Knew* Ch. 98).[4] Even the manner of delivery of his final words, his lips moving against Emily's fingers, is infantile: "she laid the tips of her fingers on his lips. [. . .] at length the lips moved, and with struggling ear she could hear the sound of the tongue within" (*He Knew* Ch. 98). As Mary Hamer points out, Emily can receive absolution only

> because she is willing to take her husband as an infant, a child who has not yet learned to speak and whose signs it is up to a mother to interpret. The contact that finally satisfies her is one which brings her a sense of his mouth, the infant's primary organ, rather than his words.
>
> *(157–8)*

As Louis murmurs his dying words, his metamorphosis into an infant is complete, and Emily is left, in Hamer's words, like "the mother in a Pietà, supporting in her arms a tortured and collapsed male body" (158). However ambivalent the narrator has been about Emily as a wife, he has nothing but tenderness for her at the close of the novel.

> But if she erred, surely she had been scourged for her error with scorpions. As she sat at [Louis's] bedside watching him, she thought of her wasted youth, of her faded beauty, of her shattered happiness, of her fallen hopes. She had still her child, – but she felt towards him that she herself was so sad a creature, so somber, so dark, so necessarily wretched from this time forth till the day of her death, that it would be better for the boy that she should never be with him. There could be nothing left for her but garments dark with woe, eyes red with weeping, hours sad from solitude, thoughts weary with memory.
>
> *(He Knew Ch. 98)*

Contrast the tragic, even biblical, grandeur of this picture with the brisk dismissal of Louis: "At last the maniac was dead, and in his last moments he had made such reparation as was in his power for the evil that he had done" (*He Knew* Ch. 99). The narrator cannot muster a word of sympathy for Louis. All his lyricism and compassion are poured into the image of Emily's lonely future from which even her beloved child cannot protect her. As Simon Gatrell has noted, these pages are the climax of a "gradual emphasis of blame on Trevelyan and absolution for his wife" 114). The suggestion that both spouses are at fault that characterizes the opening chapters of the novel gives way in the end to the condemnation of the husband and the tragic victimhood of the wife.

He Knew He Was Right is a novel about a mid-Victorian couple who can find no legal relief from their misery, despite the recent liberalization of both custody and divorce laws. Indeed, in *He Knew He Was Right*, the intrusion of the language and procedures of the new Court for Divorce and Matrimonial Causes into the Trevelyans' relationship serves only to speed up its demise. As I have shown, the Trevelyans' marriage is doomed – if not from the beginning, at least from the moment Trevelyan engages Bozzle to spy on his wife. Within the protective walls of the home, there is at least the potential for flexibility. As we have seen, Kathy Psomiades argues that the novel celebrates the Nora Rowley–Hugh Stanbury, Caroline Spalding–Charles Glascock, and Dorothy Stanbury–Brooke Burgess unions as "happy modern marriages, where fully developed self-reflexive liberal subjects freely consent to a social arrangement in which command and obedience are emptied of their meaning by affect, and self-regulation makes law irrelevant" (39). Caroline Spalding, for example, realizes that Charles Glascock, her husband-to-be, is "so strong that he treated her almost as a child; – and yet she loved him infinitely the better for so treating her" (*He Knew* Ch. 81). As Deborah Morse explains, Glascock is a "nurturer," and his refusal to countenance Caroline's anxieties about their marriage is an expression not of a desire for mastery but of "authentic love" (130). The novel's commitment is finally not to "gentle patriarchy" (Jones 408) or to "companionate marriage" (Herbert 451), but to the freedom to work through emotional conflicts without interference by the law. Its cautious optimism about the marriages of the future is in stark contrast with the assumptions behind the easing of restrictions on divorce in the mid-nineteenth century. In passing the 1857 Divorce Act, Parliament expressed a view of English society in which men were seen to need rescuing from unfaithful wives, and women to need protection from adulterous, violent, and neglectful husbands. *He Knew He Was Right* offers us the story of a marriage that is destroyed by assumptions like that; but it also expresses the hope that things could and will be different. As Nora tells Lady Milborough, "I am going to marry for liberty" (*He Knew* Ch. 95). The defensive, adversarial model that emerges from the 1857 Act is supplanted by a different, more joyful version of the modern, in which marriages are resilient because the parties to them are free to disobey, to err, and to be forgiven. In a world like that, there would be no need for divorce.

Abbreviations

Act to Amend: *An Act to Amend the Procedures and Powers of the Court for Divorce and Matrimonial Causes*, 23 & 24 Vict., c. 144. *The Statutes of the United Kingdom of Great Britain and Ireland*. Google. Web.
Divorce Act: *Act to Amend the Law Relating to Divorce and Matrimonial Causes in England*, 20 & 21 Vict., c. 85. *The Statutes of the United Kingdom of Great Britain and Ireland*. Google. Web.
He Knew: Trollope, Anthony. *He Knew He Was Right*. 1869. Oxford: Oxford University Press, 1985.
Infant Custody Act: *An Act to Amend the Law Relating to the Custody of Infants*, 2 & 3 Vict., c. 54. *The Statutes of the United Kingdom of Great Britain and Ireland*. Google. Web.

Notes

1 The 1857 Act to amend the Law Relating to Divorce and Matrimonial Causes in England instructed the court not to grant a divorce in cases where the petitioner was found to have "deserted or willfully separated himself or herself from the other Party [. . .] without reasonable Excuse" (*Divorce Act*: cl. 31).
2 Priscilla: "[Men] can't suckle babies, and they can't forget themselves" (*He Knew*, Ch. 25); Charles Glascock: "Can [John Stuart Mill] manage that men shall have half the babies?" (*He Knew*, Ch. 55); Mrs Bozzle: "He can't suckle 'em, can he? I don't believe a bit of his rights" (*He Knew*, Ch. 59).
3 "Collusion" was when the couple made a secret agreement that one of them would commit, or be represented in court as having committed, an action that could lead to divorce; "condonation" was when one spouse forgave the matrimonial offense of the other; "connivance" was the consent of one spouse to the matrimonial offense of the other.
4 Helen Huntingdon in Anne Brontë's *The Tenant of Wildfell Hall* (1848) also returns to her debauched husband to nurse him in his last illness; Isabel Vane in *East Lynne* (1861) returns to her marital home in disguise and cares for her son as he dies.

Works cited

apRoberts, Ruth. "Emily and Nora and Dorothy and Priscilla and Jemima and Carry." *The Victorian Experience: The Novelists*. Ed. Richard A. Levine. Athens: Ohio University Press, 1976. 87–120. Print.

———. *The Moral Trollope*. Athens: Ohio University Press, 1971. Print.

"Belles Lettres." *Westminster Review* 36 (1869): 302–18. Web.

Ben-Yishai, Ayelet. "A Common Endeavor: Anthony Trollope and the Law." *The Cambridge Companion to Anthony Trollope*. Ed. Carolyn Dever and Lisa Niles. Cambridge: Cambridge University Press, 2011. 155–68. Web.

Brontë, Anne. *The Tenant of Wildfell Hall*. 1848. Oxford: Oxford University Press, 2008. Print.

Collins, Wilkie. *The Evil Genius*. 1886. Oxford: Oxford University Press, 2008. Print.

Cunningham, Valentine. "Anthony Trollope and Law, Laws, Legalisms and Assorted Legislations." *REAL: Yearbook of Research in English and American Literature* 18 (2002): 89–107. Print.

Devey, Louisa. *Life of Rosina, Lady Lytton*. London: Swann Sonnenschein, Lowrey, 1887. Web.

Dickens, Charles. *Hard Times*. 1854. Oxford: Oxford University Press, 2008. Print.

Gatrell, Simon. "Jealousy, Mastery, Love and Madness: A Brief Reading of *He Knew He Was Right*." *Anthony Trollope*. Ed. Tony Bareham. New York: Barnes and Noble, 1980. 95–115. Print.

Goodman, Helen. "Madness in Marriage: Erotomania and Marital Rape in *He Knew He was Right* and the *Forsyte Saga*." *Victorian Network* 4:2 (2012): 47–71. Print.

Gruner, Elisabeth Rose. "Plotting the Mother: Caroline Norton, Helen Huntingdon, and Isabel Vane." *Tulsa Studies in Women's Literature* 16:2 (1997): 303–25. Web.

Hager, Kelly. *Dickens and the Rise of Divorce: The Failed-Marriage Plot and the Novel Tradition*. Farnham: Ashgate, 2010. Web.

Hamer, Mary. "No Fairy-Tale: The Story of Marriage in Trollope's *He Knew He Was Right*." *Scarlet Letters: Fictions of Adultery from Antiquity to the 1990s*. Eds. Nicholas White and Naomi Segal. New York: Macmillan – St. Martin's, 1997. 149–59. Print.

Hammerton, A. James. *Cruelty and Companionship: Conflict in Nineteenth-Century Married Life*. London: Routledge, 1992. Print.

Hardy, Thomas. *Jude the Obscure*. 1895. Oxford: Oxford University Press, 2009. Print. Rev. of *He Knew He Was Right*, by Anthony Trollope. Spectator 12 June 1869: 706-8. Web.

Herbert, Christopher. "*He Knew He Was Right*, Mrs. Lynn Linton, and the Duplicities of Victorian Marriage." *Texas Studies in Literature and Language* 25:3 (1983): 448–69. Web.

Holmes, Ann Sumner. "The Double Standard in the English Divorce Laws, 1857–1923." *Law and Social Inquiry* 20:2 (1995): 601–20. Web.

Horstman, Allen. *Victorian Divorce*. London and Sydney: Croom Helm, 1985. Print.

House of Commons Debate. *Court for Divorce and Matrimonial Causes*. 7 February 1860. Hansard, 156, cc. 614–29. *Hansard 1803–2005*. UK Parliament. Web.

———. Second Reading of the *Custody of Infants Bill*. 14 February 1838. Hansard, 40, cc. 1114–23. *Hansard 1803–2005*. UK Parliament. Web.

House of Lords Debate. *Custody of Infants*. 30 July 1838. Hansard, 44, cc. 772–91. *Hansard 1803–2005*. UK Parliament. Web.

———. *Custody of Infants*. 18 July 1839. Hansard, 49, cc. 485–94. *Hansard 1803–2005*. UK Parliament. Web.

———. Second Reading of the *Custody of Infants Bill*. 14 February 1838. Hansard, 40, cc. 1114–23. *Hansard 1803–2005*. UK Parliament. Web.

James, Henry. "Anthony Trollope." *Partial Portraits*. London: Macmillan, 1888. 97–133. Web.

Jones, Wendy. "Feminism, Fiction and Contract Theory: Trollope's *He Knew He Was Right*." *Criticism: A Quarterly for Literature and the Arts* 36:3 (1994): 401–14. Web.

Kincaid, James. *The Novels of Anthony Trollope*. Oxford: Clarendon Press, 1977. Print.

Lacey, Nicola. "Could He Forgive Her? Gender, Agency and Women's Criminality in the Novels of Anthony Trollope." *Subversion and Sympathy: Gender, Law and the British Novel*. Eds. Martha C. Nussbaum and Alison L. LaCroix. New York: Oxford University Press, 2013. 176–204. Print.

Lansbury, Coral. *The Reasonable Man: Trollope's Legal Fiction*. Princeton: Princeton University Press, 1981. Print.

Leckie, Barbara. *Culture and Adultery: The Novel, the Newspaper and the Law, 1857–1914*. Philadelphia: University of Pennsylvania Press, 1999. Print.

Markwick, Margaret. *Trollope and Women*. London; Rio Grande: Hambledon Press, 1997. Print.

McMaster, Rowland D. *Trollope and the Law.* New York: Palgrave Macmillan, 1986. Print.

Morse, Deborah Denenholz. *Reforming Trollope: Race, Gender, and Englishness in the Novels of Anthony Trollope.* Burlington, VT: Ashgate, 2013. Print.

Nardin, Jane. *He Knew She Was Right: The Independent Woman in the Novels of Anthony Trollope.* Carbondale: Southern Illinois University Press,1989. Print.

Oberhelman, David D. "Trollope's Insanity Defense: Narrative Alienation in *He Knew He Was Right.*" *SEL: Studies in English Literature, 1500–1900* 35:4 (1995): 789–806. Web.

Phillips, Roderick. *Putting Asunder: A History of Divorce in Western Society.* Cambridge: Cambridge University Press, 1988. Print.

Polhemus, Robert. *The Changing World of Anthony Trollope.* Berkeley and Los Angeles: University of California Press, 1968. Print.

Psomiades, Kathy Alexis. "*He Knew He Was Right*: The Sensational Tyranny of the Sexual Contract and the Problem of Liberal Progress." *The Politics of Gender in Anthony Trollope's Novels: New Readings for the Twenty-First Century.* Eds. Margaret Markwick, Deborah Denenholz Morse, and Regenia Gagnier. Burlington, VT: Ashgate, 2009. 31–44. Print.

Smalley, Donald, ed. *Trollope: The Critical Heritage.* London: Routledge and Kegan Paul, 1969. Print.

Surridge, Lisa. *Bleak Houses: Marital Violence in Victorian Fiction.* Athens: Ohio University Press, 2005. Print.

Wood, Ellen. *East Lynne.* 1861. Oxford: Oxford University Press, 2008. Print.

7

LEGITIMACY AND ILLEGITIMACY

Jenny Bourne Taylor

> So I came sported into the World, a Kind of Shuttlecock between Law and Nature . . .
> Richard Savage, Preface to *Miscellaneous Poems* (1726)

> It was at this moment when he began to perceive that his fortune would return to him, when he became aware that he was knocked about like a shuttlecock from a battledore, that his pride came by its first fall. Mollett was in truth the great man, – the Warwick who was to make and unmake the kings of Castle Richmond.
> Anthony Trollope, *Castle Richmond* (1860, ch. 41)

The continuities and contrasts in Anthony Trollope's treatment and use of "illegitimacy" as a personal disability and a legal status can be seen by comparing the central figures in an early novel, *Doctor Thorne* (1858) and a late work, *Mr Scarborough's Family* (1883). In the former, the heroine Mary Thorne, a girl of no wealth and uncertain position, is revealed to the reader in the second chapter to be the child of an illicit liaison between Thomas Thorne's brother Henry, and Mary Scatcherd, the sister of a local stonemason who has now become a wealthy railway contractor and newly ennobled baronet, and who is also Squire Gresham (Frank's father's) creditor. *Mr Scarborough's Family* opens with the decision of "old Mr Scarborough," whose wealth consists of hereditary lands supplemented by industrial profit, to render his profligate elder son, Mountjoy, illegitimate by announcing that he was a prenuptial child (born before his parents' marriage), so that his wealth might pass to his second son, the priggish Augustus.

At first, these two illegitimate identities – the female child of a working-class mother seduced by a higher-ranking man, and the disinherited male heir of a landed estate (if not an actual title) – seem to represent two key long-standing stories of bastardy as they are taken up and transformed in nineteenth-century fictional narrative. The first "old story," as the workhouse doctor calls it in the opening pages of Charles Dickens's *Oliver Twist* (1838), is primarily a moral and affective one: it is the "feminised" tale of the seduced and abandoned woman whose child is both the product and sign of her mother's shame. This trope of the "ruined mother" has a range of forms and uses. It pervades nineteenth-century radical melodrama – much of the rhetoric of the movement again the 1834 New Poor Law, whose Bastardy Clauses notoriously absolved fathers of responsibility for their illegitimate offspring, drew on this figure as a synecdoche of wider class exploitation (the measure was largely repealed by the 1845 Bastardy Act). The "ruined mother" is a means of evoking and reworking modes of sentiment and sympathy in poems such as William Wordsworth's "The Thorn" (1798); or of reassessing concepts of class and moral obligation in mid-century novels such as Elizabeth Gaskell's *Ruth* (1850); and it is a central aspect of representations of the "fallen woman" that pervade mid-nineteenth-century literary and visual culture. Concealed illegitimacy is a central element of sensation fiction, too, becoming a central trope of a secret that is somehow already known, of the power of hidden memory and of the past to haunt the present, in novels such as *Little Dorrit* (1857) and Wilkie Collins's *The Woman in White* (1859).

The second narrative, usually hinging on the male bastard, also has a long cultural genealogy. This is the story of being at once defined by and excluded from land, titles, and patrilineal inheritance, which reaches back to early modern culture and beyond, in the struggles of dynastic succession in feudal kingship. As Findlay has explored, the bastard dramatized the close relationships between state and familial power in Renaissance drama – an alternatively natural or unnatural figure, either excessively profligate or virtuous, which both subverts and upholds dominant power structures. In his seminal study of Trollope's later fiction, Tracy has described Trollope's fascination with Elizabethan and Jacobean drama in detail, and as Nussbaum has noted, Trollope often knowingly alludes to the figure of the excluded bastard in his depiction of the illegitimate heir, above all in the heroic but vulnerable Ralph Newton in *Ralph the Heir* (1871), who echoes and overturns the figure of Edmund in *King Lear* (Tracy; Nussbaum; Sutherland). By the mid-eighteenth century the illegitimate son has become a prototypical figure of modernity – Henry Fielding's *Tom Jones* (1749) is an obvious instance (Schmidgen). In contrast, by the mid-nineteenth century the male bastard often represents a self-consciously anachronistic glance back to older structures of inheritance, in novels such as W. M. Thackeray's *The History of Henry Esmond* (1852) and George Eliot's *Felix Holt* (1867) and *Daniel Deronda* (1876): here Daniel's belief that he is Sir Hugo's natural son is bound up with his problematic Englishness, in contrast with the modernity of his revealed maternal genealogy. These gendered narratives are usually intertwined, but they represent two aspects of the concept of bastardy as a moral status and as legal disability.

Yet while they allude to them, both *Doctor Thorne* and *Mr Scarborough's Family* radically question and undercut these stories. As Nussbaum has recently demonstrated, *Doctor Thorne* subverts the narrative of shame and punishment that pervades, for example, Dickens's *Bleak House* (1853) or Elizabeth Gaskell's *Ruth* (1850). Instead of dying either desperately or nobly, Mary Scatcherd marries, and while her rehabilitation takes the familiar form of emigration, she goes on to have a thriving family life in America. While Mary Thorne herself is brought up in ignorance of her parentage, she suffers no sense of inherited or acquired stigma. In contrast with Esther Summerson, for example, she is self-possessed and self-confident, while Thomas Thorne is far more comfortable in his skin than is John Jarndyce – a loving figure who is "both a father [. . .] and mother" to Mary (ch. 2), and whose moral conflict is over whether Mary should be revealed as Roger Scatcherd's heir as her mother's eldest child. Indeed, Mary's formal illegitimacy is supplementary to her poverty and her gender through most of the novel, and one of its ironies is that it is finally completely overridden by her inheritance of Scatcherd's un-entailed wealth, which passes through her back to the Greshams. In contrast, the much later novel *Mr Scarborough's Family* takes the slipperiness of illegitimacy itself as a legal category to an almost absurd level, and probes the very idea of legal right and legal fiction through contrasting the dissolute but affectionate son Mountjoy to his priggish and scheming legitimate brother. Yet despite their differences, both novels share Trollope's abiding concern with property, inheritance, and the scope of testamentary freedom, and in both, formal bastardy is always shaped through, and overshadowed by, specific economic interests, motives, and values.

These two novels form part of Trollope's recurrent interrogation of the competing claims of contract, blood, and intimacy – that is, formal law, dynastic imperative, and emotional bonds – those often contradictory ties that make up the family, but which are most clearly focused though the problematically legitimate heir. The key texts here are *Castle Richmond* (1860), *Ralph the Heir*, *Lady Anna* (1874), *Is He Popenjoy?*(1878), and *Mr Scarborough's Family*, though doubtful liaisons, and their legally dubious offspring, also play less central roles in *The Belton Estate* (1866), *The Way We Live Now* (1875), *John Caldigate* (1879), and *Ayala's Angel* (1881). The question of legitimacy, in its broad as well as specific sense, has been recognised to be of crucial importance in studies of Trollope – whether of the law (Ben-Yishai; McMaster; Frank), in discussions of family, marriage, and gender (Marcus; Markwick, *Trollope and Women*; Michie; Morse, *Women*; Psomiades), of explorations of identity (including national and racial identity), or of genre more broadly (Herbert, *Culture, Trollope*; Kincaid; Letwin; Morse, *Reforming*; Taylor, "Trollope"; Tracy; Turner).

Yet while there is a mass of critical work on Trollope's engagement with the law (including marriage and family law) surveyed impressively by Ben-Yishai in this collection, specific explorations of Trollope's representation of illegitimacy as a personal status in the context of its complex social and cultural history are somewhat thin on the ground. Tracy briefly notes the shared preoccupation with legitimacy in *Lady Anna* and *Ralph the Heir*, and Frank explores more closely the intimate relationship between possession, identity, and legitimacy in *Ralph the Heir* and E. M. Forster's *Howard's End* (1910), arguing that the desire of the father to legitimise his son invokes J. S. Mill's concept of testamentary freedom in *The Principles of Political Economy* (1848) as a key marker of modernity (a point also made by Henry Maine in *Ancient Law* in 1859). "The ability to pass on one's possessions, to control them even after death, is synonymous with shaping of one's individual identity and conferring it to posterity" argues Frank; "The preservation of property was thus tantamount to a preservation of the self that is doubly confirmed by the procreation of lawful heirs of the body" (193). Her essay explores the implications of the laws of inheritance and of entail in *Ralph the Heir*, which contrasts Squire Newton's virtuous natural son Ralph Newton with his cousin and namesake, the profligate legitimate heir, and describes the squire's attempts to circumvent the entail by buying out his nephew's interest. As Frank notes, Trollope makes it clear that the attempt to manipulate old-established inheritance structures is fraught with problems; in Gregory Newton's words, "things would go terribly astray [if] the right heir [legitimate Ralph] was extruded" (vol. 1, ch. 28), and like other critics, such as Tracy, she emphasises his ultimate position, that such structures are necessary for social stability despite the individual cost. Frank contrasts the realism of Trollope's text, with its equal emphasis on the will as an empirical document and expression of personal identity, with Mrs Wilcox's unofficial will in *Howards End*, which, though only a note scrawled on a scrap of paper, nevertheless embodies the willed "transmission of cultural identity" (211) that dominates the book, and represents a more open spirit of modernity.

Ralph the Heir is a focus, too, for Nussbaum, who places it alongside *Doctor Thorne* within a broad overview of the legal and cultural history of illegitimacy. It is also one of the texts examined by my own 2009 analysis ("Bastards") of the significance of illegitimacy as a slippery legal fiction in Trollope's novels of the 1870s. Stressing that questions of political representation, legitimacy, nationality, and nationhood were becoming increasingly pressing during the late 1860s and 1870s, developing alongside debates by Henry Maine and J. F. McLennan on the origins of the family and notions of legitimate marriage, I explore how contests over legitimacy in *Ralph the Heir, Lady Anna*, and *Is He Popenjoy?* rework these wider concerns of belonging and nationhood. In particular, I read each novel as taking up elements in Eliot's *Felix Holt* (1866), a novel that hinges on hidden illegitimacy of the male heir within the contexts of struggles over political representation. I thus interpret *Ralph the Heir* as reworking the "Harold Transome" aspect of Eliot's novel;

Lady Anna as exploring the unsanctioned daughter's claim (the "Esther Lyon" story in *Felix Holt*), while the infant son in *Is He Popenjoy?* reworks the figure of the mixed-race heir of dubious legitimacy ("little Harry" in Eliot's text).

In her survey of legal culture, Ben-Yishai proposes that we need to modify our idea of the law as, in McMaster's words, a "skeleton" or stable structure underlying Trollope's fiction, in favour of an understanding of legal discourse as "a collection of disparate practices, [. . .] prescriptions and descriptions" which "come together in a dynamic, historically contingent relationship, often incompatible with each other, if not in outright contradiction" (Ben-Yishai, this volume). The complex and contradictory construction of illegitimacy is a particularly clear example of this unevenness, while demonstrating how old-established common law codes and practices could stubbornly persist. As defined by common law, the illegitimate child was *fillius nullius* or "nobody's child": not entitled to a family name, having no legal next of kin, and debarred from inheriting as a member of a family. The *fillius nullius* rule remained in place through the nineteenth century (it was finally abolished by the Legitimacy Act of 1926), though it was modified in practice by the continuing rise of testamentary freedom. Common law also followed the ancient Roman law code that ruled that children born within wedlock were legally the children of the mother's husband – a presumption based on the need for stability and continuity that came under increasing strain through the eighteenth and nineteenth centuries, as the fear that property might fall into the hands of "spurious issue" was underpinned by developments in obstetrics and medical science. At the same time, common law decreed that prenuptial children, born before their parents' marriage, should remain indelibly illegitimate. In contrast, Church or canon law (which underpinned Scottish marriage law) had defined the children of adultery as illegitimate, and reinforced the precept that bastards, as "children of sin," could not inherit. But it allowed the legitimation of prenuptial children, and, underpinned by natural law principles of European civil law, stressed the duty of parents to their children regardless of their formal legitimacy (Finn, Lobban, and Taylor, 4–8; Frank; Witte). So while children born of unmarried parents were unambiguously illegitimate within both codes, there were various cases which highlighted the slipperiness of the status. Thus Scottish and much European law allowed prenuptial children to be retrospectively legitimised, though English law (which formally pertained in many colonies) did not.

These tensions came under increasing strain during the nineteenth century as they interacted with interconnected concerns around gender, marriage, and nationality. The pressure to modify the ancient common law of coverture in debates on marriage law reform did not lead to any improvement in the legal situation of illegitimate children – indeed the 1857 Matrimonial Causes Act (which condoned the husband's, but not the wife's adultery) was underpinned by entrenched anxieties about the threat of adulterine bastardy to hereditary estates. Nonetheless, some liberal legal writers did recognise the close connections between the situation of women in marriage and that of illegitimate children, and, like many nineteenth-century novelists, saw the illegitimate child as a victim, unjustly inheriting the sins of the fathers. The unsuccessful 1857 Married Women's Property Bill, fostered by the Law Amendment Society, had been orchestrated by the feminist Barbara Leigh Smith (herself the natural daughter of a radical MP), and the arguments of her 1854 pamphlet *A Brief Summary in Plain Language of the Laws Concerning Women* had gained wide liberal support. *A Brief Summary* had been partly prompted by specific cases, such as those of Caroline Norton and Anna Jameson (Shanley, 31); specifically, though, it drew on and condensed elements of the respected barrister J.J.S. Wharton's *An Exposition of the Laws Relating to the Women of England* that had been published the previous year (Hirsch, 86). While Wharton's treatise explicitly concerned the situation of women through the legal life cycle, he sets within this framework a passionate defence of illegitimate children and a stringent attack on the commons law of *fillius nullius* – albeit one which did not appear more widely in the public domain. The section on "Infancy," for example, deals in detail with the position of, and laws defining, natural children. Wharton is highly critical of the presumption against such children in the case of trusts, stating that they are often "the sufferers of technical and distorted constructions of plain and unmistakable language" (11). "A man dying before the birth of his natural child, and honestly admitting the child to be his own [. . .]," he argues, "has his righteous intents towards his helpless and unprotected offspring set at naught by the withering authority of a cruel and absurd law" (14). He is even more scathing about the indelible illegitimacy of prenuptial children; in contrast with European civil law, "a doctrine in perfect accordance with natural justice and wholesome reparation [. . .] Our Common Law," he writes, denies "to parents an opportunity of redressing a wrong, thus visiting, in spite of everything, the sins of the fathers upon the children" (40).

Such arguments were made in the interstices of public debates on the property and personal rights of women in marriage during the 1850s, and resurfaced in the growing anxiety around the incommensurate laws governing marriage, and thus legitimate birth, between England, Scotland, and Ireland. These legal inconsistencies had been highlighted by the Yelverton bigamy case that ran through the late 1850s and 1860s, and a series of other cases of uncertain marriage, including colonial marriages, in which English common law was often at odds with local practice, giving rise to conflicts not only concerning personal legitimacy but also over nationality and legal subjecthood (Gill; Taylor, "Bastardy"). Such tensions, though, were as likely to lead to pleas for cultural relativism as much as to a call to remove discrepancies. The legal theorist and anthropologist J. F. McLennan had argued that most attempts to place rigid boundaries around diverse local customs were bound to lead to misery and confusion.

> Every course has been tried [. . .]," he wrote in 1861, "and every system has been found productive [. . .] of innumerable instances of cruel wrong done for the vindication of legal form, and of almost more cruel uncertainty arising out of the conflict between Acts of Parliament and the facts of daily life.
>
> *(197)*

The Lord Chief Justice of Scotland, too, insisted in the 1868 *Report of the Royal Commission on the Laws of Marriage* that the imposition of English common law regarding the indelible bastardy of prenuptial children would be

> to subject Scotland [. . .] to the unnatural and pernicious rule of the English Marriage Law, merely because it is the law of England, though opposed alike to the sound philosophical principles and to the practical experience which has dictated the experience of other European States.
>
> *(54)*

So while the *fillius nullius* rule remained explicitly unchallenged, indeed was frequently reinforced, it was questioned both within liberal legal opinion and through a series of cases of doubtful legitimacy, highlighted by the discrepancies between different legal systems within an increasingly globalised and modern culture, in which long-standing or local marriage laws (such as the canon law governing Scottish marriage based on verbal consent, and informal colonial partnerships) were often deemed valid in the cause of social stability.

Trollope's fiction echoes and amplified this ambivalence. While the English laws of legitimacy are seen as fictive, arbitrary, and even (as in the case of *Ralph the Heir*) going against the tenets of natural law and natural justice, his novels usually suggest they are nonetheless necessary for cultural as much as social stability and continuity. *Doctor Thorne* is an important exception here. Unambiguously *fillius nullius*, Mary, according to Wharton, would probably have been the victim of "the withering authority of a cruel and absurd law"; so that in making her Scatcherd's heir, Trollope chooses a fictional outcome that would have been theoretically possible, but in practice highly unlikely. To evade this problem of credibility, the narrator hides behind the persona of the unworldly author: "modern English writers of fiction should keep a barrister, in order that they may be set right on such legal points as will arise in their little narratives," he notes, continuing, "I can only plead for mercy if I be wrong in allotting all Sir Roger's vast possessions in perpetuity to Mary Thorne" (ch. 45). What Trollope more cannily suggests, though, is that Mary's position as a middle-class, cultured, and intelligent woman makes her an eminently suitable candidate both to inherit Scatcherd's wealth and to annul the Gresham debts. Here Trollope performs two "knights' moves" of avuncular inheritance: Mary's social and cultural identity transmitted through the displaced paternal line through her adoption by her paternal uncle; and her eventual economic wealth transmitted indirectly through the maternal line via her mother's brother.

Mary's wealth is passed through exogamous exchange to the Greshams – back to what the narrative hints is its rightful place. But to be convincing, this move needs to be part of a wider narrative pattern, and the illegitimacy plot in Trollope's novels is always developed in conjunction with other tropes and priorities, particularly those of the courtship-and-marriage plot. In *The Vulgar Question of Money*, Michie describes Mary's inheritance in *Doctor Thorne* (like the Doctor's eventual marriage to Martha Dunstable) as "a kind of symbolic money laundering" (113); both moves cleanse "contaminated" commercial wealth (though Scatcherd's has the virtue of being legitimately earned) through the exogamous exchange of the heiress. She traces this pattern in Trollope's work as part of her analysis of the classic plotline of the nineteenth-century novel of manners, in which the hero is forced to choose between the virtuous poor woman and the status-conscious heiress. Michie notes how Trollope complexifies this pattern – both here and in the Palliser novels the rich women may be virtuous, though their wealth may have more dubious provenance – and brilliantly explores how this triangular structure is renegotiated in the context of shifting understandings of the meaning of wealth and developing economic theories through the nineteenth century. Trollope's illegitimacy narratives intersect with this structure in significant ways, and in the rest of this chapter, I'll briefly raise some questions about how some of these narratives, with their focus on the instability and liminality of legitimacy as a legal status, relate to courtship-and-marriage plots. I'll suggest how they might dovetail with them, undercut them, or exert a countervailing force within a multi-plot structure, and within the broader economic, social, and political frameworks of each novel.

The congruence of the plots is closest in *Doctor Thorne*, in which Lady de Courcy insists early in the novel that "Frank [Gresham] has one duty before him. He must marry money" (ch. 4); and the counterpositions of Martha Dunstable, the wealthy ointment heiress, and Mary Thorne, Frank's long-standing love, are a key driver of the novel that is given extra spice by the hidden kinship of Mary and Scatcherd. Mary's illegitimacy, I've already suggested, is supplementary to her position as a member of the professional middle class as Thorne's adopted daughter. However, although her bastardy is superseded by her class and gender, and finally cancelled out by her acquired wealth, her very absence of legal status also gives her a privileged position as the voice of "true legitimacy" underpinned by natural law in the face of vulgar economic interest. This reinforces a cultural identity that in turn overrides the "taint" of Scatcherd's fortune, while articulating the unease that these cultural transformations imply. As Herbert argues in his seminal 1991 discussion of Trollope's ethnographic vision, *Culture and Anomie*, Mary represents an "extreme instance of anomalous social identity" (280), in a world in which modern social structures are at odds with residual cultural and symbolic values. At once a "natural" child and a "cultured" young woman, she both embodies this process of cultural transformation and internalises its tensions. These are clearly focalised through Mary's own ambivalence over her status, which echoes the long-standing duality of bastardy itself, as poised between undermining and upholding dominant structures of power: "Being, as she was herself, nameless, she could not help but feel a stern, unflinching antagonism, the antagonism of a democrat, to the pretentions of others who were blessed with that of which she had been deprived," the narrator remarks. "So to herself she spoke; and yet, as she said it, she knew that were she a man, such a man as the heir of Greshambury should be, nothing could tempt her to sully her children's blood by mating herself with anyone that was base born" (ch. 8). I would expand Herbert's argument, in the light of Michie's analysis, by suggesting that through this interplay of tension and renegotiation, the illegitimacy plot is able to be assimilated into the triangular marriage plot, as Mary is set beside Martha Dunstable. Finally, Mary's wealth, newly purified by her own liminal cultural identity, is able to revive the landed estates and Burkean patrilineal continuity that the novel so insistently highlights in its opening chapter, "The Greshams of Greshambury."

Castle Richmond, *Lady Anna*, and *Is He Popenjoy?* all use the slippery boundaries of legitimate birth and marriage to rework this paradigm of marriage and courtship that is laid out so explicitly in *Doctor Thorne*. In the process, they open up the marriage plots to wider political and social concerns, recasting that unease about illegitimacy that Mary Thorne expressed to herself so eloquently. Published in 1860, the decade in which the sensation novel emerged as a cultural phenomenon, *Castle Richmond* hinges on the well-worn devices of bigamy and blackmail, as the marriage of Lady Fitzgerald (*née* Mary Wainwright) and Sir Thomas is revealed to be invalid when her fraudulent and disreputable former husband, Talbot, returns under the name of Mollett, and Herbert Fitzgerald, the heir to Castle Richmond, is pronounced illegitimate. While sensation novels such as Mary Elizabeth Braddon's *Lady Audley's Secret* (1862) and *Aurora Floyd* (1863) hinged on the struggles of the bigamous woman to keep her secret, *Castle Richmond* focuses on the devastating effects of Mollett's blackmail on Sir Thomas (Lady Fitzgerald's position is deliberately downplayed) and the effects of apparent revealed illegitimacy on Herbert's own position – in particular, his courtship of Lady Clara Desmond, the penniless daughter of an earl. Indeed, Trollope satirises the bigamy plot as generator of narrative tension as much as highlighting the slipperiness of legitimacy, by finally revealing, through the detective work of the family lawyer Mr Prendergast, that Mollett himself had been married before his liaison with Mary Wainwright all those years ago, using one form of bigamy to cancel out the other.

Instead, the illegitimacy plot is used, firstly, to create tensions within the marriage plot, in a direct inversion of that of *Doctor Thorne*, and to subject it to various kinds of critical scrutiny. It is a young woman, Clara Desmond, who is caught up in a triangular relationship, having to choose between a richer and a poorer suitor: between Herbert, the heir to a title and large estate, and his cousin Owen Fitzgerald, the slightly dissolute but nonetheless manly and honourable owner of the lesser landed property, Hap House. Initially engaged to Owen, and then to Herbert, both choices instigated by her obsessive and controlling mother, Clara finally defies the Countess of Desmond, refusing to give up Herbert when he is pronounced illegitimate; but, in contrast to *Doctor Thorne*, the romance plot is overdetermined by various forms of suppressed desire. It is Owen, rather than the slightly feminised, cautious Herbert, who is presented as a kind of noble natural son – masculine, sexually compelling, faithful to the memory of Clara; the novel ends with the image of him as a displaced wanderer, out of place and out of time. Clara's mother, the countess, is scheming and manipulative; but the novel's three backstories (of Owen, Herbert, and Clara) include the account of her unhappy and abusive marriage to an old roué of an earl, while her motivations are clearly driven by her own half-suppressed, quasi-incestuous sexual desire for

Owen. The new earl, young Patrick Fitzgerald, too, as Markwick has noted (*New Men*, "Out"), is also irresistibly attracted to Owen; while Clara, despite her faithfulness to Herbert when he is stripped of name and property, is drawn to the marriage in part because it will bring her closer to Herbert's sister Emmeline. Herbert is in a sense the empty centre of the novel, worthy and steadfast, but not the material of romance. His key role in the novel is political and social, as a pragmatic figure of "common sense" in an Irish landscape racked by the horrors of the 1846 famine, and it is in this role that he seen as the legitimate owner by the local populace. The rapacious legacy of the old Earl Desmond is displayed not only by the toxic psychic legacy he has left his wife but also by the mismanagement of the Desmond estate, which is set in stark contrast to that of Castle Richmond. As critics of Trollope's Irish novels have emphasised, one of the most harrowing scenes of the novel comes in the chapter "The Last Stage," where Herbert encounters a starving family on the Desmond estate, and the walk he takes to inform the countess of his reduced status brings the famine-stricken landscape immediately before the reader's eye. His position brings together the public and private worlds, both representing a more modern professionalised paternalism, and highlights his own acknowledgement that "how could he repine at aught that the world had done for him, having now witnessed to how low a state of misery a fellow human being might be brought? Could he, after that, dare to consider himself unfortunate?" (ch. 33)

In *Lady Anna* the positions of Lady Fitzgerald and the Countess of Desmond are combined in the figure of Josephine Murray, another victim of an "older," vicious, patriarchal power, whose marriage to the corrupt Earl Lovel, a man who had "lived as a beast of prey among his kind" (ch. 2), had been pronounced by himself to be bigamous. The novel circles round the disputed status of the daughter of this liaison, in a sensational case which spans two generations, and is endlessly circulated and reinterpreted – in court reports, clubs, gossip columns, and drawing rooms. Josephine's fight to claim the legitimacy of her daughter Anna once again links the legitimacy and marriage plots, as Anna has to choose between the old love of her days of poverty, the radical tailor Daniel Thwaite, and the new earl, Frederic Lovel, an attractive young man devoid of aristocratic pretensions. Here, too, Trollope undercuts the polarities of established legitimacy and marriage plots. Daniel is poor, but Frederic is not wealthy either, and this reframes the courtship plot as well as foregrounding issues of heredity, race, and class. Both men, however, as Englishmen, are set against the deracinated, corrupt Earl Lovel, embodiment of an "un-English" *ancien regime*, and his Italian putative wife, and mistress. As the acknowledged daughter of an earl, Anna's ability to hold the aristocratic family together depends on her being found legitimate, so that her legal status is both performative, shaped by public opinion, and swallowed up by her status as a potentially wealthy woman whose proposed marriage to the new earl is initially supported by the Whiggish solicitor general Sir William Patterson as a pragmatic compromise. Against this narrative, in which Anna is positioned as object of exchange, is her position as deciding subject, who places her old allegiance to Daniel over her undoubted attraction to Frederic, in the face of her mother's obsessive attempts to force her into a dynastic marriage.

In *Lady Anna* the interlinked legitimacy and marriage plots are connected with wider political issues of legitimacy, representation, and reform far more inextricably than the earlier novels through this focus on Anna's choice in the face of her mother's increasingly insane manipulations. In *Castle Richmond* the famine acted as a frame for private tribulations, intersecting with the legitimacy plot crucially if awkwardly at certain moments; in *Ralph the Heir* the story of Sir Thomas Underwood's attempt to stand as a parliamentary candidate sets the modern world of post-1867 reform alongside the older established issues of legitimacy and heirship. In *Lady Anna*, the radical Thwaites' championing of the Murray cause is intimately bound up with notions of political allegiance and subjecthood. Thomas Thwaite the elder is explicitly connected to the revolutionary Romanticism of the 1790s, Daniel to the upwardly mobile, organised working class and the struggles over political representation of both the 1830s and 1860s. Indeed, the Murrays' *cause célèbre* has strong echoes of the Tichborne case, in which the obscure claimant of an estate emblematically expressed working-class fantasies and aspirations (McWilliam). As Morse (*Reforming*) has noted, Trollope wrote the novel during his voyage to Australia to visit his son Fred, and this geographical liminality, she suggests, may have created the space for the novelist to develop his vision of cross-class and implicitly transracial romance, as Daniel's darkness and swarthiness are continually noted. *Lady Anna* radically redefines the ideas of affiliation and allegiance that draw on intersecting ideas of caste and race, and in the process redraws the boundaries of legitimacy itself. The arch-conservative Miss Lovel notes of Daniel, "you can never wash a blackamoor white" (ch. 46), and the countess regards cross-class marriage with a visceral loathing, both seeing Daniel's "illegitimacy" as Anna's husband in biological terms. Conversely, Daniel's sense of class identity is based on culture and history – "We are made of different fabric, though the stuff was originally the same" (ch. 46) – and Sir William, the pragmatic voice of the law, finally blesses Anna and Daniel's marriage as the product of a reformist meritocracy, albeit one too radical, as yet, for England. The focus of symbolic legitimacy thus shifts from Anna to Daniel; but still, in a sense, embodies a form of patriarchal rule: "For a man with strong views on domestic power and marital rights always choose a Radical," Sir William notes wryly (ch. 45).

The legitimacy and marriage plots are brought together again in *Is He Popenjoy?* via the liaisons of the two Germaine brothers: the elder Marquis of Brotherton's dubious alliance with an Italian countess, and the marriage of the younger son, George Germaine, to the wealthy but socially *arriviste* Mary Lovelace. But while in *Doctor Thorne*, *Castle Richmond*, and *Lady Anna* each narrative dovetailed with and drove the other, here both are hollowed out, in one of Trollope's most thought-provoking explorations of marriage itself and the ideas of rightful ownership, primogeniture, and legitimate birth. The marriage of George and Mary comes at the beginning of the novel, and the trope of the hero's choice between rich woman and poor woman is immediately undercut. George Germaine is a weak, often contemptible figure, whose "poor" first love is not a virtuous virgin but the sexually alluring and manipulative Adelaide De Baron, with whom he carries on a quasi-adulterous relationship after they both are married. The wealthy Mary Lovelace is in a similar structural position to Mary Thorne *after* she becomes an heiress; but her role in shoring up the Germaine household leads not to joining a family of sisters to whom she is close (as with both Mary Thorne and Clara Desmond) but in becoming the youngest and least powerful member of a family group marginalised by the inequalities of primogeniture, composed of mother, younger brother, and three repressed unmarried sisters – though her eldest sister-in-law, Lady Sarah, does finally become her friend. The marquis is a version of the corrupt and "un-English" Earl Lovel, though he is cynical and sarcastic rather than rapacious, and the doubtful heir – the Popenjoy of the title – is a sickly child whose problematic legitimacy under English law rests initially on whether he is a prenuptial child, which would make him legitimate in Italy but a bastard in England, and later on whether the marquis had made a previous informal marriage. Both questions, moreover, are compounded and overshadowed by his racial ambiguity: "Dear me, how black he is!" (ch. 31) exclaims Lady Susanna. "Popenjoy," the hereditary heir, is nothing but an empty space held together by a silly name.

In all the novels I've examined, moreover, the legitimacy and marriage plots are mediated and often driven by a parental figure, who has an unambiguously benign or malign influence on their progress, and who often embodies and makes explicit the underlying economic and social interests of the novels. This influence is benign in the case of the caring, maternal uncle Thomas Thorne, with his concept of the family as affective and social bonds; malign in the cases of the Countess of Desmond and Josephine Murray, with their obsession with caste and dynasty. However, these roles are combined in Mary's father Dean Lovelace, who has risen through the ranks of the Established Church to respectability, but who still carries the taint of his commercial origins, and this too helps to generate the novel's ideological dissonance. It is the pleasure-loving but ambitious and ruthless dean who brings together the legitimacy and marriage plots: on the one hand fighting to prove the spurious status of Brotherton's son, driven by the desire for his daughter to become a marchioness and his grandson the future Marquis of Brotherton; on the other hand insisting that Mary his daughter retains her own independent property and autonomy in marriage – embodying liberal paternalism in the face of George's weak, anachronistic patriarchalism. A novel whose title suggests that it is essentially concerned with name, legitimacy, and heirship, *Is He Popenjoy?* demonstrates that legitimacy is the effect of an illusory symbolic power, held together by ideas of family, race, and national belonging, echoing the work of anthropologists, such as McLennan, on primitive family structures and marriage (Taylor, "Bastards"; Psomiades). Indeed, the affective centre of the novel is marriage itself; what begins as the standard story of the novel of manners turns into a disturbing exploration of the sexual and emotional power struggles within companionate marriage, and the idea not only that the boundaries of legitimacy are shifting and unstable but also, in the *Academy*'s words, "how very slight are the barriers which part modern civilization from ancient savagery" (Anon.).

Works cited

Anon. "Review of *Is He Popenjoy? The Academy*, June 8, 1879," in Donald Smalley (ed.) *Anthony Trollope: The Critical Heritage*. London: Routledge, 1969.

Ben-Yishai, Ayelet. "Trollope and the Law," in Carolyn Dever and Lisa Niles (eds) *The Cambridge Companion to Anthony Trollope*. Cambridge: Cambridge University Press, 2011.

Braddon, M. E. *Aurora Floyd* (1863). Ed. P. D. Edwards. Oxford: Worlds Classics, 1996.

———. *Lady Audley's Secret* (1862). Ed. Jenny Bourne Taylor and Russell Crofts. London: Penguin Classics, 1998.

Chelmsford, Frederick Thesiger. *Report of the Royal Commission on the Laws of Marriage*. London: HMSO, 1868.

Collins, Wilkie. *The Woman in White* (1860). Ed. John Sutherland. Oxford: World's Classics, 1996.

Dickens, Charles. *Bleak House* (1854). Oxford: World's Classics 2008.

Eliot, George. *Daniel Deronda* (1876). Ed. Graham Handley. Oxford: World's Classics, 1984.

———. *Felix Holt, the Radical* (1866). Ed. Fred C. Thompson. Oxford: World's Classics, 1988.

Fielding, Henry. *Tom Jones* (1749). Ed. John Bender. Oxford: World's Classics, 1996.

Findlay, Alison. *Illegitimate Power: Bastards in Renaissance Drama*. Manchester: Manchester University Press, 1994.

Finn, Margot, Michael Lobban and Jenny Bourne Taylor (eds). *Legitimacy and Illegitimacy in Nineteenth-Century Law, Literature and History*. Basingstoke: Palgrave Macmillan, 2010.

Forster, E. M. *Howards End* (1910). Ed. David Lodge. London: Penguin Classics, 2000.

Frank, Cathrine O. *Law, Literature, and the Transmission of Culture in England, 1837–1925*. Aldershot: Ashgate, 2010.

Gaskell, Elizabeth. *Ruth* (1853). Ed. Angus Easson. London: Penguin Classics, 1997.

Gill, Rebecca. "The Imperial Anxieties of a Nineteenth-Century Bigamy Case," *History Workshop Journal* 57 (Spring 2004) 58–78.

Herbert, Christopher. *Culture and Anomie: Ethnographic Imagination in the Nineteenth Century*. Chicago and London: Chicago University Press, 1991.

———. *Trollope and Comic Pleasure*. Chicago and London: Chicago University Press, 1987.

Hirsch, Pam. *Barbara Leigh Smith Bodichon: Feminist, Artist and Radical*. London: Chatto and Windus, 1998.

Kincaid, James. *The Novels of Anthony Trollope*. Oxford: The Clarendon Press, 1977.

Letwin, Shirley. *The Gentleman in Trollope: Individuality and Moral Conduct*. Basingstoke: Macmillan, 1982.

Marcus, Sharon. *Between Women: Friendship, Desire and Marriage in Victorian England*. Princeton, NJ: Princeton University Press, 2007.

Markwick, Margaret. *New Men in Trollope's novels: Rewriting the Victorian Male*. Aldershot: Ashgate, 2007.

———. "Out of the Closet: Homoerotics in Trollope's Novels," in Margaret Markwick, Deborah Denenholz Morse and Regenia Gagnier (eds) *The Politics of Gender in Anthony Trollope's Novels*. Aldershot: Ashgate, 2009.

———. *Trollope and Women*. London: The Hambleton Press, 1997.

McLennan, J. F. "Marriage and Divorce: The Law of England and Scotland," *North British Review* 35 (1861): 187–218.

McMaster, R. D. *Trollope and the Law*. Basingstoke: Macmillan, 1987.

McWilliam, Rohan. *The Tichborne Claimant: A Victorian Sensation*. London: Hambleton Continuum, 2007.

Michie, Elsie B. *The Vulgar Question of Money: Heiresses, Materialism, and the Novel of Manners*. Baltimore: The Johns Hopkins University Press, 2011.

Morse, Deborah Denenholz. *Reforming Trollope: Race, Gender and Englishness in the Novels of Anthony Trollope*. Farnham: Ashgate, 2013.

———. *Women in Trollope's Palliser Novels*. Ann Abor: UMI Research, 1987.

Nardin, Jane. *Trollope and Victorian Moral Philosophy*. Athens: Ohio University Press, 1996.

Nussbaum, Martha C. "The Stain of Illegitimacy: Gender, Law, and Trollopian Subversion," in Nussbaum, Martha C. and Alison L. LaCroix (eds) *Subversion and Sympathy: Gender, Law, and the British Novel*. Oxford: Oxford University Press, 2013.

Psomiades, Kathy Alexis. "*He Knew He Was Right:* The Sensational Tyranny of the Sexual Contract and the Problem of Liberal Progress," in Margaret Markwick, Deborah Denenholz Morse and Regenia Gagnier (eds) *The Politics of Gender in Anthony Trollope's Novels*. Aldershot: Ashgate, 2009.

Savage, Richard. Preface to *Miscellaneous Poems*, 1726. Reprinted in Samuel Johnson, *Life of Savage*, Clarence Tracy (ed). Oxford: Clarenden Press, 1971, p. 27.

Schmidgen, Wolfram. "Illegitimacy and Social Observation: The Bastard in the Eighteenth-Century Novel," *English Literary History* 69:1 (2002): 133–66.

Shanley, Mary Lyndon. *Feminism, Marriage and the Law in Victorian England*. London: I.B. Taurus, 1989.

Sutherland, John. "Introduction to Anthony Trollope," in *Ralph the Heir*. Oxford: Oxford University Press, 1990.

Taylor, Jenny Bourne. "Bastards to the Time: Legitimacy as Legal Fiction in Trollope's Novels of the 1870s," in Margaret Markwick, Deborah Denenholz Morse and Regenia Gagnier (eds) *The Politics of Gender in Anthony Trollope's Novels*. Aldershot: Ashgate, 2009.

———. "Bastardy and Nationality: The Curious Case of William Shedden and the 1858 Legitimacy Declaration Act," *Cultural and Social History* 4:2 (2007): 35–56.

———. "Trollope and the Sensation Novel," in Carolyn Dever and Lisa Niles (eds) *The Cambridge Companion to Anthony Trollope*. Cambridge: Cambridge University Press, 2011.

Thackeray, E. M. *The History of Henry Esmond* (1852). Ed. John Sutherland. London: Penguin Classics, 1985.

Tracy, Robert E. *Trollope's Later Novels*. Los Angeles: University of California Press, 1978.

Trollope, Anthony. *Ayala's Angel* (1881). Ed. Julian Thompson-Furnival. Oxford: World's Classics, 1986.

———. *Castle Richmond* (1860). Ed. Max Hastings. London: The Trollope Society, 1994.

———. *Doctor Thorne* (1858). Ed. Simon Dentith. Oxford: World's Classics, 2014.

———. *Is He Popenjoy?* (1878). Oxford: World's Classics, 1973.

———. *John Caldigate* (1879). Ed. N. John Hall. Oxford: World's Classics, 1993.

———. *Lady Anna* (1874). Ed. Stephen Orgel. Oxford: World's Classics, 1990.

———. *Mr Scarborough's Family* (1883). Ed. Geoffrey Harvey. Oxford: World's Classics, 1998.

———. *Ralph the Heir* (1871). Ed. John Sutherland. Oxford: World's Classics, 1991.

———. *The Way We Live Now* (1875). Ed. Frank Kermode. Harmondsworth: Penguin Classics 1994.

Turner, Mark W. *Trollope and the Magazines: Gendered Issue in Mid-Victorian Britain*. Basingstoke: Macmillan, 2000.

Wharton, J.J.S. *An Exposition of the Laws Relating to the Women of England*. London: Longman, Brown, Green, and Longmans, 1853.

Witte, John. *The Sins of the Fathers: The Law and Theology of Illegitimacy Reconsidered*. Cambridge: Cambridge University Press, 2009.

Wordsworth, William. "The Thorn" (1798). In Thomas Hutchinson (ed.), *Poetical Works*. London: Oxford University Press, 1967.

8
TROLLOPE AND MATERIAL CULTURE

Margaret P. Harvey

Despite the enduring interest in material culture studies of Victorian literature, very few critics have singled out Anthony Trollope as an author who uses material objects in strategic and significant ways. Unlike the works of Dickens, Thackeray, George Eliot, Gaskell, and other major Victorian authors, Trollope's novels are notably missing in major inquiries into material culture. Although Trollope certainly writes less about objects than some of these authors, there is also a tendency in Trollope studies to regard objects, when and where they actually appear in the text, as realist scene dressing. The relative scarcity of narratologically or symbolically prominent objects in Trollope novels should actually draw our attention that much more powerfully to the objects that Trollope does describe in detail. It should also show us that we must read Trollope's objects differently than we have in the past, using material culture to uncover a particularly Trollopian way of understanding and dealing with the material world. In this essay, I argue that objects and descriptions of material culture often appear around and in tandem with descriptions of female subjectivity and gendered notions of value. Careful examination of objects, such as the trousseau (or wedding chest), reveals Trollope's deep engagement with and critique of the idea of objects as repositories of self-worth, souvenirs of biographical significance, and non-market registers of value.

Trollope critic James Kincaid set the tone for the study of objects in Trollope novels when he wrote in a 1978 article that "Trollope's realism is oddly immaterial" (9). While Kincaid is to some extent delineating what he sees as formal properties of Trollope's fiction, he is also arguing for an ideological reason behind the perceived lack of objects in Trollope's fiction. He contends that Trollope is attempting to reject objectification and instead focus on human relationships, writing, "Trollope seeks for a world independent of objects" and "Trollope simply assumes a world where objects are so unimportant as not to be there" (9). The problem with Kincaid's reading is that he supposes that if he doesn't see objects they must not be there and thus must be intentionally omitted from the novels. Kincaid is not the only Trollope reader who has seen or rather felt the lack of objects (Andrew Miller makes a similar observation in his reading of *The Eustace Diamonds*, discussed ahead), and his initial observation about objects in Trollope seems to have been (and to some extent still be) the prevailing attitude of Victorian scholars to material culture in Trollope.

Juliet McMaster is one of the first major Trollope scholars to notice how Trollope often uses objects to show how a character's sense of identity is mediated by the material world. In response to Kincaid's assertion of Trollope's immateriality she argues that Trollope is "conscious of the expressive paraphernalia with which his people surround themselves, and of the extent to which clothes, props, and appurtenances are of the essence of their identity" (98–9). Trollope's "emphasis is not sensuous" in the same way that Dickens's or Thackeray's is, but, as McMaster argues, Trollope's characters are just as affected by the physical world of objects as they are by their external circumstances and human relationships (99). McMaster's impassioned defense of Trollope's object sensitivity is worth reading in full, as it encapsulates the opportunities and perspective material culture can give us in reading Trollope:

> Kincaid's statement does less than justice to the life of the novels as it may be felt through vividly imagined settings and objects, and the way in which the physical world is enlivened by the passions and aspirations and the weaknesses of the characters who inhabit it. The things are there, and are endowed with a certain life and significance by the people who encounter them.
>
> *(200)*

Trollope's things inhabit both the physical and psychological spaces of his novels, and our understanding of his prose and project is enriched when we pay attention to what they can tell us about his characters and their world.

Another investigation of the formal elements of Trollope's fiction, Michael Riffaterre's 1982 article on "Trollope's Metonymies," explores how Trollope often uses objects (or, in Riffaterre's phrasing, details) in metonymic relationships to characters and plots as "comic devices" (273). Trollope most often uses metonymy to "cause the reader to infer all sorts of moral judgements about a character from his behavior or some minor feature of physical or sartorial appearance" in a manner that Riffaterre finds "uniquely Trollopian" (273). The descriptive detail about an object or other physical element at first appears to be a function of realism, mimetically recreating the world in his text. When these details are used in metonymy, however, the detail or object is emphasized and amplified to a degree disproportionate to its material or physical function. Trollope's use of objects is therefore richly contradictory: creating a realistic effect but calling attention to the text's artifice through overemphasis and repetition. Indeed, Riffaterre concludes that objects become "subtexts" (278) or a code in Trollope's novels by which both characters and readers can understand and judge people and events. This formal reading of Trollope's objects is concerned primarily with how the language of objects is used to create a literary (specifically comic) effect, but also confirms the importance of objects in Trollope's world-making. Furthermore, objects here are intricately involved in the value systems of the novels, creating judgements both inside and outside the text about the worthiness, priorities, and self-awareness of the people and plots contained in these metonymic object relationships.

Since McMaster's and Riffaterre's readings of Trollope's things, the field of material culture has made a significant mark on the way literary critics read and reflect on objects in literature in general, and Victorian literature in particular. Jeff Nunokawa's groundbreaking study *The Afterlife of Property* studied the cultural anxiety Victorians felt about the growing commodity culture, showing how the literature of the period is almost obsessed with the idea of loss being a constituent part of modern property possession. Miller expanded on Nunokawa's work in his *Novels Behind Glass*, where he describes the strategies mid-century authors, including Trollope, used to resist the commodification of human existence and its reduction to a "display window" where desires, actions, and values were bought and sold to the highest bidder (6). These early material cultural studies show how objects were in the Victorian period, as today, receptacles of cultural fears and values.

Critics such as Elaine Freedgood and John Plotz have more recently added nuance to the way we read objects, insisting on their ambiguity and ambivalence where they appear in Victorian literature and culture. As Freedgood writes, "a host of ideas resided in Victorian things: abstraction, alienation, and spectacularization had to compete for space with other kinds of object relations – one that we have perhaps yet to appreciate" (8). Studies of Victorian material culture therefore must contend with the complex and often contradictory meanings and values assigned to objects in literature and culture; objects may signify or represent not one unified meaning or value but multiple meanings and even opposing meanings. As Plotz notes,

> certain belongings come to seem dually endowed: they are at once products of a cash market and, potentially, the rare fruits of a highly sentimentalized real of value both domestic and spiritual, a real defined by being anything but marketable. The best pieces of portable property can become, in effect, their own opposites.
>
> *(2)*

Understanding how both the Victorians and modern literary critics invest objects with certain abilities and values helps us identify and appreciate objects that are not either scene dressing or metaphorical, but both at the same time and many others things as well. What these studies have contributed to the field of Victorian literary studies has been significant and far-reaching, but many of the implications of material culture are left un- or under-applied when it comes to Trollope studies.

Although the study of material culture in literature has blossomed over the past two decades, very few critics have taken up McMaster's or Riffaterre's arguments and treated Trollope as an author who is invested in the way his characters interact with the large number of objects that crowded Victorian homes, workplaces, marketplaces, and communities. There are four notable exceptions, where major material culture studies have attended to and theorized Trollope's nuanced use of objects and material culture. All four critics (Miller, Plotz, Lindner, and Arnold) engage with Trollope's 1872 novel *The Eustace Diamonds*, the only Trollope novel named for an object and a rich resource (though not without its limitations, as we shall see) for interrogating Trollope's attitudes toward commodities, property, gender, and identity.

Miller's chapter on Trollope in *Novels Behind Glass* shares Kincaid's observation that objects are "oddly invisible" (12), but concludes that, far from seeking to obliterate the role of objects in his characters' lives, Trollope uses the *language* of objects and object relations to show the intense psychic and ideological impact objects have on his characters and their world. Miller recognizes Trollope's unique perspective on how objects contribute to and negotiate a person's sense of self. He writes,

> But if goods are oddly invisible, the language of ownership and property saturates the novel, defining characters' moral and psychological identities as well as their relation to the material environment. Trollope understands the self in terms derived from the market: identity and its parts are owned, sold, lost, and stolen. [. . .] As the language of property spirals out to shape the self, however, the futility of possession accrues new pathos: just as the possession of commodified goods is a vexed enterprise, so the possession of the self becomes troubled; like the diamonds themselves, the self becomes fugitive.
>
> *(12)*

Miller uses the term "possessive identity" to describe how objects come to define people in both their personal and public narratives. He also emphasizes how the language of possession and property, even when it is not being used to describe material objects, saturates Trollope's prose, especially in a novel like *The Eustace Diamonds*, where

> while goods appear only infrequently on the stage of Trollope's text, the language of the novel transmutes what is there, even individual character, into goods whose properties and constitution are shaped by the codes of possession. And, with people given to us as goods, social life develops into a series of exchanges – thefts, losses, gifts, inheritance.
> (Miller 170)

Miller argues that instead of focusing on material objects and how characters interact with those objects, Trollope reveals how similar to material objects his characters are: they circulate, are speculated upon, and are taken possession of (especially in marriage).

Plotz's chapter on *The Eustace Diamonds* is more attentive to how the titular diamonds function in the text as an object, or, as he specifies, a thing. He argues that diamonds are "boundary-troublers" because of their "persistent refusal to turn either into pure liquidity or pure bearers of sentimental value" (25). He agrees with Miller that the characters' sense of identity and selfhood is bound up with their relationship to objects, and demonstrates how diamonds are a particularly unstable and troubling object upon which to form or stake an identity. Lizzie Eustace's "overattachment" (35) to the disputed diamonds makes it impossible for her to realize their market value, a plot that gives Trollope an opportunity to examine how distinctions between sentimental value and exchange value might complicate a character's ability to form a stable identity or sense of self-possession. As Plotz explains, Lizzie's psychological and even physical attachment to the diamonds "demonstrates that any one relationship between an individual and a particular portable property can take on a new (and hence intrinsically narratable) life of its own" (35). Trollope thus explores and experiments with the most complex issues surrounding material culture, testing the limits of both narrative and commodity culture.

Neither Miller nor Plotz has gender stakes in his argument – that is, neither one explicitly links the experience of women and female characters to his analysis about objects and identity. However, the topic of gender is somewhat inescapable in any discussion of *The Eustace Diamonds*, which has a rich critical history of feminist readings and is considered one of Trollope's most pointed commentaries on gender and the marriage market.[1] The remaining two studies of *The Eustace Diamonds* explicitly make the connection between gender and material culture. Although their conclusions are more text-specific than those reached by Miller or Plotz, both Lindner and Arnold seize upon the issue of female property ownership and agency in a society where primogeniture and couverture still kept many women from being in control of objects or even themselves. Lindner argues that Lizzie Eustace's attempt to define herself as a valuable commodity and set the terms of her own sale ends up reinforcing the patriarchal order of the novel. Arnold sees Lizzie's defiance as a tactic used against the property laws that limited female rights but granted her, as a widow, special privileges denied to married women. Both studies are masterly readings of how gender politics collide with objects, especially personal property, in this novel.

Although there has been major development in the field of material culture and Trollope studies since Kincaid's pronouncement of Trollope's "immateriality," this development has largely been confined to our understanding of one novel, at the expense of examining the material culture in any of the other forty-six novels of Trollope's oeuvre. *The Eustace Diamonds* isn't even a very representative novel for examining Trollope's ideas about objects; although it has an object as its title, the diamonds themselves barely have a physical description or presence in the novel and operate, as Plotz argues, differently than other objects because of their status as jewelry. To base our understanding of Trollope's material culture on one novel, and one rather special object within that novel, is limiting and presents us with only a partial view of the complexities and nuances present in Trollope's fiction.

To demonstrate the possibilities for material culture readings of Trollope, I will briefly look at an object, the bridal trousseau, as it appears in three different Trollope novels to see how Trollope's treatment of objects progresses, shifts, and adapts. I contend that Trollope has a keen sense of the importance of objects in mediating issues, such as identity, gender, and class, and uses his novels to explore what he sees as the important and pressing issue of how people, especially women, operate in the expanding commodity culture of the Victorian era.

On the verge of becoming wives, Victorian women were allowed and encouraged to make and embellish items that they would use during their married lives, such as linens, lingerie, clothing, and other household items. The function of the trousseau was twofold: a woman was creating useful items with which to begin a new household under her husband's roof while also performing the symbolic labor of remaking herself into a wife. Among major Victorian novelists, Trollope seems to be the only one who depicts this cultural practice with any detail or allows the making of the trousseau to figure prominently in his novels. That it does figure so prominently in several of his novels and is referenced in at least eleven of his novels and short stories suggests Trollope's understanding and deployment of the powerful cultural, psychological, and material work being performed by the trousseau and what it could offer both his plots and characters.

Because courtship and marital rituals are so important to the women in his novels, is it not surprising that Trollope attends to how objects mediate this process, but the attention he gives to the trousseau emphasizes its importance. Trollope writes in *Framley Parsonage* that "the milliner makes the bride":

> as regarding her bridehood, in distinction either to her girlhood or her wifehood – as being a line of plain demarcation between those two periods of a woman's life – the milliner does do much to make her. She would be hardly a bride if the trousseau were not there. A girl married without some such appendage would seem to pass into the condition of a wife without any such line of demarcation.
>
> *(Framley Parsonage Ch. 40)*

Although it remains to be seen whether Trollope approves of this material initiation into wifehood (his tone here seems at least partially sarcastic), he nevertheless recognizes how society uses this object to represent the material and ontological changes experienced by a woman upon her engagement and marriage.

Trollope's primary purpose in describing a bride-to-be's trousseau is to show how she values both herself and the position to which she aspires: married woman. In *Framley Parsonage*, the emotionally and morally vacant Griselda Grantly's character is on full display as she prepares her trousseau and impending nuptials to Lord Dumbello. As a woman marrying into the peerage, Griselda understands the importance of opulent display for realizing her value as the affianced of a future marquis. Trollope describes how

> she went to work steadily, slowly, and almost with solemnity, as though the business in hand were one which it would be wicked to treat with impatience. She even struck her mother with awe by the grandeur of her ideas and the depth of her theories.
>
> *(Framley Ch. 40)*

Participating in what Veblen Thorstein in 1899 termed "conspicuous consumption," Griselda signals to her peers that she is worthy of the station to which she is being raised and will properly represent her husband's prosperity and position. The success of her trousseau-making suggests her future success as a wife and peeress: she has successfully transitioned from parson's daughter to Lady Dumbello through her strategic knowledge and skillful deployment of material culture. This is the pinnacle of achievement for Griselda because she is not concerned with or capable of understanding the emotional and moral universe in which characters such as Lucy Robarts are so deeply embedded. Her value is superficial and surface, but she is nonetheless able to realize this value through her trousseau.

Not all brides or trousseaux are as successful as Griselda Grantley at knowing and inhabiting their value position, however, and Trollope's understanding of the trousseau is manifest also in his depiction of how it often fails to perform its cultural and symbolic purpose. In *The Eustace Diamonds*, Lucinda Roanoke's psychological and physiological revulsion to her marriage to Sir George Tewett is revealed through her relationships to the material goods that have come to represent it. Lucinda complains with "terrible energy" against the making of the trousseau, arguing with her aunt that she "shall never have a house to put [the objects] into" (*Eustace* Ch. 55). Lucinda's inability to imagine a future in which the items in her trousseau are useful possessions does not portend well for her future marriage and the role she will be required to fill in her husband's household. The intense disgust she feels for her marriage is further revealed during a fitting for the items in her trousseau, when Lucinda "could hardly be got to allow the milliners to fit the dresses to her body, and positively refused to thrust her feet into certain golden-heeled boots with brightly-bronzed toes, which were a great feature among the raiment" (*Eustace* Ch. 69). The resistance of her body to the material accoutrements of marriage is a precursor to her resistance to her husband's body and sexuality. Lucinda violently rejects her potential use-value as a sexual and reproducing body; this is not only strongly hinted at by the narrator and dialogue throughout the marriage subplot but also demonstrated by the account of how

> the bride absolutely ran a muck among the finery, scattering the laces here and there, pitching the glove boxes under the bed, chucking the golden-heeled boots into the fire-place, and exhibiting quite a tempest of fury against one of the finest shows of petticoats ever arranged with a view to the admiration and envy of female friends.
> (*Eustace* Ch. 69)

Lucinda's destruction of her trousseau foreshadows her refusal to go through with her marriage, her unsuitability as a wife, and her eventual descent into madness just as Griselda's careful management of her trousseau foreshadowed her success and suitability for the sphere to which she has aspired.

That trousseaux can mean different things for different women is brought home by Trollope's depiction of two sisters competing for one man and by extension one trousseau in *He Knew He Was Right* (1869). Although Camilla and Arabella French both vie for the attentions of the Reverend Thomas Gibson, only one sister can prevail in her desire to be his wife. As his intentions shift from Arabella to Camilla, a contrast is developed between the behavior of the two marriageable girls and how they approach engagement, marriage, and, most importantly to our purposes, the trousseau.[2] Camilla becomes engaged to Mr. Gibson in a rather ruthless *coup d'état* after it seemed that Arabella, the elder sister, was to be chosen: "Camilla argued that as her sister's chance was gone, and as the prize had come in her own way, there was no good reason why it should be lost to the family altogether" (*He Knew He Was Right* Ch. 50). Camilla's ability to secure the "prize" of a betrothal, however, does not indicate a corresponding ability to become a wife and mother, which is the true purpose of an engagement. Her concerns, as the term "prize" might suggest, are almost completely material, as she begins to acquire the items for her trousseau.

Although many Victorian and indeed Trollope heroines have material concerns at the core of their marital decisions – certainly Griselda Grantly considers both her future financial and society positions before accepting Lord Dumbello – Trollope shows that Camilla is not emotionally or intellectually mature enough to know how her value on the marriage market translates to expenditure on material goods. Camilla, the second daughter of an impoverished widow, is at this point third choice of wife for a provincial clergyman but spends as if she is a Griselda marrying her own English peer. Trollope describes how "she drew with great audacity on the somewhat slender means of the family for the amount of feminine gear necessary to enable her to go into Mr. Gibson's house with something of the éclat of a well-provided bride" (*He Knew* Ch. 65). She cannot fully appreciate the role for which she has been chosen, the wife of a man of modest means, nor can she understand the cost of her mistaken sense of entitlement. Camilla's "vast arrangement which she called the preparation of her trousseau, but which both Mrs. French and Bella regarded as a spoliation of the domestic nest, for the proud purposes of one of the younger birds" (*He Knew* Ch. 74) not only puts her mother's finances in danger but also makes her look more and more unsuitable in the eyes of her fiancé. Ultimately, like Lucinda Roanoke, Camilla's marriage never comes off. While Lucinda attempts to destroy her trousseau and the value it assigns to her as a sexual object, Camilla clings to hers and the idea of her worth that it represents.

Although Camilla fails to properly transition into her role as wife via the trousseau, Arabella is able to use the symbolic work of the trousseau to her advantage. While Camilla shops and spends extravagantly, we are told, Arabella "worked diligently with her needle, and folded and unfolded as she was desired, and became as it were quite a younger sister in the house" (*He Knew* Ch. 65). The work Trollope is referring to in this passage is the marking of the linens and undergarments of the trousseau with the bride's maiden initials, a practice that originated as a practical measure for identification in communal laundries, but became a highly symbolic practice that allowed the girl to create a sense of personal property and ownership over both her household things and herself. Deborah Wynne, describing the purposes of embroidering names into fabric, emphasizes how a maiden name or initials on trousseau cloth "represents an identity of herself as a property owner, reminding her of the period before marriage when she legally owned her things" (Wynne 102). Because the trousseau was one of the few things a girl would ever be able to buy and consider (rightly or wrongly) her personal property, the marking of the trousseau shows how women used this aspect of material culture as a repository of premarital value and identity at the same time it was functioning as a tool of remaking and transformation. A marked item becomes a personal or biographical memorial, while the marking process itself teaches the kind of patience and diligence the woman will need to bring into her new role as wife and mother.

Trollope, sensitive to the ideological and emotional weight of this practice, is one of the few Victorian authors who fully explore the implications of the marking process. In *He Knew He Was Right*, it is Arabella who marks the linens for her sister's trousseau, and this labor teaches her to be dutiful and diligent – qualities that recommend her to Mr. Gibson as being much more desirable in his future wife than Camilla's unchecked spending and hoarding of material goods.[3] When Mr. Gibson transfers his marriage proposal from Camilla to Arabella, the product of Arabella's labor, the trousseau, is transferred as well. It is at this point in the text that Trollope displays his masterful understanding of how material culture can both be used to a woman's advantage and cause her downfall; after Camilla's engagement is cancelled she is forced to "pick out the marks" (*He Knew* Ch. 82) that signaled her ownership of the trousseau. In this way, she is not only obliterating her future identity as Mrs. Gibson but also symbolically destroying the value she had as a marriageable woman. Only a woman who is going to be married has value, and only a woman who has value can enshrine and mark that value with a trousseau. She loses the rights to her property that were conditional upon her marriage, and Arabella gains those same rights and indeed the exact same property when she becomes the fourth and final choice for Mr. Gibson's bride. Trollope notes how "Bella commenced her modest preparations without any of the éclat which had attended Camilla's operations, but she felt more certainty of ultimate success than had ever fallen to Camilla's lot" (*He Knew* Ch. 83). She has to change only one of the letters marked on the trousseau, a tragicomic detail that fully brings to bear the importance of the trousseau and marking to a woman's identity and relationship to material culture.

Trollope's depiction of the trousseau and the women who make and mark them is ultimately a condemnation of the commodity culture that provides a sense of worth only through the consumption of material goods. Although Trollope is certainly fascinated by the process and enjoys describing the goods in detail, none of the women whom he depicts as making a trousseau is truly realizing her worth as an individual or a human being. Although Griselda Grantly's marriage is successful, there is no indication of affection or fulfillment in her relationship with Lord Dumbello. Lucinda Roanoke and Camilla French are probably as unsuitable for married life as they are unequal to the task of preparing for it. Arabella French finally gets her trousseau and makes her mark, but only after she has been so devalued and defeated that she has been forced to make and mark her sister's trousseau when she had no hope of ever having one of her own. The use of the trousseau to both memorialize and create identities not only is an ultimately futile endeavor but also harms the women who practice it. In *He Knew He Was Right*, *The Eustace Diamonds*, and even *Framley Parsonage* there is a moment when the marriage is in doubt and the bride or her family not only is responsible for the expense of the goods acquired for the trousseau, but also must face the psychological loss of the personhood that the trousseau had come to represent. Picking out the marks is certainly one of the most violent blows to a woman's sense of self-worth and identity, and Trollope's attentiveness to and repetition of this detail in his novels reveal his distrust and rejection of the ability of material culture and commodified goods to grant women the kind of value and agency that they so desperately seek and deserve.

Notes

1 See Cohen; Psomiades; and Bredesen.
2 Two sisters fighting over a suitor and trousseau is also the plot of Henry James's ghost story "The Romance of Certain Old Clothes" (1868). The similarities between the two plots (published around the same time) provide yet another James-Trollope connection and further evidence of the physic and symbolic power of the trousseau.
3 This is not the first time Arabella demonstrates her meekness and spirit of renunciation by her use of objects. Earlier in the novel, Arabella stops wearing her chignon (a hairpiece) when Mr. Gibson expresses his distaste for it (*He Knew* Ch. 48) – yet more evidence of Trollope's attention to how objects are related to gender and value.

Works cited

Arnold, Jean. *Victorian Jewelry, Identity, and the Novel: Prisms of Culture*. Farnham, UK and Burlington, VT: Ashgate, 2011.

Bredesen, Dagni. "What's a Woman to Do? Managing Money and Manipulating Fictions in Trollope's *Can You Forgive Her?* and *The Eustace Diamonds*." *Victorian Review* 31.2 (2005): 99–122.

Cohen, William A. *Sex Scandal: The Private Parts of Victorian Fiction*. Durham, NC and London: Duke Univ. Press, 1996.

Freedgood, Elaine. *The Ideas in Things: Fugitive Meaning in the Victorian Novel*. Chicago: Univ. of Chicago Press, 2006.

James, Henry. "The Romance of Certain Old Clothes." *The Tales of Henry James*. Volume I: 1864–9. Ed. Maqbool Aziz. Oxford: Clarendon Press, 1973.

Kincaid, James. "Bring Back *The Trollopian*." *Nineteenth-Century Literature* 31.1 (June 1976): 1–14.

Lindner, Christoph. *Fictions of Commodity Culture: From the Victorian to the Postmodern*. Farnham, UK and Burlington, VT: Ashgate, 2003.

McMaster, Juliet. *Trollope's Palliser Novels: Theme and Pattern*. New York: Oxford Univ. Press, 1978.

Miller, Andrew H. *Novels Behind Glass: Commodity Culture and Victorian Narrative*. Cambridge: Cambridge Univ. Press, 1995.

Nunokawa, Jeff. *The Afterlife of Property: Domestic Security and the Victorian Novel*. Princeton, NJ: Princeton Univ. Press, 1994.

Plotz, John. *Portable Property: Victorian People on the Move*. Princeton, NJ: Princeton Univ. Press, 2008.

Psomiades, Kathy Alexis. "Heterosexual Exchange and Other Victorian Fictions: *The Eustace Diamonds* and Victorian Anthropology." *Novel* 33.1 (Fall 1999): 99–118.

Riffaterre, Michael. "Trollope's Metonymies." *Nineteenth-Century Fiction* 37, No. 3, Special Issue: Anthony Trollope, 1882–1982 (December 1982): 272–292.

Trollope, Anthony. *The Eustace Diamonds*. Ed. W. J. McCormack. Oxford: Oxford Univ. Press, 2008.

———. *Framley Parsonage*. Ed. David Skilton and Peter Miles. London: Penguin, 2004.

———. *He Knew He Was Right*. Ed. John Sutherland. Oxford: Oxford Univ. Press, 1998.

Veblen, Thorstein. *The Theory of the Leisure Class: An Economic Study of Institutions*. New York: Macmillan, 1899.

Wynne, Deborah. *Women and Personal Property in the Victorian Novel*. Farnham, UK and Burlington, VT: Ashgate, 2010.

9

"WITHIN THE FIGURE AND FRAME AND CLOTHES AND CUTICLE"

Trollope and the body

Sophie Gilmartin

How is a bit of carpet redolent of a marriage proposal? Trollope's Adolphus Crosbie finds it so in *The Small House at Allington* when he must witness his fiancée's ruthless absorption as she bargains over the hymeneal carpets that are to furnish their marital home.[1] Watching her in a great London shop he knows he has himself become shop-soiled, having sold his good looks and reputation for an aristocratic bride. In *Framley Parsonage* Lucy Robarts's mind keeps coming back to the carpets. Finally confessing that she has refused the marriage proposal of a "real live lord" (whom she dearly loves), she tells her sister-in-law,

> "Well, it was not a dream. Here, standing here, on this very spot – on that flower of the carpet – he begged me a dozen times to be his wife. I wonder whether you and Mark would let me cut it out and keep it."

And later, standing on the same piece of carpet:

> "Standing exactly here, on this spot, he said that he would persevere till I accepted his love. I wonder what made me especially observe that both his feet were within the lines of that division."[2]

For Adolphus Crosbie, the brand-new carpets that his Alexandrina haggles over bespeak future years of his and her weary tread over them: the signs of their future bodies wearing and sullying them; a shabby life. Lucy Robarts's half-joking concentration upon the carpet is focused on that "exact place" because to her imagination it bears the impression of Lufton's body as he stood seeking to touch her hand, reaching for her body. In these examples the very fibres of the carpet take bodily impressions that are then impressed upon the mind with figurative and physical weight. Materiality, sense memory or prolepsis, and the emotions are brought together in and through the body.

Elaine Scarry has written eloquently of the "reciprocal alterations between man and his world" in Thomas Hardy and other nineteenth-century novelists.[3] She reads the material record left by human bodies on a landscape, in a room, on passing through a gate, and inversely, the signs that the world leaves on men and women, especially through work. She describes skin, for example, that is cut or blistered, that receives a "film" of dirt, or that is mottled with apple pulp and sap, as is Giles Winterbourne's in his work at the cider press in Hardy's *The Woodlanders*. These markings of physical labour on the body may seem far-removed from much of Trollope's writing (although there are farmers and labourers, English, Irish, Australian and New Zealander, in his works), and Scarry does not include Trollope in her study. However, Trollope's writing is as idiosyncratic in its way as Hardy's, and as meticulous in its rendering of the body as it moves through the world, traced upon and leaving traces. Until recently there has been little critical attention to the body in Trollope studies, although there are some notable exceptions. This essay will explore scholarship on the body in Trollope's fiction, as well as putting forward some new readings.

"Indeed, one can never say where one will be," says Lord Lufton, loftily, about his movements over the coming year.[4] But with Trollope, one knows where *others* are, and we know where the bodies lie. Henry James wrote that Trollope's novels have "a spacious, geographical quality".[5] Perhaps the flow of his writing can at times obscure the fact that he rarely loses sight of where and how his characters' bodies stand, sit, move, displace space, have weight, make impressions, touch and are touched. Trollope declared in his *Autobiography* that "stories charm us . . . because we feel that men and women with flesh and blood . . . are struggling amidst their woes."[6] This corporeality is marked with the wear of those struggles and woes, as well as with joy, aging and humour; with wrinkles, dimples and bruises. In *Embodied*, William Cohen's study of the senses in Victorian literature, he argues, "In psychological terms, because 'feelings' lie in a gray zone between physical sensations and emotional responses, sensation and affective experiences can switch, blend, or substitute for one another."[7] One of the many examples of this play between the affective and the physical occurs in the scene just discussed in which Lucy Robarts stands, half-joking, on the place in the carpet where her lover had stood, leaving his impression on the carpet and on her. She tells her sister-in-law that in order to get over her lovesickness she must punish her body: she needs to "starve" or "pinch" herself; to "do some nasty work, – clean the pots and pans and the candlesticks; that I think would do the most good. I have got a piece of sackcloth, and I mean to wear that, when I have made it up."[8] Momentarily serious, she explains, "How shall I act upon my heart, if I do not do it through the blood and flesh?" Here, blood and flesh are quite literal and physiological, and the "heart" seemingly not so, but rather a trite example of that emotional/physical substitution of which Cohen writes. However, Cohen's chapter on Trollope in *Embodied*, devoted to the short story, "On the Banks of the Jordan," reads this particular tale as revealing that "Beneath the epidermis there seems to lie not spiritual depth but simply more body, ever more capable of physical distress."[9] Centuries of penitents have believed otherwise, mortifying the flesh to reach spiritual depths (or heights), and Lucy Robarts is serious enough here: she needs to feel her body rubbing harshly against the world so that she can know hunger, pain, manual work and the rough clothing of the poor. She hopes that this material record will help her to suppress a latent materialism that makes her thrill at the prospect of marriage to the wealthy Lord Lufton. More crucially, however, she needs to turn from a painful, suffocating subjectivity to the objective, everyday world. Physical striving with material things will "act upon" her heart. While the heart is the seat of emotion and spiritual feeling here and elsewhere in Trollope's writing, it is also a physical organ, a blood-regulator: Lufton's declaration of love causes Lucy to "blush ruby-red through every vein of her deep-tinted face,"[10] and Lizzie Eustace experiences "a horrid spasm across her heart, which seemed ready to kill her, so sharp was the pain"[11] when she learns that her diamonds are stolen. Lizzie of course could be said to have "no heart", and the fact that her deepest emotions are reserved for her diamonds supports Cohen's conclusion that under the skin there is simply more "surface", or flesh, organic matter, materiality. But there are many exceptions to this reading of interiority in Trollope's work. In his fiction the heart is certainly an organ, and blood rises and drains from the vessels in the skin, and the skin gives and receives the touch, rubbings and bruisings of the world, which in turn act upon the heart. The body is ever-present, but it is the seat, conductor and visible sign of psychological interiority.

In his chapter entitled "Skin", William Cohen explores that organ in Trollope's short story, "On the Banks of the Jordan". On his tour of Palestine, the narrator, "Jones", jauntily dismisses the Eastern Christian pilgrims as "savour(ing) strongly of Oriental life and of Oriental dirt."[12] Jones protects his sense of self and superiority by differentiating himself on the basis of his skin colour; it is not darkened by race or dirt. Worryingly, bathing in the River Jordan covers him in "dirt and slush", and the Dead Sea leaves a repellent, invisible "film" on his body. Cohen's chapter situates the story's preoccupation with skin colour, bathing and cleanliness within the context of racial attitudes in contemporary journalism, and also in the context of the contemporary furore over the pollution of the Thames and of water supplies generally in London. He writes, "In the context of Victorian sanitary reform, the tale's ironic desublimation of ritual cleansing seems even more irreducibly corporeal."[13] Jones puts his body through the motions of spiritual pilgrimage, but he is really a tourist, ticking sights off his list. Cohen concludes that Jones, "fails to go below the surface . . . because, Trollope suggests, there is nothing else: efforts to penetrate result not in the revelation of deep truths but in a further gliding along the surface of the skin."[14]

Of this concluding sentence Elaine Freedgood writes in a review of *Embodied*,

> If we substitute "social world" or "language" or "provincial life" for "skin," then it seems to me that Cohen describes Trollope's fictional worlds more generally and their haunting refusals of "deep connection" . . . it is surface all the way down . . .".[15]

Freedgood's insightful review runs the risk here, a risk which also accompanies Cohen's last sentence, of providing eminently quotable ammunition for those who regard Trollope's attention to the material, the contemporary and the corporeal simply as evidence of superficiality. William Cohen's chapter on Trollope's short story demonstrates how the tale opens up a depth of field in historical and cultural interpretation, but it does not argue for a spiritual or psychological depth or interiority; indeed it would be difficult to do so in the case of this particular story. While his interpretation is an interesting study of the body in reciprocity with its material and cultural context, it is hardly the best or most representative vehicle to assess more widely Trollope's success or failure in evincing psychological and spiritual depth.

"On the Banks of the Jordan" presents the reader with male bonding – often physically expressed – gone awry: Jones's travel companion is revealed finally, and much to his chagrin, to be a young woman in disguise. They have been close, and Jones has offered to tend his companion's chafed legs, scarified by long hours in the saddle. Mark Forrester considers the homoeroticism of these scenarios between Jones and Smith, but also discusses the foreign landscape itself as sexually aggressive and overwhelming. He goes so far as to claim that Jones's bathing in the Dead Sea is an experience of male rape: "the lake engulfs and then penetrates the intrusive foreign body."[16] Trollope's *London Review* editor and his readers were offended by the fact that Jones was travelling with an unmarried and unchaperoned young lady, the niece of a baronet, in considerable intimacy. However, Forrester maps the discomfort of Trollope's Victorian readers and of his intrusively foreign and blushing character Jones, onto a colonial territory where British anxieties over homosexuality and control are suppressed but rife.

Another of Trollope's stories, "The Turkish Bath" (1869), is all male bonding and naked skin. Trollope's narrator goes to bathe at the Jermyn Street hammam, and explains to the reader at some length the rituals involved in the movement and presentation of one's naked body. The deployment of the two towels provided becomes rather important.

> With an absence of all bashfulness which soon grows upon one, we had divested ourselves of our ordinary trappings beneath the gaze of five or six young men lying on surrounding sofas, – among whom we recognized young Walker of the Treasury, and hereby testify on his behalf that he looks almost as fine a fellow without his clothes as he does with them, – and had strutted through the doorway to the bath-room, trailing our second towel behind us.

He "recommends" the towel-trailing to his "young friends as being at the same time easy and oriental."[17] There is a long and very funny digression about how to look one's best when one has only skin and two towels to work with. Rather than stripping away social rituals and masks, Trollope's story reveals the codes that prevail in the presentation of the body and its relation to others, when it would seem that there is nothing left to hide.

Catherine Spooner explores these social and sartorial codes in depth as they are revealed by the deployment of the towels in "The Turkish Bath." In her view the bath towel "is presented as an object that invites interpretation, a totemic item within this complex space" of the hammam.[18] The divestment of clothing is hardly nakedness, and hardly a levelling of social station, according to Spooner: the towel can lead to all kinds of social gaffes, so that worn the wrong way, it can make one appear "too feminine, too English, or simply unable to command respect."[19] These codes are so convoluted that the narrator, a newspaper editor, takes the towelled Irishman with whom he easily chats and smokes in the hammam for a cosmopolitan gentleman, when he is in fact insane. Spooner argues that the line between madness and sanity is disturbingly blurred by the end of the story, going so far as to claim that the towel-trailing that Trollope's narrator recommends is not the way to express "nonchalance" but another kind of sign: his "obsessive concern with managing his appearance reveals the fragility of his own subjecthood."[20] While historically rich and attentive, this reading does leave one wondering if everyone who has looked at a fashion magazine or been a little body-conscious on the beach is in fact insane. Certainly physical appearance and fashion are social preoccupations that lay themselves open to that diagnosis, but they are common enough, nevertheless.

Mark W. Turner views this tale and Trollope's other stories of editors and writers as "constructions of male fantasies."[21] The power and authority of the editor create an erotically charged relationship with the writer who submits his or her manuscript. In "The Turkish Bath" this fantasy of power and desire is homosexual, according to Turner, who reads the story alongside Victorian homosexual pornography. Pamela Gilbert writes of baths in London and of this story in particular that

> the uneasy perception that the nudity of the bath concealed, rather than revealed, identity was part and parcel of the general understanding of the city as a heterogeneous space in which social contact was much less mediated than in the highly controlled social rituals of access that were common in the country or in clubs.[22]

John Potvin studies the architectural space and the rituals of the hammam as conducive to male homosociality, and especially later in its history, to homosexuality.[23] Male relationships in Trollope are often emotional and physical: as I have written elsewhere, men cry a great deal in Trollope's writing, with and for and often while holding each other.[24] Margaret Markwick's study of "new men" in Trollope's novels also explores their bodily expressions, including a "hands-on" approach to fatherhood.[25]

Thackeray, George Eliot, Hardy and other of Trollope's contemporaries often set their novels in the distant or near past, giving a comforting historical patina to the material worlds represented. But Trollope's material world is glaringly new: chignons, crinolines, the London underground, dining *à la Russe* . . . bodies are adorned and transported, eat and generally act and react to the new materials of a materialistic world. His concentration upon the body and things is so constant that it works almost subliminally; seemingly they are all just part and parcel of the everyday. But out from the accretion of gestures, limbs and things can emerge an object, body or body part that is transformed by Trollope's intense gaze from the mundane to the oddly defamiliarized.[26]

Such a transformation is comically the case when Lucy Robarts, discussed earlier, asks to cut out and keep the piece of carpet impressed by the feet of her lover. It is also the case when Mr. Harding, so familiar to readers from *The Warden* (1855), is observed by Adolphus Crosbie in *The Small House at Allington* (1864). Trollope wrote in his autobiography that his characters aged in "real time": "on the last day of each month recorded, every person in his novel should be a month older than on the first,"[27] and Mr. Harding has aged over the nine years between the two novels.[28] In this scene, Trollope emphasizes that Harding does not speak; all we know of him is told through his body and gestures.

> a little, withered, shambling old man, with bent shoulders . . . Crosbie felt that he had never seen a face on which traits of human kindness were more plainly written. But the old man did not speak. He turned his body half round, and then shambled back, as though ashamed of his intention, and passed on.[29]

Trollope performs for his readers the mild shock or disturbance of coming across a friend after several years; the body and gestures are essentially the same but have been altered or perhaps have become more prominent through the aging process. Harding, always shy, is "doubtful, uncertain", and his hand-rubbing and the half turning of his body throw into relief what he always was and did, but the emphasis on his body defamiliarizes momentarily this well-known figure. He is out of place in the later novel, too, and especially as he is seen only in the company of worldly, self-assured Adolphus Crosbie. Even Crosbie, in transit from Barchester, with ambition and to perdition at Courcy Castle, is stopped briefly in his tracks, arrested by the aura of Harding's meek holiness.[30]

In her discussion of the representation of sexuality in Trollope's writing, Margaret Markwick has noticed the number of arms creeping around women's waists, or clasping "in full abandon" almost as if these limbs have a life of their own.[31] And the frequency with which Lizzie Eustace stands "upon her two legs" can only have brought those hidden limbs more forcibly to the attention of Victorian readers. Throughout her early feminist study, *Women in Trollope's Palliser Novels*, Deborah Denenholz Morse raises Trollope's openly physical treatment of women's desire: Glencora's desperate cry in *Can You Forgive Her?*, "I could have clung to the outside of a man's body, to his very trappings", and the guilt over her sexual frustration and childlessness when she tells Alice, "I used to lie in bed and wish myself dead."[32] Sometimes the strength of sexual and emotional desire is so strong as to be harrowing for characters and the reader: Glencora can end her relationship with Burgo only by taking for herself one last passionate kiss (*Can You Forgive Her?*),[33] and the same is true for Winifred Hurtle as she makes a condition of relinquishing her engagement to Paul Montague that he give her one final weekend away together, and after that one last passionate embrace (*The Way We Live Now*).[34]

Trollope's concentration on the body and its movement and parts can heighten our awareness of the familiar so much that we have to look again, until we are less secure of what is ordinary and everyday. Galia Ofek's study of hair in Victorian literature and culture argues that hair in this period (and in some of Trollope's novels) is not only defamiliarized but also fetishized. One of the examples that she discusses is taken from *He Knew He Was Right*. It is a comic yet ghastly moment from Mr. Gibson's courtship of Arabella French. Gibson, a young vicar, is increasingly alarmed by the prospect of marriage to the domineering Arabella, and his fears become oddly involved with her fashionable chignon, made of false hair. It takes on monstrous, Gothic proportions:

> Then, as she stretched forward to ring the bell, he thought that he never in his life had seen anything so unshapely as that huge wen at the back of her head. "Monstrum horrendum, informe, ingens!" He could not help quoting the words to himself.[35]

The well-known quotation ("a monster horrendous, shapeless and huge") is from the *Aeneid*, describing the Cyclops Polyphemus, but for the vicar it becomes almost incantatory, meant to ward off evil (and it would remind him of his exclusively male classical education, too – another way to protect himself from female domination). This use of incantation accords with my argument about Trollope's defamiliarization of the body and everyday objects; this is so much the case here as to make Arabella's hairpiece uncanny. (And Freud's everyday examples of the uncanny in his own experience are often corporeal and comic: his alarmed non-recognition of himself in the mirror of a train's sleeper carriage; his embarrassment, when lost, at returning time and again to the same street of prostitutes.) Of Trollope's Mr Gibson Gail Ofek writes, "Mr Gibson seems to be a perfect study of hair-fetishism as Freud was to analyze it. Like a typical fetishist, he is both attracted to and repulsed by Arabella's chignon".[36]

False as she is, Trollope resists making Lizzie Eustace physically so. She is "very bitter" over women who wear false "headgear". Her own hair, "which was nearly black . . . she wore bound tight round her perfect forehead, with one long love-lock hanging over her shoulder."[37] Like Braddon's sensational Lady Audley, Lizzie is a consummate actress, and knows how to dress her hair and body as to appear pure and modest. But, as she tries to seduce Frank Greystock on a long journey to Scotland, he observes her hair with distaste: "he was observing that her long lock of hair was out of curl and untidy – a thing that ought not to have been there during such a journey as this."[38] Rather like the distaste that Thomas Hardy's Jude Fawley feels when he sees Arabella's long tail of false hair hanging from her dressing table, Lizzie's own lovelock works against erotic interest, and becomes a "thing", as she herself becomes objectified rather than loved.

Trollope was not as prescriptive in his coding of hair and skin colour as were many of his contemporaries. The popular associations of light hair and skin with virtue and dark hair and skin with a loose sexuality and morality do not hold in his work. Helena Michie studies the "paradoxes of heroine description" in several Victorian novelists, including Trollope. She argues that despite Trollope's often meticulous descriptions of his heroine's bodies, there are bound to be "distancing codes": "the distance between the heroine's body and the words used to describe it are not simply *différance*, but an aggravated and deeply political instance of culture intervening between a subject and its representation."[39] Rather than a cultural intervention or assumption, however, Deborah Denenholz Morse argues that Trollope's rejection of colour-coding is politically nuanced in his depiction of Emily Trevelyan in *He Knew He Was Right*. Although Emily is sexually alluring and independent-minded, she is nevertheless a virtuous wife and loving mother, much-wronged by her authoritarian and increasingly mad husband. Emily, like "some girls who come from the tropics,"[40] is dark and physically strong. Deborah Morse writes of her "colour":

> Through the resistance of her rebellious spirit, and the survival of her dark-haired, "brown"-skinned body – and that brownness is insistently recalled in the book – the

dark Englishwoman is coded as a slave who rebels against her master and usurps his authority. And this is so despite the obvious fact that Emily is the white daughter of the English colonial governor of the Mandarins.[41]

Morse analyses Emily's physical darkness in the context of the highly controversial Governor Eyre affair. At the time this novel was written, Eyre was awaiting trial in London for his violent suppression of a popular uprising in Jamaica in 1865.

Trollope's use of skin and hair colour is not of a stable or permanent dye, but he is nevertheless fascinated by colouration. In his short story of 1877 "The Telegraph Girl" he takes bodily colouring to such an extreme, and to signify interiority to such a degree, that it almost seems to mock Victorian prejudices concerning skin and hair. In this story, "brownness" is valorized, but it is not the same brownness as Trollope insists upon for the glamorous Emily Trevelyan. Lucy Graham, a young woman who works in London's Telegraph Office, is "to some eyes singularly good-looking, though no one probably would have called her either pretty or handsome":

> In the first place her complexion was – brown. It was impossible to deny that her whole face was brown, as also was her hair, and generally her dress. There was a pervading brownness about her which left upon those who met her a lasting connection between Lucy Graham and that serviceable, long-enduring colour.

The passage goes on with the theme of brownness, and concludes that this is how "she regarded her own personal binding."[42] This "binding" reminds one of Didier Anzieu's description of the "skin ego" as "a containing unifying envelope for the Self; as a protective barrier for the psyche, and as a filter for exchanges and a surface for the inscription for the first traces."[43] The durability of her brown binding protects her psychologically, filtering the exchanges with the world of work and a precarious domesticity; the buffetings of those exchanges and the hardship of want are traced on her body.

Trollope had first-hand knowledge of "telegraph girls", because this new department occupied the top floor of the Post Office building where he worked. His story exhibits sympathy and admiration for these young "unprotected" women, making their own way in the city. Not only does Lucy's skin and hair colour equip her for an independent life, but her good health, strength and limbs do as well: "She stood upon her legs, – or walked upon them – as though she understood that they had been given to her for real use."[44]

Lucy's brownness is descended from Jane Eyre's brown hair, and subdued, grey dresses. Both heroines make their way in the world (both so often by walking, with limbs made for "real use"), but, as Mary Poovey has argued, they are consigned to liminal positions because their status as both middle-class and employed would seem incommensurate and even unnatural for many Victorians.[45] This liminality is a shadowy place, where women are just glimpsed at the edges of society, in quiet colours, perhaps half-hidden by the obscurity of window curtains. Such at least was the case with Jane Eyre, one of the "anathematized race" of governesses. Trollope's depiction of a working woman in his story is as sympathetic and robust as Charlotte Bronte's. In a brown study of her strength and vitality Lucy is brought out from the shadows of Victorian attitudes to the middle-class working woman.

Trollope wrote in his *Autobiography* of a "great division" in critical and popular perception between sensation and anti-sensation novels and novelists. He found this division to be a "mistake", and that a "good novel" should be both realistic and sensational, "and both in the highest degree." He provides dramatic examples from Scott, Charlotte Bronte ("the mad lady tearing the veil of the expectant bride"), Thackeray and his own Lady Mason making her "confession at the feet of Sir Peregrine Orme" in *Orley Farm*.[46] Trollope's examples make it clear that sensation is closely connected with physical sensation and proximity; with touch, movements, gestures and instincts felt in and on the body. Jenny Bourne Taylor explains that "sensation fiction was often attacked for 'preaching to the nerves' (in Henry Mansel's phrase) but Trollope often deploys similar effects". She argues that "his multi-plotted stories . . . suggest a multi-faceted reality springing from an intense sense of the significance of detail, in which emotional extremity is often generated through immediate physical response."[47] A scene from the chapter "Another Walk in the Fells" in *Can You Forgive Her?* exhibits several corporeal aspects in Trollope's writing: a detailed description of the movement, touch and alignment of his characters' bodies; skin; wounding; and an instinctive response to fear and anger felt along the nerves.

After the reading of their grandfather's will, brother and sister George and Kate Vavasor go for a "walk on the fells." George has been disinherited in favour of his sister, and on the walk he demands that she discredit the will by lying to say that her grandfather was not of sound mind. Although devoted to her brother, she refuses to tell the lie, and he becomes increasingly threatening:

> She was aware also that in refusing him she would have to encounter him in all his wrath. She set her teeth firmly together, and clenched her little fist. If a fight was necessary she would fight with him. As he looked at her closely with his sinister eyes, her love towards him was almost turned to hatred.[48]

In the course of this scene, her brother threatens to murder her, "put(ting) his hand upon her breast up near to her throat"; gets hold of her clothes, shaking her violently and repeatedly, and finally throws her furiously upon the stones, breaking her arm. In the moment before the outbreak of this violence, Kate's instincts tell her to fear:

> They were now upon the Fell side, more than three miles from the Hall; and Kate, as she looked round, saw that they were all alone. Not a cottage, – not a sign of humanity was within sight. Kate saw that it was so, and was aware that the fact pressed itself upon her as being of importance.[49]

This is an ominously "sensational" moment, in which both the character Kate and the reader pause to catch breath and to experience fear "pressed upon" the body. The bodies of Kate and George are precisely located and arranged: geographically on the fell; in their distance from each other; in their instinctive clenching of fists, set of the teeth, grasping, harming, pushing and falling. These physiological details demonstrate the extent to which "emotional extremity is often generated through immediate physical response"[50] as Kate prepares for fight or flight.

Because they are brother and sister, sexual threat is not, apparently, an issue.[51] This serves to foreground the breaking of the bond between the two, as Kate imagines it physiologically: "her blood was the same as his, and he should know that her courage was, at any rate, as high." While the threat of incest does not ostensibly fuel this scene, it is yet the case that Kate and the reader must remember that Kate's first cousin Alice, another Vavasor, had described her terror when George shook and threatened her. Alice was engaged to him at the time, but an increasing sexual repugnance for her violent cousin meant that she could not bring herself to kiss him when that is what he had demanded. She had shuddered with horror rather than pleasure at his touch.

Sexual threat, repugnance and desire are frequently represented in daringly physical terms in Trollope, and response is felt on the bodies of both women and men. Alice's response to John Grey is entirely different to that elicited from George. Just from the touch of Grey's hand, "the fibres of her body had seemed to melt within her at the touch, so that she could have fallen at his feet."[52] In *The Eustace Diamonds*, Lucinda Roanoke is driven to mental breakdown as she is pressured into marriage with a man she loathes. On the eve of her wedding she tells her aunt, "When he touches me my whole body is in agony. To be kissed by him is madness."[53] Her aunt becomes afraid that Lucinda will actually murder him on the wedding night:

> She tried to . . . realize what might in truth be the girl's action and ultimate fate when she should find herself in the power of this man whom she so hated. But had not other girls done the same thing and lived through it all, and become fat, indifferent, and fond of the world? It is only the first step that signifies.[54]

Lucinda's aunt has driven a hard bargain in the marriage market. Lucinda's "agony" at the touch of her fiancé; the shock of her madness on the wedding morning; the possibility of murder on the wedding night; the ruthlessly mercantile consideration of marital rape: these plot aspects may seem to belong to melodrama, sensation fiction or even the Gothic. Yet Trollope convinces the reader that this is all within the provenance of the realist novel, and the realities of Victorian society.[55]

From the most familiar and "civilized" of English social rituals can emerge behaviour and bodily responses that verge on the animalistic. The ferocious competition in the marriage market could mean that the events of the London season – the balls, "at homes", riding to be seen in Hyde Park – only thinly veil a drive to compete and to survive worthy of Darwin's observation. The competition in the hunting field between Lucinda and Lizzie in *The Eustace Diamonds* results in breakneck, dangerous tumbles into ditches. In *Can You Forgive Her?* a relentless fox hunt is subtly juxtaposed with Lady Monk's ball. The juxtaposition is effected through the association of human and equine bodies. In the Edgehill hunt, a reckless Burgo Fitzgerald drives his horse so hard over the day that he kills him, forcing the exhausted animal over a "huge ditch and boundary bank":

> The animal . . . fell headlong into the ditch at the other side, a confused mass of head, limbs and body. His career was at an end, and he had broken his heart! . . . His master's ignorance had killed him.[56]

This "confused mass of head, limbs and body" is a disturbing image in Trollope's novels because he is usually very precise – even in descriptions of violence or lovemaking – about how bodies are arranged and ordered. The image looms large over a scene two volumes later in the novel, at Lady Monk's party. Instigated by political and personal revenge, Lady Monk has paid Burgo to elope with the married Lady Glencora. Glencora still loves him and is vulnerable:

> The waltzers went on till they were stopped by want of breath. "I am so much out of practice," said Lady Glencora; "I didn't think – I should have been able – to dance at all." Then she put up her face, and slightly opened her mouth, and stretched her nostrils, – as ladies do as well as horses when the running has been severe and they want air.[57]

Pamela Gilbert writes that in this period "Women's bodies . . . were the weak link in the social body; closer to nature and the animal, women were thought to be more susceptible to sensory impression, leading them to be more easily corrupted." She cites Norbert Elias as arguing that "the modern body emerges as a body concerned with closure and regulation of its openings."[58] Glencora's mouth, nostrils and pores are opened by the exercise of dancing and her body is open to Burgo's touch. While there is sympathy for the lovers, the risk is clear: Burgo will drive her to destruction and "break her heart" as he did when he killed his horse.[59] In her study of "horses and sexual/social dominance" in Victorian literature, Elsie Michie writes that in provincial and rural novels by Eliot, Hardy and Gaskell, fine horses are ridden by "men newly enriched by the commercial wealth" that was "transforming" and socially disrupting the countryside. These men "display a potential to dominate in relation to sexually magnetic women and their ability to ride and control high-spirited horses."[60] This dominance is linked to a seemingly inevitable social Darwinism: the commercial leaders will be those who are fittest to survive and prosper. Michie's views are supported here in a negative case: Burgo, who is from a noble family, but weak and penniless, drives his horse, that "poor noble beast",[61] to destruction: he is one of an effete aristocracy whose failure to survive economically and to carry on his line (ultimately he fails to be sexually selected when Glencora parts from him) is represented by his negligent treatment of his horse, and of that other noble creature, Lady Glencora. Perhaps the case of Burgo is not so simple, however: he may be negligent and socially doomed but his act of disinterested kindness in providing a meal for a malnourished prostitute is the gentlest act of the novel. It does not "produce" anything, or contribute much to the gross national product, but it is kind.

Glencora's desiring body responds to Burgo in the dance; here and later, when she exchanges a passionate extramarital kiss, she has "got out of the grooves" of proper womanhood and of the Victorian domestic novel. "Getting out of the grooves" is one of the things that Lord Lufton says he likes about Lucy Robarts (although he is probably not thinking so much of extramarital passion). But he describes it again to Lucy in spatial terms: "you go along by yourself, guiding your own footsteps; not carried hither and thither, just as your grandmother's old tramway may chance to take you."[62]

Trollope's heroes and heroines move through space and over time, accreting personal, social and historical change which is felt and marked on their changing, travelling and responsive bodies. In this "guiding of their own footsteps" they are figures for Mikhail Bakhtin's chronotope. More specifically they are aligned with "the last, realistic type of novel of emergence" to which Bakhtin devotes himself in his incomplete book on the *bildungsroman*. Bakhtin writes,

> human emergence is no longer man's own private affair. He emerges *along with the world* and he reflects the historical emergence of the world itself. He is no longer within an epoch, but on the border between two epochs, at the transition point from one to the other. This transition is accomplished in him and through him.[63]

The transition is accomplished chronotopically, through time and space, and so often in Trollope's writing it is the heroine rather more than the hero who is moving "out of the grooves," the independence of her bodily movement registering a transition between historical epochs. Lucy Robarts may declare to Lord Lufton that rather than getting out of the grooves, perhaps, "my grandmother's old tramway will be the safest and best after all."[64] But she will continue to make her own way. In *The Way We Live Now*, Hetta Carbury leaves the "tramway" of tradition to take the London underground: "That afternoon Hetta trusted herself all alone to the mysteries of the Marylebone underground railway, and emerged with accuracy at King's Cross. She had studied her geography, and she walked from thence to Islington."[65]

Hetta "emerges" historically as one of the first generation of travellers to use the London underground. "Unprotected" and in Islington, she is off the beaten track, and is also going to meet another woman who has left the path in other ways: she is meeting the American ex-lover of her fiancé, a woman dismissed by one of the more conservative characters in the novel, because that relationship began on a *train*.

These women guide themselves through cities and the wider world, their bodies "unprotected" because they are emerging in a transition between two epochs. One of the features of this transition is the forging of new ways of experiencing the body in its context of the material and technological world (the street, trains, the Underground and the telegraph office), and in its context of human relations (touch, the expression of desire and sexuality). These women are not examples of the *flaneuse*, nor are they walking with Mrs Dalloway, nor are they "New Women". Trollope instead describes new women who are less circumscribed by the distancing hoops of the crinoline, who are freer in their movements and independence, and he describes also new men who emerge in the period to meet and respond to these women in his novels of emergence. These changes are felt "within the figure and frame and clothes and cuticle, within the bones and flesh of many of us."[66]

Notes

1 Anthony Trollope, *The Small House at Allington* (Oxford: Oxford University Press, 2015), Chapter 40.
2 Anthony Trollope, *Framley Parsonage* (Oxford: Oxford University Press, 1980), pp. 316–317. Chapter 26.
3 Elaine Scarry, "Work and the Body in Hardy and Other Nineteenth-Century Novelists," *Representations*, Vol. 3 (Summer 1983): p. 94. For further reading on the marking of landscape and body, see Sophie Gilmartin and Rod Mengham, *Thomas Hardy's Shorter Fiction: A Critical Study* (Edinburgh: Edinburgh University Press, 2007, 2016), esp. Chapter 1.
4 Trollope, *Framley Parsonage*, p. 195. Chapter 16.
5 Henry James, "Anthony Trollope" in *Partial Portraits* (London: 1888; Reprinted 1894), p. 121.
6 Anthony Trollope, *An Autobiography*, ed. with an introduction by David Skilton (London: Penguin Classics, 1996), p. 147. Chapter 12.
7 William Cohen, *Embodied: Victorian Literature and the Senses* (Minneapolis: University of Minnesota Press, 2009), p. 6.
8 Trollope, *Framley Parsonage*, p. 318. Chapter 26.
9 Cohen, *Embodied*, p. 74.
10 Ibid., p. 195. Chapter 16.
11 Anthony Trollope, *The Eustace Diamonds* (London: Penguin Classics, 1986), p. 507. Chapter 52.
12 Anthony Trollope, "On the Banks of the Jordan" in *Anthony Trollope: The Complete Short Stories*, vol. 3, *Tourists and Colonials*, ed. Betty Breyer (London: William Pickering, 1991), p. 115.
13 Cohen, *Embodied*, p. 84.
14 Ibid., p. 85.
15 Elaine Freedgood, review of William Cohen's *Embodied: Victorian Literature and the Senses*, *Nineteenth-Century Literature*, Vol. 65, No. 1 (Berkeley: University of California Press, June 2010), p. 110.
16 Mark Forrester, "Redressing the Empire: Anthony Trollope and British Gender Anxiety in 'The Banks of the Jordan'", Chapter 6 in *Imperial Desire: Dissident Sexualities and Colonial Literature*, ed. Philip Holden and Richard R. Ruppel (Minneapolis: University of Minnesota Press, 2003), p. 122.
17 Anthony Trollope, "The Turkish Bath" in *Anthony Trollope: The Complete Short Stories*, vol. 2, *Editors and Writers*, ed. with an introduction by Betty Breyer (London: William Pickering, 1990), p. 2.
18 Catherine Spooner, "Masculinity, Insanity, and Clothing in Trollope's 'The Turkish Bath'", Chapter 4 in *Bodies and Things in Nineteenth-Century Literature and Culture*, ed. Katharina Boehm (Houndmills: Palgrave Macmillan, 2012), p. 67.
19 Spooner, p. 78.
20 Ibid., p. 81.
21 Mark W. Turner, *Trollope and the Magazines: Gendered Issues in Mid-Victorian Britain* (Basingstoke: Macmillan Press, 2000), p. 201. In a collection entitled *An Editor's Tales* Trollope published in May 1870 various stories that had appeared in the periodical *St Paul's Magazine* between October 1869 and May 1870 (Turner, p. 195).
22 Pamela K. Gilbert, "Popular Beliefs and the Body: 'A Nation of Good Animals'", Chapter 5 in *A Cultural History of the Human Body in the Age of Empire*, ed. Michael Sappol and Stephen P. Rice (London: Bloomsbury, 2010; Reprinted 2014), p. 138. Pamela Gilbert is currently working on a book on skin.
23 John Potvin, "Vapour and Steam: The Victorian Turkish Bath, Homosocial Health, and Male Bodies on Display", *Journal of Design History*, Vol. 18, No. 4 (Winter 2005), pp. 319–33.

24 Sophie Gilmartin, "Introduction" to Anthony Trollope, *The Last Chronicle of Barset* (London: Penguin Classics, 2002).
25 Margaret Markwick, *New Men in Trollope's Novels: Rewriting the Victorian Male* (London: Ashgate, 2007).
26 Both Margaret Markwick and Deborah Denenholz Morse note that Victor Shklovsky's concept of defamilarization in art (propounded in his *"Art as Technique"* in 1917), while often applied to the work of Henry James, is also a strong feature of Anthony Trollope's writing. See, for example, Deborah Denenholz Morse, *Reforming Trollope: Race, Gender and Englishness in the Novels of Anthony Trollope* (Farnham: Ashgate, 2013), p. 10, and Markwick, *New Men*, p. 64.
27 Trollope, *An Autobiography*, p. 233. Chapter 20.
28 Kay Heath discusses aging in many of Trollope's novels in her book *Aging by the Book: The Emergence of Midlife in Victorian Britain* (Albany: SUNY Press, 2009). See her chapter on "Trollope and Aging" in this volume.
29 Trollope, *The Small House at Allington*, p. 170. Chapter 16.
30 Deborah Denenholz Morse writes of this encounter that it is "the closest that Adolphus Crosbie comes to touching the sacred", but "its effect is only momentary." *Reforming Trollope*, p. 34.
31 Margaret Markwick, *Trollope and Women* (London: The Hambledon Press, 1997), p. 81.
32 Deborah Denenholz Morse, *Women in Trollope's Palliser Novels* (Ann Arbor: UMI Research Press, 1987), pp. 16–17 and 24.
33 Anthony Trollope, *Can You Forgive Her?* (Oxford: Oxford University Press, 1991), Chapter 67.
34 Anthony Trollope, *The Way We Live Now*, Chapters 46, 47 and 97.
35 Anthony Trollope, *He Knew He Was Right* (Oxford: Oxford University Press, 1998), p. 441. Chapter 47.
36 Galia Ofek, *Representations of Hair in Victorian Literature and Culture* (Farnham: Ashgate, 2009), p. 123.
37 Trollope, *The Eustace Diamonds*, p. 55. Chapter 2.
38 Ibid., p. 732. Chapter 76.
39 Helena Michie, *The Flesh Made Word: Female Figures and Women's Bodies* (New York: Oxford University Press, 1987), p. 84.
40 Trollope, *He Knew He Was Right*, p. 7. Chapter 1.
41 Deborah Denenholz Morse, "'Some Girls Who Come from the Tropics': Gender, Race and Imperialism in Anthony Trollope's *He Knew He Was Right*" Chapter 5 in *The Politics of Gender in Anthony Trollope's Novels*, ed. Margaret Markwick, Deborah Denenholz Morse and Regenia Gagnier (Farnham: Ashgate, 2009), p. 85.
42 Anthony Trollope, "The Telegraph Girl" in *Anthony Trollope: The Complete Short Stories*, vol. 4, *Courtship and Marriage* (London: Omnium for The Trollope Society), p. 71.
43 Didier Anzieu, *The Skin Ego*, trans. Chris Turner (New Haven: Yale University Press, 1989) p. 98. William Cohen discusses Anzieu's ideas at more length in his chapter on Trollope in *Embodied*. Steven Connor's *The Book of Skin* (Ithaca: Cornell University Press, 2004) explores skin in Western culture, and also considers Anzieu's work.
44 Trollope, "The Telegraph Girl", p. 72.
45 Mary Poovey, *Uneven Developments: The Ideological Work of Gender in Mid-Victorian England* (Chicago: University of Chicago Press, 1988). See esp. Chapter 5.
46 Trollope, *An Autobiography*, p. 146. Chapter 12.
47 Jenny Bourne Taylor, "Trollope and the Sensation Novel" Chapter 7 in *The Cambridge Companion to Anthony Trollope*, ed. Carolyn Dever and Lisa Niles (Cambridge: Cambridge University Press, 2011), p. 88.
48 Trollope, *Can You Forgive Her?*, vol. 2, p. 164. Chapter 56.
49 Ibid.
50 Taylor, p. 88.
51 However, James Kincaid argues that Kate's self-abnegation is driven by a guilty, sexualized love for her brother (James Kincaid, *The Novels of Anthony Trollope* [Oxford: Clarendon Press, 1977], p. 186). Morse agrees and discusses the theme of self-sacrifice in Trollope's treatment of both Kate and Alice Vavasor (*Women in Trollope's Palliser Novels*, pp. 35–8). Sharon Marcus, alternatively, reads an earlier scene on the fells between Kate and Alice as a marriage proposal and acceptance between Kate and Alice, with Alice more as wife than surrogate to her brother (Sharon Marcus, *Between Women: Friendship, Desire and Marriage in Victorian England* [Princeton: Princeton University Press, 2007], pp. 236–9). Marcus's attention to Kate's physicality and her imitation of the male gestures of proposal is compelling.
52 Trollope, *Can You Forgive Her?*, vol. 1, p. 383. Chapter 37.
53 Trollope, *The Eustace Diamonds*, p. 670. Chapter 69.
54 Ibid., p. 671. Chapter 69.

55 Five years after the publication of *The Eustace Diamonds*, George Eliot also wrote, in *Daniel Deronda*, of a woman's physical fear and repulsion of her husband and how it brought her to the brink of madness.
56 Trollope, *Can You Forgive Her?* vol. 1, p. 186. Chapter 17.
57 Ibid., vol. 2, p. 102. Chapter 49.
58 Gilbert, p. 129.
59 George Levine noted the horse imagery in these scenes, in "Can You Forgive Him?: Trollope's *Can You Forgive Her?* and the Myth of Realism," *Victorian Studies* (18 [1974–5]), p. 28. Morse compares Burgo's careless treatment of his horse and of Glencora to that of Vronsky's treatment of his highly bred horse and mistress in Tolstoy's *Anna Karenina* (Morse, *Women in Trollope's Palliser Novels*, p. 11–12).
60 Elsie B. Michie, "Horses and Sexual/Social Dominance", Chapter 8 in *Victorian Animal Dreams: Representations of Animals in Victorian Literature and Culture*, ed. Deborah Denenholz Morse and Martin Danahay (London: Ashgate, 2007), p. 145.
61 Trollope, *Can You Forgive Her?*, vol. 1, p. 186. Chapter 17. Harriet Ritvo writes that "Popular natural history [in the Victorian period] traditionally characterized the horse as 'noble,' and sometimes as nobler than the class of humans generally charged with its care." Harriet Ritvo, *The Animal Estate: The English and Other Creatures in the Victorian Age* (Cambridge, MA: Harvard University Press, 1987), p. 19.
62 Trollope, *Framley Parsonage*, p. 194. Chapter 16.
63 M. M. Bakhtin, "The *Bildungsroman* and Its Significance in the History of Realism (Toward a Historical Typology of the Novel)" in *Speech Genres and Other Late Essays*, trans. Vern W. McGee; ed. Caryl Emerson and Michael Holquist (Austin: University of Texas Press, 1986), p. 23.
64 Trollope, *Framley Parsonage*, p. 194. Chapter 16.
65 Trollope, *The Way We Live Now* (Oxford: Oxford University Press, 1982), vol. 2, p. 385. Chapter 91.
66 Trollope, *The Eustace Diamonds*, p. 199. Chapter 18.

Works cited

Anzieu, Didier. *The Skin Ego*. Trans. Chris Turner. New Haven: Yale University Press, 1989.
Bakhtin, M. M. "The *Bildungsroman* and Its Significance in the History of Realism (Toward a Historical Typology of the Novel)." *Speech Genres and Other Late Essays*. Trans. Vern W. McGee. Ed. Caryl Emerson and Michael Holquist. Austin: University of Texas Press, 1986.
Cohen, William. *Embodied: Victorian Literature and the Senses*. Minneapolis: University of Minnesota Press, 2009.
Connor, Steven. *The Book of Skin*. Ithaca: Cornell University Press, 2004.
Forrester, Mark. "Redressing the Empire: Anthony Trollope and British Gender Anxiety in 'The Banks of the Jordan.'" Chapter 6 in *Imperial Desire: Dissident Sexualities and Colonial Literature*. Ed. Philip Holden and Richard R. Ruppel. Minneapolis: University of Minneapolis Press, 2003.
Freedgood, Elaine. "Review of William Cohen's *Embodied: Victorian Literature and the Senses*. *Nineteenth-Century Literature*." Vol. 65, No. 1 (June 2010), pp. 108–11.
Gilbert, Pamela K. "Popular Beliefs and the Body: 'A Nation of Good Animals.'" Chapter 5 in *A Cultural History of the Human Body in the Age of Empire*. Ed. Michael Sappol and Stephen P. Rice. London: Bloomsbury, 2010; Reprinted 2014.
Gilmartin, Sophie. "'Introduction' to Anthony Trollope." *The Last Chronicle of Barset*. London: Penguin Classics, 2002.
Gilmartin, Sophie, and Rod Mengham. *Thomas Hardy's Shorter Fiction: A Critical Study*. Edinburgh: Edinburgh University Press, 2007.
Heath, Kay. *Aging by the Book: The Emergence of Midlife in Victorian Britain*. Albany: SUNY Press, 2009.
James, Henry. "Anthony Trollope." *Partial Portraits*. London: Macmillan, 1888; Reprinted 1894.
Kincaid, James. *The Novels of Anthony Trollope*. Oxford: Clarendon Press, 1977.
Levine, George. "Can You Forgive Him?: Trollope's *Can You Forgive Her?* and the Myth of Realism." *Victorian Studies*, Vol. 18 (1974–5), pp. 5–30.
Marcus, Sharon. *Between Women: Friendship, Desire and Marriage in Victorian England*. Princeton: Princeton University Press, 2007.
Markwick, Margaret. *New Men in Trollope's Novels: Rewriting the Victorian Male*. London: Ashgate, 2007.
———. *Trollope and Women*. London: Hambledon Press, 1997.
Michie, Elsie B. "Horses and Sexual/Social Dominance." Chapter 8 in *Victorian Animal Dreams: Representations of Animals in Victorian Literature and Culture*. Ed. Deborah Denenholz Morse and Martin Danahay. London: Ashgate, 2007.

Michie, Helena. *The Flesh Made Word: Female Figures and Women's Bodies.* New York: Oxford University Press, 1987.

Morse, Deborah Denenholz. *Reforming Trollope: Race, Gender and Englishness in the Novels of Anthony Trollope.* Farnham: Ashgate, 2013.

———. "'Some Girls Who Come from the Tropics': Gender, Race and Imperialism in Anthony Trollope's *He Knew He Was Right.*" Chapter 5 in *The Politics of Gender in Anthony Trollope's Novels.* Ed. Margaret Markwick, Deborah Denenholz Morse and Regenia Gagnier. Farnham: Ashgate, 2009.

———. *Women in Trollope's Palliser Novels.* Ann Arbor: UMI Research Press, 1987.

Ofek, Galia. *Representations of Hair in Victorian Literature and Culture.* Farnham: Ashgate, 2009.

Poovey, Mary. *Uneven Developments: The Ideological Work of Gender in Mid-Victorian England.* Chicago: University of Chicago Press, 1988.

Potvin, John. "The Victorian Turkish Bath, Homosocial Health, and Male Bodies on Display." *Journal of Design History,* Vol. 18, No. 4 (Winter 2005), pp. 319–33.

Ritvo, Harriet. *The Animal Estate: The English and Other Creatures in the Victorian Age.* Cambridge, MA: Harvard University Press, 1987.

Scarry, Elaine. "Work and the Body in Hardy and Other Nineteenth-Century Novelists." *Representations,* Vol. 3 (Summer 1983), pp. 90–123.

Spooner, Catherine. "Masculinity, Insanity, and Clothing in Trollope's 'The Turkish Bath.'" Chapter 4 in *Bodies and Things in Nineteenth-Century Literature and Culture.* Ed. Katharina Boehm. Houndmills: Palgrave Macmillan, 2012.

Trollope, Anthony. *An Autobiography.* London: Penguin Classics, 1996.

———. *Can You Forgive Her?.* Oxford: Oxford University Press, 1991.

———. *The Eustace Diamonds.* London: Penguin Classics, 1986.

———. *Framley Parsonage.* Oxford: Oxford University Press, 1980.

———. *He Knew He Was Right.* Oxford: Oxford University Press, 1998.

———. "On the Banks of the Jordan", in *Anthony Trollope: The Complete Short Stories.* Vol. 3, *Tourists and Colonials.* London: William Pickering, 1991.

———. *The Small House at Allington.* Oxford: Oxford University Press, 2015.

———. "The Turkish Bath", in *Anthony Trollope: The Complete Short Stories.* Vol. 2, *Editors and Writers.* London: William Pickering, 1990.

———. *The Way We Live Now.* Oxford: Oxford University Press, 1982.

Turner, Mark W. *Trollope and the Magazines: Gendered Issues in Mid-Victorian Britain.* Basingstoke: Macmillan Press, 2000.

PART III
Critical theory

10
TROLLOPE'S TRAGEDY

James Kincaid

Somebody (N. John Hall) pointed out to me that this chapter's title is susceptible to multiple (well, two) interpretations. I knew that all along, of course, and didn't need buttinski Hall pointing it out. My title artfully suggests that Trollope can indeed be read as a tragic novelist and that it is, oh yes, a tragedy that he so seldom is.[1]

By "tragedy," of course I refer not to some set of formal properties in the novels but to a way of reading. Lots of genre critics – even old standards, such as E. D. Hirsch and Wayne Booth – have conceded that genre is really only a floating "contract," which means it is what you and I make it. Here's the clincher: Aristotle, who knew, said tragedy was not so much a matter of plot and character as of audience response: tragedy is whatever evokes a catharsis of pity and fear. We have become lazy and imagine that such a reaction can come about only with *King Lear* or *Hedda Gabbler*, but of course we cannot prescribe responses or ways of reading. *Huckleberry Finn*, *Lady Windermere's Fan*, the latest memo from the dean can all be read and felt as tragic – which simply means they *are* tragic. No such thing as a misreading, naturally, as we all know, and that's very good news for some of us and also keeps issues of emphasis, form, and meaning completely open, afloat, and flexible. Tragedy, I repeat, is not a formal property but a question of how we read, construct.

I have to admit that there are many signals we might attend to in Trollope that seem to be designed to distance him from tragic ambition, to let us know that we must not expect characters who are elevated beyond other men, plots featuring catastrophic, sacrificial slaughter, and sublimity generally. "Who," he asks in his essay on Hawthorne, "would not sooner be Prometheus than a yesterday's tipsy man with this morning's sick-headache?"[2] And his narrator may often seem to treat with suspicion characters who have drawn the pattern for their lives from Sophocles or Aeschylus.

But anything "inside" a Trollope novel, as I say, is susceptible to any construction to which we might be drawn, so that's not it. I suggest that our inability to read Trollope's tragedy is due to simple, downhome laziness, as we fiddle around, we critics and me especially, inside a set of parameters drawn up by a century and a half of commentators and received by us gratefully, birds in the nest with beaks agape.

To say, as I have often done, that Trollope worked within the broad tradition of the low-mimetic comedy of manners, then, is to say only that I could not find a way to read him outside that tradition – until now. But what happens when we think of the forms of tragedy, late nineteenth-century forms particularly, and the way we might experience Trollope's work? We won't get a more accurate view, of course, but there's no such thing anyhow, so we might as well have fun. And what could be more fun than a three-way with old Tony Trollope, you, and the god Dionysus?

The clearest experiences of early modern tragic expression can probably be found in opera: in Strauss, late Verdi, Puccini, and Wagner. But you can find it anywhere, provided you are equipped with the proper lenses: try Meredith's tragic poem "Modern Love," *Jude the Obscure*, *Kim*, Stevenson's *Kidnapped*, Stoker's *Dracula*, the poems of Wilde, Dowson, Browning (both of them), or *The Pirates of Penzance*. As Bill Murray chants expressively in *Meatballs* (another powerful tragedy), "It just doesn't matter." "So, what is this Victorian/Edwardian view of tragedy?" you might be asking.

My space (drat it) is limited, so I'll be brief (suggesting that if Professor Morse gave me the room I deserve, I could go on for – oh, ever so long). Think of Schopenhauer, Nietzsche, and Wagner's Ring Cycle. Nietzsche is most familiar, so let's go there. According to him, King Midas captured the demon Silenus and forced him to answer *the* central question: what is the best and most desirable thing for human kind. Silenus finally responded, "Miserable ephemeral race, why force me to speak what it would be much more fruitful for you never to hear? The best of all things is something entirely outside your grasp: not to be born, not to be, to be nothing. But the second best thing for you is to die soon."[3] This is the core wisdom for us: it really is better not to be.

But not being or dying soon is not the only alternative offered by our new theorists of tragedy. There is also ecstasy, intoxication, love, sex, compassion, and art. Almost a century before the surrealists, Walter Pater, starting from similar premises about the absence of assurances – no permanences, no stable destinations – suggested we could find ways to expand moments and, with them, our minds and hearts. It's all, Pater says, a whirlpool – we are always vanishing and in the midst of vanishings, strangely and perpetually weaving and unweaving ourselves, reinventing our lives:

> Every moment some form grows perfect in hand or face; some tone on the hills or the sea is choicer than the rest; some mood of passion or insight or intellectual excitement is irresistibly real and attractive to us, – for that moment only. Not the fruit of experience, but experience itself, is the end. A counted number of pulses only is given to us of a variegated, dramatic life. How may we see in them all that is to be seen in them by the finest senses? How shall we pass most swiftly from point to point, and be present always at the focus where the greatest number of vital forces unite in their purest energy? To burn always with this hard, gem-like flame, to maintain this ecstasy, is success in life.[4]

If it's not the fruits of experience but experience itself that matters, what might we encounter when we hand ourselves over to tragic experience, unguarded by classroom notions of what we might learn from tragedy? We learn nothing from tragedy, from any art – they offer no lessons; they offer being – they are the experience that they allow. Most of us have picked up lots of formulae about tragedy centered on ideas of character, but for Trollope and the writers we are construing this way, there are really no persons in tragedy anyhow – just forces, unspeakable forces. There seem to be people there and plots; but Nietzsche tells us these are just screens, Apollonian illusions, that make bearable to us, in our cowardly state, the heart of all tragedy – the merging, dissolving, intoxicating god Dionysus, who invites or compels us into a powerful oneness. The illusion that we are fundamentally self-contained, alone with our isolated being, is stripped away and we are left with what? On one hand the possibility of a sublime union with everything – all things – a universal oneness.

There's Trollope for you. And if it doesn't sound like your Trollope, well then, adjust.

True, we haven't been taught to couple Trollope and Nietzsche, and it might be asking a bit much to imagine transferring to the Barsetshire Chronicles our experience of "Gotterdammerung": Brunhilde plunging with the Ring through the burning ruins of Walhalla and into the waters of the Rhine, bringing a healing and happy death to all. But there's nothing to be lost – and ever so much profit to be had – in construing our experience with so many of Trollope's novels and their energies in just that way. For one thing, there's nothing holding us back, nothing determinate in the words on the pages: the novel and its force are within us (and our cultural training), so why block the voice of Silenus, issuing from within us and our world and so many in Trollope: think of Josiah Crawley, Louis Trevelyan, Lady Laura Kennedy, Augustus Melmotte, Mrs. Proudie, the Duke of Omnium, and all your other favorites.

Or, if Nietzsche doesn't work for you, think of related Victorian art forms and experiences that might give us access to Trollope's tragic power: the dramatic monologue, for instance. Ever since Robert Langbaum instructed us long ago on a way to throw ourselves into Browning's Duke of Ferrara and other such remarkable beings,[5] losing ourselves in their "songs" and leaving behind all precautionary contextual structures, such as moral codes and conventional judgments, we have been able to find ways to make the tension between "sympathy" and "judgment" tilt decidedly toward an often unsettling participation with forms of being we have no way of controlling. So why not tune in to Scatcherd's heroic and tragic song, to John Scarborough's, to Kate O'Hara's in *An Eye for an Eye*, to so many in *Is He Popenjoy?* and *The Fixed Period*, to Kate Vavasor's, and on and on.

If that doesn't suit, think on George Eliot's argument, right at the heart of *Middlemarch*, that we are surrounded by "ordinary tragedy" so deep and so common that we must desensitize ourselves to it, lest we plunge into the Dionysian abyss, "that roar which lies on the other side of silence." If we allowed ourselves to glimpse the terrible suffering of the woman next door, our office-mate, the kids down the hall, the postman and the waitress, we could not bear it. Eliot is here giving voice to a tragic experience that is not new but that erupts throughout the nineteenth century, an internalized nightmare that never issues in grand events or forms itself into the old plot, the fall of a great man. Dorothea Brooke weeping on her honeymoon is not, Eliot's narrator bitingly says, all that unusual, "and we do not expect people to be deeply moved by what is not unusual."[6]

But one reason great novels like those of Trollope exist is precisely to push us into the roar on the other side of silence, where we are unprotected and lost, never finding the cleansing of cathartic resolution, the release of pity and fear. Those emotions are aroused, certainly, but are held there, made a part of us to deal with as best we can – never very well.

I think anyone willing to hang on this long and ready to buy the argument will have no trouble supplying examples. But I have a little room remaining in my allotment – "2,580 words, Kincaid, and not a comma more!" – so will have some fun myself.

The Rev. Josiah Crawley knows very well he has it within him to play out the tragic drama the world has set up for him, and he even runs the conventional formulae in his head: "Great power reduced to impotence, great glory to misery, by the hand of Fate, – Necessity, as the Greeks called her".[7] He enfolds himself in his misery, one might say, but that misery was brought on him by what we might regard as an exalted position: his mind was on God and his works here on earth, not on a silly banker's check. Crawley pulls us into the very heart of his being by refusing to enter into any other formula, any other way of viewing things. "It's dogged as does it," says his friend Giles Hoggett, and he is right, in terms of the grand tragedy to which Crawley is loyal.[8]

Significantly, Crawley's doggedness is echoed by that of Lily Dale, who also remains fixed on a plot that finds little response in the world around her. Like Crawley, she can be – and is, unhappily – regarded as simply perverse, but we are free to respond to her very differently: as one who does not shrink from the horror at the center of being. She and Crawley echo one another, like the reinforcing subplots in the Jacobean drama Trollope so loved.

Much like Wotan in Wagner's Ring Cycle, Crawley and Lily can never find a tragic plot, are isolated completely from their worlds. But both are true to their initial, impossible vision of heroism and both embrace the wisdom of Silenus. True, if you insist, that the plot of *The Last Chronicle of Barset* pulls Crawley (though not Lily) back into some kind of feeble and conventional comedy – or seems to do so – but plots, as Trollope very well knew, are insignificant.

And then there's Phineas Finn, the charming and lucky Irishman who meets with admiration and deep friendship wherever he turns, winning elections and hearts all over the place – most importantly, the confidence of his party and the loyalty of trusted allies. Only there is, he discovers, no such loyalty – anywhere. The Duke of St. Bungay, a wisdom figure if there ever was one, speaks the bleak truth: "all loyalty must be built on the basis of self-advantage".[9] Finn sees what really is on the other side of silence and takes us with him. Even the trial that clears him has nothing to do with him, no connection to guilt or innocence. The world he lives in operates without meaning or cause; all is empty and purposeless. Even Madame Max's warming goodness seems simply incoherent, floating without anchor in this vacant space.

But it is not always thus. Phineas suffers by being alien in his world, whereas Melmotte[10] is murdered because he is all too central, sees with absolute clarity what is going on and sets himself to play a part perfectly in accord with the prevailing climate. Melmotte knows that the world of power runs on illusion, that money itself is nothing but fakery and tawdry dreams trading hands.

He sees clearly, just as Phineas did not: and it matters not at all. Like Sir Roger Scatcherd in *Doctor Thorne*, Melmotte, imagining himself self-sufficient and the center of the enormous energy erupting, is himself only a creature of that energy, swallowed up in the purposeless power, empty at the core.

Melmotte tells his board of directors that "it" is the greatest thing of the century, and he is right. Only there is no "it" beyond a blind, nihilistic force. There is no Mexican railroad, no substance anywhere, and the financial giant controlling this bubble is both the heart of a consuming power and a mere leaf blown by a great wind, destroying small men and large in its rage. In the end, Melmotte is no superman but an illustration of the tragic illusion of selfhood. His is not a titanic fall but an ordinary tragedy, the way we live now. Being inside Melmotte is indeed hearing the grass grow and the squirrel's heartbeat.

One last thing before the hook comes out and I'm off the stage. Over and over, Trollope surrounds his tragic energies with a comic plot that we may, if we like, attend to and even take into ourselves as dominant. Sure. But we've done that for over a century now, regarding Crawley as cured, Phineas as on the mend, even the lonely Duke of Omnium as swept up in the glory of his children's marriages. But the duke is not swept up: at the very end, at the altar steps, he is consumed by waves of agony, brought on by "all that he had suffered".[11]

We've spent our spring break vacation with condescending and trivial forms of comedy. Maybe we can now go back to sporting with Dionysus.

Notes

1 I say "seldom" because I don't want to go to the bother of finding out for sure whether anyone has read him as a tragedian in the way I mean. And perhaps this is the place to say that if you've come expecting solid scholarly references in the form of footnotes, then you've hit the wrong shop. I've been in this game

for over five decades and have never yet found anything useful in a footnote: of course I am not a scholar, so perhaps I have missed something.
2 Trollope, "Hawthorne," 213.
3 Nietzsche, 23.
4 Pater, 236.
5 Langbaum, passim.
6 Eliot, 226 (both quotations).
7 Trollope, *Last Chronicle of Barset*, 62.
8 Ibid., 61.
9 Trollope, *Phineas Redux*, 5.
10 Trollope, *The Way We Live Now*.
11 Trollope, *The Duke's Children*, 80.

Works Cited

Eliot, George. *Middlemarch*. 1871–2. London: Penguin Books, 1965.
Langbaum, Robert. "Analysis of Robert Browning's 'My Last Duchess.'" *The Poetry of Experience*. New York: Random House, 1957.
Nietzsche, Friedrich. *The Birth of Tragedy and Other Writings*. Eds. Raymond Geuss and Ronald Speirs, trans. Ronald Speirs. Cambridge: Cambridge UP, 1999.
Pater, Walter. *The Renaissance: Studies in Art and Poetry*. London: Macmillan, 1910.
Trollope, Anthony. *The Duke's Children*. Oxford: Oxford UP, 1991.
———. "The Genius of Nathaniel Hawthorne." *North American Review*. 274, Sept. 1879. 203–22.
———. *The Last Chronicle of Barset*. Oxford: Oxford UP, 1984.
———. *Phineas Redux*. Oxford: Oxford UP, 1983.
———. *The Way We Live Now*. Oxford: Oxford UP, 1986.

11

"AS A MATTER OF COURSE"

Trollope's ordinary realism

Jonathan Farina

"The novels went on, of course."

(Autobiography 28)

Commonplace, ordinary, everyday: affirmations of a remarkable realism have been a perfunctory refrain in Trollope criticism since it began. Laudatory reviews appraise the unaffected honesty, fidelity, and observation manifest in his "exceedingly truthful" fictions:[1] the *Saturday Review* appreciates his "unerring truth, tact, and liveliness";[2] the *Examiner* characteristically appreciates his prosy "literalness."[3] The derogatory vein of critique meanwhile regrets Trollope's lack of striking originality: the *Westminster Review* snubs his "homely and prosaic . . . ordinary level of humdrum humanity";[4] and Thomas Carlyle more derisively declares him "irredeemably imbedded in the commonplace, and grown fat upon it" (Hall *Trollope: A Biography*, 95). Thus, while Trollope's acclaimed everydayness has evidenced his unpretentious sincerity and exacting mimesis, it has likewise belied the very fictionality of his work, as if he lacked the creativity to produce the definitive gap between reality and representation, as if his fictions were artless facts. If critics have routinely found Trollope's novels pleasurable, they have done so even as they have denied them style, depth, and originality.

Of course Trollope embraced this ambivalent distinction: he modestly claimed, "A novel should give a picture of common life enlivened with humor and sweetened by pathos"; he conceded the simplicity of his plots; and he declaimed against investing more attention to the beauty of language than to its effortless purport (*Auto* ch. 7, 12). In disavowing "genius" and the "construction" of fashionable sensation plots, he thus characterized himself – like his fictional personages – according to the realist convention of mixed or, as he calls it, "dual" character (*Auto* ch. 7, 12; *ED* ch. 18). Most of Trollope's characters exhibit conflicting propensities and propinquities.[5] The critical tradition reproduces this ambivalence in its insistence on Trollope's ordinariness and in turn demonstrates its own originality by affecting to compound the ordinariness. To wit: parodying Henry James's influential claim that Trollope's "inestimable merit was a complete appreciation of the usual" (James 100–1), D. A. Miller quips that his own critique – a Foucauldian account of how mixed characters internalize social conflict and discipline – recapitulates "the usual appreciation of his appreciation of the usual" (Miller 107). To an extent, recapitulation with deviations underwrites all scholarship, but the pattern is particularly pronounced in Trollope criticism and the question of the commonplace, ordinary, or everyday because Trollope consistently depicts ordinary feeling – "the sense of reality" (*Auto* ch. 12) – precisely as the feeling of deviating subtly from a palpable, expected, or routine course. Trollope's sense of reality is indeed inscribed in the phrases "of course" and "as a matter of course," which occur over 400 times each in many of his novels. In Trollope's fiction, everyday feeling is feeling proximate to but diverging from a prescribed route, feeling "of" but not exactly on course. This chapter embeds a survey of the critical reception of Trollope's realism, most of which has attended to content and a purported transparency of style, into a fresh analysis of the way Trollope's prose style, particularly in *Rachel Ray*, portrays the ordinary as a feeling of insignificant deviation from a presupposed regular course.

Echoing David Aitken, A.O.J. Cockshut, Ruth apRoberts, and other scholars invested in Trollope's fiction as a moral process, Laurie Langbauer describes Trollope's prose as a "loosely proverbial" admixture of "colloquialisms, mottoes, maxims, platitudes, clichés, and tag lines" (97). *Phineas Redux* reports that Lady Glencora favors "downright honest figures" like "Two and two make four; idleness is the root of all evil; love your neighbor like yourself, and the rest of it" (Ch. 12), and she is – in her appreciation for colloquialisms – a fair model for Trollope. Who knows how many times he iterates "Faint heart never won fair lady." For Langbauer, the everyday is less a matter of content (probable characters, events, or things) than "a medium, a formal quality," and the proverb "becomes for Trollope in its pith and commonness a symbol of the everyday *as* form" (96–7). But Trollope surely turns many commonplaces to uncommon account as unostentatious metaphors, and he moreover assumes a consistently ironic attitude toward this formal commonness. "Of course" performs accordingly as a gesture that regularly approximates common sense, "the way things are," or how "all the world" thinks – but more often than not as an ironic gesture that diverges from or quizzes the very truism that it simultaneously confirms.

The Last Chronicle of Barset includes 457 instances of "of course," partly because it is the sixth in a series in which so much has already been told but nevertheless recurs or bears repeating, but mostly because its characters take almost everything for granted, especially the primary contingency animating the novel: Josiah Crawley's guilt or innocence. In an infamous standoff, Mrs. Proudie trebly swipes "of course" like a rhetorical stick to beat off Crawley's heroic contumely: "Of course it needs an apology . . . Of course it will, sir . . . Of course the jury will do so" (ch. 18). The Proudies take it as a matter of course that Crawley stole the check, while the Lufton-Grantly opposition takes it as a matter of course that he did not, even when they are presented with evidence to the contrary. Throughout Trollope's fiction, "of course" masks what characters doubt. Archdeacon Grantly assumes his wife will take his son's side against him – "Of course you will take his part" (*LCB* ch. 58) – less because she opposes him than because he opposes and questions himself; he recognizes his genial inability to maintain his threats and punish his son and thereby himself. The ironic "of course" thus typifies "The Cross-grainedness of Men," the title of Chapter 58 of the *Last Chronicle of Barset*, as well as Trollope's realism: in his fiction reality does not appear exactly how "all the world" – Trollope's preferred colloquial moniker for abstract social groups – assumes it ought, but instead feels like many small, estranging, persistent demurrals from that which we nevertheless take to be "matter of course," to be normal.

Beyond mixed characters, which critics as diverse as apRoberts (moral casuistry), Levine (Darwinian variation), and Miller (Foucaultian internalization of social conflict) have correlated to Trollopean realism, Trollope's reality effect is traditionally alleged to accrue to his prodigality and comprehensiveness; his "uncommonly graphic,"[6] "unaffected"[7] description; and his conventional or muddled plots. In an adulatory obituary, Richard Holt Hutton asserts that Trollope's fictions "contain a larger mass of evidence as to the character and aspects of English society . . . than any other writer of his day has left behind him . . . [They] will picture the society of our day with a fidelity with which society has never been pictured before" (Hutton "Mr. Anthony," 1573). "Without a familiar knowledge of [Trollope]," Hutton adds, "no historian who emulated the style of Macaulay would even attempt to delineate English society in the third quarter of the present century" (ibid.). William Dean Howells likewise valorizes Trollope's novels for the "serious fidelity" of "British life and character present in them in the whole length and breadth of its expansive commonplaceness" (Howells 247; cf. Hutton "Review"). Langbauer and Christopher Herbert both discern in Trollope an ethnographic pretension to total cultural representation (Herbert 253–99; Langbauer 95–7). For the former, the repetitiveness and all-inclusiveness of everyday life match that of serial fiction, and the theoretical potential for serial novels to accumulate endlessly adheres to a notion of "culture as everything" (Langbauer 97).

The sheer volume of Trollope's fiction, routinely adduced as evidence of his lack of creative depth, is also routinely adduced as if it somehow translates his fiction into an archive of actuality, his characters into matter. This equation of fiction and actuality owes partly to the cultural currency of Trollope's characters. In 1863 the *National Review* described them as "public property," so "familiar" and "wide-spread" as "necessarily [to] form part of the common stock-in-trade with which the social commerce of the day is carried on" (Hutton "Art. II. Orley Farm," 28–9). It also owes to his serial format: the reliable succession, the serial open-endedness of Trollope's work literally made it a matter of course. Indeed, reappearing characters and repetitive plots became tedious matters of course to certain reviewers. The *Westminster* complained of reading the same lectures,[8] *Dublin University Magazine* of recycled personages.[9] But readers likewise register this potential endlessness as a source of pleasure. Elizabeth Gaskell, for instance, wrote George Smith, "I wish Mr Trollope would go on writing Framley Parsonage for ever" (Chapple and Pollard 602). Trollope well knew that even the most compelling stories become matter of course over time, and he tells the story of that process over and again. *The Last Chronicle of Barset* thus recasts the sensational history of Johnny Eames as a well-known and worn-out routine: his "entire life . . . was pervaded by a great secret . . . It had been historical for the last four or five years, and was now regarded as a thing of course" (*LCB* ch. 15): as Johnny, "comporting himself like any ordinary man," puts it to Lady Julia, it is "Nothing on earth – except the same old story, which has now become a matter of course" (*LCB* ch. 35).

Critics customarily follow Trollope's lead in affecting that he has "no style at all." In *An Autobiography* he relishes Nathaniel Hawthorne's observation (in a letter to Joseph M. Field on February 11, 1860) that his novels "are just as real as if some giant had hewn a great lump out of the earth and put it under a glass case, with all its inhabitants going about their daily business," and he denigrates writing that draws attention to itself as writing, "conceits that smell of the oil" (*Auto* ch. 8). Mechanical metaphors are rampant: James's distinctly appreciative depreciation of Trollope's fiction belittles his "gross, importunate" productivity – as if James was not prolific – and his "perceptibly mechanical process" (Hall *Trollope Critics*, 1). As Walter Kendrick explains, however, "realism is a rhetorical discourse committed to the endless repetition of the assertion that it is not rhetorical" (7). Ruth apRoberts observes that his unpoetic prose defies traditional categories of literary interpretation, like allegory, symbolism, imagery, and self-conscious stylization (11–31), which might seem true, but what of Septimus Harding's virtual violoncello? What of the extended metaphors Trollope makes of foxhunting, eating, and electioneering? What of his persistent irony, his "forte," in Kendrick's words, for "saying opposite things at the same time" (35)? Trollope does indeed employ "poetic" tropes, but instead of foregrounding them as figurative, as might Dickens or Eliot, he drily ironizes them as matter of course.

Consonant with this conventional realist disavowal of style is a habitual disavowal of plot.[10] "The story itself," says *The Times* of *Barchester Towers*, "is a mere nothing."[11] For the *Saturday Review*, "his tales have been in too great a degree mere bundles of fragments bound together by the slenderest possible fragment of a plot"[12] or "There is, as usual, no plot."[13] Margaret Oliphant regretted "he has exhausted too many of the devices of fiction to be able to find always an original suggestion for his plot"; he tediously reprises "the uncomfortable vacillation between two lovers."[14] In a Darwinian culture skeptical of Providence and design, weak plots could nevertheless be said to correspond to reality and did not necessarily preclude enjoyment. As the *Athenaeum* observes,

> "The Three Clerks" has nothing like a consecutive plot; it is as rambling and straggling in its construction as a story well can be . . . Still the book is alive, and the reader will go through with it, digressions, irrelevancies and all.[15]

Elegant plots are artificial. In fiction, extraordinary, uncommon incidents ("romance") are likewise altogether conventional, and Trollope's fictions are replete with them – jiltings, murders, affairs, assaults, duels, Cinderella marriages. Jenny Bourne Taylor explains how many conventions Trollope shares with sensation fiction:

> In his resolutely contemporary settings, his concerns with the ambiguities of marriage and the position of women; his interest in the narrowness of the boundary between the legitimate and the illegitimate, and the normal and the pathological; he challenges the critical consensus that defined higher realism against its sensational other.
>
> (97)

Trollope's insistently matter-of-fact tone subordinates sensational, sometimes quixotic acts (like Doctor Thorne befriending Scatcherd, his brother's murderer!) rather than foregrounding them as transformative, epiphanic events or ironic tableaux (like the old Duke of Omnium bowing to Lady Lufton). Lady de Courcy, for instance, repeats "of course" when lecturing Frank on that which he already knows ("Of course you must marry money"), precisely because Frank, like the protagonists of most domestic fiction, defies the mercenary prescription even though he recognizes that commercial marriages are commonly regarded as a matter of course (*DT* ch. 8).

Trollope's plots are "of" course, then, in their proximity to but narrow deviation from the conventional and ideal assumptions and trajectories they simultaneously confirm and question. They depict normal life as a series of small deviations – "small worries and small bits of happiness"[16] – from otherwise certain, if sometimes ineffable, norms. In *Barchester Towers*, "The reappointment of the old warden would be regarded by all the world as a matter of course" (ch. 8), but of course it is not, for Mrs. Proudie promises the position to Mr. Quiverful. Such is the pattern of myriad Trollopian plots and subplots. *The Spectator* wryly admitted that he "appears to possess some artistic Calculus of Variations, which gives him an infinite command over the shades and details of the different specimens."[17] Reviewing *The Bertrams*, *Bentley's Quarterly* actually puts this serial deviation from the expected as a matter of "course" central to Trollopian plotting:

> The course of the hero . . . is a perpetual conquest of the actual over the ideal – a continual abandonment of preconceived places or aims to some present temptation . . . After a successful university career, Bertram recruits his powers by a journey to the Holy Land. Full of devout aspirations he approaches Jerusalem, but enters its sacred walls cursing and sweating from the discomforts of a Turkish saddle. This is a type of his course, and perhaps what Mr. Trollope would maintain is the type of many a real course which has begun in lofty aims and sunk under mean temptations.[18]

This familiar clash of a young character's lofty ideals and the sordid eventualities of lived experience is an ancient staple of different modes of realism, but Trollope diffuses it throughout his prose. Roger Slakey, Donald Stone, and George Levine have concurred in different idioms. As Levine elegantly says,

> Trollope's prodigious capacity to fill the world with variations and modifications, and to sense the minutiae of difference that keep all these from being ultimately the same gives to his work a breadth of range within apparently narrow plot conventions that allows for an astonishing openness of observation" and "uniformitarian plodding movement" characteristic of "a Darwinian world."
>
> (201)

Trollope himself reckoned the moral influences of fiction as small, corrective adjustments rather than epiphanic transformations: in *The Eustace Diamonds*, he explains, "The true picture of life as it is, if it could be adequately painted, would show men what they are, and how they might rise, not, indeed, to perfection, but one step first, and then another on the ladder" (*ED* ch. 35). Writing of another, far less prevalent of Trollope's signature demurrals – "With such censures I cannot profess that I completely agree" – Frank O'Connor brilliantly suggests that the "favorite device" of Trollope is "to lead his reader very gently up the garden path of his own conventions and prejudices and then to point out that the reader is wrong" (O'Connor 84–5); for O'Connor, Trollope's realism inheres in how "he did not start out with a cut-and-dried system of morals and try to make his characters fit," but instead "made the system fit the characters" (85). Trollope openly admitted to writing without predetermined plots and adapting his characters and events to what he had already written. He likewise marveled at adaptation as the medium of everyday life: of the American Civil War he observed that "Nothing struck me more than their persistence in the ordinary pursuits of life in spite of the war which was around them . . . we, all of us, soon adapt ourselves to the circumstances around us" (*Auto* ch. 9).

Thus Trollope's syntax, while often noted for its "ease," is actually markedly circuitous: his sentences, perhaps more than any other British writer's but Byron's, depend on adversative deviations (but, then, and yet, nevertheless) that veer from their initial course or trail off (in dashes or ellipses); as he notes, the "ordinary talk of ordinary people is carried on in short sharp expressive sentences, which very frequently are never completed" (*Auto* ch. 12). Trollope's narratives also regularly broach a subject with one sentence and then segue into several tangential paragraphs (of preparatory backstory or description) before resuming – often enough by repeating the sentence that first introduced the subject.

This waywardness extends to Trollopian character. Like Walter Scott, Trollope composes many passive heroes who prefer to let things be, to stay the course rather than ruffling feathers, but he insistently flusters them with antagonistic reformists and reforms or discomfiting upstarts. Consider Mr. Harding with his "passive fortitude" and his special aversion to "disagreeable contact with anyone" (*W* ch. 5): "he was anxious beyond measure to avoid even a semblance of rupture with any of his order, and was painfully fearful of having to come to an open quarrel with any person on any subject" (ch. 5). When the *Jupiter* publicly condemns Harding's sinecure, Trollope articulates his discomfort as a troubled course: "It was so hard that the pleasant waters of his little stream should be disturbed and muddied by rough hands; that his quiet paths should be made a battlefield" (ch. 5). The warden's passivity is usually so pronounced that he regularly expresses his suffering through the silent strokes of his virtual violoncello playing. And yet here the warden ultimately insists on resigning, on differing from the expected course, instead of acquiescing in the tactical inaction that Archdeacon Grantly prescribes – "how odd it is that you will not see that all we are to do is to do nothing" (ch. 9). Such mutually irreconcilable, stubborn insistences on staying the course and redirecting the course are the fundamental conflicts animating Trollope's novels, and the idiom of this thematic includes all sorts of paths, ways, routes, and streams, as well as the colloquial "of course."

Trollope often accordingly presents plots as if they were foregone eventualities that "all the world" assumes in advance. In *The Last Chronicle of Barset*, Lily Dale and her mother discuss Major Grantly's financially unpropitious and potentially discreditable proposal to Grace Crawley, whose father is under suspicion of theft, and Grace's refusal as routine matter of fact:

> "He asked her to marry him, of course. We none of us had any doubt about that. He swore to her that she and none but she should be his wife – and all that kind of thing. But he seems to have done it in the most prosaic way . . . Oh, she has refused him, of course."
>
> *(LCB ch. 31)*

The particular feel of Trollope's prose here toes a surprisingly fine line between astonishment and familiarity: the most surprising or doubtful things, the strongest assertions and refusals, are received as if altogether expected. Eleanor in *The Warden*, planning her supplication to John Bold to relinquish his probe into the legality and justice of Mr. Harding's £800 income, reckons Bold's reactionary proposal and likewise her own ensuing rejection as certainties: "Of course when so provoked, he would declare his passion; that was to be expected; there had been enough between them to make such a fact sure; but it was equally certain that he must be rejected" (*W* ch. 11). Bold does declare his passion and propose, but Eleanor only manages, in what became a paradigmatic Trollopian equivocation, to affect her noble resistance before passively relenting.

Such is the everyday in Trollope: the concomitant assertion of fixed expectations and the subtle turns that life actually brings. Thus when the practical archdeacon is baffled by Harding professing his resignation plans to Sir Abraham Haphazard, the succeeding disagreement pivots on different senses of what is "of course": for Harding, it is determined by sincerity – "I told Sir Abraham that I would resign; and of course I must now do so" (*W* ch. 18); for Dr. Grantly, practicality and rhetoric trump sincerity and categorical adherence to the rule of right is absurd – "Not at all . . . Of course . . . such a declaration as that you made to Sir Abraham means nothing" (ch. 18). Trollope's fiction is replete with such exchanges, and the rudimentary ligatures of Trollope's diction inscribe the posture of concurrently upholding and resisting prevailing attitudes even into scenes of apparently tactful concession. As a matter of course, Trollope's characters and readers demur from that which they take as a matter of course.

Trollope presented *Rachel Ray* (1863) to George Eliot – who complimented him for skillfully organizing "thoroughly natural everyday incidents into a strictly related well-proportioned whole" (qtd. in Hall *Letters*, 238–9) – in direct opposition to the fashionable sensation fiction of the 1860s: "I have attempted to confine myself absolutely to the commonest details of commonplace life among the most ordinary people, allowing myself no incident that would be even remarkable in everyday life" (qtd. in Hall *Letters*, 238). And to be sure, pervading the novel is a comfortable conviction that, as Mrs. Tappitt says, everything "must all fall out after the natural, pleasant, everyday fashion of such things" (*RR* ch. 3). If *Rachel Ray* stands out as one of Trollope's most poetic novels, it consistently repackages its most metaphoric passages as matter of course – that is, as barely narratable disturbances of the ordinary. The "matter" of Luke Rowan's growing impression on Rachel Ray develops over both the confluent courses of divergent and coincident geographical routes and a syntax of diurnal, routine, natural, generic, and otherwise expected patterns. At first, "the matter had passed from her mind, and therefore she had not spoken of it"

(*RR* ch. 3). Then, after Rachel's second encounter with Luke and leading up to the unexpected third, "she had been thinking of him as we think of matters which need not put us to any immediate trouble" (ch. 3). She recalls hurrying home "with a feeling half pleasant and half painful that something out of the usual course had occurred to her. But, after all, it amounted to nothing" (ch. 3), which is to say that her novel feeling exceeded narratability: it seemed an impression lacking meaningful, because actionable, content. Affirmations of ineffable feelings are staples of nineteenth-century fiction, but the moral and metafictionally canny subordination of them as "nothing" is vintage Trollope.

> What was there that she could tell her mother? She had no special tale to tell, and yet she could not speak of young Rowan as she would have spoken of a chance acquaintance. Was she not conscious that he had pressed her hand warmly as he parted from her?
>
> (ch. 3)

Rachel's feeling is both too ordinary and too extraordinary to be communicated; it is a matter of course, rather than the shocking stuff of sensation fiction. She loves Luke, but their relationship is too incipient, too informal, and indeed too romantic in its socioeconomic disparity for Rachel to acknowledge it. And yet it is altogether foregone and formal: its romance makes it altogether generic. However new to Rachel, her story is indeed routine, both nothing new to tell and the same old thing told too many times already (indeed, compare it to Madeline Stavely in *Orley Farm*: she loves Felix Graham, who has not spoken a word of love to her, and is thus flummoxed as to what to tell her mother, Lady Stavely, because nothing has happened). Trollope thus parries the sensory impetus of sensationalist fiction, rebutting its emphasis on plot with Rachel's charged sense of plotlessness, her acute sense of the "usual course" of her "something out of the usual course."

As Rachel walks with the Tappitt girls, they discuss plans for a dance riddled with consequences and happenings that the girls take for granted. "Of course it is for a dance," says Martha, "And of course you'll come and dance with Luke Rowan," adds Cherry (ch. 3). While Rachel mulls the countermanding imperatives – that of course her imperiously priggish sister Dorothea and, therefore, her mother will oppose her attendance – Trollope threads and disturbs social, colloquial, incidental, geographical, habitual, cognitive, emotional, and affective courses: "at a sudden turn of a lane, a lane that led back to the town by another route, they met Luke Rowan himself" (ch. 3). However sudden the turn and surprising the encounter (of course, not surprising to any sensible reader), they meet it with stock responses and resume their otherwise ordinary way: "The greeting was of course very friendly, and he returned with them on their path" (ch. 3). But Rachel "had felt herself to be confused the moment she saw him, – so confused that she was not able to ask him how he was with ordinary composure"; she "could not bear herself before this young man as though he were no more than an ordinary acquaintance" (ch. 3). Unable to forget "that hand-squeezing" or "to take his words as though they signified nothing," she feels "his sudden return was a momentous fact to her, putting her out of her usual quiet mode of thought" (ch. 3). As if presciently depicting and provincializing Michel de Certeau's everyday politics of walking, whereby the urban pedestrian exhibits "surreptitious creativities" in appropriating prescriptive sidewalks with his own diagonal, meandering, or otherwise individual and illegible paths, Rachel feels her life not in the habitual acts of tea and visitations that consume much of the novel but in the subtle deviations from her familiar walks. Rachel here feels the ordinary as something extraordinary. She rebuts the dismissive reduction of everyday life to senseless mimesis and feels it intensely (de Certeau 96, see 91–102). Thus "they sauntered along . . . by a route [tellingly] opposite to the churchyard" (36), as if their dallying pace and path bespeak their (mildly, apparently) errant marital intentions. The supervening scene culminates in an almost erotically explicit, poetic exchange about clouds – "Ah! do you see the man's arm, as it were; the deep purple cloud, like a huge hand stretched out from some other world to take you?" (ch. 3). This scene of hand "touching," "full consciousness," sunset, and coincident dreams is astonishingly unique in the novel, perhaps even in Trollope's oeuvre (ch. 3). But then, in a characteristic Trollopian displacement of emotion, Rachel nevertheless tries to dismiss their shared vision as a matter of course – "All the world might have seen it had they looked" (ch. 3), she says of the sunset – but her real feeling is repeatedly marked by the pedestrian fact that she has "lingered there a moment . . . lingered" (ch. 3). "Of course" is only one exceptional marker of how Trollope feels commonplaces uncommonly and sketches an ambient, not quite conformist relation to the ordinary courses of life. Michael Riffaterre observes that *Rachel Ray* abounds in "food code," particularly metonymic iterations of tea that create a sense of diurnal repetition: "as 'tea' represents food and custom, its recurrence represents comforting continuity or the rut of boredom" (Riffaterre 281). Riffaterre contends such metonymy performs dual functions of descriptive verisimilitude (reality effect) and reductive comedy (274), and in this regard it thematizes the syntactical work of Trollope's ironic matter "of course."

In an essay on *Rachel Ray*, the *Saturday Review* disparaged verisimilitude as an inadequate critical objective and symptom of impoverished Victorian culture:

> It may seem rather hard that critics should read Mr. Trollope's representations of ordinary life and enjoy them, and then abuse them for being what they are. But this is, we believe, the exact combination of feelings which they would awaken in many minds. They are entertaining and very clever, but there is a satiety attending not only Mr. Trollope's representations of ordinary life, but all such representations, whoever may be the author. We wish fiction would do something more for us besides giving us these accurate likenesses of the common ruin of those whom we see or know.[19]

This review seems to be tired of the "common," "accurate" realism that pleases it and covetous of something new, but it does not quite imagine modernism so much as it reproduces the ordinary feeling enacted in Trollope's fiction: "representations of ordinary life" are representations of pleasure and "satiety," the comfort and the tedium of comfort. Trollope's art, I have been suggesting, lies precisely in rendering dissatisfied satiety into a pleasurable sensation.

Many critics describe the feeling of reading Trollope as soothing, comforting, quiet relief. But perhaps Michael Sadleir's paradoxical description is most exemplary: he describes reading Trollope as "a sensual rather than an intellectual experience" with an "at once soothing and exciting" effect closer to a "smell, a pain or a sound" (Sadleir 34). Trollope's books are "so featureless, so sober and so undemonstrative" and yet "few are more enthralling" (35), "so drab yet so mysteriously alive, so obvious yet so impossible of imitation" (37), "so genially disposed but fundamentally detached" (36); they generate a "queer sense of the absorbing interest of normal occupations" (37). Like so many, however, Sadleir claims that this "peculiar but elusive flavour" accrues to Trollope's "acquiescence" (Hall 34; O'Connor registers a comparable "humility and passivity," 88). Acceptance of things as they are, of the way of the world, yields what Sadleir calls "a series of unsensational sensations" (37).[20] Of course, as Sadleir says,

> Like life, [Trollope novels] are diffuse, often tedious, seldom arrestingly unusual. Their monotony is the monotony of ordinary existence, which, although while actually

passing it provides one small sensation after another, emerges in retrospect as a dull sequence of familiar things.

(37)

And yet, maybe not: following Robert Polhemus's *The Changing World of Anthony Trollope* (1968) and Deborah Morse's *Reforming Trollope* (2013) we might read Trollope's prose aright by recognizing the sarcasm, irony, and tactful but subversive demurral in his "of course."

We need not hang such claims on tone or Trollope's reputedly boisterous personality alone, for he associates them with the moral ethos of his style. Reflecting on the difficulties of fiction writing, Trollope prescribes – along with some admittedly naïve remarks on "pellucid" and effortless prose that fully articulates no more or less than the author's intended sense (*Auto* ch. 12) – a style that reconciles proper written language, which is too formal to appear real, and actual speech, which is too crass to be readable:

> The novel-writer in constructing his dialogue must so steer between absolute accuracy of language – which would give to his conversation an air of pedantry, and the slovenly inaccuracy of ordinary talkers, – which if closely followed would offend by an appearance of grimace, as to produce upon the ear of his readers a sense of reality.
>
> *(Auto ch. 12)*

This maneuvering between familiar courses extends to the moral or cultural work of novel writing. As Trollope insists, unlike Ruskin, that good prose ought not to be work for the reader – "intelligible without trouble . . . and harmonious" (*Auto* ch. 12) – he insists that his novels, although he considers them sermons (*Auto* ch. 8), must steer a course between pure truth or insight and redundant familiar commonplace. In *Thackeray* he likewise explains, "in very truth the realistic must not be true but just so far removed from truth as to suit the erroneous idea of truth which the reader may be supposed to entertain" (*T* 185). Trollope thus describes the "sense of reality," his uncanny ordinariness, neither as a function of exacting mimesis and acquiescent acceptance of things as they are nor as generic and moral idealizations of how they ought to be, but something in between, as a slight deviation from the former toward the latter. Frequently noting the presence or absence of a "touch" of this or that in Thackeray's fiction, Trollope again describes realism as a kind of tactful mediation between the writer's insightful perception of reality and the readers' assumptions about reality, a touch of the real tempered by a touch of readers' misconceptions of it:

> To produce the desired effect the narrator must go between the two. He must mount somewhat above the ordinary conversational powers of such persons as are to be represented, – lest he disgust. But he must by no means soar into correct phraseology, – lest he offend. The realistic, – by which we mean that which shall seem to be real, – lies between the two, and in reaching it the writer has not only to keep his proper distance on both sides, but has to maintain varying distances in accordance with the position, mode of life, and education of the speakers.
>
> *(T 186)*

The rhetorical practice Trollope here theorizes, maintaining a comfortable detachment – "proper distance" – between potentially abrasive, pedantic, chafing accuracy or change, on the one hand, and blithe concession to common misperceptions and ungrammatical sayings, on the other, is aptly condensed in his use of "of course." His is an ambient realism that asks us to stray from the convictions it underlines as "matters of course." Writing such an article on so routine a topic, one worries that he is merely repeating what all the world has already said, but Trollope sets a precedent for differing in shades and in manner if not always in content. Repetition with an implicit, subtle difference seems to be precisely the feeling of reading Trollope, the pleasant if anxious feeling of the ordinary made extraordinary. The history of scholarship on Trollope's realism reproduces this feeling.

Notes

1 [Anon.], review of "The Claverings," *Saturday Review* 23.603 (May 18, 1867): 638–9; 638.
2 [Anon.], "The Small House at Allington," *Saturday Review* 17.446 (May 14, 1864): 595–6; 595.
3 [Anon.], review of *Framley Parsonage*, *Examiner* 2777 (April 20, 1861): 244–5; 244.
4 [Anon.], "Belles Lettres," *Westminster Review* 25.1 (January 1864): 286–306; 291.
5 Writing about characters who inhabit an array of social classes and who exhibit dynamic, conflicting traits rather than fixed, identifiably heroic or evil identities was a dominant feature of nineteenth-century British literature: Wordsworth's preface to *Lyrical Ballads*, which justifies poetry about real people in the language they speak; Thackeray's *Vanity Fair. A Novel Without a Hero*; George Eliot's apology for Mr. Irwine in Chapter 17 of *Adam Bede*, a signal manifesto for Victorian realism. *The Saturday Review* notes, "The old notion that in the dullest and most prosaic lives there is often buried a vein of unsuspected romance or pathos has been the starting-point of more than one school of novelists. But Mr. Trollope expands the original force of the notion by contending that the ordinary idea of what romance of pathos means is far too limited, and that things commonly passed over as sordid cares or ignoble perplexities are, when rightly viewed, elements in life of the truest pathos" ([Anon.], review of *Miss Mackenzie*, *Saturday Review* 19 [March 4, 1865]: 263). Outlets like *The Cornhill* praise Trollope's characters as "human beings, with good and evil strangely mingled" ([G. H. Lewes], "Our Survey of Literature and Science: Orley Farm," *Cornhill Magazine* 6 [November 1862]: 702); others, such as the *Saturday Review*, more ambivalently report that "All are ordinary men and women, and their sayings and doings are neither above nor below the level of what we see in common and everyday life" ([Anon.], review of *Framley Parsonage*, *Saturday Review* 6 [May 4, 1861]: 451); and still others, like the *National Review*, lament that "hardly any of his personages are without some repulsive trait of character which prevents the reader from taking a cordial interest in their fate" ([R. H. Hutton], "Mr. Trollope's Novels," *National Review* 7 [October 1858]: 416): nearly all reviews note this mixed characterization as a primary feature of Trollope's realism.
6 [Anon.], review of *Barchester Towers*, *Leader and Saturday Analyst* 8.374 (May 23, 1857): 497.
7 [Anon.], review of *Doctor Thorne*, *Leader and Saturday Analyst* 9.427 (May 29, 1858), 519–20; 520.
8 [Anon.], "Belles Lettres," *Westminster Review* 20.1 (July 1861): 280–91; 283.
9 [Anon.], "A Batch of Last Year's Novels," *Dublin University Magazine* 59.352 (April 1862): 396–409; 405–6.
10 Comparative estimations of plot and character were routine subjects of nineteenth-century literary criticism, though they rose to prominence in the 1860s in debates about sensation fiction and later in the 1880s in the art of fiction exchanges. Trollope explicitly privileges character, though he explains that they are necessarily inseparable (see *Auto* 228–34).
11 [Anon.], review of *Barchester Towers*, *The Times* (August 13, 1857): 5.
12 [Anon.], review of *The Bertrams*, *Saturday Review* 7.178 (March 26, 1859): 368–9; 368.
13 [Anon.], review of *Can You Forgive Her?*, *Saturday Review* 20.512 (August 19, 1865): 240–2; 242.
14 [Margaret Oliphant], "Novels," *Blackwood's Magazine* 102.623 (September 1867): 257–80; 276.
15 [Anon.], review of *The Three Clerks: A Novel*, *Athenaeum* 1574 (December 26, 1857): 1621.
16 [Anon.], review of *The Claverings*, 638.
17 [Anon.], "Mr. Trollope's Orley Farm," *Spectator* 33.1789 (October 11, 1862): 1136–38; 1138. Cf. [Anon.], review of *Miss Mackenzie*, *Spectator* 38.1914 (March 4, 1865): 244–5.
18 [Anne Mozley], "Adam Bede and Recent Novels," *Bentley's Quarterly Review* 1.2 (June 1859): 433–72; 458.
19 [Anon.], review of *Rachel Ray*, *Saturday Review* 16.417 (October 24, 1863): 554–5; 555.
20 Sadleir's observations here echo a Victorian physiological conception of consciousness as the perception of minute deviations known as "just noticeable differences." Nicholas Dames traces the application of these "JND" to fiction in the work of George Meredith, but it is I think equally applicable to Trollope, given the history of critical observations of gradualness, subtle variation, and so on (Dames 179–82, 200–3).

Works cited

Aitken, David. "'A Kind of Felicity': Some Notes about Trollope's Style." *Nineteenth-Century Fiction* 20 (1996): 337–53.
Anon. "*Barchester Towers.*" Review. *Leader and Saturday Analyst* 8.374 (May 23, 1857): 497.
Anon. "*Barchester Towers.*" Review. *The Times* (August 13, 1857): 5.
Anon. "A Batch of Last Year's Novels." *Dublin University Magazine* 59.352 (April 1862): 396–409.
Anon. "Belles Lettres." *Westminster Review* 20.1 (July 1861): 280–91.
Anon. "Belles Lettres." *Westminster Review* 25.1 (January 1864): 286–306.
Anon. "*The Bertrams.*" Review. *Saturday Review* 7.178 (March 26, 1859): 368–9.
Anon. "*Can You Forgive Her?*" Review. *Saturday Review* 20.512 (August 19, 1865): 240–2.
Anon. "The Claverings." Review. *Saturday Review* 23.603 (May 18, 1867): 638–9.
Anon. "*Doctor Thorne.*" Review. *Leader and Saturday Analyst* 9.427 (May 29, 1858), 519–20.
Anon. "*Framley Parsonage.*" Review. *Examiner* 2777 (April 20, 1861): 244–5.
Anon. "*Framley Parsonage.*" Review. *Saturday Review* 6 (May 4, 1861): 451–2.
Anon. "*Miss Mackenzie.*" Review. *Spectator* 38.1914 (March 4, 1865): 244–5.
Anon. "Mr. Trollope's *Orley Farm.*" *Spectator* 33.1789 (October 11, 1862): 1136–38.
Anon. "Rachel Ray." Review. *Saturday Review* 16.417 (October 24, 1863): 554–5.
Anon. "The Small House at Allington." Review. *Saturday Review* 17.446 (May 14, 1864): 595–6.
Anon. "*The Three Clerks: A Novel.*" Review. *Athenaeum* 1574 (December 26, 1857): 1621.
apRoberts, Ruth. *Trollope: Artist and Moralist*. London: Chatto & Windus, 1971.
Chapple, J.A.V., and Arthur Pollard, eds., *The Letters of Mrs. Gaskell*. Manchester, UK: Mandolin, 1997.
Dames, Nicholas. *The Physiology of the Novel: Reading, Neural Science, and the Form of Victorian Fiction*. New York: Oxford University Press, 2007.
De Certeau, Michel. *The Practice of Everyday Life*, trans. Steven Randall. Berkeley: University of California Press, 1988. 91–110.
Hall, N. John, ed. *The Letters of Anthony Trollope*. Stanford: Stanford University Press, 1983.
———. *Trollope: A Biography*. Oxford: Clarendon, 1991.
———, ed. *The Trollope Critics*. Totowa, NJ: Barnes & Noble, 1981.
Herbert, Christopher. *Culture and Anomie: Ethnographic Imagination in the Nineteenth Century*. Chicago: The University of Chicago Press, 1991.
Howells, William Dean. *My Literary Passions*. New York: Harper and Brothers, 1895.
Hutton, Richard H. "Art. II. Orley Farm." Review. *National Review* 16.31 (January 1863): 27–40.
———. "Mr. Anthony Trollope." *Spectator* 55.2841 (December 9, 1882): 1573–4.
———. "Mr. Trollope's Novels," *National Review* 7 (October 1858): 416–35.
———. "Review of *Can You Forgive Her?*" *Spectator* 38.1940 (September 2, 1865): 978–9.
James, Henry. *Partial Portraits*. London: Macmillan and Co, 1888.
Kendrick, Walter M. *The Novel Machine: The Theory and Fiction of Anthony Trollope*. Baltimore: The Johns Hopkins University Press, 1980.
Langbauer, Laurie. *Novels of Everyday Life: The Series in English Fiction, 1850–1930*. Ithaca: Cornell University Press, 1999.
Levine, George. *Darwin and the Novelists: Patterns of Science in Victorian Fiction*. Chicago: University of Chicago Press, 1991.
Miller, D. A. *The Novel and the Police*. Berkeley: University of California Press, 1988.
Morse, Deborah. *Reforming Trollope: Race, Gender, and Englishness in the Novels of Anthony Trollope*. Burlington, VT: Ashgate, 2013.
Mozley, Anne. "Adam Bede and Recent Novels." *Bentley's Quarterly Review* 1.2 (June 1859): 433–72.
O'Connor, Frank. "Trollope the Realist." *The Trollope Critics*, ed. N. John Hall. Totowa, NJ: Barnes & Noble Books, 1981. 83–94.
Oliphant, Margaret. "Novels." *Blackwood's Magazine* 102.623 (September 1867): 257–80.
Polhemus, Robert M. *The Changing World of Anthony Trollope*. Berkeley: University of California Press, 1968.
Riffaterre, Michael. "Trollope's Metonymies." *Nineteenth-Century Fiction* 37 (1982–3): 272–92.
Sadleir, Michael. "The Books." *The Trollope Critics*, ed. N. John Hall. Totowa, NJ: Barnes & Noble Books, 1981. 34–45.
Slakey, Roger L. "Anthony Trollope, Master of Gradualness." *VIJ: Victorians Institute Journal* 16 (1988): 27–35.
Stone, Donald D. *The Romantic Impulse in Victorian Fiction*. Cambridge: Harvard University Press, 1980.
Taylor, Jenny Bourne. "Trollope and the Sensation Novel." *The Cambridge Companion to Anthony Trollope*, eds. Carolyn Dever and Lisa Niles. Cambridge, UK: Cambridge University Press, 2011. 85–98.

Trollope, Anthony. *An Autobiography*, eds. Michael Sadleir and Frederick Page. New York: Oxford University Press, 1999.

———. *Barchester Towers*, ed. Robin Gilmour. New York: Penguin, 2003.

———. *Doctor Thorne*, ed. David Skilton. New York: Oxford University Press, 1980.

———. *The Eustace Diamonds*, ed. John Sutherland. New York: Penguin, 2004.

———. *The Last Chronicle of Barset*, ed. Sophie Gilmartin. London: Penguin, 2002.

———. *Phineas Redux*, ed. Gregg A. Hecimovich. New York: Penguin, 2003.

———. *Rachel Ray*, ed. P. D. Edwards. New York: Oxford University Press, 2009.

———. *Thackeray*. English Men of Letters, ed. John Morley. London: Macmillan, 1879.

———. *The Warden*, ed. Robin Gilmour. New York: Penguin, 2004.

12
RETHINKING MARRIAGE
Trollope's internal revision

Helena Michie

Anthony Trollope ends the first chapter of his novel *Can You Forgive Her?* with a "fact" about his heroine, Alice Vavasor: "And now for my fact: At the time of which I am writing she was already engaged to be married" (ch. 1). Such a "fact" would, of course, end most marriage plot novels, signaling the resolution of the story. We know from the heft of the remaining pages – and from the hints offered by the title – that this "fact" may, *in* fact, be subject to revision. And indeed, Alice changes her mind about whom and whether she will marry five times in the course of the novel, oscillating between John Grey, the novel's "worthy man" to whom she is engaged as *Can You Forgive Her?* opens, and her cousin George, the "wild man" of the novel, to whom she was engaged several years before the action of the novel. The last chapters reestablish Alice's engagement to John, as the worthy engagement becomes, once again, a fact. Although Alice arguably ends up where she began, the very fact of the long novel, with its reiterative descriptions of Alice's changes of mind, makes her final situation slightly, significantly, accretively different.

Thinking of those changes of mind as a form of revision can help us to link three Trollopian peculiarities on three narrative levels: his interest in intelligent and complex female characters, his fascination with the representation of the act of thinking, and the characteristic shape of his sentences. For the purposes of this article, I want to take the first for granted[1] and start with the last. Although, thanks to recent meticulous studies of his manuscripts and the writing process they reveal, we no longer see Trollope as someone who never revised or rethought his work,[2] there is still the temptation to see his language as transparent and effortless rather than as the product of craft.[3] I will be arguing for the centrality in Trollope's work of what I call "internal revision," a process by which he uses one sentence to revise another, leaving the original sentence on the page. This results in a series of sentences that are different from one another in small but significant ways: I say "significant" in part to defend Trollope against easy accusations of padding his work to produce his daily total of words, an accounting he (in)famously celebrates in *An Autobiography* and that has caused so much damage to his reputation. I also want to emphasize, however, that internal revision produces a particular kind of realism that invites or perhaps demands attention to small differences. While it is perhaps difficult to imagine Trollope in connection with what Carol Christ has called the "finer optic" of Victorian poetry, it might be easier to connect Trollope's realist enterprise to George Eliot's, his insistence on the importance of small distinctions to her – perhaps more overtly ethically charged – project.[4] If we look at the verbal and syntactical differences between sentences in Trollope as accretive – that is, as slowly adding up over time – we can also see them as the perfect vehicle for representing the process of thinking and, in particular, the complicated and recursive logics through which people are said to "change their minds."

Trollope represents thinking on several narrative levels. While it is often hard in his work to separate the author (or implied author) from the narrator, we often see the narrative "I" that brings these levels together in the process of thinking about the work of writing and creating characters. Characters, particularly women, spend a great deal of the story time thinking: we are often told, for example, that Alice has spent "several hours" or "a whole afternoon" thinking about her situation. The preoccupation with the thinking process is even clearer in the discourse time of his novels – in the way the story is told: in many of his novels large chunks of multiple chapters are taken up with the representation of characters' thought processes, even if this means rehearsing earlier decisions or summarizing past events of the novel. Scenes of women thinking also suggest a certain relation to realism: leisure-class heroines think, in part, because they have nothing else to do. They sit in their drawing rooms, or in the rooms of other people's houses, because they cannot, as in the case of Alice, fulfill their desires for action. The representation of thought in Trollope's characters makes extensive use of the technique of free indirect discourse, in which the point of view slips back and forth between character and narrator, and even between narrator and author, in such a way that they are virtually indistinguishable.

Thinking for all Trollope characters, but especially for women, happens under a set of social and generic constraints. As we shall see, the narrator of *Can You Forgive Her?* does not approve of thinking about marriage, even though this is all he (?) can give his heroines to think about.[5] The genre of the marriage plot novels demands, and indeed produces, a binary model of thinking in which women must choose between two suitors; these suitors may represent sets of contrasting values, but the heroine's choice is always an embodied one, always reduced to a choice between this man and that man.[6] As with computational languages that generate infinitely complex cascades of decisions out of series of binary choices, Trollope heroines can produce through and in their binary thinking a rich world of ideas and feelings. The marriage plot novel, unlike the computer, however, always demands a return to the binary.

While attention to Trollope's thinking women can and should be part of a thematic investigation of his representation of women and marriage, this article begins and lingers on the level of Trollope's sentences. This focus involves, of course, a confrontation with the issue of Trollope's style. The relatively recent turn to the "new formalism" in nineteenth-century studies has begun to provide scholars with a new vocabulary for describing realism at the level of the sentence.[7] Trollope presents a particular challenge to those who would take his style seriously: as Matthew Sussman suggests, the effect that Trollope seems to be attempting is a transparent non-style, a "rhetorical invisibility" (877). For Sussman, Trollope's rhetorical transparency has traditionally been linked to narrative transparency and, thus, to the verisimilitude for which Trollope is (in) famous. Sussman proposes a cannier, more skeptical Trollope, who, by marking his sentences with the rhetorical effects of "honesty," calls into question the possibility of mimesis (878).

Sussman's exemplary work is unique in its explicit foregrounding of the Trollopian sentence.[8] Even D. A. Miller, whose work on Jane Austen demonstrates in each of his own sentences the deceptive intricacies of the Austen narrator's stylistic impersonality, seems to replicate with only the slightest sense of irony the prevailing sense that Trollope's style can (and indeed demands to) be ignored. Miller, who notices everything about Austen, sees the characteristic experience of Trollope's style as a state of not noticing. As he puts it in his famous chapter on Trollope in *The Novel and the Police*:

> In much the same way as one drops onto the easy chair that is still the most likely place to read Trollope, or sinks into that half-slumber in which his pages there may be safely

skimmed, so one falls into the usual appreciation of his appreciation of the usual. . . .
"Life is like this" and "Novels are like this, too."

(107)

We "skim" Trollope, then, in part because there is nothing to arrest us, nothing to make us sit up in the easy chair and take notice, take up a position. While Miller obviously finds Trollope's unremarkable style worth remarking, he does not linger on the mechanics of Trollope's sentences that produce the illusion of restfulness and the effect of drowsiness.

This chapter represents an experiment in noticing Trollope's style through the lens of internal revision. I will be looking at examples from three novels – *Can You Forgive Her?*, *The Bertrams*, and *The Last Chronicle of Barset* – to explore their reliance on internal revision as a mode of representing marital choice. All three novels, like many others in the Trollope canon, feature heroines who choose between two men, and whose choices are always subject to revision. While conventional marriage plot novels, like *Pride and Prejudice*, are defined by a movement forward, away from bad choices toward good ones through an education plot, Trollope novels, like the ones I will be discussing, are more recursive: heroines can move back and forth between suitors, as Alice does in *Can You Forgive Her?*; they can make bad decisions and repent of them, as Caroline Harcourt does in *The Bertrams*; or they can actively, repeatedly, and painfully refuse to change their minds, as does Lily Dale over the course of two novels, *Small House at Allington* and *Last Chronicle*.

Room to think

If we were to be alert to Trollope's style, what would we see? Let us look at the eminently skimmable passage at the beginning of *Can You Forgive Her?* in which Trollope begins what will be a three-paragraph description of the drawing room in the house shared by Alice Vavasor and her father:

> I cannot say that the house in Queen Anne Street was a pleasant house. I am now speaking of the material house, made up of the walls and furniture, and not of any pleasantness or unpleasantness supplied by the inmates. It was a small house on the south side of the street, squeezed in by two large mansions which seemed to crush it, and by which this fair proportion of doorstep and area was in truth curtailed. The stairs were narrow; the dining room was dark, and possessed none of those appearances of plenteous hospitality which dining rooms ought to have. But all this would have been nothing if the drawing room had been pretty as it is the bounden duty of all drawing rooms to be. But Alice Vavasor's drawing room was not pretty. Her father had had the care of furnishing the house, and he had intrusted [sic] the duty to a tradesman who had chosen green paper, a green carpet, green curtains, and green damask chairs. There was a green damask sofa, and two green armchairs opposite to each other at the two sides of the fireplace. The room was altogether green, and was not enticing.

(ch. 2)

The reader in the easy chair might easily find herself in a "half slumber" at this catalogue of furnishings whose individual items – chairs, sofa, curtains, and carpet – are bound together by the sleep-inducing repetition of the word "green." Indeed, it is almost as if Trollope is trying to induce that reader to "skim." The paragraph seems actively to refuse our interest, beginning as it does with it a confession of insufficiency ("I cannot say") and ending (if we get that far) with the observation that the room is "not enticing." And the long middle is insistently monochromatic.

A reader a little more awake than the one Miller imagines might want to find in the paragraph some information about the relationship between father and daughter, might want to read with the home/owner metonymy so crucial to much realist fiction. But such energy is not rewarded; the Trollope narrator seems to anticipate this gesture toward meaning and to undercut it: he promises only to speak "of the material house" and "not of the pleasantness or unpleasantness supplied by the inmates." The passage's refusal of meaning, in fact, becomes its meaning: this house is just a house, the sofa a sofa.

But what of the individual sentences that make up this paragraph? We can choose not to notice them individually, just as we might choose to skip them in aggregate. The first thing we might say about their claim to notice is that they do not seem to make a claim. On the surface at least – and this passage seems to insist on surface – we see no signs of interest: no figurative language, no unusual diction, no syntactical flourishes. If there is something worth noticing, it is in the relation of one sentence to the next; sentences are linked to those that follow through the repetition of key, but not terribly interesting, words. Take, for example, the first two sentences of the paragraph: "I cannot say that the house in Queen Anne Street was a pleasant house. I am now speaking of the material house, made up of the walls and furniture, and not of any pleasantness or unpleasantness supplied by the inmates." One could say that the second sentence is a clarification, a qualification, or, even in the idiom of the domestic interior, a revisiting of the first that repeats the initial "I" and plays upon and elaborates the word "pleasant." Another way of putting it is that the first sentence offers a lexicon for the second: it sets up the term "pleasant" while the second muses on the term. A similar but not identical process marks the last few sentences that play on (or perhaps, given the tone of the passage, work with) the key word "green." The last sentence is a summary of the previous two: we know by the time we get to it that the wallpaper, the furniture (carefully itemized), and the carpet are green; we do not need the last sentence to tell us that the room is "all green." The summary term might be particularly unnecessary if we imagine a particularly alert domestic reader, perhaps someone who herself has thought about decoration or redecoration: by the 1860s many consumers would have known about the link between green pigments in household items, particularly wallpaper, and arsenic. Like Dorothea Casaubon in *Middlemarch*, who is reminded of the trauma of her honeymoon by an image from St. Peter's Cathedral of "red drapery . . . spreading everywhere like a disease of the retine," Alice (and the reader) might experience the spreading of the color green from one piece of furniture to another, and from there to the body.[9]

We also do not need to be told that the room is "not enticing"; we have been told, from the beginning of the paragraph, after all, that it is "not pleasant." If the individual sentences of the passage look simultaneously backward and forward, the final sentence returns us, perhaps unwillingly, to the first. The paragraph, then, functions as an act of revision, taking us only so far: from "not pleasant" to "not enticing." Trollope has left standing, as it were, a paragraph full of sentences minimally different from one another. He has, in effect, shown us his work.

We can, of course, rescue the paragraph for meaning through marrying form to content. By using repetition in this way, the passage produces a feeling of claustrophobia and entrapment. This feeling is enhanced by our knowledge of Alice's desire to change her surroundings:

> But yet the drawing-room of which I speak was ugly, and Alice knew that it was so. She knew that it was ugly, and she would greatly have liked to banish the green sofa, to have re-papered the wall, and to have hung up curtains with a dash of pink through them. With the green carpet she would have been contented. But her father was an extravagant man; and from the day on which she had come of age she determined it was her special duty to avoid extravagance.
>
> *(ch. 2)*

The narrator here has established a new and bolder key term: "not pleasant" has been subject to a second standing revision and is now "ugly." The term "ugly" itself passes from the third-person narrator into Alice's consciousness: it is at the moment when we understand that Alice knows the room is ugly that she is interpolated momentarily as a knowing subject. She is not, however, fully an agent. The third sentence, which repeats with a slight difference the end of the second ("Alice knew it was so" and "She knew it was ugly"), ends with a statement of desires that are destined to remain unfulfilled. Knowledge that something is wrong – in the case of interior decoration as in the case of marriage – does not produce the power to effect change.

These heightened examples of failed decision making take place, of course, within the novel's marriage plot – and often in the ugly green drawing room of whose ugliness we have heard so much. If the description of the drawing room is a place for the narrator to enact internal revision of the descriptive process, the drawing room itself becomes a scene of revision as Alice sits alone in it, pondering the choices open to her through marriage.

Thinking too much

Before we can see the novel as a representation of Alice's thought processes, we must get past one of the novel's central ironies: that the narrator seems to disapprove of people, especially perhaps of women, thinking too much about their decision to marry. After announcing Alice's first change of mind,[10] the narrator moves out from Alice's situation to what he diagnoses as a more general problem:

> People often say that marriage is an important thing, and should be much thought of in advance, and marrying people are cautioned that there are many who marry in haste and repent at leisure. I am not sure, however, that marriage may be pondered over too much; nor do I feel certain that the leisurely repentance does not often follow the leisurely marriage as it does the rapid ones. That some repent no one can doubt; but I am inclined to believe that most men and women take their lots as they find them, marrying as the birds do by force of nature, and going on with their mates with a general, though not a perhaps undisturbed satisfaction. . . . I do not know that a woman can assure to herself, by her own prudence and taste, a good husband any more than she can add two cubits to her stature; but husbands have been made to be decently good, – and wives too, for the most part, in our country, – so that the thing does not require quite so much thinking as some people say.
>
> (ch. 11)

Ringing changes on the word "leisure," in a way that I have argued is characteristic of the narrator's own accretive arguments, the narrator undermines the careful protocols of marriage plot novels, which depend largely for their emotional satisfaction on the heroine's refusal to compromise when it comes to choosing a marriage partner. This passage that privileges not thinking depends, perhaps ironically, on Trollope's characteristic syntax of thoughtfulness: the repetition of key terms, the careful qualification and balanced clauses, the gentle flight into analogy. The passage is also gently, if somewhat oddly, gendered: the woman who thinks too much is, in effect, asking to be taller by two cubits, to become, according to the analogical calculus of the sentence, considerably taller than a man. The use of the archaic (and indeed biblical) "cubit" – the length of the forearm from the elbow to the extended middle finger – hyperbolizes the woman's ambition and grounds the analogy in the body itself. To think about marrying is then doubly to resist the "force of nature" that makes most couples mate as "birds do."

The application to Alice of the exhortation not to think (too much) immediately sets up an opposition across narrative levels between thinking and feeling: "that Alice Vavasor had thought too much about it I feel quite sure." The narrator's knowledge (however qualified) derives from his ability to "feel." This is not the more typical trumping of irrational women by rational masculine values but rather a statement in the rational periods of Trollopian syntax of the primacy of feeling for "men and women" – perhaps especially for women. Trollope's colloquial, even dismissive, reference to marriage as "the thing," in the last sentence of the passage, suggests not only the advantages but also the ubiquity of the institution – and the absurdity of spending too much (story) time on making up one's mind about it. The narrator normalizes the already normal, rejecting exceptionality as he rejects thinking too much.

Decisions, decisions

But of course *Can Your Forgive Her?*, so carefully crafted to be exceptional and to differ from the traditional marriage plot novel, depends on the depiction of thinking. There is room in this novel, as in many others by Trollope, to read against the grain of the marriage plot, to temporize as Alice does on a smaller scale when she initially asks John to put off their marriage.[11] This form of resistance means taking seriously the often very slow and tedious process by which heroines' decisions are made.[12] One example of Alice's thinking and of the internal revision that accompanies and embodies it comes during John's visit to Alice in London after he has learned from her letter of her reengagement to George. The depiction of the visit, in a chapter entitled "John Grey Goes a Second Time to London," is explicitly framed as a revisitation, an incremental revision of an earlier scene in which John visits Alice in response to her initial letter asking for a delay. As with that scene, when John leaves, Alice sits in the green drawing room to ponder what has just taken place:

> Alice sat alone for an hour without moving when John Grey had left her, and the last words he had uttered were sounding in her ears all the time, "My heart is still yours, as it has been since I knew you." There had been something in his words which had soothed her spirits, and had, for the moment, almost comforted her. At any rate, he did not despise her. He could not have spoken such words as these to her had he not still held her high in his esteem. Nay; – had he not even declared that he would yet take her as his own if she would come to him? "I cannot tell you with how much joy I would take you back to my bosom!" Ah! That might never be. But yet the assurance had been sweet to her; – dangerously sweet, as she soon told herself.
>
> (ch. 37)

The "hour" that Alice spends "alone" is spent rehearsing the scene that has just taken place. Part of that rehearsal involves an internal quotation of John's words, which, in an odd use of the continuous present, "were sounding in her ears all the time." Alice's thought process includes words that were given in direct discourse only a paragraph before, at the end of the previous chapter. Interestingly, her internal repetition of John's words is a little inaccurate: where John says, "My heart is yours now as it has been since I knew you," Alice remembers, "My heart is still yours, as it has been since I knew you"; where he said, "I cannot tell you with how much joy and eagerness I should take you back to my bosom," she recalls, "I cannot tell you with how much joy I would take you back to my bosom!" These slight changes could indicate either Trollope's carelessness as a writer or his careful (and realistic) depiction of the workings of memory. The argument for Trollope's purposiveness in representing this particular form of internal revision is bolstered by the fact that Alice's repetition of John's words also puts them in a different order: John's comments about his heart follow the comment about joy in the original scene.

If Alice revises John's words, she also revises her own: "But yet the assurance had been sweet to her; – dangerously sweet, as she soon told herself." This passage of free indirect discourse (FID) begins with what is presumably Alice's "Ah!" and continues with her revision of the word "sweet" by the addition of the dash and the adjective "dangerously." The dash and the "as she soon told herself" belong to the narrator, but the revision from "sweet" to "dangerously sweet" suggests Alice's mind at work as she struggles to protect herself from what she feels are the seductions of John's goodness.

If we look into Alice's mind, then – or at least as we look at it through the narrative available to us – we see that it is made up of a series of similar phrases and sentences, of similar words strung out along chains of heavily punctuated syntax. The accretion of words that moves us forward, the punctuation that arrests that movement, and the sentences that refer back to earlier sentences in the same paragraph or in different chapters offer us not just a picture of a mind at work but also a complicated temporality in which, through which, that work takes place. And thinking is hard work despite, or perhaps because of, the constrained choices available to Alice as a heroine in a marriage plot novel and a woman with time on her hands. Despite the narrator's injunction, thinking about marriage is women's work.

Alice's thinking temporarily arrests what I have been calling the marriage plot; in the process she famously gets called – and indeed calls herself – a "jilt." While it is the marriage plot that offers the shape of the novel, Alice's actions unfold within what is technically a courtship plot; even by the end of the novel she has not yet crossed over to what she refers to in a letter to John as the "new world" of marriage (ch. 10). Trollope's strange and less well-known *The Bertrams*, published five years before Trollope began his Palliser series with *Can You Forgive Her?*, is in some ways a higher-stakes version of a similar dilemma. Caroline Waddington also jilts the man she loves for a less savory and more ambitious man, but Caroline consummates that choice through marriage in a way that makes her less redeemable than Alice.

Caroline, like Alice, uses thinking and letter writing – and thinking about letters – to temporize. Near the beginning of the novel, she takes four days to think through the request from her fiancé, George Bertram, that she set the date for their marriage despite his uncertain financial prospects. Like Alice, she wants on some level to give in to the worthier man's request. Under the influence of her desire for George, she writes him a short note asking for time to think:

> By return of post he got three lines from her, calling him her dearest, dearest George, and requesting that he would allow her a week to answer his letter at length. It could not be answered without deep thought. This gratified him much, and he wrote another note to her, begging her on no account to hurry herself; that he would wait for her reply with the utmost patience.
>
> (ch. 17)

The narrative offers us something of George's point of view: the referent for the "this" that "gratifies" George "much" is unclear; "this" seems to refer generally to the fact of Caroline's letter, or to the promise to write again in a week rather than to the arresting "deep thought" that serves as the pronoun's direct antecedent. Caroline senses a complacency in George's response:

> It was, however, apparent in the tone of his note, apparent at least to Caroline that he judged the eloquence of his letter to be unanswerable, and that he was already counting on her surrender. This lessened the effect of it on Caroline's heart; – for when first

received it had had a strong effect. On that first morning, when she read it in her bedroom before she went down to breakfast, it certainly had a strong effect on her.

(ch. 17)

Despite George's admonition "not to hurry," from Caroline's point of view he has not taken the proposed period of thinking seriously enough. George is, in effect, counting on the overriding temporality of the marriage plot. The consequence, on the level of narrative, is an implosion of temporalities. We hear first of the "lessened effect" of the note after Caroline has thought about it for a while; we are only then told of its initial "strong effect" and, then, of the "strong effect" of what looks like the note but turns out to be George's first letter initiating the correspondence about marriage. The mention of the "first morning" takes us through a period of four days in which Caroline answers George's letter and receives his note telling her not to hurry. By playing with the temporalities of this exchange and with the different letters, Trollope scrambles cause and effect, suggesting not so much logic as willfulness on Caroline's part. As with many instances of the depiction of "deep thought," what gets represented is not the process itself but the conclusion recorded in a series of accretive terms, in this case "lessened . . . effect," "strong effect," and "strong effect" accompanied by a series of differently tensed verbs – "lessened," "had had," and "had."

Caroline's thinking defers the completion of the marriage plot, but only for a few chapters. Her marriage to the successful but ultimately hollow Sir Henry Harcourt produces a different and more subversive kind of thinking that threatens, as it were, to unthink marriage. If too much thinking about marriage before it happens is unfortunate, thinking at all about it after the fact is sinful. After a year of marriage, Caroline is thinking again:

> But there were moments in which Lady Harcourt could think of her present life, when no eye was by to watch her – no master there to wonder at her perfections. Moments! Nay, but there were hours, and hours, and hours. There were crowds of hours; slow, dull, lingering hours, in which she had no choice but to think of it. A woman may see to her husband's dinners and her own toilet, and yet have too much time for thinking.
>
> *(ch. 33)*

The "Nay" that initiates the revision of "moments" into "hours," and hours into series of hours, "crowds of hours," and "slow, dull, lingering hours" is a Trollopian signal for free indirect discourse. We might imagine the "Nay" as internal to Caroline's thought process, but it could also be part of the narrative voice that moves to the generality about "a woman" having "too much time for thinking." Caroline, interestingly, has "no choice but to think"; this formulation undermines the connection between thought and rationality, thought and liberal citizenship. "Choice," a term so central to the marriage plot and to liberal individualism, gets recast as "no choice," thinking as an obsessional act.[13]

Whether it emanates from a character, the narrator, or a narrative space in between, the "Nay" is also, of course, a sign of internal revision. In this case the impulse to revise is a temporal one that speaks directly not only to the hours that weigh so heavily on Caroline, in her role as Henry's wife, but also to the time of thinking itself. Revising, as we have seen, can be a form of thinking: in this case Trollope foregrounds the complicated relation between thinking and time, revision and marriage.

The revision of the marriage plot in *The Bertrams* comes at an even heavier cost than it does in *Can You Forgive Her?* Caroline's eventual marriage to George is made possible by Sir Henry's suicide; the courtship, which takes place five years after Sir Henry's death, is dismissed in one paragraph: George's "offer" is a "cold, sad, dreary matter," and Caroline's "acquiescence" is "melancholy" and "silent" (ch. 47). It is as if the binary structure of the marriage plot takes over, emptying the decision to marry of any agency or thought. The last recorded thoughts in the novel belong to Sir Henry as he comes to the decision to kill himself: the narrator offers three pages of internal monologue marked by the rehearsal of Sir Henry's wrongs and, indeed, of much of the action of the novel itself. Thought, then, becomes literally associated with death.

Both Caroline and Alice, in their respective places within the marriage plot, revise their thinking until they produce a form of consent. The process that gets them to consent is sometimes painfully slow and sometimes painfully abrupt. In both cases, consent itself is almost immediately subject to revision, at the cost of self-respect and, especially in Caroline's case, the respect of others. In *The Small House at Allington* and *The Last Chronicle of Barset*, however, Trollope experiments with a refusal of consent, and a marriage plot that goes nowhere.

Near the end of *The Last Chronicle*, the second long novel to follow Lily's deliberations about marriage, it looks as if Lily might, like Alice, abandon obsessive thinking for an easy and happy marriage with a deserving suitor who has loved her from the beginning. The novel prepares us for this ending by portraying in detail Lily's reassessment, more than halfway through the second novel in which Lily appears, of her bad suitor, Adolphus Crosbie:[14]

> While the untrue image of what Crosbie was, or ever had been, was present to her, she could hardly bring herself to accept in her mind the idea of a lover who was less noble in his manhood than that false picture which that untrue memory was ever painting for her. Then had come before her eyes the actual man; and though he had been seen but for a moment, the false image had been broken into shivers. Lily had discovered that she had been deceived, and that her forgiveness had been asked, not by a god, but by an ordinary human being. As regarded the ungodlike man himself, this could make no difference. Having thought upon the matter deeply, she had resolved that she would not marry Mr. Crosbie. . . . But the shattering of the false image might have done John Eames a good turn.
>
> (ch. 59)

Once again, the depiction of thinking creates a disturbance in narrative temporalities: Lily has already decided not to marry Crosbie, but we still see her in the process of deciding. We both see Lily thinking about Crosbie as she reviews their uncomfortable encounter in Rotten Row and are told that the decision not to marry Crosbie was a product of having "thought upon the matter deeply." As the passage builds toward the binary logic of the marriage plot, it suggests a movement away from thought toward something like the instinct that the Trollope narrator celebrates in *Can You Forgive Her?* To reject one suitor is to take up the other, precisely without thinking. And that suitor, ready to hand, is Johnny Eames, the man who has pursued Lily through the course of two novels.

But Lily is doomed to thinking too much. In the rest of the long paragraph just quoted, Lily's thoughts return, despite herself, to a letter she has received from a woman known only by the initials "M. D.," who asserts a prior claim on Johnny Eames and encloses a compromising note purporting to be from him. Despite her internal acknowledgment that she would be pleasing her friends and family – and perhaps even herself – should she agree to marry Johnny, Lily rehearses the sentences of the "accursed letter":

> There had been nothing against [her acceptance of Johnny] but the fact that the other man had been dearer to her; and that other fact that poor Johnny lacked something, –

something of earnestness, something of manliness, something of that Phoebus divinity with which Crosbie had contrived to divest his own image. But, as I have said above, Johnny had gradually grown, if not into divinity, at least into manliness. . . . Now had come this accursed letter, and Lily, despite herself, despite her better judgment, could not sweep it away from her mind and make the letter as nothing to her. M. D. had promised not to interfere with her! There was no room for such interference, no possibility that such interference should take place.

(ch. 59)

Unfolding as another passage of free indirect discourse, this description of Lily's obsessional thought process features words that pass between levels of discourse. The first "something," as in "something of earnestness," could be voicing Lily, while the clause about Phoebus seems to come from the narrator. The metalepsis that characterizes all free indirect discourse becomes itself a sign of Lily's obsession, as she repeats the word "interference" from M. D.'s letter, first in indirect discourse ("M. D. had promised not to interfere with her") and then in her own voice ("There was no room for such interference"). The narrator's own contributions ("as I have said above") suggest repetition, rehearsal, and ultimately stasis. Lily will be unable to forget "M. D."; she will remain "L. D." and finally become, in her own idiom, an "O. M." or "old maid," frozen into that position and revised into a pair of initials.[15]

Thinking as they (inevitably) do from within the marriage plot, Trollope's heroines are at all moments subject to narrative censure. The very act of their thinking is pathologized, although to different degrees according to their place within marriage and its literary and cultural plots. There is no approved place for them to think, no plot that approves their acts of cognition, no parlor, bedroom, or park where that process can be depicted as an act of liberal citizenship, a normal and useful response to the limitations of feminine existence, a harmless way of filling leisure hours. While it might be interesting to speculate about whether Trollope or his narrators would approve of heroines thinking about something other than marriage, this possibility is foreclosed before the opening of the novels I have discussed – and in Trollope's other novels as well. If a woman should not think about marriage, and she is not allowed to think about anything else, then their range of possible actions is narrow indeed. But Trollope heroines – these and others – continue to think and to fill the pages of Trollope's novels with their thoughts.

Perhaps more crucially, Trollope's heroines also revise: their voices enact on the level of dialogue and character Trollope's narrative project: his commitment to the accretive, the revisionary, even, one might argue, the reformist. When, as Deborah Morse points out, Lily stumbles, hesitates, and repeats herself when talking to her lover (Morse, *Women*, 20–21), she is voicing in her way the Trollopian narrator and Trollope's writing process. She lets her words stand and adds to them; they pile up behind her as she moves (or ultimately refuses to move) through the marriage plot. Likewise, the novel takes shape out of amended sentences, as earlier versions coexist with and comment on later ones.

Notes

1 For an overview of recent critical engagements with Trollope's female characters, see Morse (*Reforming*, 7–8) and Morse's essay in this book.
2 For Trollope's process of composition, see Sutherland, especially 476, where he talks in some detail about the process of Trollope "thinking" about his work.
3 For an early analysis of Trollope's style, see Clark. As far as I know this was the first serious attempt to compile and categorize Trollope's rhetoric. Walter M. Kendrick calls the book "a labor of years, and of love" (418). Clark also talks about Trollope's writing habits and processes. While through the 1970s and

1980s Trollope's "disappearing style" was a topic in much Trollope criticism (see Sussman, 893n6), the issue of style has only recently been taken up by Sussman in an article entirely devoted to the subject.

4 See Christ (123) for a definition of her "aesthetics of particularity."

5 As we shall see, Trollope's relationship to the process of Alice's thinking is very complex. Juliet McMaster sees the novel as "the most explicitly anti-feminist of Trollope's novels," in part because of the narrator's disapproval of Alice's "advanced" views that lead to her indecision about marriage (McMaster, 161). McMaster seems at times to concede that Alice has a psychological problem: Alice is "hyper-conscious, brooding, even morbidly obsessed" (22). Although McMaster attributes these problems to Alice's loneliness and inactivity, the pathologizing synonyms for thoughtfulness suggest an alignment with the more negative aspects of the Trollope narrator. One page later McMaster puts the issue more neutrally, noting, "of course the mind in the process of decision is perennially interesting to Trollope." The lovely phrase "mind in the process of decision" emblematizes for me Trollope's realism, his style, and his investment in character as they come together in his portrayal of Alice.

6 For a discussion of the ubiquity of the marriage plot and its imbrication in the history of the novel, see Boone (esp. 65). As he puts it, "the history of the English-language novel cannot really be separated from the history of the romantic wedlock ideal." The marriage plot, then, as I am using the term, is a literary device, a dominant genre, and a cultural imperative. For *Can You Forgive Her?* as an instance of the "two-suitor" novel, see Morse (*Women*, 10).

7 For what might be called new formalist approaches to nineteenth-century British authors, see, for example, Miller, Raines, and Sussman. For landmarks in the debate over the definition, importance, and newness of "new formalism," see Levine, Tucker, and Dever. Tucker's and Dever's articles are responses to Levine's "Strategic Formalism," and, along with Levine's response to them in "Scaled Up," constitute a forum on new formalism in nineteenth-century studies of poetry and the novel.

8 This is not to say that some critics have not been attentive to Trollope's language, or that there have not been close readings of Trollope's prose. Morse's reading of *Small House at Allington* in *Reforming Trollope* is a particularly striking instance of close reading in which she looks at the intricacies of Lily Dale's speech – the hesitations and repetitions and qualifications that I argue are, additionally, part of Trollope's own characteristic prose (see, e.g., Morse, *Reforming*, 20–3). I discuss Morse's reading further in the final paragraph of this chapter.

9 For a history of arsenic in domestic furnishing, especially wallpaper, see Whorton (200–12). Thanks to Margaret Markwick for this connection.

10 I substitute, for reasons that the binary logic of Trollope's passage about overthinking makes clear, the slightly awkward phrase "change of mind" for the more usual "change of heart." Trollope's point is, of course, that Alice's actual feelings for John never change.

11 The contradiction here is attributable to the complexity of the Trollope narrator. See, for example, Swingle, especially Chapter 3, where he counters what he calls the prevalent idea of Trollope's "sunny optimism" about marriage (21) by positing a skeptical and ironic narrator of Trollope's view of marriage.

12 A decision to read this way can be frustrating: access to the heroines' thought processes, while often detailed, can be strangely incomplete. It is not unusual, especially in *Can You Forgive Her?*, for the narrator to represent the heroine rehearsing at length thoughts she has had throughout the novel and then coming to a decision that is not represented in the text. Take, for example, how Trollope manages Alice's first change of heart with regard to John. She decides near the end of Chapter 6 that she will concede to John's request for an early marriage. After three chapters devoted to the Widow Greenow plot, we return to Alice only to see her writing to ask John for a delay.

13 For the connection between thinking and liberal citizenship, see Hadley (49). She argues that late nineteenth-century liberalism "relocates the generative site of rationality from the highly idealized public sphere of collaboration, debate, and circulation, to an equally idealized private site of cognition [and] metal deliberation." What would (in a man?) be signs of liberal cognition become in a married woman signs of mental illness and incapacity. For a discussion of the connection of masculine liberal cognition and place, I am indebted to Kevin Morrison, whose *Frames of Mind: The Materiality of Liberal Thought* explores the paradoxical relation to place and embodiment in the liberal tradition. While cognition was represented within liberal discourse as disinterested, disembodied, and independent of place, there were certain places – like the Athenaeum club – that served as privileged sites for (indicatively masculine) liberal thought. (See chapter 1)

14 For a detailed exploration of the relationship between Lily and Crosbie in *Small House*, see Morse (*Reforming*, ch. 1). Morse argues that the bucolically named "Lily Dale" represents an ideal of the pastoral impossible to maintain in the second half of the nineteenth century. The logic of this argument would

have Lily's instance on keeping her name throughout the two novels that tell her story indicate her commitment to the idea of the pastoral. I see the scene in the (urban) park as an ultimately failed attempt at revision of L.D.'s pastoral ideals.

15 For more on the contraction of "Lily Dale" into a pair of initials, see Michie (118–19).

Works cited

Boone, Joseph. *Tradition Counter Tradition: Love and the Form of Fiction*. Chicago: Chicago UP, 1987. Print.
Christ, Carol T. *The Finer Optic: The Aesthetic of Particularity in Victorian Poetry*. New Haven: Yale UP, 1975.
Clark, John W. *The Language and Style of Anthony Trollope*. London: Deutsch, 1975. Print.
Dever, Carolyn. "Strategic Aestheticism: A Response to Caroline Levine." *Victorian Studies* 49.1 (2006): 94–9. Print.
Eliot, George. *Middlemarch*. New York: Oxford UP, 1986. Print.
Hadley, Ealine. *Living Liberalism: Practical Citizenship in Mid-Victorian Britain*. Chicago: U Chicago P, 2010. Print.
Kendrick, Walter M. "Rev. of Trollope: His Life and Art, by C. P. Snow, and the Language and Style of Anthony Trollope, by John W. Clark." *Victorian Studies* 21.3 (1978): 417–19. Print.
Levine, Caroline. "Scaled Up, Writ Small: A Response to Carolyn Dever and Herbert F. Tucker." *Victorian Studies* 49.1 (2006): 100–5. Print.
———. "Strategic Formalism: Toward a New Method in Cultural Studies." *Victorian Studies* 48.4 (2006): 625–57. Print.
Levinson, Marjorie. "What Is the New Formalism?" *PMLA* 122:2 (2007): 558–69. Print.
McMaster, Juliet. *Trollope's Palliser Novels: Theme and Pattern*. New York: Oxford UP, 1978. Print.
Michie, Helena. *The Flesh Made Word: Female Figures and Women's Bodies*. New York: Oxford UP, 1987. Print.
Miller, D. A. *Jane Austen, or the Secret of Style*. Princeton: Princeton UP, 2003. Print.
———. *The Novel and the Police*. Berkeley: U California P, 1988. Print.
Morrison, Kevin. *Frames of Mind: The Materiality of Liberal Thought*. Manuscript.
Morse, Deborah Denenholz. *Reforming Trollope: Race, Gender, and Englishness in the Novels of Anthony Trollope*. Burlington: Ashgate, 2013. Print.
———. *Women in Trollope's Palliser Novels*. Ann Arbor: UMI, 1987. Print.
Raines, Melissa Anne. *George Eliot's Grammar of Being*. London: Anthem, 2011. Print.
Sussman, Matthew. "Trollope's Honesty." *Studies in English Literature* 53.4 (2013): 877–95. Print.
Sutherland, John A. "Trollope at Work on *The Way We Live Now*." *Nineteenth-Century Fiction* 7.3 (1982): 472–93. Print.
Swingle, L. J. *Romanticism and Anthony Trollope: A Study in the Continuities of Nineteenth-century Literary Thought*. Ann Arbor: U Michigan, 1990. Print.
Trollope, Anthony. *The Bertrams*. New York: Oxford UP, 1991. Print.
———. *Can You Forgive Her?* New York: Oxford UP, 1973. Print.
———. *The Last Chronicle of Barset*. New York: Oxford UP, 1978. Print.
———. *The Small House at Allington*. London: Penguin, 1991. Print.
Tucker, Herbert. "Tactical Formalism: A Response to Caroline Levine." *Victorian Studies* 49.1 (2006): 837–42. Print.
Whorton, James C. *The Arsenic Century: How Victorian Britain Was Poisoned at Home, Work, and Play*. New York: Oxford UP, 2010. Print.

13

AFFECTIVE TROLLOPE

Marshaling the feelings in *Orley Farm*

Suzanne Keen

This essay investigates how Anthony Trollope's fictional world-making employs representations of feelings about the self and others as construction materials. To a degree unusual among his Victorian peers, Trollope's fictive places and persons come to life in the mind of the reader within a matrix of emotions. Among the core affects of narrativity, curiosity, surprise, and suspense, Trollope privileges curiosity as a driver of his plots, but he answers narrative enigmas almost as fast as they arise. Trollope's narrator's avuncular voice reassures the reader – this is the way the world works – never troubling us with too much suspense, avoiding shocks, and consoling us that any curiosity aroused by the conundrums of the characters will soon be resolved. With Trollope as a guide readers can pleasurably surrender to the representation of others' feelings. I employ the tools of rhetorical narrative theory of fictional minds[1] and cognitive narratology[2] to investigate Trollope's methods, specifically his use of narrated monologue (free indirect discourse) and psycho-narration (thought report) for revealing characters' feelings from the inside, and his use of externalized narration (behaviorist or objective narrative) and intermental thought (communal views) to invite readers' participation in assessing those characters' feelings. It may seem perverse to delve into the narrative techniques of a writer who is sometimes regarded as lacking a consistent or rigorous manner of world-making.[3] Cognitive narratology helps reveal the sources of Trollope's affective accomplishment, first described in detail by Henry James, to whose critique and appreciation of Trollope this essay returns in conclusion.[4]

Trollope's novel titles convey his commitments to his characters and their feelings. Thirty of his novels are named for characters or their roles (e.g., *Rachel Ray* [1863]; *The American Senator* [1877]). Six have catchphrases as titles, half of which evoke emotionally fraught situations: *Can You Forgive Her?* (1864–65); *He Knew He Was Right* (1869), and *An Eye for an Eye* (1879). Ten novels bear the names of places. Trollope's Barsetshire, an enduring country of the mind, is chronicled in novels named for people (*The Warden* [1855] and *Doctor Thorne* [1858]) and places: cathedral towns, a parsonage, a small house, and a county. This emphasis inclines readers to the view that Trollope creates memorable settings, as Juliet McMaster demonstrates in her readings of the emblematic valences of the settings and the allegorical uses of locations in the Palliser novels. When he describes, McMaster observes, Trollope is often "painstaking rather than vivid," or diagrammatic in his precision about properties (182). Still, detailed depiction of places and spaces is rare in the pages of Trollope's fiction. If a major use of fictional worlds is the replacement of the world of the reader with an alternative realm of story, Trollope's fictional worlds are constructed not so much out of realized spaces as out of the imagined beings that populate them and their behavior, thoughts, motives, and feelings, and their speculations about one another's feelings. *Orley Farm* (1860–61) contains within a novel named for a place Trollope's meditation on the limits of reliable knowledge about selves and the promiscuity of people's feelings about the motives of others.

In *Orley Farm*, Trollope spends more pages on describing cast iron furniture than on the actual spaces surrounding the characters, and this in a novel centrally concerned with a dispute about land. We can visualize a field and a road, an upstairs and a downstairs, but Orley Farm as a realized space is scarcely there. It has a couple of pieces of furniture, several differentiated rooms, and one contested field, the reclamation of which from a longtime renter by the impulsive heir (who wants to experiment with fertilizers) initiates the chain of events. The real meaning of Orley Farm is its money value. Orley Farm motivates a property crime carried out by forgery because it is an income-producing valuable. Even in his *Autobiography* (1883), when Trollope identifies the original for Orley Farm, a humble but Edenic retreat to which his ruined father repaired with the family, he gestures to a John Millais drawing, the frontispiece to the novel, but eschews description of the property (*Autobiography*, ch. 1). Just look at the picture, Trollope suggests, and no words will be necessary.

According to the cognitive narratologist Alan Palmer, Trollope is a great artist of *intermental thought*, "acutely attuned to the workings of social minds" (*Social Minds* 181). As Palmer has noted in his *Social Minds in the Novel*, Trollope is among those Victorian novelists whose novels are "characterized by an assumption that characters' thought processes are frequently transparent and public" (164). Just look at them and you will know what they are thinking.[5] *Orley Farm* shows Trollope examining that assumption from the reverse position, asking, as it were, what happens when a society that believes it knows others' minds is baffled by deception in the form of a calm, beautiful lady's face. Trollope employs a counterpoint technique, setting passages of externalized, behaviorist narration and communal (mis)judgments in juxtaposition with thought report that repels direct access to minds. (Trollope rarely employs quoted monologue to reveal unfiltered interiority.) Even in the climactic scene in court, when all eyes fall upon the guilty but shortly to be exonerated Lady Mason,

> she bore it all without flinching . . . though the state of her mind at that moment must have been pitiable. And Mrs. Orme [that is the friend who stands by the accused even though she knows her guilt], Mrs Orme who held her hand all the while, knew it was so. The hand which rested in hers was twitched as it were convulsively, but the culprit gave no outward sign of her guilt.
>
> (*Orley Farm*, vol. 2, ch. 72)[6]

Notice the complications here. The narrator speculates about the state of Lady Mason's mind. Mrs. Orme knows it. Everybody in the courtroom seeks to read it from Lady Mason's unflinching face. The jury has yet to be turned. We the readers know her agony though we are barred from her innermost thoughts: no consciousness represented here! Yet the passage is rich with information about thoughts and feelings. Cognitive narratology has by and large emphasized the techniques for representations of characters' knowledge about thoughts, in supplement to earlier narrative theorizing about fictional minds. For an artist dedicated to making intermentality his central subject and source of narrativity, we can observe distinct projects in Trollope's work, summed up by the following questions. What do characters *know* about the contents of others' thoughts?[7] What do they believe about others' motives? What do they intuit about the state of others' feelings? How does group certainty expressed in intermental thought intersect with and complicate reports of individual thoughts and feelings? In this essay I show how Trollope rings the changes on these possibilities throughout *Orley Farm*. The source of suspense, provoker of curiosity, locus of surprise resides especially in Trollope's use of psycho-narration to report on emotions, but he gives the technique a twist by following the world's – or at least society's – judgments and feelings.

Victorian novelists employed a variety of techniques to represent intermental or communal thought in their fiction: the behaviorist or objective version, in which the group's interests, concerns, and conclusions emerge from details of speech and action; the double-cognitive implication of what a group of others *must* be thinking, conveyed through a character's certainty about social disapproval or suspicion (the certainty does not equate with correctness; right or wrong, it gains force through the character's belief in the others' attitudes); and overt thought report by the narrator about the community's opinions, ideas, and responses. The sense that Nathaniel Hawthorne had of Trollope's fiction as "solid and substantial . . . just as real as if some giant had hewn a great lump out of the earth and put it under a glass case, with all its inhabitants going about their daily business, and not suspecting that they were being made show of" (*Autobiography*, ch. 8) derives from Trollope's goal of offering readers characters they might recognize as "human beings like to themselves" (ch. 8). The inherent interest in Trollope's fiction, which generally speaking eschews the suspense and surprise that are the bread and butter of narrativity, lies in spurring readers' curiosity about what the characters think and feel, wrongly or rightly, about themselves and one another. As Deborah Morse writes about a different novel, Trollope's narrator shows modern consciousness as fractured: "the narrator is part of this depiction of the fissured mind, and the reader is privy to the ensuing revelations of soul" ahead of the other characters (Morse 25). Following recent work on affective experience and the techniques of fiction[8] and the extension of narrative theory into social modes for representation of group thoughts and feelings,[9] I describe in this chapter the techniques by means of which Trollope invites his readers to share the feelings and insights of his central characters and those who interact with them.

In its examination of fictional minds, cognitive narratology has established the representation of consciousness as one of the defining features of fictionality.[10] The categories and functions of these narrative techniques have recently undergone extension. To the three modes for representing fictional minds established by Dorrit Cohn in *Transparent Minds*, cognitive narratologist Alan Palmer has recently added several other categories for techniques used by Victorian novelists. For readers unfamiliar with the narratological terminology, I review the terms, older and newer, with examples from *Orley Farm*.

Narrated monologue

A celebrated quality of nineteenth-century novels lies in their widespread adoption of this double-voiced discourse that enables a narrator smoothly to move from presentation of externals of action and situation to glosses of the thought stream of the character(s) involved, preserving the tense and person of the narration (usually third person and past tense), but conveying the words of the character's mind. The technique variously named narrated monologue, free indirect discourse (FID), empathetic narration, or *Erlebte Rede*, carries the past-tense and third-person narration of the outer scene while reporting inwardly in words that seem to belong to the character's thought stream. This technique, by any of its theoretical labels, enjoys precedence as one of the most characteristic features of nineteenth-century narrative fiction. Jane Austen deftly deploys it; Henry James was to develop it into a mode for lavish expenditure of words in his central characters' perspectives. One can easily find examples of it in the third-person fiction of every major Victorian novelist, and its variations (spread out among many characters, as in Trollope, or limited to a single center of consciousness, as in James) have been detailed and examined by narrative theorists and literary historians of the form of the novel.[11]

An example from early on in *Orley Farm* shows its affordances. When Lady Mason's rights to the property she has fraudulently won for her son are being challenged by a renewed lawsuit, Trollope writes, "She knew that her enemies were conspiring against her, – against her and against her son; and what steps might she best take in order that she might baffle them" (*Orley Farm*, vol. 1, ch. 5). The tense and person of the surrounding narration preserved ("what steps might she best take in order that she might" rather than "what steps should I take to"), Trollope drops into Lady Mason's busy brain for a few phrases of thought transcript. But despite the fact that Trollope employs narrated monologue to represent the thoughts and feelings of many of his characters, not only the central ones, on this very page external cues are given priority: "Lady Mason seated herself in her accustomed chair, and all trace of the smile vanished from her face. She was alone now, and could allow her countenance to be a true index of her mind" (vol. 1, ch. 5). Lady Mason has control over whether her face reveals her mind, a quality that stands her in good stead during her courtroom appearances. Right now, in private, an external mind reader can see her agony: "She sat there perfectly still for nearly an hour, and during the whole of that time there was the same look of agony on her brow" (vol. 1, ch. 5).

Quoted monologue

Thought transcripts of first-person, present-tense discourse that could be spoken aloud with no adjustment of tense and person constitute *quoted* or interior monologue. This mode of representation of consciousness also exists in English fiction as early as the work of Aphra Behn, but it is relatively rare in nineteenth-century fiction and appears more frequently in modern and contemporary fiction, with celebrated instances in Dorothy Richardson, James Joyce, and Virginia Woolf. It presents the thought stream of the character's mind in the present tense and implicit first person, just like dialogue, from which it is sometimes distinguished by tagging "She thought," rather than "She said." While Trollope employs a great deal of dialogue and indirect speech, quoted monologue of thoughts scarcely occurs in his fictional works. In over 800 pages of *Orley Farm* the only utterances that break into present-tense and implicit first-person address (without the quotation marks indicating dialogue) belong to the narrator, not to a character.

Psycho-narration/thought report

Trollope relies very heavily on thought report, in which the narrator simply asserts what the character thinks or feels. As Cohn describes it, psycho-narration not only permits a narrator's characterization of states of mind but also admits generalizations about *feeling-states* of brief or long duration (Cohn 11–12). Psycho-narration often features imagistic analogies or metaphors for inner feelings, using words to catch subverbal aspects of inner experience, what Cohn calls psycho-analogies (37–44). Psycho-narration certainly cedes authority to the narrator over the character, as it can report conditions of the mind of which the character remains unaware, or it can deny access to characters' minds in what Cohn calls "evasion of an inside view" (23). Because of its tense and person, it blends readily with narrated monologue. It is the mode most often used to convey "diffuse feelings, needs, urges" (135). It blends smoothly with narrated monologue. Thought report lends itself to describing baffled efforts at mind reading among characters.

When the lawyer Mr. Furnival and Lady Mason consult about the dangers presented by the renewed lawsuit, which could drag her back into court and deprive her son of the property she has finagled for him, Trollope writes,

> By this time Mr Furnival had dropped the hand, and was sitting still, *meditating*, looking earnestly at the fire while Lady Mason was looking earnestly at him. *She was trying to gather from his face whether he had seen signs of danger*, and *he was trying to gather from her words whether there might really be cause to apprehend danger.* How was he to know what was really inside her mind; what were her actual thoughts and inward reasonings on this subject; what private knowledge she might have which was still kept back from him?
>
> (Orley Farm vol. 1, ch. 12, emphasis added)

In this passage we see how naturally psycho-narration blends back into the narrated monologue with which it ends, facilitated by the shared tense and person of both modes.

As this passage illustrates, and as cognitive narratologist Alan Palmer has demonstrated in his *Fictional Minds*, passages featuring prominent use of free indirect discourse (narrated monologue in Cohn's terms) actually include a great deal of thought report as well. This mode divulges characters' states of mind through the better-informed observations of an authorial narrator *about* his characters, and it can seem both controlling and antiquated. The time has come, however, to break the habit of interpreting changes in formal strategies as a progressive development. Abandoning a simplifying narrative of formal progress from thought report to free indirect discourse to interior monologue (or folktale to Jane Austen to Virginia Woolf) helps us first to observe how many nineteenth-century novelists incorporated all three modes in their handling of characters' internal states of mind. Despite the wide diffusion of narrated monologue, few novelists could do without thought report, and the two modes blend nicely in third-person past-tense narration. I concur with Palmer that more accurate assessments of the proportional deployment of the techniques of psycho-narration, narrated monologue, and quoted monologue will reveal that in third-person fiction, thought report dominates well into the twenty-first century. This project helps us to recognize that *many* Victorian novelists told *about* their characters' thoughts and feelings some of the time rather than presenting their inner discourse item by item all the time.

Trollope uses thought report copiously, especially for conveying the emotions of his characters, as when Lady Mason's steadfast supporter Mrs. Orme "felt much relieved" at her son's reassurance that he will accompany her to court (*Orley Farm*, vol. 2, ch. 64) or feels her heart sink as her supportive son drives away (243). Trollope often uses thought report to disclose one character's desire to ascertain what another character thinks, feels, or knows. Furnival, the lawyer who steadfastly supports Lady Mason, is vexed by his inability to know her mind, though others can be read: "He would soon be able to ascertain what Sir Peregrine really thought – whether he suspected the possibility of any guilt; and he would ascertain also what was the general feeling in the neighborhood" (vol. 1, ch. 25), but as for asking Lady Mason directly, "It was impossible that he should ask any such question, or admit of any such confidence" (vol. 1, ch. 25). Alternatively, thought report can be used to report on what one character intuits of another's mind. This is an example of what Alan Palmer describes as a double-cognitive narrative,[12] in which one character in a fictional world gathers, from her knowledge of his disposition and the situation, what a second character *must* be thinking. So, for example, Lady Stavely feels sure that she knows her daughter's feelings about rival suitors (vol. 2, ch. 50) before Madeline knows it herself (ibid.).

Externalized narration

Behaviorist, or objective narrative, as it is sometimes labeled, eschews representation of characters' inner states and thoughts, hewing closely to the conventions of dramatic scene and relying heavily on dialogue. Externalized narration, the opposite of thought report, involves showing rather than *telling*, and it puts the reader in the position of decoding feelings and motives from external cues. In the modern period, several stories by Ernest Hemingway, such as "Hills like White Elephants" (1927) and "The Killers" (1927), are the canonical examples cited in narrative theory. In objective narration, characters know more than the narrator reveals, which shifts the "knowing" function from the narrator to the implied author and the actively decoding reader. Though rarely sustained to the length of a whole story or novel, this dramatic technique of representing minds indirectly through pure scene composed entirely of lightly tagged dialogue does occur on some pages of many nineteenth-century novels. Though the publishing circumstances of the nineteenth century encouraged expansion and even pauses for lengthy passages of description (stretching to make the length required to fill a triple-decker novel), novelists were also familiar with dramatic conventions of dialogue and group conversation. They could and did interpolate passages of objective narrative to imply qualities of mind that could be verified or enriched using narrated monologue and psycho-narration.

Trollope frequently uses externalized narration, with minimal expansions, for dialogues between lovers. In *Orley Farm* the scenes between lovers, discussions among lawyers as they strategize on both sides of the law case, and cross-examinations during the trial include passages of pure scene composed of dialogue with just a very few elaborating expansions. Trollope invites the reader to read between the lines the emotional tenor of the exchanges. For events in private, this eavesdropping mode, closely analogous to drama, invites members of an audience to come to the conclusion that if only they could hear what the characters were saying to one another, they would understand their innermost thoughts and feelings. Indeed, it comes the closest to a naturalistic representation of human mind reading (though of course fictional dialogue differs radically from transcribed real-world conversation). For the climactic public event of the trial, the same technique of transcribed dialogue points in another direction, as Trollope invites readers to imagine not just the feelings of the witnesses but also the likely responses of jury members, manipulated by the lawyers' lines of questioning.

Intermental/Communal thought

Intermental or communal thought can be seen as the result of individual acts of mind reading, when they are pooled through gossip or shared witnessing, or it can be seen as a distinct phenomenon of group perception. Why does intermental thought, shared or communal thinking (Palmer *Fictional Minds* 218; *Social Minds* 4), possess powers that intramental thought, individual thinking, cannot achieve? When it reports the conclusions of a household, village, or (in societies with newspapers) a whole class of people, intermental thought can have a socially (and narratively) amplifying effect. Beliefs held by many can be especially consequential, though the content of communal knowledge about one individual's thoughts need not be accurate. Intermental thought can be warped by prejudice and error; wrong certainties about others can be as influential as right ones. When other characters incorrectly interpret the feelings of one who shares their story world, the ensuing misunderstandings can have drastic effects. This is especially the case when a jury is involved.

Trollope represents intramental, *individual* thought using psycho-narration and narrated monologue, but he is also a great artist of intermental thought, those groups of thoughts residing in collections of characters that suggest a crowd's view. Notoriously, Trollope reveals that Lady Mason is in fact the forger of a codicil to her late husband's will very early in the novel, so all the suspense is shifted from "whodunit" to What the World Believes about Lady Mason. The phrases "The State of Public Opinion," to which Trollope dedicates an entire chapter (*Orley Farm*, vol. 2, ch. 61), the "general sympathy of the world at large" (vol. 2, ch. 79), "the general feeling on the minds of all people" (vol. 2, ch. 53), and "a general view of the matter" (vol. 2, ch. 67) flag Trollope's reports of intermental thought. Though the professional skeptics, the lawyers, have "a very divided opinion" (vol. 2, ch. 67), society comes to its own conclusion. Eventually, everybody believes that she is guilty. Even the "last servant at The Cleeve had whispered to her fellow servant that Lady Mason had forged the will" (vol. 2, ch. 64). Subplots focused on her son and her besotted lawyer, among the last to know the truth, scrutinize the reactions of those most interested parties. Fittingly, the legal plot reveals how readily a jury can be brought to distrust the testimony of witnesses who are in fact telling the truth. In *Orley Farm* Trollope invites his reader to stop caring about the truth and to focus instead on manipulation of passionate feelings and the complex emotional aftermath (relief, grief, the pain of renunciation) in the characters closest to the guilty woman, in whom he has invested our rooting interest.

Attuned Trollope readers will be well ahead of most of the characters. Halfway through the novel, Trollope flatters readers' mind-reading abilities:

> I venture to think, I may almost say to hope, that Lady Mason's confession at the end of the last chapter will not have taken anybody by surprise. If such surprise be felt I must have told my tale badly. I do not like such revulsions of feeling with regard to my characters as surprises of this nature must generate. That Lady Mason had committed the terrible deed for which she was about to be tried, that Mr Furnival's suspicion of her guilt was only too well founded, that Mr Dockwrath with his wicked ingenuity had discovered no more than the truth, will, in its open revelation, have caused no surprise to the reader.
>
> *(Orley Farm, vol. 2, ch. 45)*

This writer has no interest in the usual drivers of narrativity, the feelings of reading that inhere in narrative itself: begone suspense and surprise! Instead, Trollope practices an art of manipulating feelings, as he acknowledges. Trollope's narrator steps in at the conclusion:

> I may perhaps be thought to owe an apology to my readers in that I have asked their sympathy for a woman who had so sinned as to have placed her beyond the general sympathy of the world at large. If so, I tender my apology, and perhaps feel that I should confess a fault. But as I have told her story that sympathy has grown upon myself till I have learned to forgive her, and to feel that I too could have regarded her as a friend.
>
> *(vol. 2, ch. 79)*

We should take this meta-narrative codicil as a rhetorical gesture, for Trollope is bragging by means of apologizing.

Trollope's pride in his mode of inviting misplaced sympathy compels interest in his technique and craft. This may seem counterintuitive to those familiar with the history of Trollope's critical reception. For some critics and theorists, Trollope condemned himself when he described his writing regime. His habit of writing without revising made him seem less than serious: "If a man knows his craft with his pen," Trollope wrote, "he will have learned to write without the necessity of changing his words or the form of his sentences" (*Autobiography*, ch. 8). This proud statement about his bureaucratic prose, honed in reports written for the Post Office, has been regarded as the sign of an unserious writer. But consider also what Trollope says about his unedited freewriting: "It is by writing thus that a man can throw onto his paper *the exact feeling* with which his mind is impressed at the moment" (ch. 8, my emphasis). Trollope's knack for throwing onto paper those *exact feelings* make him a worthwhile object of study for rhetorical narratologists interested in the complex moves involved in the transmission of affect from author to reader(s). Trollope clearly indulged in what psychologists Marjorie Taylor, Sara Hodges, and Adèle Kohányi have described as the illusion of independent agency,[13] by means of which an author's imaginary creations seem to possess lives and minds of their own. Writing about his most fruitful periods of writing, when he could wander around alone in the mountains daydreaming, Trollope recalls in *An Autobiography*, "At such times I have been able to imbue myself thoroughly with the characters I have in hand. I have wandered alone among the rocks and woods, crying at their grief, laughing at their absurdities, and thoroughly enjoying their joy" (ch. 10). Taylor et al. have suggested that writers who experience this illusion of independent agency most intensely also prosper as published authors, and Trollope certainly did well in the book market. The confession of speedy composition that follows in Trollope's account, however, notoriously damaged his reputation as a craftsman. He writes, "I have been impregnated with my own creations till it has been my only excitement to sit with my pen in my hand, and drive my team before me at as quick a pace as I could make them travel" (ch. 10).

Trollope's reputation comes to us filtered through the opinions of that most rigorous early narrative theorist, Henry James. If we think of Trollope as a writer who writes fast, inviting immersion into easy, prolonged experiences of narrative transportation and lazy empathy, only to bring us up short with plot-spoiling pronouncements, we are seeing Trollope through James. James on Trollope serves as a touchstone of the emergent exacting modern writer deploring the lax form of the older generation's loose baggy monsters. Yet the artist and advocate of the center of consciousness found much to appreciate in Trollope, and James's judgment of *Orley Farm* is worth attending to.[14] James's précis of *Orley Farm* enacts both his disdain for Trollope's management of plot and his admiration of Trollope's accomplishment as a verisimilar portraitist:

> A quiet, charming, tender-souled English gentlewoman who (as I remember the story of *Orley Farm*) forges a codicil to a will in order to benefit her son, a young prig who doesn't appreciate immoral heroism, and who is suspected, accused, tried, and saved from conviction only by some turn of fortune that I forget; who is furthermore an object of high-bred, respectful, old-fashioned gallantry on the part of a neighbouring baronet, so that she sees herself dishonoured in his eyes as well as condemned in those of her boy: such a personage and such a situation would be sure to yield, under Trollope's handling, the last drop of their reality.
>
> *(130)*

With a tip of the hat to Aristotle, James theorizes,

> There are two kinds of taste in the appreciation of imaginative literature, the taste for emotions of surprise and the taste for emotions of recognition. It is the latter that Trollope gratifies, and he gratifies it the more that the medium of his own mind, through which we see what he shows us, gives a confident direction to our sympathy.
>
> *(133)*

Though he does not use the term empathy (it is two decades from being coined), James's emphasis on the "emotions of recognition" and giving "direction" to sympathy suggests that Trollope is involving readers in the kind of transaction that I have described elsewhere as authorial strategic narrative empathy, which reaches out to evoke readers' empathy in audiences near and far.[15] The fact that we are still reading and enjoying Trollope today suggests that his strategic empathizing is of the broadcast variety, reaching, if not originally intended for, a posterity readership. James asserted quite firmly that "Trollope did not write for posterity: he wrote for the day, the moment; but these are just the writers whom posterity is apt to put into its pocket" (132).

Though he did not review the novel directly, in his *Partial Portraits* retrospective on Trollope James lumps *Orley Farm*, with *Can You Forgive Her?* (1864–65), *He Knew He Was Right* (1869), and *The Way We Live Now* (1875), as one of Trollope's "exceedingly voluminous tales" (98). James thought that Trollope's productivity would get in the way of his long-lastingness: "there is sadness in the thought that this enormous mass does not present itself in a very portable form to posterity" (133). He could not anticipate the wonderful combination of a download from Project Gutenberg and an e-reader. James acknowledges that Trollope, whose productivity and proclivity for lengthy compositions he disdains as insufficiently attuned to form and theory, nonetheless pleases his audience:

> His honest, familiar, deliberate way of treating his readers as if he were one of them, and share their indifference to a general view, their limitations of knowledge, their love of a comfortable ending, endeared him to many persons in England and America.
>
> *(100)*

Like a woman writer, James judges, Trollope has a knack for the texture of daily life: "And then he *felt* all daily and immediate things as well as saw them; felt them in a simple, direct, salubrious way, with their sadness, their gladness, their charm, their comicality, all their obvious and measurable meanings" (101). Unimaginative, neither pictorial, grotesque, philosophical, or even satirical, in James's view, Trollope possesses "great natural kindness" (102) toward the subjects of his representations: "There is something remarkably tender and friendly in his feeling about all human perplexities; he takes the good-natured, temperate, conciliatory view – the humorous view, perhaps, for the most part, yet without a touch of pessimistic prejudice" (102). Insofar as Trollope treats both his characters and his readers with kindness, "he has a wholesome mistrust of morbid analysis, an aversion to inflicting pain" (102) (James was perhaps not thinking of Trollope's tortured characters, Josiah Crawley and Louis Trevelyan).

Trollope's narrative empathy is rarely empathy for suffering, making *Orley Farm* a significant anomaly among his novels. Lady Mason suffers and readers suffer with her, even though, or because, she is guilty. In admiration of his convincing but not deep-delving psychology of character, James writes that Trollope

> had no airs of being able to tell you *why* people in a given situation would conduct themselves in a particular way; it was enough for him that he felt their feelings and struck the right note, because he had, as it were, a good ear. If he was a knowing psychologist he was so by grace; he was just and true without apparatus and without effort.
>
> *(105)*

Ironically, James faults Trollope for showing what James would have told, at length. As a plotter, James observes, Trollope eschews what we have come to recognize as the emotional drivers of narrativity. James notes that despite their "great length," Trollope's stories "deal very little in the surprising, the exceptional, the complicated" (106). As is well known, James disapproved of Trollope's self-referential revelations and little "slaps at credulity" (116): "He took a suicidal satisfaction in reminding the reader that the story he was telling was only, after all, a make-believe" (116). This is in its way a deeply ironic observation, coming from the great artist of narrated monologue, whose fictional technique is premised on the notion that a third-person narrator can take the reader into the center of consciousness of a Strether, for instance, where without the aid of fictionality we could never go. James's criticism of Trollope has resonated in the critical history, but his appreciation of Trollope's good ear and knowing psychology should also be noted. A watchword for easy immersion experiences, for prolonged transportation into fictional worlds, and for chatty self-interruption, Trollope creates vivid fictional worlds out of the texture of feelings, as James was among the first to recognize and praise. As to why he could not have been *more* generous, James may have been inhibited in his overt recognition of Trollope's accomplishments by his unacknowledged indebtedness to this Victorian master.

Notes

1 The founding work of contemporary narrative theory on representation of characters' consciousness is Dorrit Cohn, *Transparent Minds* (1978). I rely in this essay on her terminology of narrated monologue, quoted monologue, and psycho-narration.
2 Cognitive narratology has in recent years extended the work begun by Cohn. See Fludernik, and Palmer (*Fictional, Social*).
3 See Morse for a useful survey of those critics who have seen Trollope as a transparent, artless, apolitical writer (2–3), and those who have seen him as more complex and subtle (3–10).
4 On Trollope in comparison with Henry James, see Morse (6, 10, 168).
5 Daniel Wright has recently demonstrated that Trollope's narrators are sometimes known to sweep instances of character opacity "under the rug and replace[] it with an account of a legible set of philosophical and emotional motivations" (1122).
6 Trollope's *Orley Farm* exists in the original twenty monthly numbers published by Chapman and Hall (1860–1), in a two-volume edition that restarts pagination in the second volume (1861–2), the basis for the Oxford World's Classic edition, and in a three-volume Tauchnitz edition for distribution on the Continent (1862). For citation purposes, I refer to the Oxford World's Classics edition, indicating volume and chapter.
7 For discussions of intersubjectivity in fiction, see Butte and Pinch; for Victorians' interest in unconscious cerebration, see Ryan.
8 On Victorian fiction, see Ablow; for a philosopher's take on the narrative sense of self illuminated by study of narrative techniques, see Goldie.
9 Alan Palmer lays the groundwork for this analysis in *Social Minds in the Novel* (2010), in which he briefly mentions Trollope, focusing in depth on Austen, Dickens, and Eliot.
10 See Fludernik (3–6).
11 Critics of the novel after Percy Lubbock have often marked the development of techniques for the representation of consciousness as formal advances. See Auerbach; Booth; Pascal; and Watt.
12 In *Fictional Minds*, Palmer uses the term "embedded narrative" in a specialized sense excluding its usual meaning of a story level within a story, an interpolated document, or a text presented within a text. He has since altered his terminology, replacing "embedded" with "cognitive," to avoid confusion with the usage of embedded narrative that means interpolated text. For an explanation of the shift in terms, see *Social Minds in the Novel* (12–13). Whether labeled "double embedded narratives" or "double cognitive narratives," the terms describe how "versions of characters exist within the minds of other characters and . . . the relationships between these versions determine to a great extent the teleology of the plot" (*Fictional Minds* 15; *Social Minds* 12).
13 See Taylor et al. (76–7).
14 For a nuanced treatment of James's treatment of Trollope, see Michie, who documents Trollope's influence on James's emergent narrative theory and practice.
15 On the varieties of strategic empathizing, see Keen (142–3).

Works cited

Ablow, Rachel. Ed. *The Feeling of Reading: Affective Experience and Victorian Literature*. Ann Arbor: U of Michigan P, 2010. Print.
Auerbach, Erich. *Mimesis: The Representation of Reality in Western Literature*. Trans. Willard Trask. Princeton: Princeton UP, 1953. Print.
Booth, Wayne C. *The Rhetoric of Fiction*, 2nd ed. Chicago: U of Chicago P, 1983. Print.

Butte, George. *I Know that You Know that I Know: Narrating Subjects from Moll Flanders to Marnie.* Columbus: Ohio State UP, 2004. Print.
Cohn, Dorrit. *Transparent Minds: Narrative Modes for Presenting Consciousness in Fiction.* Princeton: Princeton UP, 1978. Print.
Dames, Nicholas. "Trollope and the Career: Vocational Trajectories and the Management of Ambition." *Victorian Studies* 45.2 (2003): 247–78. Print.
Dever, Carolyn. "Trollope, Seriality, and the 'Dullness' of Form." *Literature Compass* 7/9 (2010): 861–6. Print.
Fludernik, Monika. *The Fictions of Language and the Languages of Fiction.* London: Routledge, 1993. Print.
Goldie, Peter. *The Mess Inside: Narrative, Emotion, & the Mind.* Oxford: Oxford UP, 2012. Print.
James, Henry. "Anthony Trollope." *Partial Portraits.* London: Macmillan, 1888. 97–133. Google Book Search.
Keen, Suzanne. *Empathy and the Novel.* Oxford: Oxford UP, 2007. Print.
McMaster, Juliet. *Trollope's Palliser Novels: Theme and Pattern.* New York: Oxford UP, 1978. Print.
Michie, Elsie B. "The Odd Couple: Anthony Trollope and Henry James." *The Henry James Review* 27.1 (Winter 2006): 10–23. Print.
Morse, Deborah Denenholz. *Reforming Trollope: Race, Gender, and Englishness in the Novels of Anthony Trollope.* Farnham, UK: Ashgate, 2013. Print.
Palmer, Alan. *Fictional Minds.* Lincoln: U of Nebraska P, 2004. Print.
———. *Social Minds in the Novel.* Columbus: Ohio State UP, 2010. Print.
Pascal, Roy. *The Dual Voice: Free Indirect Speech and Its Functioning in the Nineteenth-Century European Novel.* Manchester: Manchester UP, 1977. Print.
Pinch, Adela. *Thinking about Other People in Nineteenth-Century British Writing.* Cambridge: Cambridge UP, 2010. Print.
Ryan, Vanessa. *Thinking Without Thinking in the Victorian Novel.* Baltimore: Johns Hopkins UP, 2012. Print.
Taylor, Marjorie, Sara D. Hodges, and Adèle Kohányi. "The Illusion of Independent Agency: Do Adult Fiction Writers Experience Their Characters as Having Minds of Their Own?" *Imagination, Cognition, and Personality* 22 (2002–2003): 361–80. Print.
Trollope, Anthony. *The American Senator.* 1877. Rpt. *Oxford World's Classics.* Ed. John Halperin. Oxford: Oxford UP, 2008. Print.
———. *An Autobiography.* 1883. Rpt. *Oxford World's Classics.* Ed. Michael Sadleir and Frederick Page. Oxford: Oxford UP, 2008. Print.
———. *Can You Forgive Her?* 1864–5. Rpt. *Oxford World's Classics.* Ed. Dinah Birch. Oxford: Oxford UP, 2012. Print.
———. *Doctor Thorne.* 1858. Rpt. *Oxford World's Classics.* Ed. Simon Dentith. Oxford: Oxford UP, 2014. Print.
———. *An Eye for an Eye.* 1879. Rpt. *World's Classics.* Ed. John Sutherland. Oxford. Oxford UP, 1992. Print.
———. *He Knew He Was Right.* 1868–9. Rpt. *Oxford World's Classics.* Ed. John Sutherland. Oxford: Oxford UP, 2008. Print.
———. *Orley Farm.* 1860–1. Rpt. *Oxford World's Classics.* Ed. David Skilton. Oxford: Oxford UP, 2008. Print.
———. *Rachel Ray.* 1863. Rpt. *Oxford World's Classics.* Ed. P. D. Edwards. Oxford: Oxford UP, 2008. Print.
———. *The Warden.* 1855. Rpt. *Oxford World's Classics.* Ed. Nicholas Shrimpton. Oxford: Oxford UP, 2014. Print.
———. *The Way We Live Now.* 1875. Rpt. *Oxford World's Classics.* Ed. John Sutherland. Oxford: Oxford UP, 2008. Print.
Watt, Ian. *The Rise of the Novel: Studies in Defoe, Richardson and Fielding.* Berkeley: U of California P, 1957. Print.
Wright, Daniel. "Because I Do: Trollope, Tautology, and Desire." *ELH* 80.4 (Winter 2013): 1121–43. Print.

14

FORMS OF STORYTELLING, REPETITION, AND VOICE IN ANTHONY TROLLOPE'S *KEPT IN THE DARK*

Helen Lucy Blythe

"My real mission is to make young ladies talk."[1]

Few studies on Anthony Trollope's approach to gender relations notice the heroine in *Kept in the Dark*, a short novel published a few weeks before the novelist died in December 1882. Yet at the time, some reviews expressed considerable regard and sympathy for Cecilia Western (née Holt), who in the novel's first half elaborates her struggles to tell the man she loves and marries, George Western, her story of jilting a previous fiancé when it would seem to mock his disclosure that a woman had jilted him. In the second half, she suffers further after Western learns of her past engagement from the ex-fiancé and abandons their marriage. The reviewer in the *Spectator* notes, for instance, that "we sympathize throughout with the heroine,"[2] while the *Graphic's* commentator declares that Cecilia "must in all respects retain a high place in Mr. Trollope's gallery of heroines," and that he "has certainly not often made young ladies talk better than in these pages."[3] Others responded to the story more dismissively, however, with the writer in the *British Quarterly Review* concluding that readers "never really see" the heroine, who remains a "shadow made by a fine nature on Mr. Trollope's mind."[4] This critic also declares that Trollope's story "bears no mark of progress in any respect" (501), while that in the *Spectator* describes *Kept in the Dark* as "a very pleasant little book," but "one of the least important of Mr. Trollope's works," notable only for being one of his last novels (20 Jan. 1883, *Anthony Trollope: The Critical Heritage*, 500). Such judgments have led to a dearth of material on *Kept in the Dark*, and scarcely a story to tell of the heroine's reception.

With the exception of studies by A.O.J. Cockshut, Robert Tracy, and Margaret Markwick, most Trollope criticism tends to concur with the *British Quarterly Review*, either ignoring *Kept in the Dark* or treating it as one of the collection of late novels that, as Robert Polhemus remarks, Trollope "poured out . . . many of them incredibly bad."[5] Moreover, despite the domination of the heroine's compulsive interior monologues concerning whether or how to tell her story, existing criticism on the novel deals less with her thoughts than the inner workings of her husband's mind. In fact, Trollope's depiction of Western's ruminations has led readers to view the novel as a diluted repetition of a former work, a trend established in 1947 after Michael Sadleir labeled *Kept in the Dark* "*He Knew He Was Right* in tabloid form."[6] In his larger discussion, Sadleir included the novel in a "family of 'novels of the mind,'" that drew directly on *He Knew He Was Right* (1869), but "which tended to become shorter and simpler in plot, as their author realised the impossibility of blending successfully the old manner of episodic realism with the new concentration on psychological analysis" (394).[7]

Several decades later, Cockshut declared that in *Kept in the Dark*, "the whole interest is psychological" (225) and "a serious attempt to analyse an obsession" (226); while Michael Hardwick reiterated that it returned "to the study of morbid psychology" and "the broodings of a jealous man" visible in *He Knew He Was Right*.[8] Tracy likewise treated that novel's depiction of Louis Trevelyan's "insane jealousy" and George Western's paranoid reflections in *Kept in the Dark* as forming one of Trollope's character types (63–64). By 1992, then, G. W. Pigman III merely extended a tradition in introducing the novel as a repetition of Trollope's previous study of "the themes of jealousy, obstinacy, and marital estrangement."[9] But the continuous suturing of George Western to Louis Trevelyan has obscured the narrator's preoccupation with Cecilia and her story, while ironically and even uncannily corresponding to the overwhelming desires of characters in *Kept in the Dark* to reshape and retell Cecilia's story rather than listen to her point of view and repeat only what they hear.

It is difficult not to blame Henry James for the widespread conclusion that Trollope retold the same stories, for his influential essay in *Partial Portraits* (1899) asserts that Trollope produced innumerable variations of one story on "the ravages of love," and that he "turns them out inexhaustibly, repeats them freely."[10] Yet James likely never read *Kept in the Dark* and presumably would have disagreed with Walter Benjamin that "storytelling is always the art of repeating stories."[11] Discussing the universality of stories and narratives, Hillis Miller draws on Aristotle's treatment in *Poetics* of *mimesis* or imitation as a natural human pleasure to account for our enjoyment in repeating stories, stating that we like stories because they "are rhythmic, orderly, and it is natural to human beings to take pleasure in rhythmic forms."[12] Trollope's returns to similar subjects and forms across and within his novels fit also with Miller's claim that for a narrative to become a story, it must have a central idea recurring throughout, a "patterning or repetition of key elements, for example, a trope or system of tropes" (75). Following Hugh Sykes Davies and David Aitkin, Tracy concludes that Trollope's characteristic pattern "emerges from the juxtaposition of the several distinct movements, and the novel expands into formal unity" like musical movements (66, 67). Trollope's repetitions across different novels have produced other studies associating his fiction writing with scientific or anthropological approaches to life, such as Darwin's theories of repetition and adaptation. George Levine, for instance, elaborates that "a pattern in one novel may give way to a variation on it in the next";[13] and on Trollope's common plot of triangulated love, Christopher Herbert argues that in his "imaginative laboratory the novelist . . . runs through this situation over and over in successive stories."[14]

At the same time, it could be said that Trollope's use of character types and common themes merge into a personal master-narrative, or master-plot that H. Porter Abbot defines as "stories we tell over and over in myriad forms and that connect vitally with our deepest values, wishes, and fears," arguing further that they carry significant "moral force."[15] And so while in *Kept in the Dark*, Trollope writes sympathetically about his heroine's suffering at the hands of her obsessed husband, echoing Emily Trevelyan's anguish in *He Knew He Was Right*, the comparison of the two novels diverts attention not only from Cecilia's voice and story but also from Trollope's elaboration of the processes of storytelling and competitions for narrative authority that structure the plot. The novel enters the realm of metanarrative, therefore, telling the story of the stories that characters tell one another, and, in particular, destabilizing the master-plot that is men's "story of woman" told across the centuries.[16]

***

In his leading study on Trollope's later fiction, Robert Tracy observes that at the end of his novels, Trollope introduces a spokesman for social order "appearing to end the action" (46); and intriguingly, in *Kept in the Dark*, Trollope substitutes the heroine for the spokesman in a final scene that literally gives Cecilia the last word. In contrast with *He Knew He Was Right*, *Kept in the Dark* ends happily with the reconciliation of husband and wife, during which Cecilia completely masters her husband with disarming kisses and caresses, before she entirely silences him with her voice, simultaneously refusing to submit to his demand and dominating him with her own. The novel ends with Cecilia's direct speech and the disappearance of the narrator, who otherwise would introduce her declaration with "she said." Instead, we read only: "I cannot speak the word which you shall never be made to hear. I am the happiest woman now in all England, and you must not force me to say that which shall in any way lessen my glory."[17] Left with the splendor of a woman's voice assuming narrative authority, a reader today might find Cecilia's speech calling to mind the feminist revisionist criticism initiated by Sandra Gilbert and Susan Gubar in *The Madwoman in the Attic: The Woman Writer and the Nineteenth-Century Literary Imagination* (1979) that soon extended to equally cogent studies of other marginalized voices.[18] In this context, Cecilia's triumph affirms how the novel became a place for women to become autonomous speaking subjects even in texts written by men. But this interpretation does not tell the whole story of Trollope's heroine in *Kept in the Dark*, because it is not just a matter of Cecilia simply being free to speak or remain silent, but of her being at liberty to choose what to say and when to say it. And even more significantly, Trollope embeds his heroine's reluctance to tell her story within a larger frame of her dominating as a speaking subject – at the novel's beginning as much as at the end.

Trollope's depiction of Cecilia's eloquence in *Kept in the Dark* counters, therefore, the popular articulation of women's emancipation as a linear movement from silence into speech. For decades, Gilbert and Gubar's book was a representative scholarly narrative that in Ivan Kreilkamp's view affirmed how "the novel serves at once as a constraining cage for women's voices and the form in which women find a voice of their own."[19] Kreilkamp admits the valuable contributions to studies of the novel by scholars who "have depended on an unexamined thematic of voice: of voice suppression, voice's silencing, and ultimately voice's ecstatic escape and speaking out" (17). But his project follows a different trajectory in challenging the pervasive myth on which such studies depended: that "the advent of print displaced the spoken word . . . thereby driving speech into obsolescence" (1). In Kreilkamp's view, in the nineteenth century, "voice is heterogeneous and thriving within modern print culture," and that in Victorian society, the "relationship between speech and writing" was "a topic of recurring and urgent concern" (1, 2). The narrative in Trollope's *Kept in the Dark* appears to substantiate this claim, since it does not enact a linear story of Cecilia bursting out with speech after growing up with modest female reserve or in silence.

Trollope systematically presents his heroine as forthright and unafraid to speak and yet at other times displays her as melancholic, obsessive, and reticent, which combine to contribute to the demise of her marriage with Western. In these respects, Cecilia does not properly play the part that Henry James gave to Trollope's heroine, "the English girl," who "plays her part most properly," has "not a touch of the morbid," is forever grateful, and is "delightfully tender, modest and fresh" (127). Cecilia's outspokenness and independent spirit are visible from the beginning when the narrator introduces her as growing up without a father and becoming "the most affectionate of masters" of her mother, who "seemed to be only there to obey the daughter's behests" (Ch. 1). Moreover, when Cecilia later accepts George Western's proposal of marriage, she plays an active role: "'It shall be so,' she said, putting her hand into his" (Ch. 4).[20] And as early as the second chapter, Trollope introduces a scene of Cecilia conquering a man with her voice when she breaks her engagement with Sir Francis Geraldine, rapidly overcoming any hesitation with the command: "Do not interrupt me just at present. . . . Hear me to the end, and if you have aught to say, I will then hear you" (Ch. 2). Shocked into submission, Sir Francis sits down abruptly, "arranging the nails of one hand with the fingers of the other, as though he were completely indifferent to the words spoken to him," but indicating his underlying fury at the audacity of a woman silencing him.

Cecilia entirely wins the battle for the power to speak in this scene, refusing to hear Sir Francis and terminating the meeting when he tries to ask a question: "'Then there can be no further words. If I have done you any wrong I ask your pardon. You have wronged me only in your thoughts.' . . . Then without further words of farewell she marched out of the room" (Ch. 2). The jilted Sir Francis remains in "amazed disappointment," his pride and strategy of training her into wifely submission in tatters (Ch. 2). But while she wins this round, Cecilia suffers greatly from Sir Francis, who never forgets the offense, rewriting and circulating his own version of the episode from which Trollope develops the rest of the plot. *Kept in the Dark* is devoted to elaborating the processes of narrative and storytelling with various characters turning over Cecilia's story in their minds and competing with others for control of it, countering James's accusation that Trollope lacked "a system, a doctrine, a form," and had "no 'views' whatever on the subject of novel-writing" (100). Many scholars since have contested this view, but pertinent here is Tracy's study, since in setting out to prove Trollope's "formal skill as a writer of novels," he turned to the overlooked late novels, including *Kept in the Dark*.[21]

As the author of numerous novels, Trollope knew the conventions of storytelling, thought about how to write effective stories, read reviews of his publications, and was sufficiently interested in fiction to begin a history of the genre. His autobiography, for instance, insists that in the short story, "every sentence, every word, through all those pages, should tend to the telling of the story," a strategy evident in a short novel like *Kept in the Dark*.[22] Some contemporaries noted his storytelling abilities around the time that he was conceptualizing and composing *Kept in the Dark* in August 1880. In June, a review of *The Duke's Children* in *Illustrated London News* referred to Trollope's "wonderful power of story-telling," while the day after he started writing, the *Nation* called him a "born story-teller," raising the question of whether the subjects of storytelling or reviews were in his mind.[23] Foregrounding the oral origin of storytelling, the reviews collapse the distinction between speech and written text or oral and print culture as did a *Spectator* article early in Trollope's career in 1862, which describes his talent for creating the illusion of telling rather than writing his stories, "always narrating, not conceiving, telling you how the figures look as they pass along."[24] Or as Margaret Markwick elucidates, for Trollope, "it's not the story, it's how you tell it" (*Trollope and Women*, 202).[25] And in a similar vein, David Stilton notes Trollope's belief in a "story's need 'to tell itself,'" and extensive process of cogitating on a novel before embarking on its more rapid "telling" or "execution" (134–135).

Equally relevant to a broader understanding of Trollope's *Kept in the Dark* are the commentaries on his style in earlier novels delineating the inner thoughts of characters. *A Small House at Allington* (1864), for instance, has engendered intriguing studies by David Stilton (142) and Deborah Denenholz Morse that highlight the instrumental relationship of the interior monologue form and what Morse articulates as the "complex psychology of the two major characters in a preJamesian focus upon consciousness" (*Reforming Trollope*, 14). A contemporary evaluation of *The Vicar of Bullhampton* (1870) in the *Saturday Review* observes Trollope's "familiar tricks and mannerisms," but more importantly, how his "sentences form themselves about what *he* told himself, and what *she* told herself."[26] A decade later, what characters think to themselves or declare to each other in direct speech with little authorial intrusion becomes the bare plot of *Kept in the Dark*, creating an instrumental interplay of narrative form and theme. It comes as no surprise, therefore, to find the reviewer in the *Graphic* calling the novel representative of Trollope's literary style:

> In almost all respects, "Kept in the Dark" is typically characteristic both of the special topics of its author and of his manner of dealing with them, and might be made the text of a criticism upon his style and process, generally.[27]

In this novel, Trollope establishes patterns of meaning not just through characters' conversations with themselves and others but also through building a formal and thematic rhythm with the repetitions of phrases, such as the title "kept in the dark" and "he told" and "she told."[28]

Such expressions relentlessly punctuate the speeches and thoughts of characters represented inside quotation marks, and so not immediately the province of the third-person narrator guiding readers through the narrative, and both suture Trollope's formal concern with storytelling to his psychological theme. Characters remorselessly turn over Cecilia's story in their minds, gesturing toward Freud's theory of the compulsion to repeat "with its hint of possession by some 'daemonic' power" its neurotic attempt to master a previous traumatic incident.[29] Ruth apRoberts does not cover *Kept in the Dark* in her prominent study, but viewed its predecessor *He Knew He Was Right* as the extreme example of Trollope's belief that "human behavior tends to the irrational or absurd," and it led him to create characters who "seem 'driven,' daemonic or possessed" (*The Moral Trollope*, 102). Cecilia and George Western in *Kept in the Dark* are no exception; both appear traumatized by their previous engagements, compulsively or even addictively agonizing over how to tell, or how to interpret, respectively, the story of Cecilia's past relationship: "She herself told herself" (Ch. 3), "she could not do it, she said to herself" (Ch. 4), "she told herself again and again.... She confessed to herself ... she sat and wept, and told herself how much better would have been that single life" (Ch. 13). For his part, Western "said to himself, he was altogether in the dark" (Ch. 18), and "he reminded himself over and over again" (Ch. 21). Similar and identical examples govern the story, emphasizing how people experience their lives as stories either told about them or that they tell, and Trollope provides ballast with the subplot that gives the same phrases to Sir Francis Geraldine, and Cecilia's "friend," Miss Altifiorla.[30] Not content with being relegated to the subplot, both try to move into the center of the narrative and take over Cecilia's story.

While Trollope ensures that Miss Altifiorla fails in her endeavors, he permits Sir Francis and Mr. Western to control Cecilia's story; and both cause her significant harm. Sir Francis stuns Cecilia when she ends their engagement by accusing her of having another lover, and then circulates the false story that he jilted her, driving Cecilia into isolation and from Exeter for a year, though by traveling, to be sure, she meets George Western. On learning of their marriage, Sir Francis reinvigorates what appears to be a lifelong quest for power over women, seeking revenge for Cecilia independently throwing him over "with most abominable unconcern and self-sufficiency" (Ch. 10). He sets out to achieve this goal through storytelling, of course, convincing himself that he "must tell his story" to her husband (Ch. 10). Repeating and adapting the episode in a letter to Mr. Western, he creates turmoil for the couple, because despite knowing Sir Francis's unscrupulous character, Western chooses to believe Sir Francis's letter rather than his own wife: "Though he knew that the man was a dishonest liar yet he had believed the letter" (Ch. 18), and he takes the drastic step of leaving the marriage before learning or listening to

Cecilia's story, which she ineffectually attempts to tell in letters. Western makes "the mistake," as the narrator tells us, "of drawing a false conclusion from some words written by Sir Francis, and then of looking upon those words as containing the whole truth" (Ch. 18). Cecilia's life as a story thus circulates between men without her participation while they wield control of its narrative form and substance.

Until the feminist movement of the 1970s and 1980s, scholars imagined readers to be masculine or at the least gender-neutral, according to Jonathan Culler in his 1982 reflection on feminist criticism, which notes how Geoffrey Hartman paralleled reading with "girl-watching."[31] Considering the question that feminist scholars were addressing at the time of what it might mean to read or write as a woman, Culler interrogates the critical tradition that in the words of Carolyn Lenz focused on "male characters, male themes, and male fantasies."[32] Delineating the struggles over Cecilia's story in *Kept in the Dark*, Trollope likewise draws attention to two male traditions, or master-narratives that represented women either as unfeeling and inconstant or angelic objects of perfection. Sir Francis's cynicism and desire for power over women lead him to wish to subdue Cecilia before he marries her, while Western's idealism creates his wife as a "treasure to be kept at home" (Ch. 11), a replica of Coventry Patmore's "Angel of the House,"[33] or Sarah Ellis's "daughter of England," whose mind is "impressed with the true image of '"moral beauty,"' and whose love for the man "as her protector" is "pure, trusting, and disinterested."[34]

The narrative devotes more attention to the imaginative Western than to Sir Francis since he becomes Cecilia's husband, and he tells her of his secret ambition to author a "great book" (Ch. 5). Once Western learns of her previous engagement, his mind effortlessly develops an extravagant story of Cecilia's "secret understanding with Sir Francis," "underhand plot," and "terrible mystery. . . of which he could not gauge the depth" (Ch. 12). Having established that part of Sir Francis's letter is true, "there was nothing too monstrous for him to believe" (Ch. 12); and during long walks, and in letters to his sister, Lady Grant, he conceptualizes and composes, respectively, Cecilia's story of "fraud," "deceit," and marriage for money (Ch. 16). It takes a visit from his plainspoken sister to bring him to his senses: "I tell you that you can justify yourself before no human being. . . . People will only excuse you by saying that you were mad" (Ch. 16). While Trollope attacks women's rights through the subplot detailing Miss Altifiorla's contradictions and delusions of grandeur, he portrays Lady Grant as instrumental in reconciling the couple through her forthright speeches – giving further weight to the potency of female utterance in mastering men.

For much of the narrative, however, Sir Francis and Mr. Western create Cecilia's identity for her, forming their own versions to suit themselves and repeating the two dominant stories of woman or master-plots that men have told across the epochs and that have a palpable effect on Cecilia's life. She tries to enact an independent selfhood, but still requires the vocal support of Lady Grant, and more indirectly, news of her pregnancy. But taken together, all the men and women in *Kept in the Dark* illuminate Trollope's concern with the interplay of identity, power relations, and storytelling, interactions that Monika Fludernik locates in narrative and processes of narrating:

> We do not merely tell stories about our recent experience in which we try to make ourselves look good; we also narrate and retell our lives to ourselves. In order to create continuity between past and the present, in order to lend meaning to the experiences that we have undergone, we construct a story of our life. . . . Again, in these stories it is less the plot that counts than the evaluation that is given to (often recurring) events.[35]

Forming a story with next to no plot, the narrator of *Kept in the Dark* enacts this process, representing life as a repetitive set of stories that people tell themselves and others, illustrating that

Henry James got one point right about Trollope: "All human doings deeply interested him, human life, to his mind, was a perpetual story" (104). Constructing the narrative from characters who tell or refuse to tell stories of their experiences, Trollope formally and thematically highlights the complex relationship between story, plot, narration, and authority, and, in particular, the judgments made – or stories told – concerning the lives of others.

Distinguishing Paul Ricoeur's idea of the plot as the "artful *construction* of story" from the "sjuzhet," the Russian formalist term for the "artful *disclosure* of story," or "ways in which the plot re-arranges, expands, contracts, or even repeats events of the story," H. Porter Abbot illuminates the strategies through which Trollope's characters seek authorship and possession of their stories in *Kept in the Dark*, withholding from and providing information to others and, therefore, to readers.[36] The artful constructions and repetitive disclosures that structure the novel call attention to whether women should give voice to and own their own stories when husbands or lovers likely will ignore or distort them. How can they, the novel asks, ensure that men will listen to or read the stories they disclose when traditionally men have constructed women's stories for them?

Trollope wrote *Kept in the Dark* during the debates about women's property in marriage and coincidentally commenced the novel on 18 August 1880, two years to the day before the government passed the Married Women's Property Act on 18 August 1882.[37] His novel enacts a gendered competition for narrative ownership, with its male and female characters shaping the identities of each other in conflicting stories that become abstract forms of property, and their combined struggles affirm Paul Cobley's claim that disagreements between narrative voices raise the question, "Who is the authority here?"[38] Cobley's question is uncommon in Victorian fiction, he claims, because "in the nineteenth century, the novel attempted to contain narrative and head off such questions through a zealous pursuit of realism" (87). And readers evaluating Trollope's fiction as realist overlook *Kept in the Dark* because its debate over who has mastery of the story destabilizes what Cobley articulates as the "knowledge" or truth traditionally associated with realism manifested in "a confidence in the ability to know common persons through the web of their relations within a social structure" (89). Such destabilizations leave readers, according to Cobley, "free to find authority where it is most appropriate for them, often in defiance of the narrator's dictates" (106).

In *Kept in the Dark*, repetitions of the central story concerning Cecilia's broken engagement occur in the broader community of Exeter as members decide what they think has occurred. But Trollope focuses less on the incontrovertible truth of people's exchanges than on the reverse. Highlighting forms of telling, listening to, reading, and writing stories, Trollope's characters mimic the activities of the novelist, who imaginatively builds and divulges the stories of characters within his story, rearranging, expanding, and repeating the events, and illuminating how stories are always retellings and mutations of previous ones. Even the heroine's governing difficulty becomes one of discursive repetition and adaptation, for in having been a jilt, Cecilia mirrors the woman who jilted Mr. Western. Her story is not exactly his story, therefore, which accounts for her reluctance to tell him of it, for she would have to liken "herself to the girl who had jilted him" (Ch. 4). Like Sir Francis before him, she fears that Western might create a less pleasing interpretation of her story if he knew what had transpired.

Cecilia thus remains caught in a dilemma of either telling Western the truth, or "the untrue story, the story which the world believed," circulated by Sir Francis in Exeter who implied that he had jilted her (Ch.4). On one hand, she decides that she cannot be dishonest; on the other, "the truth was not 'suitable to be told,'" and worse still, "were she to tell her story it would seem as though she were repeating to him back his own" (Ch. 4). So she remains silent, her anguished internal machinations generating the novel's central puzzle of which version of the story the heroine should tell to the hero. Should she tell her own story and risk losing his love, or rewrite her story in accord with a man's dishonest adaptation of it? In short, should she submit and deliver herself – her identity as a woman – over to men's representations of her? At the midway point, Sir Francis takes matters out of her hands with his letter to her husband, foregrounding how most people – not just novelists – manipulate words to create meanings and distort events in their telling so that the truth falls into the borderlands between each variation. The emphasis throughout on "he told" and "she told" adds to this stylistic and narrative instability, rendering readers' and characters' access to the truth almost impossible at times because everything told becomes gossip; and one person's interpretation of a past event – or the plot – is never the whole story.[39] Trollope extends the uncertainty by narrating Cecilia's and later Western's monologues in free indirect discourse, which keeps the reader's attention on the workings of the human mind, on its repetitious creative tendencies and capacity for telling stories, while preparing the ground for the stream-of-consciousness narrative and focus on language that later emerged as modernism.[40]

The contradictory stories told by characters to themselves and to others and their competing quests for narrative authority have prevented the few readers who have noticed *Kept in the Dark* from reaching a consensus on either its value or overall meaning. Writing in 1968 prior to the rise of feminist criticism, for instance, Cockshut completely overlooks Cecilia's story, creating instead a man's story out of the extreme sensitivity of George Western and Sir Francis Geraldine, which collapses their "immense differences" in a shared cruelty (227). Cockshut treats Sir Francis surprisingly sympathetically given the lack of textual evidence, since even the reviewer in the *Spectator* expressed disappointment "that Sir Francis Geraldine comes off so easily at the end" (20 Jan. 1883, *Trollope: The Critical Heritage*, 500). A century later, however, it took feminists like Gubar and Gilbert to push readers to notice the constructed "story of woman"; and so viewing *Kept in the Dark* through the lens of *He Knew He Was Right*, Cockshut observes Western's monomania and "abnormal state of mind," but not Cecilia's extensive internal machinations, and she virtually vanishes from his story of the novel. The oversight is amusing since to his credit, Cockshut criticizes Hugh Walpole for misunderstanding *Kept in the Dark*, "because he believed he knew what Trollope was going to say before he said it" (228).

By 1992, the pendulum had swung the other way, and writing in the wake of feminism, Pigman so insists on Trollope's patriarchal views that he too cannot see Cecilia's forthright self-assertions and victories in voice, concluding conversely that the novel "confronts the readers with one of Trollope's strongest prejudices, the necessity of female submission to male authority" (viii).[41] Tracy provides a more nuanced interpretation, giving equal weight to the parallel stories of Cecilia and George Western and observing their shared morbid streak (279). Yet he expresses little sympathy for Cecilia, deciding that she rejects Sir Francis because he is inattentive, whereas Trollope tells us that Sir Francis offends her by "only half-listening to her" and displaying a "light tone of contempt" for her identity (Ch. 1). Not remotely interested in his fiancée's desires, opinions, and tastes, in short, her own story, Sir Francis expresses his general disgust with women, and his lies and mischief-making lead some readers to congratulate Cecilia for breaking off their engagement. Tracy also calls Cecilia's obvious pride the reason for her downfall, noting that she refuses "to yield or share anything of herself" (281). However, Cecilia's internal monologues reiterate that her reluctance to disclose the story stems mostly from her sensitivity to Western's feelings and her fear of him rejecting her; and after all, she is proved right.

Despite these divergences, however, Tracy's study remains the most helpful in establishing the merits of *Kept in the Dark*, foregrounding Trollope's careful style, and preparing the ground for the argument that the novel's subject is the destabilizing competition for narrative authority. Discussing the parallels between the hero and the heroine, Tracy asserts that "Trollope is almost caricaturing his own analogical method," and that "an analogy between two stories is both a structural device and an explicit part of the plot, the central problem facing the characters" (277).

Many scholars have dealt with Trollope's representations of gender, but not in *Kept in the Dark*, yet the novel further supports Robert Polhemus's conclusion that in his novels Trollope was preoccupied with "the drive for female agency, voice, and authority in his changing world."[42] *Kept in the Dark* indicates how Trollope returned to and used his stories of jealousy, frustrated love, and morbid obsession as a foundation for exploring the "sjuzhet" of storytelling, and through it the discursive challenges facing Victorian women struggling with how and when to tell their stories, and control their reception and retellings.

Was Trollope drawn to the subject as an author who had no control over the reception of his novels? Or in writing a story of multiple characters freely repeating their versions of one story over and over, was he also recalling the criticisms of *Cousin Henry*, released the previous year in 1879, that he "never tells anything that we might not have heard somewhere else," and that he must be "sorely puzzled to avoid plagiarizing from himself"?[43] The task of disentangling the possible motivations behind and meanings in *Kept in the Dark* raises a final question: to whom was Trollope addressing his novel? Was it his critics, or young ladies, or both sets of readers? If it were true that Trollope wanted "young ladies to talk," then they were his ideal reader, since his autobiography presents himself as "a preacher of sermons . . . both salutary and agreeable" to girls and youth (*An Autobiography*, 146). And certainly his narrator's plea for women to understand men's reticence suggests that his imagined reader was female.

More curiously, with *Kept in the Dark*, Trollope literally was telling a young woman his story, since his niece, Florence Bland, acted as his amanuensis for most of its composition (Sadleir, 316). Trollope's storytelling process then was very different from his early literary career spent penning his novels in solitude at his writing desk. Obliged to give voice to the story while Florence listened and wrote down his spoken words, Trollope must have had an increased awareness of telling rather than writing. There must have been some poignancy too in realizing that it was a young lady to whom he was handing over control of his stories – giving her the narrative authority to turn it into text, an activity that he would never engage in again. Yet even if his ideal reader were male or gender-neutral, Trollope's story of Cecilia still asks what it means to read as a woman, what it means for a woman to be constructed, read, and interpreted by men, and how difficult it is for a woman to take control of her own story, to tell it herself instead of having others – male authors, for instance – tell it for her. Trollope thus offers a new experience of reading, aiming to achieve what Culler recommended exactly a century later in 1982, to "make readers – men and women – question the literary and political assumptions on which their reading has been based" (51).

Notes

1 Reviewing *Kept in the Dark*, the anonymous writer in *Graphic* notes of Trollope: "'My real mission is to make young ladies talk,' is one of his self-reported criticisms" (23 December 1882), xxvi, 710. (*Anthony Trollope: The Critical Heritage,* ed. Donald Smalley, London, Routledge and Kegan Paul, 1969, 499).
2 Unsigned notice, *Spectator* (20 January 1883), lvi, 88–9. *Anthony Trollope: The Critical Heritage,* ed. Smalley, 500.
3 Unsigned notice, *Graphic*, 710. *Anthony Trollope: The Critical Heritage,* ed. Smalley, 499.
4 Unsigned notice, *British Quarterly Review* (January 1883), lxxvii, 220–1. *Anthony Trollope: The Critical Heritage,* ed. Smalley, 501.
5 Robert Polhemus, *The Changing World of Anthony Trollope*, Berkeley and Los Angeles, University of California Press, 1968, 218. For discussions on *Kept in the Dark*, see A.O.J. Cockshut, *Anthony Trollope: A Critical Study*. New York, New York University Press, 1968; Robert Tracy, *Trollope's Later Novels*. Berkeley, University of California Press, 1978; and Margaret Markwick's *Trollope and Women*, London, Hambledon Press, 1997, and *New Men in Trollope's Novels*. Aldershot, UK, Ashgate, 2007.
6 Michael Sadleir, *Trollope: A Commentary*. New York, Farrar, Straus, 1947, 396.

7. Included in this collection are *An Eye for an Eye* (1879); *Cousin Henry* (1879); *Dr. Wortle's School* (1881); *Kept in the Dark* (1882); and *An Old Man's Love* (1884).
8. Michael Hardwick, *A Guide to Anthony Trollope*. New York, Charles Scribner and Sons, 1974, 104.
9. G. W. Pigman III, introduction, *Kept in the Dark*. Oxford, Oxford University Press, 1992, vii. See also Markwick's *New Men*, which notes the narrative sympathy for Cecilia's perspective, though the focus remains on Western – not surprisingly in an investigation of Trollope's male characters.
10. See Henry James, "Anthony Trollope," *Partial Portraits*. London, Macmillan and Co., 1899, 109, 107.
11. Walter Benjamin, "The Storyteller: Reflections on the Works of Nikolai Leskov," *Illuminations*, ed. and intro. Hannah Arendt, trans. Harry Zohn, New York, Schocken Books, 1969, 91.
12. Hillis Miller, "Narrative." *Critical Terms for Literary Study,* eds. Frank Lentricchia and Thomas McLaughlin, Chicago, Chicago University Press, 1995, 68–9.
13. George Levine, *Darwin and the Novelists: Patterns of Science in Victorian Fiction*. Chicago, University of Chicago Press, 1991, 195.
14. Christopher Herbert, *Trollope and Comic Pleasure*. Chicago, University of Chicago Press, 1986, 114.
15. H. Porter Abbot, *The Cambridge Introduction to Narrative*. Cambridge, Cambridge University Press, 2007, 42, 44.
16. For Trollope's moments of metafiction in *Barchester Towers* see Markwick, *New Men*, 63.
17. Anthony Trollope, *Kept in the Dark* (1882). Oxford, Oxford University Press, 1992, Ch. 24.
18. See Sandra Gilbert and Susan Gubar, *The Madwoman in the Attic: The Woman Writer and the Nineteenth-century Literary Imagination*. New Haven and London: Yale University Press, 1979.
19. Ivan Kreilkamp, *Voice and the Victorian Storyteller*. Cambridge, Cambridge University Press, 2005, 15–16.
20. During their engagement, Sir Francis half affirms Kathy Psomiades's claim that "in Trollope husbands-to-be seize wives." *The Politics of Gender in Anthony Trollope's Novels*, eds. Margaret Markwick, Deborah Denenholz Morse, and Regenia Gagnier, Aldershot, UK., Ashgate, 2009, 42. However, Sir Francis fails in his endeavor "to put his arm round the girl's waist" (*Kept in the Dark* Ch. 2), and Trollope offers an entirely different model with Western, who is "quietly joyous" (Ch. 2) at Cecilia accepting his proposal. As a wife, Cecilia gains further dominance, practically pouncing on her husband at their reconciliation: "The door was just ajar and he passed in. In a second the whole trouble was over. She was in his arms at once, kissing his face, stroking his hair, leaning on his bosom holding his arm around her own waist as though to make sure that he should not leave her" (Ch. 24).
21. The first wave of scholarly attention to Trollope's form and style began with essays including Hugh Sykes Davies, "Trollope and His Style." *Review of English Literature*. 1 (1960), 73–84; Geoffrey Tillotson, "Trollope's Style." *Mid-Victorian Studies,* eds. Geoffrey and Kathleen Tillotson, London, Athlone Press, 1965, 56–61, reprinted from *Ball State Teachers' College Forum*. 2 (1961–2), 3–6; and David Aitken, "'A Kind of Felicity': Some Notes about Trollope's Style." *Nineteenth-Century Fiction*. 20 (1966), 337–53. Interest peaked in the 1970s with Ruth apRoberts, *The Moral Trollope*. Athens, Ohio University Press, 1971, and *Trollope: Artist and Moralist*. London, Chatto and Windus, 1971; David Stilton, *Anthony Trollope and His Contemporaries: A Study in the Theory and Conventions of Victorian Fiction*. London, Longman, 1972; J. W. Clark, *The Language and Style of Anthony Trollope*. London, André Deutsch, 1975; James Kincaid, *The Novels of Anthony Trollope*. Oxford, Oxford University Press, 1977; R. C. Terry, *Anthony Trollope: The Artist in Hiding*. London, Macmillan, 1977; and finally Robert Tracy's *Trollope's Later Novels* (1978). Since then, most Trollope criticism incorporates some discussion of Trollope's style, though not his approach in *Kept in the Dark*. Key examples include Margaret Markwick's "Telling Masculinities" in *New Men*; Deborah Denenholz Morse's *Reforming Trollope: Race, Gender, and Englishness in the Novels of Anthony Trollope*. Aldershot, UK, Ashgate, 2013; Frederik Van Dam's forthcoming study, *Anthony Trollope's Late Style*, Edinburgh: Edinburgh University Press, 2016; and my comparison of the narrative techniques in *Australia and New Zealand* (1873) and Trollope's first-person novel, *The Fixed Period* (1882), in *The Victorian Colonial Romance with the Antipodes*. New York, Palgrave Macmillan, 2014. See also essays in this volume by Suzanne Keen, Jonathan Farina, and Helena Michie.
22. See Anthony Trollope, *An Autobiography*, ed. Michael Sadleir and Frederick Page, Oxford, Oxford University Press, 1992, 237.
23. Unsigned notice, *Illustrated London News* (26 June 1880), lxxvi, 622; and Unsigned notice, *Nation*. New York (19 August 1880), xxxi, 138–9. *Anthony Trollope: The Critical Heritage,* ed. Smalley, 472, 473.
24. Unsigned notice, *Spectator* (11 October 1862), xxxiii, 1136–8. *Anthony Trollope: The Critical Heritage,* ed. Smalley, 147.
25. See also Markwick's focus on Trollope "telling" stories in *New Men*, 61–82.

26 Unsigned notice, *Saturday Review* (4 May 1870), xxix, 646–7. *Anthony Trollope: The Critical Heritage,* ed. Smalley, 335.
27 Unsigned notice, *Graphic* (23 December 1882), xxvi, 710. *Anthony Trollope: The Critical Heritage,* ed. Smalley, 499.
28 See in particular *Kept in the Dark*, Ch. 14 and Ch. 18. *Kept in the Dark* is one of Trollope's shortest novels, and yet it contains over twenty examples of the title phrase "kept in the dark" or "in the dark," while "telling" or "told" occur several hundred times.
29 Sigmund Freud, *Beyond the Pleasure Principle*, ed. James Strachey, New York, W. W. Norton, 1961, 43.
30 A comic figure of womanhood, Miss Altifiorla plans to lecture on women's rights in the United States. Lecturing was the most public form of evincing the power of the female voice, and Trollope's disapproval of women's lecturers is evident in his portrayal of Miss Altifiorla as a complete fraud, yet it did not prevent him from loving the American lecturer Kate Field. And while his interest in making young ladies talk did not extend to the lecturing profession, his inclusion of Miss Altifiorla further highlights the female voice as a central theme.
31 Geoffrey Hartman, *The Fate of Reading and Other Essays.* Chicago, Chicago University Press, 1975, 248. Quoted in Jonathon Culler, *On Deconstruction: Theory and Criticism After Structuralism.* Ithaca, NY, Cornell University Press, 1982, 44.
32 Carolyn Lenz, *The Woman's Part: Feminist Criticism of Shakespeare.* Urbana, University of Illinois Press, 1980, 4. Quoted in Culler, *The Fate of Reading*, 46.
33 Coventry Patmore, *The Angel in the House.* London and Cambridge, Macmillan and Co., 1863.
34 Sarah Stickney Ellis, *The Daughters of England: Their Position in Society, Character and Responsibilities.* New York, D. Appleton and Company, 1842, 125, 224, 225. For further information on the domestic ideology determining roles in marriage, see Antony H. Harrison, "1848," in *A Companion to Victorian Literature and Culture* ed. Herbert F. Tucker, Boston, Blackwell Publishers, 1999, 30.
35 Monika Fludernik, "Identity/Alterity." *The Cambridge Companion to Narrative,* ed. David Herman, Cambridge, Cambridge University Press 2007, 262.
36 "Story, Plot, and Narration," *The Cambridge Companion to Narrative*, ed. David Heman, Cambridge, Cambridge University Press, 2007, 43.
37 The extra rights of property granted by the Married Women's Property Act 1882 enabled a wife to own, buy, and sell her separate property, and the courts were forced to recognize a husband and a wife as two separate legal entities, in the same manner as if the wife were a "feme sole." See *Women's Property Act 1882*, The National Archives n.d. Web. 1 Oct. 2015. <http://www.legislation.gov.uk/ukpga/Vict/45-46/75/enacted>
38 Paul Cobley, *Narrative*. London, Routledge, 2001, 87.
39 In "Trollope's Trollop," *Novel* (Spring 1995), 235–56, William Cohen shows a similar world of gossip and conflict over narrative authority in *The Eustace Diamonds* (1872), differentiating mutable truths derived from "the public" (249) from the immutable truth of the guiding narrative consciousness (251). In *Kept in the Dark*, the metafictional focus on storytelling and characters' competitions to tell their and other peoples' stories make it more difficult to locate an absolute truth beyond the palpable presence of Cecilia's voice and maternal desiring body.
40 See also Morse's discussion in *Reforming Trollope* on *A Small House at Allington* in which she highlights Trollope's "portrayal of modern consciousness in a Bahktinian heteroglossia of narrative voices" (28).
41 Pigman, Introduction, viii. While the novel certainly touches on female submission, it is not the whole story by any means. Trollope places the subject of gendered power relations at the center, however, presenting Cecilia conversing with Miss Altifiorla on men and the institution of marriage, and with Lady Grant on whether women should measure "a man's desires by a woman's, a man's sense of honour by what a woman is supposed to feel" (*Kept in the Dark*, Ch. 8). For his part, Sir Francis discusses the female sex disparagingly with his friend Dick Ross in dialogues further highlighting the different ways in which *Kept in the Dark* engages with The Woman Question. On one notable occasion, even the narrator pleads for a greater understanding of men's inarticulateness before women as he reports on the protagonists' marital difficulties. Markwick explores this aspect in *New Men*, concluding that Trollope's treatment of Western's "emotional illiteracy" anticipates the common debate about "men's problems at the end of the twentieth century" (154). The narrator's intrusion here also further exemplifies that Trollope's subject was the power of the voice.
42 Robert Polhemus, "(A)genda Trouble and the Lot Complex: Older Men – Younger Women Relationships in Trollope." *The Politics of Gender in Anthony Trollope's Novels*, ed. Margaret Markwick, Deborah

Denenholz Morse, and Regenia Gagnier, Aldershot, UK, Ashgate, 2009, 11. See also Polhemus's essay in this volume on the Dalrymple/Dobbs Broughton subplot in *The Last Chronicle of Barset* (1867).
43 Unsigned notice, *Spectator* (18 October 1879), liii, 1319–21. *Anthony Trollope: The Critical Heritage,* ed. Smalley, 461; and Unsigned notice, *The Times* (6 November 1879), 6. *Anthony Trollope: The Critical Heritage,* ed. Smalley, 466.

Works Cited

Abbot, H Porter. *The Cambridge Introduction to Narrative.* Cambridge: Cambridge University Press, 2002. Print.
———. "Story, Plot, and Narration." *The Cambridge Companion to Narrative,* ed. David Heman. Cambridge: Cambridge University Press, 2007: 39–51.
Aitken, David. "'A Kind of Felicity': Some Notes about Trollope's Style." *Nineteenth-Century Fiction* 20 (1966): 337–53. Print.
apRoberts, Ruth. *The Moral Trollope.* Athens: Ohio University Press, 1971. Print.
———. *Trollope: Artist and Moralist.* London: Chatto and Windus, 1971. Print.
Benjamin, Walter. "The Storyteller: Reflections on the Works of Nikolai Leskov." *Illuminations,* ed. and intro. Hannah Arendt, trans. Harry Zohn. New York: Schocken Books, 1969: 83–109. Print
Blythe, Helen Lucy. *The Victorian Colonial Romance with the Antipodes.* New York: Palgrave Macmillan, 2014. Print.
Clark, J. W. *The Language and Style of Anthony Trollope.* London: André Deutsch, 1975. Print.
Cobley, Paul. *Narrative.* London: Routledge, 2001. Print.
Cockshut, A. O. J. *Anthony Trollope: A Critical Study.* New York: New York University Press, 1968. Print.
Cohen, William. "Trollope's Trollop." *Novel* 28. 3 (Spring 1995): 235–56. Print.
Culler, Jonathon. *On Deconstruction: Theory and Criticism after Structuralism.* Ithaca, NY: Cornell University Press, 1982. Print.
Davies, Hugh Sykes. "Trollope and his Style." *Review of English Literature* 1 (1960): 73–84. Print.
Ellis, Sarah Stickney. *The Daughters of England: Their Position in Society, Character and Responsibilities.* New York: D. Appleton and Company, 1842. Print.
Fludernik, Monika. "Identity/alterity." *The Cambridge Companion to Narrative,* ed. David Herman. Cambridge: Cambridge University Press, 2007: 260–73. Print.
Freud, Sigmund. *Beyond the Pleasure Principle,* ed. James Strachey. New York and London: W. W. Norton, 1961. Print.
Gilbert, Sandra, Gubar, Susan. *The Madwoman in the Attic: The Woman Writer and the Nineteenth-Century Literary Imagination.* New Haven: Yale University Press, 1979. Print.
Hardwick, Michael. *A Guide to Anthony Trollope.* New York: Charles Scribner and Sons, 1974. Print.
Harrison, Antony H. "1848." *A Companion to Victorian Literature and Culture,* ed. Herbert F. Tucker. Massachusetts: Blackwell Publishers, 1999: 19–34. Print.
Hartman, Geoffrey. *The Fate of Reading and Other Essays.* Chicago: Chicago University Press, 1975. Print.
Herbert, Christopher. *Trollope and Comic Pleasure.* Chicago: University of Chicago Press, 1986. Print.
James, Henry. "Anthony Trollope," *Partial Portraits.* London: Macmillan and Co., 1899. Print.
Kincaid, James. *The Novels of Anthony Trollope.* Oxford: Oxford University Press, 1977. Print.
Kreilkamp, Ivan. *Voice and the Victorian Storyteller.* Cambridge: Cambridge University Press, 2005. Print.
Lenz, Carolyn. *The Woman's Part: Feminist Criticism of Shakespeare.* Urbana: University of Illinois Press, 1980. Print.
Levine, George. *Darwin and the Novelists: Patterns of Science in Victorian Fiction.* Chicago: University of Chicago Press, 1991. Print.
Markwick, Margaret. *New Men in Trollope's Novels.* Aldershot, UK: Ashgate, 2007. Print.
———. *Trollope and Women.* London: The Hambledon Press, 1997. Print.
Miller, Hillis. "Narrative." *Critical Terms for Literary Study,* eds. Frank Lentricchia and Thomas McLaughlin. Chicago: Chicago University Press, 1995: 66–79. Print.
Morse, Deborah Denenholz. *Reforming Trollope: Race, Gender, and Englishness in the Novels of Anthony Trollope.* Aldershot, UK: Ashgate, 2013. Print.
Patmore, Coventry. *The Angel in the House.* London and Cambridge: Macmillan and Co., 1863. Print.
Pigman III., G. W. Introduction. *Kept in the Dark.* Oxford: Oxford University Press, 1992. Print.

Polhemus, Robert. "(A)genda Trouble and the Lot Complex: Older Men –Younger Women Relationships in Trollope." *The Politics of Gender in Anthony Trollope's Novels*, eds. Margaret Markwick, Deborah Denenholz Morse, and Regenia Gagnier. Aldershot, UK: Ashgate, 2009: 11–29.

———. *The Changing World of Anthony Trollope*. Berkeley and Los Angeles: University of California Press, 1968. Print.

Psiomades, Kathy Alexis. "*He Knew He Was Right*: The Sensational Tyranny of the Sexual Contract and the Problem of Liberal Progress." *The Politics of Gender in Anthony Trollope's Novels*, eds. Margaret Markwick, Deborah Denenholz Morse, and Regenia Gagnier. Aldershot, UK: Ashgate, 2009: 31–44. Print.

Sadleir Michael. *Trollope: A Commentary*. New York: Farrar, Straus, and Company, 1947. Print.

Smalley, Donald, ed. *Anthony Trollope: The Critical Heritage*. London: Routledge and Kegan Paul, 1969. Print.

Stilton, David. *Anthony Trollope and His Contemporaries: A Study in the Theory and Conventions of Victorian Fiction*. London: Longman, 1972. Print.

Terry, R. C. *Anthony Trollope: The Artist in Hiding*. London: Macmillan, 1977. Print.

Tillotson, Geoffrey. "Trollope's Style." *Mid-Victorian Studies,* eds. Geoffrey and Kathleen Tillotson. London: Athlone Press, 1965: 56–61. Reprinted from *Ball State Teachers' College Forum* 2 (1961–2): 3–6. Print.

Tracy, Robert. *Trollope's Later Novels*. Berkeley: University of California Press, 1978. Print.

Trollope, Anthony. *An Autobiography*. 1883, eds. Michael Sadleir and Frederick Page. Oxford: Oxford University Press, 1992. Print.

———. *Cousin Henry*. 1878. Oxford: Oxford University Press, 2009. Print.

———. *Dr. Wortle's School*. 1881. London: Penguin Books, 1999. Print.

———. *The Duke's Children*. 1880. Oxford: Oxford University Press, 2011. Print.

———. *The Eustace Diamonds*. 1872. Oxford: Oxford University Press, 2011. Print.

———. *An Eye for an Eye*. 1879. London: Penguin Books, 1993. Print.

———. *He Knew He Was Right*.1869. Oxford: Oxford University Press, 2009. Print.

———. *Kept in the Dark*. 1882. Oxford: Oxford University Press, 1992. Print.

———. *An Old Man's Love*. 1884. Oxford: Oxford University Press, 1999. Print.

———. *The Small House at Allington*. 1864. Oxford: Oxford University Press, 2014. Print.

———. *The Vicar of Bullhampton*. 1870. Oxford: Oxford University Press, 1988. Print.

Unsigned notice. *British Quarterly Review.* lxxvii (January 1883): 220–1. *Anthony Trollope: The Critical Heritage,* ed. Donald Smalley. London: Routledge & Kegan Paul, 1969, 501. Print.

Unsigned notice. *The Graphic.* xxvi (23 December 1882): 710. *Anthony Trollope: The Critical Heritage,* ed. Donald Smalley. London: Routledge & Kegan Paul, 1969, 499. Print.

Unsigned notice. *Illustrated London News.* lxxvi (26 June 1880): 622. *Anthony Trollope: The Critical Heritage,* ed. Donald Smalley. London: Routledge & Kegan Paul, 1969, 472. Print.

Unsigned notice. *Nation* (New York). xxxi (19 August 1880): 138–9. *Anthony Trollope: The Critical Heritage,* ed. Donald Smalley. London: Routledge & Kegan Paul, 1969, 473. Print.

Unsigned notice. *Saturday Review.* xxix (4 May 1870): 646–7. *Anthony Trollope: The Critical Heritage,* ed. Donald Smalley. London: Routledge & Kegan Paul, 1969, 335–7. Print.

Unsigned notice. *Spectator.* xxxiii (11 October 1862): 1136–8. *Anthony Trollope: The Critical Heritage,* ed. Donald Smalley. London: Routledge & Kegan Paul, 1969, 146–51. Print.

Unsigned notice. *Spectator.* liii (8 October 1879): 1319–21. *Anthony Trollope: The Critical Heritage,* ed. Donald Smalley. London: Routledge & Kegan Paul, 1969, 461. Print.

Unsigned notice. *Spectator.* lvi (20 January 1883): 88–9. *Anthony Trollope: The Critical Heritage,* ed. Donald Smalley. London: Routledge & Kegan Paul, 1969, 500. Print.

Unsigned notice. *The Times* (6 November 1879): 6. *Anthony Trollope: The Critical Heritage,* ed. Donald Smalley. London: Routledge & Kegan Paul, 1969, 466. Print.

Women's Property Act 1882, The National Archives n.d. Web. 1 Oct. 2015. <http://www.legislation.gov.uk/ukpga/Vict/45-46/75/enacted>

15
TROLLOPE WRITES TROLLOPE

Margaret Markwick

"The man of letters is, in truth, ever writing his own biography."
(*Life of Cicero, vol. 1.32*)

When we come to write about Trollope as a biographer, we are hit by a double whammy, as we write about a literary form which has been only tenuously analysed, and apply it to works that have only rarely been visited.[1] We may, then, be excused for wishing to read this line from Trollope's *Life of Cicero* as a very tempting invitation to interpret his texts as direct links to the inner man, to access those parts of Trollope so tantalisingly denied to us in *An Autobiography*. This essay will explore his four forays into life writing and his autobiography to determine the degree to which we might be justified in doing so.

The formation of a body of critical theory to describe how literary biography operates is in its infancy in comparison with the well-developed schools of thought dedicated to the theory and analysis of the novel form. There is some irony in this, since biography as a literary form has been with us for well over two millennia, while the novel is a comparatively new arrival on the scene. This is not because of lack of interest in the form. As Hermione Lee points out in *Biography: A Very Short Introduction*,[2] when Petrarch compares his craft to that of a portrait painter, he is theorising about the nature of biography (Lee 3). Samuel Johnson writes about his craft in *The Rambler* and *The Idler*; Boswell discusses his ideas of where the biographer should focus his attentions; Virginia Woolf explores its chimerical volatility, both in her two essays on the form and in her fiction – her parodic biography *Flush*, and her resistant and experimental *Orlando*. Lee's chapter "Against Biography" is a lucid journey through the confusion of ideas that made up the view of biography as a sub-literate genre, so dominant in the academy in the 1970s and 1980s, starting with the aesthetics of Bloomsbury through to Barthes and the death of the author. Since then, of course, the tide has begun to turn, and there are now university schools dedicated to the study and performance of life writing. Michael Benton's *Literary Biography: An Introduction* has done much to establish the beginnings of a discipline, while Kathryn Hughes, professor of life writing at UEA, writes widely in the academic and the trade press of the latest framing of critical thinking in her field. I propose also to use Jorge Borges, and his brief essay "Borges and I," to explore Trollope's use of the first-person narrative, a technique still considered innovative in the early twenty-first century.

Thackeray

Before his untimely death, Thackeray had left instructions that there was to be no "fulsome" (ch. 1) biography.[3] Sixteen years later his daughter Annie agreed to allow Trollope to write a short memoir and appreciation of the life and work of his friend. He promises to be discreet: "I will give such incidents and anecdotes of his life as will tell the reader perhaps all about him that a reader is entitled to ask" (ch. 1). Even so, he managed to upset Annie, not by any scandalous references to Thackeray's passion for Mrs Brookfield but by his preoccupation with how much money Thackeray had made from his writing – a reflection of his own pride in his own earnings from his pen.

Few commentators have written about Trollope's *Thackeray*,[4] and J. Hillis Miller's is probably the only extensive critique. In his cogent and measured style he incisively examines chapters 2–9, which are analyses of Thackeray's writings. Miller describes them as "a forceful apology for Trollope's own theory of the novel and practice of it" (355). However, chapter 1, nearly a third of the volume, which deals with biographical material, is our focus. Factually, it contains nothing that was not widely known about Thackeray's life, though Trollope is at pains to correct the gossip about how he lost his patrimony – a failed investment, with his stepfather, in a newspaper, not gambling. Thackeray had given Trollope his biggest break when he offered him the opportunity to open the first issue of *The Cornhill* with *Framley Parsonage*. It was the beginning of a warm friendship, and Trollope was deeply saddened by his death four years later. So it is something of a shock to discover how harshly Trollope judges his friend's lack of application to his craft.

It is important to remember that Trollope wrote this memoir three years after he had written his record of his own literary achievement – how he rose at five every morning, meticulously revising the previous day's work, writing his 250 words each quarter hour, before going off to give an honest day's work to the Post Office. Now himself the grand old man of novelists, what, he seems to say, might Thackeray have achieved if he'd shown such application, if he'd written forty-seven novels instead of a dozen or so? As he reflects on thirty years of early rising, proud of the "honest stitches" he makes, with a goodly layer of sticky cobbler's wax holding him fast to his chair, and of his conscientious service to the Post Office, he comes to believe that his is the only model of hard work which deserves to bring success. However, in judging him so harshly for frittering away his time and his talents, Trollope forgets to remember that it was perhaps Thackeray's insight into himself that enabled him to create a Pendennis who could reach into his audience's heart, and that equally, without Trollope's own wilderness years, we might have lost much of the richness and depth in Johnny Eames and Charlie Tudor. He is equally critical of Thackeray's performance as editor of *The Cornhill*. He charges him with being both perfunctory in his scrutiny of the vast amount of material submitted to him for publication, and at the same time a sucker for the heart-rending appeals from impoverished would-be contributors. Trollope himself while editor of *Saint Paul's* tried to read everything that was submitted (described by John Morley as "a waste of time, absolute and unredeemed"[5]), and it is worth noting that *Saint Paul's* was always viewed as lacklustre, while *The Cornhill* was very successful.

But what seems to rile Trollope the most, as he looks back on the life and achievement of his one-time hero, is his attempts to find a sinecure in the public services which would provide him with a steady income, while demanding little of him: politics, the diplomatic service – and the Post Office. In 1848, Thackeray petitioned for the post of assistant secretary – a high-ranking position, third or fourth in command of the service. Thackeray clearly believed that it would involve little work: "What a place for a man of letters!" he wrote to his friend Lady Blessington, who had interceded as his patron in the affair.[6] It is clear from Trollope's account (ch. 1) that he took this as a very personal slight on his own commitment to give an honest day's work for an honest day's pay at his Post Office desk. What Trollope does is to hold himself up as a yardstick by which to measure a giant, and find him wanting. His retrospective seems to me to have a stubborn subtext about Trollope's own journey to recognition. In the narrative voice of *Thackeray* we can hear the young clerk at the Post Office, criticised for lack of application, fearing that the humiliations of his schooldays will dog him all his days. We hear the voice of a driven man in relentless pursuit of success.

Lord Palmerston

The authorial voice of *Lord Palmerston*,[7] while it is certainly not as personalised as that used to talk about Thackeray's life, is none the less also one that draws on Trollope's own memories and convictions. Trollope begins his account in 1851, when Palmerston was sixty-seven, when Lord John Russell expelled his foreign secretary from his government. His account does assume that the reader is familiar with the story, a gambit less problematic then than now. This allows him to deal with the episode quite briefly, in but six and a half pages. He opens his narrative by listing his sources – the three-volume *Life* by Henry Lytton Bulwer, contemporary accounts in newspapers and periodicals, his own memory – and then, almost apologetically, Sir Theodore Martin's *Life of the Prince Consort*. For it is indeed the role of Albert, and, by implication, Victoria, in Palmerston's dismissal from the Foreign Office that so challenges Trollope and his patriotic monarchist views.

Britain was, and still is, a constitutional monarchy, which denotes a process of democratic government, independent of the Throne. However, the British royal family throughout the nineteenth century, and particularly after Victoria's marriage to Albert, was closely interrelated to every royal house in Europe, where very different protocols ruled. Albert in particular found it galling that, while his views on foreign policy, imbibed from his Germanic tutors, might be listened to politely, Palmerston, for so many years foreign secretary, would choose a path independent of his advice. It caused much ill will that Victoria regularly communicated to her prime minister. The last straw came with Louis Napoleon's coup d'état in 1851. Palmerston viewed this pragmatically, and did not condemn it out of hand, a position which Albert considered flew in the face of his political teaching, and would tend to isolate Britain from the rest of Europe. The queen demanded that Lord Russell remove Palmerston from office. This he did, but Palmerston six weeks later orchestrated a rebellion against the government's plans for local militias. The government lost the vote, Russell resigned, and Palmerston was back in the cabinet inside the year, though this time at the Home Office.

Dealing with this incident in his opening chapter frees Trollope to restart his narrative at the beginning of Palmerston's life, and revisit the late 1840s and early 1850s in much greater detail, without need to refer to that interference from the Crown. In spite of taking three chapters to explore Palmerston's major causes during these years, including an entire chapter on the "Don Pacifico"[8] case, there is this time round virtually no mention of Albert's strenuous efforts to influence government policy; this reticence perhaps reflects Trollope's patriotism and loyalty to the monarchy; having made clear his admiration for Albert's many sterling qualities, he adds a caveat. "But with the verdict of the Prince, declared in regard to Lord Palmerston as Foreign Minister, I am compelled to differ" (ch. 1). This is an assertive, abrasive "I", coming very early on. It establishes authorial authority; after this, his more self-effacing "I think" and his embracing "we are" are less open to challenge. This is a narrator of strong and personal view.

As in his *Thackeray*, Trollope again emphatically refuses to countenance intrusion into his subject's private life, to the point of total denial that there was indeed anything salacious to intrude into:

> He avoided those scrapes to which men are subject, – men who come early into their fortunes, and their titles, who profess to live, if not lives of pleasure, lives to which pleasure lends all her attractions . . . The world has heard of no trouble into which he got about women.
>
> (ch. 1)

This is a remarkable statement about a man openly known in his own times as a womaniser. During his last administration, at the age of seventy-nine, a Mr O'Kane cited him as co-respondent in his divorce. A popular joke at the time was "We know she's Kane, but is he able?" Disraeli, it is said, claimed it was all a publicity stunt on Palmerston's behalf to boost his popularity in the forthcoming elections – which does imply that tales of Palmerston's sexual prowess were widely known, and went down well with the electorate.

In fairness it is hard to know how Trollope, writing in 1881–2, might have written about Palmerston's reputation with decorum. James Froude's publication of Carlyle's *Reminiscences* of Jane Carlyle's life, based on her journals and letters, in early 1881, a month after Carlyle's death, had created uproar. "The publication took place, and literary society became like a cage of parrots upset. Everyone was shrieking at the same time." As S. J. Heidt so lucidly exposes, the shock was about the extent and nature of the intimate details of the Carlyles' private lives revealed in Jane Carlyle's journals and letters.[9] Given Trollope's stated views on a writer's right to privacy, it is hardly surprising that he declines to repeat the gossip about Palmerston. However, in denying so emphatically that there is anything of note to say on Palmerston's notorious libertine habits, he by this very default draws attention to the discrepancy between what he avers and common knowledge. In this manner, the passage operates as a joke for the cognoscenti, another of Trollope's "smoking-room jokes".[10]

So much of what Trollope admires in Palmerston reads like a portrait of one of his heroes, or of himself: "He was bold, industrious, honest, strong in purpose as in health, eager, unselfish, and a good comrade" (ch. 14). He praises his "probity, truth and honesty," and continues, "Perhaps no single word goes so far in the description of Lord Palmerston as the word 'manly'" (ch. 14). I have explored Trollope's theories of manliness at length elsewhere, but in identifying "manly" as the yardstick of Palmerston's sterling qualities, he links him to his great fictional creations, where his analysis of their manly qualities segues into their definition as Victorian gentlemen. There is a cross-fertilisation between the attributes in Palmerston Trollope so admires and the sterling qualities that go to make up his "manly" heroes, particularly Plantagenet Palliser.

The Commentaries of Caesar

The political turmoil, in Europe and America, starting with the first French Revolution in 1789, right though to 1848 when there was simultaneous political upheaval in France, Germany, Spain, Italy, and Austria, polarised all reading of Julius Caesar. Trollope's interpretation of Caesar is inextricably shaped by Trollope's response to the political events of his lifetime.

Contrary to popular belief, and unlike Charlie Tudor, Trollope did not fritter away his first eight years with the Post Office in living beyond his means and flirting with young women of doubtful provenance. His grounding, in Latin at least, enabled him to learn to read Horace fluently and with pleasure during those years.[11] In 1851 and 1856 he had written very long (20,000 words) reviews of Charles Merivale's[12] monumental seven-volume *History of the Romans Under the Empire*. While his tone is largely approving, he criticises Merivale for being too adulatory of Caesar, a view increasingly popular from 1850 onwards which Trollope found disturbing. For while in the eighteenth century, Caesar, as Addison Ward so elegantly demonstrates, had largely been constructed as a figure of excessive ambition, usurping power, with a minority but insistent voice framing him as a rescuer of the people from a discredited system of government,[13] as the nineteenth century opened conventional views in Britain hardened in the wake of revolution lapping at her shores.

As a schoolboy Trollope would have imbibed the mainstream view of Caesar, promulgated by his masters, closely adhering to the line taken by Thomas Arnold, headmaster of Rugby, who wrote a series of essays on the Late Roman Commonwealth, which were published between 1823 and 1826, during Trollope's schoolboy years. On the continent by contrast, Napoleon Bonaparte was explicitly pursuing a policy of "Caesarism", defined by Marina Wyke as "rule by an individual who seizes power from an elected government, is sustained by the military, and claims a democratic legitimacy."[14] His great-nephew Louis Napoleon III wrote his *Histoire de Jules César* (described by Trollope as "that most futile book" – *Auto* ch. 18) and sponsored huge archaeological investigations into Caesar's campaigns in Gaul. In Germany, through the 1850s, Mommsen was publishing his monumental *The History of Rome*, which constructs Caesar as "the entire and perfect man", and a model for German governance. This all fostered a groundswell of revisionist readings, which Trollope was set on confronting: "No effort shall be made, – as has been frequently and so painfully done for us in late years, – to upset the teachings of our youth, and to prove that the old lessons were wrong" (C of C ch. 1).[15] We might notice here the voice of the narrator coming through, as in "done for us", and "teachings of our youth", where the use of the first-person plural embraces the writer and reader. Trollope's heightened sensitivity to the possibilities of nuance in a shifting narrative voice is clear from his observations on Caesar's narrator in Caesar's original text: "Caesar writes in the third person and is very careful to maintain that mode of expression. But he is not so careful but that on three or four occasions he forgets himself and speaks in the first person" (ch. 1). Such close attention to Caesar's narrative voice reflects the importance he placed on the modulation of his own authorial voice,[16] and the energies he put into developing its subtleties. In his *Caesar*, Trollope's manipulation of "I" and "we" enables him to draw the reader into his view of an empire-builder-turned-despot without arguing the revisionist view.

De Bello Gallico, the first of Caesar's commentaries, is his account of the extending of the boundaries of the Roman Empire through to the English Channel, and Trollope writes his commentary on Caesar's campaign at a time when the British were extending their empire over all the far-flung parts of the globe. In a style somewhat reminiscent of Gilbert à Beckett's *Comic History of Rome* (a very popular work through the 1850s), Trollope presents Caesar as a ravening wolf, bent on devouring the lamb, the tribes of Gaul. Speaking of the inevitability of this correlation in all empire-building – be it the British in India, the Spanish in South America, the United States spreading ever westwards – he comments, "But the philosophical reader perceives that in this way, and in no other, is civilisation carried into distant lands. The wolf, though he be a ravenous wolf, brings with him energy and knowledge" (ch. 2).

However, when Trollope moves on to *De Bello Civile*, we hear a dramatic shift in the tone of his narrative voice that, in spite of Trollope's claim, is not entirely a reflection of Caesar's text:

> There is in it less of adventure, less of new strange life, and less of that sound healthy joyous feeling which sprang from a thorough conviction on Caesar's part that in crushing the lamb he was doing a thoroughly good thing.
>
> (ch. 9)

What we see in the commentary on *De Bello Civile* is a conflicted Trollope who struggles to reconcile his admiration of empire-building skills with his horror of Caesar's usurping of power from what Trollope perceived as legitimate government. In Caesar's original, it is clear that while he has no qualms about slaughtering hecatombs of Gauls to achieve his ends, he is far more circumspect about spilling Roman blood. We can detect Trollope's authorial voice struggling to reconcile this admirable reticence with his view of civil war as an unqualified aberration, something that was infecting the rest of Europe, and to be resisted at all costs on British soil:

> Caesar treats his compatriots with the utmost generosity. So many conquered Gauls he would have sold as slaves, slaughtering their leaders. . . . But his conquered foes are Roman soldiers, and he simply demands that the army of Afranius shall be disbanded. . . . Never was there such clemency – or we may say, better policy!
>
> *(ch. 9)*

Thus Trollope reduces what revisionists interpret as Caesar's integrity into clever public relations.

At the end of Trollope's *Commentary* on *De Bello Gallico*, Vercingetorix, the courageous and gallant leader of the Arverni, who so nearly led the united tribes of Gaul to overcome Caesar, taken prisoner, held captive for six years, and then strangled to honour Caesar in his first celebratory triumph as dictator, is both subjugated in justifiable empire expansion and executed to entertain a power-mad self-justifying dictator. Vercingetorix becomes the paradigm of Trollope's irreconcilable beliefs on empire and revolution.

Life of Cicero

The two-volume *Life of Cicero*[17] is the big baggy monster of Trollope's foray into life writing. It had been a long time in the making. When he wrote the lengthy reviews of Merivale's *History* in 1852, he had cut a large section on Cicero which was superfluous to the review, but which had seized his imagination. More than twenty years later he took Cicero's works with him to Australia, and it was there he resolved to write his *Life*, spurred on to the challenge by his perceived need for a rebalanced view of his hero: "A score of men have taken it upon themselves of late to belittle the great patriot: Merivale, Mommson, Beesly, and now Froude."[18] Their sin was their "attempts which are made to rewrite history on the base of moral convictions and philosophical conclusion" (vol. 1, ch. 9). For them, Caesar was the charismatic leader of a reformist movement. Beesly went one further, casting Catiline as the first great, if flawed, founder of the people's revolutionary party, with Caesar as his heir; Trollope associates such views with the French Revolution, and sees the Roman appetite for reform as the manifestation of over-vaunting egos of power-hungry freebooters.

His *Life of Cicero* attacks all four of these scholars for their uncritical praise for Caesar, which is always at Cicero's expense. Indeed Trollope's scrupulously worked book could well be subtitled "*Death by Footnote*", so assiduously does he critique them line by line. In an extended footnote in volume 1, chapter 9, he criticises Merivale for his biased "little work on the two Roman triumvirates". Trollope incorporates a swipe at Beesly in the same footnote. "The Dean's [Merivale] sympathies are very akin to those of Mr Beesly, but he values too highly his own historical judgement to allow it to run on all fours with Mr Beesly's sympathies." Using the bestial metaphor of "running on all fours" downgrades both Merivale and Beesly's work to something less than pedestrian.

The *Life of Cicero* is not so much a biography as a study of Cicero's writings in the context of his life. In this he is well ahead of his time. As Lytton Strachey so scathingly observes,[19] Victorian biographies tended to be three-volume panegyrics, a cradle-to-grave approach that lasted till the mid-twentieth century, when more creative and exploratory ways to examine a life emerged, led by Virginia Woolf and A.J.A. Symons in the 1930s, to Peter Ackroyd and Anne Wroe at the end of the century. Trollope's use of new biographical techniques causes a defamiliarisation which is strikingly modern.

It has, for a start, a very powerful "I" narrator, far more assertive than in his three earlier works. This "I" digresses into other commentators' interpretations, both textual and factual, into parallels in contemporary politics, into extended appraisal of Cicero's guiding principles, which so often sound like character outlines for Plantagenet Palliser. It is worth remembering here that his first writings on Cicero predate his success as a novelist. And as we saw in his *Caesar*, he uses fluidity between "I" and "we" to both assume and enforce commonality with his reader. Thus the "I" of the very first sentence, "I am conscious of a certain audacity in thus attempting to give a further life of Cicero which I feel I may probably fail in justifying by any new information," is a confident voice, in spite of the modesty of "I feel I may probably fail." It declares there will be no new information about the facts of Cicero's life, with the implication that the work will be more about interpretation. We can contrast this with a passage where the "I" becomes "we", as he answers critics who accuse Cicero of being self-seeking in his readiness to side with Pompey when it suited him:

> We cannot but be angry when we read the words though we may understand how well he understood that he was impotent to do anything for the Republic unless he could bring such a man as Pompey to act with him.
>
> *(vol. 2, ch. 1)*

Here the "we" incorporates the authorial "I" in a pact with his assumed reader. It carries an assumption of shared feeling and response.

A further innovative narrative gambit which we first saw in *Lord Palmerston* is his manipulation of chronology. Benton says, "Chronology is the great limitation of biography, at once the spinal column that holds the story together, and the straight-jacket that prevents its freedom of motion."[20] Trollope's deliberate and thoughtful understanding of that "freedom of motion" shows him grasping concepts that are only now being discussed. His treatment of the Catiline conspiracy is an excellent example of this. He could arrange his material chronologically, and narrate the conspiracy as the events arise during Cicero's consulship, a strategy that would make Catiline dominate the whole year, and overshadow all other events and achievements, or he could opt to write two accounts of Cicero's year in office, the first dealing with everything bar Catiline, the second dealing exclusively with the conspiracy, and its aftermath. And the chapters on Cicero's consular speeches again discard chronology, beginning with his oration on Murena, on 20th November, before switching back to January and his four orations on agrarian law. The agrarian law concerned the redistribution of wealth, transferring ownership of land from the ruling elite to the populace, particularly those who had fought to bring so much wealth and power to Rome, a policy foreshadowing Caesar's revolutionary reforms. Trollope's narrator calls this "the spirit of communism", "a redistribution of property" (vol. 1, ch. 8). It resurrects for him the residual horrors of the French Revolution. With his four speeches, Cicero had the new law repealed, to Trollope's perpetual and fervent admiration.

The work finishes with a chapter on Cicero's religious beliefs, where we can detect a more personal "I", an "I", occasionally a "We", which lays some claim to being very close to the existent Trollope, and which reveals Trollope's deep attachment to his subject. He identifies, particularly in *De Republica*, a Cicero who is Christian before the birth of Christ:[21] "He believed in eternity, in the immortality of the soul, in virtue for the sake of its reward, in the omnipotence of God, the performance of his duty to his neighbours, in conscience and in honesty" (vol. 2, ch. 14). From the opening words of the chapter, "I should hardly have thought it necessary . . ." to the final line, "Therefore I have written this final chapter on his religion," we find a narrator ready to compare his subject's beliefs with his own creed:

> . . . he had realised that doctrine which tells us that we should do unto others as we would they should do unto us, – the very pith and marrow and inside meaning of Christ's teaching, by adapting which we have become human, by neglecting which we revert to paganism.
>
> *(vol. 2, ch. 15)*

It may be that the assumed persona of that "We" is that of a hypothetical believer, though to my mind, it seems to lead directly into the existent Trollope. "The man of letters is ever writing his own biography," he says, in his *Life of Cicero* (vol. 1, ch. 1). This may be evidence of the truth of that.

An Autobiography

Trollope wrote *An Autobiography* in 1875–6. The "An" suggests the possibility that this is just one version of several, all of which might be equally legitimate, or otherwise. James Kincaid,[22] R. H. Super, and Robert Tracy have all written about this intriguing text, and all three analyse the element of fiction in it, from different perspectives. "In our lives, we are always weaving novels" (ch. 9) Trollope says, and Kincaid makes this central to his lucid exploration of the *Autobiography*. He compares it to *David Copperfield*, a theme picked up (and acknowledged) later by Robert Tracy, who tellingly declares fiction to be more truthful than memoir: "It is more truthful because it tells us everything there is to tell about David. . . . There is no alternative version of David's story (288)." R. H. Super's essay is a more literal exploration of truth versus fiction, as he nails Trollope's terminological inexactitudes.

Trollope had read the first volume of John Forster's *Life of Dickens* soon after its publication: "Forster tells of him things which should disgrace him, – as the picture he drew of his own father, & the hard words he intended to have published of his own mother".[23] This contrasts with his own choice to focus on his misery at school rather than his neglect at his parents' hand. Fanny Trollope, just before she decamped to the States for four years, wrote of her husband: "He is a good honourable man – but his temper is dreadful – every year increases his irritability – and also its lamentable effect on the children."[24] But this is never the focus of Trollope's narrative even though she had abandoned him when he was twelve. Samuel Smiles, of course, made much of triumph over adversity in the potted biographies which make up *Self Help*; this with the success of Dickens's *Life* might certainly convince Trollope there was much to be gained by showing he could profitably write of his childhood miseries, and without betraying his parents. Indeed, his account of his time living alone with his father, at Harrow as a day boy until his mother returned, is notable for the respect he shows his father, and his empathy for him in his distress heralds some of his greatest depictions of flawed men – Louis Trevelyan, Josiah Crawley, and Plantagenet Palliser struggling as a single parent in *The Duke's Children*. What Trollope has done is construct a narrative of his childhood that protects his family's privacy. He similarly protects his most intimate relationships when he settles into domestic life. He famously writes, "My marriage was like the marriage of other people, and of no interest to anyone except my wife and me (71)." And when Kate Field fished for intimate details of George Eliot's private life, he replied, "She was one of those whose private life should be left in privacy, – as may be said of all who have achieved fame by literary merits."[25] Trollope took practical steps to keep his and his friends' private life private. He assiduously destroyed letters sent to him; this is why we have some of his letters sent to Kate Field, but none of hers to him. He wished to preserve a veil between himself and prying eyes. We should not believe too ardently in this paragon, however; his second chapter, a mini biography of his mother and her writing career, while it praises her capacity for hard work, devotion, and appetite for fun, also analyses her talents as a novelist and finds her wanting.

Only the first seventy-nine pages could accurately be called biographical. As Kincaid remarks, "one sixth autobiography and five sixths something else" (348). Toward the end, Trollope describes it as "the record of my literary performances (362)," a theorising of novelistic technique that he extended and developed in his *Thackeray* (which similarly opens with a more strictly biographical section before segueing into "something else"). The "I" narrative of those first seventy-nine pages, with its selective focus on the misery of his schooldays, is the product of a very knowing pen, telling us what he is prepared for us to know, and shielding his more intimate memories from our gaze. His "I" is making a novelist's choices about what to share with his reader, a similar "I" to the voice that denies Palmerston was a womaniser. In the opening chapters of his *Autobiography*, as in his biographies, he accords his subject the same respect. The "I" of the other five-sixths, where he explores his art in the context of other novelists' work, comes paradoxically from closer to the heart, unmediated by any desire to keep the reader at arm's length, rather like the "we" of that final chapter of his *Cicero*.

This paradox, that the first-person account of his early life is more defended and detached than the account (of the same first person) of his literary life is mirrored in Jose Borges's short essay "Borges and I,"[26] where his narrative voice, his "I", takes issue with the existent Borges. This "I" has a spontaneity and purity distinctly lacking in his creator. This "I" relates in a direct and refreshing manner to art and nature, whereas Borges, the originator, "the one things happen to", is inevitably tainted with pretence when he tries to articulate his relationship with the same art and nature. Borges's "I" would agree, then, that the Trollope in passages dealing with events in his life, the things that "happen" to him, is more contrived than the "I" that tells of how he wrote his novels. The existent Borges, rather like Trollope's "I" in his biographical account, cannot help his "perverse custom of falsifying and magnifying things". And yet his "I" knows it is fruitless to chase after the identity of "I", since while the persona of the "I" is clearly the one with ideas and creativity, he is inextricably shackled to the existent author. This resonates, for me, with Trollope, whose "I" in his life writing as in his novels is an unstable illusion – tantalising and slippery, it is Trollope's creature; just as you think you may have found a link to his existent self, it slips away behind the screen again. Borges's "I" finishes his essay to exert an existence independent of his creator by undercutting his very ground: "I do not know who has written this", suggesting that there is, in fact, no definable boundary between them. This comes close to Trollope's own view of the relationship between biographer, subject, and "I", where he creates and adapts an authorial voice to match his subject, and acknowledges the presence of the existent author in its expression.

The trail from Trollope's *Caesar* to his *Cicero* is the path of an experienced writer learning to extend his range. From the straightforward voice of his *Caesar* to the tantalising *Autobiography*, to the defensive, self-referential *Thackeray*, to the bolder voice of *Palmerston* as he starts to use novelistic prerogative to shift the emphasis of chronological narrative, to his *Cicero*, his "magnum opus", where he can with confidence alter timelines for narrative effect, and analyse a fellow writer's oeuvre to reveal the man, Trollope shows he has an appreciation of the subtleties of the biographer's craft beyond any of his generation, as he pushes at boundaries that are only now being reached and breached.

Notes

1. Victoria Glendinning's essay in *The Cambridge Companion to Anthony Trollope* (ch. 2) is a fine exception.
2. Hermione Lee's *Biography: A Very Short Introduction* contains an exemplary bibliography.
3. Anthony Trollope. *Thackeray* 1879 (London: Trollope Society, 1997).
4. Again, see Glendinning.
5. Patricia Srebrnik, 172.
6. N. J. Hall, *Trollope*, 109.
7. Anthony Trollope, *Lord Palmerston* 1882 (London: Trollope Society, 2003).
8. A Gibraltar-born Jew who sued for compensation after an anti-Semitic attack on his home in Athens; fiercely defended by Palmerston, who sent in the British navy.
9. "The Carlyle Controversy". *Temple Bar*, August 1881, 516. Quoted Sarah J. Heidt, 29.
10. See Markwick, *New Men*, ch. 8.
11. *An Autobiography*, ch. 3.
12. Brother of his school friend John Merivale.
13. Addison Ward, 413–56.
14. Maria Wyke, 156.
15. *The Commentaries of Caesar* (London: Blackwoods, 1870).
16. See Markwick, *New Men*, ch. 3.
17. *The Life of Cicero*, 2 vols, 1880 (London: Trollope Society, 1993).
18. Letter to G. W. Rusden, *Letters*, vol. 2, 842.
19. Lytton Strachey, viii.
20. Benton, 220.
21. Also noted by Glendinning, 28.
22. James Kincaid, "Trollope's Fictional Autobiography", *Nineteenth-Century Fiction*, 37:3 (1982): 340–9. R. H. Super, "Truth and Fiction in Trollope's Autobiography", *Nineteenth-Century Literature*, 48:1 (1993): 74–88. Robert Tracy, "Stranger than Truth: Fictional Autobiography and Autobiographical Fiction", *Dickens Studies Annual*, 15 (1986): 275–90.
23. *Letters*, vol. 2, 557 (to George Eliot and George Lewes).
24. Teresa Ransome, 38.
25. *Letters*, vol. 2, 892.
26. Jorge Louis Borges, *Labyrinths, Selected Stories and Other Writings* (London: Penguin, 1970).

Works cited

à Beckett, Gilbert. *The Comic History of Rome*. (1852). Wauconda, IL: Bolchazy – Carducci, 1996.
Arnold, Thomas. *History of the Later Roman Commonwealth*. (1823–7). London: B. Fellowes, 1845.
Beesly, E. S. "Catiline as a Party Leader". *Fortnightly Review*. June 1, 1865, 167–84.
Benton, Michael. *Literary Biography: An Introduction*. Hoboken, NJ: Wiley Blackwell, 2009.
Borges, Jorge. "Borges and I". *Labyrinths: Selected Stories and Other Writings*. Eds. Donald A. Yates and James E. Irby. Trans. James E. Irby. London: Penguin, 1970.
"The Carlyle Controversy". *Temple Bar*. August 1881, 516.
Forster, John. *Life of Charles Dickens*. (1872–4). London: Dent, 1969.
Glendinning, Victoria. "Trollope as Autobiographer and Biographer". *The Cambridge Companion to Trollope*. Eds. Caroline Dever and Lisa Niles. Cambridge: CUP, 2011.
Hall, N. John, ed. *The Letters of Anthony Trollope*. 2 vols. Stanford: SUP, 1983.
———. *Trollope: A Biography*. Oxford: Clarendon Press, 1991.
Heidt, Sarah J. "The Materials for a 'Life': Collaboration, Publication, and the Carlyles' Afterlives". *Nineteenth-Century Contexts: An Interdisciplinary Journal*. 28:1 (2006): 21–33.
Johnson, Samuel. *The Rambler*. 60 Saturday October 13 (1750): 28–33.
Kincaid, James. "Trollope's Fictional Autobiography". *Nineteenth-Century Fiction*. 57:3 (1982): 340–9.
Lee, Hermione. *Biography: A Very Short Introduction*. Oxford: OUP, 2009.
Miller, J. Hillis. "Trollope's Thackeray". *Nineteenth-Century Fiction*. 37 (December 1982): 350–7.

Mommson, Theodor. *The History of Rome*. Trans. W. P. Dickson. London: Bentley, 1868.
Ransome, Teresa. *Fanny Trollope: A Remarkable Life*. Stroud: Alan Sutton, 1995.
Smiles, Samuel. *Self Help*. (1859). London: John Murray, 1905.
Srebrnik, Patricia. "Trollope as Editor". *Oxford Reader's Companion to Trollope*. Ed. R. C. Terry. Oxford: OUP, 1999. 171–2.
Strachey, Lytton. *Eminent Victorians*. 1918. London : Folio Society, 1967.
Super, R. H. "Truth and Fiction in Trollope's Autobiography". *Nineteenth-Century Fiction*. 48:1 (1993): 74–88.
Tracy, Robert. "Stranger than Truth: Fictional Autobiography and Autobiographical Fiction". *Dickens Studies Annual*. 15 (1986): 275–90.
Trollope, Anthony. *An Autobiography*. (1883). Oxford: OUP, 1980.
———. *The Commentaries of Caesar*. London: Blackwoods, 1870.
———. *Life of Cicero*. 2 vols. (1880). London: The Trollope Society, 1993.
———. *Lord Palmerston*. (1882). London: The Trollope Society, 2003.
———. "Merivale's History of the Romans" (vols. 1 & 2). *The Dublin University Magazine*. May (1851): 611–24.
———. "Merivale's History of the Romans" (vol. 3). *The Dublin University Magazine*. July (1856): 30–47.
———. *Thackeray*. (1879). London: The Trollope Society, 1997.
Ward, Addison. "The Tory View of Roman History". *Studies in English Literature 1500–1900*. 4 (1964): 413–56.
Woolf, Virginia. *Flush*. London: Hogarth Press, 1933.
———. "The New Biography" (1927), and "The Art of Biography" (1939). *Collected Essays*. Ed. L. Woolf. London: Chatto and Windus, 1966–7.
———. *Orlando: A Biography*. London: Hogarth Press, 1928.
Wyke, Maria. *Caesar: A life in Western Culture*. London: Granta, 2007.

16

TROLLOPE AND DARWIN

Lauren Cameron

Although Charles Darwin complained that in the decades following the publication of his theory, every version of evolutionism except his own seemed to be gaining cultural currency,[1] "Darwinism" became the general term by which evolutionary theory was referenced by the end of the nineteenth century.[2] Scholarship on Darwin's reception in literature came out steadily throughout the twentieth century, but the 1980s witnessed a revolution in the field, with Gillian Beer's *Darwin's Plots* (1983) demonstrating that Darwin drew on preexisting cultural tropes and story-generating words to compose an easy-to-receive theory[3] and George Levine's *Darwin and the Novelists* (1988) illustrating how Darwinism can be studied even for authors whose work preceded or lacked direct reference to Darwin's. By this point, Darwin reputedly has been written about more than any other scientist, and perhaps more than any other English figure except Shakespeare.[4]

And yet studies of Darwin and Anthony Trollope are notably lacking – regardless of whether that relationship is construed as Darwin's direct influence on Trollope's work, Darwinian tropes that impacted Victorian culture and thereby Trollope's thinking, or language and thought processes shared in common by Darwin and Trollope as members of the same cultural moment. By far the most substantial and significant work on Trollope and Darwin is George Levine's chapter entitled "The Darwinian World of Anthony Trollope" in his brilliant and influential *Darwin and the Novelists*. Levine takes Trollope as representative of mainstream Victorian realism in his gradualism and uniformitarianism, his scientific method of building narrative inductively based on detailed observation, his avoidance of generalization in favor of the specificity of the individual case, his promotion of hard work and persistence over chance and speculation, and what Levine sees as his essential conservatism. All of these traits, he argues, are also Darwinian.[5]

Keep in mind that Levine's *Darwin and the Novelists* was published in 1988. That makes over twenty-five years of no important contributions to the study of Darwin and Trollope. So much excellent work has been done in the past few decades presenting an increasingly complex and intellectually engaged understanding of Trollope, especially in relation to gender and imperial politics. Studies of Trollope and the burgeoning and influential scientific culture of the day must follow, given the increasing importance of the study of science in relation to literature and culture, and this essay is a step toward that end.

This essay seeks to demonstrate that the evidence against Trollope's awareness of Darwinism – including the sheer lack of scholarly studies – is shaky at best and should be approached critically;

instead, we should reexamine Trollope's connections to scientific theories of his time, Darwin's included, based on the circumstances that would have exposed Trollope to such theories – the kinds of circumstances that have enabled productive reception studies for other authors.[6] Hopefully more such connections will come to light in forthcoming scholarship. In the meantime, studying the Darwinian aspects of the Palliser novels, however briefly, illuminates the interesting connections between Trollope's thinking and Darwinian theory's direct and indirect implications, and helps to make sense of the Pallisers' world. Such a study should be deepened and extended, and other late works of Trollope's taken to be representative of his late worldview, such as *The Way We Live Now*, should be similarly studied. Much more could also be done with the similarities between Darwin's and Trollope's narratorial voices.

Even though the opening passage in Trollope's *Autobiography* states that he does not intend to write of his inner life and that no one can truly share everything about him- or herself, there is still a scholarly tendency to treat the book as a decisive statement of his thoughts.[7] N. John Hall, for example, in his important biography of Trollope, takes uncritically Trollope's assertion that "Of the merest rudiments of the sciences I was completely ignorant" and paraphrases it as a statement of fact extending over Trollope's life span, rather than noting that Trollope made this claim about his nineteen-year-old self or that Trollope was in fact later enmeshed in intellectual circles that contained some of the most prominent scientific thinkers of the day and could not possibly have avoided a familiarity with scientific debates in his personal, club, publishing, or lecturing activities.[8] Trollope's claims about his knowledge in the *Autobiography* and elsewhere must be approached critically as an extension of that public persona that he is understood to have crafted over the course of his life as a defense mechanism.[9]

There are two statements by Trollope that literary critics and biographers take as transparent professions of his scientific ignorance. The first is Trollope's September 1868 letter to the archeologist J. E. Taylor that reads:

Dear Sir,

I have been asked to forward to you the enclosed.
I am afraid of the subject of Darwin. I am myself so ignorant on it, that I should fear to be in the position of editing a paper on the subject.

Yours very truly

Anthony Trollope[10]

This is widely treated as an accurate portrayal of Trollope's ignorance of Darwinian theory and science of the day more generally, as well as a rejection of Taylor's manuscript. Unfortunately, this interpretation does not hold up to scrutiny. During his time as editor of *Saint Paul's Magazine*, Trollope is regularly unambiguous in his rejection of manuscripts in his surviving letters. Instead, he provides clear reasons for his decisions and does not shirk responsibility through passive constructions.[11] Thus, there are reasons to doubt that Trollope's letter to Taylor is in fact a rejection of Taylor's manuscript on Darwin without further evidence, which has not been provided in criticism, history, or biography on the subject.

The second piece of evidence supposedly demonstrating Trollope's ignorance of science is his request that "some one less wholly ignorant of philosophic research than myself" write about George Henry Lewes's scientific studies in a posthumous memoir Trollope was undertaking.[12] A closer look at the letter in question, however, shows that Trollope was begging off of the responsibility that Charles Lewes asked him to undertake, and instead was requesting that Frederic Harrison write the piece for the *Fortnightly*. Trollope offers to contribute a shorter portion on G. H. Lewes's literary work and style, which Harrison may use or exclude, but overall the letter reads more like a busy person trying politely to avoid a time-consuming task than a straightforward claim of scientific ignorance.

So much for the arguments against Trollope's awareness of – much less, engagement with – scientific ideas generally, and Darwinism specifically.[13] What evidence links Trollope with Darwin? We have some very suggestive links, which make safe the assumption that Trollope knew of Darwin's theory, at least its controversial and popular aspects. Foremost must be Trollope's social and intellectual circle. He transferred back to England from his longtime Irish station with the Post Office in December 1859, settling outside London, the intellectual hub of the British Empire in the mid-nineteenth century.[14] Darwin's *Origin of Species* was published in late November 1859, and the first run sold out on the day of publication.[15] George Henry Lewes wrote in the *Cornhill* in 1860 "Darwin's book is in everybody's hands," meaning, of course, "everybody" considered to be an educated reader at the time.[16] In 1860, Trollope made close and long-term connections with the leading thinkers of the day through the parties hosted by George Smith, publisher of *The Cornhill Magazine*, including Lewes and his wife George Eliot.[17] Trollope also met scientifically minded men at his clubs, including Alfred, Lord Tennyson at the Cosmopolitan – experiences that, Hall notes, influenced his novels, though Hall confines his discussion of such influences to politics.[18] Because of his inclusion in the *Cornhill* circle, Trollope made his way through social outlets where an ignorance of Darwinian science could have been maintained only through the most persistent and self-willed closed-mindedness.[19]

The importance of the *Cornhill* connection has been emphasized in biographies and should be stressed here.[20] Historians of science who write on the complex interrelation of science and literature in the Victorian era have argued that the strong mid-nineteenth-century periodical culture provided a common intellectual discourse for general readers to encounter current ideas.[21] Science and literature did not merely sit side-by-side on the pages of a periodical, but were often intentionally intertextual, as writers and editors alike borrowed from multiple discourses to guide readers between different disciplinary approaches to similar topics.[22] *The Cornhill Magazine* is frequently identified as embodying this intertextuality, and it overtly paired Trollope's novels with science multiple times.[23] In November 1862, for example, "Our Survey of Literature and Science" begins with Trollope's *Orley Farm* (1861–62) as a way to discuss character types and human nature and then shifts to thermodynamics, organic chemistry, biological experiments, and astronomy. Even more interestingly, an unattributed essay entitled "Food – What It Is" appears in the April 1861 issue. The essay opens with: "Civilization rests on hunger. Whatever part Mr. Darwin's *Struggle for Existence* may have played in the development of animal creation, it has certainly had no mean place in the development of man."[24] The very Malthusian meditation on food comes to rest on a vision of Darwin's entangled bank, where the seeming vitality of life relies upon constant destruction[25] – this relentless struggle and death, the writer holds, is the foundation of human thriving.[26] The article in question ends on page 472. An installment of *Framley Parsonage* begins on page 473. Thus, not only would readers have considered the relation of Darwin's theory to Trollope's fiction as a consequence of organization, but also as a savvy, market-conscious author and eventually an experienced editor, Trollope would have understood the intertextual suggestions of such a juxtaposition.[27]

Nonetheless, I take the most important site of Darwinian study in Trollope's *oeuvre* to be not *Orley Farm* or *Framley Parsonage*, as the periodicals might suggest, and not the Chronicles of Barsetshire or *The Claverings*, as Levine does, but rather the Palliser series. The Palliser novels constitute Trollope's only series entirely undertaken after the publication of *On the Origin of Species* in

1859 and concurrent with Darwin's rise to prominence as the cultural touchstone for evolutionary theory. Darwin's emphases on contingency, continuous adaptation, lengthy timescales, and the entanglement of organisms are interestingly incorporated and negotiated throughout these six books.

In the Palliser series, Trollope implements Darwinian narrative strategies that Eliot makes explicit in her texts and that critics have long identified as reflecting on evolutionary schemas.[28] For example, in the famous prelude to *Middlemarch*,[29] Eliot ponders those Victorian women whose "certain spiritual grandeur [is] ill-matched with the meanness of opportunity"; she goes on to suggest that in women's internal lives, "the limits of variation are really much wider than any one would imagine." An exploration of "the limits of variation" among individuals' thoughts and motives, particularly women's, and of the mismatch of ambition and environment is exactly what Trollope achieves in the Palliser series.[30] Only, for Trollope, this struggle to find meaning in life is not limited to a few exceptional Dorotheas, but rather is the norm among the female protagonists of the Palliser novels.[31] So, while their circumstances are different enough to make them distinct individuals, Lady Mabel Grex's fate resonates with Lady Laura Kennedy's, since they both reject the man they love for a suitor with money and end their lives prematurely aged and living in obscurity; Lady Laura, Glencora Palliser, and Alice Vavasor all ache for an involvement in politics to bring meaning to their lives and find their husbands inadequate conduits for such agency; Alice, Emily Wharton, and Mary Palliser all struggle against distant fathers to choose their own husbands,[32] but Emily gets her unsuitable match while Alice escapes her violent and controlling one and Violet Effingham tames hers. This list could go on and on – but the key point here is that Trollope explores the limits of variations and the adaptive or destructive decisions that individuals make, especially women.[33]

The Palliser series regularly shows women carrying the weight of sexual selection. Darwin defines sexual selection as "[depending], not on a struggle for existence, but on a struggle between the males for possession of the females; the result is not death to the unsuccessful competitor, but few or no offspring."[34] In *Can You Forgive Her?* (1864–65), the narrator's arguably ironic response to Alice Vavasor's question about what to do with her life, that she should marry and have two children,[35] is tinged with Malthusian doctrine, with which Trollope was clearly familiar:[36] two children is a sufficient replacement rate for population stability but does not threaten to outstrip resources and so weaken the family's chance of surviving a catastrophe, like a famine.[37] Malthus's ideas of population dynamics along with Charles Lyell's *Principles of Geology* (1830) were, of course, the primary inspirations for Darwin's work.

Phineas Finn (1869) contains a similar treatment of sexual selection to that in *Can You Forgive Her?*: women's dissatisfaction with the marriage market and their desire for influence in the world are reiterated through the characters of Lady Laura Standish, Violet Effingham, and Madame Max Goesler particularly. Phineas Finn, on the other hand, demonstrates the double standard of sexual selection's gender norms, since men are able to be freer and more adaptable than women because of the active roles that the process of mate selection grants to them.[38] Marie Goesler becomes a reproductive threat to Glencora Palliser, who expresses her worries in racialized and animalized terms, with Madame Max's presumably half-Jewish baby imagined as a yellow monkey.[39] This threat is neutralized by her eventual infertility[40] after she is paired with Finn in *Phineas Redux* (1874).[41]

The Prime Minister (1876) returns to issues of race and reproduction seen in the Phineas volumes. Emily Wharton's first husband is an ethnic transplant who adapts to his new environment, but only partially. Their hybrid child does not survive, although somehow the Wharton-Fletchers, who keep intermarrying through generations, are successfully fertile.[42] This runs dramatically counter to Darwin, who worried about his own consanguineous marriage, and who endorsed the genetic health of hybridized forms over those that self-fertilize in *Origin*, saying, "I am convinced that the young thus produced will gain so much in vigour and fertility over the offspring from long-continued self-fertilisation, that they will have a better chance of surviving and propagating their kind" and "close interbreeding lessens fertility, and, on the other hand . . . an occasional cross with a distinct individual or variety increases fertility."[43] Although Trollope frequently endorses the infusion of new blood into old families throughout his *oeuvre*, the Finns' and the Lopezes' infertility suggests a resistance to Darwinian patterns in favor of a harsh realism about social constraints: Emily tries to break out of the quasi-incestuous mating patterns of her family, but she is ultimately forced into them.[44] Victorian women are able to push boundaries but not to break them.

In *The Duke's Children* (1880), Lady Mabel Grex fails to perpetuate her distinguished family because she cannot follow through on her stated goals of capturing the most desirable male interested in her, regardless of her sexual feelings.[45] Her plotline shows the caprice with which a lineage can end suddenly, as well as implies that women can be predators and men prey – even if Mabel does not succeed because she cannot quite stomach the role, that does not rule out the possibility of other successfully married women having carried out such active mating behavior.[46] The novel and series end not just with marriages, promising fertility and the continuance of type,[47] but also with an indeterminacy about the future that is inherently Darwinian in its refusal to promise progress, provide closure, or augur future fates.[48]

Trollope's portrayal of women and gender dynamics more generally has been well explored in literary criticism, but a key connection needs to be made: the choice of mate is all-important in a Darwinian world because natural selection turns upon reproduction. Traditional comic plots, documenting the tribulations of courtship and ending with marriage, are not Darwinian. It is not enough to survive, nor is it enough to gain one's mate of choice. One must reproduce, to pass on one's adaptive traits to the next generation. Hybrids and newcomers must compete with the well-entrenched for resources, and often are more successful because of their adaptations. Progress is slow, if it exists at all, so much so that humans barely have the capacity to observe it. Chance adaptations and chance circumstances, so extensive as to be almost impossible to document fully, ultimately determine an individual's success or failure. Thus, stories that follow marriages into the bedrooms and explore reproductive difficulties, that consider the role of environmental constraints in an individual's success at adapting to preexisting patterns that have perpetuated social structures, that consider the psychological and financial struggles of marriage and the reproductive trials of those unions' offspring are truly Darwinian. All this is true of the Pallisers' saga.

And yet each individual is distinct, as is each situation. There are enough echoes and resonances among characters' experiences to establish patterns of experience, but enough distinctions to challenge such patterns. In each novel, the reader may encounter situations similar to those in past volumes, but the characters never feel repetitive or wooden as a consequence.[49] The reader is invited to consider how different individuals face the limits of variation and work successfully within them, or are crushed in the ongoing battle of the entangled bank, inevitable victims in the struggle for life. Ernst Mayr observes that, for Darwin, "evolutionary change is a two-step process: the first step consists of the production of variation, and the second, of the sorting of this variability by natural selection" – this is just the process that Trollope explores in the Palliser novels, the extent of variation among individuals and then the success or failure of each of these variations in its particular circumstances.[50] His focus on the gendered aspects of this process is Trollope's Darwinian intervention.

Notes

1. See Campbell 233; Desmond and Moore 492.
2. See Bowler.
3. See, for example, the preface to the second edition of *Darwin's Plots*, where Beer states, "Darwin drew on familiar narrative tropes (such as leaving the garden, or discovering your ancestry was not what you believed). That seemed crucial to understanding how it was possible for him to produce so many stories within his theory that could be teased out, or redesigned, by imaginative writers," which "allowed a wide public to read his work and appropriate his terms to a variety of meanings" (xxv, xxiv).
4. Wilson xvi; Levine, "Reflections on Darwin" 223.
5. See Levine, *Darwin and the Novelists* 177–210.
6. For example, Henkin notes that "Though George Meredith has been variously referred to as the 'poet of evolution,' in his novels there is no evidence that he had more than a most general knowledge of the principles of evolution. In all his writings there is no mention made of the name Darwin" (204).
7. *Autobiography* 21.
8. Trollope, *Autobiography* 52; Hall 50. Halperin makes a similar claim (2). The importance of male-only clubs in perpetuating scientific ideas in the Victorian era is noted by Endersby (316).
9. Hall 106, 509–10.
10. *Letters*, I, 447.
11. See, for example, *Letters*, I, 408, 419.
12. *Letters*, II, 804.
13. On Trollope's method as broadly scientific or experimental, see apRoberts 43–4; Herbert 114; Levine, *Darwin's Plots* 195. Trollope himself uses the term "experiment" in his *Autobiography* (243).
14. Trollope, *Autobiography* 130.
15. Five hundred copies of the first run were also sent by the publisher, John Murray, to Mudie's Circulating Library, meaning that at least four times that many subscribers likely read the work through that venue and that its absence in an individual's permanent library (including Trollope's) does not rule out his having read it (Browne 88–9).
16. Qtd. in Browne 128.
17. Hall 199, 202. On the similarities between Trollope's and Eliot's novels, see apRoberts 111–12; Hensley 156; Kincaid 51–2; and McMaster 156. On Eliot and Lewes's familiarity with Darwin, see Beer, "Lineal Descendants" 290.
18. Hall 219. Browne notes that Tennyson "ordered a copy of the *Origin of Species* in advance so that he might read it as soon as it appeared" but he found its conclusions and seemingly godless world bleak and cruel, and so was never fully accepting of the theory (188).
19. In fact, whether an individual directly read Darwin or not might be beside the point. Beer points out that those living in a post-Darwinian society must have a familiarity with the theory as we now do with Freudian ideas – assumptions, she says, form more quickly when the original material remains unread. "So the question of who read Darwin, or whether a writer had read Darwin, becomes only a fraction of the answer" (*Darwin's Plots* 3–4).
20. For Turner's study of Trollope and the *Cornhill*, particularly the relationship between the fiction and nonfiction articles, see 7–47.
21. See Choi; Dawson et al.; Ellegård; Shattock and Wolff; and Yeo 9.
22. Dawson et al. 2–3; Wynne 3.
23. Dawson et al. 2, 18; Kucich 121.
24. "Food" 460. Such a statement supports the common claim of critics that although Darwin hardly mentioned humans in *Origin*, Victorian readers quickly saw the applications of his theory to our own species; see, for example, Beer, *Darwin's Plots* 54; Bergmann 80; Richards 54.
25. As Darwin puts it, "We behold the face of nature bright with gladness, we often see superabundance of food; we do not see, or we forget, that the birds which are idly singing round us mostly live on insects or seeds, and are thus constantly destroying life; or we forget how largely these songsters, or their eggs, or their nestlings, are destroyed by birds and beasts of prey; we do not always bear in mind, that though food may be now superabundant, it is not so at all seasons of each recurring year" (*Origin* 62). For his famous, concluding image of the entangled bank (where the inherent violence is obscured more than in this initial presentation), see Darwin, *Origin* 489–90.
26. Beer notes that Victorians overwhelmingly understood natural selection as entailing an struggle for existence obtainable only by battling competitors for resources and mates – thus, "struggle," "fight," and

"battle" are terms charged with Darwinian significance post-*Origin* (*Darwin's Plots* xxi). For other newly charged words, see *Darwin's Plots* 13.

27 Darwin, who famously incorporated fictional observations into his scientific tracts, also read Trollope: his letters indicate that he shared volumes of *Orley Farm* with his children and that he took Trollope's views as consonant with his own; see *Darwin Correspondence Database*, entries 3683, 4901, and 4910. See also Browne 70.

28 See, for example, Beer, *Darwin's Plots* 139–219 and "Lineal Descendants" 290. Famously, Henry James deemed *Middlemarch* "too often an echo of Messrs. Darwin and Huxley" (428). These strategies are important because, as Levine notes, "Science enters most Victorian fiction not so much in the shape of ideas, as, quite literally, in the shape of its shape, its form, as well as in the patterns it exploits and develops, the relationships it allows" (*Darwin and the Novelists* 13).

29 Eliot 1. apRoberts refers to *Middlemarch* as "the most Trollopian" of Eliot's novels (28).

30 Olby notes that "No other topic in the *Origin* was given as much stand-alone coverage as variation" (32), which is understandable given that Darwin's chapter on natural selection defines the concept pithily as the "preservation of favourable variations and the rejection of injurious variations" (*Origin* 81).

31 This reflects Morse's groundbreaking study of "the tensions in Trollope's work which embody his ambivalent response to the Victorian ideals for womanhood" (137).

32 Such a dynamic is ironic, given Darwin's claim that "each new variety or species, during the progress of its formation, will generally press hardest on its nearest kindred, and tend to exterminate them" – he links this specifically to children exterminating their parents later in the book (*Origin* 110, 172).

33 Wright has also laid out some similarities among characters' behavior (92–7), as has Felber (54–9).

34 *Origin* 88. When he comes to redefine it twelve years later in *Descent of Man*, he uses ungendered terms ("the advantage which certain individuals have over others of the same sex and species solely in respect of reproduction" [*Descent* 243]).

35 "What should a woman do with her life? . . . Fall in love, marry the man, have two children, and live happy ever afterwards. I maintain that answer has as much wisdom in it as any other that can be given; – or perhaps more" (*CYFH*, Vol. 1, Ch. 11).

36 See *Letters*, I, 460; and Markwick, *New Men* 22–4.

37 On Trollope's ironically anti-Malthusian endorsement of contraception, see Markwick, "Devices and Desires."

38 McMaster similarly observes that Finn's success is based on his adaptability, a gendered and youthful prerogative (51).

39 *PF*, Vol. 2, Ch. 57. The Jewish people were conceived of as an evolutionary anomaly in the nineteenth century – a distinct population, but one that defied standard categorizations, as not bound to a particular region, physiologically diverse, and persistent despite seemingly overwhelming adversity (Beer, *Darwin's Plots* 189–90).

40 See Markwick, "How Many Children," on the Finns' infertility.

41 Finn, interestingly enough, comes from another population often dehumanized and presented as simian in order to demean and justify the oppression of the population: the Irish (Curtis). Such racism was promoted by scientific theories of human descent from apes – with non-European races supposedly less developed and therefore deserving of colonial control – which were seen as reinforced by Darwinian theory (Gould 60–164). Finn faces a number of moments of such racism in *PF*. See, for example, him being likened to a monkey (Vol. 1, Ch. 5). Corbett explores the gendered dynamics of Finn's Irishness, but it also bears noting that the other Irishman in the Phineas novels, Lawrence Fitzgibbon, carries a last name that suggests illegitimate descent from apes.

42 Glencora is surprised at Ferdinand Lopez's ability to marry into this insular class, which although seemingly maladaptive genetically in its mating strategies, in fact has successfully entrenched itself in its ecological and social niche (*PM*, Vol. 4, Ch. 77). For a convoluted description of the Whartons' and Fletchers' relationships, see *PM*, Vol. 4, Ch. 75.

43 *Origin* 104, 249.

44 Morse points out that Emily marries Lopez "because she needs to establish her identity. She wants to be more than a piece of property necessary to the continuance of the Whartons and Fletchers," but she discovers to her disappointment that "her husband wants to re-create her in accordance with those very ideals of feminine passivity she was trying to escape" (107, 8).

45 On Mabel's hyperawareness of gendered mating norms and her use of Darwinian hunting and battle imagery in such discussions, see *DC*, Vol. 1, Ch. 10, 16, 20; Vol. 2, Ch. 35, 39, 40, 42; Vol. 3, Ch. 55, 73, 77.

46 Kincaid notes that it is not Mabel's strategy but rather her "unsentimental" hyperawareness of "just what a woman's lot is" that leads to her expulsion from society (232).
47 On Isabel Boncassen as a recapitulated Glencora, rather than an entirely new character type, see Walton 155. Felber notes that while the Boncassen-Silverbridge marriage presages children, the Tregear-Mary wedding is suggestive of barrenness or the continuance of Glencora's frustrations (67–8).
48 Beer notes that "Nowhere does Darwin give a glimpse of future forms: and rightly so, since it is fundamental to his argument that they are unforeseeable, produced out of too many variables to be plotted in advance" (*Darwin's Plots* xix). See also Levine, *Darwin's Plots* 192.
49 See Felber's similar observations (54).
50 Mayr xvi.

Works cited

apRoberts, Ruth. *The Moral Trollope.* Athens: Ohio University Press, 1971.
Beer, Gillian. *Darwin's Plots: Evolutionary Narrative in Darwin, George Eliot and Nineteenth-Century Fiction.* 2nd ed. Cambridge: Cambridge University Press, 2000.
———. "Lineal Descendants: The *Origin*'s Literary Progeny." *The Cambridge Companion to the "Origin of Species."* Ed. Michael Ruse and Robert J. Richards. Cambridge: Cambridge University Press, 2009. 275–94.
Bergmann, Linda S. "Reshaping the Roles of Man, God, and Nature: Darwin's Rhetoric in *On the Origin of Species.*" *Beyond the Two Cultures: Essays on Science, Technology, and Literature.* Ed. Joseph W. Slade and Judith Yaross Lee. Ames: Iowa State University Press, 1990. 79–98.
Bowler, Peter J. *The Non-Darwinian Revolution: Reinterpreting a Historical Myth.* Baltimore: Johns Hopkins University Press, 1988.
Browne, Jane. *Charles Darwin: A Biography.* Vol. 2. New York: Alfred A. Knopf, 1995–2002.
Campbell, John Angus. "Why Was Darwin Believed? Darwin's *Origin* and the Problem of Intellectual Revolution." *Configurations* 11.2 (2003), 203–3.
Choi, Tina Young. "Natural History's Hypothetical Moments: Narratives of Contingency in Victorian Culture." *Victorian Studies* 51.2 (2009), 275–97.
Corbett, Mary Jean. "Two Identities: Gender, Ethnicity, and Phineas Finn." *The Politics of Gender in the Novels of Anthony Trollope: New Readings for the Twenty-First Century.* Ed. Margaret Markwick, Deborah Denenholz Morse, and Regenia Gagnier. Aldershot, UK: Ashgate Press, 2009, 117–30.
Curtis, L. Perry. *Apes and Angels: The Irishman in Victorian Caricature.* Washington: Smithsonian Institute Press, 1971.
Darwin, Charles. *Darwin Correspondence Database.* University of Cambridge, 2013. Web. 22 October 2013.
———. *The Descent of Man, and Selection in Relation to Sex.* 1871. New York: Penguin, 2004.
———. *On the Origin of Species: A Facsimile of the First Edition.* 1859. Cambridge, MA: Harvard University Press, 1964.
Dawson, Gowan, Richard Noakes, and Jonathan R. Topham. "Introduction." *Science in the Nineteenth-Century Periodical: Reading the Magazine of Nature.* Ed. Geoffrey Cantor et al. New York: Cambridge University Press, 2004. 1–35.
Desmond, Adrian, and James Moore. *Darwin.* New York: Warner Books, 1991.
Eliot, George. *Middlemarch.* 1871. Ed. David Carroll. New York: Oxford University Press, 1997.
Ellegård, Alvar. *Darwin and the General Reader: The Reception of Darwin's Theory of Evolution in the British Periodical Press, 1859–1872.* Göteborg: Gothenburg Studies in English, 1958.
Endersby, Jim. "Sympathetic Science: Charles Darwin, Joseph Hooker, and the Passions of Victorian Naturalists." *Victorian Studies* 51.2 (Winter 2009), 299–320.
Felber, Lynette. *Clio's Daughters: British Women Making History, 1790–1899.* Delaware: University of Delaware Press, 2007.
"Food – What It Is." *The Cornhill Magazine* 3.16 (April 1861), 460–72.
Gould, Stephen Jay. *The Mismeasure of Man.* New York: Norton, 1981.
Hall, N. John. *Trollope: A Biography.* Oxford: Oxford University Press, 1993.
Halperin, John. *Trollope and Politics: A Study of the Pallisers and Others.* Macmillan: London, 1977.
Henkin, Leo J. *Darwinism in the English Novel, 1860–1910.* New York: Russell and Russell, 1963.
Hensley, Nathan K. "Mister Trollope, Lady Credit, and *The Way We Live Now.*" *The Politics of Gender in Anthony Trollope's Novels.* Ed. Margaret Markwick, Deborah Denenholz Morse, and Regenia Gagnier. Burlington, VT: Ashgate, 2009. 147–60.

Herbert, Christopher. *Trollope and Comic Pleasure*. Chicago: University of Chicago Press, 1987.
James, Henry. "Review of Eliot's Novels." *Galaxy* 15 (1873), 424–8.
Kincaid, James. *The Letters of Anthony Trollope*. 2 vols. Ed. N. John Hall. Stanford: Stanford University Press, 1983.
———. *The Novels of Anthony Trollope*. Oxford: Clarendon Press, 1977.
Kucich, John. "Scientific Ascendancy." *A Companion to the Victorian Novel*. Ed. Patrick Brantlinger and William B. Thesing. Malden, MA: Blackwell, 2002. 119–36.
Levine, George. *Darwin and the Novelists: Patterns of Science in Victorian Fiction*. Cambridge, MA: Harvard University Press, 1988.
———. "Reflections on Darwin and Darwinizing." *Victorian Studies* 51.2 (Winter 2009), 223–45.
Lyell, Charles. *Principles of Geology*. London: John Murray, 1830.
Markwick, Margaret. "Devices and Desires: 19th-Century Contraception." *Trollopiana* 57 (May 2002), 4–10.
———. "How Many Children Had Madame Max?" *Trollopiana* 50 (August 2000), 9–14.
———. *New Men in Trollope's Novels: Rewriting the Victorian Male*. Burlington, VT: Ashgate, 2007.
Mayr, Ernst. Introduction to *On the Origin of Species: A Facsimile of the First Edition*. 1859. Cambridge, MA: Harvard University Press, 1964. vii–xvii.
McMaster, Juliet. *Trollope's Palliser Novels: Theme and Pattern*. Macmillan: London, 1978.
Morse, Deborah Denenholz. *Women in Trollope's Palliser Novels*. Ann Arbor: University of Michigan Research Press, 1987.
Olby, Robert. "Variation and Inheritance." *The Cambridge Companion to the "Origin of Species."* Ed. Michael Ruse and Robert J. Richards. Cambridge: Cambridge University Press, 2009. 30–46.
"Our Survey of Literature and Science." *The Cornhill Magazine* 6.35 (November 1862), 702–14.
Richards, Robert J. "Darwin's Theory of Natural Selection and Its Moral Purpose." *The Cambridge Companion to the "Origin of Species."* Ed. Michael Ruse and Robert J. Richards. Cambridge: Cambridge University Press, 2009. 47–66.
Shattock, Joanne and Michael Wolff, eds. *The Victorian Periodical Press: Samplings and Soundings*. Toronto: University of Toronto Press, 1982.
Trollope, Anthony. *An Autobiography*. London: Williams & Norgate, 1883 (rptd. 1946).
———. *Can You Forgive Her?* 1864–5. Ed. Dinah Birch. Oxford: Oxford University Press, 2012.
———. *The Duke's Children*. 1880. Ed. Katherine Mullen and Francis O'Gorman. Oxford: Oxford University Press, 2011.
———. *Phineas Finn*. 1869. Ed. Simon Dentith. Oxford: Oxford University Press, 2011.
———. *Phineas Redux*. 1874. Ed. John Bowen. Oxford: Oxford University Press, 2011.
———. *The Prime Minister*. 1876. Ed. Nicholas Shrimpton. New York: Oxford University Press, 2011.
Turner, Mark W. *Trollope and the Magazines: Gendered Issues in Mid-Victorian Britain*. New York: St. Martin's Press, 2000.
Walton, Priscilla L. *Patriarchal Desire and Victorian Discourse: A Lacanian Reading of Anthony Trollope's Palliser Novels*. Toronto: University of Toronto Press, 1995.
Wilson, Edward O. Foreword to *The Cambridge Companion to the "Origin of Species."* Ed. Michael Ruse and Robert J. Richards. Cambridge: Cambridge University Press, 2009. xv–xvi.
Wright, Andrew. *Anthony Trollope: Dream and Art*. London: Macmillan, 1983.
Wynne, Deborah. *The Sensation Novel and the Victorian Family Magazine*. New York: Palgrave, 2001.
Yeo, Richard. *Science in the Public Sphere: Natural Knowledge in British Culture 1800–1860*. Aldershot, UK: Ashgate, 2001.

PART IV

Illustration studies

17
TROLLOPE AND ILLUSTRATION

Paul Goldman and David Skilton

Illustration studies, in the sense of the systematic study of how illustrated works produce meanings by the complex interaction of text and image, has only become a serious scholarly discipline in its own right in the twenty-first century,[1] and it is still exploring its territory and developing its methods. Illustration in the works of Trollope is one of many topics demanding sustained study. Recent scholarship has gone beyond earlier critical models, which centred on the attractiveness and appropriateness of the illustrations, and on what is known about their commissioning and execution. Some accounts included advice on the collectability of the plates. What is new in the approach which is now called "illustration studies" is that while noticing issues of attractiveness and fidelity, it takes it as given that the meaning of an illustrated work is generated by both its verbal and visual elements. Nowadays we devote attention to the meanings which the images generate by interaction with the text. Illustration researchers also question inherited assumptions, such as that the text rules supreme over the images, and that illustration is a one-way process, in which the images draw from verbal text but do not feed back into it. To avoid these fallacies, we use terms which clearly express that the illustrated text exists in two media simultaneously – that is, that it is a "bimedial" text. Furthermore illustration as a phenomenon consists of three parts: the image in the book, the text and/or the portion of the text to which the image relates, and the caption or title which designates the image. The scholar should consider all three parts: they may be mutually supportive or they may set up enriching or damaging uncertainties of meaning.

Illustration in Trollope's works presents two particular problems: the bimedial material itself has not been thoroughly examined in all its literary, aesthetic and social contexts, and there are few ready-made methods to guide the researcher. A good number of Trollope's novels were illustrated on first appearance, and such was the relationship between word and image in Trollope's illustrated novels that it no longer seems defensible to study the words alone without reference to the images. The rich combination of text and image in the novels is what was presented to the reader at the time of first publication, and produced and still produces a reading experience qualitatively different from the reading of an unillustrated edition. Trollope makes a good case for study, being a distinctly "modern" novelist, on whose behalf publishers could call upon leading artists of the day to co-produce his bimedial, verbal-visual works for an unprecedentedly large readership. The economic conditions which made this possible are those which ushered in the age of consumerism in the second half of the nineteenth century.[2] The study of Trollope and illustration therefore locates his work at the centre of its age socially as well as artistically.

Trollope's best illustrator, the painter John Everett Millais, worked closely with him over a number of years. Their artistic relationship defines these joint ventures and at their best they effectively produce a joint narrative. Rather than read the verbal texts and then glance at the images, we should be careful to "read the entire book", including all the images it contained on its first publication, whether in a periodical, in parts or in volume form.[3] This kind of illustrated novel is a Victorian phenomenon, earlier prose fiction having attracted little illustration. Although the period also saw a rapid rise in children's literature, it is wrong to suppose that illustration originated as an aid to the reading of verbal texts. The best illustration complicates verbal meanings and requires a high degree of literacy. Understanding the relation of Millais's images to Trollope's verbal narrative requires attentive reading and a sure grasp of Trollope's narrative method.

Publishing and techniques of reproduction

Dickens and his first illustrators are often credited with bringing good novel illustration to the masses with the publication in cheap monthly parts of *The Posthumous Papers of the Pickwick Club* (1836–7) and the serialization of *Oliver Twist* in *Bentley's Miscellany* (1837–9). Before 1830 illustrated books had largely been the preserve of the well-to-do, but new modes of publication made them available to a mass readership for the first time. George Cruikshank regarded himself as at least the equal of the novelists he illustrated, and it was Dickens's popular triumph which established in the public's mind that novelists were in charge, and that illustrators had to follow their lead. There was a variety of illustrated fiction before Trollope published *his* first, *Framley Parsonage*, in 1860–61, and it ranged from Reynolds's lurid and hugely popular *Mysteries of London* in the 1840s, to Thackeray, Trollope's favourite living novelist, who illustrated much of his own work, and who, as the editor of the *Cornhill Magazine*, commissioned *Framley Parsonage* in 1859.

The dominant style of illustration was changing radically at this time, and from the late 1850s onwards high-quality wood-engraved illustration became the norm for bourgeois literature. Costs went down, so that a shilling a month – the price of one part of *Pickwick* – now bought a magazine with more than one serial novel, plus poetry, factual essays and of course profuse illustration, often drawn by well-known artists and cut by the great engraving firms of London.

With change of medium coincided stylistic change. Dickens's chief illustrators, Hablôt K. Browne ("Phiz", 1815–82) and George Cruikshank (1792–1878), drew in a comparatively "theatrical" or "comic" style, using a wiry line, generalised facial features and exaggerated dramatic gesture and posture. The "dark plates" by Phiz in *Bleak House* (1852–53) are notable exceptions, and are the plates in which Phiz exploits the full possibilities of the vertical orientation of images which are bound in a book the same way up as the text, something in which Millais later excelled.

Dickens's illustrations, like his novels, were far more widely disseminated than Trollope's. Phiz's Mr Pickwick from 1836 was and remained recognisable by the population at large, rather like Charlie Chaplin a century later. Nothing like this occurred with Trollope's characters. In Millais characters are usually portrayed full-length from a rather short distance, which puts the reader in the same fictional space. He often concentrates on single figures ruminating, on two figures interacting in a significant way, or on small groups in whose conversations the reader could almost take part. To his contemporaries he drew with a seriousness appropriate to his subjects, and his characters, while not enduring icons, came to be regarded by the public as social acquaintances rather than fictional constructions. His designs are meaningful additions to the texts, co-operating in the responsibility of the narrative, and drawing readers actively into examining the complex decisions facing the characters. Millais himself is often a narrator of the story as much as Trollope.[4]

Wood-engraved plates, like Millais's, are larger, more darkly printed and more robust than the earlier etchings and steel engravings. Because the block can be set up within the same press as the type, very fast production is possible. There was more freedom in page layout, including the "wrapping" of text around vignettes. Moreover whole pages of type and woodblock could be saved as plaster stereotypes or, by 1860, in metal by electrotyping for later reprinting. Millais and the other artists of the 1860s drew their designs directly onto the boxwood blocks or onto paper, from which it could be transferred to the wood by a variety of processes, before being cut by the great wood-engraving firms in London, chief among them the Dalziel Brothers and Joseph Swain. In this sort of wood-engraving, the engravers or "woodpeckers" followed the artist's lines exactly as drawn. There was another type of wood-engraving in which the engravers were presented with pictures in any medium, including oil-painting or pen and wash, and used their skills to "translate" them into the lines of wood-engraving, using a repertoire of techniques which, because they replaced colour and tone by black-and-white textures, such as hatching, belonged to what was called in French "gravure d'interpretation" (interpretative engraving). The Dalziel Brothers, in contrast, followed Millais's lines meticulously.

The hierarchy of artistic forms inherited from the Italian Renaissance put etching above wood-engraving because in the former the artist both drew and etched the plate (hence the term "autographic"), while in wood-engraving the designs were nearly always cut by unsung craftsmen and women, their names subsumed by the firms employing them. A prejudice against this mode of working is nonsensical since the woodcut designs of masters like Dürer and Holbein were cut by members of trade guilds and rarely by the artists themselves.[5]

The bimedial text

The images of Phiz and his contemporaries lack borders and the images fade gently into the paper surrounding them. Except for a very interesting set of small vignettes for the initial capital letter of each instalment of *The Small House at Allington*, Millais mainly produced full-page illustrations with defined borders. Decisions on format and medium were largely made by the publishers of the magazines in which the fiction appeared, so that the model for Trollopian illustration was laid down by George Smith, the founder of the *Cornhill Magazine*. He emphasised the production of meaning by visual means as opposed to decoration.

George Eliot's *Romola* (1862–63), which ran alongside *The Small House at Allington* in the *Cornhill Magazine* for twelve months, was also furnished with plates and a vignette at the opening of each instalment by Frederick Leighton. Smith spared no expense for his star novelists: Millais and Leighton each rose to become president of the Royal Academy. Their vignettes relate to their texts more than most critics recognise, Leighton's constituting a through-running impression of renaissance Florence. Millais used his vignettes in the *Small House* to reinforce the theme of the marital fortunes of the two Dale sisters by picturing them together as a matching pair, reminding us that Trollope's first choice of title had been "The Two Pearls of Allington", which was dropped because a similar title had just been used by another novelist. The initial letter vignette facing "'And You Love Me!' said she" (Ch. 4, October 1862, page 552) shows the young women at croquet, which is an integral part of the courtship rituals in the novel. This vignette increases the pictorial coverage of the fictional world, and enlarges the visualisation of the text. Millais's vignette of Lily and Crosbie as children on rocking horses at the head of Chapter 13 confirms the narrator's hints that their illusions may later be disappointed, and must remind the contemporary reader of Thackeray's similar satirical image in the initial capital letter to Chapter 59 of *The Virginians* (1857–9), not to mention the image of Rawdon and Becky flying a kite in the initial capital to Chapter 36 of *Vanity Fair* (1847–8). A full study of these small images, perhaps in relation to those of Thackeray and to those of Leighton, is overdue. When the *Small House* and *Romola* were republished in two and three volumes respectively, the vignettes were not reprinted.

Millais's full-sized illustrations to Trollope almost always enlarge the narrative, sometimes rivalling the importance of the text. "Please Ma'am, Can We Have the Peas to Shell?" in the *Small House* (*Cornhill Magazine*, September 1862, facing page 364) contributes a memorable and brooding beauty to Mrs Dale's dilemma as to whether to give up the Small House, with the loss of her garden, like a second Eden, along with its produce and its flora, which Millais represents by an evocative spray of a climber hanging into the top of the image. The image reminds the reader that the emotional suffering of a woman of Mrs Dale's age is as interesting as the love troubles of her young daughters. A second reading of the novel in volumes must have been punctuated by regular recognition of the well-loved images.

Millais had a complete grasp of the Trollopian world and understood the significance of his characters' slightest words or smallest social manoeuvres – "the moral 'hooks and eyes' of life", as the *Spectator*'s reviewer of the *Small House* put it.[6] So his designs often contribute notably to the impact of the action. The first example is "Guilty" in *Orley Farm*, where Lady Mason confesses to Sir Peregrine that she is guilty and cannot marry him. When he asks her of what she is guilty, she finds the name of her crime literally unspeakable, and exclaims, "'Guilty of all this with which they charge me.' And then she threw herself at his feet, and wound her arms round his knees" (Ch. 44). Millais's spare design graphically reinforces the impact of Trollope's lines in this incident, which, by the social conventions of the age, is startling when it occurs in a realistic text as opposed to a melodrama. Trollope himself hoped that "Lady Mason as she makes her confession at the feet of Sir Peregrine Orme" was one of the most strikingly sensational scenes in English fiction, in a novel which was not of itself an example of "sensation fiction."[7] We find another highly emotive moment illustrated in "Let Me Beg You to Think over the Matter Again" in *The Small House at Allington*, when the squire tries to reason with Mrs Dale to persuade her against leaving the Small House. The squire's posture, leaning forward, clasping and unclasping his hands, gives the scene an understated visual as well as verbal intensity well calculated to reverberate with the middle-class readership, whose withers would be wrung by the plight of the widow and her daughters.[8]

In all Millais illustrated *Framley Parsonage* (1860–61), *Orley Farm* (1861–62), *The Small House at Allington* (1864) and *Phineas Finn, The Irish Member* (1867–69), and provided frontispieces to a one-volume cheap seventh edition of *Rachel Ray* in 1864 and another for *Kept in the Dark* in 1882.[9]

Other artists who provided designs for Trollope during his lifetime

None of Trollope's other illustrators equalled Millais's achievements in terms of either volume or quality, but this does not mean that they should be discounted. See N. J. Hall for an account of them.[10] Phiz (Hablôt Knight Browne 1815–1882) and the little-known Miss E. Taylor (dates unknown) made designs for *Can You Forgive Her?*, which originally appeared monthly in twenty shilling parts from January 1864 until August 1865, Trollope having insisted that Phiz be sacked as unsuitable for this type of fiction (Sadleir 56–62). The two artists produced images in jarringly different styles, Phiz in the style which was suitable for Dickens but dated when applied to Trollope's fiction of modern life, taking the reader's attention away from the predicament of the individual in a social context and transferring it to the social context itself. Taylor's designs somewhat recall Millais, though lacking in his draughtsmanship and flair.[11] "Great Jove" (Hall 99), for example, shows her competence in a typical 1860s style. As Hall perceptively remarks, "Whatever Miss Taylor's limitations, she attempted to illustrate in the Millais fashion. There is no caricature here . . . Her work is stiff, excessively pretty, too serious, but it is not satiric in Browne's fashion" (Hall 98). Hall suggests that Browne's work often looks satirical even when the text barely demands it, and is quite unsuitable for Trollope. An exception is the scene in which the glamorous Burgo Fitzgerald has a moment of touching human contact with a street prostitute whom he takes for a drink in a public house. Burgo's social flight when he fails to persuade Lady Glencora to run away with him has reduced him to the insignificance of one of Phiz's little figures in a large world. His social origin and his beauty are overshadowed by the size of the barrels behind the bar.

With Mary Ellen Edwards (1839–c. 1910), however, we reach a considerable and underrated designer, who produced sixteen separately printed plates and one vignette (not reprinted in the first book edition) for *The Claverings* in the *Cornhill Magazine* from February 1866 to May 1867. Edwards's designs are stately and elegant and no fewer than eight feature the chief woman character, Julia Brabazon Ongar. The female figures are well drawn and the groupings are harmonious, but the engraving by Horace Harral is inadequate. Edwards is in sympathy with the text, and her feeling for and understanding of the significance of contemporary dress are always sure-footed. Given that publication in the *Cornhill* was delayed by two years it might be worth considering how exactly contemporary the female fashions are. The male figures are somewhat stock characters but well drawn throughout. This is among the best thing the artist ever did in the field.

George Housman Thomas (1824–1868) illustrated *The Last Chronicle of Barset*, which appeared in thirty-two weekly sixpenny parts from 1st December 1866 to 6th July 1867, with sixty-four wood-engraved designs, half full-page plates and half vignettes. The vignettes were included in the book edition – an honour not accorded Millais's far superior vignettes for *The Small House at Allington*. George Housman Thomas was prolific but little more than a journeyman illustrator, and his designs workmanlike but mundane, while William Thomas's engraving is not up to standard. A typical example is "'A Convicted Thief' Repeated Mrs Proudie." A dullness and lack of psychological penetration have been commented on, and the features and facial expressions are somewhat generalised. Admittedly a certain caution is required in making such a judgment, since close scrutiny of the Millais illustrations reveals that some of his faces are not constructed in any detail, and it may be that in the plates containing several figures, the postures and the overall design are sufficiently eloquent for the viewer to overlook the lack of physiognomic specificity.[12] G. H. Thomas has relied too much upon his facial expressions, and has failed to reach the grade.

Marcus Stone's designs for *He Knew He Was Right* (1869) are the finest after Millais's (Hall 124). There were sixty-four wood-engraved designs with exactly half being full-page and half vignette (Sadleir 92–103). Trollope himself had mixed feelings over the choice of illustrator but the fact that he himself felt that of all his novels this one was "nearly altogether bad" may have obscured Stone's virtues from him. In *An Autobiography* Trollope is inclined to rate the success of his novels in terms of critical comment and sales, and *He Knew He Was Right* was the worst casualty of this approach. Stone's designs are pleasingly spare with strong characterisations, elegant figure drawing and sensitive treatment of facial expression and body language. The story hinges on the marital relationship of Louis and Emily Trevelyan, and the former's suspicions that Emily may be having an affair with the older Colonel Osborne. The dislocation between the couple is well captured in such scenes as "Shewing How Wrath Began", where we see the two protagonists standing apart, with Louis looking across the room as if poised to leave, while Emily turns away from the table and gazes at him with a gesture of intense irritation. Stone's method in this illustration might be compared with Orchardson's later depictions of marital coldness or hostility in the 1880s.[13] Similarly in "Trevelyan at Casalunga" the estranged husband broods in a posture, albeit theatrical, expressive of a man who cannot quite believe what has happened. The landscape setting, which echoes Trollope's description, is very expressive, with its sparse foliage and merely suggested forms providing elements which echo Trevelyan's own sense of isolation, unsoftened by warmth or comfort. "The Rivals", showing Norah Rowley and Caroline Spalding, refers to lighter plot elements and is utterly different in sense and feeling. Here, in contrast with the two previous images there is instead a lighter, almost frothy depiction of the two young women in their elegant gowns, engaged more in banter than real conflict. Stone's lines themselves are appropriately airy and sketchy, in contrast with "Trevelyan at Casalunga", where heavier, darker lines underline the character's gloom and despair. This style is wholly apt, since this is the novel in which Trollope most obviously displays his technique of following the thoughts – often the obsessive thoughts – of a person in what the narrator calls "long, unspoken soliloquies" (Ch. 40). Trollope is here grappling with the sorts of problems which made Henry James, James Joyce and others adopt methods such as "stream-of-consciousness". Marcus's designs show throughout that he has a better understanding of the novel than did the reviewers, who attacked it so violently that Trollope himself came to believe that the work, now one of his most respected, was an abject failure.

The illustrators to the later novels were, with the odd exception, of relatively little merit. Henry Woods provided twenty-three plates and twelve vignettes for *The Vicar of Bullhampton*, which appeared in twenty shilling numbers between July 1869 and May 1870; F. A. Fraser illustrated *Ralph the Heir* in nineteen monthly sixpenny parts from January 1870 to July 1871; Fraser appears again in the eight-volume *Chronicles of Barchester* of 1878, for which he contributed the frontispieces; and Frank Holl drew for *Phineas Redux* (*Graphic* 19th July 1873 to 10th January 1874). Fine designs though these last are, they conform to the journalistic style which pervades this periodical, and owe much to the example of artists such as Hubert von Herkomer – in many ways an artist of reportage and social issues, which are dealt with in a washy but forceful style unsuited to Trollope's style of writing, full as it is of subtle ironies, indirections, implications and multiple viewpoints. In addition, in correcting the long-held belief that Luke Fildes illustrated *The Way We Live Now* (February 1874–September 1875), Hall identifies the designs instead as being the work of an amateur, Lionel Grimstone Fawkes (1849–1931). These he rightly castigates as "the absolute nadir of illustration in the Trollope canon" (Hall 145). No critic since has found reason to disagree with this verdict.

The Struggles of Brown, Jones, and Robinson, by One of the Firm, which ran in the *Cornhill* from August 1861 to March 1862, is a comic story of modern marketing and advertising in a new London haberdashery store, Magenta House, and is so unlike the fiction for which the author was best known that it was and has remained largely ignored. As a serial it was without illustrations, and, uniquely among Trollope's novels, it was not immediately brought out as a book in Britain, until it was printed in 1870 with what N. J. Hall dismisses curtly as "four undistinguished plates by an unidentified hand". The artist has since been identified as A. R. Fairfield.[14] There were in fact three plates including a frontispiece, and an illustrated title page, all engraved by Swain.[15] A case might be made for them on the grounds of their suitability to the un-Trollopian subject matter and style. In their "dashed-off" style of drawing, they are not without a certain expressiveness, and the title page which shows the opening of the new store strongly evokes what Trollope's contemporaries condemned as the "vulgarity" of this and other scenes in the book. In "Brisket Makes Himself Useful", showing the butcher putting butter and ale into a frying pan over the open fire, the way the three figures all turn their heads to look straight out at the narrator and the reader is arrestingly striking.

The other interpretative contexts

The remainder of this chapter will concentrate on the main issues which arise when Millais's illustrations to Trollope are examined more closely in the context of the broad sweep of Victorian visual culture, not neglecting socio-economic factors. This approach requires us to examine each image as a work in its own right, linked supportively to a particular moment or moments in the text, and then as part of a sequence of images relating to the entirety of the novel in question, and finally as it relates to the cultural environment in which it was produced and consumed. Treating it not only as an independent creation but also as an inseparable part of the "whole book", it is first necessary to tease out exactly the "moment" on which Millais concentrates. This is not always easy to do since his designs do not inevitably relate to a passage on the facing page of text, or indeed on any passage anywhere. Sometimes a complex set of human relations is pointed up by an illustration, such as "Bread Sauce Is So Ticklish" (*Orley Farm* vol. 2, 1862, opposite page 48).

Other factors involved can be seen from a more detailed discussion of Millais's illustrations to *Framley Parsonage*. This was Trollope's first illustrated novel, his first serial novel, and it contains the manageable number of only six illustrations. The factors identified here may or may not be present in each and every illustration to Trollope, and there is no alternative to scrutinising each on its own terms with considerable care. This scrutiny will extend into comparison with other images, other Trollope novels, the work of other writers and artists, and into considerations of the wider visual culture of the period, from the popular to the élite.

DETAILED EXAMINATION OF A SAMPLE OF MILLAIS'S ILLUSTRATIONS FOR TROLLOPE: FRAMLEY PARSONAGE

Table 17.1 Location of Millais's plates in *Cornhill Magazine* (*CM*) and 1st editions

Lord Lufton and Lucy Robarts	*CM* no. 4; Vol. 1 p. 217*
"Was It Not a Lie?"	*CM* no. 6; Vol. 1 p. 333
The Crawley Family	*CM* no. 8; Vol. 2 p. 103*
Lady Lufton and the Duke of Omnium	*CM* no. 10; Vol. 2 p. 254
"Mark," She Said, "The Men Are Here"	*CM* no. 13; Vol. 3 p. 238*
Mrs Gresham and Miss Dunstable	*CM* no. 15; Vol. 3 p. 12

* Note: These plates are frontispieces to the three volumes of the first edition. The page reference gives the location of the relevant portion of text in that edition, and it was usual practice to indicate this in the list of illustrations in the front matter of a novel, as an instruction to bind the plate in facing the page indicated. This list can be valuable evidence.

Figure 17.1 Lord Lufton and Lucy Robarts, by John Everett Millais
Wood engraving, engr. Dalziel Brothers
In *Framley Parsonage, CM* no. 4; vol. 1 (1861) p. 217

Lord Lufton and Lucy Robarts

There is obvious visual symbolism here: the gateway for the opening of a relationship, doves for love, and the dead pheasant prefiguring the possible fate of an inexperienced young woman like Lucy at the hands of a young nobleman. A melodrama of betrayal seems possible, following the pattern of plays and popular novels in which the aristocrat seduces and abandons the poor, young commoner. The fact that Trollope's story does not follow this pattern is of enormous importance in understanding his work. How closely does the image follow the text? The couple meet inside the walled garden in the text, and Millais takes them outside to allow the gateway to take on a symbolic significance. Millais also adds the circling doves, which are not indicated in the text. The whole image of course follows social conventions of the period, having the tall lord look down on the short commoner, whose eyes are, as is proper at the time, cast bashfully down. The image is also a close copy from an earlier wood engraving by Millais's friend and mentor, John Leech, the figures of Lufton and Lucy resembling in detail those of Jupiter and Semele in Leech's illustration to "Jupiter's Junket" in the *Illuminated Magazine* 1 (1843), 93, except that they are in mirror image. "Jupiter's Junket" is a burlesque of a Greco-Roman myth in which the chief god is taken by the charms of a young mortal woman, who, in the burlesque, is serving wine at a village fête. The original story, as every classically educated middle-class man would know, ends with the death of Semele, whose mortal frame cannot endure the intensity of intercourse with an immortal, and combusts. "Jupiter's Junket", following Victorian conventions, hides the physical aspect of the sexual attraction, and the derivation of Millais's image from this already shielded version of the story allows the sexual nature of the threat to Lucy to be hinted at in a discreet but effective way. To the alert and knowledgeable reader the image implies grave danger facing the young woman. Leech's image is an example of the mid-Victorian game of burlesquing classical works or myths, in which Trollope often participates, and this image complicates the presentation of the fictional situation. It is typical of Trollope that he avoids the cliché of the wicked baronet (or in this case baron) of popular drama, and his illustrator collaborates brilliantly by the visual cross reference to Leech, which alludes to it ironically – that being the nature of burlesque. A serious point is made in such a way that one cannot tell whether to take it seriously.

The passage which is of principal relevance to this illustration is on page 150 of the *Cornhill Magazine* 1 (April 1860), and on volume 1 page 217 of the first edition; and there is a further passage five chapters later, in which Trollope confirms the collaboration of novelist and artist by referring back not to his earlier text but to this image which accompanied it, when we read that Lucy now has the upper hand: "the game was at her feet now" (211). So, instead of being a later addition, an embellishment and something separable from the verbal text, this illustration is integral to the novel. It is not that the image helps interpret the text, but that a complete interpretation of the text is dependent on the image. As we shall see, there is another, even more prominent example of a similar phenomenon in *Orley Farm*, when the narrator explicitly refers the reader back to a plate published months earlier, and elaborates the description of this earlier scene by means of ecphrastic extrapolation from Millais's image.

Returning to the world of *Framley Parsonage*, we find that a few years later in *The Last Chronicle* there is a reference back to this same image two novels earlier in the *Barsetshire Chronicles*. Chapter 55 of the *Last Chronicle* is entitled "Framley Parsonage". Major Grantly, a wealthy widower, is in love with Grace Crawley, the penniless daughter of a very poor clergyman. She is staying with the Robarts family at Framley Parsonage while her father is on trial for a theft which he did not commit. The image of the dove resurfaces. Mark Robarts, the vicar of Framley, is speaking to Lord Lufton, now married to Lucy Robarts: "'Where is Grantly?' asked the vicar. 'I don't know where he is,' said his lordship. 'He has sloped off somewhere.' The major had sloped off to the

Figure 17.2 "Was It Not a Lie?" by John Everett Millais
Wood engraving, engr. Dalziel Brothers
In *Framley Parsonage, CM* no. 6; Vol. 1 p. 691

parsonage, well knowing in what nest his dove was lying hid . . ." A parallel situation is evoked, and the same topography is implied in this passage, which is linked to *Framley Parsonage* by several factors: the parsonage at Framley itself, the cast of characters involved who all derive from the cast of *Framley Parsonage*, and the subject of socially unequal love and marriage, involving a rich man and a poor bride. Moreover the conventional use of doves as symbols of love which occurs in the *Framley* illustration but not in the text stands out because it is very unusual in Trollope's oeuvre. Trollope's texts could easily (though laboriously) be searched for instances of doves. Searches of digitised literary texts often enable us to get a clearer view of the use of a particular word, and if at some later date we have databases of Victorian literary illustration in which the images are iconographically coded and as easily searchable as words now are, we shall, instead of guessing about dove symbolism in the period, be able to make statements on the subject based on real evidence. The results will sometimes be very predictable, but at other times they will force new interpretations on us. A new type of database of illustrated literature which can be searched for words and images with equal facility is badly needed, but is still far off.

"Was It Not a Lie"

Trollope thoroughly disliked this plate when he first saw it:

> I can hardly tell you what my feeling is about the illustration . . . It would be much better to omit it altogether . . . The picture is simply ludicrous, & will be thought by most people to have been made so intentionally.

Then he withdrew his objection seven weeks after the illustration was published, because, he says, "I saw the *very pattern of the dress* some time after the picture came out" (*Letters*, vol. 1, pp. 104 and 111). The conclusion usually drawn from this second letter is that the mere possibility that such a dress could exist in the "real" world was for the author adequate justification for the design. Yet despite this ostensible, almost ostentatious concession to things as they are, the fact is that the image was and remains inappropriate. Perhaps Trollope, newly arrived on the London literary scene, is deliberately deferring to his famous, well-established illustrator. The dress as Millais pictures it is very expensive, both in the amount of dress material and of needlework, and far beyond the means of Lucy on both counts. (Typically Trollope has told us her income, and how she spends it.) It is also quite inappropriate to Lucy's modest life and character. On the day in question she is going to visit a farmer's wife who has recently given birth. This is not the dress for winding baby Podgens. Such considerations of cost and appropriateness often arise in Trollope's fiction, where characters' behaviour and social morality are moulded by income and the cost of living, and their morality is revealed by the way in which they negotiate the practical problems they face in their lives. Millais seems to have made a mistake in this instance.

This incident speaks volumes about the relationship between the two artists, but it is up to individual researchers to decide how to use such speculations in the context of their wider approach to their subject. Consistent principles are essential. Nevertheless, given that illustrators were usually given uncorrected proofs to guide them, it is tempting to wonder whether Millais had read that particular instalment of the novel he was illustrating. An attentive reader could hardly have imagined this dress belonged to Lucy. Because the caption does not indicate the character, it may be that Millais imagined the young woman throwing herself on her bed in despair to be not Lucy but the very different Griselda Grantly, who is determined to marry into the aristocracy, and whose dresses and accoutrements are the subject of intense scrutiny in the novel and among its contemporary readers. As an anonymous critic in the *Saturday Review* of the

4th of May 1861 put it, "no London belle dared to pretend to consider herself literary, who did not know the latest intelligence about the state of Lucy Robarts' heart, and Griselda Grantley's [sic] flounces". Millais, it might be, has accidentally conflated the two, and pictured the flounces where Trollope was revealing the heart. We cannot know, but in any case the illustration is not "faithful" to the text, as the expression runs. On the other hand it responds accurately to the status of the *Cornhill Magazine* and *Framley Parsonage* as fashionable cultural products. Tennyson, whose poem "Tithonus" immediately followed the second instalment of *Framley Parsonage* in the *Cornhill*, thought that it was "a flashy modern novel".[16] Although there is no evidence that he actually read it, he was reacting to the look of it as a symptom of the consumerism of the age. We must not build too much on the probabilities outlined earlier, but so long as we register that they are probabilities and not certainties, we may speculate on whether Trollope forgives Millais because he needs to gain his respect in order to rise in the London literary scene, because he recognises the artist made a mistake or because they are already becoming the fast friends they were to remain until Trollope's death.

Whatever their initial differences, Trollope and Millais became linked in the fashionable phenomena which were the *Cornhill Magazine* and Trollope's first serial fiction, *Framley Parsonage*. Writing years later in *An Autobiography*, Trollope speaks very warmly of the man and his illustrations:

> An artist will frequently dislike to subordinate his ideas to those of an author, and will sometimes be too idle to find out what those ideas are. But this artist was neither proud nor idle. In every figure that he drew it was his object to promote the views of the writer whose work he had undertaken to illustrate, and he never spared himself any pains in studying that work so as to enable himself to do so. I have carried on some of those characters from book to book, and have had my own early ideas impressed indelibly on my memory by the excellence of his delineations.
>
> (Ch. 8)

The researcher is faced with a topical decision at every point in the study of specific illustrations about which evidence to rely on as fact, which to discount, and how to assess the probabilities attached to other clues. The exegetic methods, the assessment of the probability of a certain given proposition being correct, and the discrimination of which evidence it is scholarly to adduce – all these are to be negotiated anew on almost every occasion.

We can look for examples of this dress in the 1860s to see whether Millais was copying the latest fashion, or whether he and Trollope (even though not working in unison in this case) created the conditions which brought the dress to life. Picture research into the fashions of that year suggests that this style appeared a little *after* Millais's illustration, and therefore may have come originally from his pencil. It was for example worn by Princess Mary of Cambridge in a photographic *carte de visite* a number of weeks after the relevant instalment of *Framley Parsonage* had appeared. Princess Mary's dress bills were notoriously large, and her taking up this style confirms that this was not a dress for Lucy, and also suggests that it was copied from Millais's wood engraving. After all it was not uncommon to give a dressmaker an image to follow, although that image came more often from a fashion magazine than a novel.

Analysing the image itself in the context of Millais's other graphic works, we find that the pose of a woman slumped over in grief recurs in his illustrations. The pose is found in his illustration to Tom Taylor's poem "Magenta" in *Once a Week*, and to Tennyson's "Mariana in the Moated Grange" in the Moxon edition of his poems, 1857 (Skilton, "Centrality"; Thomas *Reflections*). This pose itself, particularly when intensified by Millais's repetition and visual quotation, carries

Figure 17.3 The Crawley Family, by John Everett Millais
Wood engraving, engr. Dalziel Brothers
In *Framley Parsonage, CM* no. 8; Vol. 2 p. 103

emotions of loss, regret, mourning or endurance, as clearly as would a verbal quotation, such as Tennyson's lines:

> He cometh not," she said;
> She said, "I am aweary, aweary,
> I would that I were dead!
>   (ll. 10–12)[17]

Broader iconographic research might show that the pose was used by artists long before Millais's time, or it may be that Millais's repeated use of it serves to generate and attach this meaning to it. Of course Trollope knew this Tennysonian reference, and is confident that his readers will recognise "The Moated Grange" in chapter 59 of *John Caldigate* (1878–9). The fact that Tom Taylor himself had already quoted these lines from Tennyson in his play *Still Waters Run Deep*, produced at the Olympic Theatre in 1855,[18] might spur us on to include illustrations in the web of meanings which quotation and intertextuality set up in Victorian (as in all other) literature.

The Crawley family

Here Lucy Robarts is in appropriate daily dress, visiting the family of a very low-paid clergyman, Josiah Crawley, perpetual curate of Hogglestock. Millais is now on target. He highlights her human warmth and tact, and sets up the iconography of a particular kind of "genteel poverty" which afflicts the family of this very well-educated clergyman, who is a far better scholar than his more prosperous clerical neighbours. The visual signs of poverty and book learning emphasise the shocking contrast between Crawley's poverty and his education. He has been disturbed while teaching his daughters. In a total reversal (we might nowadays say "transgression") of normal social expectations at the time, the elder daughter, Grace, is learning both Greek and Latin, and ends up proficient in both. There are themes here in text and image together well worth following up.

A figure is seen at a half-opened door in the background, either watching or entering. There is no time for an explication of it in this case, but the detail gains further significance if we examine its recurrence in Millais's illustrations to Trollope, in the total of his graphic works and easel paintings, and indeed in the visual arts in general over the centuries. There are several examples in Millais's illustrations to *Orley Farm*. Does it derive from the old masters or from the stage or from both, and what range of meanings does it produce across all its manifestations, from pleasurable expectation to possible revelation or betrayal, or for the moment an equivocal mixture of several possibilities? Millais is responding to an important feature of Trollope's narratives: that the reader is shown many things with apparent openness, but has actively to assess their significance in her own mind, at least for the nonce. In the novels of the 1850s and 1860s, Trollope's narrator often goes on to give a full explanation, but nonetheless the passive reader is not a true reader of Trollope, and Millais stimulates readerly activity.

Lady Lufton and the Duke of Omnium

The fact that Trollope or his publisher, George Smith, or both, chose to have Millais illustrate this scene in which Lady Lufton, a conservative and highly moral lady of Tory persuasion, shows her disapproval by ironically curtseying to the dissipated and immensely rich Whig Duke of Omnium, highlights the importance of the question of rank and moral standing to the readers

Figure 17.4 Lady Lufton and the Duke of Omnium, by John Everett Millais
Wood engraving, engr. Dalziel Brothers
In *Framley Parsonage, CM* no. 10; Vol. 2 p. 254

Figure 17.5 "Mark," She Said, "The Men Are Here," by John Everett Millais
Wood engraving, engr. Dalziel Brothers
In *Framley Parsonage, CM* no. 13; Vol. 3 p. 238

of the *Cornhill Magazine*. Such scenes of social engagement (in the military sense) between characters of different socio-moral characteristics occur regularly in illustrated literature at the time. The present image is striking but not unique in its subtlety and effectiveness. Here is an obvious but far from trivial research topic, which might utilise the *Spectator*'s judgment that Trollope is expert in the "social weapons" used in the "moral engagements between the different characters."[19]

A shirt-front in this picture buttons up the wrong way, either because Millais forgot that his drawing would be reversed in the process of cutting and printing, or because he mistook the process by which the drawing was to be transferred to the woodblock. The technicalities of reproduction must never be forgotten.

"Mark," She Said, "The Men Are Here"

This scene is calculated to fill the middle-class reader with dread, as the bailiffs descend on the comfortable vicarage to distrain on the Robartses' possessions. "Lord Lufton and Lucy Robarts" showed Millais deriving his poses from an earlier artist. Two years later George Elgar Hicks drew on this illustration by Millais for *Bad News*, the central image in his triptych, *Woman's Mission*, of 1863. In the Millais, the husband is the weaker partner, but when Hicks adopted Millais's iconography of the hearth and mantelpiece, and composition of the relation between the figures, he melodramatically reversed their roles, giving a strain of sentimental desperation to the wife, quite unlike Fanny's more robust attitude, which Millais captures completely. Millais has set up an iconographic paradigm worth copying, but a comparison of the two shows Millais and Trollope to share a far more "modern" and less sentimental attitude to marriage and a woman's place in it than Hicks, who better meets the criteria for public display in the Royal Academy Summer Exhibition.

Mrs Gresham and Miss Dunstable

This is a fairly common picture type in Millais, containing two contrasting characters in contrasting poses, with a suggestion of some sort of awkwardness or difficulty in communication, which it is often the business of the story to overcome. Some larger significance seems to be hanging in the air, hinting at how Millais would further develop situations requiring decoding by the reader/viewer, and leading to his invention of the "problem picture" (Skilton, "Centrality").

These illustrations to *Framley Parsonage* were inexpertly copied for an unauthorised edition by Harper & Brothers of New York in 1861. A comparison of the two sets shows up the high standard, and by implication the high cost, of the illustrations which Trollope's London publishers commissioned.

Other issues raised by close reading

This discussion of *Framley Parsonage* shows strands of meaning in word and in image closely intertwined, and meanings moving between the verbal and visual, and between fictional life and the "real" world. There is no reason to suppose that the remaining eighty-plus of Millais's Trollopian illustrations are less complex than these six.

Here are some further issues to consider. Trollope is emphatic in his approval of Millais's illustrations. "I am fond of *Orley Farm*," he wrote, "and am especially fond of its illustrations, by Millais, which are the best I have seen in any novel in any language" (*Autobiography*, p. 110). We might wonder whether these authorial memoirs are sufficient guarantee of quality, were it not

Figure 17.6 Mrs Gresham and Miss Dunstable, by John Everett Millais
Wood engraving, engr. Dalziel Brothers
In *Framley Parsonage, CM* no. 15; Vol. 3 p. 12

that in *Orley Farm* Trollope's narrator integrates word and image in an instruction to the reader to consult a particular illustration in order to visualise a later scene:

> In an early part of this story I have endeavoured to describe how this woman sat alone, with deep sorrow in her heart and deep thought on her mind, when she first learned what terrible things were coming on her. The idea, however, which the reader will have conceived of her as she sat there will have come to him from the skill of the artist, and not from the words of the writer. If that drawing is now near him, let him go back to it. Lady Mason was again sitting in the same room – that pleasant room, looking out through the verandah on to the sloping lawn, and in the same chair; one hand again rested open on the arm of the chair, while the other supported her face as she leaned upon her elbow . . .
>
> (Ch. 43)

As N. J Hall points out, Trollope imagines a reader reading part 15 of *Orley Farm*, and sends "him" to the second part, published thirteen months earlier and shelved elsewhere, perhaps, or, if reading the two-volume edition from a volume published 25th September 1862 to the first, published nine months earlier: "in the earlier description we read simply that Lady Mason 'seated herself in her accustomed chair'; the details mentioned in the latter passage are in fact a description of Millais' drawing". We ignore self-consciousness in the illustrated novel at our peril (Hall 44).

Never Is a Very Long Word

This is movement back and forth through time as defined by the publication schedule. Here is an example of an illustration, "Never Is a Very Long Word", which is not unequivocally attached to any particular moment in the "narrated time" of *Orley Farm*. Chapter 50 contains a conversation between Lady Staveley and Peregrine Orme, in which he asks Lady Staveley what her daughter, Madeleine, has reported about his proposal of marriage the day before. The mother answers, "She told me that she had declined the honour that you had offered her; – that she did not regard you as she must regard the man to whom she would pledge her heart."

> "But did she say that she could never love me?" And now as he asked the question he stood up again, looking down with all his eyes into Lady Staveley's face, – that face which would have been so friendly to him, so kind and so encouraging, had it been possible.
> "Never is a long word, Mr. Orme."
> "Ah, but did she say it?"

The illustration is not of the later conversation which is presented in the verbal narrative in this chapter, but of an earlier conversation between Madeleine and her mother, of which Trollope's description is not closely followed in the illustration. The caption, however, is taken from the later conversation, complicating how the reader is to understand what is happening. Peregrine seeks certainty from where he cannot receive it. Madeleine's mother cannot betray her daughter by giving her true assessment of the daughter's feelings, even if she knows them. The nearest she can come to openness is, "Never is a long word", which is Victorian code for "Why not try again after a while?" The instruction in the list of illustrations to bind the plate in opposite page 77 of volume 2 is correct in that that is where it needs to be read and that is the page from which the caption is taken, but that page does not describe the scene which Millais draws. The plate

Figure 17.7 Never Is a Very Long Word, by John Everett Millais
Wood engraving 169 × 106 mm, engr. Dalziel Brothers
In *Orley Farm* vol. 2 (1862) recto opp. p. 77

Figure 17.8 Monkton Grange, by John Everett Millais
Wood engraving 169 × 106 mm, engr. Dalziel Brothers
In *Orley Farm* vol. 1 (1861) recto opp. p. 216

illustrates narrative complication and the problems of Victorian discourse on love and marriage, as much as an identifiable event in the novel. A number of plates, such as "Sir Peregrine and His Heir" and the two entitled "Farewell" go further and show events not covered by Trollope's narrative, even if they may be reasonably inferred from it. Such singularities may seem to suggest that illustration can validate the independent existence of a fictional world when it is not actually being narrated, and hence reinforce some of the more extreme claims of literary realism. In fact the difficulty disappears as soon as the novel is recognised as a bimedial text, these otherwise interpolated events being adequately narrated visually, if not verbally.

Monkton Grange

"Monkton Grange" shows Millais breaking new ground in artistic subject matter. This is thought to be the first representation of a hunt about to move off, rather than in the field. It also creates an atmosphere which is simultaneously very "modern" and expressive of a myth of timeless Englishness at the same time, since the architecture of Monkton Hall is the historic style many landowners strove for, but which they usually had to create for themselves in simulacrum, since most Tudor and Jacobean houses had by then been altered beyond recognition. The image secretly expresses the paradox that what was fashionable was the appearance of age but with all modern conveniences. It is also a brilliant use of the "portrait" orientation of an image which might have been produced in "landscape". It is a tour de force which, by positioning the observing eye at a slight distance and at the height of an adult's eye, draws the reader in with unparalleled power.

There are also images in *Orley Farm* which cannot be understood from their captions, such as "Your Son, Lucius, Did Say Shopping", or "Bread Sauce Is So Ticklish". These require an extensive acquaintance with the verbal text, and are too involved to be analysed here.

"It's All the Fault of the Naughty Birds"

Faced with the characteristically Victorian difficulty of presenting a highly intelligent young woman with satirical views on the behaviour of men, Millais has it both ways in this illustration to chapter 7 of the *Small House*. He shows the Dale sisters demurely veiled behind a group of men who have returned empty-handed from a shooting trip, yet he pictures the discomfiture of the men as though seen through Lily's satirical gaze. This is the female gaze made socially acceptable. The double perspective here is fascinating. The men are seen in Lily's terms, while she is demurely veiled at the back of the group. Despite conventionally occupying a female place, she usurps the role of narrator and hence of the construction of social judgment.

Summing up

Clearly no complete guidance can be given to new researchers in this field, as scholars are only just coming to terms with the richness of cultural reference in illustration, and because of the diversity of approaches which are appropriate in different cases. Besides there are limits to what can usefully be written about illustrations in the absence of their images. Certainly close attention has not yet been paid to all the illustrations to Trollope. The onus has to be on the researcher to decide which information or conjecture is relevant and acceptable in the type of research being undertaken. Meaning production by word and image interacting in illustration is the closest sort of study to traditional literary criticism. Many other matters come under the heading of the History of the Book. Ideally work on Trollope illustration should intersect with larger projects

Figure 17.9 "It's All the Fault of the Naughty Birds," by John Everett Millais
Wood engraving 158 × 102 mm, engr. Dalziel Brothers
In Anthony Trollope, *The Small House at Allington*, *Cornhill Magazine* 6 (November 1862), verso facing p. 663

on the work of artists, engravers and publishers, to the enrichment of both. The same is true of the linkage between the illustrative images and other visual art or visual cultural products. Perhaps the general rule can be expressed as the necessity to maintain a sound theoretical scrutiny of the principles involved, without surrendering to a catch-all theory of illustration which, although not the product of empirical evidence, pronounces on the status of all images in all books at all times and in all places. Very many cases seem to be special cases both in how images interact with the text and in how the illustrations came into being in the first place. One writer commissions an artist to illustrate her writing. Another has an unsuitable artist foisted on her by the publisher. Some writers vet their illustrations in detail. Others appear to be content to let them be embellishments to attract buyers. Often we have no information on the subject at all. It is best to remain open-minded about all such things until hard evidence comes to light.

However, we end with the plea that whatever research is undertaken, due attention will be paid to accurate bibliographical description and other metadata, to allow the subject to advance. And researchers should never think they have examined an illustration thoroughly until they have scrutinised it through a magnifying glass.

Literature review

The systematic study of literary illustration is a relatively recent development, and work on Trollope's illustrations largely concentrates on those by John Everett Millais, which are generally judged to be the best.

Armstrong, Walter, *Sir John E. Millais, Bart: Royal Academician, His Life and Work* (London: Art Journal Office, 1885) contains the first attempt at critical commentary on Millais's illustrations to Trollope.

Bennett, Mary, *PRB Millais PRA*, exhibition catalogue (Liverpool: Walker Art Gallery and London: Royal Academy), 1967, pp. 64–65, items 143–154: useful on the preparatory drawings.

Dalziel Brothers – *The Brothers Dalziel: A Record* (London: Methuen, 1901): a rambling account of the activities of the firm, including their relations with Millais; contains a brief mention of Trollope on p. 81.

Goldman, Paul, *Beyond Decoration: The Illustration of John Everett Millais* (London: British Library, Pinner, Middx; New Castle, Delaware: Private Libraries Association, 2005): a general catalogue and survey, including passages from the texts which are immediately related to the illustrations. All the designs are carefully reproduced.

Goldman, Paul (with an essay by Tessa Sidey), *John Everett Millais: Illustrator and Narrator* (Aldershot: Lund Humphries, 2004): advances the argument that Millais is a storyteller in his own right and examines the narrative elements in his work.

Hall, N. J. (ed.), *The Letters of Anthony Trollope* (Stanford, CA: Stanford University Press, 1983) 2 vols paginated as one: an essential source of factual information.

Hall, N. John, *Trollope and His Illustrators* (London: Macmillan Press 1980): discusses nearly all the illustrations in fine detail, with special attention to those by Millais; an essential companion for students of the subject. (Dismisses those to the 1870 British first edition of *The Struggles of Brown, Jones and Robinson* as unworthy of attention.)

Life, Allan Roy, "The Periodical Illustrations of John Everett Millais and Their Literary Interpretation", *Victorian Periodicals Newsletter* 9 (June 1976), 50–68: a useful, early exploration.

Mason, Michael, "The Way We Look Now: Millais' Illustrations to Trollope", *Art History* 1, no. 3 (September 1978), 309–40: a pioneering analysis of the designs.

Reid, Forrest, *Illustrators of the Sixties* (London: Faber and Gwyer, 1928). The Trollope illustrations are examined briefly but penetratingly in chapter 5, section 6: the first but now very dated example of modern scholarship on these designs.

Sadleir, Michael, *Trollope: A Bibliography* (London: Constable, 1928), reprinted 1964, 1977, etc.: an essential source of bibliographical information about all the illustrations.

Skilton, David, "The Centrality of Illustration in Victorian Visual Culture: The Example of Millais and Trollope", *Journal of Illustration Studies* Issue 1 (December 2007) http://jois.uis.no/articles.php (accessed May 10, 2015): closely investigates a small number of Trollope illustrations in various material and textual contexts.

Skilton, David, "The Relation Between Illustration and Text in the Victorian Novel: A New Perspective", in Peter M. Daly, Karl J. Höltgen and Wolfgang Lottes (eds), *Word and Visual Imagination: Studies in the Interaction of English Literature and the Visual Arts* (Erlangen Forschungen, vol. 43, 1988), pp. 303–25: an early attempt to establish how words and images jointly produce meanings in Victorian novels, including some of Trollope's.

Skilton, David (Gen. Ed.), Trollope Society and Pickering and Chatto editions of the collected novels in forty-eight volumes (1988–99), which reproduce most of the original illustrations.

Ullmann, Jennifer M., "'The Perfect Delineation of Character': Process and Perfection in the Book Illustrations of John Everett Millais", in Susan P. Casteras (ed.), *Pocket Cathedrals: Pre-Raphaelite Book Illustration* (New Haven: Yale Center for British Art, 1991), pp. 55–65. A useful discussion of Millais's designs with attention to the circumstances of publication.

Notes

1 Skilton "Centrality" and "Editorial", Goldman and Cooke. Earlier there is valuable descriptive work on illustration in the Victorian novel by Harvey in 1971, in Dickens by Steig in 1978 and in Trollope by Hall in 1980.
2 Flanders.
3 Skilton "Editorial"; Spinozzi "Interarts" and *Sopera*; Kooistra *Artist*; Thomas *Pictorial* and "Reflections"; Goldman *Beyond*.
4 Mason; Goldman *John*.
5 Goldman and Cooke 31–2.
6 Anon. "Review of *Small House*". It is plausibly argued that this review is by R. H. Hutton, literary editor of the paper.
7 Trollope *Autobiography*, chapter 12.
8 Goldman *Beyond*, 115 and 227.
9 Sadleir; Hall.
10 See Hall for a full account.
11 It is sometimes remarked that Millais's drawing of hands and feet can let him down.
12 It is a practice of some later comic-book artists to underplay the individuality of faces, allowing the reader more freedom to contribute to character production.
13 See Sir William Orchardson's series of three paintings about unhappy marriage, *Mariage de Convenance* (1883), *Mariage à la Mode – After!* (1886) and *The First Cloud* (1887).
14 By Bethan Stevens, in a private email to Skilton.
15 An unauthorised US edition in the Library of Select Novels, New York, in 1862 was unillustrated.
16 Tennyson *Letters*, ii, p. 252.
17 John Everett Millais, "Mariana", wood engraving engr. Dalziel Brothers, in Tennyson *Poems*.
18 Taylor.
19 Anon. "Review of *Small House*".

Works cited

Anon. 'Jupiter's Junket', *Illuminated Magazine* 1 (1843), p. 93.
Anon. 'Review of *Framley Parsonage* (anon.)', *Saturday Review* 11 (4 May 1861), pp. 451–2.
Anon. 'Review of *Small House at Allington*', *Spectator* 37 (9 April 1864), pp. 421–3.
Flanders, Judith. *Consuming Passions: Leisure and Pleasure in Victorian Britain* (London: Harper, 2006).
Girouard, Mark. *The Victorian Country House*, revised edn (New Haven, CT: Yale University Press, 1979), p. 71.
Goldman, Paul. *Beyond Decoration: The Illustrations of John Everett Millais* (London: British Library, 2005).
———. *John Everett Millais: Illustrator and Narrator* (Farnham: Lund Humphries and Birmingham Museums and Art Gallery, 2004).
———. *Victorian Illustrated Books 1850–1870: The Heyday of Wood-Engraving* (London: British Museum Press, 1995 and Boston, MA: David Godine, 1995).
Goldman, Paul, and Cooke, Simon (eds). *Reading Victorian Illustration 1855–1875: Spoils of the Lumber Room* (Farnham, England: Ashgate, 2012), pp. 13–32.
Hall, N. John. *Trollope and His Illustrators* (London: Macmillan Press, 1980).
Harvey, John. *Victorian Novelists and Their Illustrators* (New York: New York University Press, 1971).

Kooistra, Lorraine Janzen. *The Artist as Critic: Bitextuality in Fin-de-Siècle Illustrated Books* (Aldershot: Scolar, 1995).

———. *Poetry, Pictures, and Popular Publishing: The Illustrated Gift Book and Victorian Visual Culture 1855–1875* (Athens: Ohio University Press, 2011).

Leighton, Mary Elizabeth, and Lisa Surridge. 'The Plot Thickens: Toward a Narratological Analysis of Illustrated Serial Fiction in the 1860s', *Victorian Studies* 51, no. 1 (Autumn 2008), pp. 65–101.

Mason, Michael. 'The Way We Look Now: Millais' Illustrations to Trollope', *Art History* 1 (1978), pp. 309–40.

Sadleir, Michael. *Trollope: A Bibliography* (London: Constable 1928 and reprint Folkestone, Kent: William Dawson 1964, 1977).

Skilton, David. 'The Centrality of Illustration in Victorian Visual Culture: The Example of Millais and Trollope, 1860–64', *Journal of Illustration Studies* 1 (December 2007), http://jois.uis.no/articles.php?

———. 'Editorial', *Journal of Illustration Studies* 1 (2007), http://jois.uia.no/articles.php?article=42.

———. The Relation Between Illustration and Text in the Victorian Novel: A New Perspective. In P. M. Daly, J. K. Höltgen and W. Lottes (eds), *Word and Visual Imagination: Studies in the Interaction of English Literature and the Visual Arts. Erlangen Forschungen* (Erlangen, Germany: Universitätsbibliothek Erlangen-Nürnberg, 1988), pp. 303–25.

Spinozzi, Paola. 'Interarts and Illustration: Some Historical Antecedents, Theoretical Issues, and Methodological Orientations', *Journal of Illustration Studies* (December 2007), http://jois.uia.no/articles.php?article=43 21 Mar 2014

———. *Sopera il reale: Osmosi interartistiche nel Prefraffaellitismo e nel Simbolismo inglese* (Florence: Alinea editrice, 2005).

Steig, Michael. *Dickens and Phiz* (Bloomington: Indiana UP, 1978).

Taylor, Tom. *Still Waters Run Deep*. In Martin Banham (ed.), *The Plays of Tom Taylor* (Cambridge: Cambridge University Press, 1985), p. 26.

Tennyson, Alfred. *The Letters of Alfred Lord Tennyson*, ed. Cecil Y. Lang and Edgar F. Shannon, Jr., 3 vols. (Cambridge, MA: Harvard University Press, 1981), ii, p. 252.

———. *Poems* (London: E. Moxon, 1857).

Thomas, Julia. "Happy Endings: Death and Domesticity in Victorian Illustration". In Goldman P. and S. Cooke (eds), *Reading Victorian Illustration 1855–1875: Spoils of the Lumber Room* (Farnham: Ashgate, 2012), pp. 79–96.

———. *Pictorial Victorians: The Inscription of Values in Word and Image* (Athens: Ohio University Press, 2004).

———. 'Reflections on Illustration: The *Database of Mid-Victorian Wood-Engraved Illustration (DMVI)*', *Journal of Illustration Studies* 37 (December 2007). <http://jois.uia.no/articles.php?article=37> accessed 21 Mar 2014

Trollope, Anthony. *An Autobiography*, ed. David Skilton (Harmondsworth: Penguin Books, 1996).

———. *The Letters of Anthony Trollope*, ed. N. John Hall, 2 vols paginated as one (Stanford: Stanford University Press, 1983).

18
TROLLOPE'S PICTURESQUE CHRONICLETTE AND JOHN MILLAIS
Portrait of the artist as a young swain

Robert Polhemus

The picture was progressing, and so also, as it had come about, was the love-affair between the artist and his model.[1]

Prologue

Anthony Trollope was a "titanic" talent,[2] but a writer so prolific that it's hard to see and keep in mind the full range of his accomplishment. With his forty-seven novels – most of them good – plus all those stories and nonfiction books, who can read it all, much less take it in with the attention it deserves? Like filmmaker Woody Allen or novelist Philip Roth, Trollope is a master who just keeps on keeping on and doing it well. But people fall behind, can't keep up, and so invent reasons not to. The big critical problem in dealing with major artists who never stop is not that they repeat themselves, but that they don't: they move on, try new things, and upset conventional takes and easy generalizations. Lack of "close reading" often leads to the sloppiness of *closed* reading. It's hard to describe the sprawling big picture of Trollope's whole wordy world without oversimplifying – without distorting or missing the rich complexities and contradictions of his genius.

So how can we take in what still seems to matter in him and hold on to his "best things"? One way might be to think *small* – to pick out relatively little-known chapters, unexpected episodes, "untypical" characters, and surprising dialogue in those multi-volume prose avalanches, look hard at them in and of themselves, without having to relate and diffuse them into some spurious organic whole of an 800-page novel – and thereby discover in a few relatively obscure spots *fresh* aesthetic brightness that can teach and delight.

In *The Last Chronicle of Barset*, there's a supposedly minor section that's actually a major piece of fiction, and it involves Trollope's close friend and sometime illustrator John Everett Millais.[3] Though usually ignored or dismissed,[4] this resonant subplot, set behind the scenes of the Victorian art-world culture – not a milieu that pops first to mind regarding Trollope and Barset – features a Pre-Raphaelitish painter, Conway Dalrymple, his love life fused with his art, and the dramatic making and fate of his grand portrait *Jael*.[5] The chroniclette is no *roman à clef*, but

Trollope uses Millais as his main source for this "Jael" tale and for Dalrymple, who, like Millais, marries his freedom-seeking model. It's a brilliant prelude for late-Victorian "art-for-art's-sake" concerns and the massive art versus bourgeois morality themes flooding twentieth-century fiction (e.g., Proust's *Remembrance of Things Past*, Joyce's *Ulysses*, Galsworthy's *Forsyte Saga*).

In Barsetshire, Trollope made the English clerical community a fitting subject for popular fiction, and in this chroniclette[6] he does a similar thing for an artist-centered milieu. If in *Barchester Towers*, we see Trollope's secular and comic faith displacing – or supplanting – theological, supernatural faith, here we see him featuring worldly aesthetic faith and the explicit vocation of an artist in creating and preserving what makes people value life. My goal is to focus on this resonant, neglected piece of fiction – virtually a detachable short novel – and, as something I see fine, new, and exciting in Trollope, make it better known. Centered on a painting, it has tremendous analogical power and suggests rich, allegorical meaning for anyone interested in erotic or aesthetic faith.

The chroniclette

The story in chapters 24, 25, 26, 38, 51, 60, 64, 65, 75, and 84 of *The Last Chronicle* at first may look simple: *artist meets girl, artist paints girl, artist marries girl*. He falls in love with his "striking" model for a would-be masterpiece and changes both their lives for the better – a basic marriage plot. But in fact the chroniclette love story is unique in Trollope – and as complex, subtle, and fascinating as any he wrote. Very close to John Millais when writing *The Last Chronicle* (in 1866), the novelist is working in new territory for him, exploring the where, how, and why of the processes that produce art. The episode puts the value of a distinguished work of art in question when its very being both depends upon and comes in conflict with subjective morality, love, and marriage. He portrays the volatile relationship of the making of art to – among other things – scripture, eroticism, myth, history, elitism, beauty, money, comedy, high-class consumerism, sexism, faith, and mood-swinging psychology. These packed chapters depict an ambitious, talented painter finding work and "true" love, but they also feature two upper-class women looking for fuller, better lives through the effects of art and the artist. One woman is Conway's ex-model, the other he takes as a new model, and, though very different figures, they both need and look for cultural capital and meaning to fill the emptiness of their prescribed female roles.[7] And both convey the historic importance of women as *models* – objects and mutable subjects of art and desire in their world.

Right away in the chroniclette, Trollope makes art a subject, specifying what kind of painter Conway is (thus showing his own interest in the linkup of pictures and words, visual images and storytelling):

> It was the peculiar merit of his pictures, – so at least said the art-loving world, – that though the likeness was always good, the stiffness of the modern portrait was never there. There was also ever some story told in Dalrymple's pictures over and above the story of the portraiture. [*à la John Millais*]
>
> *(ch. 24)*

An urban atmosphere of sexual and gender tensions, passion for art, moral dilemma, and economic fixation defines this part of the novel. In it Trollope makes clear the tangled, changing desires of its artist Dalrymple, the *Jael* project's main patron (Maria, Mrs. Dobbs Broughton), and its magnetic, tough-minded model Clara Van Siever, oppressed by her money-mad mother, but "a young woman with a will and purpose of her own" (ch. 51). His portrait of the fluid relationship between art and life here shows how the particular motives of individuals involved in creating a picture bring it about *and* how the work of art itself comes then to shape the desires and actions of these figures: art determines the way these characters live in their evolving *now*. The creation of art depends on the literal turning of people into words, pictures, and songs, but then words, pictures, and music form real lives.

The subplot

Conway Dalrymple accepts a dinner invitation from his "very beautiful" friend, Maria (Mrs. Dobbs Broughton). A rising, hot painter "whom the rich English world was beginning to pet and pelt with gilt sugar-plums" (ch. 24), he first appears as a charming womanizer. He knows erotically two women at the party: crucially, his hostess, but also the melodramatic Madalina Demolines, a sleaze queen in the Victorian marriage mart (he knows her love life well enough to advise Johnny Eames she'll do anything for money). Maria wants Dalrymple to meet Clara Van Siever, daughter of the tyrannical but filthy rich mother who's trying to marry her off to the grubby "man of business," Musselboro. Maria's own, speculator husband has paid Conway lots for a stunning triple portrait of his trophy wife as "The Three Graces," and while she modeled for him, the painter "won" her "heart" (ch. 24). At the episode's start, she and Conway are having a love affair (a *publishable* Victorian affair – i.e., a liaison between two pleasure-seeking people – heavy verbal petting, no explicit sex, but much implied). But Maria, in danger from her intimacy with Dalrymple and a sottish spouse getting jealous, decides to beef up her weak will, stop things before she's a fallen woman, and preserve her marriage – which, after all, has so far "paid off." So she plots to fix up the man she thinks she loves with a suitable wife, Clara:

> "There's no telling how much she'll have," said Mrs. Dobbs Broughton, in the warmth of her friendship. . . . You might offer to paint her, you know. She'd make an excellent picture. So much character". . . .
> And now he had come to meet Miss Van Siever, and now was seated next to her at table.
>
> *(ch. 24)*

Such a scene and talk might seem to preview either scathing comic satire (see *The Way We Live Now*) or the highbrow, bottom-feeding moral world of Henry James novels, but in fact both the artist and his ditsy lady-friend, though sometimes foolish, selfish sex teases, generally mean well – "good-enough" people in their ethically mixed-up world. Conway is no cynical cad, but before seeing Clara, love hasn't mattered much to him. What drives the story is discontentment that Miss Van Siever, a gorgeous, smart, serious female powerhouse trapped by her mother's mammonism, needs the kind of liberation that art can sometimes offer.

Gazing at her before they exchange a word, the artist mentally portrays her handsome but off-putting features; they both enthrall and repel him. He sees her as a scary girl, with whom he could never, ever mate (ch. 24). But immediately, a passion to paint her as one of the Bible's female man-killers seizes him – as "Judith" the head-chopper or as "Jael." The artist's mind goes to work, and everything follows from his idea of making a shocking portrait by fusing a violent scriptural figure with a stern Victorian beauty. It's a painting and not a woman that Conway first wants, and out of that desire come the narrative and its themes.

Trollope imagines that when Conway conceives his Jael painting in this *not-love-at-first-sight* meeting, he wants it to portray faith in his art over love and career over relationships. He picks his subject as though to convey for his era a vivid (though stereotyped) anti-feminist view (i.e., *a strong woman can be a menace*). In the beginning, Clara means for him a professional device: paint, not flesh; pose, not intimacy; artifice not reality.

I want to stress Trollope's focus on the subject of *Jael*, the circumstances in which it gets painted, and its fate. It's a sensational story, and for Trollope, like Dalrymple, *Jael* hangs over his imagination and shapes it. In the *Book of Judges* (4: 17–21), the married woman Jael drives a spike through the head of Sisera, the sleeping enemy general she's seduced. She does it to free her "chosen people" from their foes and thus fulfills proto-feminist prophet Deborah's claim that a woman shall win this victory (*Judges*, 4 and 5). As a living parable *Jael* symbolizes both projections of a raw, violent desire in women to kill off the man-imposed system of gender bondage *and* the dread of males at losing domination over the female sex they have so depended on, adored, and exploited.

Using *Jael*, Trollope shows how an artist's choice of subject can and does reverberate in particular lives and ultimately in the world at large. Pun and metaphor help define the chroniclette and its analogical direction: *the artist must go to Jael and then get out of Jael and so must his model*. The idea of *Jael* and a strong woman's quest for power must both live and be transformed in modernity, and Trollope makes *Jael* the occasion for new love, change, and the release of the artist and his model from the obsessions of their past.

The ménage portrait

He imagines an extraordinary *ménage à trois* portraiture featuring Dalrymple, Mrs. Dobbs Broughton, Miss Van Siever, and their confused, shifting relationships. It's filled with implications and questions not just about Victorian painting and modeling but about all art history: for example, *Who's your model and why? What's your subject? What, how, and why do male artists project on women? How does the creative process work out for the people involved in it? What can an image from the mythic past have to do with the present? What's more important, a person or a masterpiece?*

Conway has to get both Mrs. DB and Clara to agree to his project. He needs Maria to provide a secret setting in her house where he can paint *Jael* without art-hating Mrs. Van Siever forbidding it or jealous Dobbs Broughton and gossipy outsiders knowing about it. And he must somehow persuade Clara to pose for him.

As for Maria, she has to deal with the mind-split between her rational scheme to marry him off and her "fevered" (ch. 25) longing to hang on to him. She plays a loopy, but big part in these chapters. The artist's memorable painting of her has made Mrs. Dobbs Broughton for a time socially prominent. Conway likes her; she likes him, and she loves the glamorous touch of renown his art has brought her. Through her, Trollope gets at the influence of the mutable psychology and goals of patrons and onlookers in aesthetic history.

In Conway and his vocation, Maria finds for a time release, relief, and bouts of joy from the life that her gender, she believes, dooms her to lead: "submitting to that ill-usage which is the ordinary lot of woman" (ch. 64). That unforgettable phrase fits all the women of the *Jael* subplot – even the obnoxious Madalina and Mrs. Van Siever, both caught up in the culture's wealth idolatry. By the end, what sounded like privileged whining becomes Maria's truth: her unloved soused spouse goes broke and widows her with a gunshot suicide in the City's cash jungle, and Conway, seeing her heartless reaction to Dobbs's death, loses respect and affection for her (ch. 64). He helps Maria, now single, in her crisis, but makes it plain he has chosen Clara for good. (In both Trollope and his friend Millais, as in so much writing, music, and painting of the last two centuries, that "ordinary lot of women," "ill-usage," often forms the basis of their work.)

Early on Dalrymple needs Mrs. Dobbs Broughton's help in getting Miss Van Siever to model, and he gets it. With Clara present, he shows Maria his Jael sketch:

"It is very good,"... said Mrs. Dobbs Broughton. "I do not for a moment doubt that you would make a great picture of it.... And then the pose of the woman would be so good, so much strength, and yet such grace!.... No painter living tells a story so well as you do."

Conway Dalrymple knew that the woman was talking nonsense to him, and yet he liked it, and liked her for talking it. [*That sentence spells out telling words about artists and the effect of their relationships and amatory history on their work – words, that is, not just about Dalrymple but also about Trollope and Millais (ch. 26).*8]

When he turns to Clara to persuade her to pose, we see the power she's gained over his imagination:

"But Mr. Dalrymple can paint his Sisera without making me a Jael," said Miss Van Siever....

"But I never will," said the artist. "I conceived the subject as connected with you, and I will never disjoin the two ideas...."

"I know I never shall do it.... I don't know why Mr. Dalrymple wants it."

"Want it!" said Conway. "I want to paint a striking picture."

"But you can do that without putting me into it."

"No; – not this picture."....

It did not take much persuasion on the part of Conway Dalrymple to get the consent of the younger lady to be painted, or of the elder to allow the sitting to go on in her room.

(ch. 26)

Why such an easy sell for the painter here? Later he asks Clara: "I wonder what it was that first induced you to sit?" "Oh, I don't know. I took a fancy for it" (ch. 38).

The chroniclette shows her modeling Jael because the life she leads lacks inspiration, purpose, and genuine erotic spark. When Conway asks her why she's never had her portrait painted, she answers:

"[M]y mother ... hates pictures."

"Hates pictures!"

"And especially portraits. And I'm afraid, Mr. Dalrymple, she hates artists."

".... If everyone was like your mother, how would the artists live?"

"'There would be none."

"And the world, you think, would be none the poorer?"

"I did not speak for myself. I think the world would be very much the poorer. I am very fond of ancient masters"...

"Perhaps you don't care for modern pictures?"

"Not in comparison, certainly. If that is uncivil, you have brought it on yourself."...

"I find I have come across a real critic."

"I hope so, at any rate, I am not a sham one" and Miss Van Siever as she said this looked very savage.

(ch. 24)

Trollope, it seems, could see how the expression of taboo impulses simmering in female consciousness might appeal to women old and young – conventional or rebellious. Participating in

Jael for a bright girl who likes art could mean taking part in a quest for aesthetic value but also a vicarious project of sublimated gender resentment. The artist wins Clara over by appealing to her radical sympathies – in essence: *you are a singular woman perfect for modeling a righteous, female will*. He valorizes defying her authoritarian, philistine mother by casting Clara as the key figure in a fierce, ambitious portrait. And – decisively – he tells her that for him, London's star young artist, she is indispensable.

The art of love

Here is the first image of Trollope's uniquely erotic *Jael* portraiture-a-trois:

> On the first of March Conway Dalrymple's easel was put up in Mrs. Dobbs Broughton's boudoir upstairs, the canvas was placed upon it on which the outlines of Jael and Sisera had been already drawn, and Mrs. Broughton and Clara Van Siever and Conway Dalrymple were assembled with the view of steady art-work.
>
> *(ch. 38)*

Behind this passive-voice, understated prose, the situation is wild – wild and unpredictable like the whole concept and contingency of artistic endeavor. In this site of romantic intrigue we get a rendering of the genesis of art out of fluid, dynamic erotic concerns – conscious or not.

"The picture was progressing, and so also, as it had come about, was the love-affair between the artist and his model" (ch. 51). That sounds like – and finally *is* – the flow of Trollope's plot, but page by page what he unfolds are the snarly twists and turns of luck and life that make the creation of paintings, marriages, and art history such a wondrous mockery of common sense and free will. The seeming harmony of the twin progress between the *Jael* picture and the Conway-Clara love in fact belies profound conflicts within characters' selves and story.

Intimate with both women, Conway conveys Eros to each, but as he goes on painting Clara, his libido pushes him to marry her – Maria's exact plan. But Maria's supposed "success" turns her into a zany mistress of contradiction; ogling them from her boudoir couch, her mind turns madly – entertainingly – schizoid:

> In one moment she resolved that she would hate Clara as woman was never hated by woman; and there were daggers, and poison-cups and wrangling cords in her eye. In the next she was as firmly determined that she would love Mrs. Conway Dalrymple as woman never was loved by woman; and then she saw herself kneeling by a cradle and tenderly nursing a baby, of which Conway was to be the father and Clara the mother.
>
> *(ch. 51)*

Of course the whole operation *is* her baby. (Such Freudian bouts of poetic frenzy will seem crazy only to those who never lost "the big one that got away" or – my key point – *those who know little of painters' biographies or disparage and ignore how they relate to the processes of art*.) Trollope sums up her conflict in her three words to Conway: "Go. But stay." That makes a neat epithet for a basic, unavoidable contradiction in criticism: *stay focused on the work of art, not on the loose rigmarole of the artist's life – except, of course, when you need it to illuminate the process and meanings of the artwork*.

In Clara – "Miss Van Jael" (ch. 25) – Trollope gets at conflicts that drive modern Jael psychology. Impressed that Conway so wants to paint her, she still can't quite believe he cares about her except as a vocational tool. Even when she accepts him, she's still skeptical about love, though as his model, she finds herself "in truth" in love with him. She argues with Conway, disdains the way he patronized her, and won't flatter him. Trollope, however, never patronizes *her* as he does all the other women in *The Last Chronicle*.⁹ What's important in making his love story convincing is the intelligent, morally serious, and often ironic dialogues from which artist and model learn about one another and themselves. When they talk, they surprise and interest each other.

Right away Dalrymple's patronizing manner sets loose fatal barbs of intelligence from Clara – fatal because she's sharp enough to pierce both the artist's mind and heart. She shows him she knows and cares about his ruling passion and is a would-be devotee to art herself, but she won't put up with the preening of male superiority.

After working so closely and staring at her hour after hour, the tone of his talk changes:

"I do so hope you will like the picture. . . ."

"I don't think I shall. But you will understand that it is natural that a girl should not like herself in such a portraiture as that." [*Trollope puts one theme clearly here: if you're in "Jael," with all that can mean, sometime you'll need to get out.*]

"I don't know why. I can understand that you specially should not like the picture; but I think that most women in London in your place would at any rate say that they did."

"Are you angry with me?"

"What; for telling the truth? No indeed." [*Trollope the master of subtle dialogue: Conway reflects hurt vocational pride, but also his sense that Clara is honest and thoughtful, different from the other women he sees – and she's more solicitous than before. He's sorting out what he really wants most now: it's her.*] . . . It will have been a prosperous picture to me . . . if it leads to the success of which I am ambitious."

"I am told that all you do is successful now, – merely because you do it. That is the worst of success. . . . When won by merit it leads to further success, for the gaining of which no merit is necessary."

Their dialogue is alive with both "felt life" and "thought life," and it leads a hot Dalrymple on to the impetuous climax of their story.

"I will slit the canvas from top to bottom – if you will let me."

"For heaven's sake do nothing of the kind! Why should you?"

"Just to show you that it is not for the sake of the picture that I come here, Clara."

(ch. 51)

Later, on the final day of Clara modeling, with Conway in the midst of proposing to her, Mrs. Van Siever bursts in. She forbids the project, threatens to disinherit her daughter, and tells the painter she'll sue him to keep the picture from being shown:

Dalrymple deliberately opened his penknife and slit the canvas across, through the middle of the picture each way. Clara, as she saw him do it, felt that in truth that she loved him.

(ch. 60)

Love, it may seem, triumphs over art; when Conway stabs the portrait, we see how the marriage plot has been hammered home by a recast Jael nail. By imagining Clara as a Jael avatar, he came to see her, know her, and learn to care for her, but Trollope shows he needed to get rid of that now inapt analogy. How to free Clara (and himself) from the pejorative *Jael* text with which he began: *cut it out*.

But – especially in an era of art-for-art's-sake theory and fierce disputes about aesthetic faith, religious faith, and political faith – vandalizing a major painting opens up tough critical issues. Destroying art is an act of symbolic power and meaning. Does the crux of this happy love story merely promote sentimental bourgeois morality: that is, *"you're worth more to me than any old picture"*; *"real, living people matter more than art"*; *"love loves to love love"*; *"I never saw a picture as pretty as you,"* and so forth?

The point of the chroniclette, however, is not that love always comes first, but that sometimes it must. As the surprising but logical end of the chroniclette will make clear, Dalrymple's romantic, sacrificial act for love doesn't at all mean giving up on his "striking" picture.[10] In Trollope's Conway-and-Clara plot, there's no ultimate need to choose between love and art since neither can flourish without the other.

Clara's disdain for the self-deceiving bromides and platitudes of her world shapes and firms her mind, but Trollope also shows how her critical alienation could become a vacuum sucking the joy from her youth. After she accepts Conway's proposal, Trollope, fully aware of that "lot" of "ill-usage" that must worry any woman, writes for her a last, quietly moving internal discourse:

> Clara Van Siever was left to her reflections. She had never before had a lover. She had never had even a friend whom she loved and trusted. Her life had been passed at school till she was nearly twenty, and since then . . . vainly endeavouring to accommodate herself . . . to her mother. Now she was about to throw herself into the absolute power of a man who was nearly a stranger to her! But she did love him, as she had never loved any one else; – and then, on the other side, there was Mr. Musselboro!
>
> (ch. 65)

The change from living with authority that worships money but despises art to marrying a dedicated painter specifies the gist of Clara's story and its social and historical focus. For her, Trollope shows, embracing art means finding both an internal and an external heart. Glib or schmaltzy as that might sound, her vision in her last two sentences cuts right through any sentimentality to her common vulnerability as a young woman whose married well-being depends on always dicey amorous faith and luck: deciding whom to marry often becomes a test in how to choose the lesser evil. The pacification of the Jael myth is a lasting historical project. In Trollope, the modern Jael has powerful significance and brings a sense of a woman's force, courage, and intelligence, but she, like the painter, must be redeemed by a new testament of love.

A happy ending: the embrace of life, art, and love

In a subplot switch Trollope makes the happy ending of his *Jaelites* not a wedding made from the sacrifice of painting but the harmony of a good marriage and a famous picture hanging for all London to see. When Dalrymple and Clara return from their honeymoon, on the penultimate page of *The Last Chronicle*, we get this: "The picture of Jael and Sisera was stitched up without any difficulty, and I daresay most of my readers will remember it hanging on the walls of the exhibition" (ch. 84).

It hung, that is, at an elite exhibition of the Royal Academy, like so many paintings of John Millais. Mind-boggling Trollopean irony: *Here YOU are, that is, most of you, a large public, have seen this distinguished picture, care about art enough to patronize it, and therefore are literally part of the*

Figure 18.1   A Private View at the Royal Academy, 1881, by William Powell Frith
Private collection c/o Martin Beisly Fine Art

chroniclette world and what a painting can become. Mind-boggling serendipity for a critic: *A Private View at the Royal Academy, 1881,* William Frith's noted painting (Figure 18.1), features a celebrity-packed audience (everyone from Prime Minister Gladstone and Oscar Wilde to stage stars Ellen Terry and Lillie Langtry) at a special exhibition ordered by Queen Victoria for John Millais's portrait of Benjamin Disraeli. The prominent, white-bearded, top-hatted figure standing on the left writing notes is Anthony Trollope. The featured top-hatted man at the far right looking at pictures is John Millais himself.

Millais and chroniclelette background

Without Millais, there would be no "chroniclette." The painter's art, life, and friendship inspired Trollope. Millais and Effie Gray, John Ruskin's wife for five years in a marriage never consummated, fell in love while she modeled for his famed painting *The Order of Release* (1853) – and found her own release: after her annulment, the two wed in 1855. No wonder Trollope would want to write a love story about a popular young artist, an oppressed virgin posing for his picture, and how they sensationally come to marry. The experience and images – visual and psychological both – of Millais, Effie, and her sister Sophie all feed the Dalrymple–Van Siever pages and subplot.

In 1860, Millais began illustrating Trollope's fiction (*Framley Parsonage*), and in the next two decades would complete eighty-seven drawings for six different novels. The work delighted the writer,[11] and the two became fast friends. The novelist, writes John Guile Millais, the painter's son, was "one of the oldest and most intimate friends of his father"; "the friendship ended only with Trollope's death in 1882". Trollope in his *Autobiography* praises Millais and breaks through a code of Victorian understatement:

> I do not think that more conscientious work was ever done by man. . . .
>   To see him has always been a pleasure. His voice has been a sweet sound in my ears. Behind his back I have never heard a word spoken against him without opposing the

censurer [*intimating, no doubt, scandalous gossip was rampant ever after Effie left Ruskin for him, and Trollope devotedly defended him*]. These words . . . will come to him from the grave, and will tell him of my regard – as one living man never tells another.[12]

Says Trollope's friend T.H.S. Escott about their collaboration:

> J. E. Millais['s] . . . tastes, sympathies and exceptional insight into the life and characters depicted by Trollope qualified him beyond any other artist . . . to interpret with his brush the most characteristic creations of the novelist. . . . [T]he personal acquaintance . . . ripened into a lifelong intimacy.[13]

Escott's knowledge of the circles and salons in which Millais and Trollope moved helps us in seeing the background out of which the chroniclette came:

> Thoby Princep kept open house for Trollope, as for many others beneath his roof. . . . At Princep's, also he . . . met habitually the artist Millais. Trollope there made another artistic friendship, with the painter [George Frederick] Watts. . . . As Princep's guest . . . he heard all the gossip.[14]

Much of what Trollope learned about painters, models, and especially leading artist and libertine G. F. Watts fed the chroniclette, but Millais was his main filter and source.[15] He inspired Trollope's quest for meaning in *The Last Chronicle* and its focus on issues of artistic, erotic, and moral value.

These two admired each other's work, and illuminate one another. I want to conjoin a book illustration and two paintings by Millais with the chroniclette. Millais's art opens up the process and motives of Dalrymple portraying Clara Van Siever, and the chroniclette can reveal purpose and meaning in Millais's portraits – including one of his very best, *Portrait of a Girl (Sophie Gray)*.

Imagining the harmony of his aesthetic outlook with this genius artist, a dazzled Trollope said, "Should I live to see my story illustrated by Millais no body would be able to hold me."[16] But his first reaction to Millais's *Framley Parsonage* work was the exact opposite – disgust.[17] He hated the crinoline image of Lucy Robarts in the drawing "Was It Not a Lie?" (see Figure 18.2) and told his publisher they should give up on Millais for the book. "The picture is simply ludicrous . . . a burlesque."[18] *Wrong*: Biographer R. H. Super comments, "Trollope was too quick in making his judgment: . . . it is undoubtedly the most memorable of the illustrations."[19]

In 1856, a steel *cage crinoline* was patented and widely adopted,[20] and it makes a fine objective correlative for how women had to live. The *Framley* drawing with the crinoline-encaged girl illustrates the simultaneous repression and emphasis surrounding the libido of Victorian females, and their inhibited, frustrating quest for freedom through love, sex, and fertility. What makes this such a brilliant illustration is the way it gets at the fascination with women that drove Trollope and how he imagined the complex subject of sexual attraction.

The symbolic crinoline shape and cage limn his broad, evolving view of feminine experience, with its arbitrary, often rigid, but not always unyielding social constraints. He missed here the portrayal of his own analogical power and allegorical imperative: Trollope was the novelist laureate of the crinoline cage, as Millais saw. Not only does the picture show a woman's sad passion about the truth of her love life – that gendered social custom makes her feature it but suppress and lie about it – but also it shows the implicit sexual image of a woman that drives men's art and desire. Men like Dalrymple see that enticing shape and imagine that bed. Those layers upon layers of

Figure 18.2 "Was It Not a Lie?" by John Everett Millais
Wood engraving, engr. Dalziel Brothers
In *Framley Parsonage, CM* no. 6; Vol. 1 p. 691

fashionable material seem both to hide and yet to stress the presence of the body and its nether mysteries – like Clara's Jael costume does for Conway.

Indeed this crinoline cage turned out to be a favorite of readers and critics: it *is* a remarkable picture. The crinoline-exaggerated sexualized body-shape of a love-struck young woman lying face down on a bed alone, her flouncy, prominent rear posed directly before a huge vanity on the wall, can be seen to mirror the general social and psychological implications of Trollope's portraits of ladies. Frank O'Connor called Trollope's fiction the "mirror in the roadway," but Millais, just as perceptively, portrays it here as a "mirror" on the way to a marriage bed.

One quality that made Trollope a great novelist is that he kept on learning. Always curious about other points of view and rarely dogmatic, he was not ashamed to change his mind. Realizing that Millais here had better interpreted his creativity than he himself, he said, "I have had my own ideas impressed on my memory by the excellence of his delineations."[21] He could see that "the crinoline cage" was the metaphorical subject of Lucy Robarts and his book – indeed a huge subject of his fiction generally – and that Millais got its parable power down pat.

Millais had special reasons, conscious and unconscious, for having portrayed the crinoline cage. For Effie, Millais, and Effie's sister Sophie, crinoline was, *a la* Proust, the *petite madeleine* that summoned up the memory of the escape from Ruskin. Suzanne Cooper, in *The Model Wife*, describes Effie Ruskin's last conjugal moments as her husband unknowingly took her to the train on which she would leave him for good: "Taking a seat beside her sister Sophy, she avoided his eye, preoccupied with arranging the cage of her crinoline."[22] Trollope's request for a drawing of his heroine titled "Was It Not a Lie?" triggered Millais's own creativity and a drawing of the symbolic erotics of the crinoline cage in his own life.

The Order of Release

The title *The Order of Release*, words crucial to Millais and Trollope too, sums up both the autobiographical imperative for the painter *and* the Dalrymple–Van Siever plot of *The Last Chronicle*. Parallels abound, as Trollope knew. Both works feature confined figures finding release into the order of honest, moral love. Effie, modeling as a true wife of a husband who can actually father a child, falls in love with her portrayer, and Clara falls in love too with her painter, who might free her from a life without amour.

In Trollope the *The Order of Release* – meaning sequence of events – matters: the decision to paint a radical, meaningful picture; getting Clara to pose; next the procedures and form of art generating their intimacy; then the painter-in-love's act of sacrifice to show the model she's become more important than his picture; their mutual embrace of marriage no matter how risky; and finally the one-sentence epilogue fusing art back into their union and into readers' lives.

Trollope did not intend the chroniclette to depict the romantic life of Everett and Effie Millais except in the most general way, but it does treat matters that touched them deeply. Though Millais was painting a famous picture, what made it such a dominant experience for him was not that he created a work sending his reputation moon-high, but that Effie posed as his "model wife" with "the strange half-smile" and the face he came to love.[23] As Clara became more important to Conway than *Jael*, Effie was more important to Millais then than this masterwork. One thing that makes *The Order* so fascinating is that it reveals his imperative to see and use Effie's Ruskin experience in imagining a true wife as a force of freedom. *The Model Wife* puts it eloquently: "It was a bold picture, full of emotional tensions. . . . There was no prettiness, but instead a study of strength, determination, suffering. Everett had seen through her." And the model Effie Ruskin – not Scottish history – was the muse and mother of Millais's vision.

Figure 18.3 The Order of Release, by John Everett Millais
Tate Britain

Trollope's chroniclette insists that we need to see the subjectivities in the making and viewing of art to understand it, and that it can be key to know or imagine the relationship of those who create art with those portrayed. When Conway is painting Clara after he decides he wants her, we read a passage that opens up the work of Millais and hundreds of other artists (e.g., Goya and Picasso):

> There was something perplexing in the necessity which bound him to look upon the young lady before him as both Jael and as the future Mrs. Conway Dalrymple, knowing as he did that she was at present simply Clara Van Siever. A double personification was not difficult to him. He had encountered it with every model that had sat to him and with every young lady he had attempted to win. . . . But the triple character, joined to the necessity of double work, was distressing to him.
>
> *(ch. 60)*

Trollope is saying – rendering – that for many artists every person is both a real human being and a symbolic figure in their process of creation, and what's more a life potentially bound to them in a real future. And the interplay of that tripleness in their psychological and sociological selves determines not only what they choose to do and create but also what it may come to mean over time. Just as a person they use in making art does not remain static, neither does aesthetic perception of the subject, the relationship, and the meaning of the artwork. The "triple character" here includes the composite mind-flow of history that can and will form an artist's and artwork's future identity in unknowable ways. For Dalrymple, as Trollope imagines, it's hard enough to find a good subject, model, and place to work and then try to paint a picture of brilliance, without having to worry about whether your startling image of a beautiful, sexy, patriotic murderess could – 'til death do you part – make you a "good wife," a good mother (for imaginary, nonexistent children) – much less figure what later aesthetic perception will say you've done to be remembered and honored.

Modeling

The relationship of artists and models has the potential, life-changing charge of other special vocational fields in modern times where, for good or ill, complex, close relationships develop, flourish, and seize people's interest – for example, confessor and layperson, doctor and patient, psychiatrist and analysand, professor and student, boss and intern, director and movie star. Both Clara and Maria in *The Last Chronicle* embody the importance of women as models, and with Trollope's rendering of this hot topic and what it suggests about Millais's focus in *The Order of Release* and *Portrait of a Girl*, we see a new world coming – the art and era of sexual discourse.

The painter's history with Effie and his relationship with other Pre-Raphaelites and followers who fell for their models got Trollope very interested in this area of energy and moral ambiguity. Suzanne Cooper puts the subject in a spicy perspective that in the coming centuries would bring forth scandal sheets, gossip columns, and the soft porn by supermarket checkout lines:

> Victorian attitudes to models and modeling were complex. . . . What exactly went on in the intimacy of an artist's studio? It was mysterious space, where [*talented*] young men had unchaperoned access to beautiful women. Beyond the narrow world of artists and critics professional modeling was sometimes seen as little better than prostitution.[24]

Examples from the Victorian hotbed of artist-model relationships: Dante Rossetti married model and mistress Elizabeth Siddal, but he did not marry model and mistress-housekeeper Fanny Cornforth nor model and mistress Jane Burden, who did, though, marry William Morris; James Whistler's model, lover, and agent Joanna Hiffernan left him to model and become the lover of Gustave Courbet, and Whistler lived for five years with another model and mistress, Maud Franklin; G. F. Watts was intimate with many models who posed for him (including Sara Princep and sister Sophie Dalrymple), and he seduced his sixteen-year-old model Ellen Terry (she became the famous actress), whom he married briefly, though she was his junior by thirty years; Edward Burne-Jones's model Maria Zambaco tried to commit suicide by drowning herself in the Regent's Canal; even the sometimes puritanical Holman Hunt tried hard, but with no luck, to marry the model he loved. Millais, who became a model citizen of the Victorian establishment, married the wife of his patron and mentor who had asked him to use Effie as a model. And then, blessedly for portrait painting and British art, he turned his attention and puzzled libido to an extraordinary teenage model, his sister-in-law Sophie Gray.

Portrait of a Girl (Sophie Gray)

The Millais painting closest to Dalrymple's vision of Clara – very close – is not of Effie but of her fast-maturing, young teenage sister Sophie, a confidante of the lovers during their covert romance, *Portrait of a Girl* (Figure 18.4). After the marriage in 1855, Sophie modeled for him as a pubescent girl in 1856 and a post-pubescent young woman in the 1857 painting *Portrait of a Girl*. Given their relationship and age difference the portrait is startling – not a hint of the *miss-nice-girl* naïveté and passively asexual feminine norms her culture promoted – no budding *angel-in-the-houseism* here. Neither warm nor sentimental, this confrontational, erotically alive figure – anything but a child – projects an extraordinary intensity of presence and engagement. The family didn't keep or own this unique, sex-laden painting,[25] and it was not publicly displayed until after Millais's death.

Why would a portrait of Millais's sexually ripening sister-in-law, who for the rest of her sad, brief life would be hopelessly in love with him in the all-consuming, secret ways of nineteenth-century Freudian history, matter to Trollope? He had no intention of telling any tale about a presumed liaison between the artist and Sister Sophie. But the portrait features what Trollope especially wanted to – and did – convey in the chroniclette: the intense, passionate, mutable connection of artist, subject, and viewer. He makes beautifully clear that the particular face that an artist sees and then paints can matter profoundly – can, like Sophie's, radiate desire and show how infinitely influential the expression of a face can be.

I'm arguing that passages in the chroniclette make clear that Trollope knew the picture, that it hit him hard, and that he used it for all its worth – namely, to imagine what the making of an audacious portrait might mean and how it can become a living part of aesthetic, gender, and cultural history.

Pre-Raphaelite patron, artist, and collector George Boyce bought the picture and eventually hung *Sophie* next to a pendant he commissioned, the scandalous *Bocca Baciata* by Dante Rossetti, whose model was his then mistress Fanny (the title refers to the kissed mouth of a girl passed from one man to another in Boccacio).[26] The Princep bohemian crowd and the aesthetic friends who met at Little Holland House saw and knew this astonishing portrait of Sophie. Millais and Trollope in the closeness of their friendship and work often talked intimately in the early and mid-1860s when the novelist learned of the portrait. Trollope's letters don't mention paying Boyce a visit to see it, but, given its sexualized context and setting, they wouldn't – especially since Millais did not make it public.[27]

Figure 18.4 Portrait of a Girl, by John Everett Millais
Bridgeman Art Library and Peter Nahum at Leicester Galleries

Said Trollope, "How does a man learn to love a great picture? By standing in front of it till he does love it, or till he drops."[28] That's likely what he did with *Sophie Gray*. The impact of the *Portrait of Sophie* is not just the sense of a looking at a remarkable face, but of seeing an image so emotionally vital that it can color and infiltrate how we see and regard other faces.

Meditating on Millais's art, Trollope found a way of imagining, seeing, and narrating Dalrymple's developing desire and Clara's special character. He was out to create an episode where the subject and model of a picture fuse and come alive for artist and audience as Sophie does here. Looking at the portrait, he would have seen – as we do now – the girl as a *colorful character*. (I choose the words *colorful* and *character* here to stress precisely for both art history and literary history the significant interplay of the Sophie portrait and the chroniclette.) *Character* expresses the subjective narrative identity viewers inevitably find in painted figures, and *colorful* connotes the intertwining of visuality and language – the inseparable flow of perception between the arts.

Scholars now consider *Portrait of a Girl* one of Millais's finest works:

Allison Smith

In its resolute likeness, careful drawing and paint application and subtle tones, this intimate picture is one of the finest realist portraits of the nineteenth century. It also conveys a deep sense of connection between artist and subject.[29]

Jason Rosenfeld

The portrait of Sophie Gray of 1857 is alluring, haunting and far less affectedly [meaning here *insincerely*, *artificially*] sexual than anything Dante Gabriel Rossetti or Hunt would subsequently paint. . . . Only . . . George Frederic Watts approached *Sophie Gray* for the imagining of modern desire.[30]

Suzanne Fagence Cooper

It is extraordinary in its sensuality. . . . This is Sophy as Everett saw her. Her eyes are mesmerizing . . . she has a new knowing look. She is self-possessed, aware of her own loveliness and the power it brings. Her appearance is disturbingly direct and modern.[31]

Picturesque

I want to go back to the text and compare it directly to the painting. The description of Dalrymple's first sight of Clara brings home how such a picture as Millais's *Portrait of a Girl* can come into being and the explosion of passionate subjectivity and fate-driving voyeurism that a single visage – in person or picture – can set off:

> [*She*] was certainly a handsome young woman. . . . Her features were regular, and her full, clear eyes had a brilliance of their own, looking at you always steadfastly and boldly, though very seldom pleasantly. Her mouth would have been beautiful had it not been too strong for feminine beauty. . . . Her nose and chin were finely chiselled, and her head stood well upon her shoulders. But there was something hard about it all which repelled you. Dalrymple, when he saw her, recoiled from her, not outwardly, but inwardly. . . . [T]here was about her nothing of feminine softness. . . . He certainly could make a picture of her. . . . Yes, – he thought she would do as Jael.
>
> *(ch. 24)*

What Conway sees here is exactly what we can see in the portrait of Sophie: a cold, serious, not-very-friendly-looking young woman; fine features; intensity of expression – those challenging wide eyes staring us down; a beautiful, hard, unsmiling mouth; the gorgeous, stylized white neck – somehow weirdly but definitely phallic – on which "her head stood well upon her shoulders" (odd, vague descriptive remark – unless we see how it comes straight out of the portrait, which relies on the eroticism of blatant bare flesh and the aggressive stare inherent in modeling); the lack of conventional "feminine softness"; and a dramatic personal and aesthetic charisma. For the chroniclette Trollope wanted art, not love, at first sight, and *Sophie Gray* could show him erotic first sight need not be sentimental, conscious, or predictable.

But soon Trollope, celebrating the power in life of "the artist's eye," gives us more when Conway, a few days later, again focuses on the colorful figure he's about to paint:

> There was something in her countenance which seemed to declare that she could bear any light to which it might be subjected, without flinching. . . . She . . . could dare to be seen at all times. Dalrymple, with an artist's eye, saw this at once, and immediately confessed to himself that there was something great about her. He could not deny her beauty. But there was ever present to him that look of hardness which had struck him when he first saw her. . . . But not the less was she beautiful, and – beyond that and better than that, for his purpose – she was *picturesque* [emphasis mine].
>
> (ch. 26)

"For his purpose": Trollope, learning from Millais's painting, wants to show that an artist's purpose can develop and change and that, therefore, the perceived purposes of a painting (or a novel) can and will change too. "Handsome" before, she is "beautiful" here; at first "repellent," Clara in Conway's vision is now becoming "great."

Millais found something captivating about his precocious sister-in-law – something great that he had to paint. She was no longer a girl but a disturbing magnetic young woman and for a time a libidinous force in his own life. Trollope shows Dalrymple finding the same thing in Clara. The female self-possession and tough independence, which the painter first saw as a negative, become both intellectual and physical qualities that soften him and get his heart thumping.

Picturesque is the key word. It means that this character offers just what the painter's calling – his aesthetic faith – demands. She fits all the dictionary definitions of the word, *striking in an unusual way, suitable for a picture, expressive and vivid in the emotions she arouses*. But this *picturesque* evolves, and the novelist gives the word new depth. For him objective entities – a *model* and a *portrait* – become living, subjective beings. The *picturesque* is kinetic in time, and the picture – the work of art – changes in the changing world of Anthony Trollope.

Millais's *picturesque* moves beyond his own use of preexisting stories or typical character types (e.g., *figure of the past acting out history; lovely, innocent maiden; joyous youth; loyal, self-sacrificing sister; ironic victim of destined tragedy she can't see coming; etc.*). He creates an individualized, unique portrait, and can be seen doing just what Trollope imagines that Dalrymple, using Clara to revise his pre-chroniclette style,[32] wants his *Jael* painting to do – move beyond conceptual nostalgia from and for the past into a new vision that shows us the fascination and complexity of what is erotically present and to come in the artist's and his subject's desire – and what subsequent viewers will think about it. For Trollope the figure would be a picturesque emblem of the aesthetic insight and wonder that Millais's art brings to the world.

In the eyes of *Sophie*, in the mysterious gaze of intimacy with the beholder (the artist, Trollope, museum-goers, readers – *you and me*), in the marvelous tinge of both gloom and voluptuousness, we can read the unpredictability and fluidity of sexual attraction and the sheer affective power of female beauty. Gazing back, we can find strength, sexuality, and seriousness free from the rigidity of prescribed female narratives. Millais – and Trollope too – render the possibilities of fresh allegorical imperatives demanding our subjective interpretations.

Picturesque also appears here in a literal sense that shouldn't be taken for granted: Trollope has centered the chroniclette on a picture, *Jael*, that shapes the plot and characterizes its figures – a bold, innovative thing to do. Like Proust's *Remembrance of Things Past* with Botticelli forming and defining Swann's Odette, like Donna Tartt's *The Goldfinch*, like Tracy Chevalier's *The Girl with the Pearl Earring*, it makes a painting the radiating center of the fictional world.

Interplay

So Trollope helps me appreciate Millais, and Millais helps me appreciate Trollope. Nothing is better than good art and artists to make us see the quality and power of other fine artists. When I read the chroniclette and then turn back to *Sophie Gray*, Trollope shows me how to see more in it – namely, the projective force of the artist's characterization and the range of desire it suggests. And, vice versa, Sophie's eyes, mouth, and bare white neck get me to focus more clearly on the sensual immediacy and complex erotic nature implicit in the Conway-Clara portrayal scenes. I repeat – because it is the basis of a subjective but important critical methodology – Trollope's words and story help articulate visual expression and Millais's painted face clarifies and sharpens our sense of how fiction's language works.

I want to end by applying and adapting to Millais and the *Portrait* the words, tenor, and spirit of the Conway-Clara dialogue (ch. 26) I cited before when he insists that she absolutely must pose for his *Jael*. The passage shines direct light on how the personal relationship operating in any work of art can make and define it and, in particular here, how psychological motives and erotic drive could and would produce the most original, intellectually suggestive, and complex portrait of John Everett Millais's career:

> "But Everett can paint his *Portrait of a Girl* without making it me" said Sophie.
> "But I never will," said the artist. "I conceived the subject as connected with you, and I will never disjoin the two ideas."
> "I don't know why you want it?"
> "Want it!" said Everett. "I want to paint a striking picture."
> "But you can do that without putting me into it."
> "No; – not this picture."

Juxtaposing them, we see Millais and Trollope have together ripped up an old static sense of the picturesque and found a new – and daring – way to stitch it up and display it. They convey a profound sense of the personal connection between artist and subject and why it matters. And together they show us our own subjective connection to the ongoing, flowing stream of consciousness of both painting and literature – most assuredly our "love of the arts."

Notes

1 Anthony Trollope, *The Last Chronicle of Barset* (London: Penguin Classics, 2002), ch. 51, 531. For convenience I'm using this widely available edition and also providing the chapter nos. for all citations.
2 So says art historian and Tate Pre-Raphaelite curator Jason Rosenfeld, *John Everett Millais* (London: Phaidon Press, 2012).
3 See David Skilton's excellent article, "The Centrality of Literary Illustration in Victorian Visual Culture: The Example of Millais and Trollope from 1860–1864," *Journal of Illustration Studies*, December 2007,

4 N. John Hall (*Trollope and His Illustrators* [London: Macmillan, 1980]), in his fine, useful book on the illustrations in Trollope's novels, nonetheless, calls these scenes "those extraneous episodes that many readers and critics believe to have damaged Trollope's masterpiece" (121). Commentators from Frank O'Connor onwards have admired *The Last Chronicle*, but few examine the Dalrymple/Van Siever plot in any detail. Mario Praz in *The Hero in Eclipse in Victorian Fiction* is clearly struck by the subplot's narrative, since he regularly refers to it, though never analyses it, when discussing other works (313 onwards). Jerome Thale's nuanced essay on the structure of *The Last Chronicle* has no exploration of this subplot, and Geoffrey Harvey, who reads Thale's "gradual accumulations of situations and events in spatial patterns as analogous to painting or music" (82), dismisses Dalrymple's painting as "the perversion of art and history, for Dalrymple is simply pandering to the commercial man's desire to make himself heroically immortal" (94). And while Bill Overton in *The Unofficial Trollope* gives us a gratifyingly modern narratological analysis of voice in his chapter on *The Last Chronicle*, there is no exploration of any of the action at Hook's Court. R.H. Super's plot summary in *The Chronicler of Barsetshire* (Ann Arbor: University of Michigan Press, 1988) omits the subplot entirely, and Ruth apRoberts, in *The Oxford Reader's Companion*, gives Dalrymple and Clara eight words. See James Kincaid in *The Novels of Anthony Trollope* (137–9) for a contrary, though short, persuasive view finding the irony and the role of art in the subplot significant and revealing.

5 Jael in the Bible is a female assassin who killed Sisera in cold blood when he took refuge in her tent (Judges 4:17–21).

6 For convenience, I use the term "chroniclette" for this virtually self-contained *Last Chronicle* subplot.

7 Trollope writes of Mrs. DB:

> As it was she had nothing to do. She had no child. She was not given to much reading. She could not sit with a needle in her hand all day. She had no aptitude for . . . meetings, or the excitement of charitable good works. Life with her was very dull, and she found no amusement within her reach so easy and so pleasant as the amusement of pretending to be in love [*with her painter*] (ch. 38).

8 Mrs. Dobbs Broughton's chatter would seem to derive from John Millais's experience as reported by him and his wife Effie, also Trollope's friend:

> [Everett] was a frequent visitor to Little Holland House [Thoby and Sara Princep's establishment, the prime salon for the mid-Victorian art-world was leased for them by their fellow resident painter George Frederick Watts, who was intimately patronized by Sara – as Trollope's Dalrymple is patronized by Mrs Dobbs Broughton.]. . . . Effie was less comfortable in such surroundings, and wrote sharply to a friend:
>
> . . . . Poets & Artists have their own place in the world like other people but Tennyson-&-Watts-worship is very disgusting, and Everett gets it also. but dislikes it as I do. It is all such nonsense. (Rosenfeld, 132)
>
> Maybe, like Dalrymple, he didn't mind it at all. See Rosenfeld.

9 To see why the Victorian women needed some form of "Miss Van Jael" spirit, compare with Clara and Conway's interchanges this passage featuring the dialogue of the primary lovers in *The Last Chronicle*'s main "happy" marriage plot: abject Grace Crawley and rich Henry Grantley (here a self-praising laureate of benevolent sexism):

> "I do not know why you should be so good to me," she said.
> "Because I love you," he said, "better than all the world."
> "But why should you be so good to me as that? Why should you love me? I am such a poor thing for a man like you to love."
> "I have the wit to see you are not a poor thing, Grace; and it is thus that I have earned my treasure. Some girls are poor things and some are rich treasures." (ch. 82)

10 Just as the Pre-Raphaelite Dante Gabriel Rossetti's act of burying, out of guilt and homage, the manuscript of his poetry in with the corpse of his much abused mistress, model, and wife, Lizzie Siddal, did not in the end mean the sacrifice of his literary art – which he retrieved by digging up and opening the coffin of his love.

11 Except for "Was It Not a Lie?" in *Framley Parsonage* (ch. 55) – see ahead.

12 Anthony Trollope, *An Autobiography*, edited by David Skilton (Harmondsworth, England: Penguin Books, 1996), 98–9.

13 T.H.S. Escott, *Anthony Trollope: His Work, Associates and Literary Originals* (London: John Lane, The Bodley Head, 1913), chapters 8 and 11. Microfilm: https://archive.org/stream/cihm_66434#page/n9/mode/2up.
14 Escott, 140. Womanizing painter George Frederick Watts lived in Little Holland House under the Mrs. Dobbs Broughton–like patronage of Sara Prinsep, along with her much older husband, Thoby. Watt was intimate with Sara, fell in love with her sister Virginia (who turned him down), was close to another, the distinguished photographer Julia Cameron, and was involved with still another sister, Sophia Dalrymple, whom he painted together with Sara and whose name Trollope would appropriate.
15 Says N. John Hall in *Trollope, A Biography* (Oxford: Clarendon Press, 1991) in words that indicate the main information for the art chapters in *The Last Chronicle*: "One wonders how much of this sprang from talk with Millais" (215).
16 Hall, *Trollope: A Biography*, 203.
17 Hall, *Trollope and His Illustrators*, 14–15.
18 See Super, 115, for an informative discussion of the incident and why Trollope would change his mind.
19 Super, 115.
20 See crinoline: http://en.wikipedia.org/wiki/Crinoline.
21 Millais, *Life and Letters*, vol. 1, 282.
22 Suzanne Fagence Cooper, *The Model Wife: The Passionate Lives of Effie Gray, Ruskin and Millais* (London: Duckworth Overlook, 2010), 1.
23 Cooper, 88.
24 Cooper, 90.
25 For a balanced, speculative, informative account of Sophie Gray Caird and of the relationship of Sophie and John Everett, see Cooper, *Model Wife*, 206–27 (esp. 212–15). See also Mary Lutyens, *Millais and the Ruskins*, London: John Murray, 1967, Vanguard Press in USA.
26 See Cooper, 212–13.
27 Trollope was eager to get Millais to illustrate *The Last Chronicle*, and Millais, who had given up such work, indicated he was willing, but that he was then booked up solidly for months and years. (He no longer had the time or need to do illustration work.) But when the Dalrymple chroniclette appeared (very badly illustrated), Millais did quickly agree to do the pictures for *Phineas Finn*, his friend's next big novel. See Hall, *Trollope and His Illustrators*, 114–15.
28 "The National Gallery", *St James's Magazine*, 2 (Sept. 1861), 163. See Hall, *Trollope and His Illustrators*.
29 *Millais Exhibition Catalogue*, 134 (Tate Gallery, Sept. 2007–Jan. 2008), curated by Jason Rosenfeld and Alison Smith. London: Tate, 2007.
30 Rosenfeld, 94–6.
31 Cooper, 213.
32 "There was . . . ever some story told in Dalrymple's pictures over and above the story of the portraiture" (ch. 24).

Works cited

apRoberts, Ruth. *Trollope: Artist and Moralist*. London: Chatto and Windus, 1971.
Cooper, Suzanne Fagence. *The Model Wife: The Passionate Lives of Effie Gray, Ruskin and Millais*. London: Duckworth Overlook, 2010.
Escott, T.H.S. *Anthony Trollope: His Work, Associates and Literary Originals*. London: John Lane, The Bodley Head, 1913.
Hall, N. John. *Trollope: A Biography*. Oxford: Clarendon Press, 1991.
———. *Trollope and His Illustrators*. London: Macmillan, 1980.
Harvey, Geoffrey. *The Art of Anthony Trollope*. London: Weidenfeld and Nicolson, 1980.
Kincaid, James. *The Novels of Anthony Trollope*. Oxford: Clarendon Press, 1977.
Lutyens, Mary. *Millais and the Ruskins*. London: John Murray, 1967.
Millais, John Guile. *The Life and Letters of John Millais*. London: Methuen, 1899.
Overton, Bill. *The Unofficial Trollope*. Brighton: Harvester Press, 1983.
Praz, Mario. *The Hero in Eclipse in Victorian Fiction*. Trans. Angus Davidson. London: Oxford University Press, 1956.
Rosenfeld, Jason. *John Everett Millais*. London: Phaidon Press, 2012.
Rosenfeld, Jason, and Allison Smith. *Millais*. London: Tate, 2007.
Skilton, David. "The Centrality of Literary Illustration in Victorian Visual Culture: The Example of Millais and Trollope from 1860–1864," *Journal of Illustration Studies*, 1 (December 2007).

Super, R. H. *The Chronicler of Barsetshire*. Ann Arbor: University of Michigan Press, 1988.
Thale, Jeremy. "The Problem of Structure in Trollope," Nineteenth Century Fiction, 15:2 (1960), 147–57.
Trollope, Anthony. *An Autobiography*. Ed. David Skilton. London: Penguin Books, 1996.
———. *The Last Chronicle of Barset*. London: Penguin Classics, 2002.
———. "The National Gallery," *Saint James's Magazine*, 2 (September 1861), 163–76.

PART V
Trollopian preoccupations

19

"FIERY SHORTHAND"

Trollope's Irish novel

Robert Tracy

> For now that it was gone, it all seemed
> Far stranger: more fantastical than Pharaoh.
> – Seamus Heaney, "After the Fire", a translation of Rilke's "Brandstätte"

Anthony Trollope arrived at Banagher, County Offaly, in September 1841, as surveyor's clerk for a postal district including Connaught, Ireland's western province. He was "to travel about the country," inspecting the Irish postal system (*Autobiography* ch. 3). He "entered on his Irish employment with a firm persuasion . . . to commence novelist as soon as he had . . . enough material for his first chapter." Popular novels by Charles Lever and Samuel Lover had recently appeared, featuring comic Irish characters: Lever's *Confessions of Harry Lorrequer* (1839) and *Charles O'Malley, the Irish Dragoon* (1841), Lover's *Rory O'More* (1837). Lever emphasized Connaught's lawlessness and how Irishmen spoke English; "Why . . . should not Anthony himself find some class of the community" to write about? Why not "the daily doings of the people among whom for the present his lot was cast?" (Escott 53). His mother had written *Domestic Manners of the Americans* (1832); he would examine the domestic manners of the Irish, governed from Britain but very foreign – John Bull's "*Other*" island. In the years immediately preceding "*Gorta mor*," the "Great Hunger," the Potato Famine of 1845–49, Trollope recognized a simmering resentment underlying the picturesque speech and behavior in a poor and dangerously overcrowded country with economic and political systems that no longer worked.

Connaught, with few "Big Houses" of Ascendancy (Anglo-Irish Protestant) landowners and a large population of their Irish-speaking and poverty-stricken Catholic tenants, was considered Ireland's Wild West, violent and openly rebellious in 1798, when French soldiers landed and proclaimed the Connaught Republic; thousands of peasants joined them against British troops. During the Famine poverty and the primitive state of roads would make Connaught particularly vulnerable; over 400,000 people were lost to hunger, typhus, or emigration.

"I had learned to think that Ireland was a land flowing with fun and whisky," Trollope later recalled, where "irregularity was the rule of life, and . . . broken heads were looked upon as honourable badges" (*Autobiography* 62). In 1916 Lord Dunraven nostalgically remembered Connaught's "hard riding, hard drinking, dueling, lavishly hospitable landed gentry, ruling over contented tenants . . . dependents and hangers-on, in a country where the King's writ did not run

... The clan system still existed" (Dunraven vii). In "The Man for Galway," Lever had defined a proper Connaught gentleman:

> To drink a toast,
> A proctor roast,
>   Or bailiff, as the case is;
> To kiss your wife,
> Or take your life
>   At ten or fifteen paces;
> To keep game cocks, to hunt the fox,
> To drink in punch the Solway,
> With debts galore, but fun far more;
> Oh, that's "the man for Galway".
>   (Lever, *Charles O'Malley* 1:6:29)

William Gregory of Coole Park, County Galway, Trollope's Harrow contemporary, made him welcome, and Coole Park became his

> second home ... and a most instructive school for the study of Irish life and character ... in the heart of a district literally overflowing with the local colour, incidents, and personages ... [of] his earliest novel ... the old picturesque, lawless *régime* ... had not been effaced by the modern Anglicising dispensation. In his little park, full of retainers who would have risen as one man to repel any invasion of his ancestral roof, William Gregory lived a patriarchal life ... proper to a stock rooted in the soil from mythical times.
>
> *(Escott 49–50)*

Trollope expected Escott would be his biographer, and shaped his narrative. Coole Park was already an "encumbered [mortgaged] estate," but Gregory would not let "the gaieties" he hosted be "interfered with by irregularly paid rents" (Escott 49–50). Writing in 1884, Gregory recalled an 1836 Galway ball: "three glorious days ... the fun ... fast and furious, and the drinking steady ... riotous license ... the dying out flicker of old Irish revelry" (Gregory 40–43).

Trollope's first novel, *The Macdermots of Ballycloran* (1847) depicts Ireland as he saw it in the early forties: "a good novel," he declares in *An Autobiography*, "worth reading by anyone who wishes to understand what Irish life was before the potato disease, the famine, and the Encumbered Estates Bill" (*Autobiography* 71). Completed in 1845, *The Macdermots* shows how well and how rapidly Trollope had come to know Ireland. There are comic scenes, but the doomed Macdermots are prisoners of Ireland's past and present. Trollope already understood why Irish stories often ended in "political despair and Celtic fatalism ... evil triumphant ... good crushed" (Yeats, *Stories from Carleton* xvii). A deep sadness underlay the lively banter, the picturesque squalor, the sudden shocking violence of Irish life. Trollope was sure that he never made another plot "so good – or, at any rate, one so susceptible of pathos" (*Autobiography* 70): a story of extravagance, waste, secret societies, brutality, seduction, murder, and betrayal.

The earliest Irish novelists, Yeats suggested, "tried to make one see life plainly, but all written down in a kind of fiery shorthand that it might never be forgotten" (*Letters* 143). In *Castle Rackrent, an Hibernian Tale* (1800), Maria Edgeworth initiated the Irish novel as national, in content, intention, and attitudes unlike the novels of what Bishop Berkeley called "a neighboring island." Lady Morgan, Gerald Griffin, and William Carleton soon followed, for Yeats precursors of the literary revival he was already planning. "If you would know Ireland – body and soul – you must read its poems and stories," Yeats insisted in 1891, introducing stories by Edgeworth, Griffin, and Carleton; "They came into existence to please nobody but the people of Ireland . . . They are Ireland talking to herself" (*Representative Irish Tales* 1:3). Trollope studied these Irish predecessors to learn how to portray this strange country. What situations, character types, and themes distinguished Irish fictions? With *The Macdermots* he became the last of those whose "fiery shorthand" transcribed the violent, improvident, melodramatic pre-Famine Ireland he had come to know. He finished *The Macdermots* in July 1845. On 9 September the *Dublin Evening Post* reported the first signs of potato blight. Six days later, Trollope signed the contract to publish his novel – itself to become a victim of the Famine. When it appeared in 1847, readers were tired of Irish misery. Like Trollope's other Irish novels, *The Macdermots* found few readers, then or since.

Trollope read *Castle Rackrent* before coming to Ireland. In Gregory's library at Coole he discovered other stories "racy of the soil" (did Trollope read *The Nation*?): Lady Morgan's "vivacious pages," Gerald Griffin's *The Collegians*, William Carleton's *Traits and Stories of the Irish Peasantry*, and of course Lover and Lever. Trollope drew on them all in *The Macdermots*, but he criticized Lover's and Lever's "traditional misrepresentation" of Irish characters: ignorant, quarrelsome, speaking comic English (Escott 52–4). As Carleton pointed out, the Irishman's tendency to "impress the idiom of his own language upon" English is why "bulls and blunders" are "attributed to him" (*Traits* 1: ii).

A tale of "extravagant" landlords and their "debt, embarrassment, despair, and ruin," *Castle Rackrent* became for Trollope "the usual story . . . of Connaught gentlemen" (*Macdermots* 3), his basic model for *The Macdermots*. Edgeworth had invented an Irish genre, the "Big House" novel, about a landowning family, their estate, servants, tenants, possessions, and the house itself with its traditions. Elizabeth Bowen, like Edgeworth the daughter of a Big House, defines the genre: "hermetic solitude . . . the autocracy of the great country house, the demonic power of the family myth, fatalism, feudalism, and the 'ascendency' outlook" (Bowen 101). Like Castle Rackrent, Trollope's Ballycloran (*Baile Cloichrean*, stony townland) is an impoverished Big House and estate. Edgeworth adopted the *persona* of Thady Quirk, the Rackrent steward and butler, to describe how four successive heirs mismanage the estate, until Sir Condy loses it. Thady praises their follies as aristocratic open-handedness, like William Gregory's lavish entertainments despite his unpaid rents.

"Having out of friendship for the family . . . undertaken to publish the Memoirs of the Rackrent Family," he begins, "I think it my duty to say a few words . . . concerning myself." Though he is "poor Thady," his son Jason is "attorney Quirk . . . a high gentleman" with "better than 1500 a-year" and a "landed estate" (Edgeworth 7–8). When Sir Condy dies penniless, Jason takes possession of Castle Rackrent. Thady eavesdrops on the Rackrents, encourages their weaknesses, and guards his perks as steward/butler. He has picked up the language of his employers and Jason's legal terms. Edgeworth anticipated skepticism about his "legal knowledge." "They all love law, " she points out; "It is a kind of lottery . . . every man, staking his own wit or cunning against his richer neighbour's property, feels that he has little to lose and much to gain" (Edgeworth 108–11). Edgeworth knew how servants and tenants watched the gentry, ready to profit at any sign of improvidence or profligacy. She understood what the Irish call "cute," an acute awareness of one's own interests and of possible advantages in the careless behavior of others.

Castle Rackrent is really about how Thady tells and controls the story, and is its principal character. "I began to write a family history as Thady would tell it," Edgeworth recalled; "he seemed to stand beside me and dictate; and I wrote as fast as my pen could go, the characters all imaginary" (Edgeworth xi). She imagines an oral performance by a traditional storyteller, a *shanachie*, who tells about "old times": local families and their doings, local history, genealogy, gossip, encounters with ghosts or fairies. Writing in English, Edgeworth let her readers hear an Irish voice for the first time, using turns of phrase to suggest Irish usage and speech patterns, and providing a glossary. "Happy the man who could get a sight of the hearse!" Thady exclaims, describing Sir Patrick's funeral; "Out of forty-nine [law] suits which [Sir Murtagh] had, he never lost one but seventeen" (Edgeworth 11, 15).

Edgeworth insisted that "the race of the Rackrents has long been extinct in Ireland" (Edgeworth 4–5). But "in the early forties" Trollope often encountered landlords "Down at heels, out at elbows, with no clothes in his wardrobe, and nothing but an overdraft at his bankers . . . rough, thriftless." He opposed the Encumbered Estates Act of 1849, which bought them out, warning that speculators with no traditional bond to the tenants would replace them, speculators interested only in profits and likely to provoke agitators (Escott 51).

Trollope begins *The Macdermots* with an evening stroll in Drumsna, County Leitrim, on the Shannon's east bank. Passing a ruined Big House, he reads in it the "usual story" he is to write, of extravagance, debt, and ruin (*Macdermots* 3). Edgeworth imagined Thady dictating her story; Trollope attributes his tale to a *shanachie*, authenticating it as Irish and experienced as an oral performance, modestly adding, "reader, if I ever thought it would be your good fortune to hear the history of Ballycloran from the guard of the Boyle coach, I would recommend you to get it from him, and shut my book forthwith" (*Macdermots* 7). Trollope admitted that he "fabricated" his "plot while still among the ruined walls and decayed beams" of an abandoned house near Drumsna (*Autobiography* 70). In *The Wild Irish Girl* (1806), an epistolary novel by Lady Morgan, Trollope found a name for his doomed family and his theme for *The Macdermots*: the uncertain status of old Irish families, proud, poor, Catholic, socially isolated, still retaining a remnant of their former estates, and some hereditary loyalty among the peasantry, but disdained by the Ascendancy.

The Wild Irish Girl made Lady Morgan, then Miss Owenson, famous. Adopting the red cloak and white gown of Glorvina, her heroine, and playing the harp, she gained the patronage of the Duchess of Abercorn, and a titled husband. Lady Morgan defended the Irish against the scornful condescension of the English, Scots, Welsh, and especially the Ascendancy. When Horatio's father banishes him to a family estate in Connaught for "presiding . . . at . . . nocturnal orgies of vitiated dissipation" in London (Morgan 1: vi–vii), Horatio disdains the Irish as "turbulent, faithless, intemperate, and cruel; formerly destitute of arts, letters, or civilization, and still but slowly submitting to their salutary and ennobling influence" (Morgan 1: 36–7). His letters record his changing attitude as he learns about contemporary Ireland and the Irish past. He is amazed at the prosperity and neatness of Dublin, touched by the intelligence and kindness of peasants he meets. After he meets Glorvina, daughter of The Macdermot, Prince of Inismore, she lectures him on Ireland's history, antiquities, traditional literature, scenic beauty, and general excellence. *Castle Rackrent* showed little interest in Irish history or traditions, but Lady Morgan, with unabashed pride, made Glorvina an idealized self-portrait and a celebrator of the Irish past.

Glorvina's "forefathers" were "true Milesians bred and born . . . not a drop of *Strongbonean* [English blood] flowed in their Irish veins agrah! . . . the family flourished . . . until . . . the poor old Prince was put to death . . . by one of Cromwell's English Generals." Horatio realizes that the Cromwellian general was his ancestor. His father's estate once belonged to the Macdermots. The present Macdermot prince, "descended from the Kings of Connaught," is as aristocratically impractical as the Rackrents. He "would never let it come near him, that things were not going on well . . . it did not become him to look after such matters"(Morgan 1: 113–15). Sir Condy lost Castle Rackrent to his lawyer; the prince mortgaged the mansion he could not afford, and such land as was left, and was dispossessed by the "spalpeen steward" employed by Horatio's father.

Now he lives in half-ruined Inismore castle, "keeps up the old Irish customs and dress, letting nobody eat at the same table but his daughter, not even his Lady, when she was alive." The peasantry love Glorvina,

> a great *physicianer* . . . curing all the sick and maimed . . . so proud that divil a one soul of the quality will she visit . . . though she will sit in a smoky cabin for hours . . . to talk to the poor . . . will sit for hours at her Latin and Greek, after the family are gone to bed, and yet you will see her up with the dawn, running like a doe among the rocks; her fine yellow hair streaming in the wind, for all the world like a mermaid.
> *(Morgan 1: 125–26)*

Horatio attends mass in the castle chapel, suspecting she will be "*Red headed*, a pedant, and a romp", but hoping her "amiable and intelligent; as she must be simple and unvitiated" (Morgan 1: 129).

The Macdermots of Ballycloran, also poor, are proud, old Irish gentry dispossessed by penal laws against Catholics. Like the Prince of Inismore, Larry Macdermot's father "planned, ordered, and agreed for a house, such as he thought the descendant of a Connaught Prince might inhabit without disgrace." Ballycloran House, "half-finished," is still unpaid for. The estate – "six . . . bad acres" – is mortgaged to the builder, who offered Larry his daughter, the house to be her dowry. But Larry refused her as not his equal in blood, and married "a Milesian . . . of true descent." Now Keegan, an attorney like Jason Quirk, holds the mortgage on Ballycloran (*Macdermots* 8). Larry shares the prince's pride in his ancient blood, his inability to live within his means. Another recluse, he cannot leave the house, lest he be arrested for debt. His children, Thady and Feemy, are trapped by their pretensions and their poverty.

Like Glorvina, Feemy (Euphemia) Macdermot is descended from Irish kings, "Tall, dark . . . with that bold, upright, well-poised figure, which is so peculiarly Irish. She walked as if all the blood of the old Irish Princes was in her veins; her step, at any rate, was princely" (*Macdermots* 11). Horatio attends mass, where Glorvina appears as a

> sylphid elegance of spheral beauty . . . in a robe of vestal white . . . with a narrow girdle embossed with precious stones . . . a mantle of scarlet silk, fastened . . . with a silver bodkin . . . the fine turned head was enveloped in a veil of point lace, bound round the brow with a band, or diadem, ornamented with the same description of jewels as encircled her arms . . . Such was the *figure* of the Princess of Inismore!
> *(Morgan 1:147–49)*

When we meet Feemy, her hair is in soiled curlpapers, "her dress . . . the very picture of untidiness . . . the tuck of her frock was all ripped and torn " with "a dreadful gap . . . showing some article beneath . . . by no means as white as it should be," her shoes "down at heel . . . stockings woefully dirty," reading a "thumb-worn novel" (*Macdermots* 103). She is shabby but believable, unlike Glorvina in her "vestal white," speaking French and reading Greek and Latin.

After mass, Horatio hears "a low wild tremulous voice . . . o'er the harp's responsive chords." Climbing a wall, he sees the prince listening to "the chords of his country's emblem . . . the pathos of his country's music – breathed from the lips of his apparently inspired daughter . . . moon-light . . . played round her fine form." Then he tumbles off the wall – to awaken inside the castle, the prince and the chaplain in attendance, "Glorvina, her looks pale and disordered . . . preparing bandages" (Morgan 1:159–63). Horatio's convalescence keeps him there for some time, while Glorvina lectures him at length on Irish history, and they fall in love. Lady Morgan's ending unites Catholic and Protestant, Gael and Sassenach, Irish woman and English man, to share the estate the Macdermots once ruled. Glorvina will be an English countess as well as an Irish princess. She brings Horatio a traditional Irish right to estates that will be his under English law. As an English earl and Prince of Inismore, their son will embody the 1800 Act of Union.

Her flowing hair, white robe, and harp make Glorvina a national symbol, that Caitlín Ní Uallacháin (Cathleen Ní Houlihan) traditionally evoked by Irish poets to represent Ireland as dispossessed victim or as the Ireland that someday will regain sovereignty and independence. In Yeats's *Cathleen Ní Houlihan* (1902), Maud Gonne portrayed her as the poor old woman robbed of her land who becomes a young girl with "the walk of a queen" when the French land in 1798 (Yeats, *Plays* 57). In the 1916 *Proclamation of the Irish Republic* she "summons *her* children to *her* flag and strikes for *her* freedom" (Townshend xx). Gerald Griffin, William Carleton, and, in *The Macdermots*, Trollope depict her as an Irish victim of sexual aggression, a metaphor for Ireland under British rule.

In Gerald Griffin's *The Collegians: A Tale of Garryowen* (1829) Trollope found a wider social *milieu* than Edgeworth and Lady Morgan portrayed. Again the focus is on Big House families and their servants, but Griffin, from Limerick's rising Catholic urban middle class, includes magistrates, soldiers, landowners, servants, and peasants, all interacting comically, tragically, but also believably, in a panorama of Irish life. The Limerick gentry are as incompetent as the Rackrents, as proud and extravagant as the Prince of Inismore, as violent as Lever's "Man for Galway." Garryowen was notorious for rowdy drinkers, "fierce . . . mirth" and "scenes of strife" (Griffin 1: 1: 2–3). In their anthem, "The Boys of Garryowen," who "beat the bailiffs out of fun . . . make the mayor and sheriffs run," are "the boys no man dares dun." Their drunken harassment of Eily O'Connor and her father sets Griffin's story in motion, and establishes its atmosphere of violence. Mrs. Chute, "a very wild girl," gave Tom Chute three choices: a duel with pistols, a horsewhipping, or a proposal to her (Griffin 1: 3: 43). At Roaring Hall, Barnaby Cregan's companions are Hepton Connolly, who consumes "a prodigious quantity of whisky-punch at a sitting" and "Hyland Fireball Creagh . . . notorious duelist" (Griffin 1: 6: 120, 116–17). Myles-na Coppaleen, Myles of the ponies, an itinerant horse-trader, is comic, shrewd, and sympathetic, but an unconvincing Irish peasant. Cregan promises that Myles's first entrance will be "'as good as a play'" (Griffin 1: 9: 180), he only heralds another stage Irishman.

Hardress Cregan must marry Anne Chute, whose money will save his family's estate. But he has secretly married Eily O'Connor, a rope-maker's daughter, attracted by her artless simplicity. Soon tiring of Eily and "that brogue" (Griffin 1:15: 329), he imagines her "bashfulness . . . homeliness of speech and accent" among his own class, "peeling a potato with her fingers! . . . during dinner" (Griffin 2: 20: 101). Sequestering Eily in a remote cabin, he courts Anne Chute. When he orders his servant, Danny Mann, to take Eily to America, "master and man exchanged a look of cold and fatal intelligence" (Griffin 2: 20: 101). Danny, who prides himself on anticipating his master's wishes, murders Eily. Hardress is out with the local hunt when the hounds unearth Eily's rotting corpse.

Griffin's social range allows sudden shifts between comic, melodramatic, and darkly tragic – inconsistencies of tone reflecting the inconsistencies of Irish life. When Danny is suspected of the murder, the legal proceedings become a comic sketch of "the closeness, the affected dullness, the assumed simplicity, and all the inimitable subtleties of evasion and of wile which an Irish peasant can display" in court (Griffin 3: 39: 179–80). But grim intensity immediately resumes. Visiting Danny's cell, Hardress insists he never ordered Eily's death: "'I did not say for death . . . Did I not warn you not to touch her?'" "'Your eye looked murder when you said it,'" Danny replies; "'de sign of death was on your face dat time, whatever way your words went'" (Griffin 3: 40: 204–5).

On the eve of Hardress's marriage to Anne, Danny confesses Eily's murder to a magistrate, naming Hardress as instigator:

> "A gentleman will have a bloody longing, an' he'll hide it for fear of shame . . . A gentleman will buy the blood of his innemy for goold, but he'll keep his own clane gloves and slender fingers out of it . . . a gentleman – besides his being a murderer – is a decaver an' a coward."
>
> *(Griffin 3: 42: 245)*

Danny denounces the system that supports "gentlemen" and suppresses protest:

> "I knew your laws of old. It isn't for nothing that we see the fathers of families, the pride an' the strength of our villages, the young an' the old, the guilty an' the innocent, snatched away from their own cabins, an' shared off for transportation an' the gallows. It isn't for nothing our brothers, our cousins, an' our friends are hanged before our doores from year to year. Dey teach us something of the law, we tank 'em."
>
> *(Griffin 3: 42: 245–46)*

Convicted of murder, Hardress is transported to Australia. Danny Mann is hung.

Eily O'Connor is another Cathleen Ní Houlihan, Ireland as female victim. So is Trollope's Feemy Macdermot. She is often visited by Captain Ussher, a representative of British rule, who is zealously arresting illicit distillers, most of them also Ribbonmen, members of a secret society opposed to landlords and the government. When Father John, the parish priest, asks if Ussher intends to marry Feemy, Thady responds,

> "I wish Feemy had never set eyes on him . . . can't you be doing better than coupling her name with . . . his, that way? and he a black Protestant, and filling her head up with nonsense . . . and don't the country hate him for the way he's riding down the poor?"

"'Is it not that you fear the young man won't marry Feemy, rather than that he will?'" Father John asks;

> "people begin to say . . . Captain Ussher thinks too much of himself to take a wife from Ballycloran, and that he has only been amusing himself with your sister . . . I fear . . . that he's taking advantage of her ignorance and quietness."
>
> *(Macdermots 56–58)*

Feemy refuses to listen, though anxious that Ussher will not name a marriage date.

As in Griffin's *Collegians*, Trollope's social range includes peasants, the middle class, duelists, and hard-drinking local gentry. Ballycloran is impoverished, tense, ready to erupt into violence. Petty squires and their hangers-on drink themselves into insensibility before the Carrick races. They torment a newcomer until he lies in the street at 4:00 a.m., "his face dreadfully bleeding" (*Macdermots* 318). Trollope also introduces humorous episodes illustrating Irish customs and manners: Father John's discussion about Denis McGovery's marriage (*Macdermots* 45–55), the cow that didn't calve, and the pigs that will be the bride's dowry; the McGovery-Brady wedding celebration.

The Quirks betrayed Sir Condy Rackrent, and Danny Mann betrayed Hardress. Lawyer Keegan will make Pat Brady, Thady Macdermot's "trusty servant," his "chief informer" if he helps Keegan to seize Ballycloran by involving Thady in a plot to murder Ussher. Brady's "friends" are eager to kill Thady's enemies, Ussher and Keegan (*Macdermots* 205–208). Denis McGovery's wedding party gives Brady an opportunity to arrange Ussher's murder, end the harassment of illicit distillers, and implicate Thady. Thady and Ussher will be wedding guests, along with Ribbonmen who hope Thady will "'lend a hand to punish the murthering ruffian as have got half the counthry druv into gaols, and as is playing his tricks now with his own sisther,'" and "'join wid us to rid the counthry'" of Ussher (*Macdermots* ch. 9).

At the wedding, scenes of "universal and incessant . . . fun" (*Macdermots* 221) alternate with hints that something ominous lurks behind the revelry. Thady arrives furious and already drunk: Keegan has insulted Feemy, struck Thady with a shillelagh, and delivered an ultimatum: the Macdermots must accept a pittance to leave Ballycloran, or foreclosure will force them to go. Thady is ready to join the Ribbonmen, "who, he knew, were meeting with some secret plans for proposed deliverance from their superiors" (*Macdermots* 170). Denis McGovery warns Ussher of danger; Ussher warns Thady that Pat Brady is helping Keegan to banish the Macdermots from Ballycloran. When the Ribbonmen promise to kill Ussher and Keegan if Thady takes the Ribbon oath, he drunkenly agrees. Later Thady and Ussher quarrel over Feemy until Father John intervenes, spoiling Brady's plot to kill Ussher that night, and implicate Thady. Sober the next day, Thady refuses the Ribbon oath.

Already pregnant, Feemy agrees to elope, hoping Ussher will "afterwards . . . give her what reparation a tardy marriage could afford" (*Macdermots* 285). When Ussher arrives at Ballycloran by night to collect her, Thady hears the carriage, and then an angry man's voice urging haste: "'This is d – d nonsense, Feemy! You know you must come now.' These were the last words he ever uttered" (*Macdermots* 371). Believing that Feemy is being abducted against her will, Thady strikes the captain with his heavy knobbed stick, killing him. Horrified and confused, he summons Pat Brady, who improvises another incriminating plot, advising Thady that the Ribbonmen will "get him out of harm's way . . . up in the mountains . . . where the police would never be able to find him" (*Macdermots* 374). Thady briefly flees, but returns to consult with Father John and surrender to the police. While he awaits trial at Carrick, Ribbonmen intimidate Ussher's successor.

Increasing violence alarms the authorities. When Keegan forecloses on Ballycloran, and rides there to collect his rents, three men knock him from his horse:

> he came to himself . . . lying on the road; the man who had stopped his horse was kneeling on his chest; a man, whose face was blackened, was holding down his two feet . . . a third, whose face had also been blackened, was kneeling on the road beside him with a small axe . . . Keegan's courage utterly failed him . . . he began to promise largely if they would let him escape . . . before the first sentence . . . was well out of his mouth, the instrument fell on his leg, just above his ankle . . . the second cut the flesh, and grated against the bone . . . a third, and a fourth, and a fifth descended, crushing the bone, dividing the marrow, and ultimately severing the foot . . . they left him on the road.
>
> (*Macdermots* 446–447)

Before Thady's trial begins, Trollope shows us another Irish courtroom: evasive witnesses, cat-and-mouse cross-examinations, a witness ridiculed for not behaving like a "'Connaught man'" (*Macdermots* 519). The mood darkens when Thady is tried for conspiring with Ribbonmen to murder a police officer.

"'The peace of your country – the comfort of your hearths – the safety of your houses – the protection of your property,'" the prosecutor tells the jurors, depend on convicting Thady. That a landowner joined with Ribbonmen "'greatly increases the magnitude of his presumed crime'" (*Macdermots* 538–539). Pat Brady, the chief prosecution witness, testifies that, after killing Ussher, Thady said, "'he would be off at once to the mountains,'" with "the boys," adding,

> "But shure, yer honour knows the thing had been talked over."
> "What thing had been talked over?"
> "Why, the Captain's death."
> "You mean to say by that, that arrangements had been made by certain persons to kill Captain Ussher?"
> "I don't know about arrangements; but there war boys through the counthry determined to have a fling at him . . . I've heard the boys say he would be undher the sod that day six months . . . I don't know that they ever said death or murder; they don't spake out that way; av they war going to hole a chap, it's giving him his *quiatis* or his *gruel* they'd be talking about."
>
> *Macdermots* 542–543

Brady's testimony weaves Thady into a seditious conspiracy. At the McGovery wedding, "the boys" swore to prevent Keegan from seizing Ballycloran if Thady would "'jine them in putting down the peelers and the Captain . . . there war a dale of shilly-shallying – but at last the masther said as how he would jine the boys in ridding the country of the Captain, and he thin agreed to come . . . the next night . . . to get the secret signs and the pass-words. And to take the oaths'" (*Macdermots* 544–546). Pat Brady's Irish English, with its comic associations, his pretence of not understanding questions, his "confidence and self-assurance," convinces the jurors. They find Thady guilty of murder and of joining an illegal society. He is hanged a week later.

No other Irish fiction "proved so useful to Trollope" as William Carleton's *Traits and Stories of the Irish Peasantry* (1829–33), and *Fardorougha the Miser* (1839) (Escott 54). Carleton understood the smoldering resentment that made the attack on Keegan believable. Ireland's first peasant novelist, he grew up among Irish-speakers, knew how people spoke and *thought* in Irish, giving his accounts of Irish life unique authority. "I found [the peasantry] a class unknown in literature, unknown by their own landlords, and unknown by those in whose hands much of their destiny was placed," he wrote;

> If I became the historian of their habits and manners, their feelings, their superstitions, and their crimes; if I have attempted to delineate their moral, religious, and physical state, it was because I saw no person willing to undertake a task which surely must be looked upon as an important one . . . I was anxious that those who ought, but did not, understand their character, should know them – not merely for selfish purposes, but that they should teach them to know themselves and appreciate their rights, both moral and civil, as rational men, who owe obedience to law, without the necessity of being slaves either to priest or landlord.
>
> (*Tales of Ireland* x–xi)

Yeats called "secret societies" and "the *agent provocateur*" Carleton's persistent theme (*Stories from Carleton* xv). Ribbon lodges often aroused and directed the violence that had become normal in Irish life. In "The Battle of the Factions" his narrator explains how to make a cudgel a deadly weapon. Faction fights are "'an agreeable recreation . . . truly comical and facetious . . . every one knows that fighting is our national amusement'" (*Traits* 1:143, 141, 132). That is Carleton's point. His narrator admires Ribbon arsonists and abductors, glories in the violence that Carleton implicitly condemns by satirizing the peasant view of violence as heroic and amusing, perhaps imitating the Ascendancy's admiration for hot-tempered duelists.

In "Wildgoose Lodge," Ribbonmen meet at midnight in a chapel, where their captain distributes whisky as a sacrilegious communion. He sets Wildgoose Lodge on fire, ordering that no one is to escape. When a woman begs that her baby be spared, he bayonets mother and child, thrusts them into the flames. "'Remember . . . what you've sworn this night, on the book 'an altar of God – not on a heretic Bible,'" he reminds his men; "'You may hang us; but let me tell you . . . that if you do, there is them livin' that will take care the lase of your own lives will be but short.'" Carleton's footnote assures us that his story is true. Wildgoose Lodge burned because an inhabitant refused to take the Ribbon oath. The captain was hanged, and then left in chains; "The peasantry . . . frequently exclaimed, on seeing him, 'Poor Paddy!' A gloomy fact that speaks volumes!" (*Traits* 2: 362).

Carleton showed how secret societies, originating in a culture of violence and injustice, intimidated landlords by threatening that

> all belonging to them . . . would be a heap of ashes . . . they would be as cunning as foxes . . . If one of them wanted a wife, it was . . . find out the purtiest and the richest farmer's daughter in the neighborhood . . . march into her . . . house, at the dead hour of night, tie and gag every mortal in it, and off with her . . . Then what could be done? If the . . . parents didn't . . . give in, their daughter's name was sure to be ruined . . . no other man would think of marrying her.
>
> *(Carleton, Traits 1:118)*

Trollope found Carleton's "longest, most ambitious [novel]" *Fardorougha the Miser or, The Convicts of Lisnamona* (1839) "really stimulating" (Escott 53). Fardorougha (*fear dorcha*) means "the dark or swarthy man," perhaps a secretive, even malignant man; it can also mean a blind man. Fardorougha Donovan wears his coat like a cloak, saving the sleeves from wear. He claims to be amassing money for Connor, his only child, but fails to see how avarice nearly robs him of his son. Rich by local standards, he will not give Connor the farm he needs to marry Oona O'Brien. Despising Fardorougha's parsimony, Oona's parents reject the match. Bartle Flanagan, the local Ribbon captain, hates Fardorougha, who foreclosed his family's farm, and considers Connor his rival for Oona. Bartle and his Ribbonmen burn O'Brien's haggard because he refuses to purchase their protection, but the raid is also intended to destroy Fardorougha and Connor. Bartle borrows Connor's shoes; their distinctive footprints will identify Connor as one of the arsonists. When Bartle and some of his men testify that Connor was near O'Brien's farm that night, the shoes convict him, and he is transported to penal servitude in Australia. With Connor gone, Bartle attacks O'Brien's farm to abduct Oona, but abducts her maid instead. When O'Brien's tenants capture the Ribbonmen, Bartle's plots are exposed. Connor is pardoned, and marries Oona. Fardorougha dies, warning Connor "'against lovin' the wealth o' this world too much'" (*Fardorougha* 20: 226).

Pat Brady's schemes in *The Macdermots* show how thoroughly Trollope understood the shadowy world of Ribbonism, and why informers and betrayals flourish where landowners and government fear secret societies. He denounces "the treachery which" the informer system

> creates – the feeling of suspicion which it generates – but above all, the villainies to which it gives and has given rise, in allowing informers, by the prospect of blood-money, to give false informations, and to entrap the unwary into crimes – are by no means atoned for by the occasional . . . punishment of a criminal . . . secret informers . . . have

greatly increased crime in many districts . . . the result must be to create suspicion of each other among the poor, and fearfully to increase instead of diminishing crime.

(Macdermots 174–175)

Like Carleton, Trollope recognized Ireland's social and political fragility and unsustainable economy, just as it was about to collapse in the Great Famine. With *The Macdermots*, he joined the conversation about Ireland that Maria Edgeworth began. Griffin and Carleton taught him to avoid sentiment and achieve what Yeats calls Carleton's "clay-cold melancholy" (Yeats, *Stories from Carleton* xv–xvii). Trollope would return at intervals to Ireland in four later novels, but never again with so sure a touch, such confident insight.

Works cited

Bowen, Elizabeth. *The Mulberry Tree*. Ed. Hermione Lee. London: Virago Press, 1986.
Carleton, William. *Fardorougha the Miser, or, The Convicts of Lisnamona*. Dublin, 1839. Ed. Benedict Kiely. Belfast: Appletree Press, 1992.
———. *Tales of Ireland*. Dublin: W. Curry, 1834.
———. *Traits and Stories of the Irish Peasantry*. Dublin, 1843–4. 2 vols. Reprint. Ed. Barbara Hayley. Gerrards Cross: Colin Smythe, 1990.
Dunraven, Earl of. Introduction to W. H. Maxwell's *Wild Sports of the West* (1832). Reprint, New York: Frederick A. Stokes, 1916.
Edgeworth, Maria. *Castle Rackrent*. Ed. George Watson. London: Oxford University Press, 1964.
Escott, T.H.S. *Anthony Trollope, His Public Services, Private Friends, and Literary Originals*. 1913. Reprint. Port Washington, NY: Kennikat Press, 1967.
Gregory, Lady, ed. *Sir William Gregory, K.C.M.G., Formerly Member of Parliament and Sometime Governor of Ceylon: An Autobiography*. London: J. Murray, 1894.
Griffin, Gerald. *The Collegians*. 3 vols. London: Sanders and Otley, 1829.
Lever, Charles. *Charles O'Malley, the Irish Dragoon*. 2 vols. New York: Atheneum, n.d.
———. *The Confessions of Harry Lorrequer*. New York: Atheneum, n.d.
Lover, Samuel. *Rory O'More: A National Romance*. Boston: Little Brown, 1903.
Morgan, Lady (Sydney Owenson). *The Wild Irish Girl*. 1806. 3 vols. Reprint. New York: Garland, 1979.
Rilke, Rainer Maria. "After the Fire." Trans. Seamus Heaney. In *District and Circle*. London: Faber, 2006, p. 16.
Townshend, Charles. *Easter 1916: The Irish Rebellion*. London: Allen Lane, 2005.
Trollope, Anthony. *An Autobiography*. London: Oxford University Press. 1950.
———. *The Macdermots of Ballycloran*. 1847. Ed. Robert Tracy. Oxford: Oxford University Press, 1989.
Trollope, Frances. *Domestic Manners of the Americans*. New York: Oxford University Press, 1984.
Yeats, W. B. *Collected Plays*. New York: Macmillan, 1953.
———. *Letters*. Ed. Allan Wade. London: Rupert Hart-Davis, 1954.
———, ed. *Representative Irish Tales*. New York & London: G.P. Putnam's Sons, 1891.
———, ed. *Stories from Carleton*. London: Walter Scott, 1889.

20

"THE CLEVER SON OF A CLEVER MOTHER"

Anthony and Frances Trollope

Elsie Michie

> "In short, cleverness is a sort of genius for instrumentality. It is the brain in the hand."
> *Samuel Taylor Coleridge, The Friend*

For Victorian critics cleverness functioned as the kind of minor aesthetic category that Sianne Ngai has recently identified in the culture of modernism. Like cuteness in its relation to beauty, cleverness was typically opposed to the higher category of genius, as when a reviewer of Wilkie Collins explains that "[w]e should . . . prefer to assign to [the author] overflowing cleverness rather than genius" (Page 264). Consigning an author to a secondary status, cleverness had the double function Ngai finds in cuteness, allowing critics to convey a pleasurable response to a work of art while at the same time insisting on the work's limited importance. Functioning as "the means by which one judges under cover of describing" (40), such categories mark an uneasy awareness of the link between capitalism and aesthetic production. But while Ngai has associated such uneasiness primarily with modern artistic practices, an exploration of cleverness allows us to locate it also in the Victorian novel, which was born at the moment Thomas Carlyle identified with the emergence of the "cash nexus." To track this connection, I turn to Frances and Anthony Trollope, whose practice, reviews, and novels allow us to analyze changes that took place in the uses of cleverness between the 1830s and 1840s, when Frances became a famous author in the years that also marked the beginning of Charles Dickens's career, and the 1860s and 1870s, when the Victorian novel took its most distinctively complex form in the late works of Anthony Trollope, as well as Charles Dickens and George Eliot.

The Trollopes understood cleverness to be an equivocal rather than a purely negative category. As Aristotle explains in the *Nicomachean Ethics*,

> cleverness is a certain faculty . . . the nature of which is to be able to do, and to attain those things which conduce to the aim proposed. If . . . the aim be good, [it] is praiseworthy; but if it be bad, it becomes craft.
>
> *(173)*

Anthony's *An Autobiography* makes clear that both he and his mother valued the "focus . . . [on] efficiency and productivity" (Kristjansson 89) characteristic of cleverness. Describing Frances as someone who "was at her table by four in the morning, and had finished her work before the world had begun to be aroused" (25) and "continued writing up to 1856, when she was seventy-six years old, – and had at that time produced 114 volumes, of which the first was not written till she was fifty" (32), Anthony provides a model for his own goal-driven writing. "It was my practice to be at my table every morning at 5:30 am" (271);

> I have allotted myself so many pages a week. The average number was about 40. It has been placed as low as 20, and has risen to 112. . . . And as page is ambiguous here, my page has been made to contain 250 words.
>
> *(119)*

Both Trollopes were also aware of the negative connotations of the term clever, particularly as it was used in reviews, yet both chose to embrace it as a self-definition. Endlessly deprecated by reviewers as merely a clever woman, Frances Trollope eventually wrote a novel entitled *The Life and Adventures of a Clever Woman* (1854), a phrase Pamela Neville-Sington used as the subtitle of a 1998 biography of Frances. In his autobiography Anthony cheerfully asserts that "I never fancied myself to be a man of genius" (ch. 7), and insists that, in idealizing adolescent daydreams, "I never was a learned man, nor even a philosopher. But I was a very clever person, and beautiful young women used to be fond of me" (ch. 3).

As becomes clear in Frances's and Anthony's strikingly similar novels *The Lottery of Marriage* (1849) and *The American Senator* (1877), both Trollopes explored the negative implications of cleverness through the fictional figure of a crafty woman. Indeed in his posthumous assessment of Anthony Trollope's career, the novelist's favorite critic, Richard Holt Hutton, associates "the dread which he evidently entertained for the craftiness of women" with "the deep study he had given to all the tactics of social life" (Smalley 505–6). As Hutton put it in an 1864 review of *The Small House at Allington* (1864) in which he attempted to define the ineffable pleasures of reading Anthony's novels:

> Mr. Trollope's intellectual grasp of his characters, as far as he goes (which is only now and then below the surface), is nearly perfect; but then he chooses to display that grasp most exclusively in the hold they get or fail to get over other characters, and in the hold they yield to other characters over them. It is in his command of what we may call the moral "hooks and eyes" of life that Trollope's greatest power lies.
>
> *(Smalley 198)*

Referencing grasping, holding, and hooking, Hutton echoes the etymological history of the word clever, which was likely derived from the "Middle English *clivers* 'claws, talons, clutches' in the sense [of] 'nimble of claws, sharp to seize'" (*On-line OED*). Linking the abilities of the author to those of his characters, Hutton shows that both display, for good or for bad, the tactile imaginative practices that Coleridge identifies with "the brain in the hand." Central also to Frances Trollope's novels, those were the practices Anthony would eventually claim as crucial to the Victorian novel as an art form.

Frances Trollope

Born four years after Jane Austen and growing up in the same milieu as her more famous precursor, Frances began her writing career shortly before Charles Dickens was to publish his first novel. Developing an Austenian marriage plot in a world increasingly dominated by the cash nexus, her novels of the 1830s and 1840s show England to be becoming a place where, as she had observed of America in her 1832 work *Domestic Manners of the Americans*, "every bee in the hive is actively employed in search of that honey of Hybla vulgarly called money" (38). As Frances's reviews and novels demonstrate, this social change transformed the connotations of the word cleverness, which for writers who preceded her seemed fairly benign, as when Emma Woodhouse is defined as "handsome, clever, and rich" (Austen 1). In Austen's novel cleverness is associated with wealth, and has a somewhat pejorative tinge, since Emma's privileged position will lead to a series of misprisions. Nevertheless, because in that novel, social status, though beginning to change, is still anchored firmly in hierarchy, clever remains a fairly innocuous adjective.[1] By the time Frances Trollope began her career, cleverness carried with it a much more powerful pejorative edge, as becomes clear in her reviews. They are, as Gerard Genette puts it, "persuasive or valorizing descriptions that bridge the abyss between fact and value *without becoming too conspicuous*" (quoted in Ngai 40). "Semi-descriptive and semi-judgmental" (40), they acknowledge the pleasure of reading Frances Trollope while simultaneously condemning her. As the critic for *The New Monthly Magazine* put it in 1839, "[n]o other writer of the present day has been at once so much read, so much admired, and so much abused" (quoted in Ayres 1).

That equivocal response typically centered on the term clever, which made possible the "yes but" rhetorical structure that recurs insistently throughout her reviews, which open with praise, followed by and intertwined with critique. Reviewing her 1836 abolitionist novel *The Life and Adventures of Jonathan Jefferson Whitlaw*, the *Literary Gazette and Journal of Belles Lettres* describes her as "a clever woman, with a quick eye for observation, and a smart, keep-moving style of narrative. Her great fault is exaggeration" (420). In reviewing her 1837 anti-Evangelical novel *The Vicar of Wrexhill*, the *Athenaeum* characterizes her as "a clever woman, quick of eye, ready of hand, heedless of utterance – not devoid of taste for what is beautiful, refined, and luxurious, – though she seems, from choice, to delight in subjects which are painful and repulsive" ("Vicar" 708). Assessing her career in 1839 *The New Monthly Magazine* calls her "a clear-seeing and clever woman, who surprises us with the extent, the variety, and the lucidity of her visions," but whose "clairvoyance is a skilful delusion" ("Mrs. Trollope" 551). Clearly fully aware of these value judgments, Frances responded by embodying them in the characters she created. Repeatedly seen as a writer whose "wit trenches on caricature"("Female Novelists" 21), she imagines in *The Lottery of Marriage* the husband-hunting antiheroine Cassandra de Laurie, who is both one of those "accustomed to make the external fictions of society their study" (47) and a painter of caricatures, "clever atrocities in which her spirit luxuriated" (49). Using terms from one of the earliest reviews of her novels, which critiqued her for "luxuriat[ing] with a congenial zest . . . in painting the vulgar, the half-bred, or better still the under-bred" (quoted in Heineman 120), Frances points to what the entire structure of *The Lottery of Marriage* reveals to be true: that cleverness emerges as a negative but useful talent at the moment when traditional social hierarchies began to be undermined by the power of money.

Both Frances's *The Lottery of Marriage* (*LM*) and Anthony's *The American Senator* (*AS*) tell the story of a set of matchmakers who surround a landed and titled figure who seems to embody all the values society used to hold dear. In Frances's world, the central representative of the landed aristocracy, Lord Wigton, is described as "[t]he admiration of every female eye, and the hope of every female heart" (*LM* 59). In Anthony's novel, Lord Rufford is similarly characterized as possessing "everything . . . money, rank, fashion, and an appetite for pleasure. And he was handsome, too, and good humoured" (*AS* ch. 36). Both characters are aware that this privileged position means that they will be relentlessly pursued by marriageable women, hunted, as Wigton says of himself, "with as little ceremony as if I were a fox or a badger" (*LM* 200). In Anthony's novel, Rufford is similarly aware that "[a]s for the hunting, that was a matter of course. He was as much born and bred to be hunted as a fox" (*AS* ch. 45). But, as Frances's novel makes clear, this situation forces the lord to experience himself not as having a secure position within a social hierarchy but as caught up in a series of social interactions in which he must play a particular role. As Wigton exclaims, in trying to justify his propensity to lure the women who pursue him on and then abandon them, leaving only expensive gifts in his place, such actions are part of "the whole tissue and network of the society in which I have lived!" (*LM* 120). Echoed in reviews of *The Lottery of Marriage*, which describe it as depicting "the whole web . . . of drawing-room strategies" ("The New Novels" 208), this phrase underscores Frances's association of cleverness with the experience of society as a network in which, as Bruno Latour has argued in terms reminiscent of Hutton's description of Anthony's writing, "the action is distributed among agents" (50).

In Frances's novel, this new experience of society as a network rather than a hierarchy is shown to undercut the mental abilities of those who possess status while fostering cleverness in those who lack such social guarantors. As one of Frances's characters realizes, land and wealth mean that there is a "tax levied upon the intellect. A man may have a hundred thousand a year and be an honest man, a pious man, a benevolent man, notwithstanding – but he cannot be a wise man" (*LM* 284).[2] In *The Lottery of Marriage* it is the fortune hunters who use their intelligence: Cassandra de Laurie, her matchmaking mother Lady de Laurie, and the penniless Augustus Oglevie, "one of the best worked up sketches ever depicted by Mrs. Trollope's clever and satirical pen" ("Mrs. Trollope's 'Lottery of Marriage'" 262). The first scheming character to appear in the novel, Augustus uses his handsome appearance and aristocratic demeanor combined with his propertied cousin Julian's disinterest in wealth to create the impression that he is the one who owns the family estate "the Bush," when it actually belongs to Julian. Cleverness is the attribute that allows its possessor to assume the semblance of possessing what he or she lacks through the successful use of both people and things to achieve one's ends. Writing this novel in 1849, as Anthony was just two years into his novelistic career, Frances was already emphasizing the talent that Hutton found to be characteristic of Anthony's later work: the hold characters achieve over one another.

Secretly engaged to the daughter of the local squire as *The Lottery of Marriage* opens, Augustus proves able to court in the presence of his fiancée a woman he believes to possess more wealth than she. Exercising his "habitual power . . . to display as much as he chooses of his real feelings and no more" (*LM* 38), he plays adeptly with the feelings of others. As the narrator observes,

> it was part of the *social* tactics of Augustus Oglevie, never to converse with a pretty woman, without giving her reason to believe that he was becoming every moment more and more captivated by every look she looked, and by every word she said.
>
> (*LM* 43)

His strategies are met and matched by the novel's female fortune hunters, Lady de Laurie and her daughter Cassandra, who also manipulate the signs "indicative both of wealth and status" (*LM* 104). A peripatetic pair, with no money and no fixed residence, they carry with them "a wonderful variety of articles, approaching more nearly to the properties, decorations, and scenery belonging to a company of strolling players" (*LM* 51) that allow them to convert "an ordinary lodging-house into an abode, the fanciful elegance of which might strike every beholder at first sight" (*LM* 52). Acquired during the career of Lady de Laurie's late husband, an army general, who traveled the world with his wife on various military campaigns, these objects are explicitly connected with tactics, in the original meaning of the term as arranging objects so as to achieve a military advantage. Transferring these strategies to the drawing room, Cassandra de Laurie uses cosmetics, false hair, a stately bearing, and skills at chess and waltzing to make herself into an avatar of wealth and beauty so mesmerizing that even the clever Augustus,

> one of the least frank, the most skeptical, the least confiding, and the most selfish of created men, was positively brought to believe by the glance of an eye that the showy, worldly, satirical woman before him was ready to sacrifice anything and everything for him.
>
> *(LM 105–6)*

Yet despite these negative characterizations of Cassandra, Frances exhibits a curious sympathy for her crafty woman character, having her narrator explain that

> Though Cassandra de Laurie of my tale is a real living human being, there are features of her character which it may be difficult to trace with such clearness, and such freedom from exaggeration as may give my sketch the value of a portrait.
>
> *(LM 48)*

Insisting that there is something real even in portraits that seem exaggerated, Frances both incorporates and counters critiques of her work that insist, as her son Anthony put it in his autobiography, that "in her attempts to describe morals, manners, and even facts, my mother was unable to avoid the pitfalls of exaggeration" (ch. 2). Anthony Trollope will similarly incorporate both sympathy and critiques of his own work in his portrait of Arabella Trefoil, the crafty woman who dominates the plot of *The American Senator*, whom he presents with what James Kincaid calls "a sort of fascinated respect without approval" (238), and with what Robert Tracy calls "compassion" (220). In Anthony's own words, as he wrote to fellow novelist Anna C. Steele,

> I have been, and still am, very much afraid of Arabella Trefoil. The critics have come and they will tell me that she is unwomanly, unnatural, turgid, – the creation of a morbid imagination, striving after effect by laboured abominations. But I swear I have known the woman, not one special woman . . . but all the traits, all the cleverness, all the patience, all the courage, all the self-abnegation, – and all the failure.
>
> *(Letters II. 710)*

Echoing the wording of an early critic of *The Warden* (1855) who added "a gentle word of rebuke at the morbid condition of the author's mind" (*Autobiography* ch. 5), Anthony follows his mother in associating the crafty woman with himself as an author. This personal investment explains why both Frances and Anthony express sympathy for characters that critics experienced as unpleasantly bitter. As the reviewer for the *Examiner* argued of *The American Senator*, its author "must keep a special inkstand supplied with gall, for use when describing fashionable society" (Smalley 430). This passage reiterates the 1839 description of Frances's "ink" as "abounding in gall" and the author as "dipping deeply as ever in the gall of her ink" ("Mrs. Trollope," 550, 555).

Anthony Trollope

Nowhere acknowledging his mother's influence directly, Anthony Trollope signals his knowledge of her work throughout his career by allusive references embedded in proper names.[3] When, for example, he entitles his novel *The Eustace Diamonds* (1872), he echoes his mother's anti-Catholic novel, *Father Eustace* (1847), which opens with the theft of diamonds. When he gives the father of Emily Trevelyan, the unhappy wife in *He Knew He Was Right* (1869), the first name Marmeduke, he echoes the name of the abusive husband, Sir Marmaduke Wentworth, in *One Fault* (1840), Frances's novel about the decay of a marriage in which a husband attempts and fails to control his wife. In *The American Senator*, he evokes his mother through the story of the senator who reverses the trajectory of Frances's career, which began with the dramatically successful publication of *Domestic Manners of the Americans* (1832), by coming from America to England in order to write a book that critiques English manners. When the novel ends with the senator being told, "I don't know how far it is wise for a man to tell another man, much less a nation, of all its faults" and him replying, "You English tell us of ours pretty often" (*AS* ch. 78), nineteenth-century readers would have recognized a sly dig at Frances's work, which was famous for its virulent criticisms of American manners. But Anthony also nods to his use of a particular Frances Trollope novel, *The Lottery of Marriage*, by naming the inn at which a number of the novel's characters congregate "the Bush," the title of an estate in Frances's novels, and calling the mother of his calculating fortune hunter Lady Augustus.

Like Lady de Laurie, "an extremely clever woman in many ways" who aims "to make as much use of everybody and everything as possible" (*LM* 17), Lady Augustus and her daughter Arabella Trefoil adeptly manipulate social appearances to create the impression of wealth; "how it was that the two ladies lived so luxuriously was a mystery to their friends, as for some time past they had enjoyed no particular income of their own" (*AS* ch. 12). Moving from one family to another as guests, on a "lengthened cruise among long-suffering acquaintances" (*AS* ch. 20), they make themselves seem rich through clothes that Arabella wins on bets and by sending letters that appear to come from exclusive hotels where they are not actually staying. Like Cassandra de Laurie, Arabella uses her natural beauty, the artificial aids of powder and paint, and her deportment to create the impression that she is an irresistible object of desire. And, like Augustus Oglevie, she enters *The American Senator* engaged to one person and then decides to pursue another of higher station and greater wealth, a situation that, as in Frances's novel, drives the clever individual to exploit social tactics to the utmost. As Arabella puts it of herself,

> No girl could make better use of her time; but think of the difficulties! All that she did would have to be done under the very eyes of the man to whom she was engaged, and to whom she wished to remain engaged, – unless, as she said to herself, she could "pull off the other event."
>
> (*AS ch. 20*)

But this sentence also marks the difference between Frances's and Anthony's novels; in the latter cleverness is a mode of consciousness as much as a use of strategies. In Anthony's world, social tactics involve less intentional deception than the astute manipulation of materials that become available, materials that derive not only from the conventional social interactions that Augustus and Cassandra use in *The Lottery of Marriage* but also from arbitrary, even unpredictable events. When, for example, Arabella and Lord Rufford are hunting and Major Canebake falls and is kicked so badly he eventually dies, she is "quite conscious . . . that the poor major's misfortune, happening as it had done, just beneath her horse's feet, had been a godsend to her" (*AS* ch. 23). The accident allows her to establish an emotional intimacy with Rufford, which would not otherwise be possible. Watching the interaction, Rufford's sister exclaims, "That girl is very clever" (*AS* ch. 23), understanding cleverness to mean tactically arranging not just the physical objects so important to Frances's characters but also unforeseen events and strong involuntary emotions like grief and fear to further one's aims. While Rufford's retort, that Arabella "is very much excited rather than clever at this moment" (*AS* ch. 23), might seem to reflect his gullibility, in fact the novel repeatedly shows that its crafty heroine can and indeed must be both excited and calculating at the same time. In a later scene as Arabella swoons in Rufford's arms after a long day of hunting that has actually exhausted her, the narrator emphasizes that

> For a few minutes she lay there, and as she was lying she calculated whether it would be better to try at that moment to drive him to some clearer declaration, or to make use of what he had already said without giving him the opportunity of protesting that he had not meant to make her an offer of marriage.
>
> *(AS ch. 39)*

Insisting that she "was conscious, but hardly more than conscious, that he was kissing her; – and yet her brain was at work" (*AS* ch. 39), Anthony defines cleverness as a joint or split response that involves simultaneous thinking and feeling. He would return to this stance in the first two chapters of his autobiography, "My Education" and "My Mother," which he wrote immediately after completing *The American Senator*. There he explains of his mother that

> I have written my novels under many circumstances; but I doubt much whether I could write one when my whole heart was by the bedside of my dying son. Her power of dividing herself into two parts, and keeping her intellect by itself clear from the troubles of the world and fit for the duty it had to do, I never saw equaled.
>
> *(ch. 2)*

This may have been a peculiarly powerful experience for Anthony since he was recalling an event that he did not himself witness. As Leonard Shengold notes, "His mother did not summon him to attend the funerals in Bruges of his brother Henry and then of his father, although she asked Tom and Cecilia, who also were in England, to come" (93). Perhaps feeling the pain of that exclusion, which may have recaptured his experiences as a child, when he was tormented at Winchester School while all the rest of his family was in America, Anthony notes that he, like his mother, had a curious ability to think while feeling, explaining that

> It is now more than forty years ago, and looking back over so long a lapse of time I can tell the story, though it be the story of my own father and mother, of my own brother and sister, almost as coldly as I have often done some intended scene of pathos in fiction; but that scene was indeed full of pathos.
>
> *(ch. 3)*

Anthony comes closest to pointing to his own pathos in his account of his experiences as a boy at Winchester, where he became "a Pariah" (ch. 1), disdained by the students who came from the ranks of the wealthy and titled. Learning to "appreciate to its full the misery of expulsion from all social intercourse" (ch. 1), he stresses the pain of social exclusion, explaining that "I coveted popularity with a coveting which was almost mean. It seemed to me that there would be an Elysium in the intimacy of those very boys whom I was bound to hate because they hated me" (ch. 1); "they seemed to me to live in a social paradise, while the desolation of my Pandemonium was complete" (ch. 9). Yet this account conveys less pain than one might expect, in part because Anthony had rehearsed a similar scene of social exclusion at the end of *The American Senator*. When Arabella confronts Lord Rufford one last time, trying to force him to marry her, she is effectively asking to be fully accepted into the classes that tormented Trollope in his childhood. Though Rufford rejects her, he realizes that there is no reason why he should; "[s]he was very beautiful in her present form, – more beautiful, he thought, than ever. She was the niece of a duke, and certainly a very clever woman. He had not wanted money, and why shouldn't he have married her?" (*AS* ch. 67). Arabella is, as Tracy notes, "a victim of that dangerous combination from which Trollope himself suffered in childhood, 'poverty and gentle standing'" (221). Characterizing her as "the odious woman" (*Letters* II.710) in his letters, Anthony associates his character with the repulsiveness he assumes others found in his child self, whom he says became "odious in the eyes of those I admired and envied" (*Autobiography* ch. 1).

By locating that shame in a fictional character, Anthony is able in both novel and memoir to write in such a way as to think while feeling. In the novel, he evokes the powerfully negative feelings that must have overwhelmed him as a child and attaches them to a character whose sufferings he can watch with some detachment. In the memoir, he can narrate those childhood experiences directly but shorn of the feelings that would make it most difficult for him to achieve the intellectual distance necessary to write. This is the stance that in both novel and memoir he associates with cleverness, an ability that he is able in *An Autobiography* to rescue from its negative associations with money grubbing to make a virtue exemplified in his own career. Describing Arabella as having "thought that she might climb up to the glory of wealth and rank while [other women] would have to marry hard-working clergymen and briefless barristers" (*AS* ch. 75), he represents her as incapable of valuing the virtues he praises in her in his letters when he writes, "Think of . . . how she works, how true she is to her vocation, how little there is of self-indulgence or idleness" (*Letters* II.710). In his case hard work allows him to overcome the social stigma he experienced at Winchester. As he explains at the memoir's end, the successful novelist "is, if not of equal rank, yet of equal standing with the highest . . . He without money can enter doors which are closed to all but him and the wealthy" (ch. 11). Asserting that "gradually I became known . . . almost as though I had been an Essex squire, to the manner born" (ch. 9), he shows cleverness to have become gradually more acceptable as Victorian culture moved toward values grounded in work and intellectual accomplishment rather than inherited wealth and title.

But in *An Autobiography* Anthony does more than redeem his own work, as he implicitly suggests that cleverness runs the machinery of all Victorian novels, even ones like those written by Charles Dickens that seem full of the pathos from which Anthony Trollope distances himself in recounting his own past. As a number of critics have noted, Dickens seems to have been on Trollope's mind when he wrote his autobiography. Reading Forster's posthumous biography of Dickens in 1872, Trollope expressed his dislike in a letter to George Eliot and George Henry Lewes, exclaiming that "Forster tells of him things which should disgrace him, – as the picture he drew of his own father, & the hard words he intended to have published of his own mother" (*Letters* II.557). Understanding that Victorian critics could easily view Dickens, particularly in the moment of his death, as a genius, Trollope insists that "Dickens was no hero; he was a powerful, clever, humorous, and in many respects wise man" (*Letters* II.557). For Trollope Dickens's revelations about his childhood experience show that the novelist was cleverly conscious of the way he used emotions both in novels like *David Copperfield* and even in reserving that autobiographical fragment to be published after his death.

To grasp this reading of Dickens in terms of the clever women who fascinate Frances and Anthony Trollope in *The Lottery of Marriage* and *The American Senator*, one might turn to the famous scene in *Great Expectations* where Pip first finds himself at Miss Havisham's. That scene has such an extraordinarily powerful and immediate emotional impact on both the novel's child hero and its reader that one forgets that the objects on Miss Havisham's dressing table and elsewhere did not, in fact, naturally come to be in the positions in which Pip sees them.[4] In Coleridge's words "some brain in the hand" must have stopped and reset the clocks and moved shoes and brushes to create the impression the scene later makes. The effectiveness of that scene depends on the talent exhibited by Lady de Laurie and her daughter as they arrange pieces of furniture to create the impression that they are wealthier than they actually are. It depends on the talent that allows Arabella Trefoil to manipulate traumatic events like Major Canebake's death to elicit a particular emotional response in Lord Rufford. From Anthony's point of view, the writer is endlessly, like the crafty woman, conscious of how he uses emotions even as he feels them, strategically deploying everything that comes to his hands to create the effects that engender the success of the novel. The difference between Trollope's autobiography and Dickens's biography, between Trollope's novels and Dickens's, is that Trollope refuses to allow readers to ignore the novelist's use of social tactics. Particularly through the voice of the intrusive narrator that Henry James so disliked, Trollope insistently reminds us that he is thinking about the details he includes in his stories, thereby "outing," in Carolyn Dever's words, "the open secrets of realist convention" (861), the fact that the novel depends on the cleverness its critics deplore.

Reading the careers of Frances and Anthony Trollope as a sequence that runs from 1832, when she published her first book, to 1882, when he died while working on novels that would be published posthumously, provides a window onto transmutations in the uses of cleverness over a fifty-year period. In the years before and after the beginning of the Victorian period, when Frances began publishing, clever took on an increasingly pejorative connotation, as it came to be associated with the social changes resulting from the collapse of traditional patterns of hierarchy and deference and the emergence of a culture based more clearly on the pursuit of wealth. By the mid-1850s, cleverness had become more acceptable, as the tone of Anthony's reviews reveals. Like his mother, he was relentlessly described as clever. The word appears fourteen times in the *Critical Heritage* (ed. Smalley) reviews covering his publications from 1855 to1858.[5] It opens reviews of *The Warden* (1855) and *Barchester Towers* (1857), and by 1860, "it is a matter of course, that *Castle Richmond*, being written by Mr. Trollope, is very clever and amusing" (114); "[w]e need not tell our readers that *Castle Richmond* is a clever and amusing novel, for its author's name is warrant enough for that" (Smalley 115). As the reference to the name suggests, these reviewers were explicitly reading Anthony as, in the words of an 1862 review of *Framley Parsonage*, "the clever son of a clever mother" (Smalley 115). But, as the tone of these comments makes clear, by the time Anthony's career took off, in the mid-1850s, cleverness no longer bore the extreme disgust or odium conveyed in the reviews of Frances's work.

Though Anthony's reviewers also use the "yes but" construction characteristic of Frances's, the qualification that follows cleverness does not point to exaggeration but its opposite, the way in which Anthony's novels are almost too ordinary. As the reviewer for the *Examiner* put it of *Orley Farm* in 1862, "[t]he author writes cleverly and pleasantly but at the simple level of the better sort of conversation" (Smalley 154). The tenor of that comment is reiterated in an 1869 review of *Phineas Finn*, which argues that, "clever novels bid fair to become as ephemeral as the daily paper" (Smalley 318). This shift in usage marks the movement from the 1830s and 1840s to the 1860s and 1870s. In that earlier period, as evidenced in Frances Trollope's novels, the cleverness associated with the collapse of social hierarchy and the relentless pursuit of wealth is defined as vulgar and exaggerated, something that readers enjoy, because they recognize it from their own experiences, but also know they should deplore. But by the time we get to the 1860s, the world in which individuals from a variety of classes pursued their own aims was acknowledged to be an everyday experience. By the 1870s and 1880s, cleverness could, as Anthony's biography shows, be redeemed as a positive quality associated with the valuing of work and intellectual accomplishments. Yet, even with the gradual acceptance of cleverness as a useful social skill, it remained, by and large, a dismissive critical term. Frances and Anthony challenged this usage, demonstrating that the cleverness that allowed individuals to negotiate changing social structures was a version of the practical ability, the "brain in the hand," that allowed Victorian novelists to construct narratives that were complex social networks. From this point of view, the conditions that disgust reviewers in Frances's novels, their focus on the vulgar middling classes, are those out of which the Victorian novel arises, as writers like Dickens learned to develop a form in which strategically placed myriad objects, characters, and emotions create the ineffable effects that readers remember to this day.

Notes

1 Susan Ferrier's *Marriage* (1818) uses clever in a similarly ambivalent manner. It is positive when the novel's heroine is described as clever and a suitor critiqued for not being clever enough. But it is negative when a character exclaims, "There is nothing more insupportable than one of your clever women" (482).
2 Lord Rufford in *The America Senator* is a similarly impaired figure, "an empty neutrality," that lacks the aristocracy's "vaunted substantial instincts" (Kincaid 238). This is especially clear when he reappears in *Ayala's Angel* (1881).
3 For discussions of Frances's influence on Anthony see Teresa Ransom, Pamela Neville-Sington, Leonard Shengold, Kay Heath, Deborah Morse, and Elsie B. Michie.
4 David Kurnick first drew my attention to this dynamic in his comments during an MLA panel on Dickens and the Theater.
5 In *Anthony Trollope: The Critical Heritage* there are twelve references to clever between 1851 and 1865, another thirteen between 1865 and 1875. After the publication of *The Way We Live Now* (1875), cleverness virtually disappears.

Works cited

Anonymous. "Female Novelists. No. V—Mrs. Trollope." *New Monthly Magazine* 96 (1852): 19–27.
Anonymous. "*The Life and Adventures of Jonathan Jefferson Whitlaw*." *The Literary Gazette and Journal of the Belles Lettres* 1015 (1835): 420–2.
Anonymous. "Mrs. Trollope." Reprinted from *New Monthly Magazine*, *The Eclectic Magazine of Foreign Literature (1844–1898)* 27.4 (Dec. 1852): 550–6.
Anonymous. "Mrs. Trollope's 'Lottery of Marriage.'" *New Monthly Magazine* 86.142 (June 1849): 261–2.
Anonymous. "The New Novels." *Bentley's Miscellany* 26 (1849): 207–12.
Anonymous. "The Vicar of Wrexhill." *Athenaeum* 517 (1867): 708.
Aristotle. *The Nicomachean Ethics of Aristotle*. Trans. Robert William Browne. London: George Bell and Sons, 1889.
Austen, Jane. *Emma*. Ed. Stephen M. Parrish. New York: Norton, 2000.
Ayres, Brenda. *Frances Trollope and the Novel of Social Change*. Westport, CT: Greenwood Press, 2000.
Carlyle, Thomas. *Chartism*. New York: Wiley and Putnam, 1847.
"Clever," adj. and adv. *Online Oxford English Dictionary*. http://dictionary.oed.com.
Coleridge, Samuel Taylor. *The Friend: The Collected Works of Samuel Taylor Coleridge*. Vol. 4, Pt. 1. Ed. Barbara E. Rooke. London: Routledge and Kegan Paul, 1969.
Dever, Carolyn. "Trollope, Seriality, and the 'Dullness' of Form." *Literature Compass* 7/9 (2010): 861–6.
Ferrier, Susan. *Marriage*. New York: Penguin-Virago, 1986.
Heath, Kay. *Aging by the Book: The Emergence of Middle Age in Victorian Britain*. Albany: SUNY Press, 2009.
Heineman, Helen. *Mrs. Trollope: The Triumphant Feminine in the Nineteenth Century*. Athens: Ohio University Press, 1979.
Kincaid, James. *The Novels of Anthony Trollope*. Oxford: Clarendon, 1977.
Kristjansson, Kristjan. *Aristotle, Emotions, and Education*. Aldershot: Ashgate, 2007.
Latour, Bruno. *Assembling the Social: An Introduction to Actor-Network Theory*. Oxford: Oxford University Press, 2005.
Michie, Elsie B. "Frances Trollope's *One Fault* and the Evolution of the Novel." *Women's Writing* 18.2 (2011): 167–81.
Morse, Deborah Denenholz. *Reforming Trollope: Race, Gender, and Englishness in the Novels of Anthony Trollope*. Farnham: Ashgate, 2013.
Neville-Sington, Pamela. *Frances Trollope: The Life and Adventures of a Clever Woman*. New York: Viking, 1998.
Ngai, Sianne. *Our Aesthetic Categories: Zany, Cute, Interesting*. Cambridge, MA: Harvard University Press, 2012.

Page, Norman, ed. *Wilkie Collins: The Critical Heritage.* London: Routledge and Kegan Paul, 1974.
Ransom, Teresa. *Fanny Trollope: A Remarkable Life.* New York: St. Martin's Press, 1998.
Shengold, Leonard. *Is There Life After Mother?: Psychoanalysis, Biography, Creativity.* Hillsdale, NJ: Analytic Press, 2000.
Smalley, Donald, ed. *Anthony Trollope: The Critical Heritage.* London: Routledge and Kegan Paul, 1969.
Tracy, Robert. *Trollope's Later Novels.* Berkeley: University of California Press, 1978.
Trollope, Anthony. *The American Senator.* Ed. John Halperin. Oxford: Oxford University Press, 1991.
———. *An Autobiography.* Ed. Michael Sadleir and Frederick Page. Oxford: Oxford University Press, 1980.
———. *Ayala's Angel.* Ed. Julian Thompson-Furnival. Oxford: Oxford University Press, 1986.
———. *The Letters of Anthony Trollope.* 2 vols. Palo Alto: Stanford University Press, 1983.
———. *The Way We Live Now.* Ed. John Sutherland. Oxford: Oxford University Press, 1991.
Trollope, Frances Milton. *Domestic Manners of the Americans.* Ed. Pamela Neville-Sington. London: Penguin, 1997.
———. *Father Eustace: A Tale of the Jesuits.* London: Henry Colburn, 1847.
———. *The Life and Adventures of a Clever Woman.* London: Hurst and Blackett, 1854.
———. *The Lottery of Marriage.* Ed. Elsie B. Michie. *The Widow and Wedlock Novels of Frances Trollope.* Ed. Brenda Ayres. Vol. 4. London: Pickering and Chatto, 2011.
———. *One Fault.* London: Richard Bently, 1840.

21
LEGAL CULTURE

Ayelet Ben-Yishai

There are many reasons for readers of Trollope and Victorian culture to turn to the law, just as there are reasons for scholars of law and legal history to turn to Trollope. Indeed, it is probably safe to say that every one of the political, social, or cultural aspects of Trollope's oeuvre – thematic or formal – discussed in scholarship over the years has legal manifestations, representations, consequences, or underlying structures. "The law," writes R. D. McMaster of Trollope's fiction, "is a sort of skeleton, underlying it, giving it shape, allowing for possibilities of action and setting limitations" (11).

While I tend to agree with this quotation, I also think it reveals some of the problems common in law-and-lit scholarship (and not restricted to the Trollopian variety). Note that "the law" here is regarded as a priori and permanent. It precedes fiction, it is stable ("skeleton"), and the novels are structured upon it; the law is a constant with which literature engages, whether to uphold or critique. This is indeed a common view of the law, when approached from a humanities-based perspective. But as any practitioner of the law knows, and as recent legal scholarship has shown, "the law" is but a collection of disparate practices, ideas, doctrines, texts, genres, structures, prescriptions, and descriptions. These come together in a dynamic, historically contingent relationship, often incompatible with each other, if not in outright contradiction. Regarding "the law" as constant rather than dynamic, or as uniform rather than multiple, is thus not only to misunderstand the law but also to miss out on much of what the interdiscipline of law and literature has to offer.

In fact, it seems that no one understood this better than Trollope. His novels present a keen awareness of Victorian legal plurality and its dynamic nature. This awareness, I would like to argue, also explains his obsession with the law, akin as it is with the plurality and dynamic nature of Englishness itself. The first sustained examinations of Trollope and the law, written in the early 1980s, tended to relate his fascination with legal form and content to his biography as the son of a (failed) Chancery lawyer and barrister, and his long experience in the civil service (McMaster; Lansbury).[1] But while McMaster focuses on the connections between the fictional instances and their probable origins in Trollope's life and family history, he also already recognizes that they are also connected on a broader, cultural level. "In the law, Trollope finds not only a machinery for the practical functioning of society but an expression of spiritual principles integral to the English way of doing things" (x). Indeed, if we understand the common law's role in preserving and maintaining the idea of Englishness itself, and Trollope's deep-rooted concern over the rapid and substantive changes that this idea was undergoing, then we understand the importance of law to Trollope, staunchly committed as he was to the idea of Englishness, at the same time as he deftly exposed its always-shifting complexities and contradictions (Ben-Yishai, "Common Endeavor").[2]

Trollope's acute understanding of legal plurality also explains lawyers' well-documented fascination with his fiction (McMaster; Cunningham). This mutual interest goes back a long way – to Trollope himself and to his contemporaries from the legal world, who seemed to turn to each other in a mutual effort to figure out the ways in which words and actions accrue meaning and effect in a changing world. And indeed, Trollope's legal plots have famously been found so challenging as to serve lawyers and legal scholars as "legal hypotheticals," cases through which a student or scholar of the law can try out his or her knowledge and skills of legal analysis (Windolph; Gardner; Roth). This legal scholarship ranges from a simple use of Trollopian plot summaries as legal hypotheticals, through questions of legal doctrine, to an examination of the novels as an "interpretive resource in legal and social history" (Lacey 599). The fact that the same novels that have figured as legal hypotheticals are those that have been central to more historical, social, or formal analyses only goes to show that the novelistic or cultural concerns were closely related to the legal ones, to the point of being inextricable.[3]

A central figure in Trollope's fiction through which we can explore this plurality is that of the lawyer and/or barrister, without whom (almost) no novel is complete.[4] Lawyers in Trollope are sometimes gentlemen, sometimes their auxiliaries or extensions (especially in the form of the "family lawyer," such as the Eustaces' Mr. Camperdown), and sometimes both. As consummate outsider/insider figures, they often personify the schism between what is legal and what is just, "between finding the truth and promoting the interests of their clients" (Dolin, *Fiction and the Law* 99). Even more importantly for my argument, they tend to be painfully aware of that schism, one that is often portrayed through the common-law distinction between solicitors and barristers.

As opposed to barristers, who are almost uniformly vilified, family lawyers or solicitors are complexly and variously portrayed. Since they are extensions of the gentleman and his family (and family name) solicitors are often involved in the case at hand and have a personal stake not only in the professional, moral, or ethical dilemma but also in the family name and fortune; Mr. Furnival of *Orley Farm* and Mr. Boltby in *Sir Harry Hotspur of Humblethwaite* are but two additional examples of this involvement (Arkin). Barristers, on the other hand, are portrayed as loyal to none but their profession; they uphold no values but are solely concerned with winning their case – with its formal features, strategy, and odds of success. The result is a portrayal of a mercenary professional who might be brilliant, but is always somehow sullied (often literally so). This might account for the reason that Trollope's early reviewers often complained that he judged the entire profession too severely (Lyons 14). Many of Trollope's courtroom scenes (and even more commonly, scenes of consultation between solicitors, barristers, and their clients) show the tension between the rival worldviews and values of client/gentleman, lawyer/solicitor, and barrister (most prominently portrayed in *Orley Farm*, *The Warden*, and *The Eustace Diamonds*). Though the three are ostensibly on the same side, their stakes in the matter at hand are different, as are their ethics and the way they understand "the law." But because the three figures ultimately work together, Trollope uses these encounters to challenge superficial dichotomies often generated by legal themes: us/them, right/wrong, good/bad. Rather than pitting the novel's complexity against the law's ostensible superficiality, Trollope foregrounds the fact that complexity is inherent in the law, and widely understood by its professionals.[5]

Following Trollope's lead, I would thus like to suggest that divining what Trollope thought about "the law" is not as productive a venture as is an engagement with his novels' legal themes to bring out the complexities that *challenge* a monolithic understanding of the law, or of culture, for that matter (Pettitt 75). This approach I am advocating foregrounds an understanding of legal plurality that is lacking from much scholarship. David Sugarman and Gerry Rubin argue that scholars, even legal historians, pay too little attention to the significant divergences between legal prescription and actual legal practice (4). They emphasize the flexibility and plurality of legal culture and legal institutions (state and non-state) thus "extending our knowledge of the uses and limits of the law" (48; 111).[6] Understanding this, we must thus ascertain that our work is ever attuned to the historical specificity of the various legal practices, rather than to the universality that pervades much (academic) legal discourse. This is the kind of practice Kieran Dolin promotes in his commitment to what Gillian Beer has called "the historical moment" and to the multiplicity of meanings that are generated through the intersections of diverse professional, cultural, and social activities at a certain time and place (Dolin, *Critical Introduction* 10).

In fact, Margot Finn argues that law and literature scholarship, when it is historically knowledgeable and nuanced, could help bring out the plurality of legal practice in the Victorian era. She suggests that literary critics writing about the law need to keep triangulating their disciplinary intersection with that of legal history, otherwise running the risk of remaining "wedded to precisely the conventional paradigms that recent legal histories have been at pains to subvert" (Finn 142).

This approach also means letting go of the disciplinary separation implied by the conjunction in "law *and* literature" and to stop viewing the two through the disciplinary specters the disciplines themselves have created of and for each other (Peters 448).[7] Focusing on the striking similarities and telling differences between law and literature of the nineteenth century, while fascinating in its own right, runs the risk of consolidating them as abstract categories rather than opening them up to scrutiny. Even when attuned to the particularities of historical context, much law-and-lit scholarship is weakened by the tendency to categorize law and literature as "competing" institutions, reifying rather than questioning common conceptions and misconception about both law (that it is narrow, authoritative, pragmatic) and literature (copious, complex, more equitable) (Pettitt 75–76). Moreover, in order to maintain this distinction between law and literature, scholars tend to rely uncritically on a set of deceptively distinct oppositions: between character and identity, private and public, romantic and realistic, empirical and non-empirical.

Reading legal and literary texts together, not as two discourses on opposite sides of an imaginary divide but as two discourses and practices taking part in a shared endeavor, enables an exciting investigation of the relationship between a local, individual occurrence and its larger institutional and philosophical meanings and implications. To do so we need to continue following Trollope, for whom both law and literature were strategies of representation of real life, a way of understanding and regulating the complexities of social and personal relations and structures. To bear this out, I now turn briefly to the legal regulation of property in the novels, pointing out both the substantial existing scholarship in the field and themes and approaches that could be further explored.

Trollope's legal themes and questions rarely focus on crime or criminality, and when these questions do arise, they seem secondary to that which looms largest in Trollope: property and family law. In fact, one might argue that all of Trollope's legal questions, whether about inheritance, contract, divorce, or legitimacy, are derivative of an overarching concern with property.[8] As Frederik Van Dam has argued, the alienation of property is at the heart of Trollope's fiction (801). This alienation is of course a social one: after all, property does not designate one's relation to a thing, but rather one's relation to others. Thought about in this way – as Trollope evidently did – property, and especially landed property, becomes an overdetermined nexus of social organization and structure, a way of communal and cultural regulation. Moreover, property, its regulation, circulation, and transmission (whether through commerce or along the lines of kinship), was a synecdoche of Trollope's aforementioned grand obsession with what it meant to be English in a period in which the meaning and value of Englishness were shifting.

One of the most productive locations where this dynamic between law, property, and Englishness plays out is in the congested relationship between property (landed and portable) and the English gentleman. Trollope's novels betray a repeated anxiety over the elusive meanings and manifestations of the English gentleman: writing in his *Autobiography*, Trollope insists on the superiority (albeit embattled) inherent in the English gentleman. At the same time, he is at a loss to describe or define this quality: "A man who publicly claims exclusive rights (and commissions) to being a gentleman," writes Trollope, "would be defied to define the term [gentleman], and would fail should he attempt to do so. But he would know what he meant, and so very probably would they who defied him" (38). Although novels such as *The Way We Live Now* and *The Prime Minister* seem to recognize that a gentleman need no longer be defined simply by his ownership of land, they repeatedly return to a gentleman's relationship to property, which in one way or another always holds the key to his identity. In other words, even when a gentleman is defined by his behavior or lineage, landed property, though often lost or diminished, can never be far behind (Ben-Yishai, "Common Endeavor" 161–2). Discussions of property and its legal regulation are thus always discussions of individual (gentleman) and collective (English) identity, a nexus to which Trollope returned repeatedly and that scholars have yet to explore fully (Gilmour; Letwin).

And yet, Trollope's preoccupation with property is most powerfully and irrevocably connected to the legal regulation of family relations. After all, ownership of property can be transferred primarily in two main ways: through commercial transactions with strangers or through kinship. According to the separate spheres logic of nineteenth-century classical liberalism, commerce and the family belonged to discrete realms and the law was to avoid intervening in the latter.[9] Family law – largely concerned with inheritance and marriage, the two primary means through which property is non-commercially reassigned – is an important and knotty exception to this ideal. And indeed, family law, and especially the regulation of the transfer of property along the lines of kin, brings up some of the most vexed questions in Victorian culture, connecting, as it does, the private and the public, the intimate and the social. These issues were thus at the heart of some of the most important legislative reforms of the Victorian period, reflecting and constructing the changing relations between men and women, the transformations in English identity and commonality, and what Henry Maine famously identified as the shift "from status to contract." Not surprisingly then, though with some important examples to the contrary, Trollope's novels address these questions at their thorniest by dealing primarily with the complications arising from the transfer of landed property due to structures of kinship and family, rather than through commercial transactions.[10]

For example, Aviva Briefel shows how *The Eustace Diamonds* responds to the anxieties surrounding married women's emerging status as property holders and the reform of the married women's property laws beginning in the late 1860s. Dagni Bredesen addresses similar concerns in *Can You Forgive Her?* and *The Eustace Diamonds* through the doctrine of *couverture*, the legal "covering" of a wife by her husband.[11] *He Knew He Was Right* not only unsettles the definitions of marriage but also – as Wendy Jones shows in her analysis of marriage as a contract – raises the increasingly visible specter of divorce.[12]

Moreover, gender- and family-based transfer of property ownership was not reserved to marriage but also prominent in the laws and practices that governed inheritance. The many examples of entailment (whether through primogeniture or other arrangements) as well as the rights of widows to property left them, by bequest or by law, by their husbands were all expertly explored by Trollope. Indeed, as Frank shows, a will is not only a way of transmitting material property between generations but also a way of transmitting culture: in the early Victorian period the will became a nexus for the construction of identity and character and for imagining the relationship of these private dimensions with a social order and economy founded on property (*Law Literature, and the Transmission of Culture*).

The anxiety over inheritance and kinship explains yet another major concern of the period, that of illegitimacy (Finn, Lobban, and Taylor). The dilemma raised explicitly in *Ralph the Heir*, which pits an illegitimate yet deserving heir against a legitimate and undeserving one, comes up repeatedly, if more obliquely in his later fiction (Taylor). For Trollope, it seems, the problem was often not one of legal illegitimacy (being born out-of-wedlock), but of otherwise arriving illegally or sometimes simply unconventionally at a more equitable allocation of property (see Deborah Denenholz Morse on the inheritance of Wharton Hall in *The Prime Minister*, as well as similar conundrums in *Orley Farm*, *Doctor Thorne*, and *The Way We Live Now*). Echoing yet again Maine's transition "from status to contract" Trollope examines the viability and legitimacy of traditional status-based modes of inheritance, such as primogeniture and other forms of entail. The theme of illegitimacy thus reflects on a larger ethical question: the legitimacy of an ethical result got at by illegitimate means (Luban). The fact that the more equitable result is usually made clear and the reader knows who the deserving party is does not make the solution to the moral dilemma any easier to come by. At the same time that his novels advocate for a more equitable result, so are they invested in the continuity and constancy engendered by adhering to legal procedure.

Trollope is thus far from voicing a simplistic critique of rigid legal proceeding in favor of a larger understanding of justice and morality. Indeed, his writing resists this very opposition. As is evident from novels as early as *The Warden*, rather than depicting the moral in opposition to the formal and procedural, Trollope insists that the two are often the same. He thus repeatedly asks his characters and readers to debate the merits and demerits of formal justice and substantive justice (insisting that both are, indeed forms of justice) though not necessarily to come to a definitive conclusion.

Most crucially, all of these examples serve to show that the law – for Trollope, and in Trollope's work – is not a separate sphere of influence but one that is a necessary and inextricable part of the reality both he and his characters inhabit. The law can no longer be considered simply as a set of rules and decisions but a living, dynamic construct containing disparate entities in varying degrees of tension with each other, one that I here call "legal culture" and that is akin to what Patricia Ewick and Susan Sibley call "legality":

> Legality consists of cultural schema and resources that operate to define and pattern social life. At the same time that schemas and resources shape social relations, they must also be continually produced and worked on – invoked and deployed – by individual and group actors. Legality is not inserted into situations; rather, through repeated invocations of the law and legal concepts and terminology, as well as through imaginative and unusual associations between legality and other social structures, legality is constituted through everyday actions and practices.
>
> (*Ewick and Sibley* 43)

Legal culture is thus not only plural and dynamic, as I have already claimed earlier, but also more capacious than we normally think of it, encompassing much that is outside the narrower confines of what we tend to call "the law."

In this understanding, Trollope's novels neither reflect legal culture nor stand in contrast to it. Rather, they participate in that culture in what Ewick and Sibley identify as a "mediating process through which social interactions and local processes aggregate and condense into institutions and powerful structures" (38). In other words, reading Trollope allows us to understand the very process by which a legal culture is constructed. Attention to legal culture as a practice thus

> attempts to keep alive the tension between structure and agency, constraint and choice. . . . Every time a person interprets some event in terms of legal concepts or terminology – whether to applaud or criticize, whether to appropriate or resist – legality is produced. The production may include innovations as well as faithful replication. Either way, repeated invocation of the law sustains its capacity to comprise social relations.
>
> *(Ewick and Sibley 45)*

Trollope, I thus suggest, not only understands legal culture but also participates in it; his fiction does not (or not only) represent or critique "the law" but is an active agent in the British legal culture of the mid-Victorian period.

Understanding this, we can bring more strands of a legal culture to bear on each other, especially those that are not immediately or obviously part of this culture. For example, Frederik Van Dam examines jurisprudence – the way that Trollope engages with the philosophical aspects of the law – and Trollope's use of free indirect discourse in *The Eustace Diamonds* and *John Caldigate* to articulate an alternate understanding of conscience, conceptualized through a popular understanding of equity. These new insights enable a return to the complex questions of morality explored earlier by scholars such as Ruth apRoberts, Geoffrey Harvey, and R. D. McMaster, connecting ideas, social practices, cultural form, and local historical behavior. They also add another dimension to Trollope's fascination with and repeated scrutiny of other, not expressly legal institutions, such as the Church of England, the British government, and the political system.

Van Dam's example brings me to the final point I want to make, and to what I regard as the most exciting aspect of Trollope scholarship today – namely, the questions of literary form and the various ways it takes part in constructing (and being constructed by) the legal culture with which it engages. Turning to the language of his fiction, Coral Lansbury argues that the "reasonable" and "rational" world presented by the legal form of his novels can be ascribed not to Trollope the lawyer (which he wasn't) but rather to Trollope the civil servant, one who spent as much time writing official reports as he did novels. She traces this legal form to John Fredrick Archbold's 1821 *A Digest of the Law Relative to Pleading and Evidence in Actions Real Personal and Mixed*, a treatise that had been adopted by the secretary to the Post Office in Trollope's time, Sir Francis Freeling. The legalistic style it advocated was strictly imposed on all Post Office employees, including Anthony Trollope, who learned to write statements that were "certain, positive, and true," in a style that was "plain, simple and unadorned," and based on an implicit "reliance upon a complete and honest rendering of the evidence" (Archbold qtd. in Lansbury 15; 16; 20).

Lansbury was but the first to relate the law in Trollope to form rather than theme, a tendency that has lately been revisited and expanded. For example, recent scholarship, including my own, explores the epistemology of Trollope's realism: the ways his characters, narrators, and implied readers understand what is truthful and what is real. These studies pay close attention to the (narrative and non-narrative) forms through which law gains its authority and conviction: how lawyers plead, how precedent is invoked, how wills are written and constructed as authoritative. Combining these formal analyses with similar ones in the literary realm allows us to relate, for example, Victorian legal empiricism to the epistemology that also undergirds the realist novel (Ben-Yishai, *Common Precedents*; Frank, *Law, Literature and the Transmission of Culture*; Krueger;

Schramm; Van Dam).[13] Similar questions regarding the forms of evidence and the ways in which Trollope constructs his narratorial authority could lead to an important reconsideration of the forms and ethics of realist narration and of literary realism more widely.

To exemplify this approach briefly let us turn to *Is He Popenjoy?*, a novel whose plot of illegitimacy brings up many of the concerns I have already raised here, most prominently the question of legal plurality, as the identity of the next Lord Popenjoy rests on several different laws and jurisdictions. In addition, as Jenny Bourne Taylor has already expertly showed, "legitimacy is always an effect of an essentially illusory symbolic power" (57); the legal question is but a nexus of the perceived plight of the waning aristocracy, of the ability of money to buy rank, and of the Victorian social anxiety about the infiltration of the foreign and different. In marking the middle ground of propriety between the weak, noble George Germain and his social-climbing and greedy father-in-law, the dean of Brotherton, the lawyer Mr. Battle serves as the novel's commonsensical center. Note that the legal question, "is he Popenjoy?" makes adversaries of the infant foreign child and the dean, both of whom demand recognition from the family ensconced, almost barricaded, within Manor Cross. The family members try to figure out which of the two outsiders is more threatening to them: "the daughters, though they had at first been very strong in their aversion to the foreign mother and the foreign boy, were now averse to [the dean] also, on other grounds" (Ch. 49). Their allegiances constantly shift during the novel, betraying the slippery foundation on which these questions of status stand, even in this highly conservative novel.

But what these shifting allegiances betray most surprisingly, perhaps, is the similar formal foundation of illegitimacy and the realist novel: that both are based on a presumption of the way things are: "I think one always does take things for granted till somebody proves that it is not so," says Mrs. Houghton (Ch. 53). She is speaking about the presumption of legitimacy of her cousin's son, but might as well be talking about the novel, for this presumption, like other legal presumptions and like realist fiction, marks the normal mode of things, the way things could be and most probably are. By showing the way that different characters at different points in the novel adhere (or not) to the legal presumption, the novel reveals the inherent instability of "taking things for granted." And yet the social order depends on these legal conventions, if only to mark a deviation that reinforces its norm, just as the realist novel depends on conjecture and probability to establish the truthfulness of its fiction. Presumption paradoxically comes to anchor the foundations of stability in the legal and textual culture of the novel.

Throughout this essay, I have proposed that those writing about Trollope and the law consider his writing as a form of participation in a legal culture, thus challenging more monolithic conceptions of the law. By ending with the implications of Trollope's legal culture for reading literary form, I hope to have made clear that in so doing, this kind of scholarship has the potential not only to promote a more capacious understanding of the law but also to challenge our own assumptions about Victorian literary form, about realism, about culture, and about the way we make meaning in the world.

Notes

1 Some even relate to the way that Trollope's novels were brought back to him in cases in which he appeared as witness for the Post Office (Cunningham).
2 In referring to Englishness, I mean something more capacious than just English nationality. Indeed, for Trollope, Englishness was an ever-elusive quality, as desirable as it was shifting. See, most recently, Deborah Denenholtz Morse's *Reforming Trollope: Race, Gender and Englishness in the Novels of Anthony Trollope*.
3 In his magisterial compendium, *Everyone and Everything in Trollope*, George Newlin lists and discusses five novels in the section "Family Law": *Orley Farm* (1861), *Ralph the Heir* (1871), *John Caldigate* (1879),

Cousin Henry (1879), and *Mr. Scarborough's Family* (1882). Other novels that are also often discussed in legal Trollope scholarship are, most prominently, *The Eustace Diamonds* (1872) and its Palliser companions, *Can You Forgive Her?* (1864–65), *Phineas Finn* (1869), *and Phineas Redux* (1874), as well as *The Warden* (1855), *He Knew He Was Right* (1869), and *The Macdermots of Ballycloran* (1847).

4 Cunningham estimates that the novels feature over 100 lawyer characters (93).
5 Interestingly, Albert D. Pionke registers the competition between law and literature, mentioned earlier, as a **professional** one, between lawyers and novelists, a rivalry over "professional stature and a finite amount of charismatic authority in Victorian England" (130). On the representation of lawyers as representing others, see also Paula Jean Reiter's discussion of *Orley Farm* and the infamous Bartlett case.
6 For another discussion of legal plurality in Trollope see my discussion of common law, positive law, and natural law in "A Common Endeavor."
7 While Peters's description is persuasive, her analysis of the field necessitates ignoring much of the more historically nuanced and culturally based scholarship in recent years that engaged both legal and literary texts to great effect, such as much of the scholarship cited here. For more on this see the introduction to my book (4).
8 For further discussion of Trollope and property see, among others, Elsie Michie, Andrew H. Miller, Jeff Nunokawa, and John Plotz. The case of *Phineas Redux* is an important exception – politics and, as Cathrine O. Frank has shown, the not-unrelated legal question of divorce are at stake here, rather than property ("Trial Separations").
9 In her work on Victorian liberalism, Anat Rosenberg challenges this division; she shows how *The Way We Live Now* problematizes the separation of spheres demanded by liberal contract theory by juxtaposing marriage promises with their ostensible opposite – commercial promises.
10 Focusing on the world of commerce and finance and not on landed property, TWWLN is arguably the most important of these contrary examples. Note, however, that Melmotte's final downfall is precipitated by his attempt to purchase an estate for himself, to clinch his status as an Englishman.
11 For more on the societal roles of autonomous women and changing definitions of marriage in *Can You Forgive Her?* see also Sharon Marcus, and more generally Christine Higgins.
12 See also Frank, "Trial Separations." Also more generally, if from another disciplinary perspective, see Janette Rutterford and Josephine Maltby in the *Accounting Historians Journal*.
13 See also more generally Alexander Welsh, and Jonathan Grossman.

Works cited

apRoberts, Ruth. *The Moral Trollope*. Athens: Ohio University Press, 1971. Print.
Arkin, Marc. "Trollope and the Law." *The New Criterion* (October 2007): 23–7. Web.
Ben-Yishai, Ayelet. "A Common Endeavor: Anthony Trollope and the Law." *The Cambridge Companion to Anthony Trollope*. Ed. Carolyn Dever and Lisa Niles. Cambridge: Cambridge University Press, 2011. 155–68. Print.
———. *Common Precedents: The Presentness of the Past in Victorian Law and Fiction*. Oxford: Oxford University Press, 2013. Print.
Bredesen, Dagni. "'What's a Woman to Do?': Managing Money and Manipulating Fictions in Trollope's *Can You Forgive Her?* and *The Eustace Diamonds*." *Victorian Review* 31.2 (2005): 99–122. Web.
Briefel, Aviva. "Tautological Crimes: Why Women Can't Steal Jewels." *NOVEL: A Forum on Fiction* 37.1/2 (2003): 135–57. Web.
Cunningham, Valentine. "Anthony Trollope and Law, Laws, Legalisms and Assorted Legislations." *REAL: Yearbook of Research in English and American Literature* 18 (2002): 89–107. Print.
Dolin, Kieran. *A Critical Introduction to Law and Literature*. Cambridge: Cambridge University Press, 2007. Print.
———. *Fiction and the Law: Legal Discourse in Victorian and Modernist Literature*. Cambridge: Cambridge University Press, 1999. Print.
Ewick, Patricia, and Susan S. Sibley. *The Common Place of Law: Stories from Everyday Life*. Chicago Series in Law and Society. Chicago: University of Chicago Press, 1998. Print.
Finn, Margot. "Victorian Law, Literature and History: Three Ships Passing in the Night." *Journal of Victorian Culture* 7.1 (2002): 134–46. Web.
Finn, Margot, Michael Lobban, and Jenny Bourne Taylor, eds. *Legitimacy and Illegitimacy in Nineteenth-Century Law, Literature and History*. Palgrave Studies in Nineteenth-Century Writing and Culture. New York: Palgrave Macmillan, 2010. Print.

Frank, Cathrine O. *Law, Literature, and the Transmission of Culture in England, 1837–1925*. Aldershot: Ashgate, 2010. Print.

———. "Trial Separations: Divorce, Disestablishment, and Home Rule in *Phineas Redux*." *College Literature* 35.3 (2008): 30–56. Web.

Gardner, Simon. "Trashing with Trollope: A Deconstruction of the Postal Rules in Contract." *Oxford Journal of Legal Studies* 12 (1992): 170–94. Web.

Gilmour, Robin. *The Idea of the Gentleman in the Victorian Novel*. London: Allen & Unwin, 1981. Print.

Grossman, Jonathan H. *The Art of Alibi: English Law Courts and the Novel*. Baltimore, MD: Johns Hopkins University Press, 2002. Print.

Harvey, Geoffrey. "A Parable of Justice: Drama and Rhetoric in *Mr. Scarborough's Family*." *Nineteenth Century Fiction* 37.3 (1982): 419–29. Web.

Higgins, Christine. "The Woman Business: Mill, Trollope and the Law." *Law Text Culture* 1.1 (1994): 63–80. Web.

Jones, Wendy. "Feminism, Fiction and Contract Theory: Trollope's *He Knew He Was Right*." *Criticism* 36.3 (Summer 1994): 401–414. Web.

Krueger, Christine L. *Reading for the Law*. Charlottesville: University of Virginia Press, 2010. Print.

Lacey, Nicola. "The Way We Lived Then: The Legal Profession and the 19th-Century Novel." *Sydney Law Review* 33 (2011): 599–621. Web.

Lansbury, Coral. *The Reasonable Man: Trollope's Legal Fiction*. Princeton: Princeton University Press, 1981. Print.

Letwin, Shirley Robin. *The Gentleman in Trollope: Individuality and Moral Conduct*. London: Macmillan, 1982. Print.

Luban, David. "A Midrash on Rabbi Shaffer and Rabbi Trollope." *Notre Dame Law Review* 77 (2001–2002): 889. Web.

Lyons, Paul. "The Morality of Irony and Unreliable Narrative in Trollope's *The Warden* and *Barchester Towers*." *South Atlantic Review* 54.1 (1989): 41–54. Web.

Maine, Henry. *Ancient Law*. London: J.M. Dent, 1917. Print.

Marcus, Sharon. "Contracting Female Marriage in Anthony Trollope's *Can You Forgive Her?*" *Nineteenth-Century Literature* 60.3 (2005): 291–325. Web.

McMaster, Rowland D. *Trollope and the Law*. New York: Palgrave Macmillan, 1986. Print.

Michie, Elsie. "Buying Brains: Trollope, Oliphant and Vulgar Victorian Commerce." *Victorian Studies* 44.1 (2001): 76–97. Web.

Miller, Andrew H. *Novels Behind Glass: Commodity Culture and Victorian Narrative*. Cambridge: Cambridge University Press, 2008. Print.

Morse, Deborah Denenholz. *Reforming Trollope: Race, Gender and Englishness in the Novels of Anthony Trollope*. Burlington: Ashgate, 2013. Print.

———. *Women in Trollope's Palliser Novels*. Ann Arbor: University of Michigan Research Press, 1987. Print.

Newlin, George. *Everyone and Everything in Trollope*. Ed. George Newlin. Vol. 1–4. Armonk, NY: M. E. Sharpe, 2005. Print.

Nunokawa, Jeff. *The Afterlife of Property: Domestic Security and the Realist Novel*. Princeton, NJ: Princeton University Press, 1994. Print.

Peters, Julie Stone. "Law, Literature, and the Vanishing Real: On the Future of an Interdisciplinary Illusion." *PMLA* 120.2 (2005): 442–53. Web.

Pettitt, Clare. "Legal Subjects, Legal Objects: The Law and Victorian Fiction." *A Concise Companion to the Victorian Novel*. Ed. Francis O'Gorman. Malden: Blackwell, 2008. 71–90. Print.

Pionke, Albert D. "Navigating 'Those Terrible Meshes of the Law': Legal Realism in Anthony Trollope's *Orley Farm* and *The Eustace Diamonds*." *English Literary History* 77.1 (2010): 129–57. Web.

Plotz, John. *Portable Property: Victorian Culture on the Move*. Princeton: Princeton University Press, 2008. Print.

Reiter, Paula Jean. "Husbands, Wives, and Lawyers: Gender Roles and Professional Representation in Trollope and the Adelaide Bartlett Case." *College Literature* 25.1 (1998): 41–62. Web.

Rosenberg, Anat. "The Promise of Liberalism: The Victorian Novel and Contract Law." Diss. University of Tel Aviv, 2010. Print.

Roth, Alan. "He Thought He Was Right (But Wasn't): Property Law in Anthony Trollope's *The Eustace Diamonds*." *Stanford Law Review* 44.4 (1992): 879–97. Web.

Rutterford, Janette, and Josephine Maltby. "Frank Must Marry Money: Men, Women and Property in Trollope's Novels." *Accounting Historians Journal* 33.2 (2006): 169–99. Web.

Schramm, Jan-Melissa. *Testimony and Advocacy in Victorian Law, Literature, and Theology*. Cambridge: Cambridge University Press, 2000. Print.

Sugarman, David, and Gerry Rubin. "Towards a New History of Law and Material Society in England, 1750–1914." *Law, Economy and Society, 1750–1914: Essays in the History of English Law*. Ed. G. R. Rubin. Abingdon, England: Professional Books, 1984. 1–123. Print.

Taylor, Jenny Bourne. "Bastards to the Time: Legitimacy as Legal Fiction in Trollope's Novels." *The Politics of Gender in Anthony Trollope's Novels: New Readings for the Twenty-First Century*. Ed. Margaret Markwick, Deborah Denenholz Morse, and Regenia Gagnier. Surrey, England: Ashgate, 2009. 45–59. Print.

Trollope, Anthony. *An Autobiography*. Oxford World's Classics. Oxford: Oxford University Press, 2009. Print.

———. *Is He Popenjoy?* Oxford World's Classics. Oxford: Oxford University Press, 1986. Print.

Van Dam, Frederik. "Victorian Instincts: Anthony Trollope and the Philosophy of Law." *Literature Compass* 9.11 (2012): 801–12. Web.

Welsh, Alexander. *Strong Representations: Narrative and Circumstantial Evidence in England*. Baltimore, MD: Johns Hopkins University Press, 1992. Print.

Windolph, Francis Lyman. *Reflections of the Law in Literature*. Philadelphia: University of Pennsylvania Press, 1956. Print.

22
TROLLOPE AND AGING

Kay Heath

Of all Victorian novelists, Anthony Trollope may have been the most attentive to issues of age. His emphasis on "the necessity of progression in character, – of marking the changes in men and women which would naturally be produced by the lapse of years" (*Autobiography* ch. 17) reveals an interest not merely in old age itself but aging as a process. Instead of focusing on the elderly pensioners of Hiram's Hospital, *The Warden* centers around Septimus Harding wondering in his fifties whether he and his sinecure are outmoded. *Miss Mackenzie*'s questionable marriageability intrigued Trollope, as a thirtyish spinster considered too old to be wooed – until she inherits money. Trollope especially was drawn to liminal moments that test whether youthfulness can be sustained. Trollope penned few fictional words about actual agedness, instead depicting characters' relational challenges as marriageability and profession decline and the young become competitors. Writing about his own potential obsolescence in letters and his autobiography, he posited decline only to qualify or even deny the possibility. Trollope's works are sensitive to aging as an aspect of lived experience, reflecting and questioning how culture defines age.

Scholars will find Trollope's novels rich ground for age studies, yet few sustained examinations of his approach to aging have appeared. Karen Chase's *The Victorians and Old Age* and my own *Aging by the Book* are the first book-length studies to consider Victorian constructions of advancing age, and both return repeatedly to Trollope.[1] While I consider Trollope's gendered depictions of midlife anxiety, Chase explores the surprising agency across a wide variety of his older characters. Beyond these two books, aging remains a relatively untouched area of Trollope studies though his oeuvre offers a rich and detailed picture of Victorian consciousness about aging.[2]

Aging may have been so significant to Trollope because he wrote a majority of his fiction – thirty-two of forty-seven novels – after his fiftieth birthday, roughly the point at which he began to describe himself as "old." In his late forties, Trollope felt at the height of his powers, recalling in his autobiography that at forty-seven, after two decades working in Ireland and then returning to England, where he excelled in the dual career of novelist and postal surveyor: "I now felt that I had gained my object. . . . a position among literary men, and . . . an income on which I might live in ease and comfort" (*Autobiography* ch. 9). Two years later, however, turning forty-nine, Trollope applied to be assistant secretary of the Post Office and was passed over for a man eight years his junior. He confesses to "a feeling existing at that time that I had not been altogether well treated," in part, as he explains, because "I did not . . . wish that any younger officer should . . . pass over my head" (*Autobiography* ch. 15). At fifty-two, he retired from the Post Office to devote more time to writing and editing, his decision influenced by the lost promotion (*Autobiography* ch. 15). He also attributed his unsuccessful run for Parliament a year later to aging: "fifty-three was too late an age at which to commence a new career" (*Autobiography* ch. 16).

As his sense of aging began to solidify, Trollope regularly described himself as old while simultaneously resisting the descriptor. At fifty-seven, he wrote to George Eliot and G. H. Lewes, "I am beginning to find myself too old to be 18 months away from home," but continues, "Not that I am fatigued bodily; – but mentally I cannot be at ease with all the new people and the new things" (Hall, *Letters* 557). At fifty-eight and suffering from hearing loss, Trollope wrote, "For such troubles a man ought to be prepared as he grows old," but then lamented, "Why should anything go wrong in our bodies? . . . Why should there be decay? – why death?" (Hall, *Letters* 599) – his characteristic approach to decline.

In his autobiography, Trollope claims to write from "the garrulity of old age" during his sixties, yet he also posits and then denies authorial obsolescence (*Autobiography* ch. 1). Recalling that friends advised "at fifty-five I ought to give up the fabrication of love stories" (*Autobiography* ch. 19), he mentions *Ralph the Heir*, written at fifty-four, as weak enough "almost to have justified" their claims (*Autobiography* ch. 19) but then counters that *The Eustace Diamonds*, completed at fifty-five, proves them wrong: "There is not much love in it, but what there is is good" (*Autobiography* ch. 19). He also conjectures that the Palliser novels would determine his reputation, written from forty-eight into his sixties (*Autobiography* ch. 20), and he touts experience over youth, concluding, "many young fail also because they endeavor to tell stories when they have none to tell" (*Autobiography* ch. 12).

Trollope also resisted the physical limitations of aging. At fifty-six, he describes his "half fear that I may never hunt any more" (Hall, *Letters* 543), and by his early sixties, confessed, "I am . . . now old for such work." He then adds, however, "But I ride still after the same fashion, with a boy's energy" and describes having "gone through a long run to the finish, keeping a place, not of glory, but of credit among my juniors" – a vision of mature competence that contrasts sharply with his boyhood misery (*Autobiography* ch. 10). The furious pace and boisterous personality characteristic of Trollope from early maturity until death continuously imbued his entire adult life with youthful energy (Hall, *Biography* 508–9).

Trollope's fascination with and sensitivity to age are apparent in his fiction. Victorian aging norms differed significantly from current Western constructions: women were considered middle-aged in their thirties, at least a decade earlier than men, while old age began in the late fifties to sixties for both, dependent on a variety of factors, including physical fitness (Heath 10–12). Men and women appear in Trollope's love plots long past the years conventionally associated with romance in Victorian culture.

Critics frequently have commented on Trollope's remarkable ability to depict the challenges of Victorian womanhood, a skill evident when he employs and then critiques ageist stereotypes. Richard Mullen and James Munson note that Trollope's spinsters portray a Victorian reality – during Trollope's mid-thirties, 8 percent of British women were spinsters, but by his death in 1882, the number had doubled (471). Some of his characters struggling with age are surprisingly young due to spinsterhood's constraints. Like other Victorian novelists, Trollope represents spinsterhood beginning around age thirty, proclaimed forthrightly by Mrs. Burton in *The Claverings*: "I think I'd feel ashamed of myself to have a daughter not married, or not in the way to be married afore she's thirty" (*Claverings* ch. 4; Mullen and Munson 471). However, Trollope frequently resisted the convention that spinsters' lives were grim. In *Mr. Scarborough's Family*, fortyish Matilda Thoroughbung happily relinquishes her brief engagement, preferring to retain her money and her housemate, Miss Tickle. In the same novel, Dolly Grey, though she appears decades older than her thirty years, rejects a marriage proposal to remain contentedly with her father (Mullen and

Munson 470). Trollope did famously asseverate "the best right a woman has is the right to a husband" (*North America* 262), but in characters like these Trollope recognized spinsterhood's pleasures.

However, Trollope also was sympathetic to women's fear of looming spinsterhood. Mary Gresham identifies a vicious double bind, telling her friend Martha Dunstable in *Framley Parsonage*, "All unmarried women are necessarily in the market, but if they behave themselves properly they make no signs" (*Framley* ch. 38). In *The Way We Live Now*, Georgiana Longestaffe equates the dire consequences of marriage market failure with drowning:

> Twelve years had been passed by her since first she plunged into the stream . . . and she was as far as ever from the bank; nay, farther. . . . [and] must strike out with rapid efforts, unless, indeed, she would abandon herself and let the waters close over her head.
>
> (*Way We* ch. 95)

Trollope poignantly demonstrated spinsterhood's perils in Lady Mabel Grex of *The Duke's Children* as "a tragic figure" (Morse, *Women* 125). Keenly aware she's a burden to her father, Lady Mabel waffles between sincere love for penniless Frank Tregear and the necessity of marrying for money. She voices frustration at the social hypocrisy forcing women to "work hard" at husband hunting while accusing them of "sinning against their sex" when they do (*Duke's Children* ch. 10), and she eventually "equates marriage with . . . suicide" (Morse, *Women* 127). Realizing too late that love should trump money, she loses Frank to another, and Trollope leaves her isolated in a ramshackle Scottish estate, mourning, "A girl unless she marries becomes nothing, as I have become nothing now" (*Duke's Children* ch. 77).

Trollope combines censure with guarded admiration of Arabella Trefoil in *The American Senator* as she desperately connives to marry the richest suitor. Her mercenary husband hunting is grueling work against the clock:

> she remembered her age, her many seasons, the hard work of her toilet, those tedious, long and bitter quarrels with her mother, the ever-renewed trouble of her smiles, the hopelessness of her future should she smile in vain to the last, and the countless miseries of her endless visitings.
>
> (*American Senator* ch. 32)

Arabella is manipulative and false, from her fake hair to her heavy makeup, and Trollope asserts that in her, he "wished to express the depth of [his] scorn for women who run down husbands" (Hall, *Letters* 702). Yet he understands her dilemma: "How might she best avoid the misfortune of poverty for the twenty, thirty, or forty years which might be accorded to her?. . . . She must live" (*American Senator* ch. 49). He writes, "The critics . . . will tell me that she is unwomanly, unnatural," but continues, "Think of her virtues; how she works, how true she is to her vocation, how little there is of self indulgence, or of idleness" (Hall, *Letters* 710–11). Marrying her to a civil servant with whom she anticipates a tedious life in Patagonia, Trollope admonishes her mercenary attitude but honors the work ethic behind her necessary quest.

Trollope also contravenes the spinster stereotype by showing that, given property, such women could be marriageable, and he bestows love matches on several. Martha Dunstable in *Framley Parsonage*, "neither young nor beautiful" (*Framley* ch. 3), with inherited wealth from sales of the lowly "Oil of Lebanon," a patent medicine, is pursued by several suitors and ultimately settles into a happy, loving marriage with Dr. Thorne. Trollope stated his intention to write *Miss Mackenzie* "without any love," by writing about "a very unattractive old maid" (*Autobiography* ch. 10).

When the confirmed spinster of thirty-five becomes an heiress, however, she is pursued by several suitors, and then, Trollope quips, "even she was in love before the end of the book and made a romantic marriage with an old man" (*Autobiography* ch. 10). With John Ball, an "old man" in his mid-forties, she enjoys a sexually charged union (Heath 151–5).

Trollope also critiqued Victorian expectations that aging women, especially mothers, should give up on love. The quintessential midlife woman was a sacrificial mother who, presumably postmenopausal and therefore non-reproductive, directed her energies toward her children's marital quest.[3] The Widow Dale declares in *The Small House at Allington*, the "theory of her life . . . [was] that she should bury herself in order that her [marriageable] daughters might live well above ground" (*Small House* ch. 3). Similarly, "The Courtship of Susan Bell" describes a timid widow who "longed for . . . [love] as well as feared it; – for her girls, I mean; all such feelings for herself were long laid under ground" ("Courtship" 18–19). Trollope's metaphors of live burial expose the deathlike nature of idealized, sexless matronhood, and he proclaims that the Widow Dale was "wrong" not to let herself "be young in spirit at forty" (*Small House* ch. 3). Lady Desmond in *Castle Richmond*, Lady Carbury in *The Way We Live Now*, and Lady Mason in *Orley Farm* all are midlife mothers who become romantically involved.

While matrons were encouraged to mentor the young, Trollope faults aging women who meddle in the lives of younger people, refusing to relinquish control. Philip Launay in "The Lady of Launay" sums up Trollope's usual approach to intergenerational power struggles: "It is the old story. . . . Young people and old people very often will not think alike: but it is the young people who generally have their way" ("Lady" 829). Though his mother demands he marry within the peerage, Philip "felt that he had a right to marry whom he pleased . . . any dictation from his mother in such a matter was a tyranny not to be endured" ("Lady" 823). As he predicted, Philip triumphs, marrying a commoner. Similarly, Lucy Robarts must win over her future mother-in-law, Lady Lufton, in *Framley Parsonage*, and Lady Arabella Gresham (née de Courcy) in *Doctor Thorne* opposes her son's marriage until illegitimate Mary Thorne inherits a fortune. The widowed Countess Lovell in *Lady Anna* prefers her daughter die rather than marry a lowly tailor, first disowning her, and then trying to kill her sweetheart – which, as Morse points out, "is Trollope's final argument for the derangement of her ideas" (*Reforming* 58). In *Mr. Scarborough's Family*, Trollope suggests such women ultimately regret their despotism. Mrs. Mountjoy, acquiescing to her daughter's choice, writes her own candidate, an inveterate gambler, "It has been the longing of my heart that you two should live together. . . . But such longings are, I think, wicked, and are seldom realized" (*Mr. Scarborough's* ch. 61).

Aging women especially transgress their duty by becoming involved with their protégée's suitor. In *The Last Chronicle of Barset*, Mrs. Dobbs Broughton contrives a courtship between Clara Van Siever and the painter Conway Dalrymple with whom she has conducted a flirtation herself. Only in her mid-thirties, Broughton is a self-imposed matchmaker for Clara, helping her avoid her mother's choice, Mr. Musselboro. By the time Clara marries the artist, Broughton is a widow, and she then weds Musselboro. Artificial and manipulative in comparison to the sincere, natural Clara, Maria is an unseemly spectacle as she takes her protégée's leavings for herself.

Though Trollope denounces meddling mothers and competitive duennas, he also depicts the most unseemly with compassion. *Castle Richmond*'s dowager countess of Desmond disapproves when Owen Fitzgerald courts her daughter, because "though . . . an unfit suitor for an earl's daughter, it might still be possible that he should be acceptable to an earl's widow" (*Castle* ch. 4). Owen is fifteen years younger than her thirty-eight years, but people assume they'll wed. When Owen pursues seventeen-year-old Clara instead, the countess is jealous, thinking bitterly that Owen "had regarded [her] merely as the mother of the woman he loved," as "old and wrinkled and ugly" (*Castle* ch. 16). Despite this unsavory scenario, Trollope asks the reader for understanding rather than judgment. While Lady Desmond prefers the rugged, Celtic man, daughter Clara weds the good-natured, steady Herbert Fitzgerald. Trollope grants the countess a godly veneer when she tells Owen, "I swore on my knees that I would love you only as my son, – as my dear, dear son. Nay, Owen, I did; on my knees before my God" (*Castle* ch. 43). He seeks the reader's mercy with biblical allusions: "Unfortunate girl, marred in thy childhood by that wrinkled earl with the gloating eyes; or marred rather by thine own vanity! Those flesh-pots of Egypt! Are they not always thus bitter in the eating?" (*Castle* ch. 43). However, Lady Desmond is no angel – she shuns her daughter, lamenting, "Owen was lost to them both, lost through her child's fault" (*Castle* ch. 44). Though Lady Desmond is an unnatural mother who betrays her most sacred trust, she is also pitiable.

Trollope celebrates the duenna-turned-rival in *Can You Forgive Her?* when an amorous midlife widow transforms from comedic husband hunter to genuinely valorized bride (Heath 126–39).[4] Initially, Arabella Greenow is satirized for husband hunting in her forties. Instead of seeking suitors for her niece Kate, she overshadows her young protégée:

> Kate Vavasor became immediately aware that a great sensation had been occasioned by their entrance, and equally aware that none of it was due to her . . . How many ladies of forty go to church without attracting the least attention! But it is hardly too much to say that every person in that church had looked at Mrs. Greenow.
>
> (*Can You* ch. 7)

Mrs. Greenow also blatantly transgresses her duty when she promotes a romance between Kate and Samuel Cheesacre, a prosperous farmer, but then takes him as her own suitor. Kate's indifference to Cheesacre only heightens the comedy as Mrs. Greenow toys with a man she initially intended for her niece and then chooses another.

Trollope differs from most Victorian novelists by frankly depicting sexuality in midlife women. Eventually, Mrs. Greenow becomes a genuinely attractive woman whom Trollope allows to forthrightly admire "a well-made man," right down to the "exquisite shapes of his . . . trousers" (*Can You* ch. 8). She accepts the proposal of Bellfield, a handsome rake, who kisses her on the high road, and the narrator comments, as "neither he nor his sweetheart were under forty, perhaps it was as well that they were not caught toying together in so very public a place" (*Can You* ch. 65), a detail of courting unusual in aging Victorian characters.[5] *The Way We Live Now* offers a similar situation when fiftyish Nicholas Broune steals kisses from fortyish Lady Carbury. The narrator describes their blatant and therefore self-consciousness sensuality: "It is not that Age is ashamed of feeling passion and acknowledging it, – but that the display of it is, without the graces of which Youth is proud, and which Age regrets" (*Way We* ch. 99).[6] In Trollope, passion can be a normal part of older women's lives.

Aging men in Trollope's fiction face complicated problems because their dominance, a primary marker of Victorian masculinity, was threatened by decline. Males' wider range of marriageability offered them unique chances for failure, greater property rights carried the challenge of making wise bequests, and professional preeminence eventually brought about tough retirement decisions. Unlike many writers of his time, Trollope did not "regard a man of forty as very much too old for falling in love" nor did he "make a similar mistake as to men of fifty" – charges he levels against young Lawrence Twentyman in *The American Senator* (ch. 6). Because unmarried men were not subject to the injustices of spinsterhood and retained fertility longer than women, Trollopian suitors in their forties and fifties often seek younger women yet fear they're too old and grapple with new paradigms of manliness as younger rivals threaten to supplant them.[7]

It's easy to conjecture that Trollope wrote from his own experience about older men attracted to younger women. Scholars note his regard for Kate Field, twenty-three years his junior, an

American friend of both Anthony and Rose.[8] In 1876, after he and Kate had been close for fifteen years, Trollope writes in his autobiography that aside from family members, she is his "most chosen friend" and "one of the chief pleasures which has graced my later years" (*Autobiography* ch. 17). He acted as a father figure, advising her on her career, counseling her to marry, repeatedly emphasizing their age difference, and calling himself "old" in his letters, but their correspondence also suggests his unconsummated love for Kate. Closing a letter with "a kiss that shall be semi-paternal – one-third brotherly, and as regards the small remainder, as loving as you please," Trollope allows himself a portion of romance (Hall, *Letters* 438).[9]

Many of Trollope's older suitors are in love with younger women, and he forthrightly defends such attractions in "Mary Gresley," which is based on Trollope's experience as an editor,[10] and in which he advises behavior like his toward Kate. The editor, married and in his fifties, details the guilty pleasure of his temptation toward a young protégée who has asked for his help as a writer: "In love with Mary Gresley, after the common sense of the word, we never were, nor would it have become us to be so. . . . Nevertheless we were in love with her. . . . We loved her, in short, as we should not have loved her" – which the editor defends as "a wholesome and natural condition" ("Mary" 532–3). Trollope endorses his right to such feelings by criticizing Thackeray's vehement condemnation of Laurence Sterne's affair with the unnamed Eliza Draper, a married woman thirty years his junior (Keymer xv). The editor/narrator argues, "The love which he declared when he was . . . a worn out wreck of a man, – disgusts us, not because it was felt, or not felt, but because it was told" ("Mary" 533).

Arguing such desire "cannot be killed" but only "may be controlled," the editor advocates admiration from afar, and silently harbors his irresistible attraction ("Mary" 534). He insists such a love cannot be denied due to "age, nor crutches, nor matrimony, nor position of any sort," emphasizing by its place first on the list that age does not quash passion ("Mary" 533). He ends his tale with a fond memory of their only kiss, dockside, as bids her good-bye, his love chastely untold, and she sails to Africa – to marry a missionary and die. Robert Polhemus argues that the narrator voices intimate feelings Trollope elided from his autobiography, perhaps in regard to Kate Field (26).

Managing age-disparate romance poses a challenge for Trollope's older suitors as each confronts a crisis of masculinity. Victorian ideals of manliness changed as the Reform Acts and "gospel of work" conferred new respect on labor. Timothy Ziegenhagen points out that in *Doctor Thorne* the de Courcy family shows its ideas have become "outmoded" when they insist a gentleman does not work (168). A focus on physical toughness – from "muscular Christianity" to emerging sports and scouting organizations – highlighted physical brawn rather than elite social status as markers of masculinity (Tosh 88, 95). In addition, the growing science of sexology also brought unprecedented attention to virility waning with age. Under these pressures, the aging Victorian gentleman could find himself hard pressed to compete,[11] and older men feared they were too outmoded to make good husbands. In *Framley Parsonage*, Dr. Thorne, at fifty-five physically fit enough to ride cross country, visiting his patients, feels "almost ashamed of himself" when he considers proposing to Martha Dunstable: "How could he be such an ass at his time of life as to allow the even course of his way to be disturbed by any such idea?" (*Framley* ch. 8).

Trollope portrays the older suitor, even when ultimately successful, plagued by age anxiety as he endures the splendors of a younger rival. In "Lotta Schmidt," the angst-ridden Herr Crippel, a musician in his mid-forties, competes with twenty-five-year-old Fritz Planken for a young woman. She initially rejects Crippel, opining, "Surely a girl may know a man old enough to be her father without having him thrown in her teeth as her lover" ("Lotta" 462), and she criticizes his inept aging:

> I should not mind his being bald so much, if he did not try to cover his old head with the side hairs. If he would . . . declare himself to be bald at once, he would be ever so much better. He would look to be fifty then. He looks sixty now.
>
> *("Lotta" 466)*

In contrast to Crippel's sad combover, young Fritz, handsome to the point of dandification, frequently runs his fingers through his luxuriant hair and "inflicts unutterable agonies on the hearts of the Herr Crippels of the world" ("Lotta" 467). Yet, eventually Lotta rejects Fritz for his insecure manhood when he defies her request to be his only dance partner. The older man's superior sexual prowess is implied as Planken merely toys with his amber-headed cane while Crippel draws music from a curvaceous violin. Crippel's experience becomes an advantage: Lotta knows he has long supported his aged mother, earns a good salary, and owns theater shares. Untainted by youthful ego, Crippel ardently pursues her. After a concert, she claims she'll marry him "all because of the zither" ("Lotta" 477): his accomplished fingering and passionate maturity outshine Fritz's overly dapper posturing. Though Crippel triumphs, the older suitor's age angst provides Trollope abundant opportunity for humor.[12]

Trollope also is sensitive to the crisis of confidence endured by men caught between the roles of father and lover. In *The Way We Live Now*, Roger Carbury, "not much short of forty" (ch. 6), pursues his cousin Henrietta, "barely twenty-one" (ch. 2). Old-fashioned and slightly mystified by the modern world, Roger is bested by Paul Montague, whose manly, urban energy more than compensates for his youthful inexperience. Roger steps aside, proclaiming he'll remain a bachelor father to Hetta, but his struggle is evident as he bitterly asks,

> what should he do? Annihilate himself as far as all personal happiness in the world was concerned, and look solely to their happiness, their prosperity, and their jobs? Be as it were a beneficent old fairy to them, though the agony of his own disappointment should never depart from him?
>
> *(Way We ch. 8)*[13]

In *An Old Man's Love*, fifty-year-old William Whittlestaff courts his ward, Mary Lawrie, twenty-five, but is outdone by John Gordon, a man not only twenty years younger but also, according to Mary, "the personification of manliness" (*Old Man* ch. 10). Next to Gordon's fortune made in South African diamond mines, Whittlestaff appears effete, his daily routine reading poetry and awaiting the postman. As he continually wonders whether to be Mary's father or lover, he's further undermined by his housekeeper badgering him to be more masterful. Mary weds Gordon, and Whittlestaff calls himself her father, aware he falls short of the new masculine paradigm Gordon so amply embodies (Heath 63–71).[14] In these plots, Trollope illustrates the emasculation older men suffer when losing to a younger rival.

Aging men in Trollope also face complicated challenges when a prospective son-in-law exposes their waning powers. John Bold, a hardworking doctor, doesn't directly challenge his sweetheart's father, but Mr. Harding doubts the ethics of his highly paid, leisurely sinecure as a by-product of Bold's reformist zeal. Though Eleanor convinces Bold to protect her father by stopping his campaign, the warden resigns, and the tiny scope of his new parish emphasizes his downgrade to outdated artifact. Obadiah Slope later tells Harding, "Work is now required from every man who receives wages. . . . New men . . . are now needed and are now forthcoming in the church, as well as in other professions" (*Barchester* ch. 12). As Morse points out, Trollope's sympathies are with Harding, a pinnacle of integrity and Christ figure who offers "a kind of Last Supper" to his Bedesmen before leaving Hiram's Hospital (*Reforming* 32), while the narrator pillories Slope. Despite his love of Harding, however, Trollope describes the manly, young professional, John Bold, eclipsing the middle-aged warden.

In *The Duke's Children*, Plantagenet Palliser objects to both his children's sweethearts, but his daughter's especially heightens his sense of decline when he parallels Frank Tregear with Burgo Fitzgerald, his recently deceased wife's lover. He notes that Frank is "a very handsome man" like the "almost abnormally beautiful" Burgo for whom Glencora nearly left him, and he dwells on his conviction that Mary is mistreating him as her mother did (*Duke's Children* ch. 24; Markwick, *New Men* 168; McMaster 138; Tracy 66–7). As Morse describes it, "Mary seems to love a reincarnation of Burgo . . . to be replicating Glencora's gift of 'her early spring of love,' given to Burgo, not to the Duke" (Morse, *Women* 124; *Duke's Children* ch. 7). Struggling to control Mary as he did his wife, he informs her, "you were not entitled to give your love to any man without being assured that the man would be approved of by – by – by me" (*Duke's Children* ch. 8), his hesitation revealing both insecurity and discomfort at his own heavy-handedness. When his son also rebels, Palliser wavers, asking, "What power had he over Silverbridge, – or . . . even over his own daughter? They had only to be firm and he knew that he must be conquered" (*Duke's Children* ch. 61). William A. Cohen notes that though they fail to follow his advice, "the younger generation wishes to remake itself in his image – as aristocrats who serve in Parliament" (55). As he wishes them happiness, his goodwill is tinged with self-pity because he feels he has not gotten his way in anything – the next generation, too, has injured and will supplant him (Tracy 68).

In *Mr. Scarborough's Family*, Trollope illustrates trouble caused by men who cling to their power of bequest. Attempting to manipulate the entail, Scarborough has married his wife twice – before the birth of each of his sons – so either can qualify as the first-born legitimate heir. He changes his favor from son to son, disinheriting one for gambling and the other for greed. A parallel plot features Peter Prosper, a fiftyish bachelor who, having taken his nephew as legatee, then decides to marry and produce his own heir. When Peter's fiancée, Matilda Thoroughbung, shows an independent streak, he reinstates Harry, a subplot resolved when Harry marries his sweetheart. Scarborough's story ends without such happy closure, however – neither the gambler nor the avaricious son has a secure future. Setting brother against brother, Scarborough has left his family in shambles. This novel, written a year before his death, illustrates Trollope's sensitivity toward the difficulty elders face when releasing control.

Trollope also highlighted retirement as a unique challenge for aging men. He believed the aged should work, writing at sixty-one, "As to that leisure evening of life, I must say that I do not want it. I can conceive of no contentment of which toil is not to be the immediate parent" (Hall, *Letters* 691). A week before his sixty-third birthday, he expressed this conviction to his brother-in-law, Sir John Tilley, who contemplated retiring as the secretary general of the Post Office. Trollope argues that, barring physical impairment, "I do not think the mere fact of your age should induce you to leave" and also inquires, "What future employment do you propose for yourself" after retirement? (Hall, *Letters* 773). For Trollope, retirement simply was not a possibility; work was a prerequisite for happiness in every life stage.

Trollope experienced aging at a time when older workers began to feel pressure to retire, a new concept in Victorian England. Traditionally, laborers had worked until death, but as profession became a marker of middle- and upper-class identity, retirement became a possibility. In 1881, a year before Trollope's death, 73 percent of men sixty-five or older reported that they still were employed (Macnicol 20), but by the 1891 census, the retired were listed as a separate and growing category. Karen Chase notes that Trollope associates retirement with death and insanity (95), an attitude evident in his fiction. In *Mr. Scarborough's Family*, lawyer John Grey, duped by his client's frauds, believing himself outmoded and fit only to retire, laments, "A man cannot leave his work forever without some touch of melancholy" (*Mr. Scarborough's* ch. 58). When daughter

Dolly hears his plan, she echoes Trollope's advice to Tilley, insisting he "find out some employment" in retirement (*Mr. Scarborough's* ch. 62).

As in his personal musing on age, Trollope's fiction sometimes proposes and then withdraws the possibility of obsolescence. Such is the professional path of his favorite character, Plantagenet Palliser. No longer prime minister in *The Duke's Children*, Palliser is approached by the Duke of St. Bungay to form a new Liberal Ministry, who argues, "a man such as you . . . as long as health and age permits . . . cannot recede without breach of manifest duty" (*Duke's Children* ch. 22). Palliser, nearing fifty and prematurely aged since Glencora's death, refuses and retires. He later realizes, however, "if anything could once again make him contented it would be work" (*Duke's Children* ch. 78), and he becomes president of the new Liberal government's cabinet. Trollope leaves his beloved character in reversed retirement, happily and perpetually working.

In *The Fixed Period*, Trollope parodies compulsory euthanasia, championing productive old age. Trollope satirically points out that legislating death for aging is not only barbaric but also illogical because people decline at different rates. Crasweller, the first person to be exterminated at the assigned age of sixty-eight, is physically and mentally fit. The colonial setting emphasizes the law's outlandishness – the British, too civilized to countenance such a proceeding, send a warship to countermand the law. While many readers have been unsure how seriously to take *The Fixed Period* (Chase 99), Trollope himself claimed, "It's all true – I *mean* every word of it" (Hall, *Biography* 487).

Trollope's later life is an exemplar of productive aging. He spent his last years reading intensely (hoping to complete all English plays written through 1625), playing weekly whist games, and, of course, writing (Hall, *Biography* 415). The year before he died, Trollope told an admirer, "I now am an old man, 66, and shall soon have come to the end of my tether" (Hall, *Letters* 903), but the end of Trollope's tether was a remarkably busy and productive place. In his last year, suffering from various ailments, he merely slackened his pace, writing six rather than twelve pages a day (Hall, *Biography* 500). He traveled twice to Ireland, researching *The Landleaguers*, and finished forty-eight of sixty planned chapters (Hall, *Biography* 502–6).

Trollope never ventured beyond the threshold of old age, only sixty-seven when he died in 1882. He was listening to his beloved niece Edith read aloud after dinner from a popular comic novel, F. Anstey's *Vice Versa*, in which a fiftyish father magically switches bodies with his son and finds youth is not the idyll he remembered (Hall, *Biography* 514). Guffawing boisterously at an elder-turned-schoolboy blundering through adolescent trials like his own, Trollope suffered a stroke from which he never recovered, dying a month later.

To the end of his life, Trollope appreciated the protean nature of aging, not only resisting its intrusions with his furious work schedule but also on his last lucid day, laughing over its vicissitudes. Trollope's interest in aging endured throughout his career, as he challenged the inevitability of decline in his characters and his life, presenting many faces of age in Victorian England. Further age studies that examine Trollope's works promise not only to offer a clearer understanding of shifting Victorian age constructions but also to challenge our own assumptions about the inexorable workings of time.

Notes

1 See also Polhemus 11–30.
2 One exception is criticism on Trollope's *The Fixed Period*, though scholars often focus on issues other than age. For age studies treatments of the novel see Andrea Charise, "'Let the Reader Think of the Burden': Old Age and the Crisis of Capacity," *Occasion: Interdisciplinary Studies in the Humanities*, 4 (2012): 1–16 and Sam Silverman, "Trollope's the Fixed Period: A Nineteenth-Century Novel Revisited." *Illness, Crisis, & Loss*, 12.4 (2004): 272–83.

3 Tilt calculated the average age of menopause in the mid-forties (12). See also Heath 79–81.
4 See also Noble 184–5.
5 Nardin notes the widow's uncensored interest in sex (134). Markwick argues that Trollopian women are sexual beings and Mrs. Greenow's plot is "an open acknowledgment that being in love and desiring to marry is about wanting to touch someone in an intimate way, and about enjoying being touched" (*Trollope and Women* 80). Morse comments on Mrs. Greenow's "obvious sexuality" (9) and the increased "sexual possibility" with her second husband in contrast to her first elderly one (*Women* 10). See also Heath 126–39.
6 See also Heath 157.
7 See also Heath 27–35.
8 For example, see Hall *Biography* 209–12 and Polhemus 18–24.
9 See Hall *Biography* 211–12.
10 See Niles 82–3.
11 See also Heath 25–34.
12 See Niles 71–84.
13 See also Heath 59–63; Chase 69–70.
14 See also Chase 68–9.

Works cited

Charise, Andrea. "'Let the Reader Think of the Burden': Old Age and the Crisis of Capacity." *Occasion: Interdisciplinary Studies in the Humanities* 4 (2012): 1–16.
Chase, Karen. *The Victorians and Old Age*. Oxford: Oxford UP, 2009.
Cohen, William A. "The Palliser Novels." *The Cambridge Companion to Anthony Trollope*. Ed. Carolyn Dever and Lisa Niles. Cambridge: Cambridge UP, 2011. 44–57.
Hall, N. John, ed. *The Letters of Anthony Trollope*. 2 vols. Stanford: Stanford UP, 1983.
———. *Trollope: A Biography*. New York: Oxford UP, 1991.
Heath, Kay. *Aging by the Book: The Emergence of Midlife in Victorian Britain*. Albany, NY: State University of New York Press, 2009.
Keymer, Tom. *The Cambridge Companion to Laurence Sterne*. Cambridge: Cambridge UP, 2009.
Macnicol, John. *The Politics of Retirement in Britain, 1878–1948*. Cambridge: Cambridge UP, 2002.
Markwick, Margaret. *New Men in Trollope's Novels: Rewriting the Victorian Male*. Farnham and Burlington, VT: Ashgate, 2007.
———. *Trollope and Women*. London: Hambledon Press, 1997.
McMaster, Juliet. *Trollope's Palliser Novels: Theme and Pattern*. New York: Oxford UP, 1978.
Morse, Deborah Denenholz. *Reforming Trollope: Race, Gender, and Englishness in the Novels of Anthony Trollope*. Farnham and Burlington, VT: Ashgate, 2013.
———. *Women in Trollope's Palliser Novels*. Ann Arbor: UMI Research P, 1987.
Mullen, Richard and James Munson. *A Penguin Companion to Trollope*. London: Penguin, 1996.
Nardin, Jane. *He Knew She Was Right: The Independent Woman in the Novels of Anthony Trollope*. Carbondale: Southern Illinois UP, 1989.
Niles, Lisa. "Trollope's Short Fiction." *The Cambridge Companion to Anthony Trollope*. Ed. Carolyn Dever and Lisa Niles. Cambridge: Cambridge UP, 2011. 71–84.
Noble, Christopher S. "Otherwise Occupied: Masculine Widows in Trollope's Novels." *The Politics of Gender in Anthony Trollope's Novels*. Ed. Margaret Markwick, Deborah Denenholz Morse, and Regenia Gagnier. Farnham and Burlington, VT: Ashgate, 2009. 177–90.
Polhemus, Robert M. "(A)genda Trouble and the Lot Complex: Older Men-Younger Women Relationships in Trollope." *The Politics of Gender in Anthony Trollope's Novels*. Ed. Margaret Markwick, Deborah Denenholz Morse, and Regenia Gagnier. Farnham and Burlington, VT: Ashgate, 2009. 11–30.
Silverman, Sam. "Trollope's *The Fixed Period*: A Nineteenth-Century Novel Revisited." *Illness, Crisis, & Loss* 12.4 (2004): 272–83.
Tilt, Edward John. *The Change of Life in Woman, in Health and Disease*. 4th ed. Philadelphia: P. Blakiston, 1883.
Tosh, John. *Manliness and Masculinities in Nineteenth-Century Britain: Essays on Gender, Family and Empire*. Harlow, England: Pearson Longman, 2005.
Tracy, Robert. "Trollope Redux: The Later Novels." *The Cambridge Companion to Anthony Trollope*. Ed. Carolyn Dever and Lisa Niles. Cambridge: Cambridge UP, 2011. 58–70.

Trollope, Anthony. *The American Senator*. 1877. Ed. John Halperin. Oxford: Oxford UP, 1999.

———. *An Autobiography*. 1883. Eds. Michael Sadleir and Frederick Page. Oxford: Oxford UP, 1999.

———. *Barchester Towers*. 1857. Ed. John Bowen. Oxford: Oxford UP, 2014.

———. *Can You Forgive Her?* 1864–5. Ed. Andrew Swarbrick. Oxford: Oxford UP, 2008.

———. *Castle Richmond*. 1860. Ed. Mary Hamer. Oxford: Oxford UP, 1989.

———. *The Claverings*. 1867. Ed. David Skilton. Oxford: Oxford UP, 1999.

———. "The Courtship of Susan Bell." *Tales of All Countries*. First Series. 1861. London: Penguin, 1993.

———. *Doctor Thorne*. 1858. Ed. David Skilton. Oxford: Oxford UP, 2000.

———. *The Duke's Children*. 1880. Ed. Katherine Mullen and Francis O'Gorman. Oxford: Oxford UP, 2011.

———. *The Eustace Diamonds*. 1871–2. Ed. W. J. McCormack. Oxford: Oxford UP, 1983.

———. *The Fixed Period*. 1881–2. Ed. David Skilton. Oxford: Oxford UP, 1993.

———. *Framley Parsonage*. 1861. Ed. David Skilton and Peter Miles. London: Penguin, 1985.

———. *Lady Anna*. 1874. Ed. Stephen Orgel. Oxford: Oxford UP, 1990.

———. "The Lady of Launay." 1878. *Later Short Stories*. Ed. John Sutherland. Oxford: Oxford UP, 1995.

———. *The Last Chronicle of Barset*. 1866–7. Ed. Stephen Gill. Oxford: Oxford UP, 1980.

———. "Lotta Schmidt." 1867. *Later Short Stories*. Ed. John Sutherland. Oxford: Oxford UP, 1995.

———. "Mary Gresley." 1869. *Later Short Stories*. Ed. John Sutherland. Oxford: Oxford UP, 1995.

———. *Miss Mackenzie*. 1865. Ed. O. A. J. Cockshut. Oxford: Oxford UP, 1988.

———. *North America*. New York: Harper, 1862.

———. *An Old Man's Love*. 1884. 2 vols. New York: Arno Press, 1981.

———. *Orley Farm*. 1861–2. Ed. David Skilton. Oxford: Oxford UP, 1985.

———. *Ralph the Heir*. 1870–1. Ed. John Sutherland. Oxford: Oxford UP, 1990.

———. *Mr Scarborough's Family*. 1882–3. Ed. Geoffrey Harvey. Oxford: Oxford UP, 1989.

———. *The Small House at Allington*. 1862–4. Ed. James Kincaid. Oxford: Oxford UP, 1980.

———. *The Warden*. 1855. Ed. Robin Gilmour. New York: Penguin, 2004.

———. *The Way We Live Now*. 1874–5. Ed. John Sutherland. Oxford: Oxford UP, 1986.

Ziegenhagen, Timothy. "Trollope's Professional Gentleman: Medical Training and Medical Practice in *Doctor Thorne* and *The Warden*." *Studies in the Novel* 38.2 (2006): 154–71.

23

TROLLOPE AND LITERARY LABOUR

Kate Osborne

Anthony Trollope's wife, Rose, complained that she wished her husband was not a writer. But her frustration was really that Trollope wrote too much: "He never leaves off, and he always has two packages of manuscript in his desk, besides the one he's working on, and the one that's being published" (Hawthorne, 227). Of all the ways in which Trollope's literary contemporaries might have irritated their marital partners, few could have plagued them with such industry as Trollope demonstrated. Over the course of his career, Trollope produced forty-seven novels, forty-four short stories, five works of travel writing, three biographies, four privately printed lectures, four collections of 'Sketches', two plays, a *Commentary* on *Caesar's Commentaries*, one book of social criticism and his *Autobiography* – and countless essays and reviews.[1] He also had a full-time and, in due course, high-ranking position at the Post Office for thirty-three years, co-founded *The Fortnightly Review* and for three years edited *Saint Paul's Magazine*. By anyone's standards, this productivity is exceptional. It certainly seemed so to his contemporaries. At a lunch party hosted by George Eliot and her partner, G. H. Lewes, "Trollope described writing every morning at 5:30 for three hours, with his watch on his desk, pushing on with his 250 words every quarter of an hour." George Eliot 'positively quivered' with dismay, volunteering that "there were days on end when she could not write a line". Trollope, rather generously, informed her that "with imaginative work like yours that is quite natural; but with my mechanical stuff it's a sheer matter of industry. It's not the head that does it – it's the cobbler's wax on the seat and the sticking to my chair!" (Hall, 63).

Trollope insisted on authorship as a profession that required regularity and rigour, at a time when writing novels for money could not securely be considered respectable. His writing practices, which he describes in detail in his *Autobiography* (1883), were heavily informed by the routine of his administrative work at the Post Office. Consistency was key. Trollope advised "young men who look forward to authorship as the business of their lives [. . .] to seat themselves at their desks day by day as though they were lawyers' clerks" (ch. 7). He was fond of quoting Latin mottoes on the importance of writing daily. "*Nulla dies sine linea* [trans: 'no day without a line'] [. . .] *Gutta cavat lapidem non vi, sed sæpe cadendo* [trans.: 'constant dripping wears away a stone']" (ch. 20). So was efficiency. He designed and had fitted up a portable desk so that he could write on the train. Seasick on a voyage between Marseilles and Alexandria, he wrote "in between rushing away to be sick in the privacy of [his] state room" (ch. 7). Despite Rose's protests that he wrote incessantly, he claimed that "three hours a day will produce as much as a man ought to write" (ch. 7), although he did concede that such proficiency required assiduous practice. By the later stages of his career, the manuscripts he submitted to his editor were so neat – barely revised and with a consistent number of words per page – that John Sutherland briefly speculates he may have written out a new copy from an original draft, before concluding that the chances are "almost nil" ("Trollope at Work", 486). He did not have time.

Trollope's extraordinary hard work and his insistence on authorship as labour – perspiration over inspiration, the pocketbook over the Muse – played a considerable role in his critical neglect. Orthodoxy holds that Trollope's loss of literary stature began when his *Autobiography* was published shortly after his death. It is certainly true that the *Autobiography* provided lots of material for critics determined to interpret what Trollope presented as "mechanical" as perfunctory, arbitrary and vulgar. However, as early as 1858, reviewers were beginning to find him "guilty of the bad taste of counting quantity before quality" ("Mr. Trollope's Novels", 88). Like Rose, these reviewers did not wish he would stop writing so much as that he would more habitually leave off. Then came the *Autobiography*, full of blunt and sometimes repetitive avowals of his systematic working methods, in which Trollope once again designated his work "mechanical" rather than "imaginative" and repeated his maxim of the cobbler's wax sticking him to his chair. For decades, the *Autobiography* was a rather embarrassing liability for Trollope supporters. Chauncey Brewster Tinker in 1947 was sympathetic, claiming that "Trollope's inexhaustible abundance [. . .] contributes to his popularity" even if he was "fool enough to tell about it" (67). But even in 1956, Frank O'Connor judged there to be "a difference between honesty and uncouthness" (167). Donald D. Stone observes that by the 1970s criticism on Trollope had shaken off the apologetic tone that characterized previous studies (Stone, 132), and broadly this is true, but still Trollope's work ethic was often ignored, or noted before being dismissed. Gerald Warner Brace was an exception when he defiantly concluded in 1961 that "The *Autobiography* contains the most useful advice to writers that I know of" (106). Trollope's heavy emphasis on labour might have been tackled by a strand of Marxist criticism in the 1970s that considered authorship as a means of production. However, what has often been read as a conservative embrace of the demands of the literary marketplace, and what was considered a tendency toward "bourgeois empiricism", as Terry Eagleton put it (181), made him an unattractive proposition in which to read ambivalence or resistance.

The 1980s saw disapproval or omission of Trollope's methods give way to explication. Susan L. Humphries, Andrew Wright, John Sutherland and, most significantly, Mary Hamer reconstructed his writing practices in tones ranging from neutral to admiring. But while Hamer calmly noted that in writing novels Trollope was seeking self-approval, Walter M. Kendrick designated him obsessive. Kendrick's *The Novel Machine* (1980) argues that Trollope, the titular machine, is more interested in producing novels and in their subsequent consumption than in the novels themselves. Others sought to identify a psychological lack that gave rise to his unflagging work ethic, taking his fiction to be a substitute for or an enactment of this lack. Trollope's *Autobiography* provided plenty of material for psychoanalytic and biographical readings by D. A. Miller, Patricia A. Vernon and Lawrence Jay Dessner. Andrew Wright and J. Hillis Miller both take as their starting point Trollope's account of daydreaming as a child to escape the misery of his social exclusion. Wright goes on to examine the ontological limits of his fiction, but J. Hillis Miller uses the *Autobiography* as his primary text, concluding that Trollope's writing obsessively reiterates an unassailable moral code. More recently, Richard Dellamora has argued that Trollope's fiction re-enacts the shame of his childhood, overcast by bullying and jibes of effeminacy.

Although the accuracy of Trollope's *Autobiography* should be treated with caution, some degree of reliance on the *Autobiography* is hard to avoid when discussing his representation of literary labour. It is immensely quotable. Trollope usually eschews figurative language, as David

Aitken has noted (350–351), but Trollope's counter to those who claimed that he published too frequently at the expense of quality is particularly suggestive:

> When my work has been quicker done, – and it has sometimes been done very quickly – the rapidity has been achieved by hot pressure, not in the conception, but in the telling of the story. [. . .] I have been impregnated with my own creations till it has been my only excitement to sit with the pen in my hand, and drive my team before me at as quick a pace as I could make them travel.
>
> *(ch. 10)*

Passages such as this provide plenty of material for critical work on Trollope's representation of authorial subjectivity, and there have been significant contributions on this subject, often contextualised by the feminization of novel-reading, and by Trollope's relationship with his mother, Frances. Like Anthony, Frances Trollope was a prolific author in a variety of genres. He adopted her writing practices as his own,[2] and she helped him get his first book published, giving *The Macdermots of Ballycloran* to her London publisher, Thomas Cautley Newby. But Trollope found association with her embarrassing and did his best to distance himself from it.[3] Humiliatingly, Newby tried to convince the public that Frances wrote *The Macdermots*, and for a long time her career continued to overshadow his. Andrew Dowling takes the *Autobiography* as a whole to be configuring literary labour as decisively masculine. Rachel Ablow argues for Trollope's construction of an alternate subjectivity for paid labour, in order to find a secure model for masculine authorship (118–144). J. Hillis Miller and Kate Thomas conclude from Trollope's image of impregnation that the blurring of gender in the metaphor of childbirth and the separation of the writing hand – Trollope's "team" – from the author present a subjectivity that is not decisively gendered but split, abstracted or anonymous (Hillis Miller 93–5; Thomas 74–98).

More recently, criticism has moved toward contextualising Trollope's literary output rather than pathologizing it. While there is still focus on the *Autobiography* as a primary text – Richard D. Aguirre and Silvana Colella read it as a critique of unregulated capitalist markets and as economic theory, respectively – there is also more focus on his fiction. Research on material culture and on the history of the book has identified in the nineteenth-century novel a recognition of its existence as a commodity. Trollope's openness about the market forces shaping his work has seen him taken up by Nicholas Dames, Daniel Hack, Jennifer Ruth, Kate Thomas, Christina Crosby and Susan E. Colón, who seek to place him in the context of economic and professional discourses. There has been a spate of work on the influence of Trollope's career at the Post Office on his fiction by Kate Thomas, Ceri Sullivan and Laura Rotunno. These critics often seek to clarify the rhetorical function of Trollope's repeated references to the labour that has gone into his novels. The rise of the novel, and the type of influence the novelist might have over an increasingly literate population, caused considerable anxiety during the nineteenth century. Trollope's *Autobiography* noted that

> There are many who would laugh at the idea of a novelist teaching either virtue or nobility, – those, for instance, who regard the reading of novels as a sin, and those also who think it to be simply an idle pastime.
>
> *(ch. 8)*

Questions of the integrity of the novel and the novelist especially pertain to the kind of fiction Trollope produced, containing elements of realism and of satire. Trollope's fiction often questions the capacity of language to depict its subject faithfully. He regrets that "no mental method of daguerreotype or photography has yet been discovered", that the author's experience of composition is that

> his words forsake, elude, disappoint, and play the deuce with him, till at the end of a dozen pages the man described has no more resemblance to the man conceived than the sign-board at the corner of the street has to the Duke of Cambridge.
> (*Barchester Towers*, ch. 20)

Yet while he might not feel himself equal to conveying reality, he often chooses not to. Trollope knows that it is in the nature of the satirist to exaggerate, that while "the spirit which produces the satire is honest enough [. . .] the very desire which moves the satirist to do his work energetically makes him dishonest" (ch. 20).

One way to insist on the value of authorship was to insist on the author's capacity to demonstrate and instil moral principles in the reader. Trollope compares himself to both a preacher and a teacher. The novel is a "pulpit [. . .] both salutary and agreeable" (ch. 8); later, "if my writings be popular, I shall have a very large class of pupils" (ch. 12). Another is to insist on writing's rigour and routine, relating authorship to other professions that were more immediately practical. Trollope compared his work variously to that of cobblers, upholsterers, shoemakers and coffin-makers – as Hillis Miller notes, the occupations are often "working-class (and pre-industrial) [. . .] in which there is a relatively easy measure of the value of the commodity produced" (Hillis Miller, 88). It wasn't until 1841 that the Copyright Amendment Act gave authors legal rights to protect their work from reproduction by profiteers, and the debate around this informed Trollope's views on the text as a product and its ownership by the author as a moral question, as Andrew H. Miller has discussed (184–88). As Cathy Shuman argues, building on work by Henry N. Rogers, for Trollope the question of how authorship should be valued can be answered only by that which is tangible – the texts "the author-as-craftsman" produces (94–122). In 1861 in an address to his colleagues at the General Post Office he dismissed the notion that payment for any kind of labour, including that of the author, might be an act of charity rather than simply one of exchange: "authors sued humbly, cap in hand, to the great lords, praying for some fee in return for a dedication. All that is nearly over now" ('The Civil Service as a Profession', 217).

Just as he compares authors with worthy intentions to more conventional workers, Trollope draws parallels between less scrupulous authors and prostitutes, beggars and criminals. As John Sutherland has noted, there is "something uncomfortably close to carnal prostitution" in the way in which *The Way We Live Now*'s Lady Carbury employs her feminine wiles to further her literary career ('Introduction,' x). Trollope's unusually cruel satire of her pointedly differentiates his type of novel from hers. Daniel Hack argues that Trollope is particularly interested in distinguishing his writing from begging letters (128–133), while, to much the same end, Karen Odden contends that Trollope likens trashy potboilers like Lady Carbury's to the get-rich-quick schemes of fraudulent railway barons.

Some of the best critical work on Trollope's representation of his own labour derives from studies of his narrative voice, particularly consideration of the "visibility" of the author in the narrative. Few sum up Trollope's narrative presence better than Frank O'Connor, who remarks that Trollope likes to "lead his reader very gently up the garden path of his own conventions and prejudices and then to point out that the reader is wrong" (167–8). As Juliet McMaster notes, Trollope's techniques for introducing himself into his own novels range from unsympathetic caricatures of himself to authorial intrusions, which draw attention to his construction of the novel.

> A late writer, wishing to sustain his interest to the last page, hung his hero at the end of the third volume. The consequence was that no one would read his novel. And who

can apportion out and dovetail his incidents, dialogues, characters, and descriptive morsels so as to fit them all exactly into 930 pages, without either compressing them unnaturally, or extending them artificially at the end of his labour? Do I not myself know that I am at this moment in want of a dozen pages, and that I am sick with cudgelling my brains to find them?

(*Barchester Towers*, ch. 51)

These intrusions have been so polarizing in the history of Trollope studies that James Kincaid defines them as "the Trollope problem" (196). They have found many detractors – Trollope's supporters have not quite exorcised Henry James's contempt for Trollope's "suicidal satisfaction in reminding the reader that the story he was telling was only, after all, a make-believe" (535), if frequent citation is any indication. Defenders of his authorial intrusions – such as Paul Elmer More, O'Connor, R. Anthony Arthur and Samuel F. Pickering – have always existed, but generally in smaller numbers. Now the more conventional position is to view these moments as a hallmark of his narrative sophistication. Critics such as Margaret Markwick, Deborah Denenholz Morse and Mary Poovey conclude that these interludes are "Trollope writing metafiction" (Markwick, 63), that his reflexivity is an indication of the dexterity with which he can flit between the real world and the multiple layers of his fictions, his reader following all the while. While Trollope in these moments flaunts his power over the plot, what is particularly interesting about the passage quoted in this paragraph is that it simultaneously undermines that power. Trollope's artistic authority is trumped by a commercial imperative to defer to his readership. Is this a sign of nervousness? Or a clever trick performed in total security of the author's narrative power? If it is the former, this deference might sting all the more in view of Leah Price's analysis of the fascination in Trollope's fiction with the inattentive reader, who uses the book as a physical barrier between themselves and others (45–71).

Trollope's work is acutely sensitive to the varying conventions and demands of each literary form. Mary Hamer has demonstrated how Trollope found the fixed spatial dimensions of serialized fiction "paradoxically liberating" (ix). The form that Trollope claimed to find particularly oppressive was that of the novel in three volumes, known as the triple-decker, or three-decker. Twenty-one of Trollope's novels were published as triple-deckers. Authors publishing in this form were sometimes under contract to deliver a pre-agreed, non-negotiable number of pages. Trollope was not subject to such a contract but he set himself a target before beginning, calculating prospective page and word counts, and held himself to it, just as Lady Carbury does: "the length of her novel had been her first question. It must be in three volumes, and each volume must have three hundred pages" (365). As Mark W. Turner has demonstrated, Trollope also paid attention to the character of each publication his work appeared in, tailoring it to take into account the gendered and religious readerships of different periodicals. In *He Knew He Was Right*, the political content of the newspaper is registered in its material culture. Hugh Stanbury's aunt, Jemima, on discovering that he has written for what she mistakenly supposes is a radical newspaper, declares more than once that she will not "have [her] house crammed with radical incendiary stuff, printed with ink that stinks, on paper made out of straw" (ch. 7). Later: "And I'm told that what they call ink comes off on your fingers like lamp-black. I never touched one, thank God; but they tell me so" (ch. 12).

While the author is always on the defensive, Trollope represents other occupations involving literary labour as endowed with power – generally over the author. Through gullibility or lack of options, the writers in Trollope's novels are at the mercy of their editors. In *The Three Clerks* (1858), Charley, a foolish young man attempting to earn extra income by writing for a periodical named the *Daily Delight*, tells his friend, "I'm only to be allowed ten paragraphs for each number, and I am expected to have an incident for every other paragraph for the first four days" (ch. 19). A collection of Trollope's short stories, *An Editor's Tales* (1870), is a fictionalized account of an editor's working life that was published in *Saint Paul's Magazine*, which Trollope edited for three years.[4] The editor in these stories is much gentler than Charley's. Although he encounters some minor obstacles, to hold an editorship is to generally distribute the "butter-boat of benevolence" to poverty-stricken authors ("The Turkish Bath", 42). The critic is a far less sympathetic figure who wields power over the author. Trollope's fiction never inhabits the mind of a critic, although his authorial intrusions sometimes imagine or preempt their reaction to his work. In his fiction the critic is savage and anonymous, and his savagery is facilitated by his anonymity. For this very reason, Trollope argued against anonymous reviews in the pages of the *Fortnightly Review*.[5] In *The Way We Live Now*, Trollope imagines one of the "sharp-nailed subordinates [. . .] set upon" Lady Carbury's novel by Mr Alf, a newspaper editor:

> his name was Jones [. . .] He must have been a man of vast and varied erudition, and his name was Jones. The world knew him not, but his erudition was always there at the command of Mr. Alf, – and his cruelty. The greatness of Mr. Alf consisted in this, that he always had a Mr. Jones or two ready to do his work for him.
>
> (ch. 11)

Mr Alf even has in his possession "one special Jones [. . .] entirely devoted to the Elizabethan drama." That Lady Carbury's novel deserves its critical mauling doesn't lessen the cruelty of Mr Jones, determined to attack to order regardless of quality, because "the crushing review is the most popular, as being the most readable" (ch. 11).

Trollope's representation of the author as subordinate to editor, critic and reader suggests a clear-eyed critique of the ways in which the whims of the market leave the author vulnerable. Taking up Kendrick's characterization of Trollope as a novel machine, Andrew Miller claims that, conceiving of his identity as a producer of commodities, Trollope understands the self only in market terms (159–177). However, recent attention to the construction of gender in Trollope's novels suggests that Trollope sees the damage that abstracting the self into a market value can do. Deborah Denenholz Morse's analysis of *Ayala's Angel* draws out Trollope's critique of a marriage market that treats women as easily moveable objects of quantifiable value (91–108). William A. Cohen's demonstration of the parallels between the literary and the marriage markets in *The Eustace Diamonds* also points toward Trollope's critique of the limited agency these markets allow women and authors. Miller's portrayal of Trollope also ignores the ways in which he intervened in and disrupted the literary market. His position on the board of the Royal Literary Fund from 1861 until his death gave him a considerable say in the selection of recipients of the grants the fund handed out to struggling writers.[6] After the death of fellow author and editor (and friend) Robert Bell, Trollope cancelled the auction of Bell's library so that he could buy it himself at above market price, in order to provide for Bell's financially struggling widow, reportedly saying, "We all know the difference in value between buying and selling books" (Hall, 303). Trollope also published *Nina Balatka* (1867) and *Linda Tressel* (1868) anonymously and, consequently, for a lesser price – although Trollope's distinctive style quickly gave the game away. Judith Knelman takes at surface value Trollope's assertion that he wanted to prove that the literary market was harsher on unestablished authors, but Mark W. Turner points out that the publisher was fully aware of Trollope's identity; Trollope wanted to test the power of his brand, and the genuineness of his reviewers (130). In either case, Trollope's desire to separate the value of his brand and that of his content suggests that his faith in the market to reward literary merit was not quite as straightforward as Miller makes out.

Trollope's rigorous and systematic approach to authorship has played an important role in framing his critical reputation, but there is still plenty of room for more work on this subject. The recent trend for considering his representation of authorship as related to other forms of labour could be extended to forms of literary labour beyond authorship. I have already indicated editing and literary criticism – there is also publishing. Trollope often became frustrated with the publisher Longman over misprints of his work and insufficient remuneration for his work. He later became a director of Chapman and Hall, which published work by Trollope and Dickens among others, and obtained a partnership there for his elder son, Henry.[7] Focus on the *Autobiography* has also left a wealth of material in Trollope's lesser-known novels and his short stories that might be explored to this end. I am thinking particularly of Trollope's short stories 'The Panjandrum', which hinges on whether a piece of work should be classified as a novel or a short story, and 'Miss Polly Puffle, or The Story of a Pseudonym', which features an author bearing a remarkable resemblance to George Eliot, as Victoria Glendinning has noted (489). The *Autobiography* is now generally read with attention to the self-consciousness of its construction, rather than as a touchstone by which to clarify his fiction. Consequently, there is room for a more thorough investigation of the divergences between his fictional authors and the way he reports his own literary efforts. "There is perhaps no career of life so charming as that of a successful man of letters", Trollope tells us in his account of his life (ch. 11). Yet although they are occasionally allowed some modest degree of success, the comfort Trollope describes proves elusive for his characters with literary ambitions.

Notes

1 Both plays were never performed. Trollope was advised by a family friend who was formerly manager of the Covent Garden Theatre that *The Noble Jilt* (1851) wasn't good enough for the stage. Trollope was asked to write *Did He Steal It?* (1869) by the manager of the Gaiety Theatre, London, but the play was subsequently rejected. Trollope claimed not to remember why, but it was probably on the grounds of quality (Super, *The Chronicler of Barsetshire*, 215). The book of social criticism, *The New Zealander*, would remain unpublished until 1972.
2 Frances rose early and "sat at her writing table until the allotted task of so many pages was completed", which was usually achieved before breakfast (Terry, *Interviews*, 19).
3 For more on Frances Trollope's life, work and relationship with Anthony, see Elsie B. Michie and Jane Nardin.
4 For more on Trollope's editorship, see Patricia Thomas Srebrnik; and Turner, 141–7. Hack offers some analysis of editorship in Trollope's short stories (131–3).
5 See Trollope, 'On Anonymous Literature', *Fortnightly Review* 1 July 1865: 491–8.
6 For a history of Trollope's involvement with the Royal Literary Fund, see Super, "Trollope at the Royal Literary Fund."
7 Henry Trollope remained there for three and a half years, with mixed success (*Autobiography*, ch. 18).

Works cited

Ablow, Rachel, *The Marriage of Minds: Reading Sympathy in the Victorian Marriage Plot*. Stanford, CA: Stanford University Press, 2007.

Aguirre, Robert D., "Cold Print: Professing Authorship in Anthony Trollope's an Autobiography." *Biography*. 25 (2002): 569–92.

Aitken, David, "'A Kind of Felicity': Some Notes About Trollope's Style." *Nineteenth-Century Fiction*. 20.4 (1966): 337–53.

Arthur, R. Anthony, "Authorial Intrusion as Art in *The Last Chronicle of Barset*." *Journal of Narrative Technique*. 1.3 (1971): 200–6.

Brace, Gerald Warner, "The World of Anthony Trollope." *The Trollope Critics*. Ed. N. John Hall. London: Macmillan, 1981. 99–109.

Cohen, William A., "Trollope's Trollop." *NOVEL: A Forum on Fiction.* 28.3 (1995): 235–56.

Colella, Silvana, "Sweet Money: Cultural and Economic Value in Trollope's Autobiography." *Nineteenth-Century Contexts: An Interdisciplinary Journal.* 28:1 (2006): 5–20.

Colón, Susan E., *The Professional Ideal in the Victorian Novel the Works of Disraeli, Trollope, Gaskell, and Eliot.* Basingstoke: Palgrave Macmillan, 2007.

Crosby, Christina, "Trollope's Addictive Realism." *The New Economic Criticism: Studies at the Intersection of Literature and Economics.* Ed. Martha Woodmansee and Mark Osteen. New York: Routledge, 1999. 293–305.

Dames, Nicholas, "Trollope and the Career: Vocational Trajectories and the Management of Ambition." *Victorian Studies.* 45.2 (2003): 247–78.

Dellamora, Richard, "Stupid Trollope." *Victorian Newsletter.* 100 (2001): 22–6.

Dessner, Lawrence Jay, "The Autobiographical Matrix of Trollope's The Bertrams." *Nineteenth-Century Literature.* 45.1 (1990): 26–58.

Dowling, Andrew, *Manliness and the Male Novelist in Victorian Literature.* Aldershot: Ashgate, 2001.

Eagleton, Terry, *Criticism and Ideology: A Study in Marxist Literary Theory.* London: New Left Books, 1976.

Glendinning, Victoria, *Trollope.* London: Hutchinson, 1992.

Hack, Daniel, *The Material Interests of the Victorian Novel.* Charlottesville, VA: University of Virginia Press, 2005.

Hall, N. John, *Trollope: A Biography.* Oxford: Oxford University Press, 1991.

Hamer, Mary, *Writing by Numbers: Trollope's Serial Fiction.* Cambridge: Cambridge University Press, 1987.

Hawthorne, Julian, *Shapes That Pass: Memories of Old Days.* London: John Murray, 1928.

Hillis Miller, J., *The Ethics of Reading: Kant, de Man, Eliot, Trollope, James and Benjamin.* New York: Columbia University Press, 1987.

Humphries, Susan L., "Order – Method: Trollope Learns to Write." *Dickens Studies Annual.* 8 (1980): 251–71.

James, Henry, "Anthony Trollope." *The Century Magazine.* July 1883: 97–133. Rept. in *Anthony Trollope: The Critical Heritage.* Ed. Donald Smalley. New York: Barnes and Noble, 1969. 525–45.

Kendrick, Walter M., *The Novel Machine: The Theory and Fiction of Anthony Trollope.* Baltimore: Johns Hopkins University Press, 1980.

Kincaid, James, "Trollope's Narrator." *The Trollope Critics.* Ed. N. John Hall. London: Macmillan, 1981. 196–209.

Knelman, Judith, "Trollope's Experiments with Anonymity." *Victorian Periodicals Review.* 14.1 (1981): 21–4.

Markwick, Margaret, *New Men in Trollope's Novels: Rewriting the Victorian Male.* Aldershot, England: Ashgate, 2007.

McMaster, Juliet, "The Author in His Novel." *The Trollope Critics.* Ed. N. John Hall. London: Macmillan, 1981. 210–15.

Michie, Elsie B., *The Vulgar Question of Money Heiresses, Materialism, and the Novel of Manners from Jane Austen to Henry James.* Baltimore: Johns Hopkins University Press, 2011.

Miller, Andrew H., *Novels Behind Glass: Commodity Culture and Victorian Narrative.* Cambridge: Cambridge University Press, 1995.

Miller, D. A., "The Novel as Usual: Trollope's Barchester Towers." *Sex, Politics, and Science in the Nineteenth-Century Novel: Selected Papers from the English Institute, 1983–84.* Ed. Ruth Bernard Yeazell. Baltimore: Johns Hopkins University Press, 1986. 1–38.

More, Paul Elmer, "My Debt to Trollope." *The Trollope Critics.* Ed. N. John Hall. London: Macmillan, 1981.

Morse, Deborah Denenholz, *Reforming Trollope: Race, Gender, and Englishness in the Novels of Anthony Trollope.* Aldershot: Ashgate, 2013.

"Mr. Trollope's Novels," *National Review,* 1858. *Anthony Trollope: The Critical Heritage.* Ed. Donald Smalley. New York: Barnes and Noble, 1969. 80–9.

Nardin, Jane, *He Knew She Was Right: The Independent Woman in the Novels of Anthony Trollope.* Carbondale: Southern Illinois University Press, 1989.

O'Connor, Frank, "Trollope the Realist." *The Mirror in the Roadway: A Study of the Modern Novel.* New York: Knopf, 1956, 165–83.

Odden, Karen, "Puffed Papers and Broken Promises: White-Collar Crime and Literary Justice in *The Way We Live Now.*" *Victorian Crime, Madness and Sensation.* Ed. Andrew Maunder and Grace Moore. Aldershot: Ashgate, 2004. 135–45.

Pickering, Samuel F. Jr, "Trollope's Poetics and Authorial Intrusion in 'The Warden' and 'Barchester Towers.'" *The Journal of Narrative Technique.* 3.2 (1973): 131–40.

Poovey, Mary, "Trollope's Barchester Novels." *The Cambridge Companion to Anthony Trollope*. Ed. Carolyn Dever and Lisa Niles. Cambridge: Cambridge University Press, 2010. 31–43.

Price, Leah, *How to Do Things with Books in Victorian Britain*. Princeton, NJ: Princeton University Press, 2012.

Rogers, Henry N., "Trollope's Fourth Clerk: 'Crinoline and Macassar' in *The Three Clerks*." *Publications of the Arkansas Philological Society*. 13.2 (1987): 81–99.

Rotunno, Laura, *Postal Plots in British Fiction, 1840–1898: Readdressing Correspondence in Victorian Culture*. Basingstoke: Palgrave Macmillan, 2013.

Ruth, Jennifer, *Novel Professions: Interested Disinterest and the Making of the Professional in the Victorian Novel*. Columbus: Ohio State University Press, 2006.

Shuman, Cathy, *Pedagogical Economies: The Examination and the Victorian Literary Man*. Stanford, CA: Stanford University Press, 2000.

Smalley, Donald, ed., *Anthony Trollope: The Critical Heritage*. New York: Barnes and Noble, 1969.

Srebrnik, Patricia Thomas, "Trollope, James Virtue, and Saint Pauls Magazine." *Anthony Trollope, 1882–1982*. Spec. issue of *Nineteenth-Century Fiction*. 37.3 (1982): 443–63.

Stone, Donald D., "Critical Opinions of Trollope: 1951–80." *Oxford Reader's Companion to Trollope*. Ed. R. C. Terry. Oxford: Oxford University Press, 1999. 131–3.

Sullivan, Ceri, *Literature in the Public Service: Sublime Bureaucracy*. Basingstoke: Palgrave Macmillan, 2013.

Super, R. H., *The Chronicler of Barsetshire: A Life of Anthony Trollope*. Ann Arbor: University of Michigan Press, 1990.

———, "Trollope at the Royal Literary Fund." *Anthony Trollope, 1882–1982*. Spec. issue of *Nineteenth-Century Fiction*. 37.3 (1982): 316–28.

Sutherland, John, "Introduction." *The Way We Live Now*. Oxford: Oxford University Press World's Classics Series, 2008, vii–xxviii.

———, "Trollope at Work on *The Way We Live Now*." *Anthony Trollope, 1882–1982*. Spec. issue of *Nineteenth-Century Fiction*. 37.3 (1982): 472–93.

Terry, R. C. ed. *Trollope: Interviews and Recollections*. New York: St Martin's Press, 1987.

Thomas, Kate, *Postal Pleasures: Sex, Scandal, and Victorian Letters: Sex, Scandal, and Victorian Letters*. Oxford: Oxford University Press, 2012.

Tinker, Chauncey Brewster, "Trollope." *The Trollope Critics*. Ed. N. John Hall. London: Macmillan, 1981. 66–74.

Trollope, Anthony, *An Autobiography*. Oxford: Oxford University Press World's Classics Series, 2008.

———, *Barchester Towers*. Oxford: Oxford University Press World's Classics Series, 2008.

———, *Nina Balatka/Linda Tressel*. Ed. Robert Tracy. Oxford: Oxford University Press, 1991.

———, "The Civil Service as a Profession." Address. General Post Office, London. 4 Jan. 1861. published in *Cornhill Magazine*. 3rd Feb. 1861: 214–28.

———, "On Anonymous Literature." *Fortnightly Review*. (1 July 1865): 491–8.

———, *The Three Clerks*. Oxford: Oxford University Press World's Classics Series, 1943.

———, "The Turkish Bath." *An Editor's Tales*. London: Strahan, 1870. 1–47.

———, *The Way We Live Now*. Oxford: Oxford University Press World's Classics Series, 2008.

Turner, Mark W., *Trollope and the Magazines: Gendered Issues in Mid-Victorian Britain*. Basingstoke: Macmillan, 2000.

Vernon, Patricia A., "The Poor Fictionist's Conscience: Point of View in the Palliser Novels." *Victorian Newsletter*. 71 (1987): 16–20.

Wright, Andrew, *Anthony Trollope: Dream and Art*. Chicago: University of Chicago Press, 1983.

———, "Trollope Revises Trollope." *Trollope Centenary Essays*. Ed. John Halperin. New York: St. Martin's, 1982. 109–33.

24
TROLLOPE AND FIELD SPORTS

Heather Miner

From the early nineteenth century onwards, British field sports acted as a political symbol, an instrument of community relations, and a metaphor for public morality. The popularity of field sports underscores the increased access to the countryside in Victorian Britain, but, according to John Lowerson, this alone cannot account for the growing status of hunting in the Victorian era (171). Examining the social relations involved in foxhunting engages with quintessential, and competing, Victorian structures of feeling. At the heart of this contested culture space in mid- and late-Victorian Britain lie Anthony Trollope's novels, monographs, and editorials, arenas in which Trollope uses the hunt as a narrative backdrop and as a means of exploring a set of complex but coherent social values. This essay surveys the ethos ascribed to Victorian hunting as Trollope assimilated and transmitted them in his work, and emphasizes the role he, in turn, played in shaping Victorian attitudes toward emergent animal-rights discourses.

Sport historians Mike Huggins and Callum McKenzie have identified the central ways that field sports are commonly treated in Victorian leisure studies.[1] The first might be described as the antiquarian mode, in which nineteenth-century field sports are treated as social expressions of a desire to find order and discipline in the practice of a seemingly timeless British pastime. Accordingly, hunting could be seen as one of many "traditions" invented by Britons to symbolize continuity and articulate cultural ideology (Hobsbawm 1–15). A second, related, view of hunting stresses the role of sports in forming middle-class masculinity. The ideals ascribed to field sports, according to Linda Colley, expressed "the new patriotic, patrician machismo" of the Victorian middle-class: hunting seemingly enhanced the body, the mind, and the character (172). Moreover, the cost of field sports limited participation while distancing participants from increasingly disreputable working-class sports.

The critical regard for Trollope's portrayal of field sports show that his ongoing interest in recreation, which is sustained throughout his corpus, contains some of Trollope's most challenging and thought-provoking approaches to the cultural concerns of his day, making his treatments of sport more than merely escapist or nostalgic. Field sports are referenced in most studies of Trollope, but scholarship focusing specifically on Trollope's obsession with hunting has emerged only recently, encouraged, in part, by Christopher Herbert's reading of Trollope through the semiotics of culture, focusing on traditional economic relations and morality, and Laurie Langbauer's critical interrogation of the assumption that "the everyday" life in Trollope's work is ideologically fixed (Herbert 253–99; Langbauer 87). Scholarship on Trollope and hunting is thus conceptually diverse, from Gordon Bigelow's study of conservatism in the Irish novels to Jen Sattaur's focus on horses as commodity objects in *The Eustace Diamonds*.[2] In this essay, I emphasize noteworthy trends in the emergent work on Trollope and field sports by first reviewing the Barsetshire novels, in which hunting is frequently invoked to articulate the concerns of rural communities and social cohesion. I then survey Trollope's mid-career novels, in which hunting is emblematic of Victorian modernity in the urbanizing nation, and conclude by contextualizing these fictional treatments within the national controversy over hunting in 1869/1870. As this essay demonstrates, critical work to bring Trollope's writings into conversation with Victorian historiography has helpfully expanded our understanding of both fields.

Trollope certainly provided a wealth of material for critical fodder; hunting scenes proliferate in Trollope's novels, beginning with *The Kellys and the O'Kellys* (1848). In this novel about rural Ireland, Trollope portrays hunting society both as an encompassing moral community and an exclusive coterie. Lord Ballandine is Master of the Hunt and keeper of the hounds, who confers with an Anglican clergyman about the dogs, who in turn consults with local Catholic tenants.[3] The hunting field presents a comforting portrait of Anglo-Irish hunting society as essentially inclusive, even to a despised middleman, Barry Lynch (Berol 113). Yet this society is also protective: during the hunt, Lynch tramples a dog that must then be killed, causing the group to condemn Lynch; this exile from the hunt foreshadows Lynch's later exile from the district. This expression of communal feeling, and the power of exclusion the community wields, was part of what allowed supporters of field sports to affirm the structures of feeling embedded in hunting society.

This social power of the hunt in rural communities is even more central to the Barsetshire series, as *The Last Chronicle of Barset* well shows. Hunting is a constant presence in this series; for Trollope, Barsetshire was a place known by "its members of Parliament, and the different hunts which rode over it. I knew all the great lords and their castles, the squires and their parks, the rectors and their churches."[4] The central plot of *The Last Chronicle*, the concluding Barsetshire novel, gathers together these tropes through concern for the impoverished perpetual curate, Mr. Crawley, who has been accused of theft. Mr. Crawley's crime, however, is not the only one in the novel: a local gamekeeper has committed the crime of vulpicide, the killing a fox outside of the purview of the hunt. According to J. Jeffrey Franklin, the novel's focus on circulation and capital exchanges "constitutes the plot structure" of the "representative" Barsetshire novel (503–4). Franklin's examination of the plot structure, however, occludes mention of the vulpicide plot. In fact, this subplot's focus on hunting mores is a subtle reworking of the novel's central ideological argument for collaboration and moral conservancy. The inherent unification of local land management issues and patrilineal relations in the vulpicide plot provides an ancillary to the nomadic movement of community actors across the globe elsewhere in the novel: masculine representatives of the local community determine and affirm their relationality by returning to values shaped by the hunt. The discussion of sport links Barsetshire clergy to the Barsetshire squirearchy and thereby becomes symbolically representative of the common and communal ground for local gentry identity.

The hunting plot is sustained by the pre-Tractarian clergyman, Archdeacon Grantly, a non-hunting character through whom Trollope represents the widespread concern with fox-hunting in the community. The propriety of a clergyman's involvement in the hunt was a recurrent issue in the Barsetshire series (see, e.g., *Framley Parsonage*) and in Trollope's nonfiction study of hunting "types," *Hunting Sketches*. By the mid-Victorian era, Raymond Carr notes, the "ecclesiastical climate had turned against fox hunting. Ritualists might only object to hunting in Holy Week; Evangelicals thought it wicked whenever practiced and revived a long Protestant tradition that disapproved, above all, of a hunting clergyman" (176). Trollope reflected this widely held view in *Hunting Sketches*: "The world at large is very prone to condemn the hunting parson, regarding him as a man who is false to his profession, and, for myself, I am not prepared to say that the world is wrong" (ch. 6).

Yet in *The Last Chronicle*, Grantly's concern is not with hunting per se, but with community stewardship; his hunting values are part of the rural society's ethics and masculine cultural. Grantly's accumulation of property over the course of the Barsetshire series allows him to move the church hierarchy to the landowning gentry and in this context, "saving" a fox for the hunt is a secular demonstration of his religious function, as both roles demand a responsibility to tend to and develop the resources of local places and people. His preservation of foxes is presented as the natural inclination of a man who "had lived all his life among gentlemen in a hunting county" (ch. 33). The "crime" of vulpicide draws together various members of what David Skilton has called Barsetshire's exclusive "social masculinity," including Grantly, landowners Wilfred Thorne and Frank Gresham, two gamekeepers, and tenant farmers (134). Foxhunting men form a group that mediates between the poles of local society, but ultimately the crime is solved through polite correspondence between property owners: the archdeacon writes to Mr. Thorne, who "had confessed the iniquity, had dismissed the murderous gamekeeper, and all was serene" (ch. 83). Hunting is a means through which the homosocial community, and particularly the gentry, is connected.

In the Barsetshire series, the trope of hunting is thus used to represent both discursive and social means through which rural societies identify, even when scenes of hunting are absent. Rather, through characters such as Major Grantly and Frank Gresham, Trollope helped construct the masculine hunting type in the Victorian popular imagination; the hunting gentleman also occupied a prominent place in the works of authors such Charles Lever, Robert Surtees, and George Henty. The hierarchy of rural communities, in which male comradeship and social unity reached their full expression, found their complement, according to Trollope, in the masculine sphere of field sports – a sphere in which the hunt itself is often secondary to the performance of social roles. Yet these fictional representations obscure the economic and political changes occurring in the countryside in the final decades of the century, when the agricultural depression spreading across most of rural Britain was well under way. As Elizabeth Helsinger points out, "After 1870, it was clear . . . that [England's] countryside would not again play the same central role in nourishing her own or Great Britain's inhabitants" (6). The agricultural depression was central in the transformation of agriculture communities from national to symbolic importance.

As economic structures changed across Britain in the 1870s and 1880s, Trollope's portrayal of hunting increasingly became metaphoric of struggles for representational and societal power. Rural affairs were increasingly integrated into primarily urban novels, as Trollope traces similar economic and cultural concerns in both spaces. In *The Way We Live Now* (1875) and *The Prime Minister* (1876), Trollope focuses on London's financial networks, coupled with a growing sense that traditional patterns of ownership and culture are crumbling. As Trollope grew increasingly interested in competition and speculation, his representation of hunting in *Phineas Finn* (1869), *The Eustace Diamonds* (1872), *Phineas Redux* (1874), and *Ayala's Angel* (1881) perhaps inevitably became more concerned with gender and the marriage market.[5] Indeed, in the Palliser novels, Plantagenet Palliser shows little interest in foxhunting; rather, the hunting discourse is often maintained by Glencora, who worries over the "Lying-in Hospital for the foxes," and, like Lizzie Eustace, is aware of the social cachet associated with hunting (*PR* ch. 69). In *The Eustace Diamonds*, the hunt functions as a sign of the courtship field in which Lizzie must prove her capability.[6] Lizzie is delighted by "her horse [that] galloped with her as though his pleasure was as great as her own" (ch. 38). Participation in the hunt and Lizzie's interaction with her horse are signs of Lizzie's wealth and independence, and, as Elsie Michie has shown, offered Victorians an image of "dominion over the natural world" (146).[7]

However, Trollope's representation of hunting as a bastion of British life did not go unchallenged, as Victorians increasingly defined themselves in opposition to blood sports.[8] Edward Augustus Freeman, clergyman and professor of history at Oxford, and Trollope play a significant role in this transforming attitude toward animals. In 1869, Freeman sparked a national controversy by publishing "The Morality of Field Sports" in the *Fortnightly Review*. As the debate spread to other journals, issues of class and gender came to structure the interactions between animal-rights and pro-hunting supporters, following a (now common) thread in animal-rights debates; as Morse and Danahay note, "The discourse on animal rights inevitably invokes political battles over human rights" ("Introduction" 5).[9] Freeman's argument was primarily based in progressive ideas of the modern Englishman: "What connexion is there between the savage amusements of ancient heathens or low ruffians among ourselves and the manly and gallant sports of high-minded and refined English gentlemen?" (367). In Freeman's evolutionary rhetoric, blood sports, from gladiatorial contests in ancient Rome to cockfighting in eighteenth-century Britain, had been banned as sport become responsive to progressive morality. Accordingly, Freeman anticipated "a day coming when an English gentleman will look with the same disgust on the diversions of the present age" (367). Freeman's argued that not only was cruelty to animals in sport antiquated but also that the modern Englishman should have compassion for the hunted, rather than for the hunter. Freeman voices an emergent structure of feeling in Victorian society: progressive, middle-class Englishness identity is formed through a species relationship; the human and humane are defined in relation to each other in sympathy with the animal and against the transgressions of history.

Trollope was an obvious candidate to respond to Freeman: apart from being an avid hunter and a founder of the *Fortnightly Review*, Trollope had also gained prominence in the sporting press with his monographs *British Sports and Pastimes* (1868) and *Hunting Sketches*. In his response, however, Trollope returned to a topic familiar in his fiction, hunting and masculinity. The crux of Freeman's argument depended on a masculine type who disassociated himself from cruelty.[10] Trollope, conversely, portrayed foxhunters as embodiments of refinement:

> Men are thrown together who would not otherwise meet, and converse on all subjects common to men. Politics are discussed, and agriculture, social habits, the affairs of the country, the preservation of foxes, the enmity of this enmity to the sport, and the devoted friendship of that friend. . . . A community is formed in which equality prevails.
>
> *("Mr. Freeman" 618)*

Trollope claims that the chivalrous community formed through the hunt is aligned with contemporary metropolitan taste and not with rustics who "think that a London club means drunkenness, gambling, and wickedness" ("Mr. Freeman" 618). Instead, Trollope claimed the hunting field as a unique space in which "City-men learn country lore, and country-men are told the ways of cities" ("Mr. Freeman" 618). Trollope attempts to drive a wedge between hunting and animal cruelty, stigmatizing Freeman's perspective as an enfeebled provincialism.

Though at first confined to the *Fortnightly Review*, the "morality of hunting" issue soon spread to the mainstream periodical market, and many of the London literati defended Freeman, if not the means through which Freeman reached his conclusion. In an editorial, John Ruskin condemned hunting not because of animal cruelty ("reprobation of fox-hunting on the ground of cruelty . . . is entirely futile"), but because hunting distracted the upper classes from agricultural labor and leadership (314). John Stuart Mill privately wrote that Freeman had "broken ground against field sports, a thing I have been often tempted to do myself" (374). Helen Taylor believed that the "pleasure of the chase . . . to be the real attraction of fox-hunting and to be demonstrably cruel in its own nature, and degrading in its effect on human character" (67). John Morley, the *Fortnightly* editor, anonymously defended Freeman in *The Pall Mall Gazette*, as did commentators in the *Spectator, Daily Telegraph, Saturday Review*, and *The Times*. The influential support of Ruskin, Mill, Taylor, and Morley lent Freeman celebrity and cosmopolitan approbation. Yet this response from the metropolitan elite hints at the burgeoning divide between city and country that was becoming ever more pronounced in mid- to late Victorian culture. By engaging the foxhunting community, the intellectual elite, and the general public, the terms of the modern debate on animal cruelty and recreation had been defined.

Trollope's representation of hunting proceeding and following the field sports controversy was written in distinct social and economic climates, but it did little to dim Trollope's continued preoccupation with the subject. *The American Senator*, in particular, turns on a defense of field sports: the hunt is repeatedly figured in the novel's tangled courtship plots as ground for erotic play and as an arena of socialization. The novel rehashes many of Freeman's arguments against foxhunting (as does *Marion Fay*) in order to attack "philanimalists," "the small knot to self-anxious people" who pretend to condemn foxhunting for cruelty but, instead, condemn recreation and community.[11] Returning to the hunt is represented as a man's prodigal return to his communal position after a period of masochistic seclusion. The themes are, by now, familiar: studying hunting in Trollope's work shows that, for him, field sports continued to be a marker of modernity and social ethos. Yet, for modern readers, looking backwards at Trollope's discourse on hunting, alone and in the context of changing norms over animal-human relations, allows us access to a more complete, if more splintered, understanding of Victorian social relations.

Notes

1 The following summary is indebted to McKenzie, "The Origins of the British Field Sports Society," and Huggins.
2 See also Hughes, Miner, and Trotter.
3 See Berol for a discussion of the novel's Anglican-Catholic politics.
4 *Autobiography*, Ch. 8.
5 *Ayala's Angel* is unique in portraying the death of the fox as problematic. For a discussion of this novel and Victorian taste, see Morse, *Reforming*, 91–111.
6 For a discussion of the hunt as a sexual metaphor, see Markwick, 95–127, and Morse, *Women*, 39–84.
7 For a study of horses in nineteenth-century literature, see Dorre.
8 This began with the suppression of bullbaiting in 1835; see Thomas and Ritvo.
9 See *Victorian Animal Dreams* for a longer discussion of human dominion over animals and analysis of contemporary perspectives.
10 See Boddice.
11 *American Senator*, Ch. 73.

Works cited

Berol, Laura. "The Anglo-Irish Threat in Thackeray's and Trollope's Writings of the 1840s." *Victorian Literature and Culture* 32.1 (2004): 103–16. Print.
Bigelow, Gordon. "Trollope and Ireland." *The Cambridge Companion to Trollope*. Ed. Carolyn Dever and Lisa Niles. Cambridge: Cambridge UP, 2011. 196–209. Print.
Boddice, Rob. "Manliness and the 'Morality of Field Sports': E. A. Freeman and Anthony Trollope, 1869–71." *The Historian* 70.1 (2008): 1–29. Print.
Carr, Raymond. *English Fox Hunting: A History*. London: Weidenfeld and Nicolson, 1976. Print.

Colley, Linda. *Britons: Forging a Nation, 1710–1800*. New Haven: Yale UP, 1992. Print.

Dorre, Gina M. *Victorian Fiction and the Cult of the Horse*. Aldershot: Ashgate, 2006. Print.

Franklin, J. Jeffrey. "Anthony Trollope Meets Pierre Bourdieu: The Conversion of Capital as Plot in the Mid-Victorian British Novel." *Victorian Literature and Culture* 31.2 (2003): 501–21. Print.

Freeman, Edward A. "The Morality of Field Sports." *Fortnightly Review* 6.34 (1 October 1869): 353–85. Print.

Helsinger, Elizabeth. *Rural Scenes and National Representation: Britain, 1815–1850*. Princeton: Princeton UP, 1996. Print.

Herbert, Christopher. *Culture and Anomie: Ethnographic Imagination in the Nineteenth Century*. Chicago: U of Chicago P, 1991. Print.

Hobsbawm, Eric. "Introduction: Inventing Tradition." *The Invention of Tradition*. Ed. Eric Hobsbawm and Terrance Ranger. New York: Cambridge UP, 1983. 1–15. Print.

Huggins, Mike. "Second-Class Citizens? English Middle-Class Culture and Sport, 1850–1910: A Reconsideration." *International Journal of the History of Sport* 17.1 (March 2000): 1–35. Print.

Hughes, Robert. "Trollope and Fox-Hunting." *Essays in Literature* 12.1 (1985): 75–84. Print.

Langbauer, Laurie. *Novels of Everyday Life: The Series in English Fiction, 1850–1930*. New York: Cornell UP, 1999. Print.

Lowerson, John. *Sport and the English Middle Classes, 1870–1914*. Manchester: Manchester UP, 1988. Print.

Markwick, Margaret. *Trollope and Women*. London: Hambledon Press, 1997. Print.

McKenzie, Callum C. "The Origins of the British Field Sports Society." *International Journal of the History of Sport* 13.2 (August 1996): 177–91. Print.

Michie, Elsie. "Horses and Sexual/Social Dominance." *Victorian Animal Dreams: Representations of Animals in Victorian Literature and Culture*. Ed. Deborah Denenholz Morse and Marin A. Danahay. Aldershot: Ashgate, 2007. 145–66. Print.

Mill, John Stuart. Letter. "To W. B. Dawkins, Esq." 20 Dec. 1869. Rpt. in *The Life and Letters of Edward A. Freeman*. Ed. W.R.W. Stephens. 2 vols. London: Macmillan, 1895. 1.374. Print.

Miner, Heather. "Trollope and the Hunt for West Country Identity." *Victoriographies: A Journal of Nineteenth-Century Writing, 1790–1914* 1.2 (2011): 221–42. Print.

[Morley, John?]. "Morality of Field Sports." *Pall Mall Gazette* (7 Jan. 1870): 8. Print.

Morse, Deborah Denenholz. *Reforming Trollope: Race, Gender, and Englishness in the Novels of Anthony Trollope*. Aldershot: Ashgate, 2013. Print.

———. *Women in Trollope's Palliser Novels*. Ann Arbor: UMI, 1987. Print.

Morse, Deborah Denenholz, and Martin A. Danahay. "Introduction." *Victorian Animal Dreams: Representations of Animals in Victorian Literature and Culture*. Ed. Deborah Denenholz Morse and Marin A. Danahay. Aldershot: Ashgate, 2007. 1–12. Print.

Ritvo, Harriet. *The Animal Estate: The English and Other Creatures in the Victorian Age*. Cambridge: Harvard UP, 1987.

Ruskin, John. Letter. "The Morality of Field Sports." *Daily Telegraph* 15 Jan. 1870. Rpt. in Ruskin, John. *Arrows of the Chace*. Boston: Dana Estes, 1880. 313–14. Print.

Sattaur, Jen. "Commodities, Ownership, and *The Eustace Diamonds*: The Value of Femininity." *Victorian Literature and Culture* 38.1 (March 2010): 39–52. Print.

Skilton, David. "The Construction of Masculinities." *The Cambridge Companion to Anthony Trollope*. Ed. Carolyn Dever and Lisa Niles. Cambridge: Cambridge UP, 2011. 128–41. Print.

Taylor, Helen. "A Few Words on Mr. Trollope's Defence of Fox-Hunting." *Fortnightly Review* 7.37 (1 Jan. 1870): 63–8. Print.

Thomas, Keith. *Man and the Natural World: Changing Attitudes in England 1500–1800*. London: Allen Lane, 1983. Print.

Trollope, Anthony. *The American Senator*. Ed. John Halperin. New York: Oxford UP, 1986. Print.

———. *An Autobiography*. Ed. Nicholas Shrimpton. New York: Oxford UP, 2014. Print.

———. *Ayala's Angel*. Ed. Julian Thompson-Furnival. New York: Oxford UP, 1986. Print.

———. *British Sports and Pastimes*. London: Virtue, 1868. Print.

———. *The Eustace Diamonds*. Ed. Helen Small. New York: Oxford UP, 2011. Print.

———. *Framley Parsonage*. Ed. Katherine Mullin and Francis O'Gorman. New York: Oxford UP, 2014. Print.

———. *Hunting Sketches*. London: Chapman and Hall. 1865. Print.

———. *The Last Chronicle of Barset*. Ed. Helen Small. New York: Oxford UP, 2015. Print.

———. "Mr. Freeman on the Morality of Hunting." *Fortnightly Review* 7 (1 December 1869): 616–25. Print.
———. *Phineas Finn*. Ed. Simon Dentith. New York: Oxford UP, 2011. Print.
———. *Phineas Redux*. Ed. John Bowen. New York: Oxford UP, 2011. Print.
———. *The Prime Minister*. Ed. Nicholas Shrimpto. New York: Oxford UP, 2011. Print.
———. *The Way We Live Now*. Ed. John Sutherland. New York: Oxford UP, 2009. Print.
Trotter, Jackson. "Foxhunting and the English Social Order in Trollope's *The American Senator*." *Studies in the Novel* 24.3 (1992): 227–41. Print.

PART VI

Creed and cant

25
RETHINKING TROLLOPE AND ANTI-SEMITISM
Gender, religion, and "the Jew" in *The Way We Live Now*

Anna Peak

There is a wide critical consensus that Anthony Trollope was anti-Semitic and that his later novels especially are notable for the ugliness of their anti-Semitism.[1] This view has its roots in the assumption that Trollope was a conservative whose views either never changed or became more reactionary as he got older and in the anxiety of critics to condemn Trollope for anti-Semitism in order to establish their own purity. Yet the argument that Trollope was anti-Semitic has been built almost entirely upon one novel, *The Way We Live Now* (1875), and almost entirely upon the portrayal of one character (Augustus Melmotte) in that novel – a narrow foundation that is unfortunately in keeping with a consistent critical tendency to make sweeping statements about all of Trollope's works based on a few of them.[2] The critical condemnation of Trollope as an anti-Semite has also rested upon an assumption that Trollope's narrative technique is uni-layered and that all quotations from his novels can therefore be taken at face value, despite a growing body of scholarship that suggests Trollope's narrative technique is in fact complex and embodies a moral relativism.[3] More troublingly, in making their case that Trollope was anti-Semitic, critics have leaned upon an implicit definition of "the Jew" as male. Further, critics have assumed that the Victorians constructed Judaism exclusively in terms of race without regard to religion; this critical reluctance to deal with Victorian religiosity, for fear of being thought religious, has served to elide discussion of the relations between racism and religious belief. In fact, Trollope's Christian Protestant views undercut his own attempts to deconstruct prejudice, but if we reconsider *The Way We Live Now* in light of the sophistication of its narrative technique and include in our consideration the novel's portrayal of multiple characters, including female ones, we can see that the novel also satirizes anti-Semitism and deconstructs "the Jew" as a male racial Other in order to argue for greater tolerance of both religious conviction and female independence.

When Jewish characters are portrayed negatively in the novel, it is often in ways that subvert the relations between nineteenth-century anti-Semitism and domestic ideology. Nadia Valman has demonstrated that while nineteenth-century English literary texts usually construct male Jews as "racially repellent, socially intrusive, or politically subversive," female Jews are portrayed as being "in every way the opposite. . . . [I]n English literary culture the Jewess was idealized rather than exoticized, a model for rather than a foil to bourgeois femininity" (Valman, "Bad Jew/Good Jewess," 150–151). For Valman, this is the result of a domestic ideology that saw women of all backgrounds as inherently nurturing and spiritual. Female Jewish characters were generally portrayed as "inherently spiritual and ardent, and also particularly oppressed by the archaic Jewish legal code – calling out for aid to [their] Christian sisters" ("Bad Jew/Good Jewess" 152). Such portrayals, common throughout the nineteenth century, nurtured a conservative Christian sense of women's innate angelhood while paradoxically suggesting that Christianity is the superior religion because it grants women more freedom.

In contrast, the portrayals of Marie and Madame Melmotte in *The Way We Live Now* resist these particular stereotypes. Neither woman's identity is justified by an ardent desire to convert to Christianity, even though the two women do convert, in a sense; when Melmotte moves them from Germany, where they had lived as Jews, to France, "there they were all Christians" (Ch. 11). Yet while the swiftness of the "conversion" suggests its expediency, as does the family's lack of Christian identity when they move again to England, there are two sorts of insincerity involved here: while Mr. Melmotte is presumably attempting to rise in the world, his wife and daughter more likely convert in obedience to his orders, for it is at this same period, we are told, that Melmotte begins to beat both women (Ch. 11). The women's false conversion is thus portrayed sympathetically, as deserving of forgiveness, while the novel simultaneously suggests that a wife's or a daughter's submissiveness to a male head is problematic precisely because male heads are imperfect and submitting to them may mean insincerity in religion – a serious matter. The novel thus suggests that the Jewish woman who converts is not an object of admiration but of pity, and that far from receiving aid from Christians, Christianity becomes a means of bullying them.

Similarly, both women's interest in money is portrayed as a legitimate seeking of power. When Mr. Melmotte dies, his wife can feel only relief, and both she and Marie are primarily interested in the money that Melmotte leaves behind and the freedom that it brings them. While not exactly admirable, their interest in money is a sad commentary not on them but on the man who was such a poor father and husband that his death forever improves the lives of his family. Again, during their periods of suffering neither woman "calls out for aid to her Christian sisters," who despise them, for to do so would imply a structure in which Jewish women depend on Christian ones, and in which Christianity is therefore superior. Instead, the novel suggests that what these women – all women – need is to become more independent altogether. After a girlhood of obedience that has earned her only beatings, Marie begins to think for herself, a change that is portrayed as admirable rather than disobedient: her father is unworthy of obedience and Marie's independence is associated with courage (Ch. 11). Dependence is portrayed as the result of cruelty, and independence as the result of good treatment: "There was, too, arising within [Marie's] bosom a struggle to be something in the world, an idea that she, too, could say something, and have thoughts of her own, if only she had some friend near her whom she need not fear" (Ch. 17). Valman argues that Marie's assertion of herself is a spiritual defiance that mimics the defiances of English literature's other spiritual Jewish heroines and in so doing reinforces traditional domestic ideology, but in fact Marie's self-assertion is self-centered and practical rather than selfless and spiritual – and is portrayed as justifiable just the same, suggesting that all women should have greater independence of thought and deed.

One could argue that the novel still ultimately demonizes "the Jew" because both women have been oppressed by Mr. Melmotte and the "archaic Jewish code" he represents. But there is nothing archaic about Melmotte's abuse of his wife and daughter. And, despite the fact that early scholarly critics of the novel confidently asserted that Melmotte is definitely a Jew,[4] the novel tells us only that "it was suspected by many . . . that Melmotte had been born a Jew" (Ch. 56). Other critics have argued that this very uncertainty proves that Melmotte would have been read as a Jew; Bryan Cheyette, for example, argues that Melmotte is a "wandering" and "slippery" figure (39) who would therefore have been read as both Jewish and threatening. According to this line of thought, though not identified as a Jew in the novel, Melmotte is for that very reason "not just *a* Jew but rather *the* Jew" (Freedman 83).

The argument that Melmotte represents "*the* Jew" is, however, problematic for several reasons. First, it has relied too little on textual evidence; Melmotte is in fact revealed at the very end of the novel to have been most likely an American Irishman (Ch. 98), a fact that has so far been ignored by critics,[5] despite the wide body of scholarship on the portrayal of Americans and the Irish in Trollope and in English literature generally. Second, the case for Trollope's anti-Semitism has relied too much on critics' own use of suggestive wording to make their case in lieu of textual evidence. Cheyette, for example – who also misspells the name of Mr. Brehgert as "Brehgart" throughout, although perhaps that is an editorial error – bases his case that Melmotte is an "ultimately unknowable semitic 'other'" (42) largely on single words that are often placed in quotation marks but that are not in fact quotations from the novel. He argues, for example, that Melmotte's "romantic 'wanderings'" (39) suggest that he is Jewish. The word "wanderings" here implies, *petitio principii*, the argument that is going to be made, but the word choice and typography are misleading for they suggest that Trollope himself evokes the image of the Wandering Jew with his word choices, when in fact he does not (the word "wandering" and its variants appears in the novel only in reference to Sir Felix and Roger Carbury).

Perhaps most significantly, the argument that Melmotte embodies a demonized Jew relies heavily on assumptions regarding how Victorian readers would have read the novel and fails to take into account what Victorian readers themselves said about how they read the novel. Contemporary reviews of the novel (the only evidence we have unless and until new diaries or letters turn up) do not read Melmotte as a Jew, or even as a particularly bad character. While Mr. Brehgert is invariably identified in these reviews as a Jew (of which more later), Melmotte is usually described simply as "a swindler" (*Saturday Review* 88) or "a vulgar City swindler" (*The Spectator* 825). The reviewer for the American *Lippincott's Magazine* is eager to claim Melmotte for the Americans by pointing out that while Melmotte is "said by some to be a German Jew, by others [he is said to be] a New York Irishman" (644). Further, contemporary reviewers, while finding his character "unpleasant" (*The Spectator* 825), do not find Melmotte to be significantly worse than any of the other characters in the book. Indeed, one of the charges leveled against the novel was that its atmosphere is too generally one of "sordid baseness" (*The Spectator* 825) and that, in a novel "[w]here everybody else is mean, abject, toadying, sunk in sloth, [Melmotte's] gigantic knavery and boldness rise almost into virtues" (*Saturday Review* 88). Melmotte is considered notable not because he is portrayed as sinister but because his character is "always ably, and sometimes powerfully, drawn" (*Saturday Review* 88) to the possible moral detriment of readers who might be tempted to sympathize over-much with Melmotte. Trollope's readers may have feared Melmotte, but what they fear about him is that Trollope asks that we see Melmotte with a measure of respect and sympathy.

Further working against the idea that Marie and Madame Melmotte are oppressed by Judaism is the way the novel continually suggests that Melmotte's behavior is driven by his desire to be treated as a man, implying that it is a certain type of masculinity that results in the oppression of his wife and daughter, not some Jewish legal code. Melmotte wishes to be treated according to English society's rules for how gentlemen should be treated, and, perceiving a link between manhood and money, believes that he can buy manhood as well as gentlemanhood. This is why, for example, Melmotte is angry when Sir Felix comes to him to ask for Marie's hand in marriage (Ch. 23); he knows that it is customary to ask the father's permission first, and he tells Sir Felix that his money ought to have bought him that privilege (Ch. 23). Melmotte believes that if he accrues enough money, he will finally be treated as a man, and he is angry to find that he is wrong. Likewise, when he wants to assert himself as the head of his household, he uses either physical violence or his financial power over his family to do so, taking advantage of English legal codes that work to deny women financial independence.

Likewise, the novel's major Jewish character, Mr. Brehgert, is a better man than Melmotte because he adopts a less oppressive and in some ways more feminized style of masculinity. Mr. Brehgert's manliness is focused on the courage that is required to be continually open and honest, rather than on trying to buy respect with bills or blows; he is a man of "single-minded genuine honesty" (Ch. 79) who is openly and matter-of-factly Jewish despite the fact that his faith and his identity lead to his being ill-treated. Further, when he realizes that his fiancée, the Christian Georgiana Longestaffe, looks down on him for being a Jew and is marrying him only for his money, he writes her a letter breaking off the engagement. The breaking of engagements is normally considered the prerogative of the lady and not the behavior of a gentleman, but in this case Georgiana's prejudice forfeits her that consideration and Brehgert's honesty and self-respect make his feminine behavior fully justified and simultaneously manly because it is "particularly sensible" (Ch. 79). The reason Melmotte is worse than Brehgert is thus that Melmotte exemplifies an overly violent form of masculinity while Brehgert embodies what Margaret Markwick has termed Trollope's "New Man."

Brehgert's goodness and decency, in fact, have long posed a problem for those critics who have argued that *The Way We Live Now* is an anti-Semitic novel; if the novel supposedly defines Jewishness in terms of a "wandering" or "slippery" identity, what are we to make of this man whose identity and sense of self are quite certain? As Brehgert does not easily fit this argument, he has been largely ignored by critics, or dismissed as being admirable only because he knows his place (Cheyette, 41; Valman, "Trollope," 713). Critics have assumed that Brehgert breaks off his engagement to Georgiana in acknowledgment of Georgiana's superiority and that the narrator "concurs" with her father Mr. Longestaffe's relief (Cheyette 41). No textual evidence is cited by these critics for any of these statements, unfortunately, and in fact, Brehgert does not know his place; he breaks his engagement to Georgiana Longestaffe when she makes it plain that she believes herself fundamentally superior to him as "a Christian lady of high birth and position giving herself to a commercial Jew" (Ch. 79) precisely because he is not willing to accept such treatment or the place to which Georgiana ascribes him. It is Georgiana, not the narrator, who thinks that Mr. Brehgert will know his place, and she receives a sharp lesson that her assumption is flatly wrong. Further, Brehgert, in retracting his offer of marriage, censures Georgiana for her prejudice. The narrator, in one of the novel's touchstone moments, tells readers that this is a "plain-spoken, truth-telling" (Ch. 79) letter, and it is in this letter that Mr. Brehgert writes, with the narrator's implicit seal of approval, that

> Fifty years ago, whatever claim a Jew might have had to be as well considered as a Christian, he certainly was not so considered. Society was closed against him, except under special circumstances, and so were all the privileges of high position. But that has been altered.
>
> (Ch. 79)

Society, in this novel, may have opened its doors for the wrong reasons, but it does not follow that its doors were closed for the right reasons. Because the novel criticizes "the way we live now," critics have almost universally assumed that it must therefore glorify the way we lived once; but that does not follow. In fact, like Abraham in Trollope's short story "The Telegraph Girl," the novel suggests that "Some things seem right because people have been wrong so long" (95). Anti-Semitism is part of the problem with the way we live now.

To see this, we must engage not only with the actual text and how it was read by Victorian readers, but also with the question of Trollope's narrative technique. Reading Trollope as an anti-Semite has depended heavily on ignoring the ways that the narrative voice in *The Way We Live Now* constantly shifts into and out of free indirect discourse. Earlier critics tended to assume that Trollope's novels employ a reliable, omniscient narrator; more recent critics have argued that the Trollopian narrator is in fact unreliable because of the novels' frequent use of indirect discourse.[6] In fact, as J. Hillis Miller briefly points out in *Literature as Conduct* (105–106), Trollope habitually employs both third-person indirect discourse and an omniscient narrator. These shifts force the reader to make a continual effort to distinguish between third-person free indirect discourse and third-person omniscient narrator without the aid of grammatical cues. Readers must instead assess statements by their relations to each other in a continual series of "if-then" judgments that refer back the touchstone statements (often clearly signaled by a phrase such as "in truth" or "in fact") of the omniscient narrator ("If this statement is true, then character X is right to do Y; but since she is 'in truth' wrong, then this statement is not to be taken as true but rather as the expression of her point of view"). The reader is thus asked to adopt an intensely logical state of mind that is simultaneously speculative and open, and that also requires the reader to be constantly ready to understand and empathize even with points of view they might otherwise find abhorrent (thus contemporary reviewers' uneasiness with the novel). A consistent use of indirect discourse, without those touchstone moments from the omniscient narrator, would make the novel more "psychological" and "modern" at the expense of these subtleties and demands on the reader.

With these facts in mind, it becomes clear that the novel's expressions of hostility toward or stereotyping of its Jewish characters generally come from the perspective of (nominally) Christian characters whose opinions are portrayed as projections of their own shortcomings. When Sir Felix Carbury visits Mr. Melmotte to ask for Marie Melmotte's hand in marriage, for example, the conversation quickly devolves from Sir Felix's point of view, as Melmotte insists on asking some perfectly predictable questions about a prospective son-in-law's financial position. As Sir Felix becomes more and more uncomfortable, Melmotte is described in the third person in ever more unflattering terms that reflect not so much Melmotte's actual character but Sir Felix's growing embarrassment and anger. The narration states at one point that Melmotte "ought not to ask questions about trifling sums of money" (Ch. 23) – but of course they are not trifling sums; the novel has been quite clear that Sir Felix is a cad; and neither Trollope nor his readers would have thought a father wrong to ask such a question – we are in Sir Felix's mind here so that we can observe what drives prejudice. As the conversation goes on and Sir Felix first prevaricates and then outright lies, Melmotte continues to press for a straight answer and Sir Felix becomes angry: "[He] felt his own position. Was he not a baronet, and a gentleman, and a very handsome fellow. . .? If this surfeited sponge of speculation, this crammed commercial cormorant, wanted more than that for his daughter why could he not say so without asking disgusting questions" (Ch. 23)? While critics such as Jonathan Freedman have taken this speech at face value (84), its Dickensian panache, its over-alliteration, is clue enough that we are not to take this view of Melmotte seriously, and when Melmotte closes the conversation by suggesting, "Perhaps you will get your lawyer to write to me," the narration adds a final sarcastic touch: "'Perhaps that will be best,' said the lover" (Ch. 23). The tremendous evil that Melmotte represents in this passage – and even in his mind Sir Felix, to give him his due, never thinks a specifically anti-Semitic slur – is simply the creation of a sulky, work-averse young souse; it is Sir Felix, not Melmotte, who is the "lover" of money, and it is Sir Felix, not Melmotte, who is described in the novel as "wandering" and unreliable.

Such satire of Christian characters' attitudes and projections regarding Jewish ones – or characters whom Christians think might be Jewish – is pervasive, and one of Trollope's particular targets is the way that Christians racialize Jews in terms of their appearance. Mr. Brehgert's appearance, for example, is a constant source of horror and disgust to his fiancée and to all the Longestaffes. Georgiana thinks of him as a "fat, greasy man of fifty, conspicuous for hair-dye" (Ch. 60), and the narrator confirms this description by describing him as "a fat, greasy man" but, however, "good-looking in a certain degree. . . . The charm of his face consisted in a pair of very bright black eyes, which were, however, set too near together in his face for the general delight of Christians" (Ch. 60). Significantly, Mr. Longestaffe is described in terms very similar to the description of Mr. Brehgert. Mr. Longestaffe is a "tall, heavy man of about fifty, with hair and whiskers carefully dyed" (Ch. 13). Despite the way each man's appearance mirrors the other's, no Longestaffe seems concerned with the idea of Georgiana figuratively marrying her father; they are concerned that she is planning to marry someone they define as being different based on looks that are not different. This is part of a more general strategy in the novel of applying anti-Semitic stereotypes to Jewish and non-Jewish characters – Mr. Longestaffe is not only a fat old man with dyed hair but also the head of a family deeply concerned with money and with problems of assimilation and comingling. The Longestaffes define otherness in terms that would equally well fit themselves; they are physically no different from Mr. Brehgert or any other Jew they despise, and stereotypes and fears regarding the supposed social climbing of the Other apply to these gentile characters, not Mr. Brehgert.

Again, one of the problems with "the way we live now," as Everett Carter has suggested, is anti-Semitism; the characters' prejudices are part of a romanticization of the past that serves to elide the faults of the present. Mr. Longestaffe's anti-Semitism is a reflection of his own mindlessness and a projection of his own inability to deal with the present:

> [I]f he had ever earned for himself the right to be called a Conservative politician by holding a real opinion of his own, – it had been in that matter of admitting the Jews into parliament. When that had been done he was certain that the glory of England was sunk for ever. And since that time, whenever creditors were more than ordinarily importunate, when Slow and Bidewhile could do nothing for him, he would refer to that fatal measure as though it were the cause of every embarrassment which had harassed him.
>
> *(Ch. 60)*

When Mr. Longestaffe discovers that his daughter is engaged to Mr. Brehgert, he demands confirmation of Mr. Brehgert's Jewishness from his daughter, asking the question "with as much thunder as he knew how to throw into his voice" (Ch. 65), before going on to ask her if Brehgert is indeed "that old fat man"; having ascertained these important facts, he returns to the realm of the truly crucial: "And a Jew?' He again asked the horrid question, and again threw in the thunder" (Ch. 65). Anti-Semitism is portrayed here as an artificial thing, sustainable only by contrived efforts, and feeble at that, at "thunder," and one that finds its home in the hearts of the superficial and the silly so that they may have a convenient whipping boy on hand on whom to place their own faults.

But frustration is not the only root of prejudice; so also is a muddled and uncertain understanding of Christianity. Later, Mr. Longestaffe finds it necessary to deal with Mr. Brehgert in matters of business, and the two get along quite well, mostly because Mr. Brehgert is "singularly good-natured and forbearing after the injuries he had received" (Ch. 88). Once Mr. Longestaffe has actually associated with Mr. Brehgert as a person rather than as a symbol, he "absolutely formed a kind of friendship for that gentleman" (Ch. 88). But when Mr. Brehgert has the temerity to speak of his former engagement to Georgiana, because he "didn't quite like that the matter should be passed over as if I was in any way ashamed of myself" (Ch. 88), then Mr. Longestaffe stops thinking of Brehgert the person and resumes thinking of him as the Jew to whom his family might have been allied. His latent prejudice resurfaces:

> As soon as [Brehgert] was gone Mr. Longestaffe opened the door and walked about the room and blew out long puffs of breath, as though to cleanse himself. . . . He told himself that he could not touch pitch and not be defiled!
>
> (Ch. 88)

The reference to Ecclesiasticus is no accident; in times of stress and emotion, Mr. Longestaffe reverts not only to prejudices and projections but to the proverbs he believes to be part of his religion,[7] which he understands to justify his anti-Semitism. His wife, Lady Pomona, goes further; her understanding of Christianity is such that it not only justifies but actually requires anti-Semitism, without regard to considerations of race. It is the Bible – or her rather shaky understanding of it – and not Darwin that grounds Lady Pomona's prejudice. Rousing herself from her posture of horrified prostration brought on by the dreadful tidings of her daughter's engagement, Lady Pomona tells Georgiana, with ominous earnestness,

> It seems to me it can't be possible [for a Christian to marry a Jew]. It's unnatural. It's worse than your wife's sister.[8] I'm sure there's something in the Bible against it. You never would read your Bible, or you wouldn't be going to do this. . . . An accursed race, think of that, Georgiana, – expelled from Paradise.
>
> (Ch. 78)

Despite Lady Pomona's invocation of Christianity, contemporary readers understood that the novel in fact suggests that such intermarriage is not necessarily a problem; in fact, it was this suggestion that *The Saturday Review* found particularly abhorrent (88). Lady Pomona's own uncertainty about her claims ("I'm sure there's something") is not an encouraging sign, and her proofs undermine them further. Her reference to the question of the lawfulness of marrying a deceased wife's sister reveals how Lady Pomona has confused custom and law with Christianity, of which she appears to know nothing, not having heard that there is no Jew or Greek. She is also confused regarding who was expelled from Paradise in the Bible – not the Jews but Adam and Eve – that is, all of humanity. Once again, the Longestaffes construct as Other what is in fact human and true of themselves in order to avoid the truth about themselves. Lady Pomona ends her peroration with the statement, "as for Mr. Brehgert – I can't bear to have his name mentioned in my hearing" (Ch. 78), a contradiction that reinforces for readers the fact that she is a flighty fool who has no logical or certain beliefs, only emotions that manifest themselves in confused and contradictory uncertainties.

Indeed, one of the novel's primary targets is uncertainty of belief. This is another reason why Brehgert is a better man than Melmotte: not that he is a submissive known quantity, as has been previously argued (Valman, "Trollope," 713), but that he is a man of assertive and genuine religious beliefs. He is for that reason a better model of manhood than Melmotte, who sees religion as a financial and political tool and is willing to adopt any religion that he thinks will help him get ahead. This is why Melmotte's religious views keep changing. His daughter Marie's first memories are of living in a "dirty street in the German portion of New York"; no religion is mentioned, but when the "hardly-treated woman who had been her mother" dies, Melmotte marries "her present mother in Frankfort" and Marie is told that "from henceforth she was to be a Jewess" (Ch. 11). The Melmottes remain Jewish as long as they are in Germany, but "there had soon come another change. They went from Frankfort to Paris, and there they were all Christians" (Ch. 11). Melmotte's identity and religious views are definite (if expediently insincere) as long as he is living in either Germany or France. In America and England, however, his views are considerably less clear; this uncertainty is a reflection of the uncertain identity, not of Melmotte – he is happy to be whatever people want him to be – but of these countries.

Melmotte's identity in England is uncertain precisely because the English lack religious conviction; they see religion, as Melmotte does, as a political tool to be bought and sold. When Melmotte begins to establish himself in politics, he has to make two important decisions: whether he will run as a Liberal or a Conservative – a decision he makes purely with a view to which views will best help his career – but also what religion he should adopt, again with a view to helping his political career. The latter decision proves difficult; Melmotte at first believes that he can gain both the Catholic and the Protestant vote (Ch. 56) by giving money to both groups, and is content to be considered a Protestant by Protestants and a Catholic by Catholics. Later, however, Melmotte learns that "though catching the Catholic vote would greatly help a candidate, no real Roman Catholic could hope to be returned" (Ch. 56). Melmotte therefore considers declaring himself to be not Catholic but Protestant, but his advisors tell him that no one will believe that as the Catholics believe he is a Catholic pretending to be a Protestant and the Protestants have decided he is probably really a Jew (Ch. 56). In moving from America to Germany, Melmotte was content to establish a definite identity for himself as a Jew; in France as a Christian; but in England Melmotte can only convince Catholics that he is Catholic, and that will not help him get ahead. Accordingly, he decides to drop religion altogether. The fact that even muddled, nominal, and heterogeneous religious belief can have the strength to defeat a Melmotte suggests something about the strength of Trollope's own faith in religion.

That very faith brings up the possibility that Trollope, despite his efforts to combat racist anti-Semitism, might still consider Jews inferior with regard to religion. Historians of anti-Semitism, such as Gavin Langmuir,[9] have argued that the late nineteenth century saw a shift from a centuries-old anti-Judaism that had its origins in Christianity to a newer, even more virulent anti-Semitism that had its origins in racism. *The Way We Live Now* stands at this crossroads of anti-Judaism and anti-Semitism. Thus, even if the novel deconstructs the newer, racist anti-Semitism, it is still possible that Trollope's own certainty of religious belief undermines both his attempts to deconstruct the idea of the Jew as a racial male other and his suggestion that genuine religious conviction deserves respect.

In the conversations between the Catholic Father Barham and the Anglican Bishop of Elmham, the novel seems to suggest that there is a hierarchy of religions where the newest is both best and truest. When Father Barham suggests that Catholics are superior to Protestants because Catholics are "chiefly the poor" and it was "chiefly the poor who at first put their faith in our Saviour'" (Ch. 16), the bishop responds that "'We are speaking of those who are still attached to an old creed. Our Saviour was the teacher of a new religion'" (Ch. 16). In this paradigm, the "old" religion is Catholicism and the new, Anglicanism; but the old religion displaced by "Our Saviour" is Judaism more than it is Catholicism. And while the bishop is imperfect, he is also "an unselfish man, who loved his neighbor as himself," who labors for the social good (Ch. 16) and does not vulgarly impose his views on others. These facts suggest that the bishop is an admirable and trustworthy Christian whose views deserve respect, and in fact neither Trollope nor his Victorian readers were likely to disagree with the evolutionary view of religion he puts forth. There seems a clear ranking: the comparatively new Anglicanism; below that, the older religion of Roman Catholicism; and, by extension, below that, the even older and therefore presumably even more inferior religion of Judaism. Other Trollope novels similarly suggest that there is a difference between older and newer Jews – for example, the narrator contrasts the "ancient type" (Ch. 2) of Mr. Chaffanbrass with the modern, good-looking Mr. Aram in *Orley Farm* (1862) – perhaps suggesting that Jews are worthy of respect only if they evolve away, racially and religiously, from Judaism.

Yet in his nonfiction Trollope expresses a determined sense that Jews and gentiles should be considered as equals. In *North America* (1868), for instance, Trollope writes,

> Any patriotism must be poor which desires glory, or even profit, for a few at the expense of the many, even though the few be brothers and the many aliens. As a rule, patriotism is a virtue only because man's aptitude for good is so finite that he cannot see and comprehend a wider humanity. He can hardly bring himself to understand that salvation should be extended to Jew and Gentile alike.
>
> (96)

Trollope does not elaborate on his thoughts here; it is possible that he means that only "saved" Jews – that is, converts who have evolved toward a newer religion – should be considered as equals. Yet Mr. Brehgert's quietly determined faith suggests that he has not evolved away from Judaism in the least, and is all the nobler for it. The hierarchy of religions is also undercut by the fact that Mr. Brehgert and the bishop both are portrayed much more sympathetically than the Catholic Father Barham.

Future discussions of Trollope's portrayal of Jews would do well to investigate further Trollope's evolving views on religion more generally, which could usefully be placed in the context of the considerable body of scholarship on the history of anti-Judaism and anti-Semitism that exists in the fields of both history and Jewish studies. Future criticism should also take gender into account in discussing the portrayals of both male and female characters in Trollope's novels. Trollope will not always come out of such investigations looking pure, particularly in his earlier novels written when he was a younger and more conservative man. Still, we can give Trollope credit for being, like Roger Carbury, if not always perfectly generous or just, still "struggling . . . to be generous, passionately fond . . . of justice" (Ch. 93).

Notes

1 See, for example, Brantlinger, Cohen, Freedman, Goodlad, and Rosenberg. A quick search of Google Books for "Anthony Trollope" and "anti-Semitism" also reveals that Trollope is held up as the type of Victorian anti-Semitism in a number of encyclopedias on anti-Semitism and Jewish studies.
2 For further discussion of this phenomenon, see Morse, *Reforming Trollope*, especially page 9.
3 See, for example, apRoberts, Markwick, and Morse.
4 See Cohen, and Rosenberg.
5 The two exceptions here are Everett Carter, who acknowledges that Melmotte is at best only possibly a Jew, and, after a fashion, Jonathan Freedman. While Freedman acknowledges that Melmotte's Jewishness is therefore not exactly established, he goes on to argue that in a way it is because of the novel's "invocation of anti-Semitic topoi . . . , . . . its conscious rescripting of the Shylock / Jessica scenario from the *Merchant*, [and] most fully of all [with its] culturally contumacious habit of linking a Jew to the structures of affect that circulate in the marketplace" (86). The singular Jew in question, however, appears to be Melmotte, which makes this reasoning contumaciously circular as well as avoiding the question of Mr. Brehgert's definite Jewishness and wholly different and honest relation to the marketplace. Further, the rescripting of the Shylock/Jessica scenario is not one in which a bad Jew bullies a would-be Christian Jewess, but one in which a daughter has been ordered into one religion after another by a man of no religion at all (of which more later). Finally, by the "invocation of anti-Semitic topoi" Freedman appears to mean the way that Melmotte is "embodied" (85), but Freedman's reading of how Melmotte is embodied depends on taking Sir Felix as reliable and trustworthy (84), a very doubtful assumption that again begs the question.

6 For a comprehensive overview of how critics have historically read Trollope's narrative techniques, see Markwick, 1–14, and Morse, *Reforming Trollope*, 1–12.
7 Ironically, Ecclesiasticus or Sirach is part of neither the Jewish nor the Protestant canon, thus undercutting the authority of the quotation and highlighting the lack of genuinely Biblical support for Mr. Longestaffe's prejudice.
8 For a complete discussion of this bill, see Corbett.
9 See, in particular, Langmuir's *Toward a Definition of Anti-Semitism* (Berkeley: University of California Press, 1990) and *History, Religion, and Anti-Semitism* (Berkeley: University of California Press, 1990), which received the National Jewish Book Award in 1991.

Works cited

apRoberts, Ruth. *Trollope: Artist and Moralist*. London: Chatto and Windus, 1971. Print.

Brantlinger, Patrick. *Fictions of State: Culture and Credit in Britain, 1694–1994*. Ithaca, NY: Cornell UP, 1996. Print.

Carter, Everett. "Realists and Jews." *Studies in American Fiction* 22.1 (Spring 1994): 81–91. Print.

Cheyette, Bryan. *Constructions of 'the Jew' in English Literature and Society: Racial Representations, 1875–1945*. Cambridge: Cambridge UP, 1993. Print.

Cohen, Derek. "Constructing the Contradiction: Anthony Trollope's *The Way We Live Now*." *Jewish Presences in Literature*. Ed. Derek Cohen and Deborah Heller. Montreal: McGill-Queen's UP, 1990. 61–75. Print.

Corbett, Mary Jean. *Family Likeness: Sex, Marriage, and Incest from Jane Austen to Virginia Woolf*. Ithaca, NY: Cornell UP, 2008. Print.

Delany, Paul. "Land, Money, and the Jews in the Later Trollope." *SEL: Studies in English Literature, 1500–1900* 32.4 (1992): 765–87. Print.

Freedman, Jonathan. *The Temple of Culture: Assimilation and Anti-Semitism in Literary Anglo-America*. Oxford: Oxford UP, 2000. Print.

Goodlad, Lauren M. E. "Anthony Trollope's *The Eustace Diamonds* and 'The Great Parliamentary Bore.'" *The Politics of Gender in Anthony Trollope's Novels: New Readings for the Twenty-First Century*. Ed. Margaret Markwick, Deborah Denenholz Morse, and Regenia Gagnier. Farnham: Ashgate, 2009. 99–116. Print.

Ikeler, A. Abbott. "That Peculiar Book: Critics, Common Readers, and *The Way We Live Now*." *College Language Association Journal* 30.2 (December 1986): 219–40. Print.

Langmuir, Gavin. *History, Religion, and Anti-Semitism*. Berkeley: University of California Press, 1990. Print.

———. *Toward a Definition of Anti-Semitism*. Berkeley: University of California Press, 1990.

Markwick, Margaret. *New Men in Trollope's Novels: Rewriting the Victorian Male*. Aldershot: Ashgate, 2007. Print.

Miller, J. Hillis. *Literature as Conduct: Speech Acts in Henry James*. New York: Fordham UP, 2005. Print.

Morse, Deborah Denenholz. *Reforming Trollope: Race, Gender, and Englishness in the Novels of Anthony Trollope*. Farnham: Ashgate, 2013. Print.

Rosenberg, Edgar. *From Shylock to Svengali: Jewish Stereotypes in English Fiction*. Stanford: Stanford UP, 1960. Print.

Skilton, David. "'Depth of Portraiture': What Should Distinguish a Victorian Man from a Victorian Woman?" *The Politics of Gender in Anthony Trollope's Novels: New Readings for the Twenty-First Century*. Ed. Margaret Markwick, Deborah Denenholz Morse, and Regenia Gagnier. Farnham: Ashgate, 2009. 207–20. Print.

Trollope, Anthony. *North America*. Vol. 1. Philadelphia: J.B. Lippincott, 1863. Print.

———. *Orley Farm*. 1862. Reprint. Oxford: Oxford UP, 2008. Print.

———. "The Telegraph Girl." *Anthony Trollope: The Complete Short Stories, Vol. IV: Courtship and Marriage*. Ed. Betty Jane Slemp Breyer. Fort Worth: Texas Christian UP, 1982. 69–106. Print.

———. *The Way We Live Now*. 1875. Reprint. Oxford: Oxford UP, 2008. Print.

Valman, Nadia. "Bad Jew/Good Jewess: Gender and Semitic Discourse in Nineteenth-Century England." *Philosemitism in History*. Ed. Jonathan Karp and Adam Sutcliffe. Cambridge: Cambridge UP, 2011. 149–69. Print.

———. "Trollope, Anthony (1850–82)." *Antisemitism: A Historical Encyclopedia of Prejudice and Persecution*. Ed. Richard S. Levy. Santa Barbara: ABC-CLIO, 2005. 712–13. Print.

"The Way We Live Now." Rev. of *The Way We Live Now*, by Anthony Trollope. *Lippincott's Magazine of Popular Literature and Science* 16 (November 1875): 644–5. *Google Books*. Web. 31 Aug. 2013.

"The Way We Live Now." Rev. of *The Way We Live Now*, by Anthony Trollope. *The Saturday Review* 40.1029 (17 July 1875): 88–9. *C19: The Nineteenth Century Index*. Web. 31 Aug. 2013.

"The Way We Live Now." Rev. of *The Way We Live Now*, by Anthony Trollope. *The Spectator* 48.2452 (26 June 1875): 825–6. *C19: The Nineteenth Century Index*. Web. 31 Aug. 2013.

26

CAN YOU FORGIVE HIM?
Trollope, Jews, and prejudice

Steven Amarnick

Anthony Trollope wrote several dozen novels in which no Jewish characters appear – leaving a generous supply of others in which, to give a quick sampling, we hear about "a nasty, greasy, lying, squinting Jew preacher; an imposter,"[1] "a greasy Jew adventurer out of the gutter,"[2] "a nasty, stuck-up, greasy Jew,"[3] "an impudent low Jew,"[4] a "small, and oily, and black-haired, and beaky-nosed" man who speaks with a "lisping fiendish sound" and who is "[o]f the modern Hebrews a most complete Hebrew,"[5] and "a thin, black-browed, yellow-visaged woman with ringlets and devil's eyes, and a beard on her upper lip, – a Jewess."[6] They are "[a]n accursed race,"[7] and members of "an alien nation; a nation expressly set apart and separated from all people – a peculiar nation distinct from all others."[8] As one Madame Zamenoy puts it in *Nina Balatka*, "Oh, I hate them! I do hate them! Anything is fair against a Jew."[9]

Such hostility would hardly seem to fit the persona Trollope creates with his genial narrator – guiding us, nudging us along, playing the part of the wise and warm-hearted friend. A 2001 "Talk of the Town" piece in *The New Yorker*, about a lecture at the New York Bar Association co-sponsored by the Trollope Society, ends with the exasperated speaker wondering why Trollope, despite his obvious anti-Semitism among other unappealing qualities, manages to snooker such a devoted group of readers. "Some of it is a fetish about England – an extraordinary love of Englishness," he decides. "Trollope can get away with murder. He can do no wrong. But then you do just sink into the arms of Trollope."[10]

Often, of course, readers still admire the work of authors who are known to have especially repellent views. It is arguably not so difficult to praise, say, "The Love Song of J. Alfred Prufrock" or "The Waste Land," no matter how prickly or prejudiced we believe its author to be. But Trollope's fiction succeeds to the extent that he seems to let us embrace his personality, not escape it. If we become convinced that Trollope's vaunted worldliness and tolerance are a mask for ignorance and narrow-mindedness, we may find it difficult to read him with any pleasure at all.

As it happens, the startling quotations several paragraphs earlier all come from characters in Trollope's novels, not the narrator – as we shall see, a crucial distinction. It goes without saying that in many of his novels Trollope exposes the distaste, and sometimes outright disdain, many nineteenth-century British people felt for Jews. But exposure and endorsement are hardly the same thing, and a close reading of Trollope shows that there is nothing in his representation of Jews to make us question the sincerity or thoughtfulness of his own declared politics.

****

"I consider myself to be an advanced, but still a conservative Liberal," Trollope writes in his autobiography.[11] As he explains, the conservative sees inequalities in society and is committed to preserving them; though the conservative realizes that there are tendencies at work to reduce those inequalities, he looks upon such changes as an evil that he must at least slow down if he cannot stop altogether. On the other hand, the Liberal "is alive to the fact that these distances are day by day becoming less, and he regards this continual diminution as a series of steps towards that human millennium of which he dreams."[12] The conservative Liberal believes the changes must occur gradually so as to take hold properly; and though Trollope in this book never explains his use of "advanced," it is apparently meant to warn off those who will see too much of the conservative in his views. "Conservative," as an adjective not a noun, has to do only with the speed of change; he is an advanced Liberal, then, because he is not lukewarm about what are sometimes radical goals.[13]

"By no amount of description or asseveration," Trollope says, "could I succeed in making any reader understand . . . how frequently I have used [my characters] for the expression of my political and social convictions."[14] If we consider, then, just how serious Trollope was in promoting his views as an advanced conservative Liberal, it becomes even more difficult to ignore his representation of Jews, whose progress in British society would seem to be an obvious step toward lessening distances. Even if we decide that on the Jewish question Trollope was no worse than most of his contemporaries, it still becomes hard to reckon why he is not better. Trollope acknowledged in one of his later travel books, *South Africa*, that he had "invariably found Jews to be more liberal than other men" – which he meant as a compliment.[15] To regard Jews as more liberal *and* more odious would seem inexplicable for someone with Trollope's worldview – unless his distaste was so ingrained, so reflexive, that it survived any mere observations.

It has not helped Trollope's case that most of his controversial portrayals of Jews came late in his career, so that it can plausibly be said that he was reacting to the gradual changes taking place in British society. Two books from the 1990s, Bryan Cheyette's *Constructions of "the Jew" in English Literature and Society: Racial Representations, 1875–1945*, and Michael Ragussis's *Figures of Conversion: "The Jewish Question" & English National Identity*, make this argument. According to Cheyette, even at his tolerant best Trollope

> constructs the racial origins of "the Jew" as a problem that, only after thorough investigation, can be situated in a narrowly defined "English" nation. Within these constraints, Trollope's "Jews" either regulate their own racialized behaviour or are excluded from an idealized, homogeneous England. By the 1870s, however, an increasingly pessimistic Trollope began to lose faith in the capacity of "the Jews" to regulate their worst excesses and in his mode of realism to adequately "know" the dark intentions of the semitic "other."[16]

Ragussis is even harsher, focusing on what he sees as Trollope's antipathy to those like Disraeli who convert to Christianity or those who try to hide their Jewish origins; for Trollope, these acts "facilitated the Jew's invasion of English culture."[17] The result of Trollope's obsession with the threat: "a series of novels whose anti-Semitism is unparalleled in the nineteenth century."[18]

Trollope certainly would not be the first whose stated views contradicted those he actually practiced; indeed, one of the better books on his work, *The Unofficial Trollope*, by Bill Overton, claims that while there are many "official" views in Trollope's writing – including some run-of-the-mill anti-Semitism – meant to reflect the commonsense opinions of the common reader in Victorian England, there is an "unofficial" Trollope as well, "working beneath and at times contradicting the beliefs he maintained explicitly."[19] Overton's argument is unassailable when it comes to questions of gender; Trollope's characters are too varied, too vibrant, to match the occasionally stereotyped pronouncements the author makes about masculinity and femininity. But in looking at Trollope's representations of Jews, one can argue that there is no "official" portrayal in his novels at all – no narrow-minded comments by the narrator that seem to mimic Victorian prejudices. There are certainly some unappealing Jewish characters, and nasty remarks about Jews from various characters too; and Trollope's narrator does not swoop in to lecture the reader on the proper way to react to such characters and remarks. Perhaps it could be said that Trollope was willing to be subtle in his presentation of Jews, and was thus willing to allow some misreadings; or that if he had been more passionate in his desire to combat what we now call anti-Semitism, he would have been careful to avoid, say, the occasional stereotyped Jewish moneylender.[20] Yet there should be no mistaking how he tried to nudge his readers toward more enlightened stances.

Overton's book, published in 1982, offers a brief but useful overview of the debate about Trollope and anti-Semitism. He agrees with those who say that "Trollope plainly associated Jews with his pet obsession: dishonesty in commerce and politics." But he also argues that Trollope "oscillated between prejudice and understanding" and that there is a strong case to be made by those who emphasize the latter.[21] Since then, some have made the case for a stridently anti-Semitic Trollope (see, most notably, Ragussis earlier), while others have argued the exact opposite, as Graham Handley does in his entry in the *Oxford Reader's Companion to Trollope*; he states flat out that "Trollope is warmly sympathetic to Judaism and the Jews."[22] Paul Delaney offers a mixed verdict, saying that "Trollope bases his anti-semitism on the long association between Jews and finance capital," but also that some "critics have assumed too easily that Trollope marginalizes and stigmatizes all Jews." Rather,

> Trollope extends to Jewish manners and aspirations a certain novelistic sympathy; and he has an acutely dialectical sense of how Jews are assigned an identity by the host society, even as they play a crucial role in transforming it into something else.[23]

Everett Carter argues that while Trollope did exhibit some prejudice "against the manners of some Jews, [he] was free of malicious racial antipathy," and goes on to show how the "sometimes casual, sometimes vicious" anti-Jewish prejudices of his characters are "satirized . . . subtly but surely."[24] Clara Claiborne Park tells us that "Trollope has a thing about grease" and is willing "to invoke the ugliest of Jewish stereotypes," but she also writes in depth about positive portrayals of Jews in other Trollope novels, including those I discuss ahead.[25] Recently, Ann Marlowe grants that "there is nasty anti-Semitism in Trollope's depictions of Jews, but there is also identification." As the title of her article indicates, it is the identification that is paramount.[26]

N. John Hall, like many others, takes a middle ground. He notes that Trollope "had many of the prejudices of most of his upper-middle-class contemporaries" and that "Jews in his stories are often unattractive, especially in the minor roles of usurious money-lenders." At the same time, Hall points to a number of positive portrayals of Jews, and says that in *Nina Balatka* especially "Trollope presented an unequivocal indictment of anti-Semitism."[27] Yet there is perhaps false equivalence in arguments such as this one. After all, *Nina Balatka*, set in Prague and published in 1867, is the only novel in which Trollope makes anti-Semitism central to his plot; it's the only time he attempted anything like a definitive statement on the subject. Considerable attention should be given to what he says in this novel and how he says it.

Anton Trendellsohn and Nina Balatka wish to marry, despite their different religions, and the entire book is about the obstacles that face them. Anton is a proud Jew who comes up against the bitter hatred of Nina's family and friends. And while Nina is not hated by Anton's family and friends, they still object to the idea of him marrying a Christian. At the end Anton and Nina do wed, but they must move to another country, where they "will not be ashamed to be known."[28] Neither one plans to convert; within their own union, the couple will attempt to carry out Anton's larger ideal for how Jews and Christians can intermingle: living "as one man should live with his fellow-men – on equal terms, giving and taking, honouring and honoured."[29] The happy ending is a muted one, but not because of the mixed marriage; rather, we are made to question whether love can conquer all, if it means that both husband and wife are permanently cut off from their own communities and incapable of forming part of a new one. Their ideal, then, is a noble one; whether they will succeed in carrying it out is left open. That it's a worthy ideal, though, is made apparent in many ways, not the least of which is Trollope's identification with Anton by giving the character his own initials. There is nothing coincidental or unconscious about this; at one point, he has Anton sign a letter "A. T.," which is how Trollope ended some of his own letters.[30]

Trollope's cosmopolitan vision is readily apparent by the end of *Nina Balatka*. What is particularly crafty about the novel is the way he ensures that we keep reading the book so that we are receptive to its message. By "we" I actually mean "they," Trollope's targeted audience: the middle-class Victorian reader likely to harbor negative feelings about Jews. Rather than scare off such readers by signaling too soon what the message will be, Trollope holds on to them by making it unclear for a long time whether Anton is a villain. And so, for instance, early in *Nina Balatka* we are told that Anton has a "greedy" mouth.[31] It is not until a third of the way through that his greed is explained in positive terms; it is here too that for the first time we become convinced of his devotion to Nina:

> To be a Jew, always a Jew, in all things a Jew, had been ever a part of his great dream. It was as impossible to him as it would be to his father to forswear the religion of his people. To go forth and be great in commerce by deserting his creed would have been nothing to him. His ambition did not desire wealth so much as the possession of wealth in Jewish hands, without those restrictions upon its enjoyment to which Jews under his own eye had ever been subjected. It would have delighted him to think that, by means of his work, there should no longer be a Jews' quarter in Prague, but that all Prague should be ennobled and civilised and made beautiful by the wealth of Jews. Wealth must be his means, and therefore he was greedy; but wealth was not his last or only aim, and therefore his greed did not utterly destroy his heart. Then Nina Balatka had come across his path, and he was compelled to shape his dreams anew.[32]

Still, Anton's heart is not safe. Nina's aunt, Sophie Zamenoy, cares nothing for Nina but refuses to have her family stained by Nina's marrying a Jew. She orchestrates a plan that culminates in Anton finding documents supposedly proving that Nina has been trying to cheat him. The efforts to break up the marriage are so relentless, and often so vile, that if we step back it is understandable that Anton begins to doubt Nina's constancy. But because the narrator has used his omniscience to tell us how trustworthy Nina is, we may still be inclined to blame Anton for his suspicions; and readers who are already inclined to be suspicious of Anton because he is Jewish may wonder if Anton's truest nature is beginning to emerge. Near the climax of the story, Nina herself at her lowest moment begins to think that the accusations against Anton are true, and "that a Jew was, of his very nature, suspicious, greedy, and false."[33] Only at the end are we fully assured of Anton's nobility; he will give up his high standing in the community, his chance for easy riches, his chance to marry an entirely worthy Jewish woman, because he loves Nina. Moreover, that other woman, Rebecca Loth, after being introduced as someone who perhaps will stoop to anything to prevent his marrying Nina, emerges as self-sacrificing and loving; she nurtures

Nina back to health after Nina's suicide attempt. As the short-story writer Frank O'Connor once wrote, Trollope's "favorite device is to lead his reader very gently up the garden path of his own conventions and then to point out that the reader is wrong."[34] It is a path that Trollope takes us up twice in *Nina Balatka* with the two major Jewish characters.[35]

Though *Nina Balatka* is Trollope's most sustained meditation on prejudice against Jews, he made similar points in *Rachel Ray*, a comic novel published two years earlier. The main plot is simple enough. Luke Rowan, an outsider from London, has inherited a portion of a brewery in a rural town. He decides to move there to improve the business – mainly, to start making beer that is not foul-tasting. The other owner, Mr. Tappitt, tries to prevent him from taking over. Battles ensue, but Luke finally prevails. He is also ultimately successful in marrying the vibrant Rachel Ray.

The Tappitt brand is universally admitted to be disgusting, but it's been around so long no one had even thought of trying to improve it. Even those who admit how bad the beer is and refuse to drink it tend to be against Luke, for he comes across as too arrogant: "they were jealous that a change should come among them with any view of teaching them a lesson or improving their condition."[36] It is a lesson, as we saw with *Nina Balatka*, for the novelist as well: if you really want to *teach* people, rather than confirm what they already know, you'd best not be heavy-handed.

When Mr. Hart, a Liberal candidate for Parliament, drinks a pint of the beer, he demonstrates that "he knew well how to canvass";[37] as a Jew running for office, he needs all the good publicity he can get. Mr. Hart barely appears as a character in his own right, but there is plenty of debate about him. For instance, Mr. Tappitt, though a Liberal himself, at first vows to abstain; he cannot bring himself to vote for "an impudent low Jew."[38] When Mrs. Cornbury, the wife of the Conservative candidate, visits him to court his vote, she argues that he is too good a Christian to vote for a Jew. Offended not by her argument but by her presence in his home, Mr. Tappitt asserts that he is duty-bound to support his political party, whereupon she says,

> Exactly; but which is your party? Isn't the Protestant religion of your country your party? These people are creeping down into all parts of the kingdom, and where shall we be if leading men like you think more of shades of difference between Liberal and Conservative than of the fundamental truths of the Church of England? Would you depute a Jew to get up and speak your own opinions in your own vestry-room?[39]

She goes on, coming up with other scenarios of improbable Jewish invasions, and by the time she leaves, Mr. Tappitt is a staunch supporter of Mr. Hart. It's bad enough that his own wife has started to push him around too much; sexism will trump anti-Semitism as he refuses to let yet another woman manipulate him.

It is especially fascinating that Luke himself seems to go along with the prejudice against Mr. Hart. In articles for the town newspaper, he argues that, while it should be legal for a Jew to run for Parliament, it would be wrong for people to actually elect a Jew. At the end of the book, though, he admits that he had partaken in plenty of "soft sawder"[40] on behalf of the election, not to be taken seriously. Ironically, the argument Luke had used is that only "their nearest neighbours"[41] should be voted for, that Mr. Hart was too much of an outsider to merit consideration. This argument had come at a point when public opinion was beginning to turn, finally, in Luke's favor, when the town was finally willing to make him part of the community instead of forcing him to remain an outsider himself. Luke's "soft sawder" has enabled him to consolidate his position.

It may not be a particularly admirable maneuver, but from the beginning Luke has been presented to us as flawed: a good-hearted, energetic man who is also "conceited, prone to sarcasm, sometimes cynical, and perhaps sometimes affected."[42] His electioneering may have been cynical, though it is clearly practical too. But by the end of the book, we are told something that may come as a surprise, though it makes sense as we think more carefully about his character: Luke is that rare breed, an advanced conservative Liberal. Trollope does not use those exact words; and instead of "advanced," he uses "radical":

> He was a radical at heart if ever there was a radical. But in saying this I must beg my reader to understand that a radical is not necessarily a revolutionist or even a republican. . . . It is in this that he is a radical; that he desires, expects, works for, and believes in, the gradual progress of the people. No doctrine of equality is his. Liberty he must have, and such position, high or low, for himself and others, as each man's individual merits will achieve for him. The doctrine of outward equality he eschews as a barrier to all ambition, and to all improvement. The idea is as mean as the thing is impracticable. But within, – is it in his soul or in his heart? – within his breast there is a manhood that will own no inferiority to the manhood of another. He retires to a corner that an earl with his suite may pass proudly through the doorway, and he grudges the earl nothing of his pride. It is the earl's right. But he also has his right; and neither queen, nor earl, nor people shall invade it. That is the creed of a radical.[43]

Luke's "soft sawder" comment is as close as he comes to a recantation of what he said during the election. And while his pandering to prejudice is reprehensible, in this comic novel we are given to understand that Mr. Hart can more than take care of himself, as he shows when he so cheerfully survives the stomach-turning beer. "Let me have a small glass of brandy at once," Mr. Hart says when he is alone with his servant";[44] and since he has a strong constitution, he recovers within half an hour. As for Luke, he may have some rough edges, but his marriage to Rachel will surely bring out his best self, so that he can outgrow his youthful indiscretions.[45] For it is Rachel's spirit that ultimately prevails; hers is the life force that quietly comes to dominate the novel. Throughout, Rachel has never said anything directly about Mr. Hart, but she does speak out, at the end of the book most emphatically, against those "who talk most of Christian charity" yet who "think evil of people."[46] Trollope shows the range and folly of pinched and narrow-minded thinking, yet he does so without preaching. The parts about anti-Semitism are seamlessly woven into a narrative that touts true "h(e)art" and "rays" of light.

Despite depicting some nasty behavior in *Rachel Ray*, Trollope maintains a genial, comic tone throughout as he leads his tale to a happy ending, and so this novel might seem to have little in common with the somber *Nina Balatka*. But Anton Trendelsohn, like Luke Rowan, is headstrong, ambitious, and full of himself. The worst sin both men commit is disappearing for a long time after opposition to the marriages becomes pronounced; though neither man intends to sever the engagement, neither realizes the suffering he causes his beloved through his silence. With both men, however, the good far outweighs the bad – once we more fully come to know them. And while both men are glad to make money, they do not care about money for its own sake. Luke really does want to make the world better by making better beer and running a more modern business, and Anton wants to make a better world in which everyone benefits from opening their hearts and minds to Jews. Both men are outsiders who are glad to become a part of their new community – though not at the cost of their own notions of integrity. But while Luke finally does become part of the community, the prejudice against Anton is such that he must reluctantly move far away.

Trollope uses similar techniques to explore similar themes in his later novels. When Madame Max Goesler is first introduced to us in *Phineas Finn* (1869), we are prepared for her to be a villain.

She is exotic and dangerous-looking, with that telltale sign in Trollope that something is deeply amiss: perfect teeth. She is a foreigner of whom almost nothing is known, though rumor has it that she is Jewish. As we come to know her well, we see that she never does the wrong thing; no character in Trollope has as fine-tuned a sense of morality and integrity. Yet even if Madame Max turns out to be, essentially, flawless, she is still very much human, for after much wandering, she hungers for real companionship and community. While she understands that there are compromises to be made, she is adamant about not compromising her integrity – hence, her purposely exotic attire, which is so different from what other women wear: not only "unlike in make, unlike in colour, and unlike in material," but also "unlike in form for any other purpose than that of maintaining its general peculiarity of character."[47] As it turns out, she is probably not Jewish, even though "[h]er enemies say that her father was a German Jew,"[48] for in one of her internal monologues, we learn that the only real complaint high society could have against her father is that he was a "small country attorney."[49] Yet she never issues any denials, never stooping to her accusers' level by declaring that her blood is "pure," and never saying a word against her late husband, who was indeed Jewish. And later, when she tries to prove that Yosef Mealyus, aka the Reverend Joseph Emilius, is a murderer, she never stoops to anti-Semitic invective, unlike Glencora, who wishes she could "rake up every wicked thing that horrid Jew has done since he was born."[50]

When, in *Phineas Redux* (1874), Phineas is accused of the murder that was committed by Emilius, both Madame Max and Glencora fight passionately to help acquit him. However, there is a crucial difference in their motivation. Glencora's support is based on faulty instinct that has no real discernment, whereas Madame Max is able to look beyond his handsome face and come to know Phineas. In some harrowing scenes, Phineas sits alone in jail and questions what an acquittal would be worth, for despite his many years in London at the center of Liberal Party politics, he is devastated by how readily people either believe him to be the murderer or, even worse, believe him capable of doing the deed and then also lying about it. Only Madame Max understands, to some degree because she sees that he too has been an outsider – a Roman Catholic from Ireland, one who has fumbled his way toward assimilating himself honorably into English society.[51]

Liking someone for the right reasons goes hand in hand with disliking someone for the right reasons, too. That Emilius/Mealyus was born Jewish does indeed become a factor in why he is so odious – just as one suspects that Trollope's disdain for Disraeli is exacerbated by the latter's Jewish origins. But it has nothing to do with anything inherently Jewish. What Trollope rails against is rank opportunism, the sense that a grossly ambitious person will do anything – including a professed change in religious beliefs – to succeed. A Jew who converts to Christianity for career advancement is a fraud. Trollope's fiction contains a gallery of Protestant and Catholic religious frauds, too, most famously Mr. Slope in *Barchester Towers*; Emilius/Mealyus is one more variation of the familiar type. As for those who have deep religious convictions and who strive to do genuine good, Trollope always endows them dignity, whether they are Christian (Mr. Harding in *The Warden* is the best-known example) or, as we saw particularly with Anton Trendelssohn, Jewish.

In *The Prime Minister* (1876), the fifth novel of the Palliser series, Ferdinand Lopez, born in Portugal, has gotten down all the moves to perfection. He is handsome and well-mannered and acts like a gentleman, but acting is all it is. Unlike Luke Rowan, who wants to make substantial changes in his new community, or Anton Trendellsohn, with his radical notions of Jewish-Christian equality, Lopez has no agenda other than to amass wealth and power and to completely fit in. Emily Wharton, daughter of a wealthy barrister, falls in love with him, and is hardly the only one to believe that he must be good; Glencora, now the Duchess of Omnium, whose husband has reluctantly become the nation's prime minister, also tries to use her influence on his behalf.

In the first part of the novel, Emily's father tries mightily to prevent Lopez from marrying his daughter. Looking for excuses, he first detects hints of "Jewish signs"[52] in Lopez's face; soon he believes Lopez to be a "probable Jew"[53] and then a definite one, a "swarthy son of Judah"[54] and a "Jew-boy."[55] Nonetheless, Emily's persistence causes her father to give in; he won't exactly bless the marriage but he does drop his opposition. He gives the couple some money, but not as much as Lopez had expected; and as Lopez's business speculations fail, he gets more and more desperate – and mean. Emily comes to realize that she has made a terrible mistake; luckily for her, Lopez ends up committing suicide and she eventually marries the man who had loved her all along, the virtuous, and slightly dull, Arthur Fletcher.

It may seem obvious enough that Wharton was right. But only a crude reading would allow us to see the novel as endorsing his vituperative anti-Semitism. In the early part of the novel, Wharton is vicious. Notably, though, he does not intensify his attacks as his son-in-law's villainy becomes evident; indeed, he makes no further anti-Jewish remarks at all. Flailing around for some excuse, any excuse, why his daughter should not marry Lopez, despite the man's impeccable looks and manners, Wharton had resorted to his heavy-handed denunciations; foolishly he thought that his noble-minded daughter could be swayed by such an argument. Once the real evidence of Lopez's wickedness is apparent, Wharton never dredges up the "fake" evidence – the idea that there is something about Jewish blood that makes Lopez inherently no good.[56]

In his effort to give Emily a happy ending, Trollope takes care to show her genuinely falling in love with Arthur – which entails distinguishing Arthur somewhat from the rest of the family. His mother is prejudiced enough to think that the widowed Emily is tainted by her association with Lopez and at first opposes the marriage to her son, while the elder brother resorts to occasional anti-Jewish slurs when speaking about Lopez. Arthur himself, however, never strays from his devotion to Emily, and earlier in the book, while he does look down on Lopez for not having "those solidities," like land, "to which such as the Whartons and Fletchers are wont to trust,"[57] he does not consider Lopez's supposed Judaism as a factor. When he asks himself, before Lopez and Emily are married, if "the man [was] necessarily unworthy because his name was Lopez, and because he had not come of English blood,"[58] the implicit answer is that this is not an adequate reason for shunning the man. Arthur here is shown to be struggling with his prejudices; but from all indications he at least understands that anti-Semitism is wrong.[59]

One could argue that Trollope struggled too – that he wouldn't have dared to be so subtle about prejudice toward Jews if he had cared deeply and unequivocally about their cause in the way that, say, George Eliot did when she wrote *Daniel Deronda* (1876). Two passages from the early 1860s hint at his awareness of own limitations – and his determination to surpass those limitations. He writes, "There is much that is higher & better & greater than one's country. One is patriotic only because one is too small & too weak to be cosmopolitan," and that

> As a rule patriotism is a virtue only because man's aptitude for good is so finite, that he cannot see and comprehend a wider humanity. He can hardly bring himself to understand that salvation should be extended to Jew and Gentile alike.[60]

Trollope does not exclude himself from being "small and weak," yet we know that he was eager to teach about "a wider humanity." Preaching would not succeed; the challenge was to continue to find ways to push and prod his readers, so that they might actually learn something. Matthew Arnold in *Culture and Anarchy* exhorted his audience "to see things as they really are."[61] And with his own prodigious body of work, Trollope tried as hard as any Victorian not only to live up to the Arnoldian ideal but also to bring his readers along with him. To be sure, there are issues on which Trollope had what we now may deem his blind spots – and he was modest enough to recognize that no human being, even an author who plays God in the creation of his omniscient novels, can fully succeed in reaching the ideal. Yet if he understood that he too could be limited in what he saw and understood, that even he might not always be as "cosmopolitan" as he would wish, he was not so falsely modest as to equate his own shortcomings with those of his typical readers. Through a combination of will and perseverance and talent, Trollope *did* see more than almost anybody else. And well before most of his contemporaries, he scrutinized what he saw as the folly of prejudice against Jews.[62]

Notes

1 Anthony Trollope, *The Eustace Diamonds*, 1872 (Oxford: Oxford University Press, 1983), Ch. 73.
2 Anthony Trollope, *The Prime Minister*, 1876 (Oxford: Oxford University Press, 1983), Ch. 15.
3 Anthony Trollope, *The Landleaguers*, 1883 (London: Penguin Books, 1993), Ch. 7.
4 Anthony Trollope, *Rachel Ray*, 1863 (Oxford: Oxford University Press, 1988), Ch. 17.
5 Anthony Trollope, *Mr. Scarborough's Family*, 1883 (Oxford: Oxford University Press, 1989), Ch. 11.
6 Anthony Trollope, *Phineas Finn: The Irish Member*, 1869 (Oxford: Oxford University Press, 1982), Ch. 11.
7 Anthony Trollope, *The Way We Live Now*, 1875 (Oxford: Oxford University Press, 1982), Ch. 78.
8 Anthony Trollope, *The Three Clerks*, 1858 (Oxford: Oxford University Press, 1989), Ch. 35.
9 Anthony Trollope, *Nina Balatka*, 1867 (Oxford: Oxford University Press, 1991), Ch. 6.
10 Rebecca Mead, "Lawyers Who Love Trollope," *The New Yorker*, April 16, 2001.
11 Anthony Trollope, *An Autobiography*, 1883 (Oxford: Oxford University Press, 1980), Ch. 16.
12 *An Autobiography*, Ch. 16.
13 That the speed of change could indeed be very slow is wittily emphasized in *The Prime Minister*, when Plantagenet Palliser (now the Duke of Omnium) explains his political beliefs to Phineas Finn – beliefs nearly identical to Trollope's own. "We can only do a little and a little," he says, so little that his wife, Glencora, won't much notice the difference. As she comes near, the Duke tells Phineas: "Here is her ladyship and the ponies. I don't think her ladyship would like to lose her ponies by my doctrine." Ch. 68.
14 *An Autobiography*, Ch. 10.
15 Anthony Trollope, *South Africa*, third edition (London: Chapman & Hall, 1878), Ch. 1.
16 Bryan Cheyette, *Constructions of "the Jew" in English Literature and Society: Racial Representations, 1875–1945* (Cambridge: Cambridge University Press, 1993), p. 14.
17 Michael Ragussis, *Figures of Conversion: "The Jewish Question" & English National Identity* (Durham: Duke University Press, 1995), p. 13.
18 Ragussis, p. 234. A more recent book, Anthony Julius's *Trials of the Diaspora: A History of Anti-Semitism in England* (Oxford: Oxford University Press, 2010), devotes only a few pages to Trollope, but gives a verdict that is also severe.
19 Bill Overton, *The Unofficial Trollope* (Sussex: Harvester Press, 1982), p. xi.
20 See Edgar Rosenberg, *From Shylock to Svengali: Jewish Stereotypes in English Fiction* (Stanford: Stanford University Press, 1960), for a discussion of how Trollope and other nineteenth-century novelists made use of the centuries-old myth of the "Jew-villain." Rosenberg argues that the literary deployment of such myths may or may not be indicative of "personal bias toward the Jews" (p. 13) – that indeed in many cases it is impossible to know. In his detailed and appreciative exploration of *The Way We Live Now* (Rosenberg is forthright about calling Trollope a major artist, a view that was not widely shared by critics of his era), he shows how Trollope both upholds and subverts stereotypes.
21 Overton, pp. 8–9.
22 R. C. Terry, ed., *Oxford Reader's Companion to Trollope* (Oxford: Oxford University Press, 1999), p. 283.
23 Paul Delany, "Land, Money, and the Jews in the Later Trollope." *Studies in English Literature, 1500–1900*, 32.4 (Autumn 1992), pp. 774.
24 Everett Carter, "Realists and Jews." *Studies in American Fiction*, 22.1 (Spring 1994), pp. 81–91.
25 Clara Claiborne Park, "Grease, Balance, and Point of View in the Work of Anthony Trollope." *The Hudson Review*, Autumn 2007, pp. 435–44.

26 Ann Marlowe, "Why Anthony Trollope Is the Most Jewish of the Great English Novelists." *Tablet*, April 24, 2015, online.
27 N. John Hall, *Trollope: A Biography* (Oxford: Clarendon Press, 1991), pp. 287–8.
28 *Nina Balatka*, Ch. 14.
29 *Nina Balatka*, Ch. 6.
30 *Nina Balatka*, Ch. 8. Though Trollope initially published *Nina Balatka* anonymously, he did not intend to hide his authorship indefinitely; and in 1871 he gave permission to Blackwood to publish the novel with his name on it (Hall, *Trollope: A Biography*, p. 308).
31 *Nina Balatka*, Ch. 1.
32 *Nina Balatka*, Ch. 6.
33 *Nina Balatka*, Ch. 12.
34 Frank O'Connor, "Trollope the Realist," in *The Mirror in the Roadway: A Study of the Modern Novel* (New York: Knopf, 1956), p. 168.
35 In his fine introduction to *Nina Balatka* for Oxford World's Classics (Oxford: Oxford UP, 1991), Robert Tracy writes that though Trollope is sympathetic to his male protagonist, he "cannot refrain from endowing Trendelssohn with certain stereotypical traits" (p. xiv). In my view, Trollope very deliberately gives Trendelssohn those traits in an effort to lure the unsuspecting (and anti-Semitic) reader.
36 *Rachel Ray*, Ch. 18.
37 *Rachel Ray*, Ch. 24.
38 *Rachel Ray*, Ch. 17.
39 *Rachel Ray*, Ch. 17.
40 *Rachel Ray*, Ch. 29.
41 *Rachel Ray*, Ch. 24.
42 *Rachel Ray*, Ch. 4.
43 *Rachel Ray*, Ch. 26.
44 *Rachel Ray*, Ch. 24.
45 For an extended discussion of Luke's character, and how he "unites the integrity of heart and hearth with morality in the market place" (p. 82), see Margaret Markwick, *New Men in Trollope's Novels: Rewriting the Victorian Male* (Aldershot, UK: Ashgate, 2007).
46 *Rachel Ray*, Ch. 29.
47 *Phineas Finn*, Ch. 40.
48 *Phineas Finn*, Ch. 41.
49 *Phineas Finn*, Ch. 61.
50 Anthony Trollope, *Phineas Redux*, 1874 (Oxford: Oxford University Press, 1983), Ch. 54.
51 For more on Madame Max's exemplary behavior, see Mary Jean Corbett, "Two Identities: Gender, Ethnicity, and *Phineas Finn*, in *The Politics of Gender in Anthony Trollope's Novels: New Readings for the Twenty-First Century* (Aldershot, UK: Ashgate, 2009), and Deborah Denenholz Morse, *Women in Trollope's Palliser Novels* (Ann Arbor, MI: UMI Research Press, 1987). See also Shirley Robin Letwin's discussion of Madame Max as Trollope's "most perfect gentleman" (p. 74) in *The Gentleman in Trollope: Individuality and Moral Conduct* (Cambridge, MA: Harvard University Press, 1982).
52 *The Prime Minister*, Ch. 3.
53 *The Prime Minister*, Ch. 3.
54 *The Prime Minister*, Ch. 3.
55 *The Prime Minister*, Ch. 4.
56 Trollope uses a similar strategy in his final (unfinished) novel, *The Landleaguers*. Early in the book, the singer Rachel O'Mahoney makes a number of foul-mouthed, blatantly anti-Semitic comments about her Jewish manager, Mahomet Moss. However, when she emerges as a far more admirable figure, her diatribes stop. In the main plot, crude group thinking of any sort – all Protestants against all Catholics, all tenants against all landlords – is shown to lead to dangerous fanaticism. It is perfectly fine for Rachel to despise Moss – but only as an individual, not as representative of an entire group.
57 *The Prime Minister*, Ch. 33.
58 *The Prime Minister*, Ch. 15.
59 Everett Carter notes that "[t]here are about twenty references to Jews in the novel; only one is authorial, and that lone example is [only] modestly derogative." While we are surely meant to dislike Lopez, Trollope "fashions his other characters' response to [him] so that English society's attitude towards the outsider is faithfully recorded and implicitly condemned" ("Realists and Jews," p. 84).

60 The first quotation is from a letter written August 23, 1862; the second is from his nonfiction book, *North America*, also from 1862. I first came across these passages, side by side, in Ruth apRoberts's seminal work, *The Moral Trollope* (Athens: Ohio University Press, 1971), p. 175.

61 Matthew Arnold, *Culture and Anarchy*, 1869 (London: Oxford University Press, 1971), Ch. 5.

62 I am grateful to Nicholas Birns, Regenia Gagnier, Lauren Goodlad, Margaret Markwick, and Deborah Denenholz Morse for their comments on an earlier draft of this chapter, and to the questions and comments of the audience at the Trollope Society in New York, where I presented a version of the chapter for the annual fall lecture.

Works cited

apRoberts, Ruth. *The Moral Trollope*. Athens: Ohio University Press, 1971. Print.

Arnold, Matthew. *Culture and Anarchy*, 1869. Oxford: Oxford University Press, 2009. Print.

Carter, Everett. "Realists and Jews." *Studies in American Fiction* 22.1 (Spring 1994): 81–91. Web.

Cheyette, Bryan. *Constructions of "the Jew" in English Literature and Society: Racial Representations, 1875–1945*. Cambridge: Cambridge University Press, 1993. Print.

Corbett, Mary Jean. "Two Identities: Gender, Ethnicity, and *Phineas Finn*." *The Politics of Gender in Anthony Trollope's Novels: New Readings for the Twenty-First Century*. Ed. Margaret Markwick, Deborah Denenholz Morse, and Regenia Gagnier. Aldershot, UK: Ashgate Press, 2009. Print.

Delaney, Paul. "Land, Money, and the Jews in the Later Trollope." *Studies in English Literature, 1500–1900* 32.4 (Autumn 1992): 765–87. Web.

Hall, N. John. *Trollope: A Biography*. Oxford: Clarendon Press, 1991. Print.

Handley, Graham. "Judaism and the Jews." *Oxford Reader's Companion to Trollope*. Ed. R. C. Terry. Oxford: Oxford University Press, 1999. Print.

Julius, Anthony. *Trials of the Diaspora: A History of Anti-Semitism in England*. Oxford: Oxford University Press, 2010. Print.

Letwin, Shirley Robin. *The Gentleman in Trollope: Individuality and Moral Conduct*. Cambridge, MA: Harvard University Press, 1982. Print.

Markwick, Margaret. *New Men in Trollope's Novels: Rewriting the Victorian Male*. Aldershot, UK: Ashgate Press, 2007. Print.

Marlowe, Ann. "Why Anthony Trollope Is the Most Jewish of the Great English Novelists." *Tablet* (April 24, 2015): N. pag. Web.

Mead, Rebecca. "Lawyers Who Love Trollope." *The New Yorker* (April 16, 2001): 31. Web.

Morse, Deborah Denenholz. *Women in Trollope's Palliser Novels*. Ann Arbor, MI: UMI Research Press, 1987. Print.

O'Connor, Frank. *The Mirror in the Roadway: A Study of the Modern Novel*. New York: Knopf, 1956. Print.

Overton, Bill. *The Unofficial Trollope*. Sussex: Harvester Press, 1982. Print.

Park, Clara Claiborne. "Grease, Balance, and Point of View in the Work of Anthony Trollope." *The Hudson Review* (Autumn 2007): 435–44. Web.

Ragussis, Michael. *Figures of Conversion: "The Jewish Question" & English National Identity*. Durham: Duke University Press, 1995. Print.

Rosenberg, Edgar. *From Shylock to Svengali: Jewish Stereotypes in English Fiction*. Stanford: Stanford University Press, 1960. Print.

Tracy, Robert. "Introduction." *Nina Balatka/Linda Tressel*. Oxford: Oxford University Press, 1991. vii–xxv. Print.

Trollope, Anthony. *An Autobiography*. 1883. Oxford: Oxford University Press, 1980. Print.

———. *The Eustace Diamonds*. 1873. Oxford: Oxford University Press, 1983. Print.

———. *The Landleaguers*. 1883. London: Penguin Books, 1993. Print.

———. *Mr. Scarborough's Family*. 1883. Oxford: Oxford University Press, 1989. Print.

———. *Nina Balatka/Linda Tressel*. 1867 & 1868. Oxford: Oxford University Press, 1991. Print.

———. *Phineas Finn: The Irish Member*. 1869. Oxford: Oxford University Press, 1982. Print.

———. *Phineas Redux*. 1874. Oxford: Oxford University Press, 1983. Print.

———. *The Prime Minister*. 1876. Oxford: Oxford University Press, 1983. Print.

———. *Rachel Ray*. 1863. Oxford: Oxford University Press, 1988. Print.

———. *South Africa*, third edition. London: Chapman & Hall, 1878. Print.

———. *The Three Clerks*. 1858. Oxford: Oxford University Press, 1989. Print.

———. *The Way We Live Now*. 1875. Oxford: Oxford University Press, 1982. Print.

27

ANTHONY TROLLOPE'S RELIGION

J. Jeffrey Franklin

> I have regarded my art from so different a point of view that I have ever thought of myself as a preacher of sermons, and my pulpit as one which I could make both salutary and agreeable to my audience.
> – Anthony Trollope, *An Autobiography* ch. 8

> It is very hard to come at the actual belief of any man. Indeed how should we hope to do so when we find it so very hard to come at our own? How many are there among us who, in this matter of our religion, which of all things is the most important to us, could take pen in hand and write down even for their own information exactly what they themselves believe?
> – Anthony Trollope, *Clergymen of the Church of England* ch. 10

It is ironic, in a characteristically Trollopian way, that we can claim such limited certainty about the religious beliefs of a man who became famous as *the* novelist of the Church of England clergyman.[1] While thousands of contemporary readers felt that his novels accurately captured Anglican clergymen and their wives, Trollope stated that "no one at their commencement could have had less reason than myself to presume himself to be able to write about clergymen," that he "never lived in any cathedral city, – except London, never knew anything of any Close, and at that time had enjoyed no peculiar intimacy with any clergyman" (*Autobiography* ch. 5). He was being falsely modest here, since "besides seven clerical ancestors by birth and seven clerical ancestors by marriage, [he] had at least nine clerical relatives sharing his surname and 14 other clerical relatives by marriage in his collateral family" (Durey 1). From boyhood he was more knowledgeable about and more interested in the ecclesiastical and political controversies that surrounded the Anglican Church than were the majority of Britons. He was deeply committed to maintaining the historical centrality of the Church of England to British society and culture. Moreover, no single fictional clergyman from the dozens portrayed in his novels fully represents either the author's personal beliefs or an exclusive stance concerning Church politics. Perhaps the strongest public statement of faith that he ever made was in reference to the founding editorial principles of *The Fortnightly Review*, that "nothing should appear denying or questioning the divinity of Christ" (*Autobiography* ch. 10). However, he accompanied this with a statement more broadly representative of his views: "The matter on which we were all agreed was freedom of speech, combined with personal responsibility. We would be neither conservative nor liberal, neither religious nor free-thinking, neither popular nor exclusive" (*Autobiography* ch. 10). This sort of dialectical balancing act – call it the Trollopian dialectic – is quintessential throughout his writings, but his oppositions seldom resolve into a comfortable synthesis but rather maintain an oscillation of positions while creating an occupiable space between them. Thus all attempts to pigeonhole him as High Church or Broad Church (Low Church never having been a serious contender) have ended in undecidability, and even where one can discern his leanings in regards to these positions his personal beliefs remain undisclosed. Trollope chose to keep his private thoughts on religion largely private, and this privateness is itself part of his position on religion.[2] Thus the Trollopian dialectic, combined with his choice to maintain a separation between the public and the private in these matters, has made the question of what he actually believed an enduring one.

Trollope wrote during a period of upheaval in the Church of England and in British Christianity in general. In short, "during the period from about 1800 to 1870 the Church of England underwent a transformation more rapid, dramatic and enduring than any which it had experienced since the Reformation" (Knight 1). It appeared to Trollope and to those of his contemporaries in the Broad Church in particular that the Church of England was threatened simultaneously by dissolution from without and by violent schism from within, given the ongoing political action by Nonconformists for separation of the "establishment" Church from the state, the highly publicized scrutiny of ecclesiastical "abuses" within the Church in the distribution of clerical positions and benefits,[3] and the bitter doctrinal and legal disputes between the High Church or Anglo-Catholic Tractarians of the Oxford Movement and the Low Church evangelicals. Trollope was painfully aware of these disruptive currents, which appear throughout his writing but especially in those most concerned with religious characters and issues: *The Warden* (1855), *Barchester Towers* (1857), *The Bertrams* (1858), *The Clergymen of the Church of England* (1866), *The Last Chronicle of Barset* (1867), and *The Vicar of Bullhampton* (1870). He wrote these contemporaneously with three of the most earth-shaking books of the nineteenth century: *The Origin of Species* (1859) by Charles Darwin, *Essays and Reviews* (1860) by a list of latitudinarian Oxbridge clergymen, and *The Pentateuch and Book of Joshua Critically Examined* (1862) by John William Colenso, Anglican Bishop of Natal, South Africa. *Essays and Reviews*, which

> initiated what was arguably the great theological and religious controversy of the Victorian era … called for a thoroughly historical and critical approach to the Bible, for recognition of the moral and spiritual worth of religious traditions outside the Bible, and for acceptance of the findings of science concerning both the age of the earth and its geological history, and the possibility (or impossibility) of miracles.
>
> (Parsons 40, 42)

This was widely greeted by British Christendom, as here in the Methodist *London Review*, as a harbinger of "'the steady onward and downward course of latitudinarianism, scepticism, infidelity, and the darkness without'" (qtd. in Shea and Whitla 29).

Religious heroes in *The Vicar of Bullhampton*

My choice of *The Vicar of Bullhampton* as a test case for the foregoing observations is predicated upon the fact that it is an under-analyzed novel with significant religious concerns about which there are conflicting interpretations. Jill Felicity Durey reads this novel as one among the later novels, including *The Eustace Diamonds* (1872) and *The Way We Live Now* (1875), that chart Trollope's "growing disillusionment with the Church as an institution, despite his remaining a devout member of it," and his "vision of a downward moral spiral in society, if not in the Church" (Durey 12, 37). In her reading, Vicar Frank Fenwick is representative of a type that "indicates through their weaknesses that the gentleman clergyman of the late 1860s does not command the same respect as his predecessor, and that he probably does not deserve it" (Durey 101). In this reading, Fenwick is an example of a weak if not failed religious leader.

In contrast, William Cadbury argues that

> because of Frank Fenwick's central part in the novel, because of his character, because of his concerns, and because of the emphasis on values [in their substance] rather than choices [by characters between competing sets of values] . . . , *The Vicar of Bullhampton* is Trollope's most religious novel.
>
> (Cadbury 154–5)[4]

He continues:

> Unlike his handling of clerical life in *Barchester Towers*, presented only in terms of the social problems of being in holy orders, Trollope here treats of the central problems of religion in the world, and most successfully creates a character who is both clergyman and man.
>
> (Cadbury 155)

By "man" Cadbury means something like "regular male member of the community" who therefore relishes defending himself with physical force against assault by would-be robbers and who is willing to join with local community in worldly pleasures, even to "let his pastoral dignity go" by playing at rat-catching with a favored young parishioner, Sam Brattle (*Vicar* 116). It is this sort of behavior that Durey interprets as a failure of the codes of the gentleman and the clergyman, supported in the text by Fenwick's closest friend, Squire Harry Gilmore, who asks Fenwick if rat-catching is not beneath his proper role. Durey overlooks the fact that Gilmore proves to be unmanly and that Fenwick is the epitome of the "manly Christianity," championed by the "muscular Christianity" movement and represented in Charles Kingsley's *Westward Ho!* (1855) and Thomas Hughes's *Tom Brown's Schooldays* (1857), that held "particular resonance for Trollope" (Vance 7; Markwick 35).

Trollope being Trollope, *The Vicar of Bullhampton* is provoking on the topic of heroes, and this is a small but significant key to the novel. The titular character is of course not named as the hero, though he is the unifying figure who connects the three primary subplots (combining seven distinct subplots). Fenwick also is proven right, if with equivocation, on three counts: in advocating for the forgiveness of Carry Brattle's sin as a fallen woman; in advocating for the innocence of Sam Brattle, her brother, who is implicated in a murder; and in representing his and the Church's position relative to Mr. Puddleham and his Methodist congregation, which has "a very strong holding" in Fenwick's parish (ch. 1). The first two of these threads constitute the "fallen woman/fallen man subplot," which also encompasses Fenwick's relation to the Brattle family, in particular the father, Jacob Brattle. Jacob is the village miller who is portrayed as a stern patriarchal judge of sin, especially in the cases of his children, but who is described throughout as an "Old Pagan, going to no place of worship, saying no prayer, believing in no creed" (ch. 5). It is for this subplot that the novel has been considered a "fallen-woman novel," and Trollope stated that he wrote it "chiefly with the object of exciting not only pity but sympathy for a fallen woman," especially among middle-class women readers, but in fact Carry is a minor character and hers is not the primary subplot in the novel (*Autobiography* 329). Perhaps Trollope did not have the same intention or perhaps courage on this subject as did George Eliot, Elizabeth Gaskell, or Thomas Hardy.[5]

The second primary subplot is the "religion subplot," the Fenwick-Puddleham or Church-Nonconformist contest with which the novel opens. Puddleham brings the contest for congregation members into Fenwick's backyard, or rather literally into his front yard by beginning to erect a Methodist chapel across the lane from Fenwick's gate. Puddleham is aided in this insult to and assault upon the Established Church by the Marquis of Trowbridge, the largest landowner in the parish. His daughters have Low Church evangelical sympathies, which align them with the Methodists, and he is insulted by Fenwick's lax treatment of such sinners as Carry and Sam Brattle and by Fenwick's presumption of equal footing as a gentleman with himself, who expects deference and fealty. The Fenwick-Trowbridge contest is an offshoot of the religion subplot, as is Fenwick's relationship with Jacob Brattle in that Brattle's "paganism" is a significant religious position competing with Fenwick's as well as with the others in the novel.

The primary subplot is the "romance subplot," involving a triangle of Mary Lowther, Harry Gilmore, and Walter Marrable. Frank and Janet Fenwick, friends with both Gilmore and Mary, attempt to compel Mary to wed Gilmore for reasons of community (with them) and practicality – she has modest resources, he is a wealthy landowner – even or especially after Mary falls in love with Walter, a dashing but not financially independent captain. The novel ultimately shows the Fenwicks and Gilmore to be wrong and Mary to be right in not marrying for practicality but rather for heartfelt love. Trollope created Mary as one of the most self-reflective and self-determining of his characters, with clearer vision than any of her elders, and in certain ways she is the real hero of this novel. However, she is a young woman, and so the text perversely adopts romance convention by naming Gilmore as "our hero, – or at least one of two," when Trollope has him squander the reader's sympathy for his heartache by becoming a maudlin stalker who tries to pressure a woman who does not love him into marriage (ch. 1). Walter is "another hero," likeable and honest enough to qualify, but he does not save Mary – she saves herself, and perhaps him as well – and really does nothing very heroic (ch. 13). That throws the reader back upon Fenwick as perhaps our hero and upon consideration of what other characters might be heroic, in a modest modern novelistic sense. I believe that Trollope intended this challenge for his readers, and, regardless of authorial intention, the text invites us to compare and contrast the relative heroism of characters representing different religious positions, which is a persuasive reason to consider this Trollope's novel most concerned with religion.

The clergymen in the novel are of course the obvious representatives of religion. Puddleham is disqualified as religious hero on multiple counts: he is a Nonconformist, not a gentleman, a toady to the marquis, and an unforgiving judge of Carry's sin. But he is true to his beliefs and his congregation. When finally defeated in his plan to locate the new chapel across from Fenwick's gate, he preaches that "it did not matter where the people of the Lord met . . . so long as they did meet to worship the Lord in a proper spirit of independent resistance to any authority [i.e., the Church] that had not come to them from revelation" (ch. 72). Puddleham functions primarily as a foil against which Fenwick demonstrates his tolerance, moderation, and Christian ethics in Broad Church fashion. Fenwick feels that "Mr. Puddleham's religious teaching was better than none at all; and he was by no means convinced – so he said, – that, for some of his parishioners, Mr. Puddleham was not a better teacher than himself" (ch. 17). The "so he said" is the sign that Trollope's narrator may not fully trust Fenwick's latitudinarianism. The reader knows that Fenwick in actuality does not much care for Puddleham or his religion. While he works upon commendable principles to avoid denominational squabbles in his parish, asking "was it not his special duty to foster love and goodwill among his people?", there is a touch of "hypocritical good humour" in Fenwick's public face about the ugly brick chapel going up opposite his house (ch. 35). The narrative leaves the reader uncertain whether to applaud Fenwick's turning the other cheek or to shake him from his assumed "willingness to regard Mr. Puddleham's flock as being equal to his own in the general gifts of civilization" (ch. 34). Puddleham serves both to recommend by contrast and to cast doubt upon Fenwick's suitability for the role of religious hero.

Far from being a religious hero, Parson John Marrable is the uncle to cousins Walter Marrable and Mary Lowther and is the rector of Loring Lowtown. He is "a kindly-hearted, good, sincere old man, – not very bright, indeed, nor peculiarly fitted for preaching the gospel, but he was much liked, and he kept a curate, though his income out of the living was small" (ch. 13). He is the example of what Trollope portrays with some sympathy but very unflatteringly as "The Town Incumbent": "located among the growing outskirts of a manufacturing town," he is overworked without financial reward commensurate to the number of his parishioners and without the pastoral lifestyle benefits of the country vicar, "probably a very good man" who "probably fails" (*Clergymen* ch. 6). With neither High nor Low Church fervor, Parson John is worldly and overly tolerant of Walter's reprobate father, Colonel Marrable, and "yet the man was a clergyman, preaching honesty and moral conduct, and living fairly well up to his preaching, too, as far as he himself was concerned!" (ch. 16). The latter phrase and exclamation mark again signal the narrator's judgment. Parson John also is an inveterate bachelor, in part out of financial necessity, and sour on marriage; contrary to his intentions, he therefore serves as an example of why Mary's hesitation about marrying Walter under less than optimal financial conditions is problematic and why her final choice to marry him in faithfulness to her own deepest feelings is right (though Trollope eases her decision by having the finances come right too).

The next potential candidate for religious hero is Rev. Henry Fitzackerley Chamberlaine, a more complex but hardly more heroic cleric. He visits Bullhampton to dispense advice to Gilmore, his nephew, about the foolishness of romantic fixation on Mary and to Fenwick about the foolishness of his tolerance for a fallen women, the foolishness of not tolerating the pretensions of a marquis, and then, when it is proved that the marquis does not own the land on which the Methodist chapel is being erected, the foolishness of tolerating its presence. He arrives in his own carriage and pair of horses and has highly refined tastes in wine, coffee, and ideas. He is "a prebendary of the good old times" who owns a stall at Salisbury Cathedral "worth £800 a year and a house" (ch. 24). In addition, he is "incumbent of a living in the fens of Cambridgeshire, which he never visited," upon which Trollope's narrator pointedly adds, "his health forbidding him to do so," when it is clear that he is in good health (ch. 24). Even though he donates money from the incumbency back to that parish, he is an exemplar of the abuses into which the Ecclesiastical Commission was probing at the time. Chamberlaine approaches the type of Dr. Grantly, but then he lacks Grantly's engaging pugnacity; he approaches the type of Mr. Arabin, but then he lacks both the spiritual devotion and the openness to female tutelage of Arabin. While Grantly and Arabin are thoroughly married, Chamberlaine, like Parson John, is an inveterate bachelor, a sign of unmanly self-centeredness for Trollope.

Though the novel is not explicit about Chamberlaine's refined ideas, we are told that "it suited his tastes and tone of mind to adhere to the well-bred ceremonies of life," which points to ritualism (ch. 24). As Fenwick describes him, "'He is the most perfect philosopher I ever met . . . and has gone to the very centre depth of contemplation. In another ten years he will be the great Akinetos,'" a genuine pagan (ch. 24). This marks him as an example of the high-and-dry Church and of a kind with the "Normal Dean of the Present Day," whose duties are "difficult to define," who "shall have shown a taste for literature in some one of its branches," and who "is a gentleman who would probably not have taken orders unless the circumstances of his life had placed orders very clearly in his path" (*Clergymen* ch. 3). He has "great gifts of preaching, which he would exercise once a week during thirteen weeks of the year," and "many applications were made to him to preach here and there, but he always refused" (ch. 24). His definition of "work" is not Trollope's. Thus the narrator comments that while he is considered a great man of the Church he "was only a prebendary, was the son of a country clergyman who had happened to marry a wife with money, and had absolutely never done anything useful in the whole course of his life" (ch. 24). The novel's final judgment of him is sealed when he heartlessly responds to Fenwick's attempts to rehabilitate Carry and bring her back to her father's house and to the community by saying, "'There are penitentiaries and reformatories, and it is well, no doubt, to subscribe to them'" (ch. 27).

This leaves among the clergymen only Fenwick as candidate for religious hero. He would seem to qualify on the basis of Christian compassion and charity, in particular in working to save Carry. The problem from the perspective of Mr. Puddleham and his congregation, the marquis and his daughters, and even Fenwick's own more traditional parishioners is that he seems less concerned with saving her soul than with saving her in the worldly ways of body, family, and community. To Puddleham, who believes she must be cast out and allowed to suffer the full consequences of such a heinous sin, Fenwick responds in a Mauricean vein:

> Have we not all so sinned as to deserve eternal punishment. . . . Then there can't be much difference between her and us. . . . If she believe and repents, all her sins will be white as snow. . . . Then speak of her as you would of any other sister or brother, – not as a thing that must be always vile because she has fallen once.
>
> (ch. 17)

On the one hand, Fenwick is only enacting his author's participation in an historical trend that was especially compatible with Broad Church principles. There was a movement throughout the century, even among evangelicals, away from the Calvinist emphasis on fallenness, a

> shift of emphasis from the death of Christ to the life of Christ – from a theology centred on the Atonement to one centred on the Incarnation – and a shift from the wrath and judgement of God to the love and Fatherhood of God.
>
> (Parsons, 109)

Jacob Brattle, the marquis, and Mr. Puddleham, though very different, each practice the wrath of God. In contrast, and on the other hand, Fenwick practices liberality in the extreme, even within the historical trend. Janet Fenwick, in writing to Mary about the Jobian suffering of Jacob Brattle, asks,

> Can it really be that the man is punished here on earth because he will not believe? When I hinted this to Frank, he turned upon me, and scolded me, and told me I was measuring the Almighty God with a foot-rule.
>
> (ch. 14)

For Fenwick, Brattle is not excluded from God's love even in his apostasy. Thus the marquis refers to Fenwick throughout, up until their final reconciliation, as an infidel, "and if an infidel, then also a hypocrite, and a liar [in claiming allegiance to the *Thirty-Nine Articles*, as required], and a traitor, and a thief" of the parish's tithes to the Church (ch. 26).

It only further weakens Fenwick's case in the eyes of those around him when he variously acknowledges sexuality as a natural human act, even for women; points out the greater culpability of men than women, as well as the double standard by which women even so are more harshly judged; and minimizes the severity of it as a sin, as when he says,

> Think how easy it is for a poor girl to fall, – how great is the temptation and how quick, and how it comes without knowledge of the evil that is to follow! How small is the sin, and how terrible the punishment! Your friends, Mr. Brattle, have forgiven you worse sins than ever she has committed.
>
> (ch. 27)[6]

Reminding people of their equal culpability and, worse, of their hypocrisy about it does not strengthen one's case, though it is clear that Trollope's narrative favors Fenwick's greater tolerance on religious issues and on women's issues.

Meanwhile, Fenwick has hypocrisy and credibility issues of his own. The novel foregrounds this first in relation to Fenwick's fishing and rat-catching with Sam Brattle, which is known throughout the parish and casts doubt upon his objectivity concerning Sam's innocence of murder and upon his fitness for his office. The marquis and his family are under the impression that the vicar and Sam spend "the best part of their Sundays" in these sports, and though Trollope does not substantiate this claim he intimates it in order to bring in one of his pet peeves about evangelicals, which is their strict Sabbatarianism (ch. 17). Fenwick says to Gilmore on the subject,

> I understand it all, old fellow . . . and know very well I have got to choose between two things. I must be called a hypocrite, or else I must be one. I have no doubt that as years go on with me I shall see the advantages of choosing the latter.
>
> (ch. 17)

Being a hypocrite means here both engaging in an activity one loves even if beneath the dignity of a vicar and, by implication at least, breaking the Sabbath, according to stringent Sabbatarians (such as Mrs. Proudie), even when training and norms compel one to preach observance of it. Trollope raises the latter issue in "The Clergyman Who Subscribes for Colenso," whom he describes thus:

> Now the special offence of the liberal preacher on this occasion was a thing conveyed in a sermon that the fourth commandment ["Remember the Sabbath Day to keep it holy"] in its entirely is hardly compatible with the life of an Englishman in the nineteenth century.
>
> (*Clergymen* ch. 10)[7]

Indeed, hypocrisy is the special cross to be borne by the liberal clergyman: "He is one who, without believing, cannot bring himself to think that he believes, or to say that he believes that which he disbelieves without grievous suffering to himself. He has to say it, and does suffer" (*Clergymen* ch. 10). It may be that Fenwick is a clergyman who, like Trollope, subscribed for Colenso.

The crisis of hypocrisy and credibility comes home for Fenwick in his relationship to Carry. Carry bears the burden of beauty, and Fenwick is not quite self-reflexive enough to fully understand the complexity of his own motives or the risk that he is taking in the eyes of the community. Thus we read:

> He thought for a moment that he would tell her that the Lord loved her; but there was something human at his heart, something perhaps too human, which made him feel that were he down low upon the ground, some love that was nearer to him, some love that was more easily intelligible, which had been more palpably felt, would in his frailty and his wickedness be of more immediate avail to him than the love even of the Lord God.
>
> *(ch. 25)*

Indeed. While the novel approves the Broad Church toleration that facilitates Fenwick's genuine Christian charity, it also expresses an ambivalence around that latitude, which occurs at the interface between the spiritual and the temporal, in the form of Fenwick's natural human frailty and the observance of it by his critics in the community. Fenwick's temporal frailty is a commentary on the frailty of his spiritual position, and it is in this way that Trollope participates in the general discourse of his time about spiritualism versus materialism, though only indirectly, given his reticence on spiritual topics.

The text enacts this ambivalence as an oscillation in the narrator's commentary. The narrator first observes that "perhaps it was a fault with [Fenwick] that he never hardened his heart against a sinner, unless the sin implied pretence and falsehood" (ch. 25). Then, when in discussing with his wife Brattle's casting away of Carry, Fenwick says, "It is very difficult to make crooked things straight," the narrator comments, "It is probably the case that Mr. Fenwick would have been able to do his duty better, had some harsher feelings toward the sinner been mixed with his charity" (ch. 26). The narrative appears to be aligning itself with Brattle's harsh judgment, though with the qualification of "perhaps" and "probably." A hundred pages later, the same question arises:

> Was it a fault in him that he was tender to her because of her prettiness, and because he had loved her as a child? We must own that it was a fault. The crooked places of the world, if they are to be made straight at all, must be made straight after a sterner and a juster fashion.
>
> *(ch. 40)*

Yet, when the narrative returns to this topic it comments, "The straight-going people of the world, in dealing with those who go crooked, are almost always unreasonable" in expecting the crooked to embrace with gratitude the harsh corrective measures sanctimoniously offered (ch. 52). This is the Trollopian dialectic, the "characteristic doubling mind" of his "subversive" or "slippery" narrator, the canny structuring through which the "narrative voices establish a dialogue between themselves while playing a teasing game with the reader, so quintessential of Trollope, [and] feels decidedly modern" (Swingle 112; Kincaid 155; Morse, *Reforming* 7; Markwick 81).

It would appear that Trollope, like his age, was divided. "Isn't the world a better place if we all live by the example of Jesus' love," he seems to be saying, but then, in the same instant, "Wouldn't the straight path be easier to discern if God's law and the method of following it were universally clear for all to follow?" Trollope says something quite similar in *Clergymen of the Church of England*, referencing the clergyman who subscribed for Colenso:

> If one could stay [with non-modernized Christianity], if one could only have a choice in the matter, if one could really believe that the old shore is best, who would leave it?

Who would not wish to be secure if he knew where security lay? But this new teacher, who has come among us with his ill-defined doctrines and subrisive smile, – he and they who have taught him, – have made it impossible for us to stay. With hands outstretched towards the old place, with sorrowing hearts, – with hearts which still love the old teachings which the mind will no longer accept, – we, too, cut our ropes, and go out in our little boats, and search for a land that will be new to us. . . . Who would not stay behind if it were possible to him?

(Clergymen ch. 10)

There is some genuine pathos here. Trollope knew that neither he nor, ultimately, Christianity itself could remain on the old shore but rather must follow the new clergyman who "had, by the subscription, attached himself to the Broad Church with the newest broad principles, and must expect henceforth to be regarded as little better than an infidel . . . by the majority of his brethren of the day" (*Clergymen* ch. 10). "Infidel" is the word used repeatedly by the Marquis of Trowbridge for Mr. Fenwick.

The Vicar of Bullhampton thus enacts the competing historical pressures inherent in what Victor Shea and William Whitla, commenting upon *Essays and Reviews*, describe as the "Broad Church compromise" (124).[8] This was the rhetorical maneuver by which first the literalness of the Bible is disproved and the necessity of accommodating it to "modern criticism" and to science is established, but then "these discrepancies are swept away and a faith position is asserted" (Shea and Whitla 110, 125). That "faith position" was based upon the felt rightness of awe before God and of adherence to Christian morality. Matthew Arnold employed this argument to posit the essence of Christianity as "righteousness," "not simply *morality*, but *morality touched by emotion*," meaning God's immanence verified by the common human experience of right and wrong (Arnold 176).[9] The Broad Church compromise was the resolution that resulted from the "juggling of these two factors, the emotional, located in the truth of the human heart, and the rational, located in the critical faculties of the mind analyzing history and language" (Shea and Whitla 124). In *The Vicar of Bullhampton*, all three of the primary subplots – the fallen women/fallen man, religious, and romantic subplots – enact the ascendency of the "truth of the human heart" and a compromise with rationality, and Trollope's artistic mastery resides in part in his design of the implicit parallels between Fenwick's choices in the former two subplots and Mary's choices in the latter one.[10]

The Broad Church compromise actually was between three, not two, positions: faith, unbelief, and "morality touched by emotion." Faith, according to Broad Church proponents, was implicit in or folded into morality/emotion, but, according to some Broad Church opponents, was therefore effaced and lost. For the Broad Church, morality/emotion was, to use non-phenomenological language, the deconstructing third term; it kept faith alive by not opposing it irreconcilably to the rationality or worldliness that might lead to unbelief. *The Vicar of Bullhampton* represents all three of these religious positions. Put simply, Fenwick and Mary each represent morality/emotion and faithfulness to one's deeply held emotional truths, whether in religion or in love. They demonstrate the compromise needed to balance spirituality with temporality, as do all of Trollope's sympathetic clerical characters.

The two most lionized religious figures in this novel are none of the clergymen but rather Fanny, Carry's sister, and Jacob, her father. They stand respectively for faith and unbelief of a particular kind. Fanny is the unbeautiful, selfless, pious sister, but she is neither simpering nor sanctimonious. She reflects upon "the strange destiny of women" by which her beautiful sister has been ruined and she is likely to have no lovers and continue as "a homely, household thing," but she does this without judgment or self-pity (ch. 53). She stands true to both her sister and her brother. It is she who has the will to admit Carry into the house against her father's edict. It is she who cares for Carry's physical needs for food and clothing and, when those are met, asks, "will you kneel here and say your prayers as you used to?" (ch. 53). She is emblematic of the old shore of faith, the unmodernized Christianity, but compassionate rather than judgmental, and still free from doubt.

Jacob Brattle, working-class, almost primitive, "pagan," is more than a match for Fenwick, who, while pugnacious to robbers and noblemen alike, says that Brattle "is the only person in the world of whom I believe myself to be afraid" (ch. 26). While he may be a non-practitioner, he practices a rigorous but unforgiving Christian morality. Fenwick wonders whether he should be working harder to bring Brattle into the fold, but "of what use could it be to preach repentance to one who believed nothing":

> he could tell the man, no doubt, that beyond all this there might be everlasting joy not only for him, but for him and the girl together; – joy which would be sullied by no touch of disgrace. But there was a stubborn strength in the infidelity of this old Pagan which was utterly impervious.
>
> *(ch. 63)*

Nevertheless, in ways that no doubt concerned Trollope's devout readers, Brattle is the religious hero of the novel: "about the miller there was a stubborn constancy which almost amounted to heroism" (ch. 50). The novel opens and closes with Brattle, and on the last page one reads that "Death, when it came, would come without making the old man tremble" (527).

Brattle's character represented a radical religious statement. It reflects Trollope's recognition of what was to come, that in the last quarter of the century "it would hardly be an exaggeration to say that it was the agnostics rather than the orthodox who had the sense of being official, an intellectual establishment more powerful than the church establishment" (Cockshut 11). It is as if Trollope foresaw that "by 1900, the question 'What do Anglicans believe?' [would] become, in any straightforward sense, impossible" (Parsons 62), that the history in which he was living would be

> the story of how the unity represented by the Established Church of England gave way to religious pluralism and diversity and of how Britain adapted to this pluralistic society through the growth of religious tolerance and a more religiously neutral polity.
>
> *(Melnyk 155)*

Trollope deeply regretted this, but he was a realist, as is Fenwick when, visiting London, he reflects upon "the Sunday occupations of three millions of people not a fourth of whom attend divine service" (ch. 68). He worked to ameliorate this trend, to swing public attention away from the divisive in-fighting between ritualists and evangelicals, and to shore up the Church as still the authentically British platform for genuine religious practice and the best institutional structure for a civil, ethical, and caring society.

N. John Hall observes that the

> segment of the Church of England informally denominated 'broad' suited Trollope nicely; he could pretty much dismiss the Old Testament, admire the moral teachings of Christ, and keep up an ill-defined belief in a supreme being and a vague hope of some kind of immortality.
>
> *(Hall 184)*

While not inaccurate, this seems mildly dismissive, untrue to the complexity of Trollope's struggles over religion, and presumptive on questions of faith about which Trollope chose to remain silent. I too have argued that Trollope came down somewhere within the Broad Church, though I do not disagree with Amanda Anderson's nuanced conclusion that "it certainly cannot be claimed that Trollope unequivocally supports a liberal ideal, even one tempered by sober realism or anchored by exemplary character," because "there is a genuine tension between his liberalism and his persistent valuing of traditional forms of life in the face of what for him are the negative dimensions of modernity" (Anderson 531). Trollope's upbringing and tastes predisposed him to High Church traditionalism, but he opposed both its dogmatic and elitist elements and was enough of a true Protestant to bridle at the paternal mediation of a priesthood between individual and God. Though he sometimes tarred evangelicals, it could be argued that he shared their characteristic allegiance to individual choice in questions of faith and individual responsibility for moral decisions. Yet, he saw the proliferation of "brands competing in the religious marketplace" and the swelling culture of "consumer-consciousness" in religious choice as destructive to the Church, to Christianity, and to English culture and society (Melnyk 135). In contrast to a fully "modern Christianity" of Protestant persuasion, which might be said to stand on individualized faith but in a public arena (of evangelical testimony), Trollope's Christianity, modified by a gentlemanly reticence on questions of faith, was at once private and communal, private faith within community practice, which may characterize one type of modern Anglicanism.[11] Trollope being Trollope, he famously described his political position as "an advanced, but still conservative Liberal" (*Autobiography* ch. 16). A similar statement might apply to the religious position he fashioned for himself, which was more multifaceted and contingent than the primary categories of High, Broad, and Low. At the periphery of the center of nineteenth-century British religious discourse, Trollope occupied a position between all others.

Similarly, there is and can be no singular religious hero in Trollope's fictional world, nor, he believed, in his society. His heart was with heart, the morality/emotions that he believed must serve as the mediating factor between unquestioning faith and unbelieving rationality, between spiritual commitment and temporal interests. Morality/emotions – the faith of the Broad Church – must be the compass between individual choices and communal responsibilities, but Trollope well understood that this is a human instrument, even if created and potentially guided by God, and so is fallible, frail, unavoidably self-interested, and influenced by desires beyond reliable control. Thus Fenwick cannot be fully suitable as the novel's religious hero, given that he demonstrates also the natural frailty of the human heart, and this fact is the sign of Trollope's strain to believe even in its unerring rightness or to hold any faith not based upon morality/emotion monitored by rationality. Rather, Fanny Brattle, Jacob Brattle, and Frank Fenwick (paralleled by Mary Lowther) form a trinity of partial religious heroes, each incomplete without the others, representing faith, righteous unbelief, and the morality/emotions that must balance the other two. The highly Trollope-like commentary of the narrator is required to hold this trinity in unsettling but vital community.

Notes

1 apRoberts, 13, also observes this.
2 Mullen and Munson, 433, make a similar observation about Trollope's privateness on religion.
3 The Ecclesiastical Commission had been launched in 1836 to regulate the distribution of the "11,600 total benefices in England and Wales" (Melnyk 7). The most common "abuses" were nepotism (favoritism in distributing incumbencies), pluralities (clergy holding multiple incumbencies), and absenteeism (clergy not in residence at one of their held parishes), all of which Trollope's novels represent.
4 For a similar observation, see Kincaid, 155.

5 On Trollope's treatment of fallen women, see Morse, *Women in Trollope's Palliser Novels*.
6 "In regard to a sin common to the two sexes, almost all the punishment and all the disgrace is heaped upon the one who in nine cases out of ten has been the least sinful" (*Autobiography* ch. 18).
7 Trollope acknowledged that he "worked always on Sundays, – as to which no scruple of religion made me unhappy" (*Autobiography* ch. 15). Also see the article he published in *The Fortnightly Review* titled "The Fourth Commandment."
8 The Broad Church compromise may have echoed the Tudor settlement between church and state at the founding of the Church of England; see Shea and Whitla 76. The working out of the resulting conflicts between church and state is present behind all of Trollope's writings about clergymen.
9 See Franklin, 820.
10 There is a more specific parallel between Carry and Mary (as their names imply), and Trollope's complex and subtle point is this: the fact that Carry has committed a sin of passion and perhaps love (and that Fenwick's motivations in relation to her are mixed for similar reasons) does *not* mean that Mary should not marry with consideration for passion and love but rather that she should do just that. This is the Trollopian dialectic.
11 For some nineteenth-century conceptions of fully "modern Christianity," see Patterson, Sabatier, and Walker.

Works cited

Alford, Henry. "Mr. Anthony Trollope and the English Clergy." Rev. of Clergymen of the Church of England, by Anthony Trollope. *The Contemporary Review* (June 1866): 240–62.
Anderson, Amanda. "Trollope's Modernity." *ELH* 74.3 (2007): 509–34.
apRoberts, Ruth. "Introduction." In Anthony Trollope, *The Clergymen of the Church of England*. 1866. Ed. Ruth apRoberts. Leicester: Leicester University Press, 1974, 9–49.
Arnold, Matthew. "Literature and Dogma, An Essay Towards a Better Apprehension of the Bible." In *The Complete Prose Works of Matthew Arnold*. Vol. 6. *Dissent and Dogma*. Ed. R. H. Super. Ann Arbor: University of Michigan Press, 1968, 139–411.
Bankert, M. S. "Newman in the Shadow of *Barchester Towers*." *Renascence* 20.3 (1968): 153–61.
Cadbury, William. "The Uses of the Village: Form and Theme in Trollope's *The Vicar of Bullhampton*." *Nineteenth-Century Fiction* 18.2 (September 1963): 151–63.
Chadwick, Owen. *The Victorian Church*. 2 vols. Part 1. Oxford: Oxford University Press, 1966.
Cockshut, A. O. J. *Anglican Attitudes, A Study of Victorian Religious Controversies*. London: Collins, 1959.
Durey, Jill Felicity. *Trollope and the Church of England*. Houndmills, England: Palgrave Macmillan, 2002.
Franklin, J. Jeffrey. "The Influences of Buddhism and Comparative Religion on Matthew Arnold." *Literature Compass*. Special Issue: Philosophy and Literature in Nineteenth-Century Britain. 9.11 (November 2012): 813–25. <http://onlinelibrary.wiley.com/doi/10.1111/lico.2012.9.issue-11/issuetoc>. 11 November 2012.
Gilmour, Robin. *The Idea of the Gentleman in the Victorian Novel*. London: George Allen & Unwin, 1981.
Hall, N. John. *Trollope: A Biography*. Oxford: Clarendon Press, 1991.
Hughes, Thomas. *Tom Brown's Schooldays*. 1857. London: Dent, 1906. <https://babel.hathitrust.org/cgi/pt?id=coo.31924013486091;view=1up;seq=11>. 30 April, 2016.
Kimball, Roger. "A Novelist Who Hunted the Fox: Anthony Trollope Today." *New Criterion* (March 1992): n.p. <http://www.newcriterion.com/articlepdf.cfm/A-novelist-who-hunted-the-fox—Anthony-Trollope-today-4519>. 23 October 2013.
Kincaid, James. *The Novels of Anthony Trollope*. Oxford: Oxford University Press, 1977.
Kingsley, Charles. *Westward Ho!* 1855. New York: Thomas Y. Crowell & Company, 1893. https://babel.hathitrust.org/cgi/pt?id=nyp.33433074877089;view=1up;seq=9. 30 April 2016.
Knight, Frances. *The Nineteenth-Century Church and English Society*. Cambridge: Cambridge University Press, 1995.
Letwin, Shirley Robin. *The Gentleman in Trollope: Individuality and Moral Conduct*. Pleasantville, NY: Akadine Press, 1997.
Markwick, Margaret. *New Men in Trollope's Novels: Rewriting the Victorian Male*. Aldershot, England: Ashgate, 2007.
Mayne, Michael. "Introduction." In Anthony Trollope, *The Clergymen of the Church of England*. 1866. Ed. Ruth apRoberts. London: Trollope Society, 1998. vii–xix.

Melnyk, Julie. *Victorian Religion: Faith and Life in Britain.* Westport, CT: Praeger, 2008.

Morse, Deborah Denenholz. *Reforming Trollope: Race, Gender, and Englishness in the Novels of Anthony Trollope.* Farnham, England: Ashgate, 2013.

———. *Women in Trollope's Palliser Novels.* Ann Arbor, MI: UMI Research Press, 1987.

Mullen, Richard, and James Munson. *The Penguin Companion to Trollope.* London: Penguin, 1996.

Parsons, Gerald. *Religion in Victorian Britain.* Vol. 1. Ed. Gerald Parsons. Manchester: Manchester University Press, 1988.

Patterson, Charles Brodie. "The Spirit of Modern Christianity." *The Arena* 26.4 (October 1901): 384.

Perkin, J. Russell. *Theology and the Victorian Novel.* Montreal and Kingston: McGill-Queen's University Press, 2009.

Sabatier, Auguste. "Religion and Modern Culture." *The New World: A Quarterly Review of Religion, Ethics and Theology* 8 (March 1899): 91–110.

Shea, Victor, and William Whitla. *Essays and Reviews: The 1860 Text and Its Readings.* Charlottesville, VA: University Press of Virginia, 2000.

Swingle, L. J. *Romanticism and Anthony Trollope: A Study in the Continuities of Nineteenth-Century Literary Thought.* Ann Arbor: University of Michigan Press, 1990.

Terry, R. C., ed. *Trollope: Interviews and Recollections.* New York: St. Martin's Press, 1987.

Trollope, Anthony. *An Autobiography.* Ed. Michael Sadleir and Frederick Page. 1883. New York: Oxford University Press, 1950.

———. *Barchester Towers.* 1857. Oxford: Oxford University Press, 1980.

———. *Clergymen of the Church of England.* 1866. London: Trollope Society, 1998.

———. "The Fourth Commandment." *The Fortnightly Review* 17 (January 15, 1866): 529–38.

———. *The Vicar of Bullhampton.* 1870. London: Penguin, 1993.

Vance, Norman. *The Sinews of the Spirit: The Ideal of Christian Manliness in Victorian Literature and Religious Thought.* Cambridge: Cambridge University Press, 1985.

Walker, E. D. *Reincarnation: A Study of Forgotten Truth.* 1888. New York: University Books, 1965.

Wilson, Harry Bristow. "Séances historiques de Genève – The National Church." *Essays and Reviews, The 1860 Text and Its Readings.* Ed. Victor Shea and William Whitla. Charlottesville, VA: University Press of Virginia, 2000. 275–344.

PART VII

Global Trollope

28

IRISH QUESTIONS

Ireland and the Trollope novels

Gordon Bigelow

To say a thing was "Irish," in a certain strand of nineteenth-century discourse, was to say that the thing in some way stood in contradiction to itself. The *OED* preserves this sense of the word, citing among other things an 1838 letter by George Eliot.[1] Margaret Hale, in Gaskell's *North and South*, thinks to herself at one point, "If the world stood still, it would retrograde and become corrupt, if that is not Irish."[2] The usage obviously derives from the term "Irish bull," publicized by Maria Edgeworth and her father, Richard, in their essay of 1802: a witticism that rebounds in some self-cancelling way upon the wit, leaving us wondering whether we or the speaker are the ultimate butt of the joke.[3] When Thady Quirk, narrator of Edgeworth's *Castle Rackrent*, says that old Sir Condy could have been a brilliant lawyer, "if he could have borne the drudgery of that study," he is saying a great deal.[4] You can't be a lawyer of any kind if you can't bear the "drudgery," but we can never really figure out whether this is naïve and sentimental praise or knowing criticism from Thady. "Bull" existed as a term long before the Edgeworth's essay: a bull was a piece of nonsense, a contradiction, and an Irish bull was one that contained one of these particular backflips.[5] It will be useful to keep these high-stakes linguistic maneuvers in mind as we consider Trollope's relation to Ireland.

Trollope lived in Ireland between 1841 and 1851 and continued there off and on until 1859, and so from the start anyone invested Trollope's books needed to consider what he had to say about the place. But Trollope's Irish novels are, to put it in a somewhat neutral and preliminary way, strange. They are different formally and thematically from the novels that built Trollope's reading audience and that came to stand for his place in the history of the novel, however that might be construed. Their tone is often harsh and often unstable, shifting registers unexpectedly. Their plots seem to lack the affably unhurried pace of the canonical productions, and the playful but nonetheless comprehensive sense of formal unity found in the Barsetshire or Palliser novels. But even if we consider just the timing of the Irish books, they demand our attention. His first two novels were both written and set in Ireland: *The Macdermots of Ballycloran* (1847) and *The Kellys and the O'Kellys* (1848). After the commercial failure of these, Trollope essentially abandoned Ireland as a subject, dipping back in only with *Castle Richmond* (1860), and later with the novella *An Eye for an Eye* (1879). But at the end of his life he returned to the same questions that motivated the novels of the 1840s, leaving the draft of a final novel, *The Landleaguers*, about two-thirds complete at his death in 1882. Alongside these five novels, which sit so uncomfortably alongside the mainstream, we also need to consider *Phineas Finn* and its sequel, which reverse the pattern by offering typically Trollopian form with an Irish protagonist.

There is little in these novels to gratify the taste of Victorian readers for "Irish" wit, in the deprecatory sense described earlier. In general they contain no "bulls" or sly verbal "quirks," but rather a sustained examination of social and economic conflict. But it also seems clear that readers from the first found these novels in some fundamental way illegible, incomplete, or incoherent. One review of *Macdermots* argued that "the story should excite an interest which we cannot feel for the characters, either as gentry or peasants, because they belong to neither."[6] Another suggested that "such startling anomalies as are presented to us in the history of the decline and fall of the M'Dermots of Ballycloran [sic] can only be met with in Irish life."[7] *Castle Richmond*, set during the Irish Famine of 1845–50, drew similar responses. One reviewer complained about the novel's mixture of politics and romance, saying that "the milk and the water really should be in separate pails."[8]

In other words, the problem in these books is not that they are poorly conceived or poorly written. The problem is that they are, in some local sense, "Irish": defying received categories, blurring identifiable patterns, disrupting interpretation. The issue is how to read these apparently inconsistent, self-undermining, "Irish" productions. Early critics, focused largely on matters of evaluation, tended either to disparage the Irish novels or to defend their value on developmental or historical grounds. Only recently has it become possible to consider the problematic form of these texts as a legitimate critical object in itself.

Early patterns

T.H.S. Escott, Trollope's first biographer, knew the author in the last decade of his life, and subsequent writers have relied on Escott for key aspects of Trollope's early years in Ireland. In one important line of argument, Escott emphasizes the visits Trollope made to Coole Park, the country estate of his old school acquaintance William Gregory. Here, Escott asserts, Trollope was immersed in Irish fiction. He was at this point already a devoted reader of Scott and Austen, and if Escott's recollection is accurate, it was here that Trollope encountered Edgeworth and the tradition that came to be known as the Irish National Tale. He read more recent work by William Carleton with particular interest and struck up a friendship with Charles Lever, whose episodic comedy *Harry Lorrequer* had appeared in 1839.[9] When *Macdermots* was published, Escott reports, Gregory called it "the best Irish story that had appeared for something like half a century."[10] All this suggests that when Trollope wrote novels about Ireland, he did it with an awareness of a rich tradition.

But the other enduring aspect of Escott's account moves in an opposing direction, for if he points on the one hand toward deliberate study of the Irish novel, he suggests on the other a more diffusive personal transformation. In Ireland, he writes, Trollope "fancied he could see a resemblance between the condition of the country and his own state and prospects. This inspired him with a kind of sympathetic affection for the Irish people."[11] The equivocation in the term "fancied" is typical of Escott, cultivating the kind of carefully hedged neutrality that first appeared to fit him for the editorship at the *Fortnightly*, as the magazine edged away from what had been a more liberal orientation.[12]

Escott hints here that Ireland may be a matter more of biographical than literary relevance in Trollope's career, a place of personal transformation but not of lasting intellectual engagement. This line of argument reaches its logical end point in Michael Sadleir's 1927 biography, which offered the following influential judgment:

> Ireland produced the man; but it was left to England to inspire the novelist. Indeed one may go further. Ireland, having by friendliness, sport and open air saved Trollope from himself, came near by her insane absorption in her own wrongs and thwarted hopes to choke the very genius that she had vitalized.[13]

He adds the corollary proposition that when Trollope started writing about Ireland in the 1840s, the books are marred by an unaesthetic "insistence on actual political happening."[14]

He draws a bright line between these books, along with *Castle Richmond* and *Landleaguers*, and the dominant voice Trollope establishes in the 1850s. *The Warden* is thus "the first Trollopian novel," representing a substantial break from the Irish books preceding it.[15] And thus Ireland produced in Trollope's life a "queer contradictory effect."[16] The formulation is striking inasmuch as it recirculates the notion of what is "Irish" that was common in Trollope's age, and that Trollope himself was fairly careful to avoid.

Sadleir's dismissal of the Irish books was answered by Robert Donovan in a 1956 article called "Trollope's Prentice Work." Donovan makes the case that the first novels "represent an inevitable early stage in the growth toward what he later became."[17] He aims to show that *Macdermots* and *Kellys* are no more topical or "political" than any other Trollope novel, and that these early books experiment with techniques central to Trollope's later work. In establishing these continuities between the Irish and the English Trollope, Donovan has to rely a bit too much on *Kellys*, with its gently inclusive comic spirit, but the direction of the argument is significant. Donovan seeks to defend the literary character of the Irish novels in developmental terms, thus securing for them some provisional place in the great display case of Victorian masterworks.

There were still some bibliographical and textual matters in this period that needed clearing up, and publications in the 1960s and 1970s filled in the basic picture. In 1965 Helen Garlinghouse King collected the seven letters Trollope wrote to the London *Examiner* in 1849 and 1850, letters that provide an extensive and revealing analysis of the Famine and the varying government programs for relief.[18] R.C. Terry in 1972 told the story of three lost chapters from *Macdermots*, chapters that had been removed when the novel was prepared for republication in 1859.[19] John W. Clark's *Language and Style of Anthony Trollope* (1975) provided a welcome shift of focus toward the specific verbal texture of the novels, and his section on "Irish English" includes a catalogue of evidence to support his view that "Trollope was a close and loving observer of Irish speech."[20]

The 1960s and 1970s also saw increasing critical attention to the Irish novels, much of it following Donovan's lead in looking for continuities rather than radical breaks. R.C. Terry's 1977 monograph places considerable emphasis on that first novel whose lost chapters he had recovered. Terry champions *Macdermots* as a "virtuoso performance," easily deserving recognition alongside Trollope's better-known works. But this reading does not harmonize well with his overall contention that what drives Trollope's typical plots is an impulse toward social compromise.[21] A very different argument for continuity emerges in Robert Polhemus's *The Changing World of Anthony Trollope* (1968). For Polhemus, Trollope at his best is a historical contextualist, showing always the way individual action is shaped by "the clutch of history." The Irish novels thus represent only somewhat exaggerated versions of Trollope's norm.[22] E. W. Wittig takes pains to dissent from Polhemus's Marxist premise but without providing a clear alternative.[23]

The centenary

The early 1980s saw a general revival of interest in Trollope's fiction, with 1983 marking the one hundredth anniversary of his death. Two centenary anthologies appeared, each with overview chapters covering the Irish novels. Janet Dunleavy's short piece in a 1982 volume emphasizes the historical accuracy of Trollope's observations.[24] A chapter by John Cronin in a 1980 anthology provides perhaps the most sustained and careful consideration of the Irish novels to that point, with an extended critique of Sadleir's early dismissal.[25] But like Dunleavy, Cronin is still trying to bear the critical burden of canon formation, seeking reasons to release some (but not all) of the Irish novels from their critical purgatory. He reserves *Macdermots* and *Kellys* for special praise, and his work on Irish literary and social history is still of interest. He concludes nonetheless by seeking a special exception for *Landleaguers*, which he suggests "must be charitably ignored as an aberration."[26]

A somewhat different approach is adopted by John Hynes and Judith Knelman, both of whom try to piece together a coherent view of Irish politics out of the novels and the *Examiner* letters.[27] Hynes also wrote an imaginative essay about the cultural atmosphere the young Trollope would have encountered in the town of Banagher when he first arrived there in September, 1841.[28] Hynes's emphasis on local and specific conditions marks something new in the conversation. This tendency toward focused investigations was most pronounced in two essays by Robert Tracy, essays that are perhaps the most enduring contributions of the era. In "The Unnatural Ruin" Tracy expands on Cronin by looking carefully at Trollope's relation to the Irish fiction of the first half of the nineteenth century. What emerges here largely settles the question of Trollope's reading, which others had pondered over in the abstract.[29] This article provided a baseline for further research and is still a useful starting point. Tracy's essay on *Landleaguers* again sidesteps the evaluative standards that had dominated discussion of the book and provides a key to the novel's precise reflection of contemporary events.[30] Tracy's contributions here are all the more impressive given that he published widely on other aspects of Trollope's work, including an essay on "Trollope's Classicism" and a book on the late novels.[31] Tracy demonstrates the kind of border-crossing expertise in Victorian literature, Irish fiction, and Irish cultural history that seems necessary to cope with the particular problems Trollope's Irish fiction presents.

Equally detailed in its attention to the Irish cultural context, but very different in outcome, is Owen Dudley Edwards' attempt to prove that Trollope is really an "Irish Writer."[32] The details of the argument are still interesting even if contemporary readers judge the larger point moot. Where assertions of this kind rely on the critic's sense of what counts as "Irish" or "English" in some transcendent sense, contemporary readers have found it more instructive to consider the history of these categories themselves, and the largely uninventoried traces of history that formed them.

Perhaps the most expansive criticism of this era came from Christopher Herbert, and while Herbert's work touched little on the Irish Trollope, it established important directions for research that still bear significantly on the Irish novels. In *Trollope and Comic Pleasure* (1987), Herbert proposes that Trollope's "lifelong devotion to the mode of comedy" resulted in a surprising emphasis on sheer play and "purely verbal exoticism," aspects of the work typically neglected when we see Trollope as a realist.[33] And in *Culture and Anomie* (1991) Herbert expends considerable intellectual energy in hefting what could easily be seen as the lightest of the Barsetshire novels, *Doctor Thorne*. This familiar cross-class romance, in Herbert's hands, turns out to reveal an emerging anthropological view of culture, in which the term indicates nothing about organic growth or development but rather suggests a "total way of life."[34] Herbert's emphases on genre and "culture," as I will argue ahead, are both of potential use to students of the Irish novels.

The novel and the Famine

The pattern we have seen so far is one that stretches back to Sadleir's 1927 judgment that the Irish novels are different from the rest, and inferior, and Donovan's 1956 claim that they are the same, just somewhat rougher. Attention to the Irish fiction through the 1970s and 1980s generally followed Donovan's path, defending the novels from charges of incoherence or anomaly through various historical and biographical strategies. Thus *Macdermots* and *Kellys* are celebrated as the essential germ of Trollope's art, unfinished but potent, and all the books are celebrated for their historical accuracy. In the 1990s critics reject the need to "defend" the Irish novels at all. The result is further work of the kind Tracy pioneered on Irish literary contexts, and Herbert pointed to in his emphasis on genre. What is nascent here is a new and more careful attention to the history of cultural and aesthetic forms, and it is this work that has produced the most promising results to date.

The most striking example comes in a pair of readings of *Castle Richmond*, Trollope's novel of the Irish Famine. This book represents the author's first return to Irish matters since he had so resolutely abandoned them more than a decade before, but it only reinforces the question of form pressed on us by the novels of the 1840s. Its romance plot is about the sheerest of any in Trollope's oeuvre, and this thin narrative fabric is stretched to the breaking point by the grievous political and economic matters the book takes on. Its drastic shifts of tone, as it moves from the tropes of light romance to the subject of death by starvation, are shocking and unresolved.

As the 150th anniversary of the Famine arrived in the final years of the twentieth century, scholars of Irish history and culture returned to the event with renewed urgency and interest. New studies arising in the 1990s made it clear how many questions remained to be answered about this period, which saw roughly a million people die from starvation and disease, and another million emigrate – this from a total population of less than 8 million.[35] All this provided a new framework in which to consider Trollope's book. While Trollope had always been in some way understood as a political author, the sense of what this meant began to shift. Readings focused on the representation of parliamentary governance and the thematic treatment of legislative questions had dominated this conversation, as evidenced in Halperin's *Trollope and Politics* (1977).[36] Articles by Hynes and Knelman treated the Irish fiction in this way, looking for thematic content that would argue one thing or another about repeal or Famine relief or land reform. This interest in the representation of politics begins to appear untenable once the limitations of what is called "political" in this sense began to be made clear. New waves of criticism posed broader questions about authority and aesthetics and the politics of culture. Instead of looking only at what is said directly in political essays, like the *Examiner* letters, or what is conveyed thematically in the fiction, critics considered the allegiances and ideologies tangled up with matters of form, genre, and verbal texture. To use a familiar shorthand, the question shifted from the representation of politics to the politics of representation itself. In many ways these questions coalesced and crystallized in the field of postcolonial studies, as this field transformed the conversation about Irish cultural history.

Criticism in this higher key produced two landmark assessments of *Castle Richmond*. Christopher Morash's 1995 book *Writing the Irish Famine* explains the formal disruption of *Castle Richmond* as evidence of a more general tension between the generic impulses of the novel and the violence of history. He follows Lukacs's observation that the form of novel is primarily biographical, with typical plots emphasizing "the integration of the individual into the social order."[37] But this generic imperative is at odds with the optimistic liberalism Morash finds in the letters to the *Examiner*, letters that construe the Famine as a tragic but ultimately salutary correction made to a distorted social and economic system. Thus while liberal "metanarratives of progress may have made it possible to accept the 'extermination' of entire classes or categories of beings," it is impossible that novels could do so given their investment in the uniqueness of individual characters.[38] And so the tears in the novel's structure are most meaningful not as an indication of the author's own politics or skill but as evidence of the antinomies of liberal historicism itself.

Margaret Kelleher's 1997 book *The Feminization of Famine* pursues a parallel analysis of history and narrative form, emphasizing colonial contexts where Morash is somewhat more attuned to economic ideology. Surveying famine texts from the Irish crisis as well as the Bengali famine of the 1940s, Kelleher notes a marked tendency to represent the overwhelming human suffering of these events through the depiction of "female spectacle."[39] The pattern is clearly in evidence in *Castle Richmond*, confirmed in that central episode in which the protagonist, Herbert Fitzgerald, enters a tiny stone cabin where an emaciated mother has just witnessed the death of her child.[40] Images of female suffering like this one, according to Kelleher, dramatize the problem of famine but also contain it, presenting famine as "an unstoppable force" that benevolent individuals can do little to alter. Thus "Trollope's image of famine as female spectacle . . . functions to ensure that the problem of famine is at once communicated and obscured."[41]

Castle Richmond has continued to attract critics' attention since these two major readings. A 2004 special issue of the journal *Victorian Literature and Culture* on Ireland featured a reading of romance genres in *Castle Richmond* by Bridgett Matthews-Kane.[42] A 2006 essay by Margaret Scanlon continues to explore the book's "awkward lurches from the melodramatic Anglo-Irish plot to the actual disaster."[43] A revisionist reading by Jane Nardin appeared in 2003, and it questions the emphasis on formal disruption in recent studies. Nardin relies on James Kincaid's idea of Trollope's typical structure, in which the "exposition of . . . traditional values" in a central plot is typically disrupted by a "counter-exposition" or critique arising out of a subplot.[44] Thus for her the shock of the Famine depictions makes clear the "parodically artificial" character of the romance plot, as the "'background' descriptions of the famine. . . jump into the foreground."[45] The two plots in her reading are thus aligned in a kind of logical tension, or what an earlier generation of critics might have called structural irony, with the effect that romance conventions are revealed in all their ideological depth. Nardin's cautionary note is worth keeping in mind, but it doesn't lay the question to rest. The distance between plot and subplot (can we call famine a subplot?) is simply on a different scale in this text. *Castle Richmond* may attempt the same kind of narrative arrangement as any of the Barsetshire novels, but that does not mean it succeeds.

Mary Jean Corbett's 2000 book *Allegories of Union* should also be considered here given its interest in narrative structure and generic conventions. As its title suggests, the book looks at the trope of marriage as deployed in the representation of the English-Irish relationship, a trope whose hoary provenance is frequently alluded to but rarely studied. In a detailed reading of *Macdermots*, Corbett focuses on Feemy Macdermot's elopement with Myles Ussher, but the depth of her research produces a rich analysis of this "marriage plot" in the novel *as* a plot, a kind of narrative that becomes readable in relation to the young novelist's struggle to craft original plots of his own. With *Castle Richmond* Corbett looks at the way the novel continues to transform the domestic plots of the National Tale; what results for her is a complex "ambiguity at the heart of even so confidently imperial a reading of Ireland as Trollope's."[46] A similarly nuanced look at the marriage allegory informs Catherine Frank's 2008 essay on *Phineas Redux*.[47]

The problem presented by the Irish novels from the start has been a matter of form. The approach outlined in Kelleher and Morash and Corbett offers a way forward, holding out the promise that the formal problems characterizing virtually all of Trollope's Irish texts might become legible to us in a new way. They point in the direction Emer Nolan called for in a more recent study of the novel in Ireland: a way to "read the precise nature of these [formal] distortions and discontinuities in relation to the history that generates them."[48] All this helps to indicate what can be achieved through a method of reading that can consider the politics of aesthetic forms and the ideological limits imposed by particular generic conventions. This method, charted in this work on *Castle Richmond*, stands to open our view of Trollope's writing in general and to address the questions about the Irish novels that have plagued critics from the start.

The return of the political

But if our sense of what counts as "political" expanded in the 1990s, it has recently begun to contract once again. As if weary of indirect arguments about the politics of culture, critics have returned as it were to the politics of politics, bringing with them a refreshed set of critical tools. In Victorian studies this trend emerged in the reexamination of nineteenth-century liberalism, and the trend has led critics generally away from Trollope's problematic Irish novels and toward the more straightforward national allegory of *An Eye for an Eye*, and toward the *Phineas* books.

An Eye for an Eye, little discussed in twentieth-century criticism, has now attracted defenders as ardent as those who first championed the novels of the 1840s. A sympathetic 2006 article by Jill Durey scrutinizes the Old Testament allusion of the novel's title.[49] A 2004 piece by John McCourt looks at Trollope's use of Hiberno-English in the novel, concluding, in parallel with Clark's *Language and Style*, that the text "succeeds surprisingly well."[50] In another article the following year, McCourt considers the way the novel's "liminal" setting near the western Cliffs of Moher allegorizes the English-Irish conflict it depicts.[51] In a 2009 book Thomas Tracy provides a sophisticated reading of this allegory, finding in the novel a skeptical revision of Sydney Owenson's *Wild Irish Girl*.[52]

It is *Phineas Finn*, however, that gains most in this new trend. Brilliantly unproblematic in form, this otherwise seamless comedy of parliamentary life nonetheless revolves problematically around an Irish character. Trollope remarked in the *Autobiography* that it had been a "blunder" to make Phineas Irish, and this seems to have authorized readers to assume that Ireland is an accidental theme in these books, not a central subject of analysis.[53] Patrick Lonergan clears this path a bit, offering an explanation in 2004 as to why Irish matters seem somewhat tangential in *Phineas*, and quite remote in the books that follow. As Home Rule came to dominate the Irish parliamentary contingent, he suggests, it became impossible to contend that an Irish MP opposed to Home Rule could continue to serve, and thus Phineas had to be marginalized as the Palliser series goes on.[54] Two different readings in 2009 take things further, confronting more systematically the sometimes elusive issue of Phineas's Irishness. In a study of nineteenth-century realism, Geoffrey Baker argues that Ireland in the Phineas books is associated with the principle of romance, such that the story of Phineas's London career stages an encounter between romance and empiricism characteristic of the modern novel.[55] An article by Mary Jean Corbett takes seriously the question of Phineas's divided or decentered subjectivity – a matter of central concern for Trollope's narrator – arguing that the text "calls into question the naturalness" of "ethnic and gendered norms."[56]

But in or about 2010 something changed, and two critics attempted detailed contextual readings of the Irish land question in the novel. Elaine Hadley finds confirmation there of her view that mid-Victorian liberalism was more embedded in locality and land than earlier accounts emphasizing intellectual abstraction and psychic detachment have suggested. For her, *Phineas Finn* is built around the "deep presumption ... that a person draws his gendered, civic authority from his open possession of the ground on which he stands and takes a stand."[57] Hence "the liberal subject in this period, even amid its embodied abstractions, is not universal but local," and Phineas stands for this complex locality.[58] Sara Maurer is similarly concerned with the issue of property, but her reading emphasizes a distinction between the chores associated with owning land – maintaining the buildings, cultivating the foxes – and the pleasures of its use. Owning nothing but visiting in grand houses everywhere, Phineas is the novel's foremost example of this kind of "vicarious enjoyment."[59] As the emblem of enjoying without owning, Phineas then stands for a special Trollopian kind of unionism, holding Ireland in allegorical marriage to the British state. But Maurer finds this compromised vision of property to be pervasive in the period, and thus she concludes like Hadley that the characteristics associated with Phineas's Irishness are, through some paradoxical reversal, offered up in these texts as things that are, at their core, characteristically English. In Hadley's words, Phineas represents the fundamental "Irishness of liberal opinion."[60]

These arguments about the land question in the text are both gratifying to read, bringing a sustained attention and a philosophical depth to issues earlier readers mostly ignored. But for all their detailed attention to the Phineas books, both in some way feel oddly preliminary and partial. The logic asserted in both readings works through a kind of reversal or inversion of received categories, such that local and anomalous practices associated with Ireland are shown to merge through a kind of textual slippage with the things most central to Englishness itself. This is one of the legacy gestures of poststructuralism and the modes of postcolonial criticism that it sponsored. It is the gesture that unmasks the contradictions of racial binarism and the instability of colonialism's divided societies. But then, for one thing, it is odd that neither really discusses the unusual preoccupation with race in *Phineas Finn*. It is a concern that arises not directly out of the treatment of Ireland or Irish characters but from an occasional discourse on blackness. Phineas's friend Mr. Low disparages the work of party politics by saying that "it is at the best slavery and degradation."[61] When the liberal Lord Brentford is forced to vote the elimination of his own pocket borough, one of his Tory rivals chuckles, "There's nobody on earth I pity so much as a radical peer who is obliged to work like a nigger [sic] with a spade to shovel away the ground from under his own feet."[62] Blackness is figured here as labor without return, as occupation without ownership, and the pattern seems directly relevant to the land question Maurer and Hadley explore. We are returned to the sense that the word "Irish" sometimes conveyed: a self-defeating or self-cancelling assertion, an exertion that recoils back upon itself.

But beyond the Phineas novels themselves, when we unfold Hadley and Maurer's critique alongside the conversation about *Castle Richmond*, there is an odd divergence. The crucial thing about Trollope's depiction of Irishness, for Maurer and Hadley, is that it is on a certain deep level *the same* as the depiction of Englishness. The enduring debate about the rest of Trollope's Irish texts has to do with their overwhelming *difference*. The narrative structure, the verbal texture, and the tonal range of *Macdermots*, *Kellys*, *Castle Richmond*, and *Landleaguers* are so far distant from Trollope's accustomed norms after 1855 that they seem to be the products of some other imagination. We might add *An Eye for an Eye* to this list if we considered its oddly truncated form, which suggests that its problems can be illustrated only in a miniaturized and stylized allegory. The next stage in the discussion that Maurer and Hadley have begun might be to open it to this larger Irish corpus and to the question of form critics have raised there.

It certainly might be the case that the Phinead just functions in a different way from these other books, and that the very different treatment Maurer and Hadley bring is fitted to its subtle shape. But that only returns us to the original question: *why* are the other Irish books so different? These are multi-plot social novels, set in Ireland and dealing more with the economics than the politics of land, thus very unlike the metropolitan bildungsroman of *Phineas Finn*. To get at this broader problem, it will be helpful to think in terms of genre, to consider in a more wholistic way the problem of form that has troubled the discussion from the start. With Michael McKeon, I would suggest that the most revealing work on the theory of the novel emerges from and depends on a dialectical method.[63] It understands the formal structures of the novel to take shape in response to specific historical changes, advancing and contesting particular claims to social authority. Criticism like that of Kelleher and Morash on *Castle Richmond*, engaged with the epistemological or ideological limits of a given mode of representation, works in this dialectical tradition, as it seeks to understand social facts and subjective experiences that lie beyond those limits.

The work by Maurer and Hadley brings a welcome insight into the context of ideas in the Phineas books but is less engaged with the novels' form, and what might lie outside it.

A major advance in the discussion, though it appeared too late to receive the attention it deserves here, is offered by John McCourt's *Writing the Frontier: Anthony Trollope Between Britain and Ireland* (2015). It is the first monograph devoted entirely to this subject, and it shows what can be accomplished when the Irish books are considered together in relation to each other. Its focus is not on the questions of form and difference I have been tracking through the criticism here, but it presents illuminating contextual and thematic readings of the novels.

The energy injected by McCourt's book can help to bring further attention to this discussion and to the methodological divide that has characterized it. The divide itself is worth theorizing. The risk otherwise is that we fall into that trap that opened up early on in the formation of postcolonial theory, at least from Robert Young's *White Mythologies* (1991). Young's rejection of dialectical methods, which for him typify the authoritarian and assimilationist impulse of empire, reinforced Edward Said's rather blunt assertion that colonies were never really about material gain, and set the program for a postcolonial criticism that diverged from the Marxist imperatives of earlier anti-colonial movements.[64] The divide we've noticed in the treatment of Ireland in Trollope's work might be understood in the context of this allergy that postcolonial studies contracted early on to dialectical methods.

An Irish history of the novel

In a sharp introduction to a 1988 edition of *Macdermots*, Robert Tracy borrows the following aphorism to describe what Trollope had achieved: he "had not written a novel *about* Ireland; he had written an Irish novel."[65] The remark is from Thomas Flanagan's *The Irish Novelists* (1959), in a discussion of Gerald Griffin's 1829 novel *The Collegians*.[66] But what is meant here by "Irish novel"? Flanagan is trying to sum up the qualities that made Griffin's novel a mainstay of Irish popular culture. But Tracy applies the phrase to make the point that in his first novel Trollope is writing less in the tradition of Austen and Scott and more in the tradition of Griffin himself, and the other Irish novelists that Escott tells us he encountered in the library at Coole. Tracy sums up:

> The English novel appeals continually to social coherence as a goal, even when depicting injustice or agitation. Its form reflects this coherence, with characters and situations subordinated to and integrated into the total work. The Irish novel, depicting a divided society, rarely achieves such formal coherence. It tends to be episodic, a series of encounters or activities not wholly integrated into a plot ... In this, as in its insights, *The Macdermots* is an Irish novel.[67]

From the late nineteenth century, critics puzzled over the problem of why the novel seemed never to have flourished in nineteenth-century Ireland, and why this society had produced no novelist to contend with the likes of Eliot or Scott.[68] It was Flanagan who began to consider the problem in historical terms, or perhaps it is more accurate to say he began to consider history itself to be the problem. The Irish novel, he argued, is "saturated in history," committed to the working out of a disputed cultural legacy, and thus barred from the common ground of moral debate that defined the genre's dominant forms.[69]

Following this argument then, the failure of Trollope's early works begins to seem less a matter of youthful inexperience than "of the resistance of an anomalous Irish culture to modes of representation emerging into dominance."[70] The terms here are David Lloyd's, in an important 1991 essay on the problem. Lloyd describes the "dominant" strand of the nineteenth-century novel in terms of its drive toward "ethical identity."

> Ethical identity is the end of the novel in a double sense. On the one hand, [the novel] narrates the passage of an individual or people-nation from a contingent particularity to universal value. . . . On the other, it seeks to produce ethical identity as an intrinsic element of its aesthetic effect.[71]

The complex fractures of the Irish social landscape ran jagged lines through any possible space of ethical unity, thus forestalling any thoroughgoing resolution of social conflict at the level of form. Better known but ultimately less productive in advancing the discussion is Terry Eagleton's *Heathcliff and the Great Hunger* (1995). Eagleton stages the debate on the always slippery terrain of realism: "The realist novel," he writes, "is the form *par excellence* of settlement and stability, gathering individual lives into an integrated whole; and social conditions in Ireland hardly lent themselves to any such sanguine reconciliation."[72]

What both Lloyd and Eagleton were aiming at in this work from the mid-1990s is a critique of the sociology of literary forms, one that could expand the history of the novel from what had largely been a metropolitan focus. In the same way that Kelleher and Morash sought to make the fractured representations of the Famine legible in some framework that could take us beyond questions of aesthetic value or historical accuracy, Lloyd and Eagleton asked for a mode of genre criticism adequate to the formal variety and complexity of the novel's history in Ireland. However, in particular Eagleton's somewhat glib use of the "realist" template has led to confusion. Helen O'Connell, in an otherwise useful study of tract novels circulated by nineteenth-century charitable groups, charges that "a story commonly told about Irish writing is that it failed to produce realist fiction at a time when realism was flourishing in the European mainstream." The story is false, she argues, because the books she studies were "strongly didactic and assertively realistic."[73] In another valuable study of Irish novelists in the Victorian period, James Murphy writes sardonically about the "supposedly maimed nature of Irish fiction," deprecating the assertion as something "often simply asserted in a priori terms as part of a postcolonial critique."[74]

O'Connell and Murphy both add to our understanding of the novel in nineteenth-century Ireland, expanding the picture beyond the figures typically mentioned and making clear how rich and diverse this field actually was. But their objections to previous work are largely misplaced, with much riding only on how one defines the "realist" or "mainstream," as against the "maimed" character of the novel in Ireland.[75] Their reaction seems to stem from the evaluative premise their accounts embrace. Aiming to recover and celebrate the achievement of neglected writers, they regard any approach emphasizing formal discontinuity to be as invidious and as offensive as Sadleir's 1927 attack. Meanwhile, the criticism imagined in Lloyd would be something closer to what Mary Poovey has called "historical description": a kind of reading that could pose questions about form and genre while keeping at bay any normative presumption of organic unity.[76] We still need the kind of empirical account of what was published that Murphy and O'Connell call for, but we also will continue to require the kind of synthesis and explanation (or what detractors simply call "theory") that Lloyd aims at. To move toward an Irish history of the novel in this way, as Kelleher points out, we will need a more precise and flexible account of the dominant strains of English fiction.[77] Part of the problem here, as Garrett Stewart recently argued, is that "serious genre criticism . . . has been confined of late mostly to rise-of-the-novel studies in the long eighteenth century."[78] But if the aim is to study the metropolitan genres of the novel and their limits, then Trollope should be exhibit A. Trollope's books cross this limit whenever they cross the Irish sea, operating one way in Barsetshire and another way in Connaught.

A certain further spice is added to all this by Murphy's testy rejection of the premise that Trollope has anything much to teach us about Ireland, or about Irish fiction. *Macdermots*, he writes, opens "with an insouciance betokening a rejection of that interest in social and economic conditions, which in fact was typical of fiction about Ireland."[79] *Kellys* is "about individual action rather than social analysis."[80] And *Castle Richmond* "like its two predecessors... remains remote from any real sense of the evolving uncertainties concerning land in Ireland."[81] Murphy's biographical research on Irish novelists in Trollope's era has enlarged our sense of the period and opened new avenues of research. His exclusion of Trollope from the list of promising subjects should sharpen the appetite of his critical opponents.

For our purposes, it is encouraging to note that some of the best genre criticism on the British novel to emerge recently (though Stewart fails to notice it) has focused on the relation between Celtic regions and the English metropole. Katie Trumpener's *Bardic Nationalism* and Ian Duncan's *Modern Romance* both try to trace generic patterns in a complex exchange between Celtic peripheries and the London publishing world. Joe Cleary has extended the discussion, arguing that we need to consider the Scottish and Irish novel not in British or European but in global terms. What we will find, he argues, is that our usual "sense of comparative deficiency" is in fact a "regular feature of other national surveys everywhere in the colonial and non-metropolitan world from nineteenth-century South America to twentieth-century Africa, Asia, the Middle East or Eastern Europe." He continues:

> Once we accept that the development of Anglo-French realism in the nineteenth century is really the exception to the rule of the world novel, not the golden mean Eurocentric cultural historians have always assumed it to be, then the more fitful, wayward development of the nineteenth-century Irish novel must cease to be understood as any kind of aberration in wider international terms.[82]

Trollope stands at the crossroads of this unfinished debate. His "fitful, wayward" Irish productions were trapped for an unusually long time in an argument about canonical merits, one that could result only in new means of condemnation or celebration. But the same could be said for his canonical English works: a bit of a critical backwater, with critics struggling to justify their interest in what was thought to be second-rate. It may now be that we are ready to move beyond these limits. If the Irish novels are "fitful and wayward," these very aspects of their form provide a rich archive in which to study the way historical and cultural conditions shape and contend with metropolitan conventions of narrative. If Trollope's canonical form is affable and anodyne, then its very capacity to distract and to sooth offers its own archive of social conflict in the metropolitan field of vision.

In this way Trollope's work can advance our thinking about the relation of the English and the Irish novel, and perhaps our broader view of Western Europe in relation to the world history of the novel. What is required is a sociological criticism expansive enough to consider the colonial borders Trollope's oeuvre crosses. Given the scale of the problem, it may never yield to simple solutions, certainly not ones that will satisfy scholars committed to an empirical as opposed to a critical history of culture. But with Trollope, we might begin.

Notes

1 "Irish," *Oxford English Dictionary*, online ed. www.oed.com. Accessed November 28, 2013.
2 Elizabeth Gaskell, *North and South*, ed. Dorothy Collin (London: Penguin, 1970), pp. 390–1.
3 Maria Edgeworth, *An Essay on Irish Bulls*, ed. Jane Desmarais and Marilyn Butler (Dublin: U College Dublin P, 2006).

4. Maria Edgeworth, *Castle Rackrent* and *Ennui*. Ed. Marilyn Butler (London: Penguin, 1992), 125.
5. "Bull," *Oxford English Dictionary*, online ed. www.oed.com. Accessed November 28, 2013.
6. *Spectator* xx (May 8, 1847), p. 449, repr. in *Trollope: The Critical Heritage*, ed. Donald Smalley (London: Routledge, 1969), p. 547.
7. *New Monthly Magazine* n.s. lxxx (June 1847), p. 249, repr. in *Critical Heritage*, p. 552.
8. *Saturday Review* (May 19, 1860), repr. in *Critical Heritage*, pp. 113–14.
9. T.H.S. Escott, *Anthony Trollope: His Public Services, Private Friends, and Literary Originals* (Port Washington, NY: Kennikat, 1967), pp. 51–4.
10. Escott, p. 61.
11. Escott, p. 40.
12. D. George Boyce, "Escott, Thomas Hay Sweet," *Oxford Dictionary of Literary Biography*, online ed. www.oxforddnb.com. Accessed November 28, 2013.
13. Michael Sadleir, *Anthony Trollope: A Commentary* (Boston: Houghton Mifflin, 1927), p. 136.
14. Sadleir, p. 135.
15. Sadleir, p. 144.
16. Sadleir, p. 136.
17. Robert Donovan, "Trollope's Prentice Work" *Modern Philology* 53.3 (1956), p. 179.
18. Anthony Trollope, "Trollope's Letters to the *Examiner*," ed. Helen Garlinghouse King, *The Princeton University Library Chronicle* 26 (1965): 71–101.
19. R.C. Terry, "Three Lost Chapters of Trollope's First Novel," *Nineteenth-Century Fiction* 27.1 (1972): 71–80.
20. John W. Clark, *The Language and Style of Anthony Trollope* (London: Deutsch, 1975), p. 101.
21. R.C. Terry, *Anthony Trollope: The Artist in Hiding* (Totawa, NJ: Rowman and Littlefield, 1977), p. 189.
22. Robert M. Polhemus, *The Changing World of Anthony Trollope* (Berkeley: U of California P, 1968), pp. 10–23.
23. E.W. Wittig, "Trollope's Irish Fiction" *Eire-Ireland* 9.3 (1974): 97–118.
24. Janet Egleson Dunleavy, "Trollope and Ireland," *Trollope: Centenary Essays*, ed. John Halperin (New York: St. Martin's, 1982), pp. 53–69.
25. John Cronin, "Trollope and the Matter of Ireland," *Anthony Trollope*, ed. Tony Bareham (London: Vision, 1980), pp. 13–35.
26. Cronin, p. 34.
27. John G. Hynes, "Anthony Trollope and the Irish Question," *Etudes Irlandaises* 8 (1983): 212–28; Judith Knelman, "Anthony Trollope, English Journalist and Novelist Writing About the Famine in Ireland," *Eire-Ireland* 23.3 (1988): 57–67.
28. John Hynes, "Anthony Trollope's Creative 'Culture Shock': Banagher, 1841," *Eire-Ireland* 21.3 (1986): 124–31.
29. Robert Tracy, "'The Unnatural Ruin': Trollope and Nineteenth-Century Irish Fiction," *Nineteenth-Century Fiction* 37.3 (1982): 358–82. See Cronin 15–16 for a recap of the question.
30. Robert Tracy, "Instant Replay: Trollope's *The Landleaguers*, 1883," *Eire-Ireland* 15.2 (1980): 30–46.
31. Robert Tracy, "*Lana Medicata Fuco*: Trollope's Classicism," *Trollope: Centenary Essays*, ed. John Halperin (New York: St. Martin's, 1982): 1–23; Robert Tracy, *Trollope's Later Novels* (Berkeley: U of California P, 1978).
32. Owen Dudley Edwards, "Anthony Trollope, the Irish Writer," *Nineteenth-Century Fiction* 38.1 (1983): 1–42.
33. Christopher Herbert, *Trollope and Comic Pleasure* (Chicago: U of Chicago P, 1987), pp. 2–3, 29.
34. Christopher Herbert, *Culture and Anomie: Ethnographic Imagination in the Nineteenth Century* (Chicago: U of Chicago P, 1991).
35. Joel Mokyr, *Why Ireland Starved: A Quantitative and Analytical History of the Irish Economy, 1800–1850* (London: Allen & Unwin, 1983), p. 266.
36. John Halperin, *Trollope and Politics* (New York: Barnes and Noble, 1977).
37. Christopher Morash, *Writing the Irish Famine* (Oxford: Oxford UP, 1995), p. 40.
38. Morash, p. 40.
39. Margaret Kelleher, *The Feminization of Famine: Expressions of the Inexpressible?* (Durham, NC: Duke UP, 1997), p. 47.
40. Anthony Trollope, *Castle Richmond*, ch. 33.
41. Kelleher, p. 56.

42 Bridgett Matthews-Kane, "Love's Labour's Lost: Romantic Allegory in Trollope's *Castle Richmond*," *Victorian Literature and Culture* 32.1 (2004): 117–31.
43 Margaret Scanlon, "The Limits of Empathy: Trollope's *Castle Richmond*," *Hungry Words: Images of Famine in the Irish Canon*, ed. George Cusack and Sarah Gross (Dublin: Irish Academic P, 2006), p. 73.
44 James Kincaid, *The Novels of Anthony Trollope* (Oxford: Clarendon, 1977), p. 4.
45 Jane Nardin, "*Castle Richmond*, the Famine, and the Critics," *Cahiers victoriens & édouardiens* 58 (2003), p. 88.
46 Mary Jean Corbett, *Allegories of Union in Irish and English Writing, 1790–1870: Politics, History, and the Family from Edgeworth to Arnold* (Cambridge: Cambridge UP, 2000), pp. 115–28.
47 Catherine O. Frank, "Trial Separations: Divorce, Disestablishment, and Home Rule in *Phineas Redux*," *College Literature* 35.3 (2008): 30–56.
48 Emer Nolan, *Catholic Emancipations: Irish Fiction from Thomas Moore to James Joyce* (Syracuse: Syracuse UP, 2007), p. 54.
49 Jill Durey, "An Eye for an Eye: Trollope's Warning for Future Relations Between England and Ireland," *Victorian Review* 32.2 (2006): 26–39.
50 John McCourt, "An 'I' for an 'E'. An Ireland for an England. Trollope's Hiberno-English in *An Eye for and Eye*," *Etudes Irelandaises* 29.1 (2004), p. 20.
51 John McCourt, "Writing on the Edge: Trollope's *An Eye for an Eye*," *Variants: The Journal of the European Society for Textual Scholarship* 4 (2005): 223.
52 Thomas Tracy, *Irishness and Womanhood in Nineteenth-Century British Writing* (Farnham: Ashgate, 2009).
53 Anthony Trollope, *An Autobiography*, ch. 17.
54 Patrick Lonergan, "The Representation of Phineas Finn: Trollope's Palliser Series and Victorian Ireland," *Victorian Literature and Culture* 32.1 (2004): 147–58.
55 Geoffrey Baker, *Realism's Empire: Empiricism and Enchantment in the Nineteenth-Century Novel* (Columbus: Ohio State UP, 2009).
56 Mary Jean Corbett, "'Two Identities': Gender, Ethnicity, and Phineas Finn," *The Politics of Gender in Anthony Trollope's Novels: New Readings for the Twenty-First Century* ed. Margaret Markwick, Deborah Denenholz Morse, and Regenia Gagnier (Farnham: Ashgate, 2009), p. 129.
57 Elaine Hadley, *Living Liberalism: Practical Citizenship in Mid-Victorian Britain* (Chicago: U of Chicago P, 2010), p. 267.
58 Hadley, p. 285.
59 Sara Maurer, *The Dispossessed State: Narratives of Ownership in Nineteenth-Century Britain and Ireland* (Baltimore: Johns Hopkins UP, 2012), p. 136.
60 Hadley, pp. 229–90.
61 Anthony Trollope, *Phineas Finn*, ch. 5.
62 Trollope, *Phineas Finn*, ch. 50.
63 Michael McKeon, "Introduction," *Theory of the Novel: A Historical Approach*, ed. McKeon (Baltimore: Johns Hopkins UP, 2000), pp. xvii–xviii.
64 Robert Young, *White Mythologies: Writing History and the West* (London: Routledge, 1991); Edward Said, *Orientalism* (New York: Vintage, 1979).
65 Thomas Flanagan, qtd. in Robert Tracy, "Introduction," *The Macdermots of Ballycloran* by Anthony Trollope, ed. Tracy (Oxford: Oxford UP, 1989), p. xii.
66 Thomas Flanagan, *The Irish Novelists, 1800–1850* (New York, Columbia UP, 1959), p. 230.
67 Tracy, "Introduction," p. xxv.
68 Margaret Kelleher, "'Wanted an Irish Novelist': The Critical Decline of the Nineteenth-Century Novel," *The Irish Novel in the Nineteenth Century: Facts and Fictions* (Dublin: Four Courts, 2005), p. 195.
69 Flanagan, p. 16.
70 David Lloyd, "Violence and the Constitution of the Novel," *Anomalous States: Irish Writing and the Post-Colonial Moment* (Durham: Duke UP, 1993), p. 129.
71 Lloyd, p. 134.
72 Terry Eagleston, *Heathcliff and the Great Hunger: Studies in Irish Culture* (London: Verso, 1995), p. 147.
73 Helen O'Connell, *Ireland and the Fiction of Improvement* (Oxford: Oxford UP, 2006), p. 1.
74 James Murphy, *Irish Novelists and the Victorian Age* (Oxford: Oxford UP, 2011), p. 3.
75 Murphy's metaphor may be more apt that he intends; consider the severed foot of the lawyer, Keegan, in *Macdermots*, the horrific amputation of which forms a central tableau in that novel. This image of the disfigured body resonates throughout that text, as I have argued in "Form and Violence in *The Macdermots of Ballycloran*," *NOVEL: A Forum on Fiction* 46.3 (Fall 2013): 386–405. But one might also recall how

prevalent figures of disability are in the writing of Irish cultural history in general, as Mark Mossman argues in *Disability, Representation and the Body in Irish Writing* (Basingstoke: Palgrave, 2009).
76 Mary Poovey, *Genres of the Credit Economy: Mediating Value in Eighteenth- and Nineteenth-Century Britain* (Chicago: U of Chicago P, 2008), pp. 337–9.
77 Kelleher, "Wanted an Irish Novelist," p. 198.
78 Garrett Stewart, *Novel Violence: A Narratography of Victorian Fiction* (Chicago: U of Chicago P, 2009), p. 3.
79 Murphy, p. 124.
80 Murphy, p. 125.
81 Murphy, p. 127.
82 Joe Cleary, "The Nineteenth-Century Irish Novel: Some Notes and Speculations on Literary History," *The Nineteenth-Century Irish Novel: Facts and Fictions*, ed. Jacqueline Belanger (Dublin: Four Courts, 2005), pp. 210–11.

Works cited

Baker, Geoffrey. *Realism's Empire: Empiricism and Enchantment in the Nineteenth-Century Novel.* Columbus: Ohio State UP, 2009.
Bigelow, Gordon. "Form and Violence in *The Macdermots of Ballycloran*." *NOVEL: A Forum on Fiction* 46.3 (Fall 2013): 386–405.
Boyce, D. George. "Escott, Thomas Hay Sweet." *Oxford Dictionary of Literary Biography*. Online ed. www.oxforddnb.com. Accessed November 28, 2013.
Clark, John W. *The Language and Style of Anthony Trollope.* London: Deutsch, 1975.
Cleary, Joe. "The Nineteenth-Century Irish Novel: Some Notes and Speculations on Literary History." *The Irish Novel in the Nineteenth Century: Facts and Fictions.* Ed. Jacqueline E. Belanger. Dublin: Four Courts, 2005: 202–221.
Corbett, Mary Jean. *Allegories of Union in Irish and English Writing, 1790–1870: Politics, History, and the Family from Edgeworth to Arnold.* Cambridge: Cambridge UP, 2000.
———. "'Two Identities': Gender, Ethnicity, and Phineas Finn." *The Politics of Gender in Anthony Trollope's Novels: New Readings for the Twenty-First Century.* Ed. Margaret Markwick, Deborah Denenholz Morse, and Regenia Gagnier. Farnham: Ashgate, 2009: 117–129.
Cronin, John. "Trollope and the Matter of Ireland." *Anthony Trollope.* Ed. Tony Bareham. Totawa: Rowman and Littlefield, 1980. 13–35.
Donovan, Robert. "Trollope's Prentice Work." *Modern Philology* 53.3 (1956): 179–86.
Duncan, Ian. *Modern Romance and Transformations of the Novel: The Gothic, Scott, Dickens.* Cambridge: Cambridge UP, 1992.
Dunleavy, Janet Egleson. "Trollope and Ireland." *Trollope: Centenary Essays.* Ed. John Halperin. Houndmills: Macmillan, 1982: 53–69.
Durey, Jill. "*An Eye for an Eye*: Trollope's Warning for Future Relations Between England and Ireland." *Victorian Review* 32.2 (2006): 26–39.
Eagleton, Terry. *Heathcliff and the Great Hunger: Studies in Irish Culture.* London: Verso, 1995.
Edgeworth, Maria. *Castle Rackrent* and *Ennui.* Ed. Marilyn Butler. London: Penguin, 1992.
———. *An Essay on Irish Bulls.* Ed. Jane Desmarais and Marilyn Butler. Dublin: University College Dublin Press, 2006.
Edwards, Owen Dudley. "Anthony Trollope, the Irish Writer." *Nineteenth-Century Fiction* 38.1 (1983): 1–42.
Escott, T.H.S. *Anthony Trollope: His Public Services, Private Friends, and Literary Originals.* Port Washington, NY: Kennikat, 1967.
Flanagan, Thomas. *The Irish Novelists, 1800–1850.* New York: Columbia UP, 1959.
Frank, Catherine O. "Trial Separations: Divorce, Disestablishment, and Home Rule in *Phineas Redux*." *College Literature* 35.3 (2008): 30–56.
Gaskell, Elizabeth. *North and South.* Ed. Dorothy Collin. London: Penguin, 1970.
Hadley, Elaine. *Living Liberalism: Practical Citizenship in Mid-Victorian Britain.* Chicago: U of Chicago P, 2010.
Halperin, John. *Trollope and Politics.* New York: Barnes and Noble, 1977.
Herbert, Christopher. *Culture and Anomie: Ethnographic Imagination in the Nineteenth Century.* Chicago: U of Chicago P, 1991.
———. *Trollope and Comic Pleasure.* Chicago: U of Chicago P, 1987.
Hynes, John G. "Anthony Trollope and the Irish Question." *Etudes Irlandaises* 8 (1983): 212–28.

———. "Anthony Trollope's Creative 'Culture Shock': Banagher, 1841." *Eire-Ireland* 21.3 (1986): 124–31.
Kelleher, Margaret. *The Feminization of Famine: Expressions of the Inexpressible*. Durham: Duke UP, 1997.
———. "Wanted an Irish Novelist: The Critical Decline of the Nineteenth-Century Novel." *The Irish Novel in the Nineteenth Century: Facts and Fictions*. Ed. Jacqueline E. Belanger. Dublin: Four Courts, 2005: 187–201.
Kincaid, James. *The Novels of Anthony Trollope*. Oxford: Clarendon, 1977.
Knelman, Judith. "Anthony Trollope, English Journalist and Novelist Writing About the Famine in Ireland." *Eire-Ireland* 23 (1988): 57–67.
Lloyd, David. *Anomalous States: Irish Writing and the Post-Colonial Moment*. Durham: Duke UP, 1993.
Lonergan, Patrick. "The Representation of Phineas Finn: Trollope's Palliser Series and Victorian Ireland." *Victorian Literature and Culture* 32.1 (2004): 147–58.
Matthews-Kane, Bridgett. "Love's Labour's Lost: Romantic Allegory in Trollope's *Castle Richmond*." *Victorian Literature and Culture* 32.1 (2004): 117–31.
Maurer, Sara L. *The Dispossessed State: Narratives of Ownership in Nineteenth-Century Britain and Ireland*. Baltimore: Johns Hopkins UP, 2012.
McCourt, John. "An 'I' for an 'E'. An Ireland for an England. Trollope's Hiberno-English in *An Eye for an Eye*." *Etudes Irlandaises* 29.1 (2004): 7–23.
———. "Writing on the Edge: Trollope's *An Eye for an Eye*." *Variants: The Journal of the European Society for Textual Scholarship* 4 (2005): 211–24.
———. *Writing the Frontier: Anthony Trollope Between Britain and Ireland*. Oxford: Oxford UP, 2015.
McKeon, Michael. "Introduction." *Theory of the Novel: A Historical Approach*. Ed. Michael McKeon. Baltimore: Johns Hopkins UP, 2000.
Mokyr, Joel. *Why Ireland Starved: A Quantitative and Analytical History of the Irish Economy, 1800–1850*. London: Allen & Unwin, 1983.
Morash, Christopher. *Writing the Irish Famine*. Oxford: Oxford UP, 1995.
Mossman, Mark. *Disability, Representation and the Body in Irish Writing*. Basingstoke: Palgrave, 2009.
Murphy, James H. *Irish Novelists and the Victorian Age*. Oxford: Oxford UP, 2011.
Nardin, Jane. "*Castle Richmond*, the Famine, and the Critics." *Cahiers Victoriens & Edouardiens* 58 (2003): 81–90.
Nolan, Emer. *Catholic Emancipations: Irish Fiction from Thomas Moore to James Joyce*. Syracuse: Syracuse UP, 2007.
O'Connell, Helen. *Ireland and the Fiction of Improvement*. Oxford: Oxford UP, 2006.
Polhemus, Robert M. *The Changing World of Anthony Trollope*. Berkeley: U of California P, 1968.
Poovey, Mary. *Genres of the Credit Economy: Mediating Value in Eighteenth- and Nineteenth-Century Britain*. Chicago: U of Chicago P, 2008.
Sadleir, Michael. *Anthony Trollope: A Commentary*. Boston: Houghton Mifflin, 1927.
Said, Edward. *Orientalism*. New York: Vintage, 1979.
Scanlon, Margaret. "The Limits of Empathy: Trollope's 'Castle Richmond.'" *Hungry Words: Images of Famine in the Irish Canon*. Ed. George Cusack and Sarah Gross. Dublin: Irish Academic P, 2006: 66–76.
Smalley, Donald, ed. *Trollope: The Critical Heritage*. London: Routledge, 1969.
Stewart, Garrett. *Novel Violence: A Narratography of Victorian Fiction*. Chicago: U of Chicago P, 2009.
Terry, R. C. *Anthony Trollope: The Artist in Hiding*. Totawa: Rowman and Littlefield, 1977.
———. "Three Lost Chapters of Trollope's First Novel." *Nineteenth-Century Fiction* 27.1 (1972): 71–80.
Tracy, Robert. "Instant Replay: Trollope's *The Landleaguers*, 1883." *Eire-Ireland* 15.2 (1980): 30–46.
———. "Introduction." *The Macdermots of Ballycloran* by Anthony Trollope. Ed. Robert Tracy. Oxford: Oxford UP, 1989.
———. "*Lana Medicata Fuco*: Trollope's Classicism." *Trollope: Centenary Essays*. Ed. John Halperin. London: Palgrave, 1982. 1–23.
———. *Trollope's Later Novels*. Berkeley: U of California P, 1978.
———. "'The Unnatural Ruin': Trollope and Nineteenth-Century Irish Fiction." *Nineteenth-Century Fiction* 37.3 (1982): 358–82.
Tracy, Thomas. *Irishness and Womanhood in Nineteenth-Century British Writing*. Farnham: Ashgate, 2009.
Trollope, Anthony. "Trollope's Letters to the Examiner." Ed. Helen Garlinghouse King. *The Princeton University Library Chronicle* 26 (1965): 71–101.
Trumpner, Katie. *Bardic Nationalism: The Romantic Novel and the British Empire*. Princeton: Princeton UP, 1997.
Wittig, E. W. "Trollope's Irish Fiction." *Eire-Ireland* 9.3 (1974): 97–118.
Young, Robert. *White Mythologies: Writing History and the West*. London: Routledge, 1991.

29

PLACE AND TOPICALITY

La Vendée and Trollope's novels of regional change

Nicholas Birns

Scholarship review

Trollope's 1850 novel *La Vendée*, about the conservative rural resistance to the French Revolution in the early 1790s, has received little attention from critics. Indeed, much of the extant analysis of the book has occurred in biographies of Trollope, which have had to cover the book both out of comprehensiveness and due to its early place in the Trollope oeuvre and its pivotal role in his development as novelist. R. H. Super pointed out that, for all that the novel "failed" (57) it was nonetheless the first Trollope novel "in which he gave titles to his chapters" (56), an important formal feature of his mature work. Super (58) castigates *La Vendée* for featuring "a mass of characters" going "through a mass of events" but in truth there are no more than ten significant characters. Super also cautioned against seeing the failure of the book as that of historical fiction in general, pointing out Charles Dickens had a huge success just slightly later with *A Tale of Two Cities*. Victoria Glendinning says that *La Vendée* "was not to be the lucky shot" (173) that would put Trollope's career map, although she does acknowledge that the novel foreshadowed Trollope's political interests. N. John Hall (112) refers to a "one-sidedness" in the book, but that is something that Trollope arguably tries but fails to achieve there.

There has also been a limited if significant amount of critical essays devoted to the novel. Few have seen the book positively, from the unsigned 1850 review in the *Examiner* that called the topic of the book "a hackneyed subject for the romanticist" (Smalley 558) and said that Trollope was "hardly . . . successful," including too much of "the phlegm of history", to Robert Polhemus's assertion, over a century later in 1966, that the move "fails" because "the characters are not interesting in themselves." Karen Faulkner (175) comments that *La Vendée* comes as close as Trollope ever does to "maintaining an ideological position." Yet Polhemus, conversely, noted that Trollope's depiction of Robespierre shows a glimmering of the "balanced tolerance" of his later range of characterization (22). This response was seen as early as the unsigned *Athenaeum* review of 1850, which saw the character of Denot as both "renegade and repentant" (Smalley 559), expressing psychological ambiguity.

Thomas Escott felt otherwise, saying that Trollope committed to showing "the French royalists at their best" (86) and to argue against "the progressive removal of ancient landmarks" (89). Almost a century later, Jane Nardin added to this sense of conservatism when she stated that "Trollope accepted conventional views of women" (10) in this book. Ellen Moody states "*La Vendée* is a failure" whereas *The Macdermots of Ballycloran* is "very great" (13), indicating that

Trollope's greater familiarity with Ireland helped him in his earlier novel. *La Vendée*, though, underwent a certain rehabilitation in the 2000s from students of the historical novel. Jonathan Pitcher states that the novel's "historical vision is one we are unwilling to describe" (102), that the lack of academic currency of monarchism and traditionalist conservatism makes us blind to the novel's intermittent virtues.

Themes of counterrevolution in *La Vendée*

"Counterrevolutionary" as a term emerged in the wake of the French Revolution to denote not just those opposed to radical social change but also those who manifested a palpable opposite agenda. Trollope, though at first leaning toward the counterrevolutionary in his perspective on social change, became more reformist in his views in the course of his career. Trollope's deployment of place can be seen as an index of this tendency toward reform and liberalism.

That Trollope devoted his first non-Irish novel, *La Vendée* (1850), to the subject of the counterrevolutionary reaction in the west of France to the French Republic of 1793. *La Vendée*'s relation to place is in essence a *counterrevolutionary* one. Place was conceived after the upheavals in France after 1789 as a site of resistance to revolution. This became nationalized, with English and German specificities being used as rhetorical counters to French revolutionary universalism, and the ad hoc disorganization of Spanish *guerrillas* acting as a conceptual as well as military counter to Napoleonic martial regularity. Even in France itself, a sense of locality, of place, was seen as a node of opposition to revolution. This occurred most famously in the "La Vendée" uprising of 1793, where rural peasants in west central France refused to accept the overthrow of the monarchy and rallied against the Republican forces then assuming power. This struck both observers and later historians, as peasants were acting against their presumed class interests, supporting a hierarchical institution instead of rallying to egalitarian doctrines that seemingly would have directly benefitted them. There were surely sociological reasons for this. Barrington Moore speculated that the Vendée peasants lived on "isolated individual farms" (93) and thus were less susceptible to mass revolt. But a perspective interested in the rhetoric of counterrevolution as an ideology will give stress to how certain individuals gravitate to ideological causes for utopian reasons, not ones of mere self-interest.

That Trollope wrote *La Vendée* in the wake of the revolutions of 1848 across Europe ties the rhetoric of place in Trollope's fiction to ideas of resisting progress, blocking the centralizing innovations of the new and urban. But, Trollope being Trollope, this tie is not unproblematic or even ideologically reliable. If partisanship, political or ecclesiological opposition, plays a leading role in one way or another in most Trollope fictions, as in the Palliser and Barchester novels, this partisanship is nonetheless not always deployed in strict right-or-wrong terms. Trollope writes about people who act polemically, but this does not mean he writes polemically.

Trollope's relationship to France was significantly more tenuous than his to Ireland, where he is capable of writing about complicated class, religious, and historical divisions without taking sides. But in *La Vendée* Trollope clearly seems to be taking sides. The protagonists of the revolt – most of whom in some way are historical characters – are paladins: Larochejaquelin, Cathelineau, de Lescure. This sympathy transcends class identity: the lowly postillion Cathelineau is the most virtuous of all. Adolphe Denot, the closest the book comes to a villain, is depicted as having a moral valence corollary to what degree he is on the side of the rebels. Trollope clearly prefers monarchy as the ideal form of government in France, and – writing just after the July Monarchy of Louis-Phillipe was overthrown in 1848 – predicts, in the very last sentence of the book, that monarchy will return to France in 1865. This of course never happened, France seeing a 'farcical' (*qua* Marx in the *Eighteenth Brumaire*) emperor and then a republic. But Trollope has played his cards: monarchy for him is the way for France, and those who support it are to be admired. The changes in France during the middle of the nineteenth century – the overthrow of Louis-Philippe; the brief Second Republic out of which Napoleon's nephew emerged with a plebiscitary mandate and then declared himself Napoleon III; the overthrow of the Second Empire in the aftermath of defeat in the Franco-Prussian War and the establishment of the Third Republic after various plans to restore the Bourbon monarchy did not come to fruition – left France an arena of active debate between liberalism and more conservative ideologies in a way that was not the case in England, where both the Conservative and Liberal parties – and later the Labour party – adhered to a fundamental liberal consensus. Thus there was, in the nineteenth and twentieth centuries, a lot of counterrevolutionary and reactionary feeling in France, and Trollope depicts this vividly.

Yet the novel is neither angry nor militant. For all its depiction of a struggle not only ideologically fierce but also full of bloodshed, the novel has surprisingly little sense of *parti pris*. Indeed, it might be said that Trollope exhibited many of the same humanistic traits he describes in his character de Lescure:

> A perfect man, we are told, would be a monster; and a certain dry obstinacy of manner, rather than of purpose, preserved de Lescure from the monstrosity of perfection. Circumstances decreed that the latter years of his life should be spent among scenes of bloodshed; that he should be concerned in all the horrors of civil war; that instruments of death should be familiar to his hands, and the groans of the dying continually in his ears. But though the horrors of war were awfully familiar to him, the harshness of war never became so; he spilt no blood that he could spare, he took no life that he could save.
>
> *(La Vendée 3, Ch. 1)*

Trollope writes about partisans, but even though he has sympathies, he does not himself show partisanship.

The French Revolution's literary legacy was complicated. On the one hand the spirit of liberty and of overthrowing long-established hierarchies fit right in with the romantic aesthetic. On the other hand, both the revolutionary movement itself and the subsequent dictatorship of Napoleon were highly neoclassical in aesthetic orientation, as can be seen in the paintings of Jacques-Louis David. Thus irregular, romantic aesthetics became, to a degree, a sign of resistance to the homogenizing hegemony of the French, as was true of the paintings of Francisco Goya of the *guerrilla* movement in Spain against Napoleonic occupation. Trollope describes well the disillusionment of people with the initial hopes for revolution:

> The dethronement of the King, totally severed many . . . from the revolutionary party. They found that their high aspirations had been in vain; that their trust in reason had been misplaced, and that the experiment to which they had committed themselves had failed; disgusted, broken-spirited, and betrayed they left the city in crowds, and with few exceptions, the intellectual circles were broken up.
>
> *(La Vendée 2)*

Trollope admitted he knew little about the Vendée, gleaning information from his reading and his brother Tom's French travels as well as his mother's sojourn in Paris. In his *Autobiography*, he says, "In truth, I knew nothing of life in the La Vendée country" (67). This may be plausibly extended to indicate that he had no huge ideological stake in the subject, compared, say, to a

Carlyle in *The French Revolution: A History* (1837) or even a Dickens in *A Tale of Two Cities* 2003 [1859]. Unlike G. A. Henty's more adventure-filled, juvenile version of this tale in *No Surrender: A Tale of the Rising in La Vendée* 1914 [1899], there is no English viewpoint, no protagonist mediating the French rural fighters and English readerly sensibilities.

Another unusual aspect of the book is its closeness to real history. All the major characters except for Denot and Agatha are historical, and Trollope's source for the book was the memoirs of Madame de la Rochejaquelin (the more usual spelling as opposed to the one Trollope used in the novel), which he hewed to with reasonable fidelity. The book can be seen therefore not just as the first of his overseas novels but also as the first of his travel books, or at least his first in the "nonfiction research" genre, which was later to include books on North America, Australia and New Zealand, and the West Indies. This makes the rhetoric of place all the more important.

The political movement in *La Vendée* was named after the place, and the place-name more or less began to be equivalent to the political movement, especially so after Marx's use of La Vendée as a trope for reactionary peasant revolt (see, e.g., *The Eighteenth Brumaire* 147) made it a byword among Marxists. Yet the novel's emphasis on place as such, as opposed to ideology, is strong. One of the difficult aspects of the book is that there is no single protagonist. Cathelineau, the valiant but lowborn postillion, is the closest approximation. But he dies in the middle of the book, before his love for the virtuous Agatha can be fulfilled. Larochejacquelin and de Lescure are almost too noble – in the characterological, not the social sense, although both of 'high' descent – to be protagonists. The novel looks at them from an admirable distance but does not inhabit their souls enough to render them three-dimensional. Denot, the unstable turncoat, is the most interesting character, but he presents the image of a pathology – as Super (57) calls him "too mad for love" – more than a novelistic quandary. Trollope's focus is not personal, but topographic. Trollope explores not the interior landscape of the mind – as he characteristically does – but the topography of symbolic La Vendée, the place.

Again this is strengthened for the latter-day reader by the way Marx made the word Vendée so proverbial, in the *Eighteenth Brumaire of Louis Napoleon*. Marx made the Vendée a kind of genre, a sobering reminder to ardent leftists that the rural poor who often seemed to have the most to gain from revolution were often dead-set against it. The thoughtful Marxist had to face the fact that many peasants' revolts or insurgencies seen as left-wing had Vendée-esque aspects. The Vendée became a trope for history's unwillingness to go the way the revolutionary left desired. The Vendée rebels, in their unorganized insurgency, are in essence *guerrillas*, and that very term originated in the (basically monarchist and traditionalist) resistance against Napoleon in Spain. The underlying identity of many objects of revolutionary desire may indeed be counterrevolutionary. Counterrevolutionary fiction haunts a presumed liberal consensus with its implicit grasp of this paradox.

The rhetoric of counterrevolutionary fiction

The strategic ironies of revolutionary alignment meant that Ireland, populated for the most part by pious Catholics whose religion was tied in with nationalist assertions, was aligned with the anti-clerical, revolutionary French – as seen in Thomas Flanagan's 1979 historical novel about 1798, *The Year of the French*, which notes that Humbert, the commander of the French expedition to Ireland, "gave no quarter to the peasants in the Vendée" (380). This French revolutionary–Irish rebel alignment somewhat muddies attempts such as that of W. J. MacCormack, in his introduction to the Oxford edition of *La Vendée*, to see Trollope's interest in France as an attempt to explore by analogy the ardent Catholicism of the Irish. It would be much purer from a counterrevolutionary perspective if both the 1798 Irish uprising and the Vendée had involved alliances with monarchist regimes. But the former did not. Yet there is obviously a link, and not only because there is an eerie resemblance between aspects of the two landscapes. Trollope makes the Celtic aspects of Brittany, where the insurrection anchors its last redoubt, "la Petite Vendée," clear. The Vendée itself is on the Atlantic, and proposes itself as a cultural minority in France analogous to the Celts in Britain. In the other major presence of the Vendée in English literature, Coleridge's 'Fire, Famine, Slaughter': A War Eclogue,' published in the *Morning Post and Gazetteer* (8 January 1798). Coleridge parodied *Macbeth*, his use of the Scottish play drawing on both the shared Celticness of Britain and the Vendean arena. The Vendée as a region is rural, and religious. It represents aspects of the national weal thought residual but in times of crisis becoming re-emergent. This sort of milieu is the seedbed of counterrevolutionary identity.

But a specific nomenclatural issue arises. Even though Vendée as a term quickly became less a geographical designation than a counterrevolutionary trademark, Trollope makes clear that Vendée was not the historic name of these regions, but the designation it received (from a river that ran through it) in the new, post-revolutionary classification of French regions. The very name under which the rebels were pursuing their historic and purportedly ancient grievances was thus neither historic nor ancient – a paradigmatic instance of the invention of tradition, as Trollope speaks of the area "*subsequently* called La Vendée" (10, emphasis mine). Escott speaks of the Vendée as "the new republican name" (90) of the region.

Thus the rebellion takes its name from the lexicon of the institution arrayed against it. Like any other political movement, the rhetoric involved in the verbal expression of counterrevolution tends to complicate it. This is particularly true in that Trollope, writing before Tolstoy's recasting of the historical novel as a tableau both including hundreds of fictional characters and also incorporating large swaths of literal historical narrative, has, in the manner of Sir Walter Scott, to concentrate on a delimited number of characters and to embody history primarily through plot and character.

A twentieth-century novel like Flanagan's, with its clear Tolstoy influence, shows how much easier it is to inject historicity and ideology when the marriage plot is not the main focus, an issue the first two Irish novels, particularly *The Kellys and the O'Kellys*, struggle with more or less overtly, in that there is pretty much an inverse variation therein between an actual immersion in the historical issues and the presence of the marriage plot. Because the Scott-style historical novel has to end domestically, and because women do not take a part in public life, any public, agenda – revolutionary or counterrevolutionary, conservative or liberal – is to some extent ironized.

Discrete features of *La Vendée* also constitute cruxes, as Trollope's ostensible ideology and the narrative result do not coincide. Trollope's novel contains an enormous amount of ekphrasis, verbal renderings of visual items, ornate visual descriptions of houses and churches, as if to evoke the sense of place that counterrevolutionary ideology should be able to give in a political sense but that has difficulty being plausibly evoked in the novel. The ekphrasis in *La Vendée* often dwells upon Catholic iconography or even depiction of sculptures of pagan, Greco-Roman gods to add a slight sense of exoticism for an English Protestant reading audience. The ekphrasis both gives atmosphere to the novel and registers a certain crisis, as if to resist a narrative progress that might make the novel easier to negotiate, but also parallel the same sort of social progress that the Vendéen rebels are resisting. The ekphrasis not only intrudes in the way of the plot several times but also confirms the highly visual and place-oriented frame of the novel, as seen here:

> The rooms were square, very large, and extremely lofty; the salon alone was carpeted, and none of them were papered, the drawing-room, the dining-room and the grand salon were ornamented with painted panels, which displayed light-coloured shepherds and shepherdesses in almost every possible attitude. In these rooms, also, there were

highly ornamented stoves, which stood out about four feet from the wall, topped with marble slabs, on which were sculptured all the gods and demi-gods of the heathen mythology – that in the drawing-room exhibited Vulcan catching Mars and Venus in his marble net; and the unhappy position of the god of war was certainly calculated to read a useful lesson to any Parisian rover, who might attempt to disturb the domestic felicity of any family in the Bocage.

(25, Ch. 3)

Another group of set-pieces are *La Vendée*'s several prolonged deathbed scenes, including de Lescure's, which is lengthily protracted, because, given the era, the medical prognosis is so incompetent and capricious. Agatha's palliative concern for Cathelineau is the only sort of treatment that is functional.

Sometimes Agatha sat by the window, and watched his bed, and at others, she stole quietly out of the room to see her other patients, and then she would return again, and take her place by the window; and as long as she remained in the room, so that he could look upon her face, Cathelineau felt that he was happy.

(183, Ch. 14)

Do the disorder and idiosyncrasy of counterrevolution stand so far in the way of rationalistic abstraction as to preclude aspects of life like adequate medical care, or even a way of classifying illness that can lead to an inevitable death not being a protracted ordeal for the sufferer? The absence of medical competence is an indication that an ideology that hearkens back to the pre-rational may pose problems even for its own continuance. If modern science prolongs life, might not some adulteration of the sacred truths by it be worthwhile? In other words, the very desiderata of the narrative's moral values (continued life for the protagonists) run against and abrade a counterrevolutionary or at least counter-modern thematic. Social progress would mean better health and more life for the characters, and all the picturesque regionalism in the world cannot gainsay that. Here, the counterrevolutionary impulse rubs against how the novel, as a narrative genre, is tied into modernity. For counterrevolution to work novelistically, it must somehow also be modern. Yet the more modern its aspirations, the more analogous they are to those of revolution itself.

Counterrevolution wants to negate revolution. But it cannot simply turn back the clock to an era before popular participation or consent; it must use the tools of revolutionary agitation against it. One can see this in Denot, a rank opportunist, one of life's "superficial votaries" (Escott 92) who at one point in time finds the counterrevolutionary opportune, and then just as conveniently finds the same of the revolution. Any political cause is ripe for exploitation by opportunists. Trollope's awareness of this point is what leads him to foreground the virtue of Cathelineau, who has no place in the hierarchy and earns his laurels by merit. Counterrevolution, Trollope suggests, is as or more negotiable by a *carrière ouverte aux talents* as is revolution, and is not just a narrow vendetta of the literally aristocratic. Yet the same populism that enables a man of merit like Cathelineau to achieve prominence also opens the floodgates to the impassioned mob as much as does the convulsive atheism of a Robespierre or a Danton.

Trollope also has an uneasy relationship with the anti-reason aspects of the rebellion. Trollope is not a hard-and-fast man of the Enlightenment, not a devotee of abstract reason. But he was fond of reasonability, a practical, reformist moderation that did not get too emotionally moved even on behalf of the right cause. The plot of *La Vendée* also raises the danger of the excess of the unsystematized aura of counterrevolutionary ideals. Adolphe Denot defects to the Republican cause out of weakness of character, and a too fervent love for Agatha. Yet the book's end makes clear that the other Vendéens regard Denot as at heart a man truly of their own, who repents before his death, and is simply a case of enthusiasm gone awry, much as Trollope (far more than any commentator, left or right, would today when Robespierre has become a symbol for over-fervid revolutionary zeal) depicts Robespierre as an intelligent, altruistic man gone wrong in his hyper-rationalistic vision. Trollope sees Robespierre as a psychological type with respect to whom he manifests both empathy and, more largely, disaffinity. Denot, similarly, has the excessive emotionalism, which is the inverse of Robespierre's rigid rationalism.

Denot's misbehavior is a correlate of his unbridled romanticism. His excessive affect is the flip side of valuing place. This leads to another question about counterrevolutionary resistance in *La Vendée*. How much of it is genuine, unpremeditated, and inherently loyal, and how much of it is simply a bargaining chip? If La Vendée supports the king, it will be more powerful at the end. Regionalism exists as a bargaining chip, auguring a utopian hope of regional fulfillment. The meritocratic tinge of the virtuous postillion Cathelineau suggests a social mobility even within reaction, a populist conservatism of a vaguely Disraelian sort. The Vendean revolt could, in its rhetoric of reaction, open up socially mobile opportunities for men like Cathelineau in just the same way that the storming of the Bastille did so for other meritorious but class-subordinated individuals. As in the case of the Catholic Irish supporting the atheist French Republic while the conservative French peasantry aligns with liberal, bourgeois Great Britain, there is the intrusion of expediency, self-interest, and the tactical within the seams of ostensible idealism.

Marx and Engels indicate a similar phenomenon in *Revolution or Counter-Revolution in Germany'* when they speak of Czechs rallying against German liberal revolution because the cynosure of Pan-Slavism, Czar Nicholas I, was aiding the Austrian Empire in suppressing internal dissenters as a "Vendée" that "no country in a state of revolution and external war can tolerate" (139). This moots a non-idealistic Vendée, of the Czechs not supporting German revolutionaries because they believe that the suppressor of German liberalism, the Russian emperor, will help them. This has parallels in Trollope's novel not only in the patent turncoat Denot but also in the valorous postillion Cathelineau, whose motives are pure partially because he dies so early in the book. Another scenario might have seen him living and being accused of adventitious motives, short of his love for king and church, such as wanting to court Agatha in order to marry up. Counter-revolution is not exempt from the danger of self-interest that confronts any organized political movement.

The realistic novel, with its suspicion of overarching bonds beyond individual relationships, is ill equipped to justify utopian hopes evinced within it, no matter what the personal politics of the author. If one starts with revolutionary hope, the novel will end up ironizing it. Equally, if one starts with counterrevolutionary hope, the novel will end up ironizing that. This is why Lukács disdained most fiction written from a consciously "liberal, centrist, or social democratic perspective" (Corredor 79). Lukács also disdained realism's wealth of detail (Corredor 188). In Zola, this detail occurred as substrate. In Trollope the detail unfolded as event, what the *Examiner* review called "the phlegm of history" (Smalley 558), which, as the novel proceeds, becomes the phlegm of domestic emotion, details of a private rather than public resolution.

Toward a fiction of regional change in Trollope

Trollope's favorable stance toward the Vendée counterrevolution can be inferred from the novel's sympathy for its rebel characters and its antagonism toward the French Republic. But this tendency toward endorsement of counterrevolution is not fulfilled in *La Vendée*. This is partly because Trollope is too much of an English moderate to be fundamentally committed to it. But it is also partly because the total machinery of the form in which he is writing will not really allow it. Trollope surely does not follow Denot and end up even temporarily taking the side of the revolution. But at the end of *La Vendée* he cannot be said to be a counterrevolutionary novelist. Indeed, he has become a novelist of regional change.

Trollope abandons a counterrevolutionary sense of place for two reasons. As an Englishman, he prefers negotiated settlement to any sort of revolution, counter or no. Secondly, a negotiated settlement lends itself to the ironies and contextual ties of the realist novel form in a way that counterrevolutionary energies do not. A negotiated settlement through the marriage plot precludes revolution but also, less overtly, precludes counterrevolution. Regional change occurs when revolution has not proceeded so far as to generate counterrevolution. Regional change thus replaces not only revolution but also counterrevolution, in much the same way that the square root of a positive number being both positive and negative constitutes, as Alain Badiou (199) points out, a "commutative field." Regional change satisfies the need for revolution and counterrevolution at once, while pulling back the utopian claims of both. By its very gradualism, regional change is not paralyzed by this reflexivity. Trollope's mature regionalism was a bureaucratic, perhaps even panoptic regionalism: the regionalism of a government official sent by his superiors to inspect conditions in the provinces.

Although the Barsetshire novels are necessarily intensely regional, the made-up nature of the name and the very intensity of Trollope's construction of a meticulously rendered fictional world render Barsetshire more mainstream than the regional indication would normally assert. On the other hand, the Cumberland setting of *Lady Anna*, with its Wordsworthian resonances, is fitting for the more pronounced than usual emphasis on social inequality in that novel. In *Mr. Scarborough's Family*, even though a Staffordshire setting is specifically announced, the name of the Scarborough family seat, Tretton Park, is used as a virtual synecdoche for Staffordshire, downplaying a local-color aspect that otherwise would have been more concerted. In *Rachel Ray*, though, the Devon setting is foregrounded. It is clear that the Devon milieu is meant to be *more* rustic and provincial than Barsetshire – as the *Athenaeum* review of the book called it, "a picturesque nook" (Smalley 180), like La Vendée more regionally distinctive than the mean. The rustic specificity at once provides the idyllic aspect of the novel and also is an object of critique in it, as the evangelical rigidity of the Rev. Samuel Prong is the object of critique.

Even the most conservative aspect of the novel, that chronicling the failed attempt by a Jew, Mr. Hart, to win the parliamentary seat of Baslehurst, testifies to the possibility of regional change: by the mere fact that it happens and that he loses by only one vote, with the clear hint being that at the next election, with a few older, conservative people dying off, someone of Hart's background might well prevail. A revolutionary would be very disappointed by the ending of *Rachel Ray*, with its domestic bliss, reconfirmation of the Church of England in its most conventional mode, and exclusion of the Jew from political power. But from the perspective of *La Vendée*, regional change, a slow adjustment of the rural redoubt to progressive and metropolitan norms, would certainly have been observable.

It is interesting that, both in *La Vendée* (where a family of the name of Stein is prominent on the side of the rebels, and their name's possible origin, whether German or German-Jewish, is unremarked upon) and in *Rachel Ray*, the Jew and the region are in apposition. The perhaps not-totally-reliable narrator of *Rachel Ray* says that Mr. Hart's eloquence, admittedly greater than his more liturgical rival, was a product of the "natural fluency" (283) of superficial cosmopolitanism, which glibly enunciated smooth platitudes but could only "observe rather than think, remember rather than create," and would not be true insight. The claims of the region to organic identity would seem to exclude the Jew – and that is why he loses. But Trollope's own conception of regionalism within a bureaucratic, post office matrix makes regional identity gravitate toward metropolitan abstraction – and that is why the Jew loses by only one vote. Similarly, the plot in the Somerset-situated *The Belton Estate* (1866) leads to the reclamation of that estate by the eponymous Beltons through marriage to – and thus elimination of the name of – the female scion of the family, bearing the slightly foreign, Channel Islands name of Amedroz. English regions can partially, but not entirely, accommodate diversity. On one level, identities are fixed. On another, they are migratory.

Migratory identities are also found in *Cousin Henry*. Here, Indefer Jones, a wealthy landowner, possesses an indefeasibly Welsh name but is also utterly British, perhaps even English in everything but the name. Here Welsh can be British/English and British/English can be Welsh. When Indefer Jones reads (14) "a daily copy of whatever might be the most thoroughly Conservative paper of the day" we assume it is a conservatism exactly identifiable with that which might be manifested in Devon or Staffordshire. The Welsh setting and nomenclature are a distinct feature of the book but do not give it a regional inflection that would make its content substantively different if set in an English shire. Moreover as with *Rachel Ray*, the plot of *Cousin Henry* gravitates toward slow if palpable liberalization. Indefer Jones's lineal male heir is his nephew Henry, but he far prefers his niece Isabel. There are reminiscences here of periods in English history where a female was preferred as monarch because of the ideological (i.e., religious, Catholic) unacceptability of the male rival, as during the Elizabethan period with respect to Philip II of Spain and especially the Glorious Revolution, the prototype of peaceful, evolutionary change in English history, with respect to James II. Henry Jones has every right by blood and descent – the values privileged by those who fought on behalf of the royal cause in the Vendée – but here in Wales when the community decides they do not like Henry Jones, they basically nullify his inheritance, proving through Jones's nominal attorney Mr. Apjohn and his nominal antagonist Mr. Cheeky that Indefer had not intended to leave Henry the property.

Mr. Apjohn, after Henry is disqualified as heir, advises Isabel to change her name to "Miss Indefer Jones" (344) to secure her inheritance, and then urges William Owen, upon marrying Isabel to, through "the proper changes" (344), also adopt the name Indefer Jones. This is to bolster the title to their inheritance but also indicates a good deal of transitivity and motility, as the name of Indefer Jones migrates first to a young woman and then to a male not of Jones blood. The weakening of ascribed identities and "ancient landmarks" so feared by the Vendée landowners ends up occurring here. On the other hand, the locals prefer Isabel to Henry precisely because she seems more in touch with their values, and continuity prevails at the end of the novel. But reform and progress – even as signified by the way the happy couple slip the name "Apjohn" in tribute to the lawyer who had helped them into their name of their firstborn son – also contribute to a gradual process of regional change. Whereas Trollope's first regionalism, of the "sacred" (*Vendée* 23) cannon of resistance, could end only in bloodshed and civil strife, his second regionalism, of the alert young woman and determined attorney, ends in placid reform. We should not underestimate how important even mild reform was at the time, when to be liberal in any sense was close to being truly radical.

Trollope's second regionalism thus surrenders rebellion for autonomy, albeit within a bureaucratic-administrative matrix. It substitutes moderate regional change for counterrevolution. If one contrasts this outcome to the counterrevolutionary dreams depicted in *La Vendée*, Trollope's work reveals a remarkable shift from the redoubt of opposition to the flexibility of regional change.

Works cited

Badiou, Alain. *Number and Numbers*. Trans. Robin Mackay. London: Polity, 2008.
Carlyle, Thomas. *The French Revolution*. London: James Fraser, 1837.

Coleridge, Samuel Taylor. "Fire, Famine, and Slaughter: A War Eclogue. Web. http://spenserians.cath.vt.edu/TextRecord.php?action=GET&textsid=35393. Accessed 23 April 2016.

Corredor, Eva L. *Lukács After Communism: Interviews with Contemporary Intellectuals.* Durham: Duke University Press, 1997.

Dickens, Charles. *A Tale of Two Cities.* Ed. Richard Maxwell. London: Penguin, 2003.

Escott, Thomas Hay Sweet. *Anthony Trollope: His Public Services, Private Friends, and Literary Originals.* London: John Lane, 1913.

Faulkner, Karen. "Anthony Trollope's Apprenticeship." *Nineteenth-Century Fiction*, Vol. 38, No. 2 (September 1983), pp. 161–88.

Flanagan, Thomas. *The Year of the French.* New York: Holt, 1979.

Glendinning, Victoria. *Trollope.* London: Hutchinson, 1992.

Hall, N. John. *Trollope: A Biography.* New York: Oxford University Press, 1992.

Henty, G. A. *No Surrender! A Tale of the Rising in La Vendée.* New York: Scribner, 1914.

MacCormack, W. J. "Introduction." In *La Vendée*, by Anthony Trollope. New York: Oxford University Press, 1994.

Marx, Karl. *The Eighteenth Brumaire of Louis Napoleon.* Rockville: Wildside Press, 2008.

Marx, Karl, and Engels, Friedrich. *Revolution or Counter-Revolution in Germany.* Chicago: C. H. Kerr, 1919.

Moody, Ellen. *Trollope on the Net.* London: Bloomsbury, 2003.

Moore, Barrington. *The Social Origins of Dictatorship and Democracy.* New York: Beacon, 1993.

Nardin, Jane. *He Knew She Was Right: The Independent Woman in the Novels of Anthony Trollope.* Carbondale: Southern Illinois UP, 1989.

Pitcher, Jonathan. *Excess Baggage: A Modern Theory and the Contemporary Amnesia of Latin Americanist Thought.* New York: Peter Lang, 2009.

Polhemus, Robert M. *The Changing World of Anthony Trollope.* Berkeley: University of California Press, 1966.

Smalley, Donald, ed. *Trollope: The Critical Heritage.* London: Routledge, 1969.

Super, R. H. *The Chronicler of Barsetshire.* Ann Arbor: University of Michigan Press, 1989.

Trollope, Anthony. *Autobiography.* Ed. Bradford Booth. Berkeley: University of California Press, 1978.

———. *La Vendée: An Historical Romance.* London: Chapman and Hall 1875, originally published 1850.

———. *Rachel Ray.* London: Chapman and Hall, 1875.

30
TROLLOPE AND EMIGRATION

Tamara S. Wagner

Anthony Trollope wrote several travel books that reveal his interest in, yet also his reservations about, imperial expansion through settlement. When he described settler colonies, he was particularly concerned with their suitability for British emigrants and speculated on the colonies' future within the growing empire. His novels as well as travel accounts offer critical insight into colonial policies, the conflicts between new emigrants and earlier settlers, between settlers and indigenous populations, and between the settler colonies and the imperial centre. Still, although Trollope assessed modes and means of settlement, weighed the pros and cons of rival emigration destinations, and in his fiction, exposed the implications of colonial life at these different destinations, he stopped short of questioning the expansion of British civilisation itself. Trollope, like the majority of his contemporaries, took the growth of the settler empire for granted. It seemed natural and necessary, given the population growth in Britain's metropolitan spaces, that more and more Britons would venture out and settle the growing empire. The lost colonies that had become the United States of America – colonies that, as Trollope pointedly put it, "have now, happily, passed away from us" (*South Africa* ch. 2) – necessarily occupied a peculiar position within this world map. The main emigration destination for Britons throughout much of the century, this renegade settler colony was also a rival commercial and colonising power. Hence, emigration to the U.S. became perceived as a drain of human resources. So even if certain strata of society, or types of people, were deemed "superfluous" or "redundant" (Johnston; cf. Kranidis), it was argued that they would still usefully populate the British Empire. Victorian emigration manuals reflected changing policies that urged migration within the empire, while popular fiction as well as travel writing frequently pitted rival destinations against each other. In presenting the disappointments as much as the eager expectations of emigrants and, with a peculiar dry humour that countered common sensationalist strategies of the time, the difficulties returnees faced, Trollope participated in controversial discourses on emigration and empire. Judging from his travel accounts, he was well-informed about the places he visited as well as about topical debates on emigration. Yet the representation of these places in his fiction also provided him with an opportunity to engage consciously and self-reflexively with their representation in popular culture. Trollope's fictional treatment of emigration was always as much about playing with readers' expectations as about current controversies.

There has been an important shift in discussions of Trollope's representation of emigration in literary criticism over the last decades. Early accounts tend to focus on his real-life experience of the countries he describes, including his lengthy stays at his son's settler home (Lansbury), or they either briefly referenced (Woodruff) or meticulously traced (Davidson) the movements of individual characters in several novels. J.H. Davidson's 1969 article on "Anthony Trollope and the Colonies" still provides an excellent overview, and Coral Lansbury's seminal discussion of Australia's representation in nineteenth-century British literature, *Arcady in Australia: The Evocation of Australia in Nineteenth-Century English Literature* (1970), offers an insightful account of Trollope's complex engagement with the continent. More recently, Diana Archibald's influential *Domesticity, Imperialism, and Emigration in the Victorian Novel* (2002) includes a chapter on Trollope. New interest in Victorian emigration discourses, transatlantic studies approaches, and, above all, settler colonialism has, in fact, provided an important impetus for reinvestigations of Trollope's experience and writing. Davidson was the first to observe that the "settlement colonies" were "the only ones [Trollope] was interested in" (306), but it was not until the growing revival of interest in settler colonialism that detailed discussions of Trollope's Australian and New Zealand fiction appeared outside of specialist Australian studies publications (Durey; Starck), with the notable exception of Archibald's important study. In a recent overview of Trollope's travel writing, James Buzard has discussed how "one of Trollope's leading interests was to determine how viable each region was as a site for large-scale settlement" (170), and Helen Blythe has added that Trollope was also aware of, and dedicated considerable space to, "the violent conflicts between settlers and indigenous populations, and the ethical conundrum of colonialism" (161). Several critics and cultural historians have turned to his novels to reexamine Victorian representations of emigration (Archibald; Myers; Wagner, "Settling"), settler culture in Australia (Birns; Elliot; Moore, G.) and New Zealand (Birns; Blythe), as well as of travel writing (Buzard). Critical discourses on colonialism and emigration have thus revived interest especially in Trollope's hitherto rarely discussed works, as we shall see.

***

Trollope's first travel book was *The West Indies and the Spanish Main* (1859). It was followed by *North America* (1862), *Australia and New Zealand* (1873), and *South Africa* (1877). Some of his short pieces were collected as *Travelling Sketches* (1866) and *The Tireless Traveller: Twenty Letters to the Liverpool Mercury, 1875*, published posthumously in 1941. While he documented current controversies, throughout his travel writing Trollope sought to concentrate on the factual, on statistics and figures. This becomes particularly evident in his American travels, which were presented in deliberate contradistinction to the tradition of the British travelogue on America that had influentially been shaped by his mother's notorious *Domestic Manners of the Americans* (1832), which had "created laughter on one side of the Atlantic, and soreness on the other," and which Trollope saw as "essentially a woman's book" in its interest in social arrangements (*NA* 2). But if Frances Trollope continued to lift whole scenes from her lively anecdotal travelogue to work them into her American novels,[1] her son counterpoised his factual accounts by showing how complex the narrative uses of emigration could be in fiction. Reading Anthony Trollope's novels in the context of Victorian emigration patterns and discourses, this chapter analyses his critical and often self-ironic evocation of common clichés.

Between 1815 and 1920, approximately 17 million people formed part of what New Zealand historian James Belich has termed the "vast Anglo exodus." This "exodus" was one of several global migrations, yet the unprecedented mass movement during the period 1815–60 generated a new kind of interconnectivity that shaped what Belich describes as a new anglophone settler empire or "Anglo-world" (58). Apart from the U.S., this encompassed the British settler colonies in Aotearoa/New Zealand, Australia, Canada, and South Africa. In his focus on this settler world,

Trollope expressed what was becoming an increasingly prevailing distinction, most notoriously popularised by Charles Dilke in his best-selling travelogue *Greater Britain* (1868). Dilke distinguished between "true" colonies, such as Australia and New Zealand, and "other imperial holdings such as India and Ceylon" (Buzard 174–75; cf. Bell 1–2). Yet the confining lens of traditional postcolonial studies has caused precisely this dichotomy to be obscured, or as problematically, simply to be subsumed in colonial discourse analyses that erase the distinction that was so important to the Victorians. The result has been a skewed account of the significance of settler spaces and of emigration in Victorian popular culture – a view of the Victorians' global imagination that might acknowledge, *pace* Edward Said, the British Empire's "codified, if only marginally visible, presence in fiction" (Said 63) as a whole, but which generally overlooks or dismisses the specific significance of the settler world: how it was differentiated from colonies of conquest, and what role it played in shaping nineteenth-century literature. Building on Said's much-cited argument about this visibility, Janet Myers speaks of the "seeming marginality in the Victorian novel" of characters who emigrate to, or return from, Britain's overseas settlements (Myers 3). Their representation in Victorian popular culture attests to the multifaceted roles of settler spaces in the Victorian imagination, reminding us that such marginality is only seemingly insignificant. A cursory glance at canonical fiction might well suggest that "[i]n sub-plot after sub-plot, fictional emigrants disappear into or arrive from the colonies in ways that facilitate plot development but display a reticence on the part of novelists to represent the conditions of colonial life" (Myers 3). The complex roles both of these fictional emigrants and of the places they are going to (and returning from, often after a significant failure), however, go far beyond these two main narrative trajectories. A closer look at the vast variety of nineteenth-century fiction not only exemplifies how the conditions of colonial life are represented critically and brought into contrast with the settler colonies' position in imperialist ideologies and colonial policies. It also reveals a startling centrality of emigration in the most home-centred narratives and what is often a fascinatingly deliberate play with its seeming marginality.

Trollope wrote several novels that were set to a substantial part in settler spaces or were centrally concerned with emigration and a new global mobility: *Harry Heathcote of Gangoil: A Tale of Australian Bush Life* (1874) and *John Caldigate* (1879), his two "Australian" works; his New Zealand story "Catherine Carmichael" (1878), often discussed in connection with the more symbolic function of the projected New Zealand visitor to a future ruinous London in *The New Zealander* (written in 1855, published in 1972), and also the science fiction novel *The Fixed Period* (1882), set in the fictitious island Britannula, located somewhere in the South Pacific. There are also his novels about Americans in England, including *The Way We Live Now* (1875), *The American Senator* (1877), and subplots in *The Duke's Children* (1880), and novels that foreground the impact of life in America on a returning Englishman, most prominently in *Dr Wortle's School* (1881). Similarly, the South African returnee narrative in *An Old Man's Love* (1882) rewrites earlier typical stories of disruptive return. Still, there are novels in which emigration features as a way out, like *The Three Clerks* (1857) or *Lady Anna* (1874). Such pat endings illustrate the most notorious narrative usefulness of any colonies, or former colonies, in Victorian fiction. Disruptive characters are, like Tom Gradgrind after he robs a bank in Charles Dickens's *Hard Times* (1854), quickly shipped off to America as a renegade colony that offers an appropriate place of projection, while the deserving, if unfortunate, find a new life in a largely offstage New World within the British Empire.[2] This strategy persists, but finds a counterpoise in the equally useful (in narrative terms) disruptive potential of returnee figures in mid-Victorian sensation fiction. No matter whether they are successful or not overseas, their return is always upsetting and mostly unwelcome. We only need to think of some of the better-known sensation novels of the early 1860s, such as Dickens's *Great Expectations* (1860–1) and Mary Elizabeth Braddon's *Lady Audley's Secret* (1862), novels that evoke Australia as an offstage space, a space that in the Victorian imagination is invested with several levels of sensational potential due to its history as a penal colony as well as its association with quick riches through gold digging. Indeed, the only time that emigration to the U.S. was outpaced by movement within the empire was during the mid-century gold rushes in Australia and New Zealand at a time when transatlantic travel was complicated by the outbreak of the American Civil War (Archibald 2). When Trollope, however, drew on the widespread sensationalisation of these antipodal spaces, he made the resulting rewriting an opportunity to react against sensationalism itself, while he was just as consciously reworking clichéd descriptions of specific settler colonies.

Trollope's representation of emigration in his fiction not only is well-informed, often underpinned by personal experience of the depicted destinations, and in pointed reaction to prevailing clichés in fiction and travel writing, but also forms a focal point of his genre experiments. Thus, his novella *Harry Heathcote*, one of the markedly few Victorian texts by a British writer that are exclusively set in Australia, offers an astute assessment of social conflicts within the settler colony, but also constitutes a reaction to the proliferating genre of the sentimental Christmas tale, a genre Trollope belittled for the "blatant commodity economy of Christmas publishing" (Moore, T. 104). Similarly, the American passages of *Dr Wortle's School* dismantle Wild West scenarios as popularised by the "British-authored Westerns" that Kate Flint has recently brought back to critical attention (Flint 154). Trollope, indeed, always combined his uncompromisingly realist representation of the settler colonies with an explicit reworking of genre paradigms that was just as self-conscious. A close reading of his narrative uses of emigration reveals how the representation of settler spaces in Victorian fiction is more than simply a reflection of real-life developments or the cultural mythologies forming around them. Trollope makes emigration and settler life a central theme. He critically – and at times in a curiously tongue-in-cheek fashion – engages with the colonies' impact on metropolitan culture. And precisely as he plays with already clichéd narrative uses of intruding returnee figures, he makes their conscious reworking the centre of fascinating genre experiments. A better look at some of Trollope's less frequently discussed works reveals the underestimated centrality of colonial spaces – and especially colonial settler spaces – in Victorian literature, while new attention to the changing role he gives these spaces in his fiction reveals how experimental Trollope was in self-consciously reacting against prevailing representational forms.

The Three Clerks is the first of Trollope's novels to make significant use of emigration. At first sight, the novel's ending seems straightforwardly to conform to the common use of emigration as a convenient solution to domestic problems, in and out of fiction. The exportation of troublesome, flawed, and failed characters thereby operates as a "solution to domestic conflict that surfaces in literary texts as an 'out' of sorts" (Kranidis 102). As Trollope puts it in one of his late novels, *Mr Scarborough's Family* (1883), "[w]e are apt to think that a man may be disposed of by being made to go abroad; or, if he is absolutely penniless and useless, by being sent to the colonies – that he may there become a shepherd and drink himself out of this world" (Ch. 37). How widespread this use was and how aware readers and writers were of this cliché are succinctly summed up in Douglas Woodruff's entry on "Expansion and Emigration" in G. M. Young's 1934 *Early Victorian England*:

> Victorian fiction takes, on the whole, very slight notice of the Colonies, but Victorian novels with black sheep in them could hardly fail to use emigration as a remedy. Judged on their literary remains the Early Victorians found Australia the most useful part of the Empire, and there is a majority among the writing men in favour of the Antipodes as a solution, permanent or temporary, of the difficulties in which they involve their

> characters. Those most famous emigrants, the Micawbers, and Abel Magwitch, are matched by the central figure of Charles Reade's enormously popular *It's Never Too Late to Mend*, where much of the action is boldly placed in Australia, although the author had never seen the country, by Henry Kingsley's *Geoffry Hamlyn*, and by many a minor Trollope character, as e.g. in the *Three Clerks* or *Dr. Thorne*.
>
> (Woodruff 362)

One of the titular characters of *The Three Clerks* is convicted of embezzlement and moves to Australia after serving a sentence in a London prison. Yet emigration here is not a *deus-ex-machina* device to transport an unwanted character offstage, out of sight, to a vague space of the imagination. Even in this early novel, written before Trollope's two extended sojourns in Australia and New Zealand in the 1870s, he refuses to generate just a vague space of the imagination. Instead, the detailed descriptions of everyday realities are mercilessly realist, foiling expectations of emigration as a convenient conclusion.

Emigration appears to offer itself as a way out when Alaric Tudor, the convicted clerk, seeks to find a new life for his growing family: "All hope of regaining his situation had of course passed from him, all hope of employment in England. Emigration must now be his lot" (*Clerks* Ch. 43). Britain's geographical antipodes suggest themselves, partly perhaps because Australia is successful as just such a refuge in Dickens's *David Copperfield* (1850). Although it is symptomatic that Dickens's notoriously improvident Mr Micawber can only succeed at "the antipodes," Trollope's pointed rewriting of such a pat ending also needs to be seen in the context of what Jerome Meckier has termed "the realism wars." Trollope repeatedly parodied what he considered the simplifications and exaggerations of "Mr Popular Sentiment" (i.e. Dickens). In *The Three Clerks*, Alaric's wife, Gertrude, may envisage the settler colony as a utopia, "a new land, new hopes, new ideas, new freedom, new work, new life, and new ambition," where social disgrace is left behind:

> She was eager to be off, eager for her new career, eager that he should stand on a soil where he could once more face his fellow-creatures without shame. She panted to put thousands of leagues of ocean between him and his disgrace.
>
> (*Clerks* Ch. 43)

The subsequent chapter, however, is entitled, with pointed irony, "The Criminal Population Is Disposed Of" (Ch. 44), and "The Conclusion" (Ch. 47) details how the emigrants quickly realise that this is no utopian space and no panacea to domestic problems. For one, Alaric's "history had gone with him to the Antipodes" (*Clerks* Ch. 47). Altogether, expectations in England have been overdrawn, and "[t]hat land of promise had not flowed with milk and honey when first she put her foot upon its soil" (*Clerks* Ch. 47). Trollope's debunking of standard representations of emigration is here twofold: eschewing pro-emigration propaganda and narrative uses of emigration.

Diana Archibald has made the intriguing suggestion that Trollope's depiction of the mundane dreariness of the Tudors' settler life is more realist than his subsequent representations of emigration. Far from describing a "progression from a naïve and distant view to a more complex vision informed by firsthand experience," "he seems to resort more to stereotypes *after* visiting the country. Perhaps he found the land and people more like its popular image than he anticipated" (Archibald 77). His focus certainly underwent a shift, but Archibald's point is also a good reminder not to make an analysis of literary representation hinge on the extent, or limitation, of an author's firsthand experience or to trace chronological progression alone. Instead, I shall group Trollope's fictional uses of emigration, emigrants, and returnees according to their narrative functions. The

Three Clerks and *Lady Anna* both turn on the common Victorian plot twist of emigration as an "out of sorts," although they are by no means straightforward examples of what is, without doubt, often just narrative convenience. *John Caldigate* and *Dr Wortle's School* are then read together as Trollope's most explicit engagement with the prevailing sensational treatment of returnees. These pairings illustrate the range of Trollope's evocation of emigration in his fiction. Precisely by defying any straightforward progression, emigration's changing fictional role forms part of Trollope's experimental re-presentation of prevailing clichés.

Nicholas Birns has suggested that *Lady Anna* may be read as "the first of Trollope's Antipodean novels" (182) because at the end of the novel, Lady Anna Lovel marries the tailor's son Daniel Thwaite and they emigrate to Australia. This is certainly a more classic example of the pat ending than what happens at the end of the earlier *The Three Clerks*, reminding us again to remain wary of reading Trollope's (or Victorian literature's) representation of the empire or emigration in strictly chronological terms. Still, even Lady Anna's exportation to overseas spaces that seem to entail a freer, perhaps more liberal way of life is not that straightforward. There is, of course, again the suggestion – a suggestion already debunked in *The Three Clerks* – that anything is possible at the antipodes. But the Tudors find that the replication of British civilisation includes mundane shabby gentility, and there is likewise a disturbing undercurrent in *Lady Anna* that migration will not automatically erase class differences. The couple's projected return, moreover, pinpoints several interrelated problems that complicate the novel's use of emigration as a solution.

Trollope wrote the novel on his way out to Australia in 1871, his first visit to his younger son, Frederic, who had settled on a farm in New South Wales. Looking forward to the visit and to extensive travels through Australia and New Zealand in preparation for writing a travel book, Trollope might well have imagined the New World as a space for social as well as narrative opportunities. Birns maintains that the novel's denouement "entailed an Antipodean aspect to the marriage plot" that presents Australia as a "place where the couple can be happy together and yet not outrage class norms, outside as well as within the novel" (182). Deborah Denenholz Morse further suggests that, as "Trollope nearly promises us a future novel in which the lives of Daniel and Anna will be chronicled in Australia," this yet unseen space is created as "an imaginary that might well include Trollope's remembrance of his beloved son Fred's voyages out to the Antipodes, as well as the present experience of his own writing on shipboard, en route to Melbourne" (Morse 66–7). The resulting imaginary of a more egalitarian, utopian place is crucial to the novel's critical reshaping of the marriage plot along cross-class and, Morse convincingly argues, covertly interracial lines (67). Both the idea of a return and the narrative opportunities of a novel set in Australia are toyed with at the end of the novel, although neither were realised.

But if several critics have read the novel's envisioned Australia as reflective of Trollope's view of this New World as promising more egalitarian opportunities, Jenny Bourne Taylor reminds us of the darker undercurrents that reflect Trollope's complicated attitude to empire and emigration. Bourne Taylor discusses Trollope in relation to mid-Victorian sensationalism, but I contend here that it is Trollope's insistence on describing the realities of emigration and colonial life – on providing a realist representation rather than narrative convenience – that is accountable for the "uneasy closure which many critics found unpalatable" (Bourne Taylor 93). A contemporary review in *The Times* notably remarked that "we trust that nothing may happen, even in Australia, to make Lady Anna regret that she married Daniel Thwaite the Cumberland tailor" (qtd. in Bourne Taylor 93). Bourne Taylor suggests that it is the "final twist" of Trollope's rewriting of cross-class courtship plots that "Daniel Thwaite, whom Anna finally marries and emigrates with, has all the makings of a repressive and controlling husband" (93). That there is no clear-cut resolution, or unambiguous reading, is partly the point. Trollope's uncompromising realism does not allow the reduction of emigration to either utopian or sensational narrative convenience.

Neither must we forget that *Lady Anna* is primarily set in the 1830s, reflecting English politics and attitudes before the Second Reform Bill of 1832 and hence also a different meaning of emigration. Before the opening of the Suez Canal in 1869, migration to Britain's antipodal colonies was chiefly a one-way move into a distant space. It meant taking farewell forever, as it is repeatedly put at the end of *The Three Clerks*. Trollope travelled through the canal on both his voyages to Australia, and his subsequent novels about the colonies register the radical shift in accessibility to and, by extension, the new narrative opportunities of "a post-Suez Australia" (Birns 182). Birns has suggested that this historical contingency can be seen as a crucial difference in Trollope's literary treatment of the antipodes: "The crucial difference is between a pre-Suez Australia, from which it is difficult to return, and a post-Suez Australia, from which one can return – with complications!" (Birns 182). The ending of *Lady Anna* already reflects Trollope's awareness of this change and its ramifications: for the Thwaites reaching the faraway place means severing ties with England and being offered at least the possibility of anonymity, but then this convenient offstage space does no longer exist in the world in which the novel is written and published. Return might be more easily realisable, but there is also a significant shift in what emigration means. Trollope's post-Suez novels narratively make the most of this changing meaning.

Trollope and his wife, Rose, spent eighteen months travelling across Australia and New Zealand, partly to gather material for the 1873 travel book. Trollope returned to Australia in 1875 to help his son close down his failed farming business (Starck 21). The 1874 novella *Harry Heathcote of Gangoil*, subtitled *A Tale of Australian Bush Life*, closely draws on the social stratifications that were troubling old and new settlers. Traditionally, the narrative has been seen as simply an accurate reflection of the Australian Trollopes' home and how it impressed the visiting author. Yet, Dorice Elliott has expertly read this "frontier Christmas adventure story" (24) side by side with mid-century Australian fiction concerned with everyday life in the New World, and more attention has likewise been accorded its representation of bushfires (Moore, G.). Trollope appropriates the format of the bush tale, while playing with the conventions of the traditional Christmas story. As a threatening bushfire, laid by an arsonist, and a flaming Christmas pudding appear in a tongue-in-cheek juxtaposition, *Harry Heathcote* shows how an experiment with genre confines best captures what was perceived as incongruous "back home": a domestic tale of bushlife, a heatwave in a Christmas story, a dissection of new as well as old class structures, set against the backdrop of a bushfire. While capturing social shifts in colonial Australia, the narrative also displays the shifting boundaries of different genres and how they were being transformed through their exportation throughout the anglophone settler world. *John Caldigate* similarly evokes and plays with the sensational potential of the returnee narrative, a narrative that had become much more urgent after the opening of the Suez Canal.

Harry Heathcote and *John Caldigate* are frequently paired in discussions of nineteenth-century British representations of emigration or settler life. They are generally considered Trollope's "two 'Australian' novels" (Davidson 306), although their approach to the colony's function in literature or to Australia itself could not be any more different. Instead, they exemplify and significantly reshape the two opposing trajectories in which emigration most commonly features in Victorian fiction. *John Caldigate* rewrites what had become a standard sensational narrative of disruptive return, often as the result of failed emigration (Wagner, "Settling"). It is the only one of Trollope's full-scale novels that features a settler colony at considerable length, and yet this makes up a comparatively small part in an extensive triple-decker that is concerned, first and foremost, with the empire's impact at home. Growing interest in this impact has ensured that *John Caldigate* has received extensive critical attention over the last decades. Davidson already summed up the novel's main points about the difficulties of return: how the perceived idea "that anything done in the wilds of Australia ought not 'to count' here, at home in England" (322) breaks down in the novel. Davidson addresses various discrepancies:

> A looser morality was expected in the back-blocks of the colonies, and Trollope, in exploiting this feeling and turning it to good effect in this novel, was in fact denying the validity of his observations in [his travel book]. There he never tires of commending the behaviour of the Australian working men and miners.
>
> *(311)*

Yet Trollope really debunks prevalent expectations. Those voicing stereotypical ideas about settler spaces are ridiculed, which adds to the social comedy in the domestic scenes. Simultaneously, Trollope works against sensational representational strategies. The novel contains some of the most explicit literary references to the Tichbourne Claimant, the drawn-out court case involving a fraudulent heir to an aristocratic estate who turned out to be a butcher from Australia (Wagner, "Settling" 121–2).

Briefly, *John Caldigate* is the story of a young Englishman who, like the Prodigal Son, asks for a monetary advance in lieu of his inheritance. He embarks for Australia, where we see him at first shocked by the realities of life at the diggings. But he is moderately successful, in contrast to his best friend, who succumbs to the temptations of drink. These scenes are detailed, and yet the narrator tantalisingly leaves out what Caldigate's true relationship is with a Mrs Smith he meets on the ship out. In Australia, Caldigate then decides to "make his home" in England after all, the "years of absence [having] endeared to John Caldigate a place which, while it was his home, had always been distasteful to him" (*Caldigate* Ch. 13). Once back, married and settled down as future squire, he is accused of bigamy by Euphemia Smith. Her claims turn out to be fraudulent, but the moral ambiguities and the various reactions to them form a central theme, while the fictional treatment eschews sensational mystery. As I have suggested elsewhere, the seemingly straightforward rejection of sensationalism is complicated by the narrator's initial elision of what happens in the "other" space: what exactly Caldigate and Smith have done that might constitute marriage within the notoriously slippery marriage laws of the time. As Caldigate admits, "there was so much in his Australian life which would not bear the searching light of cross-examination" (*Caldigate* Ch. 40). The gaps in the narrative rupture the confidence between omniscient narrator and familiarly addressed reader and thereby the novel's domestic realism (Wagner, "Settling" 124–5).

Myers has read *John Caldigate* side by side with emigrant letters to show how Euphemia Smith "enacts the . . . collective nightmare" of single emigrant women "as she relinquishes her identity in the colony" (66). Although Myers admits that "none of the emigrants escapes the colonial encounter unscathed" (67), she focuses on double standards, highlighting how "[t]roped as a foreigner and often referred to as an Australian woman, Mrs Smith metaphorically loses all ties to Britain" (66). Archibald has similarly read Mrs Smith as an undomestic New World woman (99), stressing how her character displays striking affinities with the pistol-wielding Wild West character Mrs Hurtle in Trollope's earlier *The Way We Live Now*. Both characters are fascinating versions of the sensational anti-heroine as well as embodiments of a lack of domesticity in the New Worlds; neither of them can be part of English society.

But as Trollope continued to rework popular representational strategies – literary sensationalism in particular – these figures received their most pointed rewriting in *Dr Wortle's School*. There, the titular protagonist realises that his assistant, an Englishman who used to teach in America, is not really married to his American wife. Trollope quickly gives away this secret, thereby ejecting its sensational potential:

> Therefore, put the book down if the revelation of some future secret be necessary for your enjoyment. Our mystery is going to be revealed in the next paragraph, – in the next half-dozen words. Mr and Mrs Peacocke were not man and wife.
> (Dr Wortle's Ch. 3)

Trollope significantly continues to call Ella Lefroy Mrs Peacocke, which clearly signals how he intends the reader to navigate the moral and legal turmoil that strikes English provincial society. As Morse has pointed out, "Scholars have historically focused upon Bowick Parish's horrified response to the discovery of bigamy in their midst in tension with the more flexible and tolerant morality of the hero" (Morse 133), with the exception of Robert Tracy's discussion of how Trollope "refuses to glamorise the type" of the post-bellum gentleman of the American South (Tracy 263). More recently, the novel has invited renewed attention to its American, or anti-American, material (Wagner, "Speculating"), and Morse has fascinatingly read Ella Peacocke as Trollope's take on the figure of the Creole to show how he negotiates "Englishness through his entry into continuing transatlantic discourse about race and the legacy of slavery" (134). What is more, even as the Peacockes' dilemma implies that returnees are likely to disqualify themselves from settling back in, the novel simultaneously demythologises the sensational potential of the embedded Wild West narrative. The Peacockes might not know that Colonel Lefroy, Ella's abusive husband, is still alive when they get married, but they do know before they move to England, ironically to seek anonymity through the transatlantic crossing. Mr Peacocke returns to America once more to prove that now Lefroy lies buried in the American West. There are bar-fights with bowie knives, and Peacocke sleeps with a pistol under his pillow, but the West is a deglamorised space, exploding the conventions of westerns that were widely circulating on both sides of the Atlantic.

Informed by new transatlantic studies approaches, developments in postcolonial studies, widening comparative analyses, and, above all, renewed attention to genre formation, new readings of Trollope's changing evocation of emigration to and return from settler spaces offer a different perspective on his fictional world. His narratively self-conscious redeployments of common clichés simultaneously show us how complex reflections on current developments were. Trollope dissected prevalent misconceptions about emigration, exposing prejudices as part of his social comedy, while nonetheless harnessing the narrative interest created by disruptive returnees. His play with popular perceptions was always also about genre experiments. Closer attention to his reworking of persistent narrative uses of emigration, therefore, prompts us to think differently about Trollope, Victorian literature, settler colonialism, and the divergent ways the Victorians thought about new forms of global mobility.

Notes

1 Frances Trollope wrote four "American" novels, *The Refugee in America* (1832), *Jonathan Jefferson Whitlaw* (1836), *The Barnabys in America; Or, Adventures of The Widow Wedded* (1843), and *The Old World and the New* (1849), although her experience in America informed several of her other works as well (cf. Ayres vol. 1, xvii).
2 The best-known examples of emigration as a fortuitous solution in Victorian fiction are probably the pastoral evocation of Canada at the end of Elizabeth Gaskell's *Mary Barton* (1848) and the successful move to Australia of quite a few characters, including the notoriously impecunious Micawbers, who succeed stunningly well once they are at "the antipodes," in Dickens's *David Copperfield* (1850).

Works cited

Archibald, Diana. *Domesticity, Imperialism, and Emigration in the Victorian Novel.* Columbia: U of Missouri P, 2002.

Ayres, Brenda. "General Introduction." *The Social Problem Novels of Frances Trollope.* London: Pickering & Chatto, 2009. Vol. 1, vii–xx.

Belich, James. *Replenishing the Earth: The Settler Revolution and the Rise of the Anglo-World.* Oxford: Oxford UP, 2009.

Bell, Duncan. *The Idea of Greater Britain: Empire and the Future of World Order, 1860–1900.* Princeton: Princeton UP, 2007.

Birns, Nicholas. "Trollope and the Antipodes." *The Cambridge Companion to Anthony Trollope.* Eds. Carolyn Dever and Lisa Niles. Cambridge: Cambridge UP, 2011. 181–95.

Blythe, Helen E. "*The Fixed Period* (1882): Euthanasia, Cannibalism, and Colonial Extraction in Anthony Trollope's Antipodes." *Nineteenth Century Contexts* 25.2 (2003): 161–80.

Braddon, Mary Elizabeth. *Lady Audley's Secret.* 1862. Ed. Lyn Pykett. Oxford: Oxford World's Classics Series, 2012.

Buzard, James. "Trollope and Travel." *The Cambridge Companion to Anthony Trollope.* Eds. Carolyn Dever and Lisa Niles. Cambridge: Cambridge UP, 2011. 168–80.

Davidson, J. H. "Anthony Trollope and the Colonies." *Victorian Studies* 12.3 (March 1969): 305–30.

Dickens, Charles. *David Copperfield.* 1850. Ed. Nina Burgis. Oxford: Oxford World's Classics Series, 2008.

———. *Hard Times.* 1854. Ed. Paul Schlicke. Oxford: Oxford World's Classics Series, 2008.

———. *Great Expectations.* 1861. Ed. Margaret Cardwell. Oxford: Clarendon, 2008.

Dilke, Charles Wentworth. *Greater Britain: A Record of Travel in English-Speaking Countries 1866 and 1867.* New York: Harper & Brothers, 1868.

Durey, Jill Felicity. "Modern Issues: Anthony Trollope and Australia." *Antipodes: A North American Journal of Australian Literature* 21 (December 2007): 170–6.

Elliott, Dorice. "Unsettled Status in Australian Settler Novels." *Victorian Settler Narratives: Emigrants, Cosmopolitans and Returnees in Nineteenth-Century Literature.* Ed. Tamara S. Wagner. London: Pickering & Chatto, 2011. 23–40.

Flint, Kate. *The Transatlantic Indian, 1776–1930.* Princeton: Princeton UP, 2009.

Johnston, H. J. M. *British Emigration Policy, 1815–1830.* Oxford: Clarendon Press, 1972.

Kranidis, Rita S. *The Victorian Spinster and Colonial Emigration: Contested Subjects.* Houndmills, Basingstoke: Macmillan, 1999.

Lansbury, Coral. *Arcady in Australia: The Evocation of Australia in Nineteenth-Century English Literature.* Melbourne: Melbourne UP, 1970.

Meckier, Jerome. *Hidden Rivalries in Victorian Fiction: Dickens, Realism, and Revaluation.* Lexington: UP of Kentucky, 1987.

Moore, Grace. "'The Heavens Were on Fire': Incendiarism and the Defence of the Settler Home." *Domestic Fiction in Colonial Australia and New Zealand.* Ed. Tamara S. Wagner. London: Pickering & Chatto, 2014. 63–73.

Moore, Tara. *Victorian Christmas in Print.* Basingstoke: Palgrave Macmillan, 2009.

Morse, Deborah Denenholz. *Reforming Trollope: Race, Gender, and Englishness in the Novels of Anthony Trollope.* Farnham, England: Ashgate, 2013.

Myers, Janet. *Antipodal England: Emigration and Portable Domesticity in the Victorian Imagination.* New York: SUNY, 2009.

Said, Edward. *Culture & Imperialism.* New York: Knopf, 1993.

Starck, Nigel. "Anthony Trollope's Travels and Travails in 1871 Australia." *National Library of Australia News* 19.1 (2008): 19–21. http://arrow.unisa.edu.au:8081/1959.8/62924 (accessed 1 October 2013).

Taylor, Jenny Bourne. "Trollope and the Sensation Novel." The Cambridge Companion to Anthony Trollope. Eds. Carolyn Dever and Lisa Niles. Cambridge: Cambridge UP, 2011. 85–98.

Tracy, Robert. *Trollope's Later Novels.* Berkeley: U of California P, 1978.

Trollope, Anthony. *Australia and New Zealand.* 1873. Cambridge: Cambridge University Press, 2013.

———. *Dr Wortle's School.* Ed. Mick Imlah. 1881. London: Penguin, 1999.

———. *Harry Heathcote of Gangoil.* 1874. Ed. Peter David Edwards. Oxford: Oxford World's Classics Series, 1992.

———. *John Caldigate.* 1879. London: The Trollope Society, 1995.

———. *Lady Anna.* 1874. Ed. Stephen Orgel. Oxford: Oxford World's Classics Series, 1990.

———. *Mr Scarborough's Family.* Ed. Geoffrey Harvey. 1883. Oxford: Oxford World's Classics Series, 1989.

———. *The New Zealander.* N. John Hall. 1855. Oxford: Clarendon, 1972.

———. *North America.* 1862. London: The Trollope Society, 2001.

———. *An Old Man's Love.* 1882. Ed. John Sutherland. Oxford: Oxford World's Classics Series, 1991.

———. *South Africa: South Africa. The Cape Colony. Natal.* 1877. London: Chapman and Hall, 1878.

———. *The Three Clerks.* Ed. Graham Handley. 1857. Oxford: Oxford World's Classics Series, 1992.

———. *The Tireless Traveller: Twenty Letters to the Liverpool Mercury, 1875.* Ed. Bradford Allen Booth. Berkeley: University of California Press, 1941.

———. *Travelling Sketches.* London: Chapman and Hall, 1866.

———. *The West Indies and the Spanish Main.* 1859. London: Cass, 1968.

Wagner, Tamara S. "Settling Back in at Home: Impostors and Imperial Panic in Victorian Narratives of Return." *Victorian Settler Narratives: Emigrants, Cosmopolitans and Returnees in Nineteenth-Century Literature.* Ed. Tamara S. Wagner. London: Pickering & Chatto, 2011. 111–27.

———. "Speculating on American Markets: Foreign Money Matters and the New British Businessman in the Victorian Novel." *Symbiosis* 14.2 (October 2010): 195–217.

Woodruff, Douglas. "Expansion and Emigration." *Early Victorian England. 1830–1865.* Ed. G. M. Young. London: Oxford University Press, 1934. vol. 2, 349–410.

31

'SO WILD AND BEAUTIFUL A WORLD AROUND HIM'

Trollope and Antipodean ecology

Grace Moore

Writing of Trollope's 1859 travelogue *The West Indies and the Spanish Main*, Claudia Brandenstein has, in an argument influenced by the work of Mary Louise Pratt, described his approach to the landscape as a type of taking possession. For Brandenstein, Trollope engages in the 'production of the monarch-of-all-I survey scene' (15), depicting landscapes that are 'feminized' and 'easily subdued' (19), stemming from a feeling of proprietorial entitlement, which is underpinned by a British imperialist sense of mastery over the West Indian colonial holdings.[1] This approach to the colonial landscape is a common feature in both painting and travel writing of the nineteenth century. Simon Ryan, for instance, has put forward a similar argument with regard to contemporary accounts of the Australian scenery. According to Ryan, explorers and other chroniclers frequently depicted the Australian countryside as 'well adapted' for settlement, deploying a European aesthetic lens of the picturesque as a means of taming its more confronting elements and uncanny vistas (74).

In the light of his somewhat conventional, totalizing approach to the West Indies, Trollope's position on Antipodean flora and fauna, as articulated in *Australia and New Zealand* (1873), is surprisingly nuanced, although that may well be because of the twelve-year distance between the two works.[2] Genuinely fascinated by the extraordinary difference of the world around him, Trollope's approach to the natural environments of both Australia and New Zealand does not always conform to prevailing ideas of mastery. At times, he explores the diverse ways in which these recent colonial acquisitions were plundered by their settler communities, while at others he writes as though nothing is more natural than that the English might help themselves to whatever they may please, anywhere in the world. Sometimes fascinated and at others aghast, Trollope proves in both his fiction and his travel writing that he was keenly concerned with ecology in the Antipodes and, in some instances, he anticipates today's debates surrounding land ownership and management. Trollope was, then, a sensitive surveyor of landscape during his time down under, although there are limits to the breadth of his vision, partly resulting from his historical situatedness and partly because of his politics. This chapter will trace some of the complexities and contradictions of Trollope's responses to the southern hemisphere, mapping his encounters with an environment that frequently challenged his aesthetic sensibilities.

Trollope visited the Antipodes twice: once between 1871 and 1872, when he based himself in Australia, but also travelled to New Zealand, and then again in 1875, when he mostly remained in New South Wales.[3] Trollope's son Frederic had settled in Australia at a young age, having, as his father puts it in his autobiography, 'resolved on a colonial career when he found that boys who did not grow so fast as he did got above him at school' (*Autobiography*, 297).[4] Trollope's representation of New Zealand is by no means as comprehensive as his depiction of Australia. Indeed, his futuristic novella, *The Fixed Period* (1882), set in the 'orderly colony' Britannula – which is generally agreed to be based on New Zealand – is remarkable for its lack of emphasis on place, dealing instead with the controversial issue of euthanasia. Equally, Trollope's travels in the colony receive comparatively scant attention in *Australia and New Zealand*.[5] While the reader is offered a state-by-state guide to Australia, the smaller New Zealand is represented by a single section in the work's second volume. His reluctance to comment is perhaps encapsulated in his introduction to the 'New Zealand' section of the book, when he remarks that, given the very large number of guidebooks, he is almost 'bound to feel that more writing would be superfluous' (*A&NZ*, 2:301). However, I would argue that his family connection to Australia makes his association with the larger colony's landscape a much more affective one.

Coral Lansbury has commented that 'Trollope found a great deal to approve in Australia and he conscientiously visited public institutions and private homes, and made the customary pilgrimage to the bush' (129). Lansbury goes on to assert that Trollope 'used Australia as a convenient device in his novels' (132), but I would argue that this position is too dismissive of the novelist's involvement in and appreciation of life in the Antipodes. While it is true that many Victorian novelists (most famously Charles Dickens) exiled difficult characters to the other end of the earth, sometimes permanently and sometimes to rehabilitate them and their fortunes, Trollope is remarkable for his sense of Australian space and place. Mastery of the land was a somewhat vexed issue for him and, as I shall explore later in this chapter, he frequently approached Australia as a vast garden that needed discipline to be imposed upon it.

In Trollope's early colonial writings, Britain's imperial holdings were presented as places to be plundered by those wishing to make a fortune. However, as he grew older, travelled extensively and learned more about life in the empire, he began to see settlement as a more permanent commitment.[6] As J. H. Davidson puts it,

> When in 1876 Disraeli argued that colonists were a fluctuating population, out to find nuggets or fleece flocks before returning 'home' to enjoy the fruits of their wealth, he was merely expressing a popular view that Trollope had once upheld . . . But as his experience of the colonies grew, he came to see that whatever might be said for gentry and professional men, most who went on that journey made it for good. Should a return trip to the Old Country be made, 'a short while sufficed to see the emigrant back in the colony again.'
>
> *(310)*

Increasingly, Trollope came to believe that occupying land involved responsibility, and while he remained deeply interested in the spectacular financial rewards that could result from hard graft in the colonies, he also understood that remaining in a place permanently involved taking some responsibility for its well-being – not just a putting down of roots but a tending to them too. This is not to suggest that Trollope never drew upon the colonial plot as the type of 'convenient device' noted by Lansbury, but rather that he did so in a way that was informed and self-conscious. The eponymous hero of Trollope's 1879 novel, *John Caldigate*, draws attention to this self-awareness when he admits to Ralph Holt of his time in Australia, 'I had to go there . . . To tell the truth, my friend, I should not have done very well here unless I had been able to top-dress the English acres with a little Australian gold' (192). This idea of Antipodean wealth as a fertilizer to the otherwise barren English fields is a compelling one that points to the mother country's growing dependency on colonial revenue. That a member of the gentry must degrade himself through manual labour on the other side of the world points to a new order, in which the considerable wealth that is earned in the colonies is more tangible and dependable than inherited means. For a wastrel who must be reformed, John's time at the diggings is also a form of penance. However, Trollope undoubtedly understood the terrible privations underpinning Antipodean work and the numerous challenges that a hostile climate could throw in the path of the most industrious worker.

Trollope's Christmas novella *Harry Heathcote of Gangoil* (1874) was written partly in tribute to his son Fred, who worked hard in his adopted country, but who failed to prosper.[7] The work is very much a novel of settlement in which the characters are committed to establishing permanent homes in Australia, albeit within a very English social framework, and in this respect it is a work that is much more steeped in Australiana than *John Caldigate*. Revolving around the seasonal threat posed by bushfires in Australia (although in this case, fires that are started through human agency), *Harry Heathcote* is a work that confronts the otherness of the Australian landscape. Set in the Queensland sugar-growing region, on one level the novella tackles uncertainties surrounding land ownership and social hierarchy in the bush. On another, though, the piece reflects settler anxieties regarding an uncertain and often hostile climate. Robert Dingley succinctly encapsulates the eponymous hero's deep apprehensions when he notes, 'Fear of disaster keeps Heathcote in a condition of constant edginess: his days are spent inspecting nervously the perimeter of his estate and he is apprehensive not only of bushfire but, within minutes of rain falling, of flood' (40).[8] While Harry's concerns are extreme, they reflect the difficulties that many settlers experienced in attempting to transpose farming skills learned in Europe to a tropical climate. Indeed, many guidebooks warned of the tribulations experienced by migrant farmers, with *Sidney's Australian Hand-Book* (1849) cautioning that agricultural schemes were little more than 'mischievous delusion[s], calculated to distract our attention from much more important objects' (*Sidney's*, 34), while the reactionary anonymous author of *The Resources of Australia* (1848) asserted provocatively that 'the pursuits of agriculture … had a great effect in retarding the prosperity of the colony' (*Resources*, 4).

For nineteenth-century settlers, farming in the bush often involved an ongoing and emotional struggle against the sprawling indigenous plant life. Heathcote's farm at Gangoil is divided into paddocks that differ from those on an English farm only in terms of their scale. However, Trollope is aware of the intense labour required to produce this illusion of a home away from home. He registers the role of land clearance (which we would today term 'deforestation') and outlines some of the challenges associated with setting up home in the bush:

> There are Australian pastures which consist of plains on which not a tree is to be seen for miles; but others are forests, so far extending that their limits are almost unknown. Gangoil was surrounded by forest, in some places so close as to be impervious to men and almost to animals in which the undergrowth was thick and tortuous and almost platted [sic], through which no path could be made without an axe, but of which the greater portions were open, without any under-wood, between which the sheep could wander at their will, and men could ride, with a sparse surface of coarse grass, which after rain would be luxuriant, but in hot weather would be scorched down to the ground.
>
> (*Harry Heathcote of Gangoil*, 6)

Trollope here points to the hostility of the climate, signalling the danger of fire that will plague Harry for most of the narrative. He also points to the damage that Europeans are inflicting upon the landscape, noting the use of axes in the undergrowth and other more serious forms of ecological vandalism.

Importantly, Trollope taps into a major controversy associated with settler land management when he raises the issue of the ring-barking of trees. Environmental historian Rory O'Brien offers insights into the wider discussion when he notes,

> In forested country, trees rather than squatters were the selector's enemy. Trees were initially regarded as an impediment rather than a resource. Ringbarking was the supreme expression of this attitude. It killed the tree with minimum labour and let in the light to encourage grass growth. Some said it dried and sweetened the soil.
>
> *(34)*[9]

Indeed, an article on the 'Nubba Prize Sheep' from the *Town and Country Journal* (24 December 1887) comments casually of the Nubba sheep farming estate in New South Wales that 'improvements have been made through ring-barking and clearing' (1327). Trollope, however, did not associate ring-barking with 'improvement', as is evidenced by his description of the corpse-like trees surrounding Gangoil:

> Further afield, but still round the home quarters, the trees had been destroyed, the run of the sap having been stopped by "ringing" the bark; but they still stood like troops of skeletons, and would stand, very ugly to look at, till they fell, in the course of nature, by reason of their own rottenness.
>
> *(Harry, 6–7)*

The fact that the character whose 'sole business was to destroy the timber after this fashion' (7) in *Harry Heathcote* is the villain, Boscobel, signifies Trollope's disapproval of this unpleasant clearance technique. Harry may have commissioned the process, but the narrative presents him as somewhat removed from it, and it is Boscobel who acts as the agent of destruction. For Trollope, Harry is a manager of the unruly terrain, while Boscobel is a dangerous instrument of death.

Trollope represents Harry as passionately attached to his new land, but his love is tinged with chronic anxiety at the prospect of fire. Robert Dingley offers helpful insights into Harry's contradictory emotional responses to his environment when he thinks in terms of 'mastery'. As Dingley puts it, 'It is not, for example, merely the possibility of being reduced to poverty that makes Heathcote terrified of fire, but the loss of "mastership" – mastership not only of the land, but of the self – that will necessarily follow' (40). Dingley is more concerned with Harry's psychological disintegration than with questions of land ownership, but he argues convincingly for points of convergence between the two, noting that

> what is, I think, distinctive about [Harry] is the way in which Trollope links causally his mental degeneration with the conditions of colonial tenure. Seeking to establish himself within clearly defined parameters, Heathcote repeatedly finds that he is the occupant of 'debatable land'.
>
> *(410)*

The land is, of course, 'debatable' not just because Harry is not its owner but also because it has been acquired forcibly. Meaghan Morris has written of what she terms the 'white panic' that pervades the Australian landscape, arguing for a 'settler terror' whereby Europeans and their descendants experience ineffable feelings of anxiety when they are in the bush (90–93). Although an aesthetic framework of the sublime goes some way to explain the settler's discomfort at the landscape's otherness, it falls short and does not account fully for the land's disturbing strangeness.[10] Harry's psychological deterioration is clearly connected to his tenuous grasp on the land he farms, leaving his mastery in some doubt, even at the tale's denouement. While the story ends with a marriage proposal and Harry's assertion that it is a 'Happy Christmas', the reader knows that – just like Christmas – the fire season will return and, as a result, Harry will never be completely at peace. His sense of triumph over the landscape is doomed to be temporary, and while the arsonist villains have been removed, it is inevitable that Harry's panic will resurface.

The later character, John Caldigate, is much more comfortable with the idea of asserting ownership over the landscape than Harry. John has a more itinerant relationship with Australia than Harry and essentially uses the environment and its spoils as a means of regaining the land for which he truly cares – his family estate, Folking. Trollope's representation of Australia in this later novel is, in some ways, much more perfunctory, in that a number of key Antipodean events (such as the cohabitation between Caldigate and Euphemia Smith) take place 'off-stage' and the Australian scenes are restricted to the early chapters.[11] Trollope, nevertheless, draws upon his travels to present a convincing depiction of life in the diggings. In particular, he captures mining's wholesale destruction of the landscape, highlighting the carelessness with which those in pursuit of swift wealth plunder the ground and move on. Caldigate and Dick Shand encounter the ravaged countryside in their quest for Mr Crinkett, who is able to extract gold from the ground at the rate of two ounces to the ton of quartz:

> They had walked about half a mile from the town, turning down a lane at the back of the house, and had made their way through yawning pit-holes and heaps of dirt and pools of yellow water, – where everything was disorderly and apparently deserted, – till they came to a cluster of heaps so large as to look like little hills; and here there were signs of mining vitality. On their way they had not come across a single shred of vegetation, though here and there stood the bare trunks of a few dead and headless trees, the ghosts of the forest which had occupied the place six or seven years previously.
>
> *(John Caldigate, 74)*

The narrator's tone here makes apparent Trollope's displeasure at the damage done by the miners. With its craters, dirt and stagnant water, the scene is that of a desolate wasteland, that is almost post-apocalyptic in its representation. While Trollope may not couch his critique in ecological terms, it is clear that he is aghast at the devastation that the miners leave in their wake. He is also deeply concerned at how life at the diggings can warp personalities, gesturing to Dick Shand's drinking and Euphemia Smith's lust for gold as examples of the toll that colonial life could exact. The appalling damaged landscape thus signifies the more widespread destruction that accompanied the imperial venture. Furthermore, when Trollope's narrator describes these scenes, the 'monarch-of-all-I-survey' perspective is conspicuous in its absence. The gaze here is aghast, not proprietorial, and what remains unsaid is just how quickly Europeans have managed to wreak devastation upon their adopted home.[12]

Trollope was, like many visitors to Australia, somewhat overwhelmed by the vista and found it difficult to accommodate the aesthetic challenges posed by the landscape, even when it was undamaged by settler hands, and particularly when it came to questions of scale. Writing of a journey to Brisbane, he complained,

> As a rule it must be acknowledged that a land of forests is not a land of beauty. Some experience in travelling is needed before this can be acknowledged, as every lover of

nature is an admirer of trees. But unceasing trees, trees which continue around you from six in the morning till six at night, become a bore, and the traveller begins to remember with regret the open charms of some cultivated plain.

(A&NZ, 1:78)

Trollope's reaction here is perhaps a response to what Jonathan Bate – following Theodor Adorno – terms 'nature's wildness'. For Adorno and Bate nature is, from the eighteenth century onwards, increasingly dominated by technology, which leads to a 'repression of wildness'. According to Bate, 'The repressed returns, but as a shiver of delight rather than a shudder of true impotence, in the frisson which eighteenth-century aestheticians called "the sublime"' (122). Trollope's idea of nature is much more akin to that rejected by George Monbiot when he complains about the ways in which sheep have come to be regarded as a natural part of the English countryside (154–60). The carefully fenced fields, complete with the livestock, that Trollope identifies as 'rural' have, of course, been carefully shaped by their owners and, as Monbiot reminds us, they are symptomatic of the enclosure of land. This cultivated, English version of the wild leaves the nineteenth-century traveller unprepared for true wilderness when s/he encounters it, and the result is often an expression of horror or the articulation of a need to 'manage' the space. Barbara Baynton's collection of short stories *Bush Studies* (1902) stages these horrified reactions to the countryside quite brilliantly, capturing the feral qualities of remote settlements, the terror of the land and the gradual degeneration of the men and women who chose to live there.[13] While Trollope may not have recognized it, his writing aligned itself with a growing convention of configuring the bush in sublime terms. Baynton also adds a heavy layer of Gothicism to her representations of the landscape – joining other Australian writers, including Marcus Clarke, Henry Lawson and Rosa Praed in adapting this European convention to convey the threatening and *unheimlich* elements of both landscapes and soundscapes. However, Trollope was either too removed from the bush's potential for terror or too pragmatic to succumb to these visceral reactions, and he continued to approach the land through a combination of wonder and disdain, seeking to assert order upon it, rather than allowing himself to be overwhelmed.

If Australia is a wilderness in need of taming, Trollope's New Zealand can be bleak and barren. John Sutherland has described his short story of life on a New Zealand sheep station, 'Catherine Carmichael', as 'a portrait of pioneer life in New Zealand so grim as to have served as a warning for any young Victorian thinking of emigration' (xxii). In this bleak short story, Trollope's narrator emphasizes the isolated desolation of the colonial landscape, most startlingly when he alludes to Peter Carmichael's assertion of his conjugal rights. Speaking of how Catherine is crushed by her loveless marriage to a 'hard, dry man', the narrator invokes a hostile, overwhelming environment in order to convey the young woman's sense of claustrophobia and despair:

When she was told that the hard, dry man would find a home for her, she had no reason to give why it should not be so. When she did not at first refuse to be taken away across the mountains, she had failed to realise what it all meant. When she reached Warriwa, and the waters in the pathless, unbridged rivers had not closed over her head – then she realised it.

(ch. 1)

The rugged landscape is, to begin with, associated with masculine authority, to the extent that Catherine's marriage to the unsuitable gold-digger and miser, Peter Carmichael, is driven by her knowledge that she 'could not live alone in that wild country!' (ch. 1).[14] Significantly, though, Peter is later killed when the river waters wash over him – an engulfing that echoes Catherine's earlier realization that the waters had not closed over her – suggesting that any assertion of mastery over the region is illusory. Interestingly, Peter's nephew and Catherine's eventual husband, John, is shown to have a very different relationship with the land, jumping in and out of a Queensland gully at will, when news of his uncle's death reaches him in the diggings. As Catherine comes to terms with her widowhood, the narrator frequently invokes her isolation and vulnerability at the rural sheep station, although these considerations evaporate rapidly when she and John reach a betrothal at the story's end. In the world of this short story, true love – and its accompanying companionship – can combat the hostilities of the wilderness.

Trollope's perplexity at the New Zealand topography reaches its zenith when he visits the hot springs at Rota Rua (Rotorua). Overwhelmed by the sulphuric odour, he feels bound to mention that the town contains only one White inhabitant. He then continues to assert that, while he had enjoyed relaxing in the waters, his overall impression was one of disappointment. He comments, rather glumly, of the geysers at Ohinemutu,

> I saw nothing of the uplifted columns of boiling water; – nor throughout the district did I see anything of the kind at all equal to the descriptions which I had read and heard. Indeed, I came across nothing which I would call a column of water thrown up and dispersed in the air. . . As to the jets of water, I was told that I was unfortunate, and that the geysers were very tranquil during my visit. I have, however, observed, all the world over that the world's wonders, when I have reached them, have been less than ordinarily wonderful.
>
> (*A&NZ*, 2:476)

Trollope's disappointment here is akin to the discomfort and boredom he articulated on his journey through the forests to Brisbane. On both occasions he speaks of feeling let down, and it would seem that his appetite for the new is not sated by his experiences. Trollope is either a traveller with extremely high expectations or one who seeks to contain difference through downplaying it, repressing both its wildness and its unknown qualities. He passes on several anecdotes regarding the boiling alive of dogs and babies with some glee, but for him, the hot springs and mud pools are the product of 'infernal chemistry'. Indeed, he notes somewhat dismissively, 'Solfataras is a very pretty name, but the thing itself is very ugly, both to the eye and to the imagination' (*A&NZ*, 2:481). The scenery's unfamiliarity (combined with an accompanying stench!) poses an artistic challenge for Trollope. Lacking the interpretive and descriptive apparatus to convey the otherness of the pools to his readers, once again he dismisses them and reaches for clichés, rather than attempting to probe the source of their 'infernal' qualities. Trollope is most comfortable when he is able to describe the environment in comparative terms that he can anchor back to the English landscape. When his experiences move beyond that aesthetic and into the realm of the unfamiliar, he is, like many other Victorian travellers, overwhelmed and his remarkable powers of description fall short.

***

While Trollope is, for the most part, fascinated by the strangeness of the southern hemisphere, his appreciation for its fauna ebbs and flows. Moving from a description of some of the world's deadliest snakes (of which he remarks, 'I do not think much of Australian snakes'; *A&NZ*, 1:186), he rather perplexingly comments, 'Australia is altogether deficient in sensational wild beasts' (*A&NZ*, 1:187). Later, he goes on to say, 'Having begun with mosquitoes I have allowed myself to be carried away into animal life generally, – a subject of which I know nothing' (*A&NZ*,

1:191), which does not, of course, prevent him from engaging in a detailed commentary thereafter. While Trollope's knowledge of Australian fauna is undoubtedly patchy, he astutely captures its endangerment at the hands of European settlers. Although at home in Britain he was a keen hunter, Trollope approaches *most* Australian wildlife with respect and curiosity.[15] He also reveals deeper insights into precarious ecological and anthropological balances in the Antipodes when he ostensibly writes of proliferating animals. Commenting of the possum,

> The opossum, – 'up a gum tree', where he is always to be found, – seems to be the most persevering aboriginal inhabitant of the country. He does not recede before civilization, but addicts himself to young cabbages, and is a nuisance. As the blacks die out there is no one to eat him, and he is prolific. He sleeps soundly, and is very easy to kill with a dog . . . But there is no fun in killing him, for he neither fights nor runs away.
>
> (A& NZ, 1:187)

For Trollope, the possum is hardy and adaptable, able to change his diet to accommodate non-native plants, like cabbages, and to adjust to the differences of settler life. The possum is, though, curiously vulnerable because of the trust he places in humans. Trollope's offhand reference to the 'blacks' dying out is repeated a few sentences later, when he notes that kangaroos are 'increasing in number, because there are no black men to eat them' (A&NZ, 1:187). The phrase 'dying out' elides the systematic persecution of indigenous Australians on the part of settler communities, suggesting a gradual process of attrition that is at odds with the historical reality. Implicit in Trollope's commentary is also the idea that the possum and kangaroo have – through their adaptability – a greater right to life than the aboriginal, whom he dismisses elsewhere in the same volume as 'ineradicably savage' (A&NZ, 1:146). Thus, Trollope's sense of an Australian ecosystem is unable to accommodate compassion for the land's traditional custodians, expressing approval only of those with what he sees as the vigour to change.

Trollope's attitude toward dingoes, the wild dogs whom he describes as 'the squatter's direct enemy' (A&NZ, 1:188), is remarkably similar to his position on indigenous Australians.[16] He regards the dingo as a pest and describes, in graphic and shocking detail, some of the attempts made to obliterate the dogs, who posed (and continue to pose) a threat to livestock and hence to livelihoods, too:

> The squatter attempts to rid himself of the dingo by poison, and consequently strychnine is as common in a squatter's house as castor oil in a nursery. On many large runs carts are continually being taken round with baits to be set on the paths of the dingo. In smaller establishments the squatter or his head man goes about with strychnine in his pocket and lumps of meat tied up in a handkerchief. Hence it comes to pass that the use of a shepherd's dog is impossible, unless he be muzzled. But the dingo likes lamb better than bait, and the squatters sometimes are broken-hearted.
>
> (A&NZ, 1:188)

The anthropologist Deborah Bird Rose has written of what she calls the 'violent unmaking' of dingoes in Australia's Northern Territory today, charting the ways in which they continue to be poisoned and treated as vermin. According to Rose, the dingo pits itself against the pastoralist, who destroys the dogs in order to assert or display dominance (93).[17] Far from being a companion species like his domesticated European counterpart, the dingo opposes himself to imported ideas of the pastoral, feeding on sheep instead of herding them; actively resisting the idea that the countryside can be parcelled up and fenced in. The dingo is, for both Trollope and Rose, what

Raymond Williams would term a counter-pastoralist – albeit a particularly feral one – who pits himself against Europeanized farming practices and ideas of property ownership. Ignoring the boundaries imposed upon the landscape by settlers, the dingo continues to treat the land as a source of 'innate bounty' (Williams, 289). Indeed, as Australian sheep stocks grew after 1850, so the number of dingoes trebled (Parker, 69). The dingo is, like the settler panic I outlined earlier, a living, plundering reminder of just how incompatible imported ideas of land ownership are with the vast and wild Australian terrain.

Toward the end of his travelogue, Trollope offers an account of a dingo hunt, which is, for him, 'great sport'. His depiction reveals how a privileged sector of settler society sought to contain – and possibly also to redefine – the dingo by treating him as they would an English fox. There are distinctions, as he explains, noting that while a fox who is shaken from a bag declines to run, the dingo is much more obliging. For the most part, Trollope focuses on the hunters themselves, recounting how they crash into fences that are too high, lose their mounts and generally prove to be unequal to the differences involved in riding to hounds in the bush. Trollope is so weary by the time he and his fellow huntsmen and women catch up with the dog that he declares, 'I cared little what it was' (*A&NZ*, 2:292). This particular dingo is taken alive, having been pursued for two miles, although what happens to him next is not reported. Most dingoes who were caught up in hunts were killed as vermin, and newspapers contain numerous accounts of the stalking of dingoes, sometimes as a blood sport and sometimes in response to the theft of sheep. *The Sydney Gazette and New South Wales Advertiser* of 2 September 1834 contained the following advertisement placed by the Sydney Hunt:

> IN consequences of the great uncertainty of finding GAME in the neighbourhood of Sydney, and from an anxiety to afford Sport, and to blood the young Hounds, the above Establishment will give Ten Shillings each for Native Dogs that have been recently caught, and are in a condition to afford a good run.
>
> (2)

The Australian reported on a meeting of the Yass Hunt on 1 October 1840: 'a dingo was unbagged on the plain, and given large field a glorious run of six miles without a check, and at a pace which admitted but four to the honors of the death' (3). While on the one hand a replication of an English country pursuit is for some an important tradition dating back to the sixteenth century, on the other the Australian version of the hunt is something more. Hunting in England is about the pursuit of an individual fox, with no sense that these enemies of the farmer might ever be eradicated through this highly ritualized chase. The hunting of dingoes, however, was part of a much more widespread and systematic process of extermination that hinged on the labelling of the wild dog as a pest. The hunt might thus be regarded as an attempt to express mastery, albeit one that fails, according to Trollope's descriptions of fallen riders and general calamity. The transposition of this aspect of English rural life to the bush is far from seamless and fails to account for the many differences between the countryside at 'home' and the much more rugged Australian terrain. In many ways, Trollope's dingo hunt highlights the numerous challenges that the land threw in the faces of migrants, challenges that were exacerbated by such wilful attempts to impose aspects of the pastoral onto a resistant environment.

Trollope allows some of the ideas that sanctioned and legitimated the dingo hunt to permeate his contribution to the debate surrounding invasive species. Once more invoking the idea of the 'pest', he remarks that 'the rabbit has become so great a plague in Victoria and parts of Tasmania that squatters in some localities are spending thousands with the hope of exterminating them' (*A&NZ*, 1:190). He notes that one farmer claims to have spent more than £15,000 in attempting to eliminate rabbits from his property, an aim which modern-day land managers know to be futile.[18] Yet while on the one hand he registers the nuisance posed by the rabbit, on the other he voices an admiration for its ability to proliferate in new climes. Trollope writes of imported European animals 'thrusting out the aboriginal creatures of this country', noting with approval that 'The emus are nearly gone. The kangaroos are departing to make way for the sheep' (*A&NZ*, 1:190). He continues to celebrate the 'numerous' sparrows, also asserting that the 'busier bee from Europe' has quickly displaced his Australian counterpart, in terms of sheer numbers, but also production of honey (*A&NZ*, 1:190). When read alongside Trollope's dismissive comments regarding indigenous Australians, remarks of this kind become inflected with contemporary notions of natural selection and racial vigour. While today's ecologists are perturbed by introduced species, for Trollope the fact that they were able to thrive in the Antipodes became a legitimation of the colonial venture and an implicit assertion of mastery. European creatures were stronger and more spirited than their Oceanian counterparts and were therefore, just like White settlers, able to displace those who had occupied the land for millennia.

Trollope's vision of a 'mastered' Antipodes is, on the whole, an ambivalent one. His extensive observations as both a travel writer and a novelist offer many instances whereby European nature or *ideas* of nature seem to have triumphed. Yet at the same time there is a transience to this triumph, and Trollope also records the settler community's ongoing struggle against the wildness of both Australia and New Zealand. Torn between admiration and disdain Trollope's engagement with the creatures, inhabitants and landscape of the southern hemisphere is uncannily prophetic in its anticipation of a number of twenty-first-century ecological concerns. Trollope's Antipodean writings thus form part of an important and ongoing environmental debate that takes in questions of invasion, adaptability and land management. That he could identify these issues in the 1870s is a testament to Trollope's sensitivity to the 'wild and beautiful world around him'. While we may not always concur with his positioning, Trollope's engagement with these environmental concerns is significant and often perspicacious. Furthermore, while dominance over the actual landscape was an ongoing battle for migrants like Fred Trollope, his father's writings attempt a different form of mastery in their efforts to capture the elusive, shifting and feral qualities of the lands down under.

Notes

1 For a detailed discussion of Trollope and the West Indies, particularly in relation to the production and consumption of food, see Michelle Mouton's chapter in this volume, '"Yams, Salt Pork, Biscuit, and Bad Coffee": Food and Race in *The West Indies and the Spanish Main*'. Mouton also offers a nuanced account of Trollope's positions on race and emancipation. Simon Gikandi questions the degree to which Trollope was able to formulate his own position on questions of race in the West Indies, asking, 'how original and independent the perceptions developed in the field really are' (Gikandi, 108), while Deborah Morse asks us to consider Trollope as a 'conflicted imperialist', a term that is highly useful in considering the author's attitudes to Australia and New Zealand.
2 See Deborah Denenholz Morse's chapter in this volume for an account of the personal and political forces which shaped Trollope, particularly in the 1860s.
3 See P. D. Edwards, 'Anthony Trollope's "Australian" Novels', *Southerly*, volume 25, no. 3, 1965, pp. 200–7, for a full account of how Trollope's travels fed into his fiction.
4 While Charles Dickens was able to dispatch two sons (Alfred and Edward) to Australia, apparently without a backward glance, Trollope wrote of the 'great pang' of his son's departure (*Autobiography*, 297). Fascinatingly, Fred Trollope and Edward Dickens knew each other for a time in Wilcannia, New South Wales, and even appeared in court together in 1885, when Fred was chief prosecution witness and Edward a police magistrate in the trial of a man named Morgan D'Arcy for animal cruelty. See P. D. Edwards, *Anthony Trollope's Son in Australia: The Life and Letters of FJA Trollope (1847–1910)* (St Lucia:

UQ Press, 1982), and Mary Lazarus, *A Tale of Two Brothers* (Sydney: Angus and Robertson, 1973), for full accounts of the interactions between Fred Trollope and the Dickens sons. Fred's colonial career was not a success and he spent much of his adult life struggling to make a living, in spite of a strong work ethic.

5 See Helen Lucy Blythe, *The Victorian Colonial Romance with the Antipodes* (Basingstoke & New York: Palgrave, 2014), for sustained discussions of both *The Fixed Period* and *Australia and New Zealand*.
6 As Edwards and Joyce remind us, by the time Trollope reached Australia, he had travelled extensively on Post Office business, taking in the Middle East, the USA and the West Indies (*Australia*, 21).
7 Trollope wrote quite emotionally of his son's misfortunes in his autobiography, noting the enjoyment of spending time with Fred and commenting with bitterness,

> I went to Australia chiefly in order that I might see my son among his sheep. I did see him among his sheep, and remained with him for four or five very happy weeks. He was not making money, nor has he made money since. I grieve to say that several thousands of pounds which I had squeezed out of the pockets of perhaps too liberal publishers have been lost on the venture. But I rejoice to say that this has been in no way due to any fault of his. I never knew a man work with more persistent honesty at his trade than he has done. (*Autobiography*, 317)

> Trollope's admiration for Fred is palpable in this fleeting reference to his son, but it is interesting that the novelist does not attempt to apportion blame for his failure. Many pamphlets extolled sheep-farming, with the anonymous author of *Australia, Van Diemen's Land, and New Zealand* (1839) noting, 'Sheep rearing *is*, and must, from the very nature and extent of the country . . . be the staple business of Australia' (13).

8 For a full account of Harry's fear of fire, see Grace Moore, '"The Heavens Were on Fire": Incendiarism and the Defence of the Settler Home' in Tamara S. Wagner (ed.), *Domestic Fiction in Colonial Australia and New Zealand* (London: Pickering and Chatto, 2014).
9 Squatters were those licensed to allow their livestock to graze on Crown land.
10 The Australian environment's uncanny qualities are partly aesthetic (the vastness of the countryside, the curious shape of the twisted eucalypts), partly auditory, and settler writers frequently blurred the ghostly cries of bush-dwelling species with their own anxieties. Ada Cambridge captures this conflation beautifully in her 1878 poem, 'By the Campfire' when she writes,

> The darkness gathered all around is full of rustlings strange and low;
> The dead wood crackles on the ground, and shadowy shapes flit to and fro;
> I think they are my own dim dreams, wandering amongst the woods and streams (70).

11 Of course, Trollope would not have been able to depict this ménage in any detail for reasons of propriety.
12 Trollope's horror ebbed and flowed. Writing of squatters, he expressed himself with a mixture of censure and envy:

> The sense of ownership and mastery, the conviction that he the head and chief of what is going on around; the absence of any necessity of asking leave or of submitting to others, – these things in themselves add a great charm to life. The squatter owes obedience to none, and allegiance only to the merchant; – who asks no questions so long as the debt be reduced or not increased. He gets up when he pleases and goes to bed when he likes. Though he should not own an acre of the land around him, he may do what he pleases with all that he sees. He may put up fences and knock them down. He probably lives in the middle of a forest, – his life is always called life in the bush, – and he may cut down any tree that he fancies. He goes where he likes and nobody questions him. (*Australia*, 132)

13 Baynton's short story 'Squeaker's Mate' offers particularly terrifying insights into the misery and darkness that could accompany life in the bush. It also, with its representation of 'quivering wail(s) from the billabong', evokes the uncanny noises that could emanate from the 'pregnant bush silence' at night (19).
14 Helen Lucy Blythe has offered an excellent discussion of the class politics associated with Antipodean life, with a particular focus on the gold diggings and what she calls the 'functional colonial body' in 'Catherine Carmichael'. See Blythe, 'The Rough and the Beautiful in "Catherine Carmichael"'.
15 Toward the end of his account, Trollope writes of participating in a kangaroo hunt and confesses that 'in the absence of fox-hunting I enjoyed it very much' (740). It is difficult for the modern reader to reconcile

the Trollope who is able to write compassionately of the cruelty of sheep shearing and its 'roughness' (309) with the man who can recount the pursuit of a mother kangaroo until she finally, in despair, throws her joey from its pouch.

16 Trollope's commentary on aboriginals elsewhere in the volume does not make pleasant reading. He speaks of indigenous Australians as a race who will inevitably die out, commenting,

> Of the Australian black man we may certainly say that he has to go. That he should perish without unnecessary suffering should be the aim of all who are concerned in the matter. But no good can be done by giving to the aboriginal a character which he does not deserve, or by speaking of the treatment which he receives in language which the facts do not warrant. (A&NZ, 1:76)
>
> While he is invested in the idea of the 'savagery' of the indigenous Australian and believes that s/he lacks the vigour to survive, he is notably more sympathetic to the New Zealand Maoris, commenting, 'Of all the people we have been accustomed to call savages, they were perhaps, in their savage condition as we found them, the most civilized' (A&NZ, 2:302).

17 In a complicated and nuanced argument that ranges from genocide in Europe to the stringing up of dingo carcasses in today's Australia, Rose situates the killing of dingoes within a broader narrative about the Western world's torture and killing of those perceived as predators (97). In particular, she explores the ways in which humanity can wilfully cause extinction.

18 The environmental philosopher Freya Mathews has documented the tensions that she has experienced as the manager of a biodiversity reserve, seeking to regenerate bush wildlife. As tenacious and fecund invaders, rabbits have posed ecological and ethical dilemmas for Mathews, who has written candidly of the impossibility of removing them from the Australian terrain. See Freya Mathews, 'The Anguish of Wildlife Ethics' in *New Formations*, 75, Spring 2012.

Works cited

'Advertisement placed by the Sydney Hunt', *The Sydney Gazette and New South Wales Advertiser*, 2 September 1834.

An Australian Colonist. *The Resources of Australia, with Special Notice of Port Philip*. London, 1841.

Australia, Van Diemen's Land, and New Zealand: Their History and Present State with Their Prospects in Regard to Emigration, Impartially Examined. London: Brittan & Reid, 1839.

Bate, Jonathan. *The Song of the Earth*. 2000. London: Picador, 2001.

Baynton, Barbara. *Bush Studies*. 1902. Melbourne: Text, 2012.

Blythe, Helen Lucy. 'The Rough and the Beautiful in "Catherine Carmichael"' in Margaret Markwick, Deborah Denenholz Morse and Regenia Gagnier (eds), *The Politics of Gender in Anthony Trollope's Novels: New Readings for the Twenty-First Century*. Burlington, VT, & Farnham: Ashgate, 2009.

———. *The Victorian Colonial Romance with the Antipodes*. Basingstoke & New York: Palgrave, 2014.

Brandenstein, Claudia. 'Representations of Landscape and Nature in Anthony Trollope's *The West Indies and the Spanish Main* and James Anthony Froude's *The English in the West Indies*' in Helen Tiffin (ed.), *Five Emus to the King of Siam: Environment and Empire*. Amsterdam & New York: Rodopi, 2007.

Cambridge, Ada (Mrs. Cross). 'By the Campfire 1878' in FRC Hopkins (ed.), *The Australian Ladies' Annual*. Melbourne: McCarron, Bird, 1878.

Davidson, J. H. 'Anthony Trollope and the Colonies', *Victorian Studies* 12:3 (March 1969), 305–30.

Dingley, Robert. 'Debatable Ground: Anthony Trollope and the Anxiety of Colonial Space' in Ken Stewart & Shirley Walker (eds), *'Unemployed at Last!': Essays on Australian Literature to 2002*. Armidale: Centre for Australian Studies, University of New England, 2004.

Edwards, P. D. 'Anthony Trollope's "Australian" Novels', *Southerly* 25:3 (1965), 200–7.

———. *Anthony Trollope's Son in Australia: The Life and Letters of FJA Trollope (1847–1910)*. St Lucia: UQ Press, 1982.

Edwards, P. D., and R. B. Joyce. 'Introduction', *Australia and New Zealand*. St Lucia: UQ Press, 1968.

Gikandi, Simon. *Maps of Englishness: Writing Identity in the Culture of Colonialism*. New York: Columbia UP, 1996.

Lansbury, Coral. *Arcady in Australia: The Evocation of Australia in Nineteenth- Century English Literature*. Melbourne: Melbourne UP, 1970.

Lazarus, Mary. *A Tale of Two Brothers: Charles Dickens's Sons in Australia*. Sydney: Angus & Robertson, 1973.
Mathews, Freya. 'The Anguish of Wildlife Ethics', *New Formations* 75 (Spring, 2012).
Monbiot, George. *Feral: Searching for Enchantment on the Frontiers of Rewilding*. London: Allen Lane, 2013.
Moore, Grace. '"The Heavens Were on Fire": Incendiarism and the Defence of the Settler Home' in Tamara S. Wagner (ed.), *Domestic Fiction in Colonial Australia and New Zealand*. London: Pickering and Chatto, 2014.
Morris, Meaghan. *Identity Anecdotes: Translation and Media Culture*. London: SAGE, 2006.
Morse, Deborah Denenholz. *Reforming Trollope: Race, Gender and Englishness in the Novels of Anthony Trollope*. Burlington, VT, & Farnham, England: Ashgate, 2013.
'Nubba Prize Sheep'. *Town and Country Journal*, 24 December 1887, 1327.
O'Brien, Rory. 'Improving' in Tom Griffiths (ed.), *Forests of Ash: An Environmental History*. Cambridge: CUP, 2001.
Parker, Merryl. 'The Cunning Dingo.' https://www.animalsandsociety.org/assets/library/642_thecunning-dingo.pdf
Rose, Deborah Bird. *Wild Dog Dreaming: Love and Extinction*. Charlottesville and London: University of Virginia Press, 2011.
Ryan, Simon. *The Cartographic Eye: How Explorers Saw Australia*. Cambridge: CUP, 1996.
Sidney's Australian Hand-Book: How to Settle and Succeed in Australia, Comprising Every Information for Intending Emigrants. London: Pelham Richardson, 1849.
Sutherland, John. 'Introduction' in John Sutherland (ed.), *Anthony Trollope: Later Short Stories*. Oxford: Oxford University Press, 1995.
Trollope, Anthony. *Anthony Trollope's Son in Australia: The Life and Letters of F.J.A. Trollope (1847–1910)*. St Lucia: UQ Press, 1982.
———. *Australia and New Zealand* (2 vols). 1873. London: The Trollope Society, 2002.
———. *An Autobiography, by Anthony Trollope*. 1883. London & New York: OUP, 1947.
———. 'Catherine Carmichael, or Three Years Running 1878' in John Sutherland (ed.), *Anthony Trollope: Later Short Stories*. Oxford: OUP, 1995.
———. *The Fixed Period*. 1882. Ann Arbor: University of Michigan Press, 1990.
———. *Harry Heathcote of Gangoil: A Tale of Australian Bush Life*. 1874. London: Dodo Press, no date.
———. *John Caldigate*. 1879. London: Dodo Press, no date.
Williams, Raymond. *The Country and the City*. 1973. London: Hogarth Press, 1993.
'Yass Gaieties Again'. *The Australian*, 1 October 1840.

32

"YAMS, SALT PORK, BISCUIT, AND BAD COFFEE"

Food and race in *The West Indies and the Spanish Main*

Michelle Mouton

Anthony Trollope opens his first published travelogue, *The West Indies and the Spanish Main* (*WISM*, 1859), by situating the reader in the initial moment, place, and circumstance of his writing – on board a trading ship between Jamaica and Cuba carrying salt fish from Canada – and with a humorously exasperated complaint about the paucity of culinary options available to him:[1]

> I am beginning to write this book on board the brig ____. . . . The marine people – the captain and his satellites – are bound to provide [for] me; and all that they have provided is yams, salt pork, biscuit, and bad coffee. I should be starved but for the small ham – would that had it been a large one – which I thoughtfully purchased in Kingston; and had not a kind medical friend, as he grasped me by the hand at Port Royal, stuffed a box of sardines into my pocket. He suggested two boxes. Would that I had taken them![2]

This opening is apt, as the travelogue is replete with descriptions of Trollope's meals, provided both to inform and entertain. He praises or condemns food served at dinner parties, at hotels and inns, on ships and railways, and even in packs made up for travel by mule. He expresses appreciation for fresh produce, a well-prepared meal, and the generosity of hosts and "friends," but also warns readers away from particular routes or hotels based on available provisions. Moreover, with an anthropological eye, Trollope observes food and food-related rituals, typically framing them as novel for his English readers: he eats shark and declares it "delicious," describes the misery of campsite cooking with multiple culinary mishaps, and marvels at the habit of White Jamaicans' drinking sherry and bitters before rather than after dinner (chs. 10, 3, and 3). These elements of the text – descriptions of the author's meals, recommendations for future travelers, and anecdotes about cultural differences relating to food and drink – might reasonably be expected of travel writing. Beyond this, however, Trollope also investigates and comments extensively on the production, processing, and transporting of food commodities, especially sugar and coffee. Trollope's 1857–1858 journey to the Caribbean isles and to Central and South America was made on behalf of the British Postal Service, his mission being to carry forward a number of initiatives that aimed at greater efficiencies, but of his official duties, Trollope reveals to readers only that his "purposed business" is "the accomplishment of certain affairs of State," and promises that this will be of no "further concern" (ch. 1). Trollope honors this promise to such an extent, and the book is so filled with references to food, that an attentive reader might reasonably guess that Trollope's assignment is to experience and propose improvements to the global *food* system rather than the British postal system.

Food studies has become in recent years a vital interdisciplinary area of inquiry, and Trollope's writings provide rich material. In 1968, Robert M. Polhemus observed that, "Like Dickens, Trollope uses the act of eating and how people look upon it to define not only the nature of particular characters but also various moral tones of his characters."[3] Despite this suggested commonality between Dickens and Trollope, scholars have been far slower to consider Trollope's works than Dickens's (and other Victorian novelists') with the critical lens of food studies. Recent work on Victorian food and literature, including Gwen Hyman's *Making a Man: Gentlemanly Appetites in the Nineteenth-Century British Novel* (2009) and Annette Cozzi's *The Discourses of Food in Nineteenth-Century British Fiction* (2010), all but omit Trollope. Of his biographers, Victoria Glendinning is most attuned to Trollope's food-related passages in fiction, nonfiction, and correspondences, and she paints a vivid picture of the food venues in London where Trollope likely ate;[4] but her interpretations of Trollope's statements about food tend toward the literal and can ignore his various rhetorical contexts and performative aims.[5] *WISM* is arguably the most pervaded by food references of all of Trollope's works. While scholars have fruitfully reexamined the text from several perspectives related to race, Englishness, and empire – including travel and tourism (e.g., Buzard, Goodlad), postcolonialism (Hall, Gikandi, Torres-Saillant), or network and mobility studies (Aguirre) – these reexaminations have had little to say about food as such. Building on these works' attention to race and empire, I argue that Trollope's racial theorizing and his demeaning and dehumanizing commentary on non-European peoples cannot fully be understood independently of his capitalist vision of a competitive and efficient global food system. Not only are Trollope's depictions of meals, of food production, and of technological developments in agriculture and in the transporting of food all racially inflected, but also Trollope's judgments of the locals he meets largely correspond to their willingness or unwillingness, as he perceives it, to take up racially appropriate roles in the emerging global food economy. Resituating passages about agricultural labor and race among Trollope's other kinds of remarks about food, and looking at them through the lens of food studies, not only opens up new ways of thinking about Trollope's work but also gestures toward the complex but foundational intersections of postcolonial and global food histories.

The timing of Trollope's trip was pivotal in relation to global food history in at least two senses. For one, technological developments – in food production and preservation, in transportation networks, and in refrigeration – would mean the emergence and acceleration of a global, industrially based food trade.[6] In the decades following Trollope's journey, the English diet would increasingly include imports enabled by these new technologies – including wheat from America, frozen meats from Australia and New Zealand, and fresh fish from northern seas – and by the end of the century would include desired fruits and vegetables imported from long distances, including the Americas.[7] In all of his travelogues, including *WISM*, Trollope actively investigates and expresses his views on emerging agricultural and food transportation technologies, thus providing a uniquely situated, if limited, snapshot of this transition. His journey's timing was pivotal in another sense too: the production of West Indian sugar was shifting from dependence on the institution of slavery to dependence on contractual labor (which would continue to rely on compulsory labor through freed slaves' so-called apprenticeship periods, and through the indentured labor of immigrants).[8] Trollope, in *WISM*, is keen to investigate differences between previously emancipated regions (English colonies and Haiti) and Spanish, slaveholding colonies' sugar production; on the mainlands of Central and South America, he continues his analysis of food production and labor. This essay suggests that the prevalence of food in Trollope's *WISM* and other travel books, if not his novels, deserves further critical attention, as Trollope's discussions illuminate the extent to which the technologically enabled, global food system emerging in the late nineteenth century was premised on colonialist and racist ideologies.

Trollope's descriptions of his own meals serve several functions, one of which is to reassure his English readers of their right to appropriate global food commodities as regular menu options. As a food critic, Trollope assumes the standpoint of a generally appreciative and good-natured traveler, but one whose views on food contrast with, and supersede in sophistication, both those of the provincial, White colonials he meets and those of his untraveled English readers; the former entertainingly prove beyond his influence, while the latter he claims to instruct. In an early chapter, Trollope explains that Cubans (referring here to the White, Anglo-Cuban population) generally are too "fond of English dishes" (ch. 2). Of his inn at Cien Fuegos, he wishes that his otherwise hospitable innkeeper "could be induced to abandon the idea that beefsteaks and onions, and bread and cheese and beer composed the only diet proper for an Englishman," and then whets his readers' appetites for West Indian produce by implicitly contrasting this list of English foods – dominated by fermented foods and ending in a monotonous, iambic rhythm constructed by monosyllabic words ("and bread and cheese and beer") – with the imagery of freshness and diversity:

> When yams, avocado pears, the mountain cabbage, plantains, and twenty other delicious vegetables may be had for the gathering, people will insist on eating bad English potatoes; and the desire for English pickles is quite a passion.
>
> (Ch. 2)

Trollope amusedly criticizes local servility to "bad English" foods again when he describes the typical breakfast of the Jamaican gentry. With a direct address to an imagined middle-class reader – English, female, married, and untraveled – Trollope explains that Jamaica "sits down . . . not to a meal, my dear Mrs. Jones, consisting of tea and bread and butter, with two eggs done for the master of the family and one for the mistress," but to the more elaborate "fish, beefsteaks – a breakfast is not a breakfast in the West Indies without beefsteaks and onions, nor is a dinner so to be called without bread and cheese and beer – potatoes, yams, plantains, eggs . . ." His use of an aside suggests uncontrollable exasperation at the inclusion of English among indigenous foods, and if this inclusion of beef steak is not bad enough already, the list ends with "a dozen 'tinned' productions, namely, meats sent from England in tin cases" (ch. 2). If Trollope's novels are, as Nathaniel Hawthorne described them, "as English as a beef-steak," the metaphor could be applied only with some degree of irony to *WISM*.[9] However, it's the very rejection of a strictly English diet that reasserts the Englishman's right to global food appropriation. Commenting that White Creoles[10] insist on importing bad English foods despite "every delicacy which the world can give them of native production" serves to distance Trollope, and his (male) readers who are more worldly than "dear Mrs. Jones," from White colonials who charmingly though misguidedly still refer to England as "home" (ch. 6). Trollope, the *genuine* Englishman and an experienced traveler, is simply interested in *good* food, whatever its source.

A common conceit of *WISM* is that the traveler has less control over his food abroad than at home, and Trollope repeatedly exploits this motif for humor. As he transgresses Victorian class, gender, and racial boundaries out of necessity in order to eat, he is able through humor to reassert an English superiority of perspective.[11] Annette Cozzi, drawing upon John Burnett's socioeconomic research on food in Victorian London, argues that "the professionalization of the middle-class gentleman . . . is defined by not only *what* one eats, but also *where*" and with whom.[12] Even as beef came to signify Englishness and thus an imagined national unity, places of eating in Victorian fiction – whether dinner parties and clubs, taverns and public houses, or the very streets of London – indicate food consumers' class (and gender) identities through a logic of exclusion, as dining locations indicate differing and exclusive levels of access to food, social networks, and power. Cozzi's (and Burnett's) taxonomy of eating venues and their socioeconomic significances could be usefully considered with respect to Trollope's novels; however, in *WISM*, travel enables Trollope to break from this set of conventions to describe meals in a variety of locations, including passenger and trading ships, railcars, the homes of local hosts, a variety of classes of hotels, lodging houses, and public houses, and even in the open air as he travels by mule to mountaintops. He shares meals with a colorful cast of characters, with estate owners, ship captains, and an English minister's secretary; but also with ill-mannered Spanish and German tourists, an American ex-filibuster, and a slaveholder in Cuba; and he is served food by and converses with "coloured" West Indian women.[13] These anecdotes, presented as the chance encounters of a tourist in need of basic sustenance, enable Trollope to provide anonymous, voyeuristic pleasure to readers. He can provide amusing observations of foreign dining practices while sharing overheard conversations.

Trollope's status nevertheless relies on pointed exclusions. In an extended anecdote, Trollope travels to Spanish Town to meet with the governor of Jamaica, and finds himself with nearly three hours to spare in the scorching heat of the day, in a town that he does not admire and that he does not know. Despite language barriers (which Trollope claims are due to his ignorance of the local vernacular, a claim undermined by his phonetic representation of the speech of the Black local residents whom he asks for directions), he at last locates a pub. He finds himself in "a miserable hole," not realizing until two hours later that there is "a better room upstairs," and climbing upwards, he is amused by what he sees and hears:

> I found there, among others, a negro of exceeding blackness. I do not know that I ever saw skin so purely black. He was talking eagerly with his friends, and after a while I heard him say, in a voice of considerable dignity, "I shall bring forward a motion on de subject in de house to-morrow." So that I had not fallen into bad society.
>
> But even under these circumstances two hours spent in a tavern without a book, without any necessity for eating or drinking, is not pleasant.
>
> (Ch. 2)

This encounter with Blackness for Trollope is uncomfortable. The social and political intellectual stature of the male speaker is unexpected because of skin color, but his words reveal his status as an elected and evidently respected lawmaker. Trollope's discomfort, and inappropriateness of their common dining area, is neutralized for the author and his readers by Trollope's facetious tone, and by the phonetic spelling of the man's utterances. Trollope, without even a book for distraction, eavesdrops upon but does not address this man he shares a dining room with. Several chapters later (titled "Jamaica – White Men," which serves as a counterpoint to "Jamaica – Black Men" and "Jamaica – Coloured Men"),[14] Trollope explains that to have a Black man at an Englishman's table in England, where it is a novelty, is quite a different thing than abroad:

> The Duchess of This and Lord That are very happy to have at their table some intelligent dark gentleman, or even a well-dressed negro, though he may not perhaps be intelligent. There is some excitement in it, some change from the common; and perhaps also an easy opportunity of practising on a small scale those philanthropic views which

they preach with so much eloquence. When one hobnobs over a glass of champagne with a dark gentleman, he is in some sort a man and a brother. But the duchess and the lord think that because the dark gentle man is to their taste, he must necessarily be as much to the taste of the neighbors among whom he has been born and bred; of those who have been accustomed to see him from childhood.

There was never a greater mistake. A coloured man may be a fine prophet in London; but he will be no prophet in Jamaica, which is his own country; no prophet at any rate among his white neighbors.

(Ch. 6)

Trollope suggests that it is the "white neighbors" in the West Indies who have no interest in cross-racial dining, but nowhere does he challenge this sentiment. Although Trollope's meals in so many unconventional locations and with so many kinds of people are *ostensibly* permissible because they are necessitated by the inconveniences of travel, they are *in fact* permissible only because he conspicuously omits descriptions of shared meals, and enabled conversations, with Black (and later, "Indian") men and women. These local residents appear in Trollope's food-related anecdotes most typically as undifferentiated servants or laborers (or, as above, as imitators of White civilization) but never as his dining companions. It is only through this exclusionary representational strategy, combined with Trollope's assumption of shared humor with White readers, that his dining situations and conversations can appear serendipitous and novel rather than improprietous and contaminating to his English readers.

If Black West Indians are absent from Trollope's staging of food consumption, they are present, but ironically only marginally so, in his representations of food production. Early in the book, traveling through the Jamaican countryside and describing the landscape, Trollope explains that sugar cane, though the primary export of Jamaica, is rarely spotted from the road, but one gains instead the occasional view of the "picturesque" provision grounds of freed slaves. Trollope compares the aesthetic quality of these gardens favorably with the more utilitarian gardens of English and Irish peasants. While the latter are filled with monotonous fields of the low-lying cabbage and the buried potato, or "other vegetables similarly uninteresting in their growth," the Jamaican gardens of freed slaves "contain cocoa-trees, breadfruit-trees, oranges, mangoes, limes, plantains, jack-fruit, sour-sop, avocado pears, and a score of others, all of which are luxuriant trees, some of considerable size, and all of them of great beauty" (ch. 3). Trollope likens the Jamaican's yam to the Irishman's potato, both of which serve as staples, except that the yam "is picturesque in its growth." This lush diversity of visually pleasing plants reinforces for English readers Trollope's appreciation of locally grown fruits and vegetables in contrast to the stereotypical English diet he is continually being served by White colonials. Moreover, the absence of people in this scene, including any laborers, suggests an Edenic image of plenty. The focus here is on food production as scenery, separated from food's uses as sustenance and as a vehicle for meaningful cultural exchange.

In contrast to the beauty of these provision grounds, Trollope finds vast swathes of cane, where he does see them, to be "ugly and by no means savoury appurtenances" (ch. 3). This sentiment is reiterated when he visits a Jamaican planter whose fields are out of sight: Trollope asserts that the Jamaican planter's occupations appear to be very like that of an English country gentleman except for the unfortunate times when he must "inspect his cane-holes, . . . a serious drawback on his happiness" (ch. 3). By the end of the book, however, Trollope's aesthetic appreciation for the gardens of ex-slaves and his dislike of cane fields will be inverted in value. The provision grounds come to signify not Eden but an unearned bounty; this bounty, in turn, signifies an innate, race-based idleness (ch. 2). Trollope asserts repeatedly and in multiple contexts that the "negro" works only when he or she must. The abundance of appealing, readily available foods (denying any labor involved in subsistence farming), and the Black person's refusal or inability to understand that "squatting" and taking food from privately owned property is stealing, means that he or she will not work for wages, at least not wages that planters can afford and at the levels necessary to sustain the sugar estates. This attitude is all the more egregious for Trollope because of the African's singular stamina for outdoor, manual labor in the tropics, in Trollope's view, whereas Europeans (and others) are subject to tropical diseases, to fatigue, and to deleterious effects of the sun. By the time Trollope sails from St. Thomas to British Guiana, taking in views along the way, then, sugar cane plants are no longer "ugly ... appurtenances," but, in contrast to labor-free provision grounds, represent the triumph of orderly civilization and of work over wilderness:

> Looking up the side of the hills [of St. Kitts and Nevis] one sees the sugar-canes apparently in cleanly order, and they have an air of substantial comfort. Of course times are not so bright as in the fine old days previous to emancipation; but nevertheless matters have been on the mend, and people are again beginning to get along.
>
> (Ch. 11)

Trollope's reference to "the fine old days previous to emancipation" may sound satirical, given that he so often claims to be opposed to slavery and undermines the nostalgic perspectives of local, White informants. Earlier, for example, Trollope had reported upon the views of Jamaican planters about labor shifts: "The complaint [of the planters] generally resolves itself to this, that free labour in Jamaica cannot be commanded [after emancipation]. . . . But the slaves! – Oh! those were the good times!" (ch. 7). Unlike here, "the fine old days" of his later remark is not set off from his words by any tag or disclaimer, as though Trollope has absorbed the planter's language into his own. In any case, if the phrasing is sarcastic, Trollope's assessment of the canes as signifiers of a productive economy and thus of the colony's "comfort" is not. By the time Trollope has toured several estates and talked with planters in Jamaica and Cuba, cane plants visually represent these islands' economic sustainability in a post-emancipation economy, and Trollope's aesthetic pleasure in provision grounds has given way to images of "the idle negro" stealing and enjoying the literal fruits of others.[15] James Buzard observes saliently about *WISM*, "Trollope sympathetically projects himself into the viewpoint of the planter; not once does it occur to him to attempt a similar exercise on behalf of the ex-slave."[16]

Buzard would be more precise, though, to say that only rarely and fleetingly, rather than never, does Trollope sympathetically assume the perspective of the ex-slave. In a couple of instances Trollope acknowledges that a refusal to do agricultural labor for wages might not be "idleness" in the sense of an innate, racial characteristic; he asks rhetorically, "who can blame the black man? He is free to work, or free to let it alone. I will not dig cane-holes for half a crown a day; and why should I expect him to do so? I can live without it; so can he?" (ch. 4). In Central America, Trollope speculates that (agricultural) work may be degrading for a recently emancipated people and incompatible with "their idea of freedom" (ch. 18). But such moments of potentially humanizing, sociological insights are overshadowed by persistent assertions of racial stereotypes, so that what could be a cross-racial commonality – a shared enjoyment in indigenous fresh foods – becomes subordinated to Trollope's liberal vision of competitive, commodity food trade among Europeans and their descendants.

Furthermore, Trollope's invocation of race and violence in relation to food production is strikingly callous toward the condition of enslavement, and toward the conditions faced by sugarcane laborers whether enslaved or "free." When a Cuban, slaveholding planter provides

Trollope with a tour of his estate, Trollope confesses, as though his desire is guiltily to experience voyeuristic, firsthand evidence of brutality, that he had been both "anxious" and "curious" to witness "coercive measures." While he does not doubt that "the whip is in use," he reports that he personally sees neither whippings nor telltale scars (ch. 10). Trollope repeatedly states his opposition to the institution of slavery in *WISM*, but commonly uses the rhetoric of slavery apologists. About his tour, Trollope explains that this planter evidently treats his slaves well. Trollope acknowledges that the long work hours (hours that would be unbearable to the English worker) may lead to a shortening of life, but likens the planter to a prudent Englishman with beasts of burden, neither of whom can afford to lose labor through poor treatment of their property. Trollope is walking a tightrope here between confirming abolitionists' stories of brutality and supporting the institution of slavery, neither of which he expressly wants to do. But if this performance leaves any question about where Trollope's sympathies lie, his acceptance of breakfast after the tour does not. The slaveholder ("my friend") humbly apologizes for having little on hand to offer but produces a sumptuous meal. Trollope's description emphasizes its appeal: "A delicious soup, made partly of eggs, a bottle of excellent claret, a paté de foi gras, some game deliciously dressed, and half a dozen kinds of vegetables." Trollope's response is, in its glibness, shockingly callous toward the people he has compared to "beasts of burden": "I had seen nothing among the slaves which in any way interfered with my appetite, or with the cup of coffee and cigar which came after the little things above mentioned." Not only does the absence of visual blood and scarring permit Trollope to indulge freely in the comforts of this meal, but he goes so far as to invite readers "to chuckle at"[17] this slaveholder's understated generosity ("these little things"). Hospitality in the form of a shared meal (as well as paid railway tickets) serves to consolidate the planter's and the English traveler's interest in sugar production, if not explicit agreement on the institution of slavery.[18]

Just as Trollope's comments on food production and consumption are racially inflected, his interest in opening up further global trade routes underscores his racial and nationalist biases. Among Trollope's several official charges by the British Post Office, he was commissioned to visit Central America in order to determine the most efficient way to move mail across the isthmus, whether via the proposed Panama Canal, by the recently built Panama railroad, or by some other means and location.[19] In a recent essay, Robert Aguirre has focused attention on those parts of Trollope's travelogue dealing with "the Spanish Main," and on Trollope's aim to find more efficient, technology-enabled transportation routes for the mail system across the Central American isthmus. The book is "the literary trace of a larger governmental project concerning the post as a key instrument in the mobility of information."[20] It is worth noting, though, that in *WISM* Trollope tracks the mobility not of information but of food. He rarely refers to the postal service. Having taken a mail boat in British Guiana, Trollope urges the governor to see to the "woeful affair" of the mail boat, "crumbling to pieces . . . in the saddest manner," and in Costa Rica he takes note of postal carriers who cross his route (chs. 12, 20). But he does not allude to the purpose of his journey by mail boat (likely to test its speed), nor does he explain why the postal carriers' pace is of interest to him. On the other hand, Trollope continually assesses infrastructures with respect to the transporting of foods. The deteriorated roads in Jamaica, where they exist at all, are not only inconvenient for travelers but also among improvements needed before the island, following emancipation, can thrive, "whatever be their produce" (ch. 3). He is firmly in favor of technological advancements in transportation. Jamaica, he speculates, could provide meat to all of the West Indies if planters could be persuaded to give up their traditional attachment to the sugar trade, and when planters object that shipping costs are too high, Trollope notes as an aside that "screw steamers" would appear there soon enough if there were significant freight to move (ch. 20). His observations are not limited to the transporting of commodity foods. Of his coffee-planter host whose house lies at the highest inhabited point of the Blue Mountain Peak, Trollope reminds readers with amazement that "every article of food" would have had to be "carried up to this place on mules' backs, over the tops of mountains, for twenty or thirty miles" (ch. 3).

Most relevant to his official duties, Trollope observes in Costa Rica the "constant traffic" of bullock carts "laden with coffee," and he is struck by the absurdity of their route, made necessary by lack of a reliable and affordable way across the isthmus (ch. 17). Coffee is grown primarily in the mountains, he explains, and even though it must "cross the Atlantic to reach its market," it is sent first down to the Pacific coast. To reach the Atlantic, then, it must go "across the isthmus railway at a vast cost" or travel by boat "around the Horn." While both routes are used, "not a grain is carried, as it should be carried, direct to the Atlantic." He explains the reason for such costly inefficiency when he crosses overland from the Atlantic to the Pacific himself by mule (ch. 20). The road he takes is at first appropriately wide and navigable, but just beyond the continental divide its construction had been abandoned by the government. His crossing from this point forward is made torturous by mud and rough terrain.

For Trollope, multiple factors are at play, including a despotic head of state, but the racially determined hindrance to greater land cultivation, infrastructure development, and capitalist progress in Latin America by the indigenous population is not idleness, as in the West Indies, but rather the local population's distinct lack of ambition and their apathy toward profit. In Costa Rica, Trollope sees bullock carts move coffee in such volumes as to suggest that "Costa Rica must be much more than sufficient to supply the whole world" with coffee (ch. 17). Despite his witnessing of this continual labor, Trollope explains to the untraveled that Costa Ricans "are a humdrum, contented, quiet, orderly race of men; . . . they have no enthusiasm, no ardent desires, no aspirations" (ch. 18). Stopping to watch a coffee transporter make "dolce," juice from sugar cane, to sweeten his coffee, and noting that the oxen primarily eat cane cut or bought by drivers, Trollope remarks, "Drivers and driven are alike orderly, patient, and slow, spending their lives in taking coffee down to Punta-arenas, and in cutting and munching thousands of sugar canes" (ch. 3). This description, particularly with the omission of the only implied "respectively" after "canes," conflates men and animals, for whom work is habitual toil rather than capitalist striving for improvement, and whose pleasures in food and drink are primitive.

In reference to recent history, Trollope laments several times that American filibusters (United States citizens in Central America who had attempted a government coup and territorial acquisition) have destroyed much local economic development, and he praises Costa Ricans for manfully ejecting them (chs. 17, 20, 21). At the same time, the lack of national ambition that Trollope observes serves to justify for him, without any apparent sense of irony, the development of Latin American land and transport routes by and for the primary benefit of Europeans. Indeed, Europeans' improvements in global trade routes are providentially scripted, and Trollope uses the whimsical extended metaphor of eating to suggest the inevitability of progress. Just as a child gradually learns to feed himself, he explains, so humanity learns gradually the most effective ways to circumnavigate the earth. Trollope likens the earth to a roast: although "we are perhaps beginning to use our own knife and fork, . . . we hardly yet understand the science of carving" (ch. 21). Having relished the fruits and vegetables available in abundance in the West Indies, this resorting to the quintessentially English metaphor of a beef roast is significant. It is the English and French whose energies, he points out, have enabled the railroads and canal proposals across the isthmus, respectively. As with his descriptions of local foods and dining practices, Trollope's assumed authority for weighing in on the most efficient and affordable of these proposals rests on his firsthand experience of the culture (unshared by his untraveled English readers) and on his disinterested observations (as compared to those of his cultural informants). However, Trollope's exclusionary rhetoric and limited experiences with both "negro" and "Indian" locals, despite his rhetoric of experientially grounded authority, reveal the limitations of his systematic vision, and the ideological underpinnings of an expanding and Eurocentric global food system developing in the later half of the nineteenth century.

Food, in *WISM*, serves multiple functions. The need for food can signify a loss of physical autonomy, one that would seem to forfeit, while ultimately shoring up, privileges allowed to the White, male English traveler. As a source of humor, food affirms English superiority of judgment and manner (even among Europeans), and solidifies Trollope's alliance with middle-class English readers more invested in England's economic progress via the colonies, than in claims of, or movements toward, racial equality. Moreover, Trollope's investigations into consumption, food production, and the distribution of food commodities (with the aid of new transportation technologies and routes) suggest his keen awareness of food as a global system. This awareness and investment in a technologically enabled global food system only deepen in later narratives: in *North America* (1862), where Trollope insists on seeing the grain-growing plains of the United States and expresses awe at the Chicago market's storage capabilities; in *Australia and New Zealand* (1873), where Trollope investigates the economics of raising livestock and witnesses developments in meat preservation and refrigeration; or in *South Africa* (1878), where he explains in wonder new artificial ostrich egg incubators. It is perhaps understandable that, having witnessed the Irish famine firsthand, Trollope would see in a global, commodity food trade the promise of a future without hunger. At its best, for Trollope, a post-emancipation, global food system would continue to feed English appetites while sustaining the health and wealth of its colonies. However, particularly in *WISP*, Trollope is only ever able to imagine food traveling in one direction, as surplus from the colonies to England; and, for all of his economic and social projections, nowhere does Trollope reflect on this growing global food trade's potential impact on local food systems and diet. Moreover, this future could occur, in the West Indian and Central American context, only with the continued manual labor of non-European, non-White, colonial subjects on Europe's behalf. *The West Indies and the Spanish Main* is important, then, both because it documents a transitional moment in food history and because the attitudes it exemplifies toward race, labor, and food would have lasting repercussions.

Notes

1 Many thanks to Devan Baty, Lynn Ikach, Catherine Stewart, and Chris Otter, as well as the editors of this volume, for readings of this essay in progress.
2 Anthony Trollope, *The West Indies and the Spanish Main* (New York: Carroll & Graf, 1999), ch. 1. See Jack Goody, "Industrial Food: Towards the Development of a World Cuisine," in *Food and Culture: A Reader*, ed. by Carole Counihan and Penny Van Esterik (New York: Routledge, 1997), pp. 339–40; Goody provides a fascinating history of "sailors' biscuit," and its place in the history of Britain's processed foods.
3 Robert M. Polhemus, *The Changing World of Anthony Trollope* (Berkeley: California U Press, 1968), p. 85.
4 Victoria Glendinning, *Anthony Trollope* (New York: Knopf, 1993), pp. 292–4.
5 See Michelle Mouton, "*Why Frau Frohmann Raised Her Prices*: Anthony Trollope, Tourism and the Nineteenth-Century Industrial Food System," *Victorians: A Journal of Culture and Literature* 128 (2015): 205–26.
6 See Yves Pehaut, "The Invasion of Foreign Foods," and Giorgio Pedrocco, "Industry and New Preservation Techniques," in *Food: A Culinary History from Antiquity to the Present* (New York: Columbia UP, 1996), for overviews of the impact of new technologies on global food trade.
7 See John Burnett, *Plenty and Want: A Social History of Diet in England from 1815 to the Present Day* (London: Scolar Press, 1979), pp. 134–5, on technology's impact on frozen meat and fresh fish imports; and pp. 286–9 on the growth of food imported to England after the 1860s. See also Jean-Louis Flandrin,

"From Industrial Revolution to Industrial Food," in *Food: A Culinary History from Antiquity to the Present* (New York: Columbia UP, 1996), p. 437, on England's importing of fresh fruits.

8 See Elizabeth Abbot, *Sugar: A Bittersweet History* (London: Duckworth, 2009), pp. 258–80 and pp. 314–22, on post-emancipation labor conditions and immigration schemes. See also Sidney W. Mintz, *Sweetness and Power: The Place of Sugar in Modern History* (New York: Viking, 1985), p. 70; Mintz suggests that through the immigration of contracted labor – a policy that Trollope favored – "the planter class sought to re-create pre-emancipation conditions – to replace the discipline of slavery with the discipline of hunger."

9 Qtd. in Deborah Denenholz Morse, *Reforming Trollope: Race, Gender and Englishness in the Novels of Anthony Trollope* (Farnham, England: Ashgate, 2013), p. 1.

10 In Chapter 11, Trollope includes this footnote: "a Creole is a person born in the West Indies, of a race not indigenous to the islands. There may be white Creoles, coloured [mixed-race] Creoles, or black Creoles. . . . The meaning of the word Creole is, I think, sometimes misunderstood." See Morse, *Reforming Trollope*, pp. 140–52, for a useful discussion of this historically contested term.

11 This conceit is most pronounced in *WISM*, where Trollope traveled alone. See *Australia and New Zealand* (London: Adamant Media, 2005), vol. 1, pp. 307–8; Trollope complains about the lack of variety in the Australian diet, but explains that the assistance of his cook, brought by Rose from England, significantly increased their "comfort" – until she "found a husband for herself when she had been about a month in the bush" (vol. 1, p. 308).

12 Annette Cozzi, *The Discourses of Food in Nineteenth-Century British Fiction* (New York: Palgrave Macmillan, 2010), p. 15.

13 Trollope records conversations with "coloured" or multiracial people in Jamaica at hotels and elsewhere, with evident pleasure in having conversations with women in particular. He argues that, as the emerging professional class and as part-descendants of Europeans, multiracial people in the West Indies have the potential for self-determination and are displacing, perhaps rightfully, in his view, the power of White elites. While Trollope's assessments of Africans and "pure" African descendants in *WISM* are highly reductive and dogmatic, his attitudes toward multiracial people and his theories regarding miscegenation are somewhat more complex. See Tim Watson, *Caribbean Culture and British Fiction in the Atlantic World, 1780–1870* (Cambridge: Cambridge UP, 2008), pp. 166–7, for a discussion of Trollope's views on miscegenation in relation to England's majority opinion. See Catherine Hall, *Civilizing Subjects: Metropole and Colony in the English Imagination, 1830–1867* (Cambridge: Polity Press, 2002), pp. 220–1, on West Indian women in *WISM*. See also Morse, *Reforming Gender*, ch. 6, on the figure of the "Creole Beauty" in Trollope's later work.

14 Trollope uses "negros" and sometimes "black" to designate people he assumes on the basis of morphography to be of strictly African descent; "coloured" to designate people of mixed African and European descent; "white" to designate people of European (usually English) descent; and "Indian" to designate people of indigenous American heritage. While this racial taxonomy required no explanation for his contemporaries, he includes a footnote on the term "Creole"; see note 13.

15 See Claudia Brandenstein, "Representations of Landscape and Nature in Anthony Trollope's *The West Indies and the Spanish Main* and James Anthony Froude's *The West Indies*," in *Five Emus to the King of Siam, Environment and Empire*, ed. by Helen Tiffin (Amsterdam: Rodopi, 2007), pp. 16–18, 20. Brandenstein argues that Trollope's text, fittingly for its historical moment, departs significantly from eighteenth-century landscape conventions; rather than surveying from mountaintops wide swathes of wilderness, land thus visually conquered, Trollope uses irony to destabilize such textual moments and appreciates instead land that was, or could be, economically exploited agriculturally.

16 James Buzard, "Trollope and Travel," in *The Cambridge Companion to Anthony Trollope*, ed. by Carolyn Dever and Lisa Niles (Cambridge: Cambridge UP, 2011), p. 173.

17 I borrow this phrase, which captures Trollope's tone in much of the travelogue with respect to his presentation of racial sentiments, from Hall, *Civilizing Subjects*, p. 221.

18 See Richard Mullen, *Anthony Trollope: A Victorian in His World* (London: Duckworth, 1990), pp. 340–2, and Hall, *Civilizing Subjects*, p. 216, on the book's positive reception, in England and (in Mullen) in America. Hall, in "Going a-Trolloping: Imperial Man Travels the Empire," in *Gender and Imperialism*, ed. by Clare Midgley (Manchester: Manchester UP, 1998), p. 181, notes that West Indian readers were "less impressed."

19 R. H. Super, *Trollope in the Post Office* (Ann Arbor: U Michigan P, 1981), p. 39.

20 Robert D. Aguirre, "'Affairs of the State': Mobilities, Communication, and Race in Trollope's *The West Indies and the Spanish Main*." *Nineteenth-Century Contexts* 37.1 (2015): 2.

Works cited

Abbott, Elizabeth. *Sugar: A Bittersweet History*. London: Duckworth, 2009.
Aguirre, Robert D. "'Affairs of the State': Mobilities, Communication, and Race in Trollope's *The West Indies and the Spanish Main*." *Nineteenth-Century Contexts* 37.1 (2015): 1–20.
Brandenstein, Claudia. "Representations of Landscape and Nature in Anthony Trollope's *The West Indies and the Spanish Main* and James Anthony Froude's *The West Indies*." In *Five Emus to the King of Siam: Environment and Empire*, edited by Helen Tiffin, 15–29. Amsterdam: Rodopi, 2007.
Burnett, John. *Plenty and Want: A Social History of Diet in England from 1815 to the Present Day*. London: Scolar Press, 1966, rev. 1979.
Buzard, James. "Trollope and Travel." In *The Cambridge Companion to Anthony Trollope*, edited by Carolyn Dever and Lisa Niles, 168–80. Cambridge: Cambridge UP, 2011.
Cozzi, Annette. *The Discourses of Food in Nineteenth-Century British Fiction*. New York: Palgrave Macmillan, 2010.
Flandrin, Jean-Louis. "From Industrial Revolution to Industrial Food." In *Food: A Culinary History from Antiquity to the Present*, edited by Jean-Louis Flandrin and Massimo Montanari, 435–41. New York: Columbia UP, 1996.
Gikandi, Simon. *Maps of Englishness: Writing Identity in the Culture of Colonialism*. New York: Columbia UP, 1996.
Glendinning, Victoria. *Anthony Trollope*. New York: Knopf, 1993.
Goodlad, Lauren. "Trollopian 'Foreign Policy': Rootedness and Cosmopolitanism in the Mid-Victorian Global Imaginary." *PMLA* 124.2 (March 2009): 437–54.
Goody, Jack. "Industrial Food: Towards the Development of a World Cuisine." In *Food and Culture: A Reader*, edited by Carole Counihan and Penny Van Esterik, 338–56. New York: Routledge, 1997.
Hall, Catherine. *Civilizing Subjects: Metropole and Colony in the English Imagination, 1830–1867*. Cambridge: Polity Press, 2002.
———. "'Going a-Trolloping': Imperial Man Travels the Empire." In *Gender and Imperialism*, edited by Clare Midgley, 180–99. Manchester: Manchester UP, 1998.
Hyman, Gwen. *Making a Man: Gentlemanly Appetites in the Nineteenth-Century British Novel*. Athens: Ohio UP, 2009.
Mintz, Sidney W. *Sweetness and Power: The Place of Sugar in Modern History*. New York: Viking, 1985.
Morse, Deborah Denenholz. *Reforming Trollope: Race, Gender and Englishness in the Novels of Anthony Trollope*. Farnham, England: Ashgate, 2013.
Mouton, Michelle. "*Why Frau Frohmann Raised Her Prices*: Anthony Trollope, Tourism and the Nineteenth-Century Industrial Food System." *Victorians: A Journal of Culture and Literature* 128 (2015): 205–26.
Mullen, Richard. *Anthony Trollope: A Victorian in His World*. London: Duckworth, 1990.
Pedrocco, Giorgio. "The Food Industry and New Preservation Techniques." In *Food: A Culinary History from Antiquity to the Present*, edited by Jean-Louis Flandrin and Massimo Montanari, 481–91. New York: Columbia UP, 1996.
Pehaut, Yves. "The Invasion of Foreign Foods." In *Food: A Culinary History from Antiquity to the Present*, edited by Jean-Louis Flandrin and Massimo Montanari, 457–70. New York: Columbia UP, 1996.
Polhemus, Robert M. *The Changing World of Anthony Trollope*. Berkeley: California U Press, 1968.
Super, R. H. *Trollope in the Post Office*. Ann Arbor: U Michigan P, 1981.
Torres-Saillant, Silvio. *An Intellectual History of the Caribbean*. New York: Palgrave Macmillan, 2006.
Trollope, Anthony. *Australia and New Zealand*. 2 vols. London: Chapman and Hall. 1873. London: Adamant Media, 2005.
———. *North America*, edited by Donald Smalley and Bradford Allen Booth. 1862. New York: Knopf, 1951.
———. *South Africa*. Vols. 1 & 2. 1878. Gloucester: Allan Sutton, 1987.
———. *The West Indies and the Spanish Main*. 1859. New York: Carroll & Graf, 1999.
Watson, Tim. *Caribbean Culture and British Fiction in the Atlantic World, 1780–1870*. Cambridge: Cambridge UP, 2008.

33

TROLLOPE AND GLOBAL MODERNITY

Mark W. Turner

Anthony Trollope understood more keenly than most the complexities of the globalizing world in the nineteenth century. An inveterate world traveller with a special interest in emerging media and communications, he wrote four detailed travel books which come out of lengthy trips abroad – *The West Indies and the Spanish Main* (1859), *North America* (1862), *Australia and New Zealand* (1873) and *South Africa* (1878) – in addition to numerous stories, some collected as *Tales of All Countries* (1861 and 1863). His travels were no less absorbed into his novels, some of which were set entirely in foreign lands (Prague, Nuremburg, Australia) or in which settings abroad are particularly significant – think of Mexico in *The Way We Live Now* (1875) or Australia in *John Caldigate* (1877). As one of the bestselling novelists of his day, Trollope's work was, of course, widely disseminated across the globe, ensuring that on his travels, he was received as a globetrotting literary celebrity. Often travelling as a government official, in his capacity as high-ranking civil servant in the General Post Office, he helped negotiate treaties related to communications routes in the service of an expanding empire. He observed, experienced and wrote about the rapid expansion of transnational networks and routes – of railway and steamship, post and telegraph, publishing centres and satellites. Trollope is, as David Skilton has recently suggested, the most recognizably 'modern' of Victorian writers.[1]

Trollope's critics have long appreciated the significance of his travelling to understanding both the man and his fiction. Michael Sadleir's pioneering *Trollope: A Commentary* (1927) notes that Frances Trollope 'handed on the travel-habit to her younger son,' who later honed the skill 'of using an official journey as a means to sightseeing, and sightseeing as a means to authorship.'[2] Bradford Booth writes of Trollope the travel writer that

> With the doggedness of the professional researcher he pursued the tangible and the intangible constituents of a foreign culture, putting poet and peasant, as well as commerce and industry, under glass for the satisfaction of his insatiable curiosity. He was a statistical Baedeker bulling his way over a strange terrain, notebook in hand, with one eye cocked, businesslike, on the economic condition of the people, while the other, that of the novelist, detected their individual and collective foibles.[3]

More recent critics have emphasized more recent concerns, particularly around questions of empire and colonialism. In this volume, essays by Gordon Bigelow, Robert Tracy, Nicholas Birns,

Tamara Wagner and Grace Moore all shed new light on Trollope's engagement with Ireland and Australia, building on a range of extant scholarship.[4]

As Daniel Headrick, David Henkin, Richard Menke and others have recently shown, the first half of the nineteenth century marked a turning point in global communications, with the development of the railway, the penny post and the telegraph, which established the nodes on the networks of global movement, whether in terms of tourist destinations, publishing and other cultural 'centres,' or economic and commercial hubs.[5] Of course, such work requires close attention to imperialism and colonialism of various kinds, and the speed of these modernizing forces was uneven and often uncertain, bringing into sharp relief questions related to local, national and other forms of identity. As Ian Baucom has observed, 'the task of "locating" English identity became ever more complex as England struggled to define the relationship between the national "here" and the imperial "there."'[6] For Laura Doyle and Laura Winkiel, the fraught realities of this globalized world require us to be attentive to the 'circuits of relation within modernity,' the ways people and texts are embedded within various circuits of communication, and to the 'local-global dialectic of inside and outside, belonging and exile, in ways that disrupt conventional poetics.'[7] David Skilton has observed that Trollope's characters are almost always creatures of the urgent present of global modernity:

> Trollope's are among the first fictional characters to live lives controlled by rapid and efficient communications. Like their author, many of them are tireless train and steamship travellers in the British Isles and abroad, they exploit the penny post, and as soon as the telegraph is available, they use that too. While Dickens and Thackeray preferred to set their novels in the past, Trollope's seemed to their contemporary readers as up-to-the-minute as the latest topical cartoon in *Punch*.[8]

Living in the present, alive to global transformations, is not always an easy place to be. Given Trollope's own experiences of the circuits of modernity (as tourist, government official and global literary celebrity), it is no surprise that his work is frequently concerned with questions of distance and proximity, borders and boundaries – whether those boundaries are in Barsetshire or the outback. In Trollope's fiction, the 'inside' is always aware of the 'outside,' the 'local' not far from the 'global.'

In transit

As he states in his first travel book, *The West Indies and the Spanish Main* (1859), Trollope makes his trip to Central America in order to attend to 'certain affairs of State', but he offers few details about his official duties. Moving through the West Indies in 1858–9 – including visits to Jamaica, Cuba, Barbados, Trinidad, Panama, Costa Rica and Bermuda – he was on a delicate mission to restructure the way the postal system in the colonies was administered, to renegotiate contracts and, generally, to inspect and improve the speed and quality of the service.[9] 'How best to get about this world which God has given us is certainly one of the most interesting subjects which men have to consider,' Trollope writes in *The West Indies*, in a chapter entitled, 'Central America – Railways, Canals, Transit,' in which he discusses new proposals for the Panama and Suez Canals:

> One of the first words of which a man has to learn the meaning on reaching these countries is "transit". Central America can only be great in the world – as Egypt can be only great – by being a passage between other parts of the world which are themselves great.[10]

Trollope and global modernity

A bit later, discussing British treaties to establish access to throughways and rights of passage in Central America, in particular a railway through Honduras, he writes that 'we are desirous of excluding no person from the benefits of this public world-road', and

> may we not boast that this is the only object looked for in all our treaties and diplomatic doings? Is it not for that reason that we hold Gibraltar, are jealous about Egypt, and resolved to have Perim in our power? Is it not true that we would fain make all ways open to all men? That we would have them open to ourselves, certainly, but not closed against any human being?
>
> (Ch. 21)

Trollope's opinions on free movement through routes (the 'public world-road') and his disregard toward spaces he sees as in-between (the 'passages' between great parts of the world) are obviously connected to a wider discourse of imperialism. In Trollope, imperialism is conflicted, sometimes contradictory, and he shifts opinions in the travel books, depending on which part of the world he's discussing.[11] For my purposes, it may be enough simply to acknowledge that Trollope's words here clearly remind us that his views are a legacy of the Enlightenment, with confident notions of technological and other forms of progress. There is a totalizing sense of things in *The West Indies*, though his thinking becomes more nuanced the more he travels. In seeing only the liberating potential of movement and flow, he certainly does not spend any time wrestling with the fact that control of communication and routes is a significant form of power in modernity and that those forms of power are frequently linked to forms of subjugation of various kinds.

Trollope kept busy in transit, always keeping to his strict writing schedule – writing aboard steamers and trains, with a specially made lap-desk, and conducting government business by writing letters and going over documents. He was writing *Doctor Thorne* during the West Indies trip, which trip he also parlayed into the travel book and five short stories, first published in magazines and later in volume form. Among other things, these stories emphasize routes, points of intersection and modes of transit, and through them we see the ways Trollope's experience of the globalizing world was registered in his fiction.[12]

'The Journey to Panama', written after his return from the Central America trip and first published in Adelaide Procter and Emily Faithfull's *Victoria Regia* in 1861, is a simple enough tale about a young penniless woman, Emily Viner, en route to marry a man she doesn't love who is based in Peru (effectively, she's been sold off and shipped off to an expatriate). On board the steamship from Southampton to Panama, she spends time with a single young man, Ralph Forrest. Nothing much happens – Emily's chaperones and the other British travellers gossip about the 'dangerous alliance' with Ralph, but she ignores them and the two become friendly, so much so that Ralph encourages her not to go through with the loveless match and to return home to England. In Panama, where Emily is due to meet up with her future husband, we learn from a letter that is handed over from a stranger that her future husband died seven days before his ship from Peru to Panama was due to sail. (In a world of good communications, the letter makes it, even if the lover doesn't!) Ralph offers to accompany her back to England, but she refuses; he heads to California and she returns home.

With its focus on the gender politics of courtship, and in particular the plight of an independent young woman with rival suitors, 'The Journey to Panama' has the makings of a longer and familiar Trollope narrative. Its brevity and location bring into striking relief some of the characteristics it shares with the novels, and the effect on the reader is a more piercing shock. The microcosm of global life on board the steamship, with its British travellers alongside Spaniards,

Germans and Danes, is a far cry from the more homogenous social landscapes of Barsetshire or London, and it seems to emphasize the isolation and loneliness which mark the story. The wanderer Ralph remains alone, and the displaced Emily unmarried. In transit, relationships between men and women are 'short lived and delusive' and 'can seldom be very lasting,' Trollope writes, and the steamship is a place of impermanence and transitory experience.[13] As one man whom Ralph befriends on board says to him upon heading his own way at St Thomas, 'I dare say we shall never see each other again. One never does.'

At the beginning of the story, Trollope has a lot to say by way of detailed description of the ocean routes his characters travel, which, in part, points to Trollope's own interests in global networks and systems:

> There are several of those great ocean routes, of which, by common consent as it seems of the world, England is the centre. There is the great Eastern line – running from Southampton across the Bay of Biscay, and up the Mediterranean. It crosses the Isthmus of Suez and branches away to Australia, to India, to Ceylon, and to China. There is the great American line, transversing the Atlantic to New York and Boston with the regularity of clockwork. The voyage here is so much a matter of every day routine, that romance becomes scarce upon the route . . . Then there is the line of packets to the African coast – very romantic, as I am given to understand; and there is the great West India route to which the present little history is attached; – great, not on account of our poor West Indian islands which cannot at the present moment make anything great, but because it spreads itself out from thence to Mexico and Cuba, to Guiana and the republics of New Grenada and Venezuela, to Central America, the Isthmus of Panama, and from thence to California, Vancouver's Island, Peru, and Chili.

This is both a familiarizing strategy, to introduce readers to a particular global map that they almost certainly do not know as well as the author, and a very specific presentation of that map. The nodes on the network here aren't significant except as points that lead to other points. There is a centre to the world – England, of course – but the movement here is outwards, continually spreading and without end. As the list of nodes continues, the centre becomes increasingly less significant. You can enter into this network at any point along the series of connections, missing out the centre altogether. This raises questions which the story naturally cannot answer: what happens when the centre becomes decentred as a result of new forms of connection? Can the centre, even an imagined or constructed one, 'hold' in a model based on continual spread?

Trollope painstakingly maps the network of steamships and packets that spread across the world, but the experience of his characters on those same routes is almost always missed connections and unrealized expectations and, as John Sutherland suggests, 'the tourist's journey is rarely worth the effort.'[14] The irony in many of Trollope's narratives is that a world of seemingly greater connectedness often leads to even greater separation. The rhythm of global modernity here is arrival and departure rather than extended connection, and the movement is imagined as spread and diffusion rather than cohesion. Upon the steamship's arrival in St Thomas, when Emily's chaperones go their way and Ralph's friend another, Trollope writes, 'And then the separation came.' Narrative closure, if it exists, is not about connection and permanence. We are left with something more unsettling: frustration, melancholy, isolation.

Another of these early stories, 'Returning Home,' published in the weekly literary supplement *Public Opinion* (1861) and then in *Tales of All Countries* (second series, 1863), is more despondent still about the dislocation from the centre, England, the 'home' of the title:

> We are all apt to think that a life in strange countries will be a life of excitement, of stirring enterprise and varied scenes; that, in abandoning the comforts of home, we shall receive in exchange more of movement and of adventure that would come in our way in our own tame country; and this feeling has, I am sure, sent many a young man roaming. Take any spirited fellow of twenty, and ask him whether he would like to go to Mexico for the next ten years. Prudence and his father may ultimately save him from such banishment, but he will not refuse without a pang of regret.
>
> Alas! it is a mistake. Bread may be earned, and fortunes, perhaps, made in such countries; and as it is the destiny of our race to spread itself over the wide face of the globe, it is well that there should be something to gild and paint the outward face of that lot which so many are called upon to choose. But, for a life of daily excitement, there is no life like life in England; and the farther that one goes from England, the more stagnant, I think do the waters of existence become.[15]

Excitement and stagnancy, stasis and spread – these are the sorts of tensions set up in the circuits of modernity. The story goes on to depict a young family, Harry and Fanny Awkright and their young baby, attempting to return home from San José, where Harry had established his business. The question early on is which of two gruelling routes to take, and they choose the Serapiqui route, which requires the family to travel by mule through pouring tropical rain and deep mud for several days, then by canoe downriver for two days, where they should catch a steamer toward Southampton. Except in this case, the journey remains incomplete. The worry throughout the journey is that Fanny, who has a foreboding sense that she won't actually make it home, will die at any moment on the mule trek in the jungle; throughout most of the story, the family is bogged down in mud that prohibits easy movement. In fact, she makes it through the jungle and just when the reader thinks there might be a happy ending to the journey, when they reach the canoe-leg of the journey, Fanny's canoe hits a fallen tree in the river and capsizes and she drowns. Harry, who survives, can't face returning home to tell Fanny's mother of her death, so he and his baby head back to San José.

'Returning Home' is a story about not returning home, a violently thwarted journey, emphasizing the tenuous nature of connectedness along the routes of global modernity. The story speaks to the difficulty and ambiguous meanings of movement in the globalizing world, in which routes do not work like clockwork, in which the British abroad find themselves alone, in danger, and caught in the gaps between the nodes on the network. Or, perhaps the phrase 'gaps in the network' isn't quite right – perhaps the fantasy of the network will also lead to stagnation and mud, to a short-circuiting. Movement, transit, spread – this may be the destiny of the British, as Trollope puts it, but it is a quality of modernity about which he registers a deep ambivalence. 'Home' may seem to be the fixed idea in Trollope, but the return journey remains incomplete, the circuit continues to spread. A great admirer of global spread, Trollope also provides us with cautionary tales of all countries.

Feedback loops

As Lisa Niles has shown, our preconceptions about the form of the nineteenth-century short story are frequently unsettled when reading Trollope, 'whose short fiction often resists closure, mediating a far more complex narrative strategy.'[16] For P. D. Edwards, Trollope's stories present us with 'a much less insulated world' than we might imagine from a narrow reading of the novels. His outward-looking sensibility in part derived from understanding that his readers were wide and far spread across the many routes he travelled. In his second travel book, *North America*

(1862), Trollope makes the emphatic point that popular authors are, in effect, global authors, writing not for a narrowly defined local market of readers but for readers spread widely across the anglophone world. 'The English author should feel that he writes for the widest circle of readers ever yet obtained by the literature of any country,' Trollope asserts, and that he writes 'not only for his own country and for the States, but for the readers who are rising by millions in the British colonies.'[17] The spread of print along emerging nodes on the imperial network – important publishing centres, such as Calcutta and Melbourne – enabled the spread of the English author abroad. As Trollope would learn at the time of his first visit to Australia in the early 1870s, an indigenous print culture had developed in that colony after the Gold Rush of the 1850s, first with local and regional newspapers and magazines, in which a whole host of English writers serialized their fiction, though much print in Australia was imported from elsewhere, not least London.[18]

When Trollope arrived in Australia in 1871, he was received as a celebrity of enormous renown; in fact, he was probably the single most famous living English novelist on the planet at that time. At virtually every stop along his travels, the Australian papers printed, and others reprinted, news of his welcome dinners, glowing speeches by local dignitaries and words of appreciation by Trollope himself. In a reported speech from the New South Wales *Bathurst Free Press*, Trollope echoes precisely the theme of the international author articulated a decade earlier in *North America*:

> that his writings circumnavigate the world, and find readers in many distant lands, he receives the greatest gratification and the highest remuneration that this world could afford him. English authors enjoy privileges which are not given to writers of any other nationality. . . . An author is better placed with an audience at a distance than one near his own door; and nothing could afford him greater satisfaction than the knowledge that his works should reach the homes of the squatter, penetrate the dwelling of the settler, and even enter the hut of the shepherd, where they might be read with an amount of pleasure and profit. It was more to him to know that his works had an importance in the estimation of the people of distant lands, than that they occupied a place upon the shelves of any of the circulating libraries of Britain (Applause).[19]

The English writer, Trollope says, holds a special place globally, perhaps offering a kind of binding, 'world literature' to global readers of English. Trollope's global awareness leads us to ask new questions of his work. For example, what might it mean to read Trollope in 'distant lands' and how do our understandings of context shift when taking into account the many sites of reception for his work? What happens to Trollope's seemingly localist mode of 'Englishness' when it's on the move in different contexts?[20]

Trollope's first trip to Australia lasted nineteen months, from 1871 to 1873. He travelled via Suez and the Indian Ocean to Australia, New Zealand, eventually Hawaii and then San Francisco, where he took a train across America. The ostensible reason for the trip was to visit his son Frederick, who, at the age of eighteen, emigrated to New South Wales, where he established a sheep station. In typical Trollope fashion, he turned the occasion of this family visit into the stuff of print, signing publishing agreements in advance. He first signed a contract for a travel book, and then approached the *Daily Telegraph*, a newspaper whose circulation, at roughly 200,000, was greater than the *Times*, for whom he agreed to publish a series of eleven letters, signed 'An Antipodean', beginning in December 1871. The headlines for the letters frequently indicate location, and include both the publication date in the newspaper and the date of Trollope's writing the letter, usually two months previous. For example, his first letter is '"England in Australia: I

Queensland," 23 December 1871 (dated October 1871)', the fifth letter is '"A Stagnant Arcadia," 5 October 1872 (dated August)'. As noted earlier, the fanfare attached to his travels across Australia was significant, as a report from the Adelaide *South Australian Register* on 8 April 1872 makes clear:

> Not the least interesting circumstance connected with the arrival of the mail steamer is the fact that it brings as a visitor the eminent novelist whose name heads this notice. Tantalized as we have been for some months with manifestations of Mr. Trollope's presence in the neighbouring colonies through the Press and the telegraph wires, we are gratified that he has not left the continent without setting foot in our "farinaceous village," which we can assure him is *not* in New South Wales.[21]

We get a sense here not only of the significance of Trollope's visits to the various regions of the colony, but also of the circuit of media reports that were picked up by other regional and local newspapers and subsequently spread round the country, tracking or mapping the famous author's movements. The readers in Adelaide were aware of the famous author's movements in the 'neighbouring colonies', building anticipation. Overwhelmingly, Trollope was received positively and feted as a great man of letters, at least to begin with. As P. D. Edwards has noted, 'after reports of his letters to the *Daily Telegraph* began to appear in the Australian papers, within a few months of his arrival, references to the visiting celebrity were often not merely unfriendly but even insulting.'[22] In other words, Trollope was writing back to the centre (London and the *Daily Telegraph*), trapped in a time lag that catches up with him when those letters from the centre get bounced back to the colonies some months later through various forms of reprints. Thus he was caught out by the *Brisbane Courier*, which reprinted at least some of Trollope's *Daily Telegraph* letters and, as a result, was far more circumspect about Trollope's recent visit than earlier media reports. Responding to Trollope's criticism in a letter a few months back, that emigrating and settling in Australia were a difficult thing, the newspaper writes,

> There is nothing in his letter to make the place "hot" for him; nothing to rouse the dislike, much less the indignation, of a single resident of this colony. On the contrary, it is on the whole rather flattering to the people here, and although it contains several grave errors, they are such that a passing visitor fresh from the old country could hardly avoid falling into, more especially under such circumstances as Mr. Trollope was placed in . . . It is unfortunate for the colony that a writer so popular and influential as Mr. Trollope undoubtedly is should have made the particular mistakes he did, because they are just those which will be most likely to frighten that particular class of emigrants from coming here which the colony most requires, and to whom we sincerely believe it offers the most solid advantages. . . . The letters of the "Antipodean," when they have done duty in the *Daily Telegraph*, will no doubt appear in the shape of a book, which will be read and accepted as literally true by tens of thousands of persons who will never see its accuracy questioned, and who would be loth to entertain a contrary opinion if it was presented to them – especially from this side.[23]

The media understands the significance of Trollope the traveller's voice to shape public opinion back in the 'old country'. Part of the initial exuberance with which he is received is because they hope to ensure good reports, which attest to the attractions of Australia, thereby encouraging further emigration. Any serious critique in his letters disrupts the message that the media hopes, in part, to help shape, in the ongoing series of letters and, perhaps more importantly, the travel book they know will follow.[24] A media feedback loop has ensnared Trollope within it, when the time lag catches up with him, but it has also ensnared the colonies who court Trollope's good words. The logic of the public world-roads of communication is one of flow in many directions – back and forth from metropole to colony, from colony to colony, spreading beyond, and not always easily controlled.

'Here' and 'there'

In addition to the letters and the travel book, there was one other interesting literary outcome from Trollope's first trip to Australia, the short novella *Harry Heathcote of Gangoil: A Tale of Australian Bush Life*, first published in the illustrated Christmas issue of *The Graphic* in 1873 in Britain and serialized between November 1873 and January 1874 in Melbourne's *The Age*. Partly inspired by the life of Trollope's son, *Harry Heathcote* depicts a young Englishman with a sheep station trying to make his way as a squatter in the colonies against all odds, which include a very un-English and hostile group of Australian neighbours, former convicts and degenerate drunkards, who try to set fire to Harry's land, during a particularly hot and dry midsummer. There's a usual Trollopian love-plot, in which Harry's sister-in-law falls in love with a newly arrived 'free selector' (those who purchase land from the government as opposed to squatters, who lease it) Giles Medlicot, another Englishman, though one less virile and robust than Harry.[25]

Midsummer in Australia is, of course, December in Britain, and the description of Christmas in Australia that opens the novel is the first of a series of defamiliarizing moments in which 'home' (England) is contrasted with the colony. Harry arrives back to the sheep station late in the evening, after a full day out, and reports, 'I never was so hot or so thirsty in my life.'[26] Shortly thereafter, the narrator tells us,

> the Christmas to which [the reader] is introduced is not the Christmas with which he is intimate on this side of the Equator – a Christmas of blazing fires indoors, and of sleet and snow and frost outside – but the Christmas of Australia, in which happy land the Christmas fires are apt to be lighted, or to light themselves, when they are by no means needed.
>
> (Ch. 1)

Trollope subtly hints at the main action of the novel here: cosy homefires of the Christmas hearth become the bush fires of colonial life, and most of the novel is taken up with Harry and his workers spending whole nights patrolling his land, in search of fire, or in search of individuals who plan to commit arson. Having dislocated Christmas for his imagined reader on 'this side of the Equator,' Trollope then goes on to dislocate Harry. He is described as 'rough to look at; but by all who understood Australian life he would have been taken to be a gentleman' (Ch. 1). Harry is both English *and* Australian, both rough and refined, a working farmer but no less a gentleman for that. We are assured of his solid English temperament when we're told that at the end of the working day 'he would lie at length upon rugs in the verandah, with a pipe in his mouth, while his wife sat over him reading a play of Shakespeare or the last novel that had come to them from England' (Ch. 1). There are further reassurances for the British reader – Harry's land is the size of 'an English county' (Ch. 1), both women in the house 'dressed for dinner . . . as they would have . . . in a country-house at home' (Ch. 1), and, we're told, Harry, though rough and colonial in his dress, 'retained the manners of a high-bred gentleman in his intercourse with women' (Ch. 7). At the same time that Trollope seeks to establish the Englishness of Harry and his family – or, as English as one can be under the circumstances of bush life – he also points to those very un-English qualities of settler life. The centre of domestic life is, in fact, outdoors, on the verandah rather than in the drawing room, and though Harry is proud of his horses, 'his stable arrangements would not have commanded respect in the "Shires"' (Ch. 1). His carriages fare no better: 'a Londoner looking at them would have declared them to be hopeless ruins' (Ch. 1).

Throughout the novel, there is a tension between, on the one hand, a comforting, recognizable Englishness coupled with a partly remembered, partly imagined homeland and, on the other hand, the colonial context which challenges English class distinctions and conventions of manliness and, arguably, reshapes masculinity in the doing. One question that emerges is: does male Englishness travel? There's a moment late in the novel, after Harry has joined forces with his former foe, the English neighbour Medlicot, in defeating the Australian ruffians who seek to burn his land, as the novel moves toward resolution, when we're told that 'There are things which can't be transplanted' (Ch. 10) and that Harry 'likes to think of the old place, though one is so far away' (Ch. 10). England – the English – is never very far away in the novel, whether imaginatively in characters' minds or in reality as one's own neighbours, though perhaps that depends where you are. Who is the imagined reader here and what difference might it make to reading the novel: is it the presumably English (or at least British) reader of the *Graphic* back 'home' or is it the reader of the serial published in the *Age* in Melbourne? Is it the reader of the *Graphic* in Australia, where that title was also published? Or, perhaps, it is the reader of the *Graphic* or the *Age* travelling somewhere else along the global flows of print and communication, perhaps a reader aboard a ship somewhere, in transit, magazine in hand.

Harry Heathcote – like other of Trollope's domestic fictions set abroad, including *Nina Balatka* (Nuremberg) and *Linda Tressel* (Prague) – is frequently said to be an unsuccessful novel, which compares unfavourably with the longer, more fully developed multi-plot novels set in England. His characters and plots, critics have suggested, do not translate well to foreign destinations. But like his short stories about dislocation and people spreading out across the globe, *Harry Heathcote* has the virtue of focusing the reader on a set of very particular questions which derive specifically from Trollope's experience of travelling to Australia for the first time to visit his expatriate son, partly from a long history of travel and interest in the spread and flow of global modernity. When Trollope writes about 'here' and 'there', 'this side of the Equator' and 'that,' he does so knowing that those seemingly stable positions – to do with nationality, place and identity – are not nearly as stable as they seem, because they are ever in relation to shifting understandings of local and global. We should think more about what's unsettling about Trollope's English people abroad, think more about what's uncomfortable to 'us', whoever 'we' are. In a world of spread, dead ends, missed connections, mediation and remediation, the act of transplanting, relocating or simply moving from 'here' to 'there' is never simply unidirectional. It is easy enough to think about how we might read and interpret a text taking into account any particular given context – much more difficult, I think, to read a text in relation to the 'circuits of modernity' of which it is a part.

Notes

1 David Skilton, 'Anthony Trollope,' in *The Cambridge Companion to English Novelists*, ed. Adrian Poole (Cambridge: Cambridge University Press, 2009), 213–15.
2 Michael Sadleir, *Trollope: A Commentary* (revised edition, London: Constable, 1945), 99 and 183.
3 Bradford Booth, ed., *The Tireless Traveler: Twenty Letters to the Liverpool Mercury by Anthony Trollope 1875* (Berkeley, CA: University of California Press, 1941), 3.
4 In addition to the essays in this volume, see important essays by James Buzard, Nicholas Birns and Amanda Clayburgh in Carolyn Dever and Lisa Niles, eds., *The Cambridge Companion to Anthony Trollope* (Cambridge: Cambridge University Press, 2011). My own essay in the *Cambridge Companion* touches on some of the concerns that I develop here.

5. Among much recent work, see Daniel Headrick, *When Information Came of Age: Technologies of Knowledge in the Ages of Reason and Revolution, 1700–1850* (Oxford: Oxford University Press, 2002), Daniel Henkin, *The Postal Age: The Emergence of Modern Communications in Nineteenth-Century America* (Chicago: University of Chicago Press, 2006), and Richard Menke, *Telegraphic Realism: Victorian Fiction and Other Information Systems* (Stanford, CA: Stanford University Press, 2008). For an epic global history of the nineteenth century in which questions of global movement and communications figure significantly, see Jürgen Osterhammel, *The Transformation of the World: A Global History of the Nineteenth Century*, trans. Patrick Camiller (Princeton: Princeton University Press, 2014).
6. Ian Baucom, *Out of Place: Englishness, Empire, and the Locations of Identity* (Princeton: Princeton University Press, 1999), 37.
7. Laura Doyle and Laura Winkiel, *Geomodernisms: Race, Modernism, Modernity* (Urbana: University of Indiana Press, 2005), 13 and 3.
8. Skilton, 214.
9. See N. John Hall, *Trollope: A Biography* (Oxford: Oxford University Press, 1991), 172ff., and R. H. Super, *Trollope in the Post Office* (Ann Arbor: University of Michigan Press, 1981), 41. On *The West Indies*, see Michelle Mouton's essay in this volume.
10. Anthony Trollope, *The West Indies and the Spanish Main* (1859; London: Dawsons, 1968), ch. 21. All citations are to this edition.
11. For a range of discussions of Trollope's liberalism and imperialist views, see Grace Moore in this volume; Amanda Anderson, 'Trollope's Modernity,' *ELH* 74, no. 3 (Fall 2007), 509–34; and Deborah Denenholz Morse, *Reforming Trollope: Race, Gender, and Englishness in the Novels of Anthony Trollope* (Farnham, UK: Ashgate, 2013).
12. The other great theme that emerges in many of Trollope's foreign tales is female independence – women in search of adventure, frequently fraught with sexual tension. See, for example, 'The Banks of the Jordan' (later titled 'A Ride Across Palestine') and 'Mrs General Talboys', both of which appear in *Tales of All Countries*, second series (1863).
13. Anthony Trollope, 'The Journey to Panama,' in Anthony Trollope, *Early Short Stories*, ed. John Sutherland (Oxford: Oxford University Press, 1994). All citations are to this edition ('The Journey to Panama,' pp. 379–96).
14. John Sutherland, 'Introduction' to Anthony Trollope, *Early Short Stories* (Oxford: Oxford University Press, 1994), xv.
15. Anthony Trollope, 'Returning Home,' in *Early Short Stories*, ed. John Sutherland (Oxford: Oxford University Press, 1994).
16. Lisa Niles, 'Trollope's Short Fiction,' in *The Cambridge Companion to Anthony Trollope*, eds. Carolyn Dever and Lisa Niles (Cambridge: Cambridge University Press, 2011), 72.
17. Anthony Trollope, *North America* (1862; Gloucester, UK: Alan Sutton, 1987), vol. 2, Ch. 15.
18. On the development of indigenous Australian print culture in the period, see David Finkelstein, 'The Globalization of the Book 1800–1970,' in *A Companion to the History of the Book*, eds. Simon Eliot and Jonathan Rose (Oxford: Blackwell, 2008), 335. Finkelstein discusses the 'flowing back' of 'raw' literary material from Australia to Britain and back to Australia and other colonies (335).
19. 'Mr Anthony Trollope at Bathurst,' *The Argus* (Melbourne), 29 Nov 1871. (Reprinted from the *Bathurst Free Press*, 18 Nov 1871.)
20. These questions are larger than the scope of this essay, but it is worth noting that other scholars have already considered the implications of Trollope's global movements to his understanding of Englishness. See Morse's provocative discussion of *Lady Anna* (1874), which Trollope completed aboard ship during his second trip to Australia (ch. 2, *Reforming Trollope*). Many of Trollope's novels were written partly in transit – *Doctor Thorne* and *The Way We Live Now*, for example. It's also worth noting that Trollope sold his house at Waltham Cross before he set sail to Australia, so he was 'homeless' while traveling abroad.
21. 'Mr Anthony Trollope,' *South Australian Register* (8 April 1872).
22. P. D. Edwards and R. B. Joyce, 'Introduction,' in Anthony Trollope, *Australia and New Zealand* (Brisbane: University of Queensland Press, 1967), 34.
23. 'Anthony Trollope in Queensland,' *Brisbane Courier* (22 March 1872).
24. The publication of Trollope's *Australia and New Zealand*, six months after his return to England, had a troubled reception in Australia, despite much praise heaped on the colonists (the Aborigines fare far less well). Partly, some Australian readers were still smarting from Trollope's *Daily Telegraph* letters, and they took exception to Trollope's accusation of Australians as 'blowers' or braggers who overstated the claims of their colony. See P. D. Edwards and R. B. Joyce, 34–5, and Hall, 375.

25 For significant discussions of *Harry Heathcote*, see especially: P. D. Edwards and R. B. Joyce, Appendix 3, 'Trollope's Australian Novels,' in *Australia and New Zealand*, 762–8; Janet C. Myers, '"Verily the Antipodes of Home": The Domestic Novel in the Australian Bush,' *NOVEL: A Forum on Fiction*, Vol. 35, No. 1 (Autumn, 2001), 46–68; and Nicholas Birns, 'Trollope and the Antipodes,' in *The Cambridge Companion to Anthony Trollope*. See also Grace Moore, '"The Heavens Were on Fire": Incendiarism and the Defence of the Settler Home,' in Tamara S. Wagner, ed., *Domestic Fiction in Colonial Australia and New Zealand* (London: Pickering and Chatto, 2014), in addition to Moore's essay in this volume.

26 Anthony Trollope, *Harry Heathcote of Gangoil: A Tale of Australian Bush Life* (London: Penguin, 1993), Ch. 1. All citations are to this edition.

Works cited

Anderson, Amanda. 'Trollope's Modernity,' *ELH*, 74, no. 3 (Fall 2007), 509–34.

Anon. 'Anthony Trollope in Queensland,' *Brisbane Courier*, 22 March 1872.

Anon. 'Mr Anthony Trollope,' *South Australian Register*, 8 April 1872.

Anon. 'Mr Anthony Trollope at Bathurst,' *The Argus* (Melbourne), 29 Nov 1871.

Baucom, Ian. *Out of Place: Englishness, Empire, and the Locations of Identity* (Princeton: Princeton University Press, 1999).

Birns, Nicholas. 'Trollope and the Antipodes,' in eds. Carolyn Dever and Lisa Niles, *The Cambridge Companion to Anthony Trollope* (Cambridge: Cambridge University Press, 2011), 181–95.

Booth, Bradford, ed. *The Tireless Traveler: Twenty Letters to the Liverpool Mercury by Anthony Trollope 1875* (Berkeley: University of California Press, 1941).

Denenholz Morse, Deborah. *Reforming Trollope: Race, Gender, and Englishness in the Novels of Anthony Trollope* (Farnham, UK: Ashgate, 2013).

Dever, Carolyn, and Niles, Lisa, eds. *The Cambridge Companion to Anthony Trollope* (Cambridge: Cambridge University Press, 2011).

Doyle, Laura, and Winkiel, Laura. *Geomodernisms: Race, Modernism, Modernity* (Urbana, IN: University of Indiana Press, 2005).

Edwards, P. D. and R. B. Joyce. 'Introduction,' in Anthony Trollope, *Australia and New Zealand* (Brisbane: University of Queensland Press, 1967).

Finkelstein, David. 'The Globalization of the Book 1800–1970,' in *A Companion to the History of the Book*, eds. Simon Eliot and Jonathan Rose (Oxford: Blackwell, 2008), 328–40.

Hall, N. John. *Trollope: A Biography* (Oxford: Oxford University Press, 1991).

Headrick, Daniel. *When Information Came of Age: Technologies of Knowledge in the Ages of Reason and Revolution, 1700–1850* (Oxford: Oxford University Press, 2002).

Henkin, David. *The Postal Age: The Emergence of Modern Communications in Nineteenth-Century America* (Chicago: University of Chicago Press, 2006).

Menke, Richard. *Telegraphic Realism: Victorian Fiction and Other Information Systems* (Stanford, CA: Stanford University Press, 2008).

Moore, Grace. '"The Heavens Were on Fire": Incendiarism and the Defence of the Settler Home,' in *Domestic Fiction in Colonial Australia and New Zealand*, ed. Tamara S. Wagner (London: Pickering and Chatto, 2014), 63–73.

Myers, Janet C. '"Verily the Antipodes of Home": The Domestic Novel in the Australian Bush,' *NOVEL: A Forum on Fiction*, Vol. 35, No. 1 (Autumn, 2001), 46–68.

Niles, Lisa. 'Trollope's Short Fiction,' in *The Cambridge Companion to Anthony Trollope*, eds. Carolyn Dever and Lisa Niles (Cambridge: Cambridge University Press, 2011), 71–84.

Osterhammel, Jürgen. *The Transformation of the World: A Global History of the Nineteenth Century*, trans. Patrick Camiller (Princeton: Princeton University Press, 2014).

Sadleir, Michael. *Trollope: A Commentary* (revised edition, London: Constable, 1945).

Skilton, David. 'Anthony Trollope,' in *The Cambridge Companion to English Novelists*, ed. Adrian Poole (Cambridge: Cambridge University Press, 2009), 210–24.

Super, R. H. *Trollope in the Post Office* (Ann Arbor: University of Michigan Press, 1981).

Sutherland, John. 'Introduction' to Anthony Trollope, *Early Short Stories* (Oxford: Oxford University Press, 1994).

Trollope, Anthony. *Australia and New Zealand* (1873; Brisbane: University of Queensland Press, 1967).

———. *Early Short Stories*, ed. John Sutherland (Oxford: Oxford University Press, 1994).

———. *Harry Heathcote of Gangoil: A Tale of Australian Bush Life* (1874; London: Penguin, 1993).
———. *John Caldigate* (1879; Oxford: Oxford University Press, 1993).
———. *Nina Balatka and Linda Tressel* (1865 and 1867; Oxford: Oxford University Press, 1991).
———. *North America*, 2 vols. (1862; Gloucester, UK: Alan Sutton, 1987).
———. *Tales of All Countries* (London: Chapman and Hall, 1861).
———. *The Way We Live Now* (1875; Oxford: Oxford University Press, 2009).
———. *The West Indies and the Spanish Main* (1859; London: Dawsons, 1968).

INDEX

Note: Italicized page numbers indicate figures and tables on the corresponding page.

Abbot, H. Porter 178, 183
Act to Amend the Law Relating to Divorce and Matrimonial Causes in England (1857) 87; *see also* Divorce Act (1857); Matrimonial Causes Act (1857)
Adams, James Eli 63
addressability 41
Adorno, Theodor 404
adultery 103
Afterlife of Property, The (Nunokawa) 112
aging studies 8, 295–303
Aguirre, Richard D. 308
Allegories of Union (Corbett) 368
Amarnick, Steven 336–46
American Senator, The (Trollope) 278–9, 297–9, 319
Anderson, Amanda 73, 357
Anglo-Catholic Tractarians 348
Anthony Trollope: A Commentary (Sadleir) 1, 51, 423
Anthony Trollope: A Victorian in His World (Mullen) 2
anti-progressive elements within modernity 72–3
anti-Semitism 8–9, 27, 325–33, 336–44
Anzieu, Didier 126
apRoberts, Ruth 28, 51, 144
Archbold, John Frederick 290
Archibald, Diana 389, 392–3
Arnold, Matthew 355
artist-model relationships 253
art of love 244–6
Austen, Jane 155, 168
Australia and New Zealand (Trollope) 399–408
authorial intrusions 309–10

Autobiography, An (Trollope): body portrayal 121, 126; cleverness narrative 274–5, 281; conservative liberalism 22, 24; English gentleman, meaning/manifestation 288; illustrations in 217–18, 247–8; introduction 1, 22; Irish theme in 369; literary labor of 307; overview 197–9; violence against women 72–3

Badiou, Alain 385
Bagehot, Walter 36, 39
Bakhtin, Mikhail 129
Barchester Towers (Trollope) 15, 17–19, 145
Bardic Nationalism (Trumpener) 373
Bastardy Act (1845) 101
Bate, Jonathan 404
Baucom, Ian 424
Baynton, Barbara 404
behaviorist narration 170
Belich, James 389
Bell, Robert 311
Benjamin, Walter 178
Ben-Yishai, Ayelet 285–94
bigamy themes 106
Bigelow, Gordon 316, 363–77
Bildungsroman 18–19, 27, 29
Biography: A Very Short Introduction (Lee) 190
Birns, Nicholas 378–87, 393
blackmail themes 106
Bleicher, Elizabeth 74
Blythe, Helen Lucy 177–89, 389
body portrayal 5, 120–30
Booth, Bradford 423

Index

Borges, Jorge 190
Bowen, Elizabeth 265
Briefel, Aviva 288
Bulwer, Henry Lytton 192
Burnett, John 414–15
Bush Studies (Baynton) 404
Buzard, James 417

Caesar, Julius (Trollope's commentary of) 193–5
Cameron, Lauren 201–9
Can You Forgive Her? (Trollope) 19–20, 128, 154–63, 299
capitalist globalization 26–8
Carleton, William 265, 271–2, 364
Carlyle, Jane 193
Carlyle, Thomas 142, 274
Carter, Everett 330, 338
Castle Richmond (Trollope): aging studies 298–9; Irish themes 363–4, 367–8, 370, 373; legitimacy/illegitimacy themes 106–7
Cathleen Ní Houlihan (Yeats) 268
centenary anthologies 365–6
Changing World of Anthony Trollope, The (Polhemus) 51, 85, 150, 365
character and metonymy 40–2
character identity through objects 111–15
Chase, Karen 295
Cheyette, Bryan 337
child custody laws 84–5
Christian Protestant views 325–6
Chronicler of Barsetshire, The: A Life of Anthony Trollope (Super) 2
Church of England 35, 41–2, 347
civic republicanism 28–9
Claverings, The (Trollope) 56–8
Cleary, Joe 373
Clergymen of the Church of England (Trollope) 354–5
clerico-political conflict 43
cleverness narrative 274–83
Cobley, Paul 183
Cohen, William 121–2, 302
Cohn, Dorrit 168
Colella, Silvana 308
Collegians, The: A Tale of Garryowen (Griffin) 268
Colley, Linda 315
comic conservatism 15
communal thought 171–5
community stewardship theme 317
configured state 42–5
Connaught Republic 263–4
conservatism Irish novels 316
conservative liberalism 21–6
"consumer-consciousness" in religious choice 357
contradictory stories, told by characters 184
Cooper, Hyson 63–71
Cooper, Suzanne 252, 255
Copley, John 84

Copyright Amendment Act (1841) 309
Corbett, Mary Jean 72–83, 368
counterrevolution fiction 381–4
counterrevolution themes 379–81
Cozzi, Annette 414–15
Crimean War (1853–1856) 38, 41
crinoline shape, symbology 248, *249,* 250
Cronin, John 366
Culler, Jonathan 182
Custody of Infants Act (1839) 84–5, 87; *see also* Infant Custody Act (1839); Law Relating to the Custody of Infants; Norton, Caroline

Daniel Deronda (Eliot) 343
Darwin, Charles 201–5
Darwinism narrative strategies 201–5
Davidson, J.H. 389, 400
destructive decisions narrative 203–4
Dickens, Charles 40, 100, 274, 281, 378, 390
Digest of the Law Relative to Pleading and Evidence in Actions Real Personal and Mixed, A (Archbold) 290
Dilke, Charles 390
"divided mind" indications 15
Divorce Act (1857) 74, 91, 97; *see also* Act to Amend the Law Relating to Divorce and Matrimonial Causes in England (1857); Matrimonial Causes Act (1857)
Doctor Thorne (Trollope) 100–1, 105, 140, 300
domestic violence 78–9
Dowling, Andrew 308
Dr Wortle's School (Trollope) 395–6
Duke's Children, The (Trollope) 302–3
Duncan, Ian 373
Dunleavy, Janet 365–6
Durey, Jill Felicity 348–9

Eagleton, Terry 307, 372
Early Victorian England (Young) 391–2
Ecclesiasticus reference 331
Edgeworth, Maria 273
Edwards, Mary Ellen 217
Edwards, Owen Dudley 366
Edwards, P.D. 427, 429
Elias, Norbert 128
Eliot, George 139, 154, 274, 296, 306, 343
emigration narratives 11, 388–96
English gentleman, meaning/manifestation 288
Escott, T.H.S. 1–2, 248, 264–6, 364, 371, 378, 382
Eurocentric global food system 420
Eustace Diamonds, The (Trollope): body portrayal 128; free indirect discourse 290; legal culture 288; material culture 113–14; mother's influence 278–9; ordinary realism 146; religious beliefs 349
Ewick, Patricia 289–90

Exposition of the Laws Relating to the Women of England, An (Wharton) 103
externalized narration 170–1
Eye for an Eye, An (Trollope) 369, 370

Farina, Jonathan 142–53
Fawkes, Lionel Grimstone 218
feedback loops 427–30
feeling narratives, about self and others: externalized narration 170–1; intermental/communal thought 171–5; introduction 6, 166–8; narrated monologue 168–9; psycho-narration/thought report 169–70, 171; quoted monologue 169
female gaze 256–7
female identity 5
feminism: critique of 182; gender and violent thought crime 54–60; introduction 6, 51–4; marital law 84–97; objects and identity 114; as satire 22; Trollope's ideological position on 80; *see also* women
Feminization of Famine, The (Kelleher) 368
feminization of novel-reading 308
Fictional Minds (Palmer) 170
field sports 8, 315–19
fillius nullius rule 104–5
Finn, Margot 287
Fixed Period, The (Trollope) 29
Flanagan, Thomas 371
Fletcher, John 37
Fludernik, Monika 182
food themes 412–20
Forester, John 197
forgery themes 78
Forrester, Mark 122
Foucault, Michel 36
Framley Parsonage (Trollope): illustration studies 219, 219–31, 220, 222, 225, 227–8, 230; material culture 115–16
Franklin, J. Jeffrey 316, 347–59
Freedgood, Elaine 113, 122
free indirect discourse (FID): introduction 6; legal culture and 290; narrated monologue 168, 170, 184; narrator revision 160–1, 163, 329; revealing characters' feelings 166; slavery concerns 78; switching point of view 155
French, Henry 63
French Revolution 380–1
Frith, William 247

Gaskell, Elizabeth 144
Gatrell, Simon 86, 96
gender relations 177–85; adultery 103; bigamy themes 106; domestic violence 78–9; female gaze 256–7; "girl-watching" 182; homosexual pornography 123; male rape 122; marital law 84–97; masculinity 63–70; misogyny theme 4, 53–60; rape themes 74; sexual assault 79; sexual maturity in female characters 18–19; sexual tension narratives 240; violent thought crime 54–60; *see also* feminism; marriage narratives; women
German liberal revolution 384
Gilbert, Pamela 123, 128–9
Gilbert, Sandra 179
Gilmartin, Sophie 120–33
"girl-watching" 182
Glendinning, Victoria 2, 55, 199, 312, 378, 413
global modernity: feedback loops 427–30; introduction 9–10, 423–4; transit 424–7
Glorious Revolution 386
Goldman, Paul 213–38
Goodlad, Lauren 15–32, 36–7
Goodman, Helen 86, 87
governance and the Victorian state 36–9
Great Expectations (Dickens) 281–2
Green, T.H. 25, 27
Gregory, William 264
Griffin, Gerald 265, 268, 371
Gubar, Susan 179

Hadley, Elaine 17, 38
Hall, N. John 2, 72, 137, 142, 338, 356
Halperin, John 15
Hamer, Mary 307, 310
Handley, Graham 338
Hardy, Thomas 120–1
Harry Heathcote (Trollope) 391, 394, 401–3, 430–1
Harvey, Margaret P. 111–19
Hawthorne, Nathaniel 414
Heath, Kay 295–305
Heathcliff and the Great Hunger (Eagleton) 372
Heidt, S.J. 193
He Knew He Was Right (Trollope): feminism 51, 52; introduction 4; marital law in 84–97; political content of the newspaper 310; trousseaux, meaning for women 117–18; women and violence 80
Helsinger, Elizabeth 317
Hemingway, Ernest 171
Hennessy, James Pope 2
Herbert, Christopher 51, 66, 73, 93–5, 144, 366
historical description, defined 372
Holmes, Ann Sumner 91
homoeroticism 52, 53, 122–3
homosexual pornography 123
Horstman, Allen 89
Howells, William Dean 144
Huggins, Mike 315
Hughes, Kathryn 190
Hughes, Robert 21
Humphries, Susan L. 307
Hunting Sketches (Trollope) 316–17
hunting trope 316–18

Index

Hutton, Richard Holt 143–4, 275, 277
Hynes, John 366

identity-as-problem 15
illegitimacy *see* legitimacy and illegitimacy
Illuminated Magazine 221
illusion of independent agency 173
illustration studies: *Framley Parsonage* 219, 219–31, *220, 222, 225, 227–8, 230*; interpretive contexts 219, *219, 220*; introduction 213–14; Millais, John Everett *219,* 219–36, *220*
Infant Custody Act (1839) 94; *see also* Custody of Infants Act (1839); Law Relating to the Custody of Infants; Norton, Caroline
institutional conformity 41
intermental thought 171–5
Ireland, as inspiration: centenary anthologies 365–6; early patterns 364–5; history of the novel 371–3; introduction 2, 363–4; Irish famine 366–8; overview 263–73; politics and 369–71
Irish Famine 366–8
Irish Novelists, The (Flanagan) 371
irony in narratives 158–9
Is He Popenjoy? (Trollope) 58–60, 69, 108–9, 291

Jael, as narrative 241–2, 246
James, Henry 51, 85, 121, 173–5, 178, 183
Jameson, Fredric 16
Jewish characters 8–9, 27, 325–33, 336–44
John Caldigate (Trollope) 394–5, 400–1
Johnson, Samuel 190
Jones, Wendy 75–6, 80–1, 86–7, 288

Keen, Suzanne 166–76
Kelleher, Margaret 368
Kendrick, Walter M. 307
Kept in the Dark (Trollope) 177–85
Kincaid, James 2, 15, 72, 86, 111–12, 137–41
Knelman, Judith 311, 366

Labour Party 21
Lacey, Nicola 86
Lady Anna (Trollope) 106, 107–8, 393–4
laissez-faire state 37
Landleaguers, The (Trollope) 3, 29
landscape narratives 399–408
Langbauer, Laurie 315–16
Langmuir, Gavin 332
language capacity questions 308–9
language of objects 113
Lansbury, Coral 290, 400
Last Chronicle of Barset, The (Trollope): art of love 244–6; community stewardship theme 317; happy ending 246–7, *247*; interplay 257; *ménage a trois* narrative 242–6; Millais, John Everett, as inspiration 247–50, *249,* 253–5, *254*; order of release 250–2, *251*; ordinary realism 143, 144,

147; overview 240–1; picturesque, as narrative 255–7; prologue 240; subplot 240–57
La Vendée (Trollope) 378–86
Law Relating to the Custody of Infants 84–5, 87; *see also* Custody of Infants Act (1839) 84–5, 87; Infant Custody Act (1839); Norton, Caroline
lawyer/barrister characters 286
legal culture 285–91
Legitimacy Act (1926) 103
legitimacy and illegitimacy 100–9
Lenz, Carolyn 182
Levine, Caroline 41
Levine, George 15, 52, 146, 178
Lewes, G.H. 296, 306
Liberal Party 21
Life and Adventures of a Clever Woman, The (Fanny Trollope) 275
Life of Cicero, The (Trollope) 19, 28, 190, 195–7,
Linton, Eliza Lynn 80
literary labour 306–12
Lloyd, David 371–2
Lonergan, Patrick 22
Lord Palmerston (Trollope) 192–3
Lottery of Marriage, The (Fanny Trollope) 277, 279
Lowerson, John 315
Lukács, Georg 16
Lyell, Charles 204

Macdermots of Ballycloran, The (Trollope) 2, 263–73, 363–4
Maine, Henry 288
male aging 301–2
male rape 122
Manful Assertions (Roper, Tosh) 63
Manliness and Masculinities in Nineteenth-Century Britain (Tosh) 64
marital law 84–97
Markwick, Margaret 86, 180, 190–200
marriage narratives: hunting trope and 317; internal revision 154–63; introduction 154–6; irony in narratives 158–9; *Jael* narrative 245–6; marital law 84–97; plot differences 159–63; skimmable passages 156–8; thinking women 155, 161–3
Married Women's Property Act (1882) 53, 183
Martel, Michael 35–47
Marx, Karl 381
masculinity 63–70
material culture 111–18
Matrimonial Causes Act (1857) 53, 103; *see also* Act to Amend the Law Relating to Divorce and Matrimonial Causes in England (1857); Divorce Act (1857)
McCourt, John 371
McKenzie, Callum 315
McLennan, J.F. 104

McMaster, Juliet: authorial intrusions 309–10; conduct-book fiction for men 69; feeling narratives 166; feminism and 51, 57; material culture 111–12; "New Man" concept 328
McMaster, Rowland 86, 88, 285
ménage a trois narrative 242–6
Meredith, George 18
metonymic relationships 112
Michie, Elsie 129, 274–84
Michie, Helene 154–65
migratory identity themes 386
Mill, Harriet Taylor 74
Mill, John Stuart: hunting trope 319; politics 21–3, 26; the state 39; testamentary freedom concept 102; violence against women 72, 74
Millais, John Everett: illustration studies 214, *219*, 219–36, *220, 222*; as inspiration 239, 240, 247; *see also* specific works
Miller, Andrew 311
Miller, D.A. 15–16, 142, 155–6
Miller, J. Hillis 178, 307, 308, 329
Miner, Heather 315–21
misogyny theme 4, 53–60
Mitchell, Timothy 40
M'Naghten Rules 87
mobility of female bodies 76
Modern Romance (Duncan) 373
Monbiot, George 404
Montague, Francis (Frank) 218
Moody, Ellen 378–9
Moore, Grace 399–411
moral principles in writing 309
Morash, Christopher 367
Morgan (Lady) 266, 268
Morley, John 21–2
Morris, Meaghan 402
Morse, Deborah Denenholz 51–62, 86, 124, 125–6, 150, 311, 393
Mouton, Michelle 412–22
Mr Scarborough's Family (Trollope) 64, 68–9, 100–1, 302–3
Mullen, Richard 2; *see also Anthony Trollope: A Victorian in His World* (Mullen)

Nardin, Jane 15, 80, 86
narrated monologue 168–9
narrative forms/strategies: cleverness narrative 274–83; Darwinism narrative strategies 201–5; destructive decisions narrative 203–4; emigration narratives 11, 388–96; introduction 6; irony in 158–9; *Jael,* as narrative 241–2, 246; landscape narratives 399–408; *ménage a trois* narrative 242–6; narrative authority of women 179; naturalistic narrative of capitalist globalization 26–8; objective narration 170; picturesque, as narrative 255–7; political settings 16–19; psycho-narration 169–70, 171; regional change narrative 384–6; repetitions of phrases in 181; sexual tension narratives 240; travel narratives 390–1; Wild West narrative 396; *see also* feeling narratives; marriage narratives
naturalistic narrative of capitalist globalization 26–8
Neville-Sington, Pamela 275
Newby, Thomas Cautley 308
New Liberalism 25
"New Man" concept 52, 53, 56, 328
New Men in Trollope's Novels (Markwick) 56, 64, 107, 123
New York Bar Association 336
Ngai, Sianne 274
Niles, Lisa 427
Nina Balatka (Trollope) 338–41
North America (Trollope) 333, 427–8
Norton, Caroline 86; *see also* Custody of Infants Act (1839); Infant Custody Act (1839); Law Relating to the Custody of Infants
Nunokawa, Jeff 112

Oberhelman, David 87
objective narration 170
object sensitivity 111–12
O'Connor, Frank 146, 250, 307
Odden, Karen 309
Ofek, Galia 125
Old Man's Love, An (Trollope) 301
Oliphant, Margaret 145
Oliver Twist (Dickens) 100
Omnium Coalition 44, 45
order of release 250–2, *251*
Order of Release, The (Millais) 247, 252
ordinary realism 142–51
Orley Farm (Trollope) 64–7, 127, 148, 167–75
Osborne, Kate 306–14
outward-looking view 10–11
Overton, Bill 337–8
Oxford Movement 348
Oxford Reader's Companion to Trollope (Terry) 338

Palliser novels: aging theme 302–3; allegorical uses of locations 166; character outlines 196–7; conservative liberalism 21–6; Darwinian aspects of 202–5; feminism and 51–3, 57, 124; field sports 317; government and the state 43, 45; heroes 193; introduction 1–6, 15–16; Ireland and 363, 369; legitimacy/illegitimacy themes 105; marriage plots 160; overview 26–8, 38, 296; parliamentary desire 19–20; prejudice in 342; regional change 379
Palmer, Alan 167, 170
Park, Clara Claiborne 338
parliamentary desire 19–21
passive heroes 146
Pater, Walter 138

Index

patriarchal views 184
Peak, Anna 325–35
Phineas Finn (Trollope) 26, 41, 341–2, 369–70
Phineas Redux (Trollope) 143, 342
picturesque, as narrative 255–7
place and topicality: counterrevolution fiction 381–4; counterrevolution themes 379–81; emigration narratives 388–96; introduction 10; regional change narrative 384–6; scholarship review 378–9
plot construction 145, 183
Plotz, John 113
Polhemus, Robert 51, 85, 150, 177, 185, 239–60, 365
political convictions in novels 337
political settings: clerico-political conflict 43; conservative liberalism 21–6; introduction 3, 15–16; in later works 28–9; narrative forms 16–19; Palliser novels 22, 26–8; parliamentary desire 19–21
Poovey, Mary 372
populism 383
Portrait of a Girl (Millais) 253–5, *254*
possessive identity of objects 113–14
Potvin, John 123
Pratt, Mary Louise 399
prejudice themes 8–9
Prime Minister, The (Trollope) 24, 43–4, 342–3
"primitive" within the civilized 79
Princep, Thoby 248
Principles of Geology (Lyell) 204
Psomiades, Kathy 80, 97
psycho-narration 169–70, 171

quoted monologue 169

race themes 412–20
Rachel Ray (Trollope) 147–8, 385
Radicalism 25–7
Ragussis, Michael 337
Raitt, Suzanne 84–99
rape themes 74, 122
Reform Bill (1866) 23
Reforming Trollope (Morse) 150
regional change narrative 384–6
religion subplot 350
religous beliefs 347–57
repetitions of phrases in narratives 181
reproduction techniques in illustration studies 214–15
Ricoeur, Paul 183
Riffaterre, Michael 112, 149
Roebuck, John Arthur 89
Rogers, Henry N. 309
romance subplot 350
romanticism 384
Romola (Eliot) 215–16

Roper, Michael 63
Rose, Deborah Bird 406–7
Rosenfeld, Jason 255
Rothery, Mark 63
Rotunno, Laura 38
Royal Literary Fund 311
Rubin, Gerry 287
Ruskin, John 318–19

Sadleir, Michael 1, 51, 149–50, 178, 364–5, 423; *see also Anthony Trollope: A Commentary*
Scarry, Elaine 120–1
secret societies 271
self-help societies 37
sentence structuring 6
settler spaces 390
sexual assault 79
sexual maturity in female characters 18–19
sexual tension narratives 240
Shengold, Leonard 280
Shuman, Cathy 309
Sibley, Susan 289–90
Sir Harry Hotspur of Humblethwaite (Trollope) 54–6
Sittlichkeit (ethical life) 25
Skilton, David 38, 213–38, 423
skimmable passages 156–8
skin ego 126
slavery themes 22, 77, 418
Small House at Allington, The (Trollope) 120, 124, 275
Smith, Allison 255
Smith, George 144, 226
Snow, C.P. 2
social convictions in novels 337
Social Minds in the Novel (Palmer) 167
society as a network 277
spinsterhood fears of women 297–8
Spooner, Catherine 123
state-funded education 25
Steele, Anna C. 278
Stern, Rebecca 73
Stewart, Garrett 372
Stilton, David 180
Stone, Marcus 217
Sugarman, David 287
Sugden, Edward 88, 92
Super, R.H. 2, 248; *see also Chronicler of Barsetshire, The: A Life of Anthony Trollope* (Super)
Surridge, Lisa 87
Sussman, Matthew 155
Sutherland, John 307, 309, 404, 426
syphilitic men 56

taboo impulses 243–4
Taylor, E. 216
Taylor, Jenny Bourne 100–10, 127, 291, 393
telegraph girls 126

440

Index

Terry, R.C. 58, 365
testamentary freedom concept 102
Thackeray, W.M. 21, 101, 126–7, 150, 191–3, 216, 300
thinking women 155, 161–3
Thomas, Kate 308
thought crime 54–60
thought report 169–70
Three Clerks, The (Trollope) 393–4
Tilley, John 302
toil/labor themes 8, 306–12
Tosh, John 63, 64
Tracy, Robert 2, 178–9, 263–73, 366
tragic constructions 137–40
Traits and Stories of the Irish Peasantry (Carleton) 271
transfer of property ownership 288–9
transit and global modernity 424–7
Transparent Minds (Cohn) 168
travel books 388–96
travel narratives 390–1
triple-decker novels 310
Trollope (Glendinning) 2, 142
Trollope: A Biography (Hall) 2
Trollope: An Illustrated Biography (Snow) 2
Trollope, Anthony: aging studies 8, 295–303; anti-Semitism and 8–9, 27, 325–33, 336–44; authorial intrusions 309–10; biographies by 190–9; body portrayal 5, 120–30; character identity through objects 111–15; commentaries of Caesar 193–5; creed and cant 8–9; critical theory 5–6; culture and gender 3–5; Darwinism narrative strategies 201–5; emigration narratives 11, 388–96; field sports 315–19; gender relations 177–85; globalism of 9–10; illustration studies 6–7; introduction 1–3; Ireland, as inspiration 2, 263–73; landscape narratives 399–408; legal culture 285–91; literary labor 306–12; material culture 111–18; mother's influence 278–83; ordinary realism 142–51; political settings 3; preoccupations of 7–8; religious beliefs 347–57; and Thackeray 21, 101, 126–7, 150, 191–3, 216, 300; as tragic novelist 137–40
Trollope, Frances (Fanny, mother) 274–83
Trollope, His Originals and Associates (Escott) 1
Trollope and Comic Pleasure (Herbert) 51
Trollope and the Law (McMaster) *see* Palliser novels
Trollope in the Post Office (Super) 2
Trollope's Palliser Novels (McMaster) 51
trousseaux meaning for women 116–18
Trumpener, Katie 373
Turner, Mark W. 52, 60, 310, 311, 423–34

Unofficial Trollope, The (Overton) 337–8

Van Dam, Frederick 15–32, 287, 290
Vicar of Bullhampton, The (Trollope) 348–57
Victorian manliness 63–70
Victorians and Old Age, The (Chase) 295
Victorian state/culture: character and metonymy 40–2; configured state 42–5; governance and 36–9; introduction 35–6; legal culture of 288; travel narratives 390–1
violence themes 54–60, 72–81, 78–9

Wagner, Tamara S. 388–98
Walpole, Hugh 184
Wandering Jew image 327
Ward, Addison 194
Warden, The (Trollope) 17–18, 147, 289
Watts, G.F. 248
Way We Live Now, The (Trollope): aging studies 297, 301; anti-Semitism in 325; body portrayal 129; religious beliefs 349; women and violence 72–81
Wells, H.G. 39
West Indies and the Spanish Main, The (Trollope) 399, 412–20, 424–5
Wharton, Alured 24
Wharton, J.J.S. 103–4
Wild Irish Girl, The (Morgan) 266
Wild West narrative 396
Williams, Raymond 408
will of one's own 78–9
Wolfreys, Julian 15
women: female gaze 256–7; misogyny theme 4; mobility of female bodies 76; narrative authority 179; sexual image of 248; society as a network 277; spinsterhood fears of 297–8; taboo impulses 243–4; thinking women 155, 161–3; trousseaux meaning for 116–18; violence and 72–81; *see also* feminism
Woolf, Virginia 190
Wright, Andrew 307
Writing the Frontier: Anthony Trollope Between Britain and Ireland (McCourt) 371
Writing the Irish Famine (Morash) 367
Wyke, Marina 194
Wynne, Deborah 117

Yeats, William Butler 264–5, 268, 271–3
Young, G.M. 391–2

Ziegenhagen, Timothy 300